RATIONAL HERDS
Economic Models of Social Learning

Penguins jumping off a cliff, economic forecasters predicting a recovery in the business cycle, financial advisors for the stock market speculating against a currency, and farmers using new seeds in India are all practicing social learning. Such learning from the behavior of others can lead to herds, crashes, and booms. These issues have become, over the last ten years, an exciting field of research in theoretical and applied economics, finance, and other social sciences. This book provides both an informal introduction and in-depth insights into the most recent advances.

The properties of social learning depend on the context in which learning and actions take place. Each chapter is devoted to a separate issue: Individuals learn from the observations of actions, from the outcomes of these actions, and from what others say. They may delay or make an immediate decision; they may compete against others or gain from cooperation; they make decisions about capital investment, crop choices, and financial investments. The book highlights the similarities and the differences between the various cases. A recurrent theme is that society may learn more if individuals are less than perfectly rational in their interpretation of others' behavior.

Christophe Chamley is Professor of Economics at Boston University and a Director of Studies at the Ecole des Hautes Etudes en Sciences Sociales, Paris. He has also held teaching or visiting positions at Yale University, the Hoover Institution, the World Bank, Universidad Carlos III (Madrid), the Université Louis Pasteur (Strasbourg), and MIT. Professor Chamley's research has appeared in the leading journals in economics, including the *American Economic Review, Econometrica,* the *Journal of Political Economy,* the *Quarterly Journal of Economics,* and the *Review of Economic Studies.* He was named a Fellow of the Econometric Society in 1995. His research interests continue to focus on the economics of information, theoretical macroeconomics, monetary economics, public economics, and public economics history. Professor Chamley received his doctorate from Harvard University.

Rational Herds

ECONOMIC MODELS OF SOCIAL LEARNING

CHRISTOPHE P. CHAMLEY

CAMBRIDGE
UNIVERSITY PRESS

PUBLISHED BY THE PRESS SYNDICATE OF THE UNIVERSITY OF CAMBRIDGE
The Pitt Building, Trumpington Street, Cambridge, United Kingdom

CAMBRIDGE UNIVERSITY PRESS
The Edinburgh Building, Cambridge CB2 2RU, UK
40 West 20th Street, New York, NY 10011-4211, USA
477 Williamstown Road, Port Melbourne, VIC 3207, Australia
Ruiz de Alarcón 13, 28014 Madrid, Spain
Dock House, The Waterfront, Cape Town 8001, South Africa

http://www.cambridge.org

First published 2004

Printed in the United States of America

Typefaces Minion 10.75/14 pt. and ITC Symbol   *System* LaTeX 2_ε [TB]

A catalog record for this book is available from the British Library.

Library of Congress Cataloging in Publication Data
Chamley, Christophe.
    Rational herds : economic models of social learning / Christophe P. Chamley.
      p.   cm.
    Includes bibliographical references and index.
    ISBN 0-521-82401-X – ISBN 0-521-53092-X (pb.)
    1. Social learning.   2. Social learning – Mathematical models.   3. Decision making.
    4. Collective behavior   I. Title: Economic models of social learning.   II. Title.
    HQ783.C47   2003
    303.3′2 – dc21   2003046180

ISBN 0 521 82401 X hardback
ISBN 0 521 53092 X paperback

To the memory of my father

Contents

Preface

Learning by individuals from the behavior of others and imitation pervade the social life. Issues related to such learning have been debated since the beginning of the social sciences, more than a century ago. However, in the last ten years or so they have stimulated a revival and very active research in economics, with extensions to other "human sciences" (sociology, psychology, political science). The purpose of this book is to give an account of these studies. Perhaps it will induce others to enter the field and provide them with some training.

The setting is one of rational agents with limited information who share that information with others through their actions. The properties of the learning process are analyzed from a theoretical point of view, but some empirical studies are discussed in relation to the theoretical results.

Special attention is devoted to the pathologies of social learning by rational agents. Herds appear to be obvious examples of failures of social learning. Indeed, herds, fads, bubbles, crashes, and booms are cited as proofs of the irrationality of individuals. However, most of these colorful events will appear in the models of rational agents studied in this book .

The assumption of rationality may seem a bit narrow. Indeed, at this stage of the evolution of research, the concept of rationality itself is beginning to be seriously investigated. In this book, the usefulness of the assumption goes beyond the standard "benchmark" justification: a recurrent issue will be that despite the rationality of individual behavior, and often because of that rationality, the process of social learning may be inefficient or fail completely. The results hint at some social benefits of nonrational behavior by individuals, but that topic is beyond the scope of the present work.

Readers

The book can be read at two levels: the first, nontechnical and the second, more formal. Both levels will demand some intellectual concentration, however.

Each chapter is devoted to a specific issue. Examples are the various channels for the transmission of information (actions, outcomes of the actions, words, and so on), the coordination of agents, and price fluctuations in a financial market. For each chapter, the results and the methodology are described in an informal introduction.

In some of the main chapters, a first section presents a reduced model that exhibits most of the essential properties. These parts of the book should be accessible to a wide audience of readers who are interested in the issues and are prepared to follow logical arguments, sometimes with a bit of formalism.

For graduate students and researchers in social sciences (mainly economics and finance, but also other social sciences), the book provides an introduction to the technical literature. The main subjects have been selected with a personal bias, and are presented in their essence. The models are analyzed rigorously without some of the baggage that is sometimes required by professional journals. In a number of cases, the analysis had to be adapted, or even rewritten, for that purpose. The techniques do not use highbrow mathematics. Most of the model manipulations use first principles.

The models are simple, but a major goal is to give the student sufficient understanding of the internal structure of these models to develop his own intuition about their "deep" properties. A model is not an exercise with cute results or a quick "validation" of some story, but it is a tool to make an argument that goes beyond its technical boundaries. It is my view that the understanding of these properties cannot be grasped from a survey, and that, in the field of social learning, it takes a considerable amount of time to develop this understanding if one has to read the technical literature. The purpose of the book is to shorten that time for the student before he goes to the frontline papers and does research about theoretical or empirical topics.

Acknowledgments

A number of people have made contributions to this book, some decisive for its completion. The project is the product of *séminaires* of the Ecoles des Hautes Etudes en Sciences Sociales at DELTA, and its realization would not have been possible without the participation of this unique group of students. Jay Surti at Boston University was an ideal Ph.D. student and made numerous suggestions. Lones Smith provided stimulating discussions. I am very much in debt to people who have been generous with their comments and their time: Markus Brunnermeier, Andrew Caplin, Benjamin Carton, Zachary Dorsey, Douglas Gale, Todd Gormley, Sanjeev Goyal, Roger Guesnerie, Ward Hanson, William Hawkins, Andrew Hertzberg, David Hirshleifer, Alan Kirman, Laurence Kotlikoff, Elie Mincer, Pierre Pestieau, Marek Pycia, Iulia Rodionova, Peter Sørensen, Christopher Udry, Xavier Vives, anonymous referees, and students in classes taught from the book at Boston University and MIT. My colleagues at Boston University provided intellectual camaraderie. The MIT Economics Department offered a stimulating setting for the last stage of the project. Scott Parris of Cambridge University Press was a strong believer from the start many years ago and never doubted.

To Mari-Cruz, Paul, and Sebastian, apologies and gratitude.

1 Introduction

Penguins are social animals. They live in groups above the water from which they get fish for food. Unfortunately, there is more than fish in the water. From time to time, killer whales (orcas) roam under the surface waiting for some prey. Penguins are aware of the danger and would like to have some information before taking a plunge. Indeed, any sensible penguin thinks that it would be very nice if some other penguin would dive first to test the water. So what is a penguin to do? Wait. Possibly some other member of the colony who is more hungry, or has other information, will go first. Is it possible that no penguin will ever go? No, because waiting becomes more costly as hunger increases. Eventually, one or more penguins will take the plunge, and, depending on the outcome, the others will either stay put or follow *en masse*. This *waiting game* is socially inefficient. It would be better if the first individual would decide to go at least a bit earlier: the first to go is, on the margin, as well off going just a little earlier; but others strictly prefer him to go a little earlier. Actually, the penguins are well aware of this social inefficiency, which they try to remedy by pushing some poor fellow off the cliff.

First-Cousin Marriages

There is a long-standing taboo against marriages between first cousins in some parts of the world. Such taboos may entail significant costs. In the United States, about thirty states have laws forbidding first cousins to marry, but on some other continents marriages between cousins are well regarded. Recent, and remarkably late, evidence shows that the risk of defects for children is marginally higher in such marriages than in the general population (Motulsky et al., 2002):

> Dr. Motulsky said that medical geneticists had known for a long time that there was little or no harm in cousins' marrying and having children. 'Somehow, this hasn't become general knowledge,' Dr. Motulsky said. 'Among the public and physicians there's a feeling it's real bad and brings a lot of disease, and there's a lot of social and legal disapproval.' Dr. Motulsky said the American laws against cousin marriage should be abolished, because they are based in part on the mistaken belief that the children of such parents will suffer from terrible physical and mental illnesses.[1]

---

[1] This quotation is from the *New York Times*, April 3, 2002.

The White-Van Frenzy

On October 26, 2002, one could read this in the *New York Times*:

> Until the final moments of the three-week reign of sniper terror in the Washington area, there was one image, one all-consuming clue, seared into the minds of a panicked public: the white van.
>
> White vans were pictured on wanted posters everywhere. Their drivers were stopped four, five, six times a day. They were forsaken by some, who rented or borrowed other vehicles because they simply could not take it anymore: the constant traffic stops, the swooping in of gun-wielding police officers, the stares from other drivers and pedestrians, the snooping around their license plates and sneaky peeks into their rear windows to check for rifles and other signs of sniping. Each shooting and each day that passed without an arrest brought a new flood of tips and witness accounts involving white vans and trucks, seemingly fed by the earliest witness accounts.
>
> Witnesses to some of the first shootings were able to describe only a glimpse at a fleeing white vehicle, information that the police quickly released and eventually used to put together composite sketches. So there was nothing but a white van and before that, a white box truck to look for. With no description of the killer, many people, gripped with fear of another attack and seizing on any detail in their personal lookout for the sniper, were in a kind of white-van haze. [. . .]
>
> For a time, the police themselves were so focused on white vans and trucks – there are roughly 100,000 on the roads of Washington and its suburbs – that they may have overlooked the vehicle they really needed to find. In fact, officers in Washington stopped the blue Caprice, ran a check on its license plates and then allowed the two men to proceed only a couple of hours before one of the sniper killings. [. . .]
>
> "Darn right I'm glad it's over," said Sinclair Skinner, who drives a white van for his dry-cleaning delivery service but parked it two weeks ago after being stopped by the police twice in one day, and rented a car. "The police were stopping people, people were asking me all kinds of questions. Finally I said: 'Look, I'm not involved in anything. I'm not the Taliban. I wasn't in the gulf war. I'm a pacifist. I listen to Pacifica Radio.'" [. . .]
>
> Meanwhile, the police, including all 1,000 officers on the Montgomery County force, the lead agency in the investigation, combed the area for white vans. When a van was stopped, several police cars often surrounded it, and officers drew their guns, sometimes telling the drivers to come out with their hands up and then ordering them to lie face down on the ground.
>
> The white van, said Officer Baliles, "was the best lookout we had."

Umbrellas

The actions of others convey some information about the state of the world. When I see other people going out with an umbrella, I take an umbrella along without checking the weather forecast. I do so because I know the decision model of others. I can then infer their private information from their action without the need to talk to them. This herding is rational. There is, however, the possibility that everyone carries an umbrella because someone carries an umbrella. The herd may be wrong.

1.1 Overview

The learning from others can operate through different channels of information (choices or results of actions, words), and in different contexts (with or without delay between actions, real or financial investment) and may be affected by externalities between the actions. The chapters are designed to study one issue at a time.

PART I: SOCIAL LEARNING

The Tools

All models will have a key random variable, which will not be observed directly: the *state of nature*. The state of nature may be the profitability of a set of new techniques, the mass of agents who are prepared to topple a government in a revolution, or the reserves of a central bank in a speculative attack against a regime of fixed exchange rate. Rational learning in this book means Bayesian learning about the state of nature.

The essential tools of analysis are presented in Chapter 2. The private information is represented by private signals, which depend on the state of nature: for example, if it will rain (if the sun will shine), two-thirds (one-third) of the agents think that rain is more likely than sunshine. To think that rain is more (less) likely is the realization of a private signal. These private signals are correct, statistically, and a large number of them, if they could be pooled directly, would bring perfect or near-perfect information.

We will use restrictive models, which will be special cases. Attempts at generality would end in futile formalism, but we will need to have a good idea whether the results of a specific model are robust or not. In most cases, these results depend on some critical assumptions. It is therefore important to know the implications of the modeling choices. Two models of private information will be used recurrently (but not exclusively): the binary model with two states ("good" or "bad"), two informations, and two actions ("investment" or "no investment"), and the Gaussian–quadratic model where all random variables are normal and the payoff is a quadratic function of the level of action (a real number). These two models are discussed in detail in Chapter 2.

The Martingale Property

The beliefs of agents are defined as their subjective probabilities about the state of nature. An agent observes a variable (aggregate investment, success or failure of an oil drilling) that depends on the state of nature. Following an observation, he updates his belief using Bayes's rule. This rule is an application of the calculus of conditional probabilities, and it generates the remarkable property of a martingale: an agent knows that he may change his belief after an observation, but the expected value of the change is nil. If that value were different from zero, the agent would change his belief right away. The martingale property, which is similar to an efficient-market equation in finance (and for good reasons), is both simple and powerful; it implies that the agent cannot change his belief forever. The martingale convergence theorem is one of the most beautiful theorems in probability theory. Its mechanism is presented here intuitively. The theorem is the most important one in Bayesian learning. It will apply in many models (but not in all of them) and facilitate the analysis of the limit properties of learning. The theorem implies that unending fluctuations of individual beliefs cannot be compatible with rational learning.

Social Learning

When an individual learns from a person's behavior, (i.e., her choice of action or her words), he learns because the person's behavior is motivated by some information that she has about a state of nature of interest to all (e.g., the example of the umbrellas). This *private information*, or private belief, is like an endowment. The process of social learning is the diffusion of the private beliefs to all individuals through the interactions of observations, learning, and action choices. The structure of the model will be dictated by the context. Actions may be more reliable than words. Some definitions of social learning restrict the learning to the observation of actions themselves (physical actions or words), but we will consider also the observation of the outcomes of actions.

In models of social learning, a large amount of (private) information may be hidden. When agents do not act, this information remains hidden. We will encounter situations where, because of some small changes, some agents will "come out of the woods," take an action, and thereby release their information and induce others to act. Long periods of low activity may be followed by a sudden boom. Inversely, a regime of high activity may be brought to a halt by a crash.

Actions as Words

When agents learn from actions, these actions are the "words" for communication. As in any language, communication is easier if there are many words. When actions can be taken from a wide set (e.g., the set of real numbers), the "message" sent by an agent can reflect his private information perfectly. When the set of actions is discrete (e.g., a farmer choosing the type of crop), the message about the private information is obviously more coarse. We begin with the case of continuous action sets.

Clustering

The model of social learning is introduced in Chapter 3: Agents are placed in an exogenous sequence of rounds; each agent chooses his level of *investment*, a real number, in his round and is observed by others. As the number of observations increases, the importance of history for individual choices grows and agents rely less, rationally, on their private information. Individual choices are *clustering*. However, any agent's action can be observed with perfect precision – in this model – and it reveals perfectly his private information. The learning from others' actions is equivalent to the direct observation of their private information. There is no information loss in social learning.

The Weight of History and Slow Learning from Others

The assumption of perfect observability requires also perfect knowledge of the decision process of each agent. However, we have all our idiosyncrasies, which make the inference from actions imperfect. When history is short, this problem is not important. When history is long, however, and it induces agents to cluster, the observation becomes dominated by the noise. This slowing down in the rate of social learning is quantified by Vives (1995) in the Gauss–quadratic model. We will find this important property of social learning in other contexts: the memory of past actions may reduce – or completely prevent – social learning.

Herds and Cascades

In Chapter 4, the set of actions is reduced to two elements (to take or not an action: fixed investment, medical procedure, new crop). This is the celebrated model of Bikhchandani, Hirschleifer, and Welch (1992), hereafter BHW. In a simple case (with binary information), they show that social learning stops completely and rapidly (at an exponential rate): Suppose two agents invest and thus reveal that they have a good signal; if the third agent has a bad signal, that signal cancels only one of the previous two signals; he should invest like the first agent, who had only one good signal to rely on; in this case, he invests even if he has a bad signal. The third agent is *herding*. His action conveys no information. In the next round, the public information is unchanged. Nothing is learned. The fourth agent is in the same position as the third. Social learning stops completely, and a *cascade* takes place.[2]

Cascades are a spectacular example of the failure of social learning due to the weight of history. Is this property robust? Careful examination shows that, technically, the property is not robust at all. Cascades depend on discrete private signals that are not generic. When private beliefs are all distinct – as in random drawings from a continuum – cascades do not exist.

On the other hand, *herds* take place for sure, eventually. A herd is defined as a situation in which all agents take the same action after some date. If all agents turn out to take the same action after some date T, there is still the possibility that an agent has a private signal that induces him to take a different action after date T. This possibility is not realized, but the very fact that it is not realized yields information, which is incorporated in the social learning (Smith and Sørensen, 2001).

The existence of a herd is an elegant application of the martingale convergence theorem: when a "black sheep" breaks away from the herd, he reveals a piece of strong private information. That information is then incorporated in the public belief, which

---

[2] See Section 1.2 for a discussion of the term "cascade".

makes a quantum jump. This event cannot occur an infinite number of times, because that would prevent the convergence of the public belief, which is a martingale.

A herd is not a cascade. However, as a herd goes on, the set of private beliefs in which an agent follows the herd grows. Social learning is very slow, because the probability of breaking the herd must be vanishingly small in order for the herd to be realized. The time profile of the evolution of beliefs is not the same as that of a cascade, where learning stops completely, but it is not very different.

An application of the model shows that a firm that introduces a new product of quality unknown to consumers should target a group willing to pay a high price, in order to establish its reputation, and then lower the price to reach a mass market.

To Forget in Order to Reduce the Weight of History

Because the weight of the information in history induces paralysis and prevents agents from conveying their information to others through their actions, the remedy is simple: partly forget the past. Indeed, Chapter 5 shows that when agents have an incomplete sample of the actions of past agents, social learning is more efficient! The inference from another individual's action is now more difficult, because the observations on which that action is based are not observable. (In Chapter 4 these observations were summarized by the public belief, which is a martingale.)

Delays Ending with a Bang or a Whimper

So far agents have made a choice in an exogenous order. This assumption cannot apply to the penguins. In Chapter 6, the setting is the same as in BHW (with arbitrary private beliefs) with the sole difference that any agent can make a decision (like plunging) at any time: each agent has an option to make one investment. This setting induces a *waiting game*, in which the more optimistic agents go first. The others know this and wait to observe how many agents plunge. A large number means that the number of optimists is large. Because private beliefs are statistically correct, the large number is a signal that the state of nature is good, and agents who were initially reluctant join the fray. A bang may take place. Events can evolve either way: there is also the possibility that the number of investors is small in an initial phase, after which investment stops completely. The game ends with a whimper (Chamley and Gale, 1994).

The waiting game has some powerful properties. The main one is the arbitrage between the cost of delay (from lost dividends) and the option value of delay (from not making a bad irreversible investment). Suppose that actions are observed through some noise. The cost of delay is not affected by the noise. Hence the information generated by the equilibrium is unaffected. The equilibrium strategy is adjusted so that more agents take action, and the net information generated by all actions is the same as without noise. The model may generate multiple equilibria with sharply different information: if most agents delay and only the greatest optimists invest, then the information generated by the equilibrium must be high (in order to induce most agents to wait). If most agents do not delay, there is little information in the equilibrium. In the cascades of BHW, there was no information. These situations are found again in the setting with endogenous delays.

In Chapter 7, the model with delays is investigated under the assumption of continuous time: agents can make a decision at any point in time. If the distribution of private beliefs admits agents with a high degree of optimism, the model does not have an equilibrium, generically. It is shown that there are essential differences between a model with periods and a model in continuous time. The properties of a model with periods do not converge to those of a continuous-time model as the period length becomes vanishingly short.

Outcomes

When agents observe the outcomes of others' actions, learning may still be incomplete if actions converge to a point where the random outcome can be explained by different states, as shown in Chapter 8. For example, the individual level of effort toward a successful economic career may converge, generically, to a value where agents cannot discriminate perfectly between the contributions of noise and chance in the outcome; or the price of a monopoly may be compatible with two types of demand schedule: the first with a high level and a high price elasticity, the second with a low level and a low elasticity.

The observation of outputs does not prevent failures in social learning: if an action is deemed superior to others, it is chosen by all agents who do not try other actions. Hence, no information can be gathered on other actions to induce a switch. A herd may take place unless some agents have very strong private beliefs that other actions may be superior. These strong believers may provide significant information benefits to others.

Networks

When agents are watching the evolution of the price of an asset, the information has a sequential structure. When they learn how to fertilize apple trees in Ghana, they rely on a network of information contacts. When a new crop (say, a high-yield variety of wheat or rice) is introduced in a region, agents make simultaneous decisions in each crop cycle, and learn from their information contacts at the end of each cycle. Networks and diffusion processes are analyzed in Chapter 9. As in previous chapters, social learning may be more efficient if the information of agents is restricted. For example, the observation of a small group (e.g., a royal family) by *all* agents could induce a cascade and a herd. The model of Bala and Goyal (1998) formalizes the description of Tarde (1900), which will be presented below.

Words

The most obvious way to communicate private information seems to be to talk. Yet, economists prefer to trust what people do. Can a financial advisor be trusted? Yes, if he has sufficient incentive to build a *reputation* for his future business. In

Chapter 10, it is shown that the reputation motive can be sufficient for truthtelling within some limits. The reputation is earned by being proven right: the receiver of the advice can verify, after a while, whether the stock that was recommended actually went up or down. However, if the public belief that the stock will go up is strong, a rational advisor who has contrary private information will maximize the chance of being right and will issue a "buy" recommendation. He is herding like any agent in the BHW model. Indeed, there is no difference between reputation herding and the herding in the BHW model, and the conditions for its occurrence are identical (Ottaviani and Sørensen, 2000). The reputation can induce people to herd and say the "politically correct" thing (Morris, 2001) or to please the boss (Prendergast, 1993). Recall the witnesses of the white van, or how the lonely juror was able to sway the others in *Twelve Angry Men* (Lumet, 1957). Who should speak first in a jury where people may herd on what others say? The analysis shows that it is not clear whether the first to speak should be among the more or the less experienced (Ottaviani and Sørensen, 2001).

PART II: COORDINATION

The issues of Part I are extended in Part II with the addition of payoff externalities between different individual actions. Agents have to coordinate their expectations about an equilibrium.

One Period without Learning

Rousseau (1762) described the problem of social cooperation in the model of the stag hunt: a hunter has a higher individual payoff if he participates in a stag hunt than if he goes on his own chasing a hare. However, the success of the stag hunt depends on the participation of all. There are two equilibria in this game with *strategic complementarity*: either all hunters participate in the stag hunt or none do. This story can be adapted to a number a situations in economics, from business cycles to speculative attacks against a fixed exchange rate, and in other social situations (e.g., revolutions).

How do agents "choose" between different equilibria? A natural first step for the analysis is to consider a one-period setting in which agents make a simultaneous decision without observing what others do. Each agent has to guess, if possible, which equilibrium agents coordinate on. Carlsson and van Damme (1993a), in their *global-game* method, build on the insight that agents do not have perfect information on each other. The removal of the assumption of *common knowledge* enables one to solve the coordination problem: agents with a low cost of investment invest, no matter what others do. With that information commonly known, agents with a slightly higher cost also invest, which is again common knowledge. A process of contagion takes place, which solves the decision problem for all agents with a cost lower than average. A similar process of *iterative dominance* induces agents with a cost higher than average not to invest. This process takes place in the heads of agents in "virtual time" and is called *eductive learning*.

A similar process of iterative dominance had been proposed previously in the context of *strategic substitutability* when, for example, farmers in a population choose their individual supplies independently and the expectations about future prices are inversely related to the total supply. In that case, there is a unique Nash equilibrium under perfect information, but the issue is the *coordination of expectations*. The analysis in Chapter 11 highlights the similarities and differences between strategic substitutability and complementarity.

A new tool, the *cumulative value function*, provides a simple intuition for the global-game method (with strategic complementarities) and enables one to solve applied models rapidly. Speculative attacks against currencies, which will reappear at the end of the book, have become a popular topic recently and are presented as an illustration.

Switching Regimes

In 1989, countries in the former Soviet bloc switched their political regimes abruptly. The opportunities for change were not apparent in the preceding winter.[3] It is the essence of oppressive regimes that a large amount of opinions remains hidden (Kuran, 1995). A turning point was the series of demonstrations in Leipzig, where protesters realized that they were a large mass. After the fall, few people seemed surprised. The story's features include a strong complementarity between the actions of agents and a large discrepancy between the common knowledge before and after the fact. These features are the main ones in the model presented in Chapter 12, which is based on Chamley (1999). The model is suggestive of regime switches in a variety of contexts of social interactions (political regimes, business cycles).

In each period, there is a new population where each agent decides whether to invest (*protest*, in a political context), or not. Investment entails a fixed cost, and the return is positive only if a sufficient mass of agents invest in the same period. The costs of agents have some unobserved distribution. Each agent knows only his own cost and observes the history of aggregate activities in the previous periods. The distribution of costs evolves slowly and randomly. The model exhibits the properties described in the previous paragraph: there are random switches between regimes of low and high activity. Most of the time, the structure of costs is such that under perfect information there would be two equilibria, with high and low activity. Under perfect information, however, the level of aggregate activity moves between a high and a low value with significant *hysteresis*, or inertia.

The inertia can be described precisely. If an outside observer had perfect knowledge about the structure of the economy, he would observe that in any period, agents

---

[3] We may tend to forget the *ex ante* beliefs before the switch of a regime. A useful reminder is found in Halberstam (1991) with an account of Henry Kissinger addressing, on February 26, 1989, the governors of the fifty states of the union: "He was condescending about what Gorbachev was doing and he was even more condescending about those poor Americans who were taking it all so seriously."

coordinate on the equilibrium that is closest to the one in the previous period. If the structure of the economy is such that low activity is an equilibrium under perfect information in periods t and $t + 1$ and is an equilibrium under imperfect information in period t, then low activity is also an equilibrium under imperfect information in period $t + 1$ (even if a switch to high activity would be possible under perfect information).

The equilibrium with random switches between high and low activity is determined by a process of iterative dominance in what is so far the only model in the literature that provides a nontrivial extension of iterative dominance to many periods. A numerical simulation illustrates an evolution of public belief that is analogous to the evolution in 1989.

Delays and Externalities

Firms that enter a new sector generate negative externalities on each other because they lower the price of the good. At the same time, they provide outsiders some information about the cost of production or the size of the demand. The prospect of more information induces delays. When the externality is positive, a small number of agents may induce others to act, and coordination may be achieved (Gale, 1995). If the number of agents is large, however, the possibility of delay may prevent coordination under imperfect information.

PART III: FINANCIAL HERDS

Since the tulip mania in seventeenth-century Holland, spectacular rises and falls have been observed in financial markets. It is easy to dismiss these as follies. An evaluation of the "irrationality" of markets can be made only with respect to properties that may be observed in a "rational" market. Part III provides an introduction to herds in financial markets with rational agents.

In the standard model of social learning (Part I), agents learn about the state of the world. The specifications of the set of actions and of the payoff externalities play a critical role in determining the properties of social learning. In financial markets, the state of the world is the fundamental value of an asset, the actions are the trades, payoff externalities arise because the gains of some are the losses of others, and timing is essential. Two market structures are considered.

Sequential Trades

The model of social learning with individuals in an exogenous sequence (Part I) becomes in financial markets the model of sequential trades between agents with different information (Glosten and Milgrom, 1985). If the learning is about a fundamental value that is a real number, beliefs updated by financial transactions with asymmetric information converge rapidly to the truth. This property is not very surprising in view of the results in Part I. Because a price can take any value in the set of positive numbers, it is a fine signal about the agents' private informations (as the actions in a continuum). In general, it seems that a state in an ordered set can be learned efficiently through financial markets.

An interesting situation occurs when the states cannot be ordered. For example, the state may be defined by the value of the fundamental and by the precision of the private informations of the agents. The updating from the history of prices does not proceed by simple upward or downward revisions. A situation may develop in which the price is incorrect for a very long time because agents interpret the history along a particular line of thought. This line of thought may become untenable after extended lack of supporting evidence. Agents are then led to switch to another interpretation, which entails a price jump (Avery and Zemsky, 1995).

No model of sequential financial trades has generated a cascade so far. However, the property of incorrect prices in protracted regimes followed by sudden and large changes – with no exogenous news – has the features of an unstable market that is apparently driven by fads.

Herds may occur when agents do not make a unique bid as in the sequential model. In this case, individual bids depend strategically on the bids of others, as in an auction. There may be an equilibrium (nonunique) that exhibits herdlike behavior (Neeman and Orosel, 1999).

Gaussian Markets and Price Jumps

The sequential model of Part I with a large number of agents, quadratic payoffs, and Gaussian random variables becomes in financial markets the CARA–Gauss model, where agents have a constant absolute risk aversion (hereafter CARA). In the standard CARA–Gauss model, which is presented here from first principles, the information from history does not slow down social learning as in Part I. Agents reduce the weight of their private information in their estimates when the information from history grows over time, as in Part I. However, there is an additional effect: because the information from history reduces the uncertainty, agents take more risk, namely a larger position, which amplifies the message about their private information. The second effect exactly cancels the first, and there is no slowdown of social learning if agents submit orders that are contingent on the trade prices (*limit orders*). If the orders are quantities to be traded at the rationally anticipated but uncertain equilibrium price (*market orders*), then social learning may slow down over time, as in Part I (Vives, 1995).

The issue of instability is modeled here by the existence of multiple equilibria. As an introduction to the vast literature, a reduced version of the model of Genotte and Leland (1990) is presented in Chapter 15. This model adds a new type of agents who are motivated by portfolio insurance: they sell some of their asset holdings when the price falls and buy when the price rises. The key argument is that agents who trade on the fundamentals (the *standard* agents) do not know that portfolio traders play an important role. (The rational expectation of the existence of such traders is assumed to be low.) The combined actions of the standard traders (who interpret, incorrectly, a price fall as bad news about the fundamentals) and of the portfolio traders (who sell when the price falls) can generate multiple equilibria. It is thus possible that small exogenous shocks induce large changes of the price.

Activity and Endogenous Information in Financial Markets

In models of social learning, a salient property is that the flow of information depends on the level of agents' activity. Typically, a higher level of aggregate activity generates more information, which feeds into the behavior of individuals. A self-reinforcing process may lead to sudden changes. Chapter 16 presents three examples of this process and indicates directions for future research.

Is it possible that in a financial market there could be two equilibria, the first with low activity associated with a high variance about the state, the second with high activity reducing the variance to a level that sustains that high activity? The answer is negative in the standard CARA–Gauss model where the state is the value of an asset, because the multiplier from the private information of an agent to his demand is independent of the precision of the public information.

The answer may be positive in a CARA–Gauss model where the state is defined by the mass of agents. There may be one equilibrium with a low price because agents are unsure about their total mass (which is positively related to the demand and therefore the asset price in the future), and another with large aggregate demand, which reduces the variance about the future (and supports the high demand by individuals); a large mass of agents who "come out of the woods" provides a strong signal about the state.

Dynamic Speculative Attacks

Speculative attacks against a fixed-exchange-rate regime and bank runs are examples of coordination games, but the people in the stag hunt do not decide one morning whether to hunt for the day or not. They watch each other; at any moment they can step in or out, depending on their observation. A one-period global game cannot take these effects into account. Chapter 16 presents a model of speculative attacks against a currency that is allowed to fluctuate within a narrow band (as in the European Monetary System before the euro). Agents face a trade-off in their timing: an early purchase of the foreign currency is made at a lower price, but the option to buy may be exercised later with a higher chance of success. On the other hand, an agent who delays faces the risk of missing the capital gain if he is beaten by others who trigger a devaluation. The model is built on the CARA–Gauss model with market orders. The monotone relation between the level of activity and information is a key property of the model: agents learn that they form a mass that is able to trigger a devaluation only if the quantity of orders is sufficiently large with respect to the noise.

The End of Speculative Bubbles

In the global-game approach to coordination, multiple equilibria are eliminated because of the lack of common knowledge among agents: all individuals know that the stag hunt would succeed, but they do not know whether others know (at some stage in the chain of reflections). In a speculative bubble, agents hold the asset with the sole purpose of capital gain. Because the capital gain, without the supporting dividends, cannot last forever, the bubble has to burst. According to the standard methodology in finance, the prospect of the eventual crash should, by backward induction, prevent the bubble. The bubble bursts only if the mass of agents selling the asset is sufficiently large. Abreu and Brunnermeier (2003) present a model in which a bubble is sustainable for some time while all agents are aware that the price is driven by a bubble, as long as this awareness is not common knowledge.

1.2 A Bit of History

CONDORCET AND VOTING FOR INFORMATION

Condorcet was the first to set the problem of aggregation of information and to present a model for analysis, in his *Essai sur l'application de l'analyse à la probabilité des décisions rendues à la pluralité des voix* (1785). His book is written in modern form. The first third (about 150 pages) sets out all the results of the analysis in words. The second part (about 300 pages) states the propositions formally with pages and pages of algebraic computations.[4]

The basic model of Condorcet is exactly the same as in any modern paper. There is a state of nature from a set of two elements, say, a person is guilty or not guilty. There is a set of individuals each with imperfect information on the state of nature. The imperfect information is modeled as a binary signal: with probability p, the person's opinion is correct. In the world of Condorcet, people expressed their true private beliefs. In our age of economists and accountants,[5] we do not trust or even hear what they say, we simply want to see what they do or what they get.

Condorcet assumes individuals express truthfully their opinion (reveal their signal, in modern jargon): they do not manipulate the process of decision; they do not let themselves be influenced by the opinion of others. Each opinion is expressed as a vote, and the decision follows the majority. This process is the same as learning from all agents with equal prior probabilities for the two events. Condorcet devoted many pages to the computation of the probabilities of the correct and incorrect outcomes, as functions of the number of polled individuals.

THE FOUNDATIONS OF SOCIOLOGY: GABRIEL TARDE AND EMILE DURKHEIM

Gabriel Tarde (1843–1904) began as a magistrate. His interests led him to become a criminologist. Crime is an activity that is quite amenable to the collection of statistics. From 1894 to the end of his life, he was director of the criminal statistics office of the Ministry of Justice (Lukes, 1972). He ended his career at the prestigious Collège de

---

[4] He was a precursor of Hicks (1939) in this respect.
[5] This famous description was applied by Burke (1790) to the executioners of Marie-Antoinette.

France.[6] Despite his academic success, Tarde was not a serious social scientist, even by generous standards. He preferred brilliance and striking insights over *Gründlichkeit*.

Tarde is interesting here because of his vision of sociology, which can be recast in modern terms. Sociology deals with groups (aggregates) of individuals who share common features in their behavior. How do these aggregates behave? How do a large number of individuals behave in similar ways? These questions are similar to those in contemporary macroeconomics (e.g., how does an economy cycle?). According to Tarde (and to Margaret Thatcher), a group as such does not exist. Individuals exist. The group is made of the aggregation of individuals. The method is the same as in the microeconomic foundation of macroeconomics. For a sociologist, human behavior includes other facets than economics, such as beliefs, language, life decision (suicide). What makes individuals in a group act in similar ways? The answer, which must be based on the individual (which for Tarde means individual psychology), is *imitation*. It is hardly stretching his view to state that a group is a collection of herding individuals.

Of course, there must be something to imitate. Indeed, some individuals do innovate. These are few. Most individuals just imitate:

> The principal role of a nobility, its distinguishing mark, is its initiative, if not inventive character. Invention can start from the lowest ranks of the people, but its extension depends upon the existence of some lofty social elevation, a kind of social water-tower whence a continuous *cascade* of imitation may descend.[7,8]

A striking expression of Tarde's view is found in a comment on Tocqueville:

> In an attentive reading of Tocqueville it may be perceived that although he never troubles himself to formulate the principle of imitation he is always running across it, and curiously enumerating its consequences. But if he had expressed it clearly and placed it at the head of his deductions, he would, I think, have been spared many errors and contradictions. He justly remarks that "no society can prosper without like beliefs, or, rather, there is none that subsists without them; for without common ideas, there is no common action, and without common action, men there may be, but not a social body." This means, at bottom, that the true social relation consists in imitation, since similarity of ideas, I mean of those ideas which are needed by society, is always acquired, never inborn. [...] Imitation, then, is the essential social action from which everything proceeds.[9]

Tarde found his "principle of imitation" at work in important fields of human activity and devoted a chapter to each in *Les Lois*: languages, religion, government, law, morals, and art. In each of these domains his insights are sometimes inspiring

---

[6] The Collège de France was founded by Francis I as the only institution of learning independent of the university (at the time essentially the University of Paris).

[7] Tarde (1900), p. 240; translation by E. C. Parsons (1962).

[8] The italics are mine. Tarde italicizes "château d'eau" (water tower), and uses the French word "cascade" beginning on p. 92 of *Les Lois de l'Imitation*.

[9] Page 309 of the translation by E. C. Parsons, where "erreurs" (p. 334 in the original text) become "minor errors."

(quite a few papers could be motivated by his remarks), sometimes very superficial, sometimes prejudiced. Unfortunately, most of the time he suggests but does not prove.

Across the rue Saint Jacques, facing the Collège de France, Emile Durkheim (1858–1917) was busy in the Sorbonne publishing dozens of articles and books before reaching sixty, and setting the foundations of sociology. He was not amused by visionary diletantism:

> But what this chapter chiefly shows is the weakness of the theory that imitation is the main source of all collective life. No fact is more readily transmissible by contagion than suicide, yet we have just seen that this contagiousness has no social effects. If imitation is so much without social influence in this case, it cannot have more in others; the virtues ascribed to it are therefore imaginary. [...]
>
> We should even be amazed at the continuing necessity of discussing an hypothesis which, aside from the serious objections it suggests, has never even begun to receive experimental proof. For it has never been shown that imitation can account for a definite order of social factors and, even less, that it alone can account for them. The proposition has merely been stated as an aphorism, resting on vaguely metaphysical considerations. But sociology can only claim to be treated as a science when those who pursue it are forbidden to dogmatize in this fashion, so patently eluding the regular requirements of proof.[10]

A proof that imitation has nothing to do with social facts is found in an analysis of suicide. One chapter of *Le Suicide* (32 pages out of 450) is devoted to imitation. It includes two maps with the frequency of suicides in each district of France and each *Land* of Germany. Durkheim discusses some of the statistical pitfalls, but such a discussion would be more elaborate in modern journals. He observes that in France,[11] the frequency of suicides by district does not exhibit circles around cities. A model of imitation would require that cities set the trends, because they make communication easier and their mass sets a stronger example. The region of highest density is to east of Paris. It would make a strange water tower for the cascades of Tarde.

1.3 How to Use This Book

For the reader who is new to the subject, Chapter 2 may be an investment that pays off later. The whole book is based on a methodology, and it may be advisable to undergo some training in it, like finger exercises before the sonatas.

The main features of social learning through the observation of actions are found in Chapter 3 and Sections 4.1.1 to 4.3 of Chapter 4. A simple model of herds and cascades is presented in Section 4.1.1, which should be widely accessible. The standard model

---

[10] Durkheim (1897), translation (1951), pp. 141–142.

[11] In Germany, there is no pattern of diffusion from cities. Five *Länder*, including the south of Switzerland, have a lower suicide rate. These regions turn out to be Catholic; the others are Protestant.

with heterogeneous beliefs is introduced in Section 4.2, and the convergence of beliefs in Section 4.3.

One may go straight from Section 4.1.1 to Section 4.2, which contains an equally simple model of social learning and delays. The standard model with delays is presented in Sections 6.2 and 6.3, which extend the standard model of herding in Section 4.2.

Chapter 8, about social learning with the observation of outcomes, is fairly independent from the others, but Section 8.3 leads to Section 9.2 in the following chapter.

Chapter 9 about networks has two distinct parts. Section 9.1, about diffusion and innovations, does not require much preparation. Section 9.2 should be read with reference to Section 5.3 (and the part of its chapter that leads to it), and also with reference to Section 8.3, as previously indicated.

Chapter 10, on reputational herding, can be read immediately after the core material on social herding (Sections 4.1.1 to 4.3 of Chapter 4). Herding by financial advisors may be studied in relation to the financial herding in Part III.

The first chapter of Part II, on coordination (Chapter 11), is different from all previous chapters. (There is only one period and therefore no learning.) The material of that chapter is necessary for the rest of Part II.

Part III, on financial markets, can be only an introduction. It does not require preliminary knowledge of finance. All the models are constructed from first principles.

The exercises at the end of some chapters proved to be useful when the material of the book was taught in formal courses.

The web site of the book contains additional material, including news, recent articles, and exercises. It is accessible at http://econ.bu.edu/chamley/rh/rh.html.

PART ONE

Social Learning

2   Bayesian Tools

Practice makes perfect.

The Bayesian framework is introduced. The main tools for the models in this book are the binary model with two states of nature and the Gaussian model with a normal distribution of information. The correspondence between private information and private beliefs is discussed. Because rational beliefs will often be martingales, the martingale convergence theorem will be used repeatedly. Its mechanism is described intuitively.

A Witness with No Historical Knowledge

In a town there are cabs of two colors, yellow and red.[1] Ninety percent of the cabs are yellow. One night, a cab hits a pedestrian and leaves the scene without stopping. The skills and the ethics of the driver do not depend on the color of the cab. An out-of-town witness claims that the cab was red. The witness does not know the proportion of yellow and red cabs in the town and makes a report on the sole basis of what he thinks he has seen. Because the accident occurred at night, the witness is not completely reliable, but it has been assessed that under similar circumstances, his probability of making a correct statement is four out of five (whether the true color of the cab is yellow or red). How should one use the information of the witness? Because of the uncertainty, we should formulate our conclusion in terms of probabilities. Is it more likely then that a red cab was involved in the accident? Although the witness reports red and is correct 80 percent of the time, the answer is no.

Recall that there are many more yellow cabs. The red sighting can be explained either by a yellow cab hitting the pedestrian (an event of high probability *a priori*) and being incorrectly identified (an event with low probability), or a red cab hitting him (with low probability) and being correctly identified (with high probability). Both the *a priori* probability of the event and the precision of the signal have to be used in

---

[1] The example is adapted from Salop (1987).

the evaluation of the signal. Bayes's rule provides the method for the updating of the probabilities. Let $\mathcal{R}$ be the event "a red cab is involved," and $\mathcal{Y}$ the event "a yellow cab is involved." Likewise, let r (y) be the report "I have seen a red (yellow) cab." The probability of the event $\mathcal{R}$ conditional on the report r is denoted by $P(\mathcal{R}|r)$. By Bayes's rule,

$$P(\mathcal{R}|r) = \frac{P(r|\mathcal{R})P(\mathcal{R})}{P(r)} = \frac{P(r|\mathcal{R})P(\mathcal{R})}{P(r|R)P(\mathcal{R}) + P(r|\mathcal{Y})(1 - P(\mathcal{R}))}.$$

The probability that a red cab is involved before the testimony is heard is $P(\mathcal{R}) = 0.10$. The probability of a correct identification is $P(r|\mathcal{R})$ and is equal to 0.8. The probability of an incorrect identification is $P(r|\mathcal{Y})$ and is equal to 0.2. Hence,

$$P(\mathcal{R}|r) = \frac{0.8 \times 0.1}{0.8 \times 0.1 + 0.2 \times 0.9} = \frac{4}{13}.$$

This probability is much less than the precision of the witness, 80 percent, because a red observation is more likely to come from a wrong identification of a yellow cab than from a right identification of a red cab. The example illustrates the fundamental principle of Bayesian learning, i.e., how prior beliefs are amended by a signal.

The example also illustrates some difficulties that individuals may have in practical circumstances. Despite these difficulties,[2] all rational agents in this book are assumed to be Bayesians. The book will concentrate only on the difficulties of learning from others by rational agents. The study of social learning between agents with limited rationality is a task for the future.

A Witness with Historical Knowledge

Suppose now that the witness is a resident of the town who knows that only 10 percent of the cabs are red. In making his report, he tells the color that is the most likely according to his rational deduction. If he applies the Bayesian rule and knows his probability of making a mistake, he knows that a yellow cab is more likely to be involved. He will report "yellow" even if he thinks that he has seen a red cab. If he thinks he has seen a yellow one, he will also say "yellow." His private information (the color he thinks he has seen) is ignored in his report.

The occultation of the witness' information in his report does not matter if he is the only witness and if the recipient of the report attempts to assess the most likely event: the witness and the recipient of the report come to the same conclusion. Suppose, however, that there is a second witness with the same sighting skill (correct 80 percent of the time) and who also thinks he has seen a red cab. That witness who attempts to report the most likely event also says "yellow." The recipient of the two reports learns nothing from the reports. For him the accident was caused by a yellow cab with a probability of 90 percent.

---

[2] The ability of people to use Bayes's rule has been tested in experiments, (e.g., Holt and Anderson, 1996). Economic rationality has also been tested in experiments, with mixed results.

Recall that when the first witness came from out of town, he was not informed about the local history, and he gave an informative report, "red." That report may be inaccurate, but it provides information. Furthermore, it triggers more information from the second witness. After the report of the first witness, the probability of $\mathcal{R}$ increased from $\frac{1}{10}$ to $\frac{4}{13}$. When that probability of $\frac{4}{13}$ is conveyed to the second witness, he thinks that a red car is more likely. (This can be shown through an exercise by application of Bayes's rule).[3] He therefore reports red. The probability according to the inspector who hears the reports of the two witnesses is now raised to the level of the last (second) witness.

The example shows how the suppression of information from one agent (the first witness) leads to improved learning by the group of agents. Social learning may fail when individuals use rationally all of their available information. The interaction between rational individual learning and learning from others (social learning) will be recurrent throughout the book. Before presenting the analysis of learning from others, we review in this chapter some properties of rational (Bayesian) learning by a single individual.

2.1 The Bayesian Framework

COMMON KNOWLEDGE

In any model of social learning, there is a set of agents, which can be finite, countable, or a continuum. All agents know the structure of the model, i.e., they have the same values for nature's probabilities of the states, and they know how private signals are determined. This information is common knowledge: each agent knows the structure, knows that each agent knows the structure, knows that other agents know that each agent knows the structure, and so on. What an agent does not know is the realizations of the state and of the private signals.

The common knowledge of the structure of the model is a rather strong assumption, which will need to be relaxed in further studies on social learning. Given the current state of the literature, this assumption will be maintained here with a few exceptions.

The models presented in this book do not aim at "generality," a futile pursuit in economics. We will have a *canonical framework* and make very specific assumptions about the structure of private information. These "examples" will be used in order to facilitate the analysis and clarify the mechanisms of social learning. The results thus obtained will be general provided that we understand the essential properties of the restrictive assumptions. We investigate now these essential properties for the two main models of private informations that will be used in this book. All models of social learning contain the following elements.

---

[3] The right-hand side is now $0.8 \times 4/(0.8 \times 4 + 0.2 \times 13) = \frac{16}{29} > \frac{1}{2}$.

a. Prior Distribution for the State of Nature θ

Nature chooses a state $\theta \in \Theta$ according to some probability distribution. Throughout the book, Θ will be a subset of $\mathbb{R}^n$. One may assume that nature's probability distribution is known by all agents, but this assumption is not necessary. It is essential, however, that all the values of θ that have positive probability[4] in nature's distribution have also positive probability in the prior distribution of the agents: an agent does not rule out *a priori* any value of θ that can be chosen by nature. If the agent thinks that some value of θ is impossible, no Bayesian learning will change that.

b. Private Information

In most models of learning, each agent has private information on the state of nature. "Private" here means "known only to the agent and not observable directly by others." To model this information, we will assume that the agent receives a signal s that is *informative on θ*: s has a probability distribution that depends on θ.

c. Bayesian Inference

The agent uses his signal s to update his distribution on θ. Formally, suppose that the agent has a prior density[5] on θ, which is denoted by $f(\theta)$, and that the distribution of s conditional on θ has a density $\phi(s|\theta)$. Following the observation of the value s, the distribution on θ is updated to $f(\theta|s)$ using Bayes's rule:

$$(2.1) \qquad f(\theta|s) = \frac{\phi(s|\theta)\,f(\theta)}{\int \phi(s|\theta)\,f(\theta)\,d\theta}.$$

We can simply state that

$$f(\theta|s) \propto \phi(s|\theta)\,f(\theta),$$

which means that $f(\theta|s)$ is proportional to $\phi(s|\theta)\,f(\theta)$. The coefficient of proportionality is such that the integral of the density is one. An equivalent formulation is that for any two states θ_0 and θ_1,

$$(2.2) \qquad \frac{f(\theta_1|s)}{f(\theta_0|s)} = \frac{\phi(s|\theta_1)}{\phi(s|\theta_0)} \frac{f(\theta_1)}{f(\theta_0)}.$$

This formulation of Bayes's rule in terms of a *likelihood ratio* is particularly useful when there are only two states of nature. Obviously, the signal s should bring some information on θ: the functions $\phi(s|\theta_1)$ and $\phi(s|\theta_0)$ should be different for some positive probability measure on s.

---

[4] The term "positive probability" is meaningful only if the distributions are discrete (atomistic). We need not dwell here on the technicalities that are required if the distributions have densities.

[5] The updating formula is similar when the distributions have points with positive probabilities. See for example the introduction to this chapter.

d. Bayesian Learning with Finite States: The Log Likelihood Ratio

Assume there are a finite number of states θ_j. The Bayesian rule for the update of the probability of the states has a simple form when probability assessments are expressed in terms of the logarithm of the likelihood ratio (LLR throughout the book). Let λ be the LLR between two states before an observation x:

$$\lambda = \log\left(\frac{P(\theta_i)}{P(\theta_j)}\right).$$

After the observation of the random variable x, which depends on the state, the LLR is updated to λ' such that

(2.3) $$\lambda' = \lambda + \log\left(\frac{P(x|\theta_i)}{P(x|\theta_j)}\right).$$

The updating term on the right-hand side is *independent* of the agent's LLR. After the observation of a random event, all the agent's LLRs are translated by the same amount.

2.2 Binary and Gaussian Information

In the simplest binary model, there are two states of nature and each individual receives his information with a binary signal. In the Gaussian model, both the state of nature and the private signals are the realizations of Gaussian (normal) random variables. The binary model is a canonical model for bounded information, whereas the Gaussian model presents nice and intuitive properties of the learning process.

2.2.1 The Binary Model

The space of the states has two elements: $\theta \in \{\theta_0, \theta_1\}$ with $\theta_0 < \theta_1$. These values can be normalized to 0 and 1, the *bad* and the *good* state, respectively. The probability distribution of any agent is characterized by one number, the probability of the good state.

The private signal of an individual takes the value 1 or 0 with probabilities given in Table 2.1. In general there will be a string of independent private signals, but in this introduction we consider a single signal.

LEARNING FROM A BINARY SIGNAL

Let $P(\theta = j)$ be the probability of state j ($j = 0, 1$) for an agent with no private signal. An agent endowed with a signal s updates his probability of θ by using Bayes's rule. Because there are two states of nature, this rule is conveniently expressed in terms of likelihood ratios:

(2.4) $$\frac{P(\theta = 1 \mid s)}{P(\theta = 0 \mid s)} = \frac{P(s \mid \theta = 1)}{P(s \mid \theta = 0)} \cdot \frac{P(\theta = 1)}{P(\theta = 0)}.$$

TABLE 2.1 The binary model

		Signal	
		$s = 1$	$s = 0$
State of	$\theta = 1$	q	$1 - q$
Nature	$\theta = 0$	$1 - q'$	q'

Following the observation of the signal s, the likelihood ratio between the good and the bad states is updated with the *updating multiplier*:

$$\frac{P(s = 1 \mid \theta = 1)}{P(s = 1 \mid \theta = 0)} = \frac{q}{1 - q'}.$$

This quantity is greater than 1 if and only if $q + q' > 1$. In that case, a signal $s = 1$ increases the probability of the good state $\theta = 1$. It is a *good* signal. One sees immediately that this definition is arbitrary. If $q + q' < 1$, the signal $s = 0$ should be called the good signal.

THE SYMMETRIC BINARY SIGNAL (SBS)

The private signal is *symmetric* if $q' = q$. Symmetry does not restrict the generality of the analysis, and it simplifies its exposition. When the signal is symmetric, then by convention $s = 1$ is good news: $q > \frac{1}{2}$. When there is a string of signals, formula (2.4) can be applied repeatedly. A symmetric binary signal will often be used in this book and will be called a SBS. The parameter q will be called the *precision* of the binary signal, for an obvious reason.

2.2.2 The Gaussian Model

The state of nature is the realization of a normal random variable or vector. For simplicity of notation, θ is a real number and its distribution is denoted by $\mathcal{N}(\bar{\theta}, \sigma_\theta^2)$. The *precision* of the distribution is the reciprocal of the variance and is denoted by $\rho_\theta = 1/\sigma_\theta^2$. In this book, when dealing with normal distributions, we will use both the variance and the precision. The choice of the variable will depend on the context.

The private signal s has a normal (Gaussian) distribution and is defined by

$$s = \theta + \epsilon,$$

where ϵ is a noise that is independent of θ and normally distributed $\mathcal{N}(0, 1/\rho_\epsilon)$.

LEARNING FROM A GAUSSIAN SIGNAL

After the signal s is received, the updated distribution of θ is normal. The updating rule will be used in one of two forms, depending on the context.

If we use variances, the distribution is updated from $\mathcal{N}(m, \sigma^2)$ to $\mathcal{N}(m', \sigma'^2)$, where[6]

$$\sigma'^2 = \frac{\sigma^2 \sigma_\epsilon^2}{\sigma^2 + \sigma_\epsilon^2},$$

(2.5)

$$m' = \alpha s + (1 - \alpha)m \qquad \text{with} \quad \alpha = \frac{\sigma'^2}{\sigma_\epsilon^2}.$$

If we use the precision (the reciprocal of the variance), the distribution is updated from $\mathcal{N}(m, 1/\rho)$ to $\mathcal{N}(m', 1/\rho')$, where

$$\rho' = \rho + \rho_\epsilon,$$

(2.6)

$$m' = \alpha s + (1 - \alpha)m \qquad \text{with} \quad \alpha = \frac{\rho_\epsilon}{\rho'}.$$

The Gaussian model is very popular because of the simplicity of this learning rule, which can be described in words: (i) after the observation of a signal of precision ρ_ϵ, the precision of the subjective distribution is augmented by the same amount; (ii) the posterior mean is a weighted average of the signal and the prior mean, with weights proportional to the respective precisions. Because the *ex post* distribution is normal, the learning rule with a sequence of Gaussian signals that are independent conditional on θ is an iteration of (2.5).

The learning rule in the Gaussian model makes precise some general principles. These principles hold for a wider class of models, but only the Gaussian model provides such a simple formulation:

1. The normal distribution is summarized by the most intuitive two parameters of a distribution, the mean and the variance (or its reciprocal, the precision).
2. The updating rules for both the mean and the precision are *linear*. This makes any computation easier.
3. The weight of the private signal s depends on the noise-to-signal ratio in the most intuitive way. When the variance of the noise term, σ_ϵ^2, tends to zero, or equivalently its precision tends to infinity, the signal's weight α tends to one and the weight of the *ex ante* expected value of θ tends to zero. The expression of α provides a quantitative formulation of the trivial principle according to which *one relies more on a more precise signal*.
4. The signal s contributes to the information on θ, which is measured by the increase in the precision of θ. According to the previous result, the increment is exactly equal to the precision of the signal (the reciprocal of the variance of its noise). The contribution of a set of independent signals is the sum of their precisions. This property is plausible, but it rules out situations where new

---

[6] To prove these expressions, use the fundamental Bayesian equation (2.1) to show that the distribution of θ conditional on s is normal and that the precision and the mean are given by the previous equations.

information makes an agent less certain about θ, a point that is discussed further below.

5. More importantly, the increase in the precision of θ is *independent of the realization of the signal s* and can be computed *ex ante*. This is handy for the measurement of the information gain that can be expected from a signal. Such a measurement is essential to decide whether to receive the signal, either by purchasing it, or by delaying a profitable investment to wait for it.

6. The Gaussian model will fit particularly well with the quadratic payoff function and the decision problem, which will be studied later.

2.2.3 Comparison of the Two Models

In the binary model, the distinction between good and bad states is appealing. The probability distribution is given by one number. The learning rule with the binary signal is simple. These properties are convenient when solving exercises. The Gaussian model is convenient for other reasons, which were enumerated previously. It is important to realize that each of the two models embodies some deep properties.

THE EVOLUTION OF CONFIDENCE

When there are two states, the probability distribution is characterized by the probability μ of the good state. This value determines an index of confidence: if the two states are 0 and 1, the variance of the distribution is $\mu(1-\mu)$. Suppose that μ is near 1 and that new information arrives that reduces the value of μ. This information increases the variance of the estimate, i.e., it reduces the confidence in the estimate. In the Gaussian model, new signals cannot reduce the precision of the subjective distribution. They always reduce its variance.

BOUNDED AND UNBOUNDED PRIVATE INFORMATION

Another major difference between the two models is in the strength of the private information. In the binary model, a signal has bounded strength. In the updating formula (2.4), the multiplier is bounded. (It is either $q/(1-q')$ or $(1-q)/q'$.) When the signal is symmetric, the parameter q defines its precision. In the Gaussian model, the private signal is unbounded and the changes of the expected value of θ are unbounded. The boundedness of a private signal will play an important role in social learning: a bounded private signal is overwhelmed by a strong prior. (See the example at the beginning of the chapter.)

BINARY STATES AND GAUSSIAN SIGNALS

If we want to represent a situation where confidence may decrease and the private signal is unbounded, we may turn to a combination of the two previous models.

Assume that the state space Θ has two elements, $\Theta = \{\theta_0, \theta_1\}$, and the private signal is Gaussian:

(2.7) $s = \theta + \epsilon$ with $\epsilon \sim \mathcal{N}(0, 1/\rho_\epsilon^2)$.

Equation (2.3), which updates the LLR between θ_1 and θ_2, becomes

(2.8) $\lambda' = \lambda + \rho_\epsilon(\theta_1 - \theta_0)\left(s - \dfrac{\theta_1 + \theta_0}{2}\right).$

Because s is unbounded, the private signal has an unbounded effect on the subjective probability of a state. There are values of s such that the likelihood ratio after s is received is arbitrarily large.

2.2.4 The Rate of Convergence of Learning

The efficiency of a learning process may be measured by the rate of convergence of beliefs to the truth. This rate will have to be compared with a benchmark: no learning process can generate more information than the (fictitious) setting where the information of others is directly observable. That setting will therefore be used as a benchmark. We now compare the rates of convergence for the binary and the Gaussian signals.

BINARY SIGNALS

There are two states of nature, 0 and 1, and the agent receives a sequence of SBSs $\{s_t\}$ with precision q: $P(s_t = \theta|\theta) = q$. By use of the Bayesian updating in (2.3), the evolution of the LLR is given by

(2.9) $\lambda_{t+1} = \lambda_t + \zeta_t$ with $\zeta_t = 2a\left(s_t - \tfrac{1}{2}\right)$, $a = \log\left(\dfrac{q}{1-q}\right) > 0.$

Assume that the true state is $\theta = 0$. The variable s_t has a mean $1 - q$. One can easily verify that the random variable ζ_t has a bounded variance and a strictly negative mean, $-\overline{\gamma}$:

(2.10) $\overline{\gamma} = a(2q - 1) > 0.$

This expression shows that the LLR, λ_t, tends to $-\infty$. The belief (probability of state θ_1) in period t is equal to

$$\mu_t = \frac{e^{\lambda_t}}{1 + e^{\lambda_t}} \leq e^{\lambda_t}.$$

Therefore, the belief μ_t tends to 0 exponentially. A precise statement is provided in the next lemma.[7]

LEMMA 2.1 *Assume* $\theta = 0$. *For any* $\gamma \in (0, \overline{\gamma})$, $\overline{\gamma} > 0$ *defined in* (2.10), *if* $\mu_t = E[\theta|s_1, \ldots, s_t]$, *then* $\mu_t = e^{-\gamma t} z_t$ *where* z_t *tends to* 0 *almost surely.*

The variance of the distribution on θ in period t is $\mu_t(1 - \mu_t)$. When $t \to \infty$, $\mu_t \to 0$ and the variance tends to 0 like μ_t, i.e., exponentially.

GAUSSIAN SIGNALS

By assumption, the state θ is drawn from $\mathcal{N}(\mu_0, 1/\rho_0)$ and the signal in period t is $s_t = \theta + \epsilon_t$ with $\epsilon_t \sim \mathcal{N}(0, 1/\rho_\epsilon)$. For simplicity, assume $\mu_0 = 0$. From the standard equation of learning in the Gaussian model (2.5),

$$E[\theta|s_1, \ldots, s_t] = \frac{s_1 + \cdots + s_t}{t} \quad \text{and} \quad \text{Var}(\theta|s_1, \ldots, s_t) = \frac{1}{\rho_0 + t\rho_\epsilon}.$$

The variance tends to 0 like $1/t$. This does not mean that the convergence in the Gaussian model is slower than in the binary model.

A COMPARISON

In the Gaussian model, the signals have to provide information on an accurate "location" of θ, which can take any value in the continuum of real numbers. In the binary model, the two possible values of θ are well separated: without loss of generality, θ is either 0 or 1.

The variance tends to 0 relatively slowly in the Gaussian model because the receiver of a signal has to distinguish between arbitrarily close values of θ. If, however, the receiver already knows that the values of θ are in a discrete set, the Gaussian signals produce very fast convergence. This can be seen by considering the model that is specified in equation (2.7). From (2.8), the LLR between the two states θ_1 and θ_0 in period t is

$$\lambda_{t+1} = \lambda_t + \zeta_t \quad \text{with} \quad \zeta_t = \left(\frac{\theta_1 - \theta_0}{\sigma_\epsilon^2}\right)\left(s_t - \frac{\theta_0 + \theta_1}{2}\right).$$

Assume for simplicity that $\theta_0 = 0$ and $\theta_1 = 1$ and the true state $\theta = 0$. The variable ζ_t is normal with a mean $-1/(2\sigma_\epsilon^2)$. The argument in Lemma 2.1 applies. The convergence of the belief is exponential.

In the Gaussian model where the prior distribution of θ is normal, the sequence of Gaussian signals also leads to exponential convergence for values of θ that are

---

[7] Choose γ such that $0 < \gamma < \overline{\gamma}$. Let $v_t = \lambda_t + \gamma t$. We have $v_{t+1} = v_t + \zeta_t'$ with $E[\zeta_t'] = -(\overline{\gamma} - \gamma) < 0$. Therefore, $v_t = v_0 + \sum_{k=1}^{t-1} \zeta_k'$. $\sum_{k=1}^{n} \zeta_k'/n$ tends to $-(\overline{\gamma} - \gamma) < 0$ almost surely. Hence, $\sum_{k=1}^{t-1} \zeta_k'$ tends to $-\infty$ almost surely. Therefore, v_t tends to $-\infty$ and e^{v_t} tends to 0, almost surely. By definition of v_t, $\mu_t \leq e^{-\gamma t} e^{v_t}$.

distant from the true value. The precise formulation of that convergence is given in the following lemma. The proof is left to the reader (Exercise 2.2).

LEMMA 2.2 *Assume that the prior distribution of θ is normal and that the agent receives a signal $s_t = \theta + \epsilon_t$ in period t. Then for any $\alpha > 0$, there exist a_1, a_2, γ positive such that*

$$a_1 e^{-\gamma t} z_t < P(|\theta - \theta_0| > \alpha | s_1, \ldots, s_t) < a_2 e^{-\gamma t} z_t,$$

where θ_0 is the actual value of θ, and z_t is a positive random variable with a stationary distribution.

YOUNGSTERS AND OLD TIMERS IN A GAUSSIAN MODEL

A nice application of the learning rules with Gaussian distributions is found in a model of Prendergast and Stole (1996). There is a state of nature θ that is drawn from a normal distribution $\mathcal{N}(0, 1/\rho_\theta)$ and fixed at the beginning of time. There are two agents A and B. In each period t, each agent receives a noisy signal on θ, $s_t = \theta + \epsilon$. All signals are independent over time, conditional on θ. The precision of the signal of agent A is ρ_A (which is the same as the precision of the noise), and that of agent B is ρ_B with $\rho_A > \rho_B$: agent A is getting signals of higher precision. We have a fast learner (agent A) and a slow learner (agent B). Before the first signal, both agents have the same zero expected value on θ and the same precision ρ_θ. Each agent observes only his own signals. The question is: how does each agent change his expected value of θ over time? Loosely speaking: how do the two agents change their minds over time?

Let an agent's opinion be his expected value of θ. When an agent receives a signal, he forms a new opinion, which is an average of his *ex ante* opinion (derived from history), and the signal. (Recall the learning rule (2.5).) During the first few periods, the fast learner changes his mind more regarding his expected value of θ, than the slow learner, because his signal has a higher precision than the precision of history. After a while, though, the weight of history becomes greater for A than for B, because agent A has accumulated information from signals of higher precision. Intuition indicates that the fast learner will change his opinion less than the slow learner after some time. Prendergast and Stole (1996) formalize this argument. They show how each agent goes through two regimes: first, as a youngster, his opinion fluctuates relatively widely as he gets more signals; second, as an old timer, his opinion is settled and not sensitive to new signals. The length of the first regime depends on the precision of the private signals he receives. An agent who keeps changing his mind reveals that he is not getting accurate signals.[8] The model is presented in the appendix (Section 2.5) and is a good exercise about the learning rules.

---

[8] The contribution of the article is to show that an agent may thus alter his actions to fool an observer who knows the model and tries to evaluate the precision of the private signal.

The result of Prendergast and Stole rests on one of the properties of the Gaussian model: as time goes on, agents are more confident about their estimates. Such an optimistic view is not embedded in the binary model, where agents may become less confident after receiving more information (p. 26). In such a model, we could observe conformist youngsters and sudden drastic changes of beliefs in middle age.

2.3 Private Signals and Beliefs

An individual's knowledge is represented by his probability estimate of the state of nature. Such a probability estimate will be called a *belief*.

DEFINITION 2.1 *A belief is a probability distribution on the set of states of nature Θ.*

PRIVATE BELIEFS

The private information is modeled in the previous sections by private signals. We have seen how an individual converts a signal into a belief. The belief that is formed from the prior probability of the state and the private signal will be called the *private belief*. This is an endowment of the agent that represents all the individual's knowledge at the beginning of time. When the number of states is finite, it is often simpler to assume directly that agents are endowed with private beliefs.

2.3.1 Equivalence between Private Signals and Private Beliefs

Assume there are two states of nature, θ_0 and θ_1, and agents receive a private signal s with a density[9] $\phi(s|\theta)$, which satisfies the *monotone likelihood ratio property* (MLRP): $\phi(s|\theta_1)/\phi(s|\theta_0)$ is monotone in s. Using a suitable convention, we can assume that this ratio is increasing. Let $\overline{\mu}$ be nature's probability of state θ_1 and $\hat{\mu}(s)$ the belief of an agent with signal s, i.e., his probability of state θ_1. From (2.2),

$$(2.11) \qquad \frac{\hat{\mu}(s)}{1 - \hat{\mu}(s)} = \frac{\phi(s|\theta_1)}{\phi(s|\theta_0)} \frac{\overline{\mu}}{1 - \overline{\mu}}.$$

Let $f(\mu|\theta)$ be the density of the distribution of private beliefs in state θ. We have

$$f(\mu|\theta) = \phi(s|\theta) \frac{d\hat{\mu}(s)}{ds} \qquad \text{with} \quad \mu = \hat{\mu}(s).$$

Substituting in equation (2.11), we find that the densities of the beliefs in the two states satisfy the following equation:

$$\frac{f(\mu|\theta_1)}{f(\mu|\theta_0)} = \frac{\phi(\hat{\mu}^{-1}(\mu)|\theta_1)}{\phi(\hat{\mu}^{-1}(\mu)|\theta_0)} = \frac{\mu}{1 - \mu} \frac{1 - \overline{\mu}}{\overline{\mu}}.$$

---

[9] The discussion is identical when the distribution is discrete.

PROPORTIONAL PROPERTY

Assume there are two states of nature θ_0 and θ_1. The densities of beliefs in the two states satisfy the *proportional property* if

$$(2.12) \qquad \frac{f(\mu|\theta_1)}{f(\mu|\theta_0)} = \chi \frac{\mu}{1-\mu} \qquad \text{where } \chi \text{ is a constant.}$$

Assume now two densities $f^1(\mu)$ and $f^0(\mu)$ that satisfy the proportional property. Define the signal $s = \mu$. The distributions of beliefs are generated by the signal s with density $f(s|\theta_i) = f^i(s)$ and the initial probability $\overline{\mu}$ of state θ_1 such that $\chi = (1 - \overline{\mu})/\overline{\mu}$. These arguments show that there is an equivalence between the endowments of private signals and the endowments of private beliefs that satisfy the proportional property.

PROPOSITION 2.1 *Assume two states θ_0 and θ_1. The specifications of a probability for state θ_1 and a signal s with densities $\phi(s|\theta_1)$ and $\phi(s|\theta_0)$ are equivalent to the specifications of two densities of beliefs $f(\mu|\theta_1)$ and $f(\mu|\theta_0)$ that satisfy the proportional property.*

This proposition may be generalized to the case of an arbitrary number of states of nature. We now provide some examples of distributions of private beliefs, which will be used later in the book.

Two distributions that satisfy the proportional property satisfy the property of first-order stochastic dominance. The proof of the next result is left as an exercise.

PROPOSITION 2.2 *Let $f(\mu|\theta_1)$ and $f(\mu|\theta_0)$ be distributions of beliefs that satisfy (2.12) in the definition of the proportional property, and F^1 and F^2 be the associated cumulative distribution functions. Then F^1 dominates F^0 in the sense of first-order stochastic dominance: for any $\mu \in (0, 1)$, $F^1(\mu) \leq F^0(\mu)$.*

2.3.2 Examples of Distributions of Beliefs with Two States

IDENTICAL BELIEFS

Assume that there are N agents and that in state θ_1, m_1 of these agents (chosen randomly) are players, whereas the number of players in state θ_0 is m_0. This structure is common knowledge (i.e., each player knows the structure, knows that the other players know the structure and that the other players know that he knows the structure, and so on). A player gets a signal on θ from his own existence: if $\overline{\mu}$ is the *ex ante* probability of the state of nature (the public belief), the belief of each agent (probability of state θ_1) is μ with

$$(2.13) \qquad \frac{\mu}{1-\mu} = \frac{m_1}{m_0} \frac{\overline{\mu}}{1-\overline{\mu}}.$$

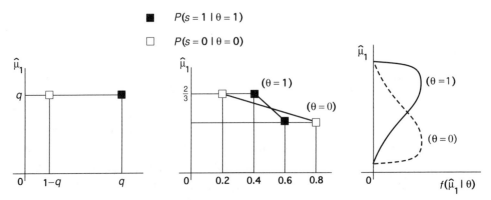

Figure 2.1 Distributions of private beliefs. The values of the private belief in the first period, $\hat{\mu}_1$, are measured on the vertical axis.

This case is convenient if we want a model with identical beliefs (as in the model with delays of Chamley and Gale, 1994). Note that the number of players is not the same in the two states of nature. Hence, the state has an effect on the real structure of the economy, and not only on the information structure. In this simple case, there is no restriction on the ratio m_1/m_0. For any such ratio and any belief μ, there is a public belief $\overline{\mu}$ such that equation (2.13) is satisfied.

TWO DIFFERENT BELIEFS AND BINARY SIGNALS

Assume now that the number of agents is independent of the state. Binary signals generate two values of the private beliefs, optimistic and pessimistic. Taking the general form of Table 2.1 and assuming a public belief $\overline{\mu}$, we find that these two values are such that

$$\frac{\mu^+}{1-\mu^+} = \frac{q}{1-q'}\frac{\overline{\mu}}{1-\overline{\mu}} \quad \text{and} \quad \frac{\mu^-}{1-\mu^-} = \frac{1-q}{q'}\frac{\overline{\mu}}{1-\overline{\mu}}.$$

We can also posit two values μ^+, μ^- and two probabilities π^1, π^0 such that the probability of being an optimist in state θ is π^θ. From Proposition 2.1, these parameters are compatible with the Bayesian construction if and only if they satisfy

$$\frac{\mu^+}{1-\mu^+} = \frac{\pi^1}{\pi^0}\frac{\overline{\mu}}{1-\overline{\mu}} \qquad \frac{\mu^-}{1-\mu^-} = \frac{1-\pi^1}{1-\pi^0}\frac{\overline{\mu}}{1-\overline{\mu}},$$

where $\overline{\mu}$ is a free parameter in the interval $(0, 1)$.

The previous two cases are illustrated in the first two panels of Figure 2.1. In the middle panel, the private signal is not symmetric: $P(s = 1|\theta = 1) = 0.4$ and $P(s = 0|\theta = 0) = 0.8$; the two states are equally likely. The case of atomless distributions with support of the densities in the interior of the interval $(0, 1)$ is illustrated in the third panel.

An important property of the information structure is whether the distribution of private beliefs is bounded or not. In an unbounded distribution, there are agents with arbitrarily strong beliefs (with μ arbitrarily close to 1 or to 0). The expression of a belief in terms of LLRs provides a simple definition.

DEFINITION 2.2 *A distribution of belief is bounded if the support of the distribution of LLRs is bounded.*

From Bayes's rule (2.3), if the distribution is bounded (unbounded) in some period, it is bounded (unbounded) in every period.

An example of an unbounded distribution with densities is generated by the private signal $s = \theta + \epsilon$, with a noise $\epsilon \sim \mathcal{N}(0, \sigma_\epsilon^2)$. Nature's probabilities of the two states θ_0 and θ_1 are identical, for simplicity. Conditional on the signal s, the LLR is $\lambda(s)$ with[10]

$$(2.14) \qquad \lambda(s) = \left(\frac{\theta_1 - \theta_0}{\sigma_\epsilon^2} \right) \left(s - \frac{\theta_1 + \theta_0}{2} \right).$$

The distributions of the LLR in the two states are Gaussian because $\lambda(s)$ is a linear function of s, which has a Gaussian distribution.

2.3.3 Other Constructions of Private Information

In all previous models of private information, the construction of private signals is in two steps: (i) the state of nature θ is drawn randomly; (ii) private signals are drawn randomly according to distributions that depend on the state θ. Some models are more tractable when the process is reversed: (i) the private signals are drawn randomly and independently; (ii) the state of nature is a *deterministic* function of the private signals. In this case, a private signal generates imperfect information about the state. The following example, which has been used by Gul and Lundholm (1995) and by Gale and Kariv (2002), illustrates the method.

Assume two agents, 1 and 2. Each agent i receives an independent signal s_i with a uniform distribution on the interval $[0, 1]$. The state is defined by $\theta = s_1 + s_2$. The structure can be generalized to a finite number of agents. This definition of the private signals may facilitate the inference when agents observe others' actions. The private belief of an agent with signal s is that θ is uniformly distributed on the interval $[s, s+1]$.

2.4 Martingales

Bayesian learning satisfies a strong property with respect to the revision of the distribution of the states of nature. Suppose that before receiving a signal s, our expected

---

[10] $\lambda(s) = \log(P(s|\theta = \theta_1)/P(s|\theta = \theta_0))$, with $P(s|\theta) = \exp(-(s-\theta)^2/(2\sigma_\epsilon^2))$.

value of a real number θ is $E[\theta]$. This expectation will be revised after the reception of s. Question: given the information that we have before receiving s, what is the expected value of the revision? Answer: zero. If the answer were not zero, we would incorporate it in the expectation of θ *ex ante*. This property is the *martingale property*. The similarity of this property to that of an efficient financial market is not fortuitous: in a financial market, updating is rational and it is rationally anticipated. Economists have often used martingales without knowing it.

The previous argument is intuitive. It is now formalized. Assume that information comes as a sequence of signals s_t, one signal per period. Assume further that these signals have a distribution that depends on θ. They may or may not be independent, conditional on θ, and their distribution is known. Define the *history* in period t as $h_t = (s_1, \ldots, s_t)$, and the expected value of θ in period t as $\mu_t = E[\theta|h_t]$. Because the history h_t is random, μ_t is a sequence of random variables, which will be shown to satisfy the martingale property.

In this book, the martingale property is defined for a sequence of real random variables as follows.[11]

DEFINITION 2.3 *The sequence of random variables X_t is a martingale with respect to the history $h_t = (s_1, \ldots, s_{t-1})$ if and only if*

$$X_t = E[X_{t+1}|h_t].$$

Suppose that an agent has a distribution on θ with mean $E[\theta]$ and receives a signal s with a distribution that depends on θ. By the rules for conditional expectations, $E\Big[E[\theta|s]\Big] = E[\theta]$, and the next result follows.[12]

PROPOSITION 2.3 *Let $\mu_t = E[\theta|h_t]$ with $h_t = (s_1, \ldots, s_{t-1})$. It satisfies the martingale property: $\mu_t = E[\mu_{t+1}|h_t]$.*

Let $\mathcal{A}$ be a set of values for θ, $\mathcal{A} \subset \Theta$, and consider the indicator function $I_{\mathcal{A}}$ for the set $\mathcal{A}$, which is the random variable given by

$$I_{\mathcal{A}}(\theta) = \begin{cases} 1 & \text{if } \theta \in \mathcal{A}, \\ 0 & \text{if } \theta \notin \mathcal{A}. \end{cases}$$

Using $P(\theta \in \mathcal{A}) = E[I_{\mathcal{A}}]$ and applying the previous proposition to the random variable $I_{\mathcal{A}}$ gives the next result.

---

[11] A useful reference is Grimmet and Stirzaker (1992).

[12] Assume for example that θ has a density $g(\theta)$, and that s has a density $\phi(s|\theta)$ conditional on θ. Let $\psi(\theta|s)$ be the density of θ conditional on s. By Bayes's rule, $\psi(\theta|s) = \phi(s|\theta)g(\theta)/\phi(s)$, with $\phi(s) = \int \phi(s|\theta)g(\theta)d\theta$. With $\int \phi(s|\theta)ds = 1$ for any θ,

$$E\Big[E[\theta|s]\Big] = \int\Big(\int \theta\psi(\theta|s)d\theta\Big)\phi(s)ds = \int\int \phi(s|\theta)\theta g(\theta)ds\,d\theta = \int \theta g(\theta)d\theta$$
$$= E[\theta].$$

PROPOSITION 2.4 *The probability assessment of an event by a Bayesian agent is a martingale: for an arbitrary set $A \subset \Theta$, let $\mu_t = P(\theta \in A | h_t)$, where h_t is the history of informations before period t; then $\mu_t = E[\mu_{t+1} | h_t]$.*

The likelihood ratio between two states θ_0 and θ_1 cannot be a martingale given the information of an agent. However, if the state is assumed to take a particular value, then the likelihood ratio may be a martingale.

PROPOSITION 2.5 *Conditional on $\theta = \theta_0$, the likelihood ratio $P(\theta = \theta_1 | h_t)/P(\theta = \theta_0 | h_t)$ is a martingale.*

This result has an interesting application. Assume two states θ_0 and θ_1, and let $\mu_t = P(\theta = \theta_1 | h_t)$. Assume further that the true state is θ_0 and that the process of learning is such that the belief converges to the truth: μ_t converges to 0. The same is true for the likelihood ratio $\mu_t/(1 - \mu_t)$. However, the previous proposition implies that $\mu_t/(1 - \mu_t)$ is a martingale. Therefore, its expected value cannot converge to 0. The likelihood ratio converges to 0, but for some histories it becomes arbitrarily large. The probabilities of these histories are vanishingly small. The interesting fact is that in some models μ_t may be bounded. In that case, learning cannot converge to the truth.

PROPOSITION 2.6 *Assume two states θ_0, θ_1, and let $\mu_t = P(\theta = \theta_1 | h_t)$. If μ_t is bounded ($\mu_t < M$ for some finite M), then μ_t cannot converge to 0 in probability if the true state is θ_0.*

The argument will be used later to show in a simple model that a selling firm managed by a sequence of myopic individuals cannot learn its demand curve (Section 8.1.1). The proof is left as an exercise.

2.4.1 Convergence of Beliefs

The martingale property is a wonderful tool in Bayesian learning because of the *martingale convergence theorem* (MCT). Consider a Bayesian rational agent who receives a sequence of signals. Let his belief be his subjective probability assessment of an event, $\{\theta \in A\}$, for some fixed $A \subset \Theta$. Can the agent keep changing his belief in endless random fluctuations? Or does this belief converge to some value (possibly incorrect)? The answer is simple: it must converge.

The belief must converge because the probability assessment is a bounded martingale. The convergence of a bounded martingale, in a sense that will be made explicit, is a great result that is intuitive. The essence of a martingale is that its changes cannot be predicted, like the walk of a drunkard in a straight alley. The sides of the alley are the bounds of the martingale. If the changes of direction of the drunkard cannot be predicted, the only possibility is that these changes gradually taper off. For example, the drunkard cannot bounce against the side of the alley: once he hits the side, the direction of his next move would be predictable.

THEOREM 2.1 (Martingale Convergence Theorem) *If μ_t is a martingale with $E[\mu_t^2] < M < \infty$ for some M and all t, then there exists a random variable μ such that μ_t converges to μ almost surely and in mean square.*

Most of the social learning in this book will be about probability assessments that the state of nature belongs to some set $A \subset \Theta$. By Proposition 2.4, the probability assessments satisfy the martingale property. They are obviously bounded by 1. Therefore they converge to some value.

PROPOSITION 2.7 *Let A be a subset of Θ and μ_t be the probability assessment $\mu_t = P(\theta \in A | h_t)$, where h_t is a sequence of random variables in previous periods. Then there exists a random variable μ^* such that $\mu_t \to \mu^*$ almost surely and in mean square.*

We can apply the previous result to the set $A = \{\theta | \theta \leq \hat{\theta}\}$ for any value $\hat{\theta} \in \mathbb{R}^n$. We have then the next result, which shows that the distribution of θ converges to a limit distribution.

PROPOSITION 2.8 *Let $F_t(\theta)$ be the cumulative distribution function (c.d.f.) of $\theta \in \Theta \subset \mathbb{R}^n$, conditional on h_t. Then there exists a function $F^*(\theta)$ such that $F_t(\theta) \to F^*(\theta)$ almost surely and in mean square.*

A Heuristic Remark on the Proof of the Martingale Convergence Theorem

The main intuition of the proof is important for our understanding of Bayesian learning. It is a formalization[13] of the metaphor of the drunkard. In words, the definition of a martingale states that agents do not anticipate systematic errors. This implies that the updating difference $\mu_{t+1} - \mu_t$ is uncorrelated with μ_t. The same property holds for more distant periods: conditional on the information in period t, the random variables $\mu_{t+k+1} - \mu_{t+k}$ are uncorrelated for $k \geq 0$. Because

$$\mu_{t+n} - \mu_t = \sum_{k=1}^{n} \mu_{t+k} - \mu_{t+k-1},$$

we have, conditional on h_t,

$$\text{Var}(\mu_{t+n}) = \sum_{k=1}^{n} \text{Var}(\mu_{t+k} - \mu_{t+k-1}).$$

Because $E[\mu_{t+n}^2]$ is bounded, $\text{Var}(\mu_{t+n})$ is bounded: there exists A such that

---

[13] The proof is given in Grimmet and Stirzaker (1992). The different notions of convergence of a random variable are recalled in the appendix (Section 2.5).

for any n, $\displaystyle\sum_{k=1}^{n} \mathrm{Var}(\mu_{t+k} - \mu_{t+k-1}) \leq A.$

Because the sum is bounded, truncated sums after date T must converge to zero as $T \to \infty$: for any $\epsilon > 0$, there exists T such that for all $n > T$,

$$\mathrm{Var}(\mu_{T+n} - \mu_T) = \sum_{k=1}^{n} \mathrm{Var}(\mu_{T+k} - \mu_{T+k-1}) < \epsilon.$$

The amplitudes of all the variations of μ_t beyond any period T become vanishingly small as $t \to 0$. Therefore μ_t converges[14] to some value μ_∞. The limit value is in general random and depends on the history.

RATIONAL (BAYESIAN) AND NONRATIONAL LEARNING

The application of the MCT to Bayesian learning is remarkable: in order to see whether the Bayesian *learning from the history* converges, one looks *into the future* and uses the fact that the future changes of beliefs must be bounded and therefore eventually tend to zero. This deep property distinguishes rational Bayesian learning from other forms of learning. Many adaptive (mechanical) rules of learning with fixed weights from past signals are not Bayesian and do not lead to convergence. In Kirman (1993), agents follow a mechanical rule that can be compared to ants searching for sources of food, and their beliefs fluctuate randomly and endlessly.

How can such an argument about the future determine a property about learning from the past? The linchpin between the past and the future is of course the martingale property itself: when the learning is rational (based on conditional probabilities), future changes that can be predicted should be incorporated in the current beliefs, which are based on learning from the past.

The next result shows that a Bayesian agent who learns from history cannot be completely wrong: if his initial probability assessment of the true state is strictly positive, then his probability assessment of the true state in period t cannot be vanishingly small. Because his probability assessment tends to some limit by the MCT, that limit cannot be zero.

PROPOSITION 2.9 (Learning cannot be totally wrong, asymptotically) *Let* $\Theta = \{\theta_1, \ldots, \theta_K\}$ *be the finite set of states of nature,* $\mu_t = \{\mu_t^1, \ldots, \mu_t^K\}$ *the probability assessment of a Bayesian agent in period t, and* $\mu_1^1 > 0$, *where* θ_1 *is the true state. Then for any* $\epsilon > 0$,

$$P(\mu_t < \epsilon) < \epsilon/\mu_1^1.$$

If $\overline{\mu}^1$ *is the limit value of* μ_t^1, $P(\overline{\mu}^1 = 0) = 0$.

---

[14] The convergence of μ_t is similar to the Cauchy property in a compact set for a sequence $\{x_t\}$: if $\sup_k |x_{t+k} - x_t| \to 0$ when $t \to \infty$, then there is x^* such that $x_t \to x^*$. The main task of the proof is to analyze carefully the convergence of μ_t.

Under Bayesian learning, if the subjective distribution on θ converges to a point, it must converge to the truth.

Proof

Consider the set A of values of μ_t^1 such that $|\mu_\epsilon^1| < \varepsilon$. Let H_t be the set of histories h_t such that $\mu_t^1 \in A$. $P(\mu_t^1 \in A) = P(h_t \in H_t)$. For any history h_t,

$$\mu_t^1 = P(\theta = \theta_1|h_t) = \frac{P(h_t|\theta = \theta_1)\mu_1^1}{P(h_t)}.$$

Therefore,

$$P(h_t|\theta = \theta_1) = \frac{\mu_t^1}{\mu_1^1}P(h_t) \leq \frac{\varepsilon}{\mu_1^1}P(h_t),$$

$$P(h_t \in H_t|\theta = \theta_1) = \frac{\varepsilon}{\mu_1^1}P(h_t \in H_t) \leq \frac{\epsilon}{\mu_1^1}. \qquad \blacksquare$$

EXERCISES

EXERCISE 2.1 Application of Bayes's rule

Assume that an agent undertakes a project that succeeds (fails) with probability θ $(1 - \theta)$, where θ is drawn from a uniform distribution on $(0, 1)$.

1. Determine the *ex post* distribution of θ for the agent after the failure of the project.
2. Assume that the project is repeated and fails n consecutive times. The outcomes are independent with the same probability θ. Determine an algebraic expression for the density of θ of this agent. Discuss intuitively the property of this density.

EXERCISE 2.2 Proof of Lemma 2.2

To prove the lemma,

1. show that $\pi_t = P(\theta > \alpha|s_1, \ldots, s_t) = (1/\sqrt{2\pi})\int_{1/2\sigma_t - \nu}^{\infty} e^{-u^2/2}\,du$, where ν is distributed $\mathcal{N}(0, 1)$ and $\sigma_t^2 = \sigma_\epsilon^2/t$;
2. find suitable upper and lower bounds of the integral for the conclusion of the proof.

EXERCISE 2.3

Prove Proposition 2.2.

2.5 Appendix

2.5.1 Some Definitions Regarding Convergence

A careful analysis of the convergence of beliefs and actions in social learning requires the construction of a probability space. Most studies avoid that task, which is cumbersome, and prefer to rely on the intuition of the reader. Notable exceptions are Easley and Kiefer (1988) and Bala and Goyal (1995).

DEFINITION 2.4 *Let X_1, X_2, . . . , X be random variables on some probability space $(\Omega, \mathcal{F}, P)$. We say that*

(a) $X_n \to X$ *almost surely, written* $X_n \overset{a.s.}{\to} X$, *if* $\{\omega \in \Omega : X_n(\omega) \to X(\omega) \text{ as } n \to \infty\}$ *is an event whose probability is* 1.

(b) $X_n \to X$ *in r th mean, where* $r \geq 1$, *written* $X_n \overset{r}{\to} X$, *if* $E[|X_n^r|] < \infty$ *for all n and* $E[|X_n - X|^r] \to 0$ *as* $n \to \infty$.

(c) $X_n \to X$ *in probability, written* $X_n \overset{P}{\to} X$, *if* $P(|X_n - X| \geq \epsilon) \to 0$ *as* $n \to \infty$.

(d) $X_n \to X$ *in distribution, written* $X_n \overset{D}{\to} X$, *if* $P(X_n \leq x) \to P(X \leq x)$ *as* $n \to \infty$ *for all points x at which $F_X(x)$ is continuous.*

The only property that requires some comment is that convergence in probability does not imply convergence almost surely. Think of a random process, say a probability assessment μ_t of some state. If $\mu_t \to 0$ in probability, the probability that μ_t is greater than some arbitrary value ϵ tends to zero. However, we could have that for any history, $\mu_t > \epsilon$ infinitely often (with the probability of that event in a period t tending to 0 as $t \to \infty$). In that case, μ_t never tends to 0. Examples of convergence in probability that do not imply convergence almost surely are simple to find. However, at this stage, there is no study of social learning with an example of convergence in probability and no convergence almost surely.

THEOREM 2.2 (Grimmett and Stirzaker, 1992) *The following implications hold: For any $r \geq 1$,*

$$\left. \begin{array}{c} (X_n \overset{a.s.}{\to} X) \\ (X_n \overset{r}{\to} X) \end{array} \right\} \Rightarrow (X_n \overset{P}{\to} X) \Rightarrow (X_n \overset{D}{\to} X).$$

If $r \geq s$, then $(X_n \overset{r}{\to} X) \Rightarrow (X_n \overset{s}{\to} X)$.

2.5.2 The Model of Youngsters and Old Timers

The expectation of an agent at the beginning of period t is defined here as $\mu_t = E[\theta | h_t]$ and depends on the history $h_t = \{s_1, \ldots, s_{t-1}\}$ of the signals he has received. It varies over time as the agent gets more signals. The variability of the expectation between consecutive periods is characterized by the variance of the expectation conditional on all the information available at the beginning of the period, $\text{Var}(\mu_{t+1} - \mu_t | h_t)$. The relation between the variability of the changes and the precision of the signals is characterized by the next result, which is proven at the end of the section.

PROPOSITION 2.10 *Let* $\mu_t = E[\theta|h_t]$, *where* $h_t = \{s_1, \ldots, s_{t-1}\}$ *is a string of independent signals with distribution* $\mathcal{N}(\theta, 1/\rho)$. *The variance of the change of the expectation* μ_t *from period* t *to period* $t + 1$, $\mathrm{Var}(\mu_{t+1}|h_t)$, *is an increasing (decreasing) function of the precision of the individual signals,* ρ, *if and only if* ρ *is smaller (greater) than the critical value* ρ^* *defined by*

$$\rho^* = \rho_\theta / \sqrt{t(t-1)}.$$

Given the precision ρ of the signals of an agent, the previous equation defines a critical value of time, $t^*(\rho)$:

$$t^*(\rho)\Big(t^*(\rho) - 1\Big) = \left(\frac{\rho_\theta}{\rho}\right)^2.$$

The periods $t < t^*(\rho)$ form the learning regime of the "youngsters" during which the variance of the change of belief increases with the precision of an agent's signal. When $t > t^*(\rho)$, the agent is an "old timer" who adjusts less when his precision is higher.

COROLLARY 2.1 *For a given* ρ, *the learning phase extends to the smallest number* t^* *such that*

$$t^*(t^* - 1) = \rho_\theta^2 / \rho^2.$$

The length of the learning phase is inversely related to ρ. The property is intuitive: an agent learns more rapidly with signals of high precision than of low precision. He changes his mind rapidly during a few periods, after which his opinion does not move very much. An agent with signals of low precision keeps changing his mind (by a small magnitude) for a larger number of periods.

From Proposition 2.10, in each period t there is a value ρ^* that separates high-precision agents (with $\rho > \rho^*$) who are in an adjusting phase from low-precision agents (with $\rho < \rho^*$) in a learning phase. The former have an *ex ante* variance of action that is a decreasing function of their precision ρ, whereas the opposite is true for the latter. Suppose now that an outside observer attempts to evaluate the precision of the private signal received by an agent. The evaluator observes only the actions taken by the agent, which depend on his estimate of θ, μ_t, and the evaluation. An agent has an incentive to change less than he would with no evaluation, because he wants to show that he already knows much (that his ρ is high). Prendergast and Stole (1996) analyze the distortion that is created by the evaluation of the agent's actions.

Proof of Proposition 2.10
By use of the learning rule with Gaussian distribution (2.5), the expected value of θ at the end of period t is $\mathcal{N}(\mu_{t+1}, \rho_{t+1})$ with

$$\mu_{t+1} = \frac{\rho}{\rho_\theta + t\rho} s_t + \left(\frac{\rho_\theta + (t-1)\rho}{\rho_\theta + t\rho}\right)\mu_t.$$

The weight on the new signal s_t increases with ρ. Note, however, that the weight does not tend to 1 as $\rho \to \infty$ (as it would in the first period), because a high ρ means that previous estimates of θ have also a high precision (because they are made with signals of high precision). At the beginning of period t, the agent knows that his end-of-period expectation is a random variable that is linear in the signal s with a variance equal to

$$\text{Var}(\mu_t | h_t) = \frac{1}{(t + \rho_\theta/\rho)^2} \text{Var}(s_t | h_t).$$

Because $s_t = \theta + \epsilon_t$,

$$\text{Var}(s_t | h_t) = \text{Var}(\theta | h_t) + \frac{1}{\rho} = \frac{1}{\rho_\theta + (t-1)\rho} + \frac{1}{\rho}.$$

Substituting in the previous expression, we obtain

$$(2.15) \qquad \text{Var}(\mu_t | h_t) = \frac{\rho}{(\rho_\theta + t\rho)(\rho_\theta + (t-1)\rho)}.$$

For $t \geq 2$, this variance is a nonmonotone function of ρ. For large ρ, the variance decreases toward 0 as $\rho \to \infty$. For a given t, because the agent has learned so much in the past ($t \geq 2$), history becomes more important compared with a new signal when ρ increases. The converse is true when ρ is small. The maximum of the variance is attained for the value ρ^*, which depends on the period t as specified in the proposition.   ∎

3 Social Learning with a Common Memory

Actions speak louder than words.

The basic model of learning from others' actions is presented. Individual actions are the means of communication between agents. When the set of actions is sufficiently large and the actions are observed perfectly, social learning is efficient. When actions are observed through a noise, the public information in history slows down social learning.

Why learn from others' actions? Because these actions reflect something about their information. Why don't we exchange information directly using words? People may not be able to express their information well. They may not speak the same language. They may even try to deceive us. What are we trying to find? A good restaurant, a good movie, a tip on the stock market, whether to delay an investment or not, etc. Other people know something about it, and their knowledge affects their behavior, which, we can trust, will be self-serving. By looking at their behavior, we will infer something about what they know. This chain of arguments will be introduced here and developed in other chapters. We will see how the transmission of information may or may not be efficient and may lead to herd behavior, to sudden changes of widely believed opinions, etc.

For actions to speak and to speak well, they must have a sufficient vocabulary and be intelligible. In the first model of this chapter, individuals are able to fine-tune their action in a sufficiently rich set, and their decision process is perfectly known. In such a setting, actions reflect perfectly the information of each acting individual. This case is a benchmark in which social learning is equivalent to the direct observation of others' private information. Social learning is efficient in the sense that private actions convey private information perfectly.

Actions can reveal private information perfectly only if the individuals' decision processes are known. Surely, however, private decisions depend on private information and on personal parameters that are not observable. When private decisions depend on unobservable idiosyncrasies, or equivalently when their observation by others is garbled by noise, the process of social learning can be much slower than in the efficient case (Vives, 1993).

3.1 A Canonical Model of Social Learning

The purpose of a canonical model is to present a structure that is sufficiently simple and flexible to be a tool of analysis for a number of issues. Most models in this book are built with the following blocks:

- the structure of information,
- the payoff function and the action set,
- the observability of others.

3.1.1 The Model

THE INFORMATION ENDOWMENTS

We want to analyze how the information of individuals is spread through the observations of their actions. In order to isolate this process, we assume that the information of all agents is given at the beginning of time. This information comes in two parts, as in the previous chapter:

1. The *state of nature* is the value of a parameter θ belonging to a set Θ: $\theta \in \Theta$. By assumption, θ is the realization of a random variable that takes values in the set Θ and cannot be observed directly by anyone. By an abuse of notation, θ denotes both the random variable and its realization.
2. There are N individuals. (In general, N is finite, but there could be a countable set of agents or even a continuum.) Each individual i has *private information* in the form of a *private signal* s_i: it is a random variable whose distribution depends on θ; the value of the signal gives some information on the true value of θ. Private signals are by definition not observable by others. Without loss of generality, private signals are independent conditional on the state of nature θ.

We saw in the last chapter how different private signals generate a diversity of private beliefs. At this stage, it may be better to model private information by a private signal. Recall that a *private belief* is an endowment and does not change over time. The *belief* of an agent in some period t will depend on his observations before that period and will be called simply his belief in period t.

ACTIONS AND PAYOFFS

Each agent i can take once an action x_i in the set Ξ, $x_i \in \Xi$. (Without loss of generality, the set of feasible actions Ξ is the same for all agents.) If the state is θ and agent i takes the action x_i, he gets the payoff $u(x_i, \theta)$. For simplicity, the function u is the same for all agents. There could be different functions for different agents, but the important assumption is that this function is known to all agents. Later, this assumption will be relaxed. When an agent makes a decision under imperfect information, he has a subjective probability on θ and his payoff is $U = E_i[u(x_i, \theta)]$, where the expectation E_i is measured on θ given all the information of agent i at the time he takes his action.

Because agents "speak" through their actions, the definition of the action set Ξ is critical. A language with many words may convey more possibilities for communication than a language with few words. Individuals will learn more from each other about a parameter θ when the actions are in an interval of real numbers than when the actions are restricted to be either zero or one.

TOOL 1: BINARY ACTIONS

Choosing a restaurant, adopting a standard, etc., imply a zero–one decision. To represent the decision process with discrete actions, we assume that the action set is reduced to two elements: $\Xi = \{0, 1\}$. The state space Θ has also two elements, $\Theta = \{0, 1\}$. (The discreteness of Θ is less important and is assumed only for simplicity.) The payoff is given by $u(x, \theta) = \theta - c$, with $0 < c < 1$.

The investment has a positive payoff in the good state ($\theta = 1$) and a negative payoff in the bad state ($\theta = 0$). Under uncertainty, the payoff of investment is $E[\theta] - c$. In general, if $x \in \{0, 1\}$, the payoff can be written as

$$(3.1) \qquad u(x) = \Big(E[\theta] - c \Big)x, \qquad 0 < c < 1, \quad x \in \{0, 1\}.$$

The binary model will be analyzed in detail in the next chapter.

TOOL 2: THE QUADRATIC PAYOFF

A standard way to model a decision process with a continuum of actions is to assume that the agent chooses a real number x that maximizes the expected value of the quadratic payoff function

$$(3.2) \qquad u(x, \theta) = -E\Big[(x - \theta)^2\Big].$$

This function has some handy properties. The first one pertains to the decision rule. The optimal value of x is obviously given by

$$x^* = E[\theta].$$

This decision rule is the same when the payoff is $u(x, \theta) = 2\theta x - x^2$. If x stands for the scale of an investment, the first term of this expression represents the productivity of the investment. The second term represents the cost of the investment.

When the payoff function is given by (3.2), the payoff of the optimizing agent is

$$U = -\mathrm{Var}(\theta).$$

The mean and the variance of the belief, which are the two most important parameters of the distribution (the only ones, if the distribution is normal), have a nice interpretation: they are equal to the optimal action and to the negative of the payoff.

PUBLIC INFORMATION AND HISTORY

In this chapter and the next, agents are ordered in an *exogenous sequence*. Agent t, $t \geq 1$, chooses his action in period t. We define the *history* of the economy in period t as the sequence

$$h_t = \{x_1, \ldots, x_{t-1}\} \qquad \text{with} \quad h_0 = \emptyset.$$

Agent t knows the history of past actions h_t before making a decision.

To summarize, at the beginning of period t (before agent t makes a decision), the *knowledge that is common to all agents* is defined by

- the distribution of θ at the beginning of time,
- the distributions of private signals and the payoff functions of all agents,
- the history h_t of previous actions.

We will assume in Chapters 3 to 7 that agents cannot observe the payoff of the actions of others. Whether this assumption is justified or not depends on the context. It is relevant for investment over the business cycle: given the lags between investment expenditures and their returns, one can assume that investment decisions carry the sole information. Later in the book, we will analyze other mechanisms of social learning. For the sake of clarity, it is best to focus on each one of them separately.

3.1.2 The Process of Social Learning

The process of social learning is illustrated in Figure 3.1. In any arbitrary period t ($t \geq 1$), the probability distribution on θ that is based solely on the public information (including the history h_t) will be called the *public belief*. Its c.d.f. is denoted by $F(\theta|h_t)$.

Agent t combines the public belief on θ with his private information (the signal s_t) to form his belief, which has a c.d.f. $F(\theta|h_t, s_t)$. He then chooses the action x_t to maximize his payoff $E[u(\theta, x_t)]$, conditional on his belief.

All remaining agents know the payoff function of agent t (but not the realization of the payoff), and the decision model of agent t. They use the observation of x_t as a signal on the information of agent t, i.e., his private signal s_t. The action of an agent is a message on his information. The social learning depends critically on how this message conveys information on the private belief. The other agents update the public belief on θ once the observation x_t is added to the history h_t: $h_{t+1} = (h_t, x_t)$. The distribution $F(\theta|h_t)$ is updated to $F(\theta|h_{t+1})$.

3.2 Efficient Learning

Social learning is efficient when an individual's action reveals completely his private information. This occurs when the action set that defines the vocabulary of social

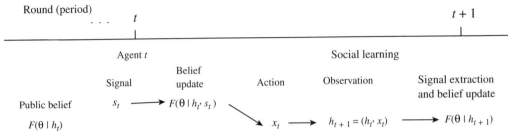

Figure 3.1 Actions and learning. The process of social learning is represented in period t. Agent t forms his belief and then chooses an optimal action x_t. The action is a message about his belief.

learning is sufficiently large. We begin with the Gaussian–quadratic model. Efficient social learning is obviously not restricted to that model, but the quadratic model will turn out to be so useful in this book that the reader had better become familiar with its analytics now.

3.2.1 The Gaussian–Quadratic Model

The model is built with the Gaussian information structure of Section 2.2.2 and the quadratic payoff in Tool 2.

- Nature's parameter θ is chosen randomly before the first period according to a normal distribution $\mathcal{N}(\bar{\theta}, 1/\rho_\theta)$. Because we focus on the social learning of a given state of nature, the value of θ does not change once it is set.
- There is a countable number of individuals, $i = 1, \ldots$. Each individual i has one private signal s_i. These signals are equal to the true value θ plus a noise :

$$s_i = \theta + \epsilon_i.$$

The noise terms ϵ_i are independent across agents and normally distributed $\mathcal{N}(0, 1/\rho_\epsilon)$. All individuals have the same payoff function $U(x) = -E[(x - \theta)^2]$. Individual t chooses his action $x_t \in \mathbb{R}$ once and for all in period t: the order of the individual actions is set exogenously.

- The public information at the beginning of period t is made of the initial distribution $\mathcal{N}(\bar{\theta}, 1/\rho_\theta)$ and of the history of previous actions $h_t = (x_1, \ldots, x_{t-1})$.

Suppose that the public belief on θ in period t is given by the normal distribution $\mathcal{N}(\mu_t, 1/\rho_t)$. This assumption is obviously true for $t = 1$ with $\mu_1 = \bar{\theta}$ and $\rho_1 = \rho_\theta$. We will show by induction that it is true in every period. In any period, the evolution of the public belief goes through the three steps illustrated in Figure 3.1: (i) the determination of the private belief of agent t; (ii) the action x_t of agent t; (iii) the inference by others from the observation of x_t and the updating of the public belief on θ for the next period.

(i) The Belief of Agent t

The belief is obtained from the Bayesian updating of the public belief $\mathcal{N}(\mu_t, 1/\rho_t)$ with the private information $s_t = \theta + \epsilon$. By using the Bayesian formulae with Gaussian distributions (2.5), the belief of agent t is $\mathcal{N}(\tilde{\mu}_t, 1/\tilde{\rho}_t)$ with

$$(3.3) \qquad \begin{aligned} \tilde{\mu}_t &= (1 - \alpha_t)\mu_t + \alpha_t s_t \qquad \text{with} \quad \alpha_t = \frac{\rho_\epsilon}{\rho_\epsilon + \rho_t}, \\ \tilde{\rho}_t &= \rho_t + \rho_\epsilon. \end{aligned}$$

(ii) The Private Decision

The agent maximizes $-E[(x - \theta)^2]$. Because the marginal payoff is $E[\theta] - x$, the agent chooses the action x_t equal to his expected value of θ: $x_t = \tilde{\mu}_t$.

From the specification of $\tilde{\mu}_t$ in (3.3),

$$(3.4) \qquad x_t = (1 - \alpha_t)\mu_t + \alpha_t s_t.$$

(iii) Social Learning

The decision rule of agent t and the variables α_t, μ_t are known to all agents. From equation (3.4), *the observation of the action x_t reveals perfectly the private signal s_t.* This is a key property. The public information at the end of period t is identical to the information of agent t: $\mu_{t+1} = \tilde{\mu}_t$ and $\rho_{t+1} = \tilde{\rho}_t$. Hence,

$$(3.5) \qquad \begin{aligned} \mu_{t+1} &= (1 - \alpha_t)\mu_t + \alpha_t s_t \qquad \text{with} \quad \alpha_t = \frac{\rho_\epsilon}{\rho_\epsilon + \rho_t}, \\ \rho_{t+1} &= \rho_t + \rho_\epsilon. \end{aligned}$$

In period $t + 1$, the belief is still normally distributed $\mathcal{N}(\mu_{t+1}, 1/\rho_{t+1})$, and the process can be iterated as long as there is an agent remaining in the game. The history of actions $h_t = (x_1, \ldots, x_{t-1})$ is informationally equivalent to the sequence of signals $(s_1, \ldots, s_{t-1})$.

Convergence

The precision of the public belief increases linearly with time:

$$(3.6) \qquad \rho_t = \rho_\theta + (t - 1)\rho_\epsilon,$$

and the variance of the estimate on θ is $\sigma_t^2 = 1/(\rho_\theta + t\rho_\epsilon)$, which converges to zero like $1/t$. This is the rate of the efficient convergence.

THE WEIGHT OF HISTORY AND IMITATION

Agent t chooses an action that is a weighted average of the public information μ_t from history and his private signal s_t (equation (3.4)). The expression of the weight of history, $1 - \alpha_t$, increases and tends to 1 when t increases to infinity. The weight of the private signal tends to zero. Hence, agents tend to *imitate* each other more as time goes on. This is a very simple, natural, and general property: a longer history carries more information. Although the differences between individuals' actions become vanishingly small as time goes on, the social learning is not affected, because these actions are perfectly observable: no matter how small these variations, observers have a magnifying glass that enables them to see the differences perfectly. In the next section, this assumption will be removed. An observer will not see the small variations well. This imperfection will slow down significantly the social learning.

EFFICIENT LEARNING WITH DISCRETE SIGNALS

Private signals that take discrete values are not as fine as those that take values in a continuum. However, the discreteness of private signals does not alter the efficiency of social learning. Modifying the previous model, assume that θ is a real number in $(0, 1)$ and that private signals are discrete with $P(s = 1) = \theta$, $P(s = 0) = 1 - \theta$. The action x_t reveals perfectly the signal s_t: an action that is higher (lower) than the public belief reveals whether the signal is good (equal to one) or bad.

3.3 Observation Noise

In the previous section, an agent's action conveyed his private information perfectly. An individual's action can reflect the slightest nuances of his information because (i) it is chosen in a sufficiently rich menu; (ii) it is perfectly observable; (iii) the decision model of each agent is perfectly known to others.

The extraction of information from an individual's action relies critically on the assumption that the decision model is perfectly known, an assumption that is obviously very strong. In general, individuals' actions depend on a common parameter but also on private characteristics. It is the essence of these private characteristics that they cannot be observed perfectly (exactly as the private information is not observed by others). To simplify, the payoff function is here parameterized by a variable that is not observable. For any agent i, the payoff depends on his action x_i, an aggregate parameter θ, and a private parameter η_i:

$$U(x, \eta_i) = -E_i[(x_i - \theta - \eta_i)^2],$$

where $E_i[\theta]$ is the expected value of θ, given the information of agent i. The optimal action is $x_i = E_i[\theta] + \eta_i$. Because the private parameter η_i is not observable, the action of agent i conveys a *noisy signal* on his information $E_i[\theta]$. Imperfect information on an agent's private characteristics is operationally equivalent to a noise on the observation of the actions of an agent whose characteristics are perfectly known.

The model of the previous section is now extended to incorporate an observation noise, according to the idea of Vives (1993).[1] We begin with a direct extension of the model where there is one action per agent in each period. The model with many agents is relevant in the case of a market and will be presented in Section 3.3.2.

---

[1] Vives assumes directly an observation noise and a continuum of agents. His work is discussed in Proposition 3.1.

3.3.1 One Action per Period

AN INTUITIVE DESCRIPTION OF THE CRITICAL MECHANISM

Period t brings to the public information the observation

$$(3.7) \qquad x_t = (1 - \alpha_t)\mu_t + \alpha_t s_t + \eta_t \qquad \text{with} \quad \alpha_t = \frac{\rho_\epsilon}{\rho_t + \rho_\epsilon}.$$

The observation of x_t does not reveal the private signal s_t perfectly, because of a noise $\eta_t \sim \mathcal{N}(0, \sigma_\eta^2)$. This simple equation is sufficient to outline the critical argument. As time goes on, the learning process increases the precision of the public belief on θ, ρ_t, which tends to infinity. Rational agents imitate more and reduce the weight α_t that they put on their private signal as they get more information through history. Hence, they reduce the coefficient of s_t in their action. As $t \to \infty$, the effect of the private signal s_t on x_t becomes vanishingly small. The variance of the noise η_t remains constant over time, however. Asymptotically, *the effect of the private information on the level of action becomes vanishingly small relative to that of the unobservable idiosyncrasy.* This effect reduces the information content of each observation and slows down the process of social learning.

The impact of the noise cannot prevent the convergence of the precision ρ_t to infinity. By contradiction, suppose that ρ_t is bounded. Then α_t does not converge to zero, and asymptotically the precision ρ_t increases linearly (contradicting the boundedness of the precision). The analysis now confirms the intuition and measures accurately the effect of the noise on the rate of convergence of learning.

THE EVOLUTION OF BELIEFS

Because the private signal is $s_t = \theta + \epsilon_t$ with $\epsilon_t \sim \mathcal{N}(0, \sigma_\epsilon^2)$, equation (3.7) can be rewritten

$$(3.8) \qquad x_t = (1 - \alpha_t)\mu_t + \alpha_t\theta + \underbrace{\alpha_t\epsilon_t + \eta_t}_{\text{noise term}}.$$

The observation of the action x_t provides a signal on θ, $\alpha_t\theta$, with a noise $\alpha_t\epsilon_t + \eta_t$. We will encounter in this book many similar expressions for noisy signals on θ. We use a simple procedure to simplify the learning rule (3.8): the signal is normalized by a linear transformation such that the right-hand side is the sum of θ (the parameter to be estimated) and a noise:

$$(3.9) \qquad \frac{x_t - (1 - \alpha_t)\mu_t}{\alpha_t} = z_t = \theta + \epsilon_t + \frac{\eta_t}{\alpha_t}.$$

The variable x_t is *informationally equivalent* to the variable z_t. We will use similar equivalences for most Gaussian signals. The learning rules for the public belief follow immediately from the standard formulae with Gaussian signals (3.3). Using (3.7), we find that the distribution of θ at the end of period t is $\mathcal{N}(\mu_{t+1}, 1/\rho_{t+1}^2)$ with

$$\mu_{t+1} = (1 - \beta_t)\mu_t + \beta_t \left(\frac{x_t - (1 - \alpha_t)\mu_t}{\alpha_t} \right)$$

(3.10)   with $\beta_t = \dfrac{\sigma_t^2}{\sigma_t^2 + \sigma_\epsilon^2 + \sigma_\eta^2/\alpha_t^2}$,

$$\rho_{t+1} = \rho_t + \frac{1}{\sigma_\epsilon^2 + \sigma_\eta^2/\alpha_t^2} = \rho_t + \frac{1}{\sigma_\epsilon^2 + \sigma_\eta^2(1 + \rho_t\sigma_\epsilon^2)^2}.$$

CONVERGENCE

When there is no observation noise, the precision ρ_t of the public belief increases by a *constant* amount ρ_ϵ in each period, and it is a linear function of the number of observations (equation (3.6)). When there is an observation noise, equation (3.10) shows that as $\rho_t \to \infty$, the increments of the precision, $\rho_{t+1} - \rho_t$, converge to zero. The precision converges to infinity at a rate slower than a linear rate. The convergence of the variance σ_t^2 to 0 takes place at a rate slower than $1/t$. The next result [proved in the appendix (Section 3.5)] measures this rate.[2]

PROPOSITION 3.1 (Vives, 1993) *In the Gaussian–quadratic model with an observation noise of variance σ_η^2 and private signals of variance σ_ϵ^2, the variance of the public belief on θ, σ_t^2, converges to zero as $t \to \infty$, and*

(3.11) $\dfrac{\sigma_t^2}{\left(\sigma_\eta^2 \sigma_\epsilon^4 / 3t\right)^{\frac{1}{3}}} \to 1.$

This result is quite remarkable. It shows that the rate of convergence is 3 times slower when there is some observation noise, and that this rate is independent of the variance of the observation noise.

When the number of observations is large, 1000 additional observations with noise generate the same increase of precision as 10 observations when there is no observation noise. The cases of noise and perfect observability for a relatively small number of observations are compared in Figure 3.2. After 10 observations, the precision is only half of that with no noise. After 100 observations, the precision is 6 times smaller, with a value of about 15. To reach a precision of 15, the number of observations must be 6 times smaller with no observation noise than with observation noise.

Proposition 3.1 shows that the standard model of social learning where agents observe others' actions perfectly and know their decision process is not robust. When observations are subject to a noise, the process of social learning is slowed down, possibly drastically, because of the weight of history. That weight reduces the signal-to-noise ratio of individual actions. The mechanism by which the weight of history

---

[2] The analysis of a vanishingly small variance is simpler than that of a precision that tends to infinity.

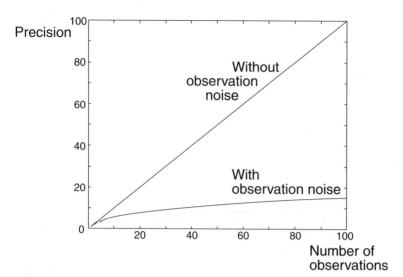

Figure 3.2 The evolution of the precision of the public belief. The parameters are calibrated to compensate for the additional noise: when there is an observation noise, the precision of the private signal, ρ_ϵ, is increased so that the increments of precision for an outside observer with observation noise and agents, acting according to their private signals and ignoring history, are the same as when there is observation noise (and observability *ex post* of the private signals). Parameters: without noise, $\sigma_\theta = 1, \sigma_\epsilon = 1, \sigma_\eta = 0$; with noise, $\sigma_\theta = 1, \sigma_\epsilon = 0.75, \sigma_\eta = 0.423$.

reduces social learning will be shown to be robust and will be one of the important themes in the book.

3.3.2 Large Number of Agents

The previous model is now modified to allow for a continuum of agents. Each agent is indexed by $i \in [0, 1]$ (with a uniform distribution) and receives one private signal *once* at the beginning of the first period,[3] $s_i = \theta + \epsilon_i$, with $\epsilon_i \sim \mathcal{N}(0, \sigma_\epsilon^2)$. Each agent takes an action $x_t(i)$ in each period[4] t to maximize the expected quadratic payoff in (3.2). At the end of period t, agents observe the aggregate action Y_t, which is the sum of the individuals' actions and of an aggregate noise η_t:

$$Y_t = X_t + \eta_t \quad \text{with} \quad X_t = \int x_t(i) \, di \text{ and } \eta_t \sim \mathcal{N}(0, 1/\rho_\eta).$$

At the beginning of any period t, the public belief on θ is $\mathcal{N}(\mu_t, 1/\rho_t)$, and an agent with signal s_i chooses the action

$$x_t(i) = E[\theta|s_i, h_t] = \mu_t(i) = (1 - \alpha_t)\mu_t + \alpha_t s_i$$

with

$$\alpha_t = \frac{\rho_\epsilon}{\rho_t + \rho_\epsilon}.$$

---

[3] If agents were to receive more than one signal, the precision of their private information would increase over time.

[4] One could also assume that there is a new set of agents in each period and that these agents act only once.

By the law of large numbers,[5] $\int \epsilon_i \, di = 0$. Therefore, $\alpha_t \int s_i \, di = \alpha_t \theta$. The level of endogenous aggregate activity is

$$X_t = (1 - \alpha_t)\mu_t + \alpha_t \theta,$$

and the observed aggregate action is

(3.12) $Y_t = (1 - \alpha_t)\mu_t + \alpha_t \theta + \eta_t.$

By use of the normalization introduced in Section 3.3.1, this signal is informationally equivalent to

(3.13) $\dfrac{Y_t - (1 - \alpha_t)\mu_t}{\alpha_t} = \theta + \dfrac{\eta_t}{\alpha_t} = \theta + \left(1 + \dfrac{\rho_t}{\rho_\epsilon}\right)\eta_t.$

This equation is similar to (3.9) in the model with one agent per period. (The variances of the noise terms in the two equations are asymptotically equivalent.) Proposition 3.1 applies. The asymptotic evolutions of the public beliefs are the same in the two models.

Note that the observation noise has to be an aggregate noise. If the noises affected actions at the individual level, for example through individuals' characteristics, they would be averaged out by aggregation, and the law of large numbers would reveal the state of nature perfectly. An aggregate noise is a very plausible assumption in the gathering of aggregate data.

3.3.3 Application: A Market Equilibrium

This setting is the original model of Vives (1993). A good is supplied by a continuum of identical firms indexed by i, which has a uniform density on $[0, 1]$. Firm i supplies x_i and the total supply is $X = \int x_i \, di$. The demand for the good is linear:

(3.14) $p = a + \eta - bX.$

Each firm (agent) i is a pricetaker and has a profit function

$$u_i = (p - \theta)x_i - \frac{c}{2}x_i^2,$$

where the last term is a cost of production and θ is an unknown parameter. Vives views this parameter as a pollution cost, which is assessed and charged after the end of the game.

As in the canonical model, nature's distribution on θ is $\mathcal{N}(\mu, 1/\rho_\theta)$ and each agent i has a private signal $s_i = \theta + \epsilon_i$ with $\epsilon_i \sim \mathcal{N}(0, 1/\rho_\epsilon)$. The expected value of

---

[5] A continuum of agents of mass 1 with independent signals is the limit case of n agents each of mass $1/n$, where $n \to \infty$. The variance of each individual action is proportional to $1/n^2$, and the variance of the aggregate decision is proportional to $1/n$, which is asymptotically equal to zero.

θ for firm i is

(3.15) $E_i[\theta] = (1 - \alpha)\mu + \alpha(\theta + \epsilon_i)$ with $\alpha = \dfrac{\rho_\epsilon}{\rho_\theta + \rho_\epsilon}$.

The optimal decision of each firm is such that the marginal profit is equal to the marginal cost:

$$p - E_i[\theta] = cx_i.$$

Integrating this equation over all firms and using the market equilibrium condition (3.14) gives

$$p - \int E_i[\theta]\, di = cX = \frac{c}{b}(a + \eta - p),$$

which, using (3.15), is equivalent to

$$(b + c)p - ac - (1 - \alpha)\mu = \alpha\theta + c\eta.$$

When both sides of this equation are divided to normalize the signal, the observation of the market price is equivalent to the observation of the signal

$$Z = \theta + c\frac{\eta}{\alpha},   \text{where}   \alpha = \frac{\rho_\epsilon}{\rho_\theta + \rho_\epsilon}.$$

The model is isomorphic to the canonical model of the previous section.

3.4 Extensions

3.4.1 Learning with a Private Cost of Information

So far, the precision of an individual signal has been exogenous. Assume now that an agent can improve this precision, at some cost. More specifically, each agent can purchase a signal s of precision q, which is defined by

$$s = \theta + \epsilon   \text{with}   \epsilon \sim \mathcal{N}(0, 1/q).$$

The cost of a signal with precision q is an increasing function, $c(q)$. Suppose for example that the signal is generated by a sample of n independent observations and that each observation has a constant cost c_0. Because the precision of the sample is a linear function of n, the cost of the signal is a step function. For the sake of exposition, we assume that q can be any real number. One agent takes one action per period, and his action is assumed to be perfectly observable by others. The payoff function of each agent is quadratic: $U(x) = E[-(x - \theta)^2]$.

Because the payoff of the optimal action is minus the variance of θ, the gain of the signal is the difference between the *ex ante* and *ex post* variances of the subjective distribution on θ:

$$V = \sigma_\theta^2 - \frac{\sigma_\theta^2}{\sigma_\theta^2 q + 1} = \frac{\sigma_\theta^4 q}{\sigma_\theta^2 q + 1}.$$

If there is an interior solution, the first-order condition for q is

$$\frac{\sigma_\theta^4}{(\sigma_\theta^2 q + 1)^2} = c'(q).$$

The proof of the following result is left as an exercise.

PROPOSITION 3.2 *Suppose that $c'(q)$ is continuous and $c(0) = 0$. If the marginal cost of precision, $c'(q)$, is bounded away from 0 (for any $q \geq 0$, $c'(q) \geq \gamma > 0$), then no agent purchases a signal after some finite period T, and social learning stops in that period.*

Note that the case of a fixed cost of information with $c(0) > 0$ is trivial. Other cases with $c(0) = 0$ are left as exercises.

3.4.2 Policy

A selfish agent who maximizes his own welfare ignores the fact that his action generates informational benefits to others. If the action is observed without noise, it conveys all the private information without any loss. If there is an observation noise, however, the information conveyed by the action is reduced when the response of the action is smaller. When time goes on, the amplitude of the noise is constant and the agent rationally reduces the coefficient of his signal in his action. Hence, the action of the agent conveys less information about his signal when t increases. A social planner may require that agents overstate the effect of their private signal on their action in order to be "heard" over the observation noise. Vives (1997) assumes that the social welfare function is the sum of the discounted payoffs of the agents:

$$W = \sum_{t \geq 0} \beta^t \left(-E_t[(x_t - \theta)^2] \right),$$

where x_t is the action of agent t. All agents observe the action plus a noise, $y_t = x_t + \epsilon_t$. The function W is interpreted as a loss function as long as θ is not revealed by a random exogenous process. In any period t, conditional on no previous revelation, θ is revealed perfectly with probability $1 - \pi \geq 0$. Assuming a discount factor $\delta < 1$, the value of β is $\beta = \pi\delta$. If the value of θ is revealed, there is no more loss.

As we have seen in (3.3) and (3.4), a selfish agent with signal s_t has a decision rule of the form

$$(3.16) \qquad x_t - \mu_t = (1 + \gamma)\frac{\rho_\epsilon}{\rho_t + \rho_\epsilon}(s_t - \mu_t),$$

with $\gamma = 0$. Vives assumes that a social planner can enforce an arbitrary value for γ. When $\gamma > 0$, the action-to-noise ratio is higher and the observers of the action receive more information.

Assume that a selfish agent is constrained to the decision rule (3.16) and optimizes over γ: he chooses $\gamma = 0$. By the envelope theorem, a small first-order deviation of the agent from his optimal value $\gamma = 0$ has a second-order effect on his welfare. We now show that it has a first-order effect on the welfare of any other individual who makes a decision. The action of the agent is informationally equivalent to the message

$$y = (1 + \gamma)\alpha s + \epsilon \qquad \text{with} \quad \alpha = \frac{\rho_\epsilon}{\rho_t + \rho_\epsilon}.$$

The precision of that message is $\rho_y = (1 + \gamma)^2 \alpha^2 \rho_\epsilon$.

Another individual's welfare is minus the variance after the observation of y. The observation of y adds an amount ρ_y to the precision of his belief. If γ increases from an initial value of 0, the variation of ρ_y is of the order of $2\gamma\alpha^2\rho_\epsilon$, i.e., of the first order with respect to γ. Because the variance is the reciprocal of the precision, the effect on the variance of others is also of the first order and dwarfs the second-order effect on the agent. There is a positive value of γ that induces a higher social welfare level.

EXERCISES

EXERCISE 3.1

Assume that (i) The distribution of the state of nature θ has a support in the set of real numbers (which does not have to be bounded); (ii) private signals are binary, symmetric, and such that $P(s = 1) = q$ with $q = \phi(\theta)$ for some monotone function ϕ that maps the set of real numbers to the open interval $(\frac{1}{2}, 1)$. An example of such a function is $\phi(\theta) = \frac{1}{4}(3 + \theta/(1 + |\theta|))$; (iii) the payoff function is $U = -E[(\theta - x)^2]$.

1. Show that the action of an agent reveals his private signal perfectly.
2. Can the history h_t be summarized by $\sum_{i \leq t-1} x_i$?
3. Analyze the rate of convergence of the public belief on θ.

EXERCISE 3.2 Endogenous private information

In Section 3.4.1, assume that $c(q) = q^\beta$ with $\beta > 0$. Analyze the rate of convergence of social learning.

3.5 Appendix

Proof of Proposition 3.1

Because we analyze a rate of convergence, it is more convenient to consider a variable that converges to zero than a variable that converges to infinity. (We will use Taylor expansions.) Let $z_t = \sigma_t^2 = 1/\rho_t$. The third equation in (3.10) is of the form

$$(3.17) \qquad z_{t+1} = G(z_t).$$

A standard exercise shows that $G(0) = 0$ and for $z > 0$, we have $0 < G(z) < z$ and $G'(z) > 0$. This implies that as $t \to \infty$, then $z_t \to 0$, which is a fixed point of F. The rest of the proof is an exercise on the approximation of (3.17) with the particular form (3.10) near the fixed point 0. Equation (3.10) can be rewritten

$$z_{t+1} = \frac{z_t\left((\sigma_\epsilon^2 + \sigma_\eta^2)z_t^2 + 2\sigma_\eta^2\sigma_\epsilon^2 z_t + \sigma_\eta^2\sigma_\epsilon^4\right)}{z_t^3 + (\sigma_\epsilon^2 + \sigma_\eta^2)z_t^2 + 2\sigma_\eta^2\sigma_\epsilon^2 z_t + \sigma_\eta^2\sigma_\epsilon^4},$$

or

$$z_{t+1} = z_t - \frac{z_t^4}{z_t^3 + (\sigma_\epsilon^2 + \sigma_\eta^2)z_t^2 + 2\sigma_\eta^2\sigma_\epsilon^2 z_t + \sigma_\eta^2\sigma_\epsilon^4}.$$

Because $z_t \to 0$,

$$z_{t+1} = z_t - \frac{z_t^4}{A}(1 + O(z_t)) \qquad \text{with} \quad A = \sigma_\eta^2\sigma_\epsilon^4,$$

where $O(z_t)$ is a term of order smaller than or equal to 1: there is $B > 0$ such that if $z_t \to 0$, then $O(z_t) < Bz_t$. Let b_t be such that $z_t = b_t/t^{\frac{1}{3}}$. By substitution in the previous equation,

$$b_{t+1}\left(\frac{1+t}{t}\right)^{-\frac{1}{3}} = b_t - \frac{b_t^4}{At}\left(1 + O\left(\frac{b_t}{t^{\frac{1}{3}}}\right)\right),$$

or

$$(3.18) \qquad b_{t+1}\left(1 - \frac{1}{3t} + O\left(\frac{1}{t^2}\right)\right) = b_t - \frac{b_t^4}{At}\left(1 + O\left(\frac{b_t}{t^{\frac{1}{3}}}\right)\right).$$

This equation is used to prove that b_t converges to a nonzero limit. The proof is in two steps: (i) the sequence is bounded; (ii) any subsequence converges to the same limit.

    (i) The boundedness of b_t: First, from the previous equation, there exists T_1 such that if $t > T_1$, then

$$(3.19) \qquad b_{t+1} < b_t\left(1 + \frac{1}{2t}\right).$$

By use of (3.18) again, there exists $T > T_1$ such that for $t > T$,

$$b_{t+1} < b_t\left(1 + \frac{1}{t}\right)\left(1 - \frac{b_t^3}{2At}\right).$$

From this inequality, there is some value M such that if $b_t > M$ and $t > T$, then

$$(3.20) \qquad b_{t+1} < b_t \left(1 - \frac{1}{t}\right).$$

We use (3.19) and (3.20) to show that if $t > T$, then $b_t < 2M$. Consider a value of $t > T$. If $b_{t-1} < M$, then by (3.19),

$$b_{t+1} < M\left(1 + \frac{1}{t}\right) < 2M.$$

If $b_{t-1} > M$, then by (3.20), $b_{t+1} < b_t$. It follows that b_t is bounded by the maximum of b_T and $2M$:

$$(3.21) \qquad \text{for } t > T, \qquad b_t < \max(b_T, 2M).$$

(ii): To show the convergence of b_t, one can extract a subsequence of b_t that converges to some limit ℓ_1. Then one can extract from this subsequence another subsequence such that b_{t+1} (defined by the previous equation) converges to a limit ℓ_2. Taking the limit, we find

$$\ell_2 \left(1 - \frac{1}{3t} + O\left(\frac{1}{t^2}\right)\right) = \ell_1 - \frac{\ell_1^4}{At}\left(1 + O\left(\frac{\ell_1}{t^{\frac{1}{3}}}\right)\right).$$

We must have

$$\ell_1 = \ell_2 \quad \text{and} \quad \frac{\ell_2}{3} = \frac{\ell_1^4}{A}.$$

Therefore,

$$\ell_1 = \ell_2 = \ell = \left(\frac{A}{3}\right)^{\frac{1}{3}}.$$

The result follows from the definition of A. ∎

4 Cascades and Herds

One million people cannot be wrong.

Each agent observes what others do and takes a zero–one decision in a preordered sequence. In a cascade, all agents herd on a sufficiently strong public belief and there is no learning. In a herd, all agents turn out to take the same decision. A cascade generates a herd, but the converse is not true. Cascades are nongeneric for atomless distributions of beliefs, whereas a herd always takes place, *eventually*. For that reason, the probability that the herd is broken must converge to zero. Hence, there is some learning in a herd (it is not broken), but the learning is very slow. The stylization of that property is the cascade.

Beliefs converge to the truth only if the distribution of private beliefs is unbounded; but the self-defeating principle in social learning implies that the convergence is slow. Because the filter imposed by discrete actions is coarse, the slowdown of social learning is much more significant than in the previous chapter. Applications for welfare properties and pricing policies by a monopoly are discussed.

A Tale of Two Restaurants

Two restaurants face each other on the main street of a charming Alsatian village. There is no menu outside. It is 6 P.M. Both restaurants are empty. A tourist comes down the street, looks at each of the restaurants, and goes into one of them. After a while, another tourist shows up, sees how many patrons are already inside by looking through the stained-glass windows – these are Alsatian *winstube* – and chooses one of them. The scene repeats itself, with new tourists checking on the popularity of each restaurant before entering one of them. After a while, all newcomers choose the same restaurant: they choose the more popular one irrespective of their own information. This tale illustrates how rational people may herd and choose one action because it is chosen by others. Among the many similar stories, two are particularly enlightening.

TABLE 4.1 Information on downloadable shareware.

Upld	Subject	Cnt	Dnld
10/16	v2.0 Space Fighter 2000 . . .	81	10/21
10/16	S.I. Magazine October Rd . . .	58	10/21
10/16	Butchenstein 2D Add-On	67	10/21
10/16	Chrono Trigger Add-On	89	10/21
10/15	Chaos Fighters Add-On	54	10/20
10/14	Wargames Add-On	92	10/21
10/14	Star Wars Magazin 2 Add-On	84	10/21
10/14	The Search For Pepe Add-On	51	10/21
10/06	Bugtown Add-On	94	10/20
10/06	v1.4 Unga Khan 4 Add-On	73	10/21

Adapted from Hanson and Putler (1996).

High Sales Promote High Sales

In 1995, the management gurus Michael Reacy and Fred Wiersema secretly purchased 50,000 copies of their business strategy book *The Discipline of Market Leaders* from stores that were monitored for the bestseller list of the *New York Times*.[1] The authors must have been motivated by the following argument: people observe the sales, but not the payoffs, of the purchases (assuming they have few opportunities to meet other readers). Of course, if the manipulation had been known, it would have had no effect, but people rationally expect that for any given book, the probability of manipulation is small, and that the high sales must be driven by some informed buyers.

The previous story illustrates one possible motivation for using the herding effect, but it is only indicative. For an actual measurement, we turn to Hanson and Putler (1996), who conducted a nice experiment that combines the control of a laboratory with a real-world situation. They manipulated a service provided by America Online (AOL) in the summer of 1995. Customers of the service could download games from a bulletin board. The games were free, but the download entailed some cost linked to the time spent in trying out the game. Some games were downloaded more than others.

The service of AOL is summarized by the window available to subscribers, which is reproduced in Table 4.1: column 1 shows the first date the product was available; column 2 the name of the product, which is informative; column 4 the most recent date the file was downloaded. Column 3 is the most important and shows the number of customers who have downloaded the file so far. It presents an index of the popularity of the product. The main goal of the study is to investigate whether a high popularity increases the demand *ceteris paribus*.

The impact of a treatment is measured by the increase in the number of downloads per day, after the treatment, as a fraction of the average daily download (for the same

---

[1] See Bikhchandani, Hirshleifer, and Welch (1998) and *Business Week*, August 7, 1995. Additional examples are given in Bikhchandani, Hirshleifer, and Welch (1992).

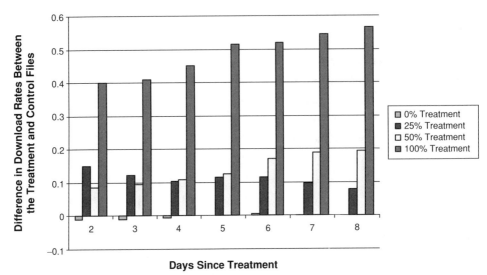

Figure 4.1 Differences between treatment and control files.

product) before the treatment. The results are reported in Figure 4.1. All treatments have an impact, and the impact of the heavy treatment (100 percent) is particularly remarkable. The experiment has an obvious implication for the general manipulation of demand through advertisements.

To ensure *ceteris paribus*, Hanson and Putler selected pairs of similar files that were offered by AOL. Similarity was measured by characteristics and popularity at a specific date. Once a pair was selected, one of the files was kept as the *control*; the other was the treatment. The authors boosted the popularity index of the treatment file by downloading it repeatedly. The popularity index was thus increased in a short session by percentage increments of 25, 50, and 100. Customers of the service were not aware that they were manipulated.

The Essential Issue and the Framework of Analysis

The previous examples share an essential common feature: individuals observe the actions of others and the space of actions is discrete. The actions are the words for the communication of information between agents. In the previous chapter, agents chose an action in a rich set: all the real numbers. Here the finite number of actions exerts a strong restriction on the vocabulary of social communication.

If there is a seminal study on social learning, it is the paper by BHW[2] (1992). They introduced the definition of informational cascades in models of Bayesian learning. In a cascade, the public belief, which is gathered from the history of observations, dominates the private signal of any individual: the action of any agent does not depend on his private information. In a cascade, all agents are herding. Because actions do not convey private information, nothing is learned, and the cascade

---

[2] Banerjee (1992) presented at the same time another paper on herding, but its structure is more idiosyncratic and one cannot analyze the robustness of its properties.

goes on forever, possibly with an incorrect action. The failure of social learning is spectacular.

A cascade generates a herd, but the concepts of cascade and herd are distinct. A herd is defined as an outcome where all agents take the same action after some period. In a herd not all agents may be herding. It is precisely because not all agents are herding in a herd that some learning takes place. The probability that the herd can be broken generates some information. However, this probability must be vanishingly small for the herd to be sustained. Hence, the amount of social learning in a herd is very small.

Cascades do not occur except in very special models, whereas herds always take place eventually. The reader may think that cascades are therefore not important. Wrong; cascades are good approximations for the properties of the generic models of learning from others' actions when those actions are discrete.

The simplest model of cascades is presented in Section 4.1. No formal mathematics is required for that section, which presents the important properties.

The general model is analyzed in Section 4.2. It is built on the models with bounded private beliefs that have been presented in Section 2.2.1. (The reader is advised to review that section if necessary.) The evolution of the beliefs is presented in a diagram, which will be used later in the book, especially in Chapter 6, where the timing of actions is endogenous. When the support is bounded, private beliefs become dominated by a public belief, which is either optimistic or pessimistic, as the number of observations increases. Such a situation actually never occurs when private beliefs have a distribution without points of positive mass (which is not just a perturbation of a distribution with such points). However, the limit behavior of the model is closely approximated by cascades.

Beliefs converge to the truth, almost surely, only if the support of the distribution of beliefs is unbounded. In this respect, the results of BHW have been criticized as not robust. Such theoretical focus on the limit beliefs is misleading. What matters is the speed of convergence.

Section 4.3 presents a detailed analysis of herds and the convergence of beliefs.[3] Herds always take place eventually, as a consequence of the MCT. There is in general some learning in a herd, but that learning is very slow. The conclusions of the simple model of BHW are shown to be extraordinarily robust. They reinforce the central message of the models of learning from others, which is the self-defeating property of social learning when individuals use public information rationally.

The Social Optimum

In an equilibrium, no agent takes into account the externality created by his action for the information of others. In a social optimum, this externality is taken into account (as in the model with actions in a continuum, Section 3.4.2). A social optimum is

---

[3] For that section, I have greatly benefited from the insights of Lones Smith, and I am very grateful to him.

constrained in that each agent "speaks" to others only through his action. An agent has a decision rule according to which his action depends on his private belief and the public belief. He can reveal his private belief only through his action. He departs from the selfish rule of using history for his own payoff only if the externality provided to others outweighs his personal loss.

In Section 4.5, it is shown that the socially optimal rule is to forget history if the belief from history – the public belief – is in some interval of values, and to herd otherwise. If the belief is outside that *interval of experimentation,* there is no social learning anymore. The socially optimal rule may be implemented by setting a price on investment contingent on the public belief.

Monopoly Pricing of a New Good

A monopolist who captures some consumer surplus will take into account the benefit of experimentation for the future. This problem is considered in Section 4.5.2. A monopoly introduces on the market a new good of imperfectly known quality. The optimal strategy is divided into two phases. The first is the *elitist phase*: the price of the good is high. Only the agents with a good signal on the good buy it, and the volume of sales raises the estimate of the other agents. When this estimate is sufficiently high, the monopoly lowers the price to reach all customers.

The incentive to learn is inversely related to the discount rate. If the discount rate is vanishingly small, the difference between the level of social welfare and the monopoly profit converges to zero. At the limit, the monopoly follows a strategy that is socially optimal. (Monopoly profits are redistributed.)

4.1 The Basic Model of Herding

Students sometimes wonder how to build a model. BHW provide an excellent lesson in methodology: (i) a good story simplifies the complex reality and keeps the main elements; (ii) this story is translated into a set of assumptions about the structure of a model (information of agents, payoff functions); (iii) the equilibrium behavior of rational agents is analyzed; (iv) the robustness of the model is examined through extensions of the initial assumptions.

We begin here with the tale of two restaurants, or a similar story where agents have to decide whether to make a fixed-size investment. We construct a model with two states (according to which restaurant is better), two signal values (which generate different beliefs), and two possible actions (eating at one of two restaurants).[4] The model is a special case of the general model of social learning (Section 3.1.2).

---

[4] The example of the restaurants at the beginning of this chapter is found in Banerjee (1992). The model in this section is constructed on that story. It is somewhat mystifying that Banerjee, after introducing herding through this example, develops an unrelated model that is somewhat idiosyncratic. A simplified version is presented in Exercise 4.3.

4.1.1 The 2-by-2-by-2 Model

1. The state of nature θ has two possible values, $\theta \in \Theta = \{0, 1\}$, and is set randomly once and for all at the beginning of the first period[5] with a probability μ_1 for the good state $\theta = 1$.
2. A finite number N or a countably infinite number of agents are indexed by the integer t. Each agent's private information takes the form of a SBS with precision $q > \frac{1}{2}$: $P(s_t = \theta \mid \theta) = q$.
3. Agents take an action in an *exogenous order*, as in the previous models of social learning. The notation can be chosen so that agent t can make a decision in period t and in period t only. An agent chooses his action x in the discrete set $\Xi = \{0, 1\}$. The action $x = 1$ may represent entering a restaurant, hiring an employee, or in general making an investment of a fixed size. The yield of the action x depends on the state of nature and is defined by

$$u(x, \theta) = \begin{cases} 0 & \text{if } x = 0, \\ \theta - c & \text{if } x = 1, \text{ with } 0 < c < 1. \end{cases}$$

Because $x = 0$ or 1, another representation of the payoff is $u(x, \theta) = (\theta - c)x$. The cost of the investment c is fixed.[6] The yield of the investment is positive in the good state and negative in the bad state. Under uncertainty, the payoff of the agent is the expected value of $u(x, \theta)$ conditional on the information of the agent. By convention, if the payoff of $x = 1$ is zero, the agent chooses $x = 0$.
4. As in the previous models of social learning, the information of agent t is his private signal together with the *history* $h_t = (x_1, \ldots, x_{t-1})$ of the actions of the agents who precede him in the exogenous sequence. The *public belief* at the beginning of period t is the probability of the good state conditional on the history h_t which is public information. It is denoted by μ_t:

$$\mu_t = P(\theta = 1 | h_t).$$

Without loss of generality, μ_1 is the same as nature's probability of choosing $\theta = 1$.

4.1.2 Informational Cascades

Agents with a good signal $s = 1$ will be called *optimists*, and agents with a bad signal $s = 0$ will be called *pessimists*. An agent combines the public belief with his private signal to form his belief. If μ is the public belief in some arbitrary period, the belief

---

[5] The reason the value of θ does not change is that we want to analyze the changes in beliefs that are caused only by endogenous behavior. Changes of θ can be analyzed in a separate study (see the bibliographical notes in Section 4.7).

[6] In the tale of two restaurants, c is the opportunity cost of not eating at the other restaurant.

of an optimist is higher than μ and the belief of a pessimist is lower. Let μ^+ and μ^- be the beliefs of the optimists and the pessimists[7]: $\mu^- < \mu < \mu^+$.

A pessimist invests if and only if his belief μ^- is greater than the cost c, i.e., if the public belief is greater than some value $\mu^{**} > c$. (If $c = \frac{1}{2}$, $\mu^{**} = q$.) If the public belief is such that a pessimist invests, then *a fortiori*, it induces an optimist to invest. Therefore, if $\mu_t > \mu^{**}$, agent t invests regardless of his signal. If $\mu_t \leq \mu^{**}$, he does not invest if his signal is bad.

Likewise, let μ^* be the value of the public belief such that $\mu^+ = c$. If $\mu_t \leq \mu^*$, agent t does not invest, no matter what the value of his private signal. If $\mu_t > \mu^*$, he invests if he has a good signal. The cases are summarized in the next result.

PROPOSITION 4.1 *In any period t, given the public belief μ_t:*

if $\mu^* < \mu_t \leq \mu^{**}$, agent t invests if and only if his signal is good ($s_t = 1$);
if $\mu_t > \mu^{**}$, agent t invests, independently of his signal;
if $\mu_t \leq \mu^*$, agent t does not invest, independently of his signal.

CASCADES AND HERDS

Proposition 4.1 shows that if the public belief, μ_t, is above μ^{**}, agent t invests and ignores his private signal. His action conveys no information on this signal. Likewise, if the public belief is smaller than μ^*, then the agent does not invest. This important situation deserves a name.

DEFINITION 4.1 *An agent herds on the public belief when his action is independent of his private signal.*

The herding of an agent describes a decision process. The agent takes into account only the public belief; his private signal is too weak to matter. If all agents herd, no private information is revealed. The public belief is unchanged at the beginning of the next period, and the situation is identical: the agent acts according to the public belief whatever his private signal. The behavior of each agent is repeated period after period. This situation has been described by BHW as an *informational cascade*. The metaphor was used first by Tarde at the end of the nineteenth century (Chapter 1).

DEFINITION 4.2 *If all agents herd (Definition 4.1), there is an informational cascade.*

We now have to make an important distinction between the herding of all agents in an informational cascade and the definition of a herd.

---

[7] By Bayes's rule,

$$\mu^- = \frac{\mu(1-q)}{\mu(1-q)+(1-\mu)q} < \mu < \frac{\mu q}{\mu q + (1-\mu)(1-q)} = \mu^+.$$

DEFINITION 4.3 *A herd takes place at date T if all actions after date T are identical: for all $t > T$, $x_t = x_T$.*

In a cascade, all agents are herding and make the same decision, which depends only on the public belief (which stays invariant over time). Hence, all actions are identical.

PROPOSITION 4.2 *If there is an informational cascade in period t, there is a herd in the same period.*

The converse of Proposition 4.2 is not true. *Herds and cascades are not equivalent.* In a herd, all agents turn out to choose the same action – in all periods – although some of them could have chosen a different action. We will see later that generically, cascades do not occur, but herds eventually begin with probability one! Why do we consider cascades, then? Because their properties are stylized representations of models of social learning.

In the present model, an informational cascade takes place if $\mu_t > \mu^{**}$ or $\mu_t \leq \mu^*$. There is social learning only if $\mu^* < \mu_t \leq \mu^{**}$. Then $x_t = s_t$ and the action reveals perfectly the signal s_t. The public belief in period $t + 1$ is the same as that of agent t as long as a cascade has not started. The history of actions $h_t = (x_1, \ldots, x_{t-1})$ is equivalent to the history of signals $(s_1, \ldots, s_{t-1})$.

Assume that there is no cascade in periods 1 and 2 and that $s_1 = 1$ and $s_2 = 1$. Suppose that agent 3 is a pessimist. Because all signals have the same precision, his bad signal cancels one good signal. He therefore has the same belief as agent 1 and should invest. There is a cascade in period 3.

Likewise, two consecutive bad signals ($s = 0$) start a cascade with no investment, if no cascade has started before. If the public belief μ_1 is greater than c and agent 1 has a good signal, a cascade with investment begins in period 2. If $\mu_1 < c$ and the first agent has a bad signal, he does not invest and a cascade with no investment begins in period 2.

In order *not* to have a cascade, a necessary condition is that the signals alternate consecutively between 1 and 0. We infer that

- the probability that a cascade has not started by period t converges to zero exponentially, like β^t for some parameter $\beta < 1$;
- there is a positive probability that the cascade is wrong: in the bad state, all agents may invest after some period, and investment may stop after some period in the good state;
- beliefs do not change once a herd has started; rational agents do not become more confident in a cascade.

PROPOSITION 4.3 *When agents have a binary signal, an informational cascade occurs after some finite date, almost surely. The probability that the informational cascade has not started by date t converges to 0 like β^t for some β^t with $0 < \beta < 1$.*

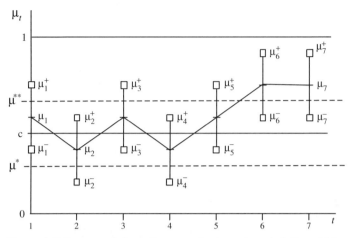

Figure 4.2 Representation of a cascade. In each period, the middle of the vertical segment is the public belief; the top and the bottom of the segment are the beliefs of an optimist (with a private signal $s = 1$) and of a pessimist (with signal $s = 0$). The private signals are $s_1 = 0$, $s_2 = 1$, $s_3 = 0$, $s_4 = 1$, $s_5 = 1$.

A GEOMETRIC REPRESENTATION

The evolution of the beliefs is represented in Figure 4.2. In each period, a segment represents the distribution of beliefs: the top of the segment represents the belief of an optimist, the bottom the belief of a pessimist, and the midpoint the public belief. The segments evolve randomly over time according to the observations.

In the first period, the belief of an optimist, μ_1^+, is above c, while the belief of a pessimist, μ_1^-, is below c. The action is equal to the signal of the agent and thus reveals that signal. In the figure, $s_1 = 0$, and the first agent does not invest. His information is incorporated in the public information: the public belief in the second period, μ_2, is identical to the belief of the first agent: $\mu_2 = \mu_1^-$. The sequence of the signal endowments is indicated in the figure. *When there is social learning, the signal of agent t is integrated into the public information of period $t + 1$.* By use of the notation of the previous chapter, $\mu_{t+1} = \tilde{\mu}_t$.

Consider now period 5 in the figure: Agent 5 is an optimist, invests, and reveals his signal, because he could have been a pessimist who does not invest. His information is incorporated in the public belief of the next period, and $\mu_6 = \mu_5^+$. The belief of a pessimist in period 6 is now higher than the cost c (here, it is equal to the public belief μ_5). In period 6, the belief of an agent is higher than the cost of investment, whatever his signal. He invests, nothing is learned, and the public belief is the same in period 7: a cascade begins in period 6. The cascade takes place because all the beliefs are above the cutoff level c. This condition is met here because the public belief μ_6 is strictly higher than μ^{**}. Now μ_6 is identical to the belief of an optimist in period 5, and the cascade occurs because the beliefs of all investing agents are strictly higher than μ^{**} in period 5. A cascade takes place because of the high belief of the last agent, who triggers the cascade. Because this property is essential for the occurrence of an informational cascade, it is important and will be discussed later in more detail.

In this simple model, the public belief $\mu_t = P(\theta = 1|h_t)$ converges to one of two values (depending on the cascade). From the MCT, we knew μ_t would necessarily converge in probability. The exponential convergence is particularly fast. The informational cascade may be incorrect, however: all agents may take the wrong decision. (See Exercise 4.2.)

BLACK SHEEP

Assume there is a cascade in some period T in which agents invest, whatever their signal. Extend now the previous setting, and assume that agent T may be of one of two types. Either he has a signal of precision q like the previous agents, or his precision is $q' > q$ and q' is sufficiently high with respect to the public belief that if he has a bad signal ($s_T = 0$), he does not invest. The type of the agent is private and therefore not observable, but the possibility that agent T has a higher precision is known to all agents.

Suppose that agent T does not invest: $x_T = 0$. What inference is drawn by others? The only possible explanation is that agent T has a signal of high precision q' and that his signal is bad: the information of agent T is conveyed *exactly* by his action.

If agent T invests, his action is like that of others. Does it mean that the public belief does not change? No. The absence of a black sheep in period T (who would not invest) increases the confidence that the state is good. Social learning takes place as long as not all agents herd. The learning may slow down, however, as agents with a relatively low precision begin to herd. The inference problem with heterogeneous precisions requires a model which incorporates the random endowment of signals with different precisions. A model with two types of precision is presented in the appendix (Section 4.8).

The simple model has served two useful purposes: (i) it is a lesson on how to begin to think formally about a stylized fact and the essence of a mechanism; (ii) it strengthens the intuition about the mechanism of learning and its possible failures. These steps need to be as simple as possible. Simplicity of the model, though, could lead to the criticism that its properties are not robust. The model is now generalized, and we will see that its basic properties are indeed robust.

4.2 The Standard Model with Bounded Beliefs

We now extend the previous model to admit any distribution of private beliefs as described in Section 2.2.1. Such a distribution is characterized by the c.d.f. $F^\theta(\mu)$, which depends on the state θ. Recall that the c.d.f.'s satisfy the proportional property (2.12) and therefore the assumption of first-order stochastic dominance: for any μ in the interior of the support of the distribution, $F^{\theta_0}(\mu) > F^{\theta_1}(\mu)$. By an abuse of notation, $F^\theta(\mu)$ will represent the c.d.f. of a distribution of the beliefs measured as the probability of θ_1, and $F^\theta(\lambda)$ will represent the c.d.f. of a distribution of the LLR between θ_1 and θ_0.

We keep the following structure: two states $\theta \in \{\theta_0, \theta_1\}$, two actions $x \in \{0, 1\}$, with a payoff $(E[\theta] - c)x$, $\theta_0 < c < \theta_1$. The states θ_1 and θ_0 will be called *good* and *bad*. We may take $\theta_0 = 1$ and $\theta_0 = 0$, but the notation may be clearer if we keep the symbols θ_1 and θ_0 rather than use numerical values.

4.2.1 Social Learning

At the end of each period t, agents observe the action x_t. Any belief λ is updated using Bayes's rule. This rule is particularly convenient when expressed in LLR as in equation (2.3), which is repeated here:

$$(4.1) \qquad \lambda_{t+1} = \lambda_t + v_t \qquad \text{with} \quad v_t = \log \left(\frac{P(x_t|\theta_1)}{P(x_t|\theta_0)} \right).$$

The updating term v_t is independent of the belief λ_t. Therefore, the distribution of beliefs is translated by a random term v_t from period t to period $t + 1$. Agent t invests if and only if his probability of the good state is greater than his cost, i.e., if his LLR λ is greater than $\gamma = \log(c/(1 - c))$. The probability that agent t invests depends on the state and is equal to $\pi_t(\theta) = 1 - F_t^\theta(\gamma)$.

The action in period t, $x_t \in \{0, 1\}$, provides a binary random signal on θ with probabilities described in Table 4.2. Because the c.d.f. F^{θ_1} dominates F^{θ_0} in the sense of first-order stochastic dominance (Proposition 2.3), there are more optimistic agents in the good than in the bad state on average. Hence, the probability of investment is higher in the good state, and the observation $x_t = 1$ raises the beliefs of all agents.

Following the observation of x_t, the updating equation (2.3) takes the particular form

$$(4.2) \qquad \lambda_{t+1} = \lambda_t + v_t \qquad \text{with} \quad v_t = \begin{cases} \log \left(\dfrac{1 - F_t^{\theta_1}(\gamma)}{1 - F_t^{\theta_0}(\gamma)} \right) & \text{if } x_t = 1, \\[2ex] \log \left(\dfrac{F_t^{\theta_1}(\gamma)}{F_t^{\theta_0}(\gamma)} \right) & \text{if } x_t = 0. \end{cases}$$

In this equation, $v_t \geq 0$ if $x_t = 1$, and $v_t \leq 0$ if $x_t = 0$. The observation of x_t conveys some information on the state as long as $F_t^{\theta_1}(\gamma) \neq F_t^{\theta_0}(\gamma)$.

Because the distribution of LLRs is invariant up to a translation, it is sufficient to keep track of one of the beliefs. If the support of beliefs is bounded, we choose the midpoint of the support, called, by an abuse of notation, the public belief. If the support is not bounded, the definition of the public belief will depend on the particular case.

THE MARKOV PROCESS

The previous process has an abstract formulation that may provide some perspective on the process of social learning. We have seen that the position of the distribution in any period can be characterized by one point λ_t. Let μ_t be the belief of an agent with

TABLE 4.2 Probabilities of observations

		Observations	
		$x_t = 1$	$x_t = 0$
States of	$\theta = \theta_1$	$1 - F_t^{\theta_1}(\gamma)$	$F_t^{\theta_1}(\gamma)$
Nature	$\theta = \theta_0$	$1 - F_t^{\theta_0}(\gamma)$	$F_t^{\theta_0}(\gamma)$

$$\gamma = \log\left(\frac{c}{1-c}\right)$$

LLR equal to λ_t. The Bayesian formula (4.2) takes the general form $\mu_{t+1} = B(x_t, \mu_t)$, and x_t is a random variable that takes the value 1 or 0 according to Table 4.2. The probabilities of x_t depend on μ_t and θ_t. The process of social learning is summarized by the equations

(4.3)
$$\mu_{t+1} = B(\mu_t, x_t),$$
$$P(x_t = 1) = \pi(\mu_t, \theta).$$

The combination of the two equations defines a Markov process for μ_t. Such a definition is natural and serves two purposes: it provides a synthetic formulation of social learning, and it is essential for the analysis of convergence properties. However, such a formulation can be applied to a wide class of processes and does not highlight specific features of the structural model of social learning with discrete actions.

4.2.2 Bounded Beliefs

Assume the initial distribution of private beliefs is *bounded*. Its support is restricted to a finite interval $(\underline{\lambda}_1, \overline{\lambda}_1)$. This case is represented in Figure 4.3. Let λ_t be the public belief in period t, i.e., the midpoint of the support, $\lambda_t = (\underline{\lambda}_t + \overline{\lambda}_t)/2$; and let $\sigma = (\overline{\lambda}_t - \underline{\lambda}_t)/2$, a constant. If λ_t is greater than $\lambda^{**} = \gamma + \sigma$, the support of the distribution is above γ and agent t invests, whatever his belief. Likewise, if $\lambda \leq \lambda^* = \gamma - \sigma$, no agent invests. In either case, there is an informational cascade. There is no informational cascade as long as the public belief stays in the interval $(\lambda^*, \lambda^{**}) = (\gamma - \sigma, \gamma + \sigma)$. The complement of that interval will be called the *cascade set*.

Figure 4.3 is drawn under the assumption of an atomless distribution of beliefs, but it can also be drawn with atoms as in Figure 4.2.

We know from the MCT that the probability of the good state, $\mu_t = e^{\lambda_t}/(1 + e^{\lambda_t})$, converges in probability. Hence, λ_t must converge to some value. Suppose that the limit is not in the cascade set. Then, asymptotically, the probability that $x_t = 1$ remains different in states θ_1 and θ_0. Hence, with strictly positive probability, the common belief is updated by some nonvanishing amount, thus contradicting the convergence of the martingale. This argument is used in the appendix (Section 4.8) to prove that λ_t must converge to a value in the cascade set.

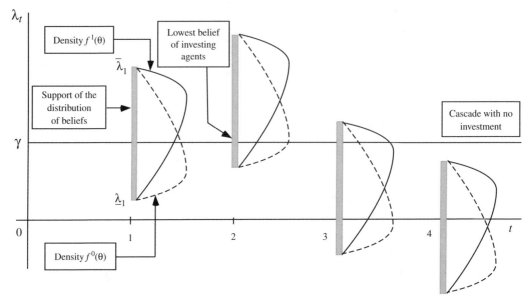

Figure 4.3 The evolution of beliefs. In each period, the support of the distribution of beliefs (LLR) is represented by a segment. The action is $x_t = 1$ if and only if the belief (LLR) of the agent is above γ. If agent t happens to have a belief above (below) γ, the distribution moves up (down) in the next period $t + 1$. If the entire support is above (below) γ, the action is equal to 1 (0) and the distribution stays constant.

PROPOSITION 4.4 *Assume that the support of the initial distribution of private beliefs is $I = [\lambda_1 - \sigma, \lambda_1 + \sigma]$. Then λ_t converges almost surely to a limit $\lambda_\infty \notin (\gamma - \sigma, \gamma + \sigma)$ with $\gamma = \log(c/(1 - c))$.*

RIGHT AND WRONG CASCADES

A cascade may arise with an incorrect action: for example, beliefs may be sufficiently low that no agent invests while the state is good. However, agents learn rationally, and the probability of a wrong cascade is small if agents have a wide diversity of beliefs as measured by the length of the support of the distribution.

Suppose that the initial distribution in LLR is symmetric around 0 with a support of length 2σ. We compute the probability of a wrong cascade for an agent with initial belief $\frac{1}{2}$. A cascade with no investment arises if his LLR λ_t is smaller than $\gamma - \sigma$, i.e., if his belief in level is such that

$$\mu_t \le \beta = \frac{e^{\gamma - \sigma}}{1 + e^{\gamma - \sigma}}.$$

When the support of the distribution in LLR becomes arbitrarily large, $\sigma \to \infty$ and ϵ is arbitrarily small. From Proposition 2.9 with $\mu_1 = \frac{1}{2}$, we know that

$$P(\mu_t \le \beta | \theta_1) \le 2\beta.$$

The argument is the same for the cascades where all agents invest. The probability of a wrong cascade for a neutral observer (with initial belief $\frac{1}{2}$) tends to zero if the support of the distribution in LLR becomes arbitrarily large (or equivalently, if the beliefs measured as probabilities of θ_1 are intervals converging to $(0, 1)$).

PROPOSITION 4.5 *If the support of the initial distribution of LLRs contains the interval $[-\sigma, +\sigma]$, then for an observer with initial belief $\frac{1}{2}$, the probability of a wrong cascade is less than 4β, with $\beta = e^{-\sigma}c/(1 - c + e^{-\sigma}c)$.*

ARE CASCADES GENERIC?

The BHW model has received considerable attention because of the simplicity of its structure and of the spectacular property of informational cascades. However, this property is essentially due to the assumption of an atomistic distribution of private beliefs. Under that assumption, the public belief moves by discrete steps. It ends in the cascade set after a finite number of steps, with probability one. For a generic class of nonatomistic distributions of private beliefs, the probability of a contrarian agent becomes vanishingly small when the public belief tends to the cascade set. Hence, because of the martingale property, the variation of the public belief converges to zero and the public belief never reaches the cascade set.

Because of the proportional property in (2.12), if the distribution of private beliefs has a density $f^\theta(\mu)$ it can be written as

$$(4.4) \qquad f^1(\mu) = \mu\phi(\mu), \quad \text{and} \quad f^0(\mu) = (1 - \mu)\phi(\mu),$$

where the function $\phi(\mu)$ has a support in $[a, 1 - a]$, and $a > 0$ because the beliefs are bounded. This distribution is generated by a two-step process in which agents draw a SBS of precision μ with a density proportional to $\phi(\mu)$. A simple case is provided by a uniform distribution of precisions where ϕ is constant. Chamley (2003c) proves that in this case, there is no cascade in any period. The result can be generalized to the case of a function $\phi(\mu)$ that does not put too much mass at either end of its support. For reasonable density functions, cascades do not occur. In this sense, the property of a cascade is not generic.

4.3 The Convergence of Beliefs

When private beliefs are bounded, beliefs never converge to perfect knowledge. If the public belief converged to 1, for example, in finite time it would overwhelm any private belief and a cascade would start, thus making the convergence of the public belief to 1 impossible. This argument does not hold if the private beliefs are unbounded, because in any period the probability of a contrarian agent is strictly positive.

4.3.1 Unbounded Beliefs: Convergence to the Truth

From Proposition 4.5 (with $\sigma \to \infty$), we have immediately the next result.

PROPOSITION 4.6 *Assume that the initial distribution of private beliefs is unbounded. Then the belief of any agent converges to the truth: his probability assessment of the good state converges to 1 in the good state and to 0 in the bad state.*

DOES CONVERGENCE TO THE TRUTH MATTER?

A bounded distribution of beliefs is necessary for a herd on an incorrect action, as emphasized by Smith and Sørensen (2001). Some have concluded that the properties of the simple model of BHW are not very robust: cascades are not generic and do not occur for sensible distributions of beliefs; the beliefs converge to the truth if there are agents with sufficiently strong beliefs. In analyzing properties of social learning, the literature has often focused on whether learning converges to the truth or not. This focus is legitimate for theorists, but it is seriously misleading. What is the difference between a slow convergence to the truth and a fast convergence to an error? From a welfare point of view and for many people, it is not clear.

The focus on the ultimate convergence has sometimes hidden the central message of studies on social learning: the combination of history's weight and of self-interest slows down learning from others. The beauty of the BHW model is that it is nongeneric in some sense (cascades do not occur under some perturbations), but its properties are generic.

If beliefs converge to the truth, the speed of convergence is the central issue. This is why the paper of Vives (1993) was so useful in the previous chapter. We learned from that model that an observation noise reduces the speed of learning from others. Because the discreteness of the action space is a particularly coarse filter, the slowing down of social learning should also take place here. When private beliefs are bounded, social learning does not converge to the truth. When private beliefs are unbounded, we should observe slow convergence.

We saw that cascades do not occur for sensible distributions of beliefs because the signal of the action (investment or no investment) is vanishingly weak when the public belief tends to the cascade set corresponding to the action. This argument applies when the distribution of beliefs is unbounded, because the mass of atoms at the extreme ends of the distribution must be vanishingly small. Hence, there is an immediate presumption that social learning must be slow asymptotically. The slow learning is first illustrated in an example and then analyzed in detail.

A NUMERICAL EXAMPLE

The private signals are defined by $s = \theta + \epsilon$, where ϵ is normally distributed with variance σ^2. An exercise shows that if μ tends to 0, the mass of agents with beliefs above $1 - \mu$ tends to zero faster than any power of μ. A numerical example of the evolution of beliefs is presented in Figure 4.4. One observes immediately that the pattern is similar to a cascade in the BHW model with the occurrence of black sheep.

For this example only, it is assumed that the true state is 1. The initial public belief is $\mu_1 = 0.2689$ (equivalent to a LLR of -1), and $\sigma = 1.5$. The actions of individuals

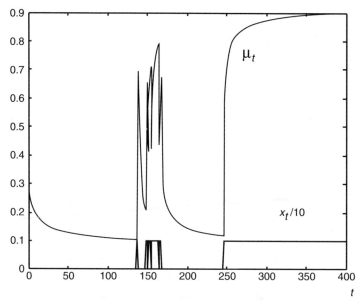

Figure 4.4 An example of the evolution of public belief. The upper graph represents the evolution of the public belief. The lower graph represents the sequence of individuals' actions. It is distinct from the horizontal axis only if $x_t = 1$.

in each period are presented by the lower schedule (equal to 0.1 if $x_t = 1$ and to 0 otherwise). For the first 135 periods, $x_t = 0$ and μ_t decreases monotonically from around 0.27 to around 0.1. In period 136, the agent has a signal that is sufficiently strong to have a belief $\tilde{\mu}_{136} > c = 0.5$, and he invests. Following this action, the public belief is higher than 0.5 (because 0.5 is a lower bound on the belief of agent 135), and $\mu_{137} > 0.5$. In the example, $\mu_{137} = 0.54$. The next two agents also invest, and $\mu_{139} = 0.7$. However, agent 139 does not invest, and hence the public belief must fall below 0.5: $\mu_{140} = 0.42$. Each time the sign of $\mu_{t+1} - \mu_t$ changes, there is a large jump in μ_t.

Figure 4.4 provides a nice illustration of the herding properties found by BHW in a model with black sheep who deviate from the herds. The figure exhibits two properties that are standard in models of social learning with discrete decisions:

(i) when μ_t eventually converges monotonically to the true value of 1 (after period 300 here), the convergence is very slow;
(ii) when a herd stops, the public belief changes by a quantum jump.

Slow Learning from Others

Assume now a precision of the private signals such that $\sigma_\epsilon = 4$, and an initial public belief $\mu_1 = 0.2689$ (with LLR equal to -1). The true state is good. The model was simulated for 500 periods, and the public belief was computed for period 500. The simulation was repeated 100 times. In 97 of the 100 simulations, no investment took place and the public belief decreased by a small amount to a value $\mu_{500} = 0.2659$. In only three cases did some investment take place, with μ_{500} equal to 0.2912, 0.7052, and 0.6984, respectively. Hardly a fast convergence!

By contrast, consider the case where agents observe directly the private signals of others and do not have to make inferences from the observations of private actions. From the specification of the private signals and Bayes's rule,

$$\lambda_{t+1} = \lambda_1 + t\left(\frac{\theta_1 - \theta_0}{\sigma_\epsilon^2}\right)\left(\frac{\theta_1 - \theta_0}{2} + \eta_t\right) \quad \text{with} \quad \eta_t = \frac{1}{t}\sum_{k=1}^{t}\epsilon_k.$$

Given the initial belief $\mu_1 = 0.2689$, $\theta_0 = 0$, $\theta_1 = 1$, $t = 499$, and $\sigma_\epsilon = 4$, we have

$$\lambda_{500} = -1 + (31.2)(0.5 + \eta_{500}),$$

where the variance of η_{500} is $16/499 \approx (0.18)^2$. Hence, λ_{500} is greater than 5.33 with probability 0.95. Converting the LLR to probabilities, we find that μ_{500} belongs to the interval $(0.995, 1)$ with probability 0.95. What a difference from the case where agents observed private actions! The example – which is not particularly convoluted – shows that convergence to the truth with unbounded private precisions may not mean much practically. Even when the distribution of private signals is unbounded, the process of social learning can be very slow when agents observe discrete actions. The cascades in Figure 4.3 are a better stylized description of the properties of social learning through discrete actions than the convergence result of Proposition 4.6. The properties of the example are confirmed by the general analysis of the convergence in Section 4.4.

4.4 Herds and the Slow Convergence of Beliefs

4.4.1 Herds

The MCT implies that the public belief converges almost surely. Assume that the distribution of beliefs is bounded. In the limit, the support of the distribution must be included in one of the two cascade sets. Suppose that on some path the support of the distribution converges to the upper half of the cascade set where all agents invest: $\underline{\mu}_t \to c$. We now prove by contradiction that the number of periods with no investment is finite on this path.

Because there is a subsequence $x_{n_t} = 0$, we may assume $\underline{\mu}_{n_t} < c$. Following the observation of $x_n = 0$, Bayes's rule implies

$$\lambda_{n_t+1} = \lambda_{n_t} + \nu_{n_t} \quad \text{with} \quad \nu_{n_t} = \log\left(\frac{F^1(\underline{\lambda}_1 + z_{n_t})}{F^0(\underline{\lambda}_1 + z_{n_t})}\right), \quad \text{and} \quad z_{n_t} = \gamma - \underline{\lambda}_{n_t}.$$

By the proportional property that was defined in (2.12), if $z_{n_t} \to 0$, there exists $\alpha < 0$ such that $\nu_{n_t} < \alpha$, which contradicts the convergence of λ_t: the jump down of the LLR contradicts the convergence. The same argument can be used in the case of an unbounded distribution of beliefs.

THEOREM 4.1 *On any path $\{x_t\}_{t \geq 1}$ with social learning, a herd begins in finite time. If the distribution of beliefs is unbounded and $\theta = \theta_1$ ($\theta = \theta_0$), there exists T such that if $t > T$, then $x_t = 1$ ($x_t = 0$), almost surely.*

This result is due to Smith and Sørensen (2001). It shows that herds take place eventually although, generically, not all agents are herding in any period!

4.4.2 The Asymptotic Rate of Convergence Is Zero

When beliefs are bounded, they may converge to an incorrect value with a wrong herd. The issue of convergence speed makes sense only if beliefs are unbounded. This section provides a general analysis of the convergence in the binary model. Without loss of generality, we assume that the cost of investment is $c = \frac{1}{2}$.

Suppose that the true state is $\theta = 0$. The public belief μ_t converges to 0. However, as $\mu_t \to 0$, there are fewer and fewer agents with a sufficiently high belief who can go against the public belief if called upon to act. Most agents do not invest. The probability that an investing agent appears becomes vanishingly small if μ tends to 0, because the density of beliefs near 1 is vanishingly small if the state is 0. It is because no agent acts contrary to the herd, although there could be some, that the public belief tends to zero. As the probability of contrarian agents tends to zero, the social learning slows down.

Let f^1 and f^0 be the density functions in states 1 and 0. From the proportional property (Section 2.3.1), they satisfy

$$(4.5) \qquad f^1(\mu) = \mu\phi(\mu), \qquad f^0(\mu) = (1 - \mu)\phi(\mu),$$

where $\phi(\mu)$ is a function. We will assume, without loss of generality, that this function is continuous.

If $\theta = 0$ and the public belief converges to 0, intuition suggests that the convergence is fastest when a herd takes place with no investment. The next result, which is proven in the appendix (Section 4.8) characterizes the convergence in this case.

PROPOSITION 4.7 *Assume that the distributions of private beliefs in the two states satisfy (4.5) with $\phi(0) > 0$, and that $\theta = 0$. Then, in a herd with $x_t = 0$, if $t \to \infty$, the public belief μ_t satisfies asymptotically the relation*

$$\frac{\mu_{t+1} - \mu_t}{\mu_t} \approx -\phi(0)\mu_t,$$

and μ_t converges to 0 like $1/t$: there exists $\alpha > 0$ such that if $\mu_t < \alpha$, then $t\mu_t \to a$ for some $a > 0$.

If $\phi(1) > 0$, the same property applies to herds with investment, mutatis mutandis.

The previous result shows that in a herd, the asymptotic rate of convergence is equal to 0.

The domain in which $\phi(\mu) > 0$ represents the support of the distribution of private beliefs. Recall that the convergence of social learning is driven by the agents with extreme beliefs. It is therefore important to consider the case where the densities of these agents are not too small. This property is embodied in the inequalities $\phi(0) > 0$ and $\phi(1) > 0$. They represent a property of a *fat tail* of the distribution of private beliefs. If $\phi(0) = \phi(1)$, we will say that the distributions of private beliefs have *thin tails*. The previous proposition assumes the case of fat tails which is the most favorable for a fast convergence.

We know from Theorem 4.1 that a herd eventually begins with probability 1. Proposition 4.7 characterized the rate of convergence in a herd, and it can be used to prove the following result.[8]

THEOREM 4.2 *Assume the distributions of private beliefs satisfy (4.5) with $\phi(0) > 0$ and $\phi(1) > 0$. Then μ_t converges in probability to the true $\theta \in \{0, 1\}$ like $1/t$.*

THE BENCHMARK: LEARNING WITH OBSERVABLE PRIVATE BELIEFS

When agents observe beliefs through actions, there is a loss of information, which can be compared with the case where private beliefs are directly observable. In Section 2.2.4, the rate of convergence is shown to be exponential when agents have binary private signals. We assume here the private belief of agent t is publicly observable. The property of exponential convergence in Section 2.2.4 is generalized by the following result.

PROPOSITION 4.8 *Assume $\theta = 0$ and $\phi(\mu)$ is constant in (4.5). If the belief of any agent t is observable, there exists $\gamma > 0$ such that $\mu_t = e^{-\gamma t} z_t$ where z_t tends to 0 almost surely.*

The contrast between Theorem 4.2 and Proposition 4.8 shows that the social learning through the observation of discrete actions is much slower, *exponentially slower*,[9] than if private information were publicly observable.

4.4.3 Why Do Herds Occur?

Herds must eventually occur, as shown in Theorem 4.1. The proof of that result rests on the MCT: the break of a herd induces a large change of the beliefs, which contradicts the convergence. Lones Smith has insisted, quite rightly, that one should provide a

---

[8] See Chamley (2003c).

[9] Smith and Sørensen (2001) provide a technical result (Theorem 4) that states that the Markov process defined in (4.3) exhibits exponential convergence of beliefs to the truth under some differentiability condition. Because the result is in a central position in a paper on social learning, and they provide no discussion of the issue, the reader who is not very careful may believe that the convergence of beliefs is exponential in models of social learning. As stated in Smith and Sørensen (2001), the convergence of beliefs to a (possibly incorrect) limit is exponential if private beliefs are bounded. The appendix of Smith and Sørensen (1996) which is the basis for Smith and Sørensen (2001), analyzes the occurence of herds with unbounded private beliefs and provides additional results. The presentation in this book has been elaborated independently from that appendix.

direct proof that herds take place for sure eventually. This is done by computing the probability that a herd is broken in some period after time t. Such a probability tends to zero, as shown in the next result (Chamley, 2003c).

THEOREM 4.3 *Assume the distributions of private beliefs satisfy (4.5) with $\phi(0) > 0$ and $\phi(1) > 0$. Then the probability that a herd has not started by date t tends to 0 like $1/t$.*

4.4.4 Discrete Actions and the Slow Convergence of Beliefs

The assumption of a fat tail of the distribution of beliefs, $\phi(0) > 0$, $\phi(1) > 0$, is easy to make mathematically, but it is not supported by any strong empirical evidence.

The thinner the tail of the distribution of private beliefs, the slower the convergence of social learning. However, if private signals are observable, the convergence is exponential for any distribution. The case of a thin tail provides a transition between a distribution with a thick tail and a bounded distribution where the convergence stops completely in finite time, almost surely.

It is reasonable to consider the case where the density of beliefs is vanishingly small when the belief approaches perfect knowledge. We make the following assumption. For some $b > 0$, $c > 0$,

$$(4.6) \qquad f^1(1) = 0 \quad \text{and} \quad \lim_{\mu \to 0} \frac{f^1(\mu)}{(1-\mu)^b} = c > 0.$$

The higher is b, the thinner is the tail of the distribution near the truth. One can show that the sequence of beliefs with the history of no investment tends to 0 like $1/t^{1/(1+b)}$ (Exercise 4.9).

The main assumption in this chapter is, as emphasized in BHW, that actions are discrete. To simplify, we have assumed two actions, but the results could be generalized to a finite set of actions. The discreteness of the set of actions imposes a filter that blurs the information conveyed by actions more than does the noise of the previous chapter, where agents could choose an action in a continuum. Therefore, the reduction in social learning is much more significant in the present chapter than in the previous one.

Recall that when private signals can be observed, the convergence of the public belief is exponential like $e^{-\alpha t}$ for some $\alpha > 0$. When agents choose an action in a continuum and a noise blurs the observation, as in the previous chapter, the convergence is reduced to a process like $e^{-\alpha t^{1/3}}$. When actions are discrete, the convergence is reduced, at best, to a much slower process like $1/t$. If the private signals are Gaussian (as in the previous chapter), the convergence is significantly slower, as shown in the example of Figure 4.4. The fundamental insight of BHW is robust.

4.5 Pricing the Informational Externality

When individuals choose their optimal action, they ignore the information benefit that is provided to others by their action. We assume that the number of agents is infinite and countable. In any period t, the value of the externality is taken into account in the *social welfare* function

$$V_t = E \left[\sum_{k \geq 0} \delta^k (\theta - c) x_{t+k} \right],$$

where δ is a discount factor $(0 < \delta < 1)$, c is the cost of investment, and x_{t+k} is the action of agent $t + k$, $x_{t+k} \in \Xi = \{0, 1\}$.

4.5.1 The Social Optimum

We assume that an agent cannot reveal directly his private information: he communicates his information through his action. The *constrained social optimum* is achieved when each agent t is *socially benevolent* and chooses his action in order to maximize the social welfare function V_t with the knowledge that each agent in period $t + k$, $k \geq 1$, likewise maximizes V_{t+k}.

The decision rule of a socially benevolent agent is a function from his information (private belief and public belief) to the set of actions. He cannot communicate his private information directly, but other agents know his decision rule and may infer from his choice some information on his private belief and therefore on the state of nature. In order to focus on the main features, let us consider the basic model: there are two states, and each agent has a SBS with precision q.

There are two possible decision rules: either the agent follows his signal and chooses the action $x = s$, or he herds, ignores his private signal, and chooses an action that maximizes his payoff given the public belief.

The social welfare at the beginning of some arbitrary period depends only on the public belief μ (probability of state 1) at the beginning of the period, $V(\mu)$. Let μ^+ and μ^- be the beliefs that are derived from the combination of the public belief μ and of a good or bad signal.[10] If the agent in the period chooses an action identical to his signal, he reveals his signal, and the function V satisfies the equation

$$(4.7) \qquad V(\mu) = \Big(\mu q + (1 - \mu)(1 - q) \Big) \Big(\mu^+ - c + \delta V(\mu^+) \Big)$$
$$+ \Big(\mu(1 - q) + (1 - \mu)q \Big) \delta V(\mu^-).$$

The first term is the expected gain from receiving a good signal and investing: the probability of the event is $\mu q + (1 - \mu)(1 - q)$; the payoff of the agent is $\mu^+ - c$; and $\delta V(\mu^+)$ is the payoff of subsequent agents who get the information μ^+. Likewise, the second term is the expected gain from receiving a bad signal and not investing.

---

[10]
$$\mu^+ = \frac{\mu q}{\mu q + (1 - \mu)(1 - q)} \text{ and } \mu^- = \frac{\mu(1 - q)}{\mu(1 - q) + (1 - \mu)q}.$$

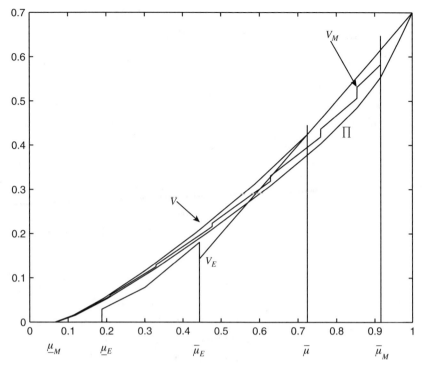

Figure 4.5 Welfare and profit with a monopoly. Parameters: $q = 0.65$, $c = 0.3$, $\delta = 0.92$. V and V_E are the levels of social welfare in the constrained optimum and in the laissez-faire equilibrium. Π is the profit of the monopoly, and V_M is the social welfare under a monopoly.

When the agent does not herd, the social welfare function $V(\mu)$ satisfies equation (4.7).

The no-herding decision requires that both herding with no investment and herding with investment be suboptimal. The first condition requires that the social welfare level $V(\mu)$ be not strictly smaller than $(\mu - c)/(1 - \delta)$, which is the social welfare level in a herd with investment. The second condition is that the social welfare level $V(\mu)$ should be positive; otherwise a herd with no investment would be optimal. In (4.7), the right-hand side defines a mapping $\mathcal{T}(V)$. Taking into account the no-herding conditions, the social welfare function satisfies the equation

$$(4.8) \qquad V = \max\left(\max\left(\mathcal{T}(V), \frac{\mu - c}{1 - \delta} \right), 0 \right).$$

The right-hand side defines an operator. The function V is a fixed point of that operator, which is computed by iteration. The optimal social welfare function is presented in Figure 4.5 by the schedule V, which is the highest curve in the figure.

The Laissez-Faire Equilibrium
The social welfare in the equilibrium where each agent acts selfishly and ignores the information externality (as in the BHW model) is represented by the schedule V_E.

It is below[11] the schedule V, and the range of experimentation $[\underline{\mu}_E, \overline{\mu}_E]$ is strictly contained in the *interval of experimentation* for the social optimum, $[\underline{\mu}, \overline{\mu}]$.

We observe some intuitive properties:

(i) There is an interval of public belief values $(\underline{\mu}, \overline{\mu})$ in which an agent does not herd and follows his private signal. In that interval the agent invests even if his payoff is negative in order to show that he has a good signal, and he does not invest even if his payoff is positive to show that he has a bad signal. It is in this sense that the interval of public beliefs $(\underline{\mu}, \overline{\mu})$ can be called the interval of experimentation. The rule for experimentation depends only on the public belief.

(ii) The interval of experimentation in the laissez-faire equilibrium is the complement of the cascade set of the public belief. That interval is narrower than the interval in the optimum, as explained before. The value of V_E is also higher than 0 and $(\mu - c)/(1 - \delta)$.

In a constrained Pareto optimum, the path exhibits two phases: (i) as long as μ is in the interval of experimentation $(\underline{\mu}, \overline{\mu})$, agents should follow their own signal and ignore the history; (ii) when μ exits the interval of experimentation, all agents should herd and either invest (if $\mu > \overline{\mu}$) or not invest (if $\mu < \underline{\mu}$). The socially optimal rule *does not call for complete learning*. If the public confidence is sufficiently high (μ sufficiently close to 1 or 0), then herding is optimal. The private cost of ignoring the public information is greater than the benefit of revealing that information. The property of the socially optimal decision rule is stated as a formal result, the proof of which is left to the reader.[12]

PROPOSITION 4.9 *In a constrained social optimum, an agent follows his own signal if the public belief is in some interval $(\underline{\mu}, \overline{\mu})$. If in some period T one has $\mu_T < \underline{\mu}$, then for all periods $t > T$, agents should herd with no investment. If $\mu_T > \overline{\mu}$, all subsequent agents should herd and invest.*

On a socially optimal path with binary private signals, a cascade eventually occurs, but this cascade occurs with a higher precision of the public belief. The behavior of the socially optimal path for an arbitrary distribution of private information remains to be analyzed. In particular, it would be interesting to compare the rate of convergence with perfect observation of the private information with the rate of convergence in the constrained social optimum.

---

[11] The discontinuities of V_E have a simple and important interpretation: the value of $V_E(\mu)$ jumps down when μ crosses $\overline{\mu}_E$. If $\mu < \underline{\mu}_E$, an agent with a low signal does not invest and reveals that information. This information is lost if $\mu > \overline{\mu}_E$, because the agent with a low signal invests like an agent with a high signal and does not reveal his information.

[12] We ignore the technicalities that arise if μ is equal to one of the bounds of the interval of experimentation.

The decision rule of a social planner depends only on the public information. Furthermore, the decision model of each agent is known. Hence, the socially optimal policy can be decentralized by incentives. A social planner can always use a subsidy (positive or negative) on investment that induces agents to act according to their private signal when the public belief is in the interval of experimentation. The role of the social planner is to take account of the information externality for better decisions in the future. In some settings, there may be agents who internalize this externality. As an example, the role of a monopoly is analyzed in the next subsection.

4.5.2 A Monopoly

A monopoly uses prices and takes into account the effect of experimentation on future profits. The extraction of his rent generates the usual distortion from the first-best, but if the discount rate is sufficiently low (and hence the value of the information externality sufficiently large), the monopoly may improve the social welfare because it takes into account the benefit of learning for the future. Here, we do not consider the distribution of income, and the profit of the monopoly is redistributed.

We analyze this problem within the framework of the BHW model, where a monopoly produces an indivisible good at a fixed cost c and faces one customer per period. In each period t, the price of the good is set at p_t by the monopoly, and a new customer either buys the good or not. The monopoly produces the good only if the customer buys the good. The objective of the monopoly is to maximize the sum of discounted profits

$$\Pi = E\left[\sum_{t\geq 0} \delta^t (p_t - c)x_t\right],$$

where x_t is equal to one if there is a sale in period t, and to zero otherwise. The other features of the model are unchanged. The good has a value $\theta \in \{0, 1\}$ to the customers, each of whom has a private signal that is binary and symmetric with precision q. The monopoly's information is the public information. As in the analysis of the social optimum, the history h_t contains all past transactions and prices.

The monopoly has an incentive to generate some social learning in order to capture the surplus of future sales. For example, suppose that the public belief μ is such that the belief of an optimist is slightly below c. In the standard model, no agent buys, and there is a herd with no purchase. A monopoly can charge a price p below the production cost c to break the herd. If the customer in the period is an optimist, the public belief increases above c and the monopoly can extract a surplus in the game that begins in the following period.

The *experimentation phase* of the game is defined as in the previous section. Suppose there is no herding: optimists buy and pessimists do not buy. Because there are only two types of customers, the demand is a step function. As in the previous section, the beliefs of optimists and pessimists are denoted by μ^+ and μ^-, respectively, when the public belief is μ. A customer buys if and only if his belief is higher than the price. Any price in the interval (μ^-, μ^+) is dominated by a higher price, which can be arbitrarily close to μ^+, and which generates the same sales and a strictly higher profit. Likewise, the price μ^- dominates any price that is lower.

If the monopolist does not want to continue the game, he sets a price above μ^+: no one buys, nothing is learned, and the game stops. Conditional on the continuation of the game, the strategy set in any period can be reduced to the two prices μ^- and μ^+, or, to be accurate, to a price vanishingly close to one of these two values and strictly smaller. To simplify, we will identify the prices with these two values. If $p = \mu^+$, only the optimists buy: the realization of a sale or no sale reveals the signal of the buyer to all agents. If $p = \mu^-$, all agents buy and there is no information: all agents herd.

Denote by $\Pi(\mu)$ the value of the game for the monopoly when the public belief is μ. If the monopoly charges μ^+, his payoff function Π satisfies the dynamic programming equation

$$(4.9) \qquad \Pi(\mu) = \Big(\mu q + (1 - \mu)(1 - q)\Big)\Big(\mu^+ - c + \delta\Pi(\mu^+)\Big)$$
$$+ \Big(\mu(1 - q) + (1 - \mu)q\Big)\delta\Pi(\mu^-).$$

This equation is identical to the dynamic equation (4.7) of the social planner.

If the monopoly charges μ^- forever and sells to all agents, there is herding with all buyers purchasing the good. In this case, the value of the game for the monopoly is

$$\overline{\Pi}(\mu) = \frac{\mu^- - c}{1 - \delta}.$$

The monopolist experiments and generates information as long as $0 < \Pi(\mu) > \overline{\Pi}(\mu)$. If $\Pi(\mu) < 0$, he charges a price higher than μ^+, and the game stops with no further sale. If $\Pi(\mu) < \overline{\Pi}(\mu)$, he chooses the lower price μ^- and sells to all agents for all periods: he reaches the mass market. The value function of the monopoly is therefore completely determined by

$$(4.10) \qquad \Pi(\mu) = \max\Big(\max\Big(\mathcal{T}(\Pi(\mu)), \frac{\mu^- - c}{1 - \delta}\Big), 0\Big),$$

where $\mathcal{T}$ is the same operator as in (4.8). The dynamic programming equations (4.9) and (4.7) are identical. Comparing the definition of Π in (4.10) with the social optimum V in (4.8), and using $\mu^- < \mu$, we have the following proposition.

PROPOSITION 4.10 *Let $V(\mu)$ and $\Pi(\mu)$ be the social welfare under a constrained Pareto optimum and the profit function of the monopoly, respectively. If $V(\mu) > 0$, then $V(\mu) > \Pi(\mu)$.*

We have seen that the social planner experiments as long as $\mu \in (\underline{\mu}, \overline{\mu})$. Likewise, the monopolist experiments as long as $\mu \in (\underline{\mu}_M, \overline{\mu}_M)$. From the previous result and definitions (4.8) and (4.10), the following inequalities hold:

(4.11) $0 < \underline{\mu} \leq \underline{\mu}_M < c.$

The monopoly requires a higher level of belief to continue the game, because his profit is smaller than the social surplus of the game.

One may conjecture that the monopoly experiments more than the social planner if the level of belief is high in order to maximize his surplus. In the example of Figure 4.5, one verifies that $\overline{\mu} < \overline{\mu}_M$.

The social welfare under a monopoly is represented in Figure 4.5. It depends on the interval of experimentation of the monopolist and is the solution of the following equations:

(4.12) $V_M(\mu) = \begin{cases} 0 & \text{if } 0 \leq \mu < \underline{\mu}_M, \\ \left(\mu q + (1-\mu)(1-q)\right)\left(\mu^+ - c + \delta V_M(\mu^+)\right) & \\ \quad + \left(\mu(1-q) + (1-\mu)q\right)\delta V_M(\mu^-) & \text{if } \underline{\mu}_M < \mu < \overline{\mu}_M, \\ \dfrac{\mu - c}{1 - \delta} & \text{if } \overline{\mu}_M < \mu < 1. \end{cases}$

Note that if μ crosses $\overline{\mu}_M$ and increases, the social welfare $V_M(\mu)$ jumps up. At this level of belief, there is too much experimentation from a social point of view: the monopolist wants to establish a higher price for the herding (which must take place eventually). When μ increases to a value above $\overline{\mu}_M$, experimentation stops and the social welfare jumps up. There are other jumps for lower values of μ because the upper end of the interval of experimentation, $\overline{\mu}_M$, may be reached, with strictly positive probability, in a finite number of steps.

A Low Discount Rate
When the discount factor increases, the monopoly has more incentives to elicit experimentation for future profits. One may conjecture that if $\delta \to 1$, the interval of experimentation of the monopolist tends to the interval $[0, 1]$ (Exercise 4.7).

DISCUSSION
1. The public belief μ_t is a martingale and therefore converges. It cannot converge to a value strictly between 0 and 1 and for which there is no herding. (That would lead to a contradiction.) Hence, the strategy of the monopoly must be to eventually choose the low price μ^- forever or to leave the market.
2. One might think that a monopolist, like a restaurant owner, would set a low price during an initial phase in order to sell more and attract new customers. This intuitive argument is not supported by the present analysis. The owner should do the opposite and set the price sufficiently high, during a first phase, to show

that "there is a flow of patrons even though the price is relatively high." Once the reputation of the restaurant has been established in this *elitist phase*, the cost of "proving oneself" by turning away customers with relatively low taste is too high with respect to the marginal improvement in reputation. The owner goes to *mass production* by lowering his price in order to make a profit on these customers as well. (Recall that their valuation μ^- is higher than the cost c of producing the meal.) An argument for an initial phase of relatively low *promotional price* would rest on a different model.

3. The previous model has the particular feature that the highest possible price generates a maximum amount of learning in that it separates perfectly the optimists from the pessimists. The binary private signal is a very special case of private information, however. An analysis with a more general model would be worthwhile.

4. Becker (1991) reflects on the well-known observation of two restaurants facing each other, one with a long queue, the other with empty seats. Why doesn't the first raise its price? Becker posits a demand $d_i(p, D)$ by individual i ($i = 1, \ldots, N$), $D = \sum d_i$. Such a demand may be rising over some range, which would induce the supplier to ration an amount $S < D$. This model is built in an *ad hoc* way to obtain a preestablished conclusion. It does not have a structural foundation, an optimizing behavior for the consumers, a dynamic analysis of learning with imperfect information, and an analysis of the history that preceeds a steady state with rationing. A proper analysis of this interesting problem remains to be done.

5. Queues may improve the efficiency of social choice. A longer queue raises the cost of the more popular restaurant, or the more popular doctor, and induces people to experiment at other places (Huynh and Rosenthal, 2000).

4.6 Crashes and Booms

The stylized pattern of a herd that is broken by a sudden event is emblematic of a pattern of "business as usual" where at first beliefs change little and then some event generates a crash or a boom, after which the new beliefs seem "obvious" in a "wisdom after the facts." This sequence has been illustrated by Caplin and Leahy (1994). Their assumption of endogenous timing is not necessary for the property.

In each period, there is a new population of agents, which forms a continuum of mass 1. Each agent has a private information on θ in the form of a Gaussian signal $s_t = \theta + \epsilon_t$, where ϵ_t has a normal distribution $\mathcal{N}(0, \sigma_\epsilon^2)$ and is independent of other variables. Each agent chooses a zero–one action $x \in \{0, 1\}$.

In period t, agents know the history $h_t = \{Y_1, \ldots, Y_{t-1}\}$ of the aggregate variable $Y_t = X_t + \eta_t$, where X_t is the mass of investments by the agents in period t, and η_t is a noise which is distributed $\mathcal{N}(0, \sigma_\eta^2)$.

If λ_t is the public LLR between states θ_1 and θ_0, an agent with private signal s has a LLR equal to

$$\lambda(s) = \lambda_t + \frac{\theta_1 - \theta_0}{\sigma_\epsilon^2}\left(s - \frac{\theta_0 + \theta_1}{2}\right).$$

Given the net payoffs in the two states, the agent invests if and only if he believes state θ_1 to be more likely than state θ_0, hence if his LLR is positive. This is equivalent to a private signal s such that

$$s > s^*(\lambda_t) = \frac{\theta_0 + \theta_1}{2} - \frac{\sigma_\epsilon^2}{\theta_1 - \theta_0}\lambda_t.$$

Let $F(\cdot;\sigma)$ be the c.d.f. of the Gaussian distribution $\mathcal{N}(0, \sigma^2)$. Because the mass of the population in period t is 1, the level of aggregate endogenous investment is

$$X_t = 1 - F(s^*(\lambda_t) - \theta; \sigma_\epsilon).$$

The level of aggregate activity,

$$Y_t = 1 - F(s^*(\lambda_t) - \theta; \sigma_\epsilon) + \eta_t,$$

is a noisy signal on θ. The derivative of Y_t with respect to θ is

$$\frac{\partial Y_t}{\partial \theta} = \frac{1}{\sqrt{2\pi}\sigma_\epsilon}(s^*(\lambda_t) - \theta) \exp\left(-\frac{(s^*(\lambda_t) - \theta)^2}{2\sigma_\epsilon^2}\right).$$

If the cutoff point $s^*(\lambda_t)$ is far to the right or to the left, the multiplier of θ on Y_t is small and the effect of θ on Y_t is dwarfed by the observation noise η_t, exactly as in the model of Vives (1993). Hence, the information content of the observation Y_t is small when most agents invest ($s^*(\lambda_t)$ is low) or most do not invest ($s^*(\lambda_t)$ is high).

Suppose that the true state is θ_0 and that the level of optimism, as measured by the LLR, is high. Most agents invest, and the aggregate activity is dominated by the noise. However, the beliefs of agents are unbounded, and the public belief converges to the true state. When the public belief decreases to the middle range, the difference between the mass of agents in the two states becomes larger and dominates the noise. The level of aggregate activity is more informative. Because the true state is θ_0, the public belief decreases rapidly and the aggregate activity falls drastically. A crash occurs.

This property is illustrated by a simulation. Two realizations of the observation shocks are considered. In the first, all realizations of the shocks are set at zero: $\eta_t \equiv 0$.

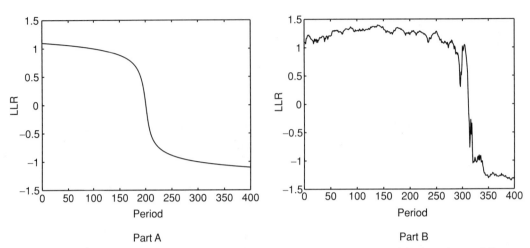

Part A   Part B

Figure 4.6 Sudden changes of beliefs. Parameters: $\theta_0 = 0$, $\theta_1 = 1$, $\sigma_\eta = 0.5$, $\sigma_\epsilon = 2$, $c = 0.5$, $\theta = \theta_1$, $\mu_1 = 0.75$. The public belief is measured as the LLR on the vertical axis. (Note that the belief is not measured by the probability of state θ_1.) The period is reported on the horizontal axis.

The evolution of the public belief,[13] measured in LLR, is represented in Part A of Figure 4.6. In Part B, the evolution of the public belief is represented for random realizations of η_t.

In Part A, the public belief evolves slowly at first, then changes rapidly in a few periods and evolves slowly after. The LLR tends to $-\infty$, but the convergence is obviously very slow.

The sudden change occurs here because of the nonlinearity of the information content of individual actions. In Part B, the changes λ_t are also sudden.

The model generates crashes and booms symmetrically. If the initial level of pessimism is low and the true state is high, eventually agents learn about it and the learning process goes through a phase of rapid changes of beliefs.

4.7 Bibliographical Notes

SOCIAL LEARNING IN A CHANGING WORLD

Throughout this chapter and the next, the state of nature is invariant. This assumption is made to focus on the learning of a given state, and it applies when the state does not change much during the phase of learning. Assume now, following Moscarini,

---

[13] The update of the public belief from λ_t to λ_{t+1} is given by Bayes's rule:

$$\lambda_{t+1} = \lambda_t + \log\left(\frac{f(x_t - (1 - F(s^*(\mu_t)) - \theta_1; \sigma_\epsilon)); \sigma_\eta)}{f(x_t - (1 - F(s^*(\mu_t)) - \theta_0; \sigma_\epsilon)); \sigma_\eta)}\right),$$

where f is the density function associated with the c.d.f. F.

Ottaviani, and Smith (1998), that the value of θ switches between θ_0 and θ_1 according to a random Markov process: the set of states of nature $\Theta = \{\theta_0, \theta_1\}$ is fixed, but between periods, θ switches to the other value with probability π.

Suppose that all agents are herding in period t. Does the public belief stay constant as in the previous sections of this chapter? Agents learn nothing from the observation of others, but they know that θ evolves randomly. Ignoring the actions of others, the public belief (probability of state θ_1) regresses to the mean, $\frac{1}{2}$. Therefore, after a finite number of periods, the public belief does not dominate the belief of some agents, in which case not all agents herd. The cascade stops. This property is interesting only if π is neither too small nor too large: if π is very small, the regression to the mean is slow and the herding behavior may last a long time; if π is sufficiently large, the expectation of the exogenous change between periods is so large that the learning from others' actions, which is driven by their information about past values of θ, bears no relation to the current value of θ. No cascade can occur.

EXPERIMENTS

The BHW model has been experimented on in the laboratory by Anderson and Holt (1996, 1997). Such experiments raise the issues of the actual understanding of Bayesian inference by people (Holt and Anderson, 1996) and of the power of the tests. An important difficulty is in separating the rational Bayesian learning from *ad hoc* rules of decision making after the observations of others' actions (such as counting the number of actions of a given type in history, or taking into account the last observed action).[14] Huck and Oechssler (2000) find that the tests of Anderson and Holt are not powerful against simple rules. More recent experimental studies include Çelen and Kariv (2002b, 2002c).

EXERCISES

EXERCISE 4.1
BHW suggest that submissions to publications may be subject to herding. Explain how herding may arise and some good papers may not be published.

EXERCISE 4.2 Probability of a wrong cascade
Consider the BHW model with parameters μ_1, c, p. Determine the *ex ante* probability of a herd on the wrong decision.

EXERCISE 4.3 The model of Banerjee (1992)
Assume that the state of nature is a real number θ in the interval $(0, 1)$, with a uniform distribution. There is a countable set of agents, with private signals equal to θ with

---

[14] This issue is raised again in empirical studies on the diffusion of innovations (Section 9.1.1).

probability $\beta > 0$, and equal to a number uniformly distributed on the interval $(0, 1)$ with probability $1 - \beta > 0$. (In this case the signal is not informative.) The agent observes only the value of his private signal. Each agent t chooses in period t an action $x_t \in (0, 1)$. The payoff is 1 if $x_t = \theta$, and 0 if $x_t \neq \theta$. Agent t observes the history of past actions and maximizes his expected payoff. If there is more than one action that maximizes his expected payoff, he chooses one of these actions with equal probability.

1. Analyze how herds occur in this model.
2. Can a herd arise on a wrong decision?

EXERCISE 4.4 The action set is bounded below (Chari and Kehoe, 2000)

In the standard model of this chapter, assume that agent t chooses an investment level x_t, which can be any real positive number. All agents have a binary private signal with precision $q > \frac{1}{2}$ and a payoff function

$$u(x, \theta) = 2(\theta - c)x - x^2 \quad \text{with} \quad x \geq 0.$$

1. Can an informational cascade take place with positive investment? Can there be an informational cascade with no investment?
2. Show that there is a strictly positive probability of underinvestment.

EXERCISE 4.5 Discontinuity of the Markov process of social learning

Take the standard model of Section 4.2, where the investment cost is $\frac{1}{2}$ with payoff $(E[\theta] - \frac{1}{2})x$, and each agent has a SBS with precision drawn from the uniform distribution on $(\frac{1}{2}, 1)$. Each agent knows his precision, but that precision is not observable by others.

1. Determine explicitly the Markov process defined by (4.3) when $\theta = 0$.
2. Show that 0 is the unique fixed point in μ if $\theta = 0$.
3. Show that $B(\cdot, 1)$ is not continuous in the first argument at the fixed point $\mu = 0$, and that therefore the partial derivative of B with respect to the second argument does not exist at the fixed point.
4. Assume that in each period, with probability $\alpha > 0$, the agent is a noise agent who invests with probability $\frac{1}{2}$. With probability $1 - \alpha$, the agent is of the rational type described before. The type of the agent is not publicly observable. Is your answer to question 3 modified?

EXERCISE 4.6 Confounded learning (Smith and Sørensen, 2001)

There is a countable population of agents. A fraction α of this population is of type A, and the others are of type B. In period t, agent t chooses between action 1 and action 0. There are two states of nature, 1 and 0. The actions' payoffs are specified in the following table (with $u_A > 0$, $u_B > 0$):

Type A	$x = 1$	$x = 0$
$\theta = 1$	1	0
$\theta = 0$	0	u_A

Type B	$x = 1$	$x = 0$
$\theta = 1$	0	u_B
$\theta = 0$	1	0

Each agent has a SBS with precision q (on the state θ), which is independent of his type. Let μ be the belief of an agent about state 1: $\mu = P(\theta = 1)$.

1. Show that an agent of type A takes action 1 if and only if he has a belief μ such that $\mu > (1 - \mu)u_A$. When does a type B take action 1?
2. Let λ be the public LLR between state 1 and state 0. Use a figure similar to Figure 4.3 to represent the evolution of the public belief.
3. Using the plot, illustrate the following cases:
   (i) an informational cascade where all agents take action 1,
   (ii) an informational cascade where all agents take action 0,
   (iii) an informational cascade where agents A take action 1 and agents B take action 0.

EXERCISE 4.7 Monopoly and herding
Consider the monopoly model of Section 4.5.2.

1. Determine the limits of the interval of experimentation of the monopoly when $\delta \to 1$.
2. Let $V_M(\mu)$ be the level of social welfare when the monopoly regulates the price of the good, $V(\mu)$ the social welfare in the Pareto optimum, $V^*(\mu)$ the social welfare in the first-best, and $V_E(\mu)$ the social welfare in the laissez-faire equilibrium. As $\delta \to 1$, analyze the limits of Π/V, V_M/V, V_E/V, and V/V^*.

EXERCISE 4.8 Rational expectations equilibrium and cascades
Following Minehart and Scotchmer (1999), assume $\theta \in \{0, 1\}$ and each agent chooses $x \in \{0, 1\}$ to maximize $E[(\theta - c)x]$. Each agent has a SBS of precision q. All agents take their decision simultaneously, knowing the decisions of the others. A *rational expectations equilibrium* (REE) is a Nash equilibrium of the game.

1. Show that in a REE, all agents take the same action. (Thus, they form a herd in the sense of Definition 4.3.)
2. Show that a REE exists if and only if nature's probability of the good state is such that in the BHW setting of sequential decisions, an informational cascade begins in the first period.

EXERCISE 4.9
Prove that if in Section 4.4.4 the densities of beliefs satisfy (4.6), then in a herd with
no investment the public belief tends to 0 like $1/t^{1/(1+b)}$. (Use the method in the proof
of Proposition 4.7.)

4.8 Appendix

4.8.1 Proofs

Proof of Proposition 4.4
Let $\underline{\mu}$ and $\overline{\mu}$ be the lower and upper bounds of the distribution of beliefs in period 1.
We assume that if $\underline{\mu} < \mu < \overline{\mu}$, then $F_1^{\theta_1}(\mu) < F_1^{\theta_0}(\mu)$. This property holds for any
period. By the MCT, λ_t converges to some value λ_∞ almost surely. By contradiction,
assume $\lambda_\infty \in (\gamma - \delta, \gamma + \delta)$. Because $F_t^{\theta_1}(\lambda_\infty) < F_t^{\theta_0}(\lambda_\infty)$, there exist $\epsilon > 0$ and
$\alpha > 0$ such that if $|\lambda - \lambda_\infty| < \epsilon$, then

$$\log\left(\frac{1 - F_t^{\theta_1}(\lambda)}{1 - F_t^{\theta_0}(\lambda)}\right) > \alpha \quad \text{and} \quad \log\left(\frac{F_t^{\theta_1}(\lambda)}{F_t^{\theta_0}(\lambda)}\right) < \alpha.$$

Because $\lambda_t \to \lambda_\infty$, there is T such that if $t > T$, then $|\lambda_t - \lambda_\infty| < \alpha/3$. Take $t > T$.
If $x_t = 1$, then by Bayes's rule in (4.2), $\lambda_{t+1} > \lambda_t + \alpha$, which is impossible because
$\lambda_t - \lambda_{t+1} < 2\alpha/3$. A similar contradiction arises if $x_t = 0$. ∎

Proof of Proposition 4.7
An agent chooses action 0 (he does not invest) if and only if his belief $\tilde{\mu}$ is smaller
than $\frac{1}{2}$, i.e., if his private belief is smaller than $1 - \mu$, where μ is the public belief.
In state θ, the probability of the event $x = 0$ is $F^\theta(1 - \mu)$. Because $F^1(\mu) < F^0(\mu)$,
the observation $x = 0$ is more likely in state 0. It is bad news and induces the lowest
possible public belief at the end of the period. The sequence of public beliefs in a herd
with no investment satisfies

$$(4.13) \quad \mu_{t+1} = \frac{\left(1 - \int_{1-\mu_t}^1 f^1(v)dv\right)\mu_t}{\left(1 - \int_{1-\mu_t}^1 f^1(v)dv\right)\mu_t + \left(1 - \int_{1-\mu_t}^1 f^0(v)dv\right)(1 - \mu_t)}.$$

Taking an approximation for small μ_t, we obtain

$$\mu_{t+1} \approx \frac{\left(1 - f^1(1)\mu_t\right)\mu_t}{\left(1 - f^1(1)\mu_t\right)\mu_t + \left(1 - f^0(1)\mu_t\right)(1 - \mu_t)}.$$

Using the condition of the proposition for the initial beliefs, we obtain

$$\frac{\mu_{t+1} - \mu_t}{\mu_t} \approx (f^0(1) - f^1(1))\mu_t = -\phi(0)\mu_t.$$

For the second part of the result, we use the previous approximation and consider the sequence $\{z_k\}$ defined by

(4.14) $\qquad z_{k+1} = z_k - a z_k^2, \qquad$ with $\quad a = \phi(0).$

This sequence tends to 0 like $1/k$. Let y_k be such that $z_k = (1 + y_k)/(ak)$. By substitution in (4.14),

$$1 + y_{k+1} = (k + 1)\left(\frac{1 + y_k}{k} - \frac{(1 + y_k)^2}{k^2}\right).$$

A straightforward manipulation[15] shows that $y_{k+1} < y_k$. Hence z_k tends to 0 like $1/k$ when $k \to \infty$. $\qquad\qquad\qquad\qquad\qquad\qquad\qquad\qquad\qquad\qquad\qquad\qquad$ ■

Proof of Proposition 4.8

The evolution of the public belief is determined by Bayes's rule in LLR:

(4.15) $\qquad \lambda_{t+1} = \lambda_t + \zeta_t \qquad$ with $\quad \zeta_t = \log\left(\frac{\hat{\mu}_t}{1 - \hat{\mu}_t}\right).$

Because $\theta = 0$, the random variable ζ_t has a bounded variance and a strictly negative mean, $-\overline{\gamma}$, such that

(4.16) $\qquad \overline{\gamma} = -\int_0^1 \log\left(\frac{v}{1 - v}\right) f^0(v)dv > 0.$

Choose γ such that $0 < \gamma < \overline{\gamma}$. Let $v_t = \lambda_t + \gamma t$. We have $v_{t+1} = v_t + \zeta_t'$ with $E[\zeta_t'] = -(\overline{\gamma} - \gamma) < 0$. Therefore, $v_t = v_0 + \sum_{k=1}^{t-1} \zeta_k'$ where $\sum_{k=1}^{n} \zeta_k'/n$ tends to $-(\overline{\gamma} - \gamma) < 0$ almost surely. Hence, $\sum_{k=1}^{t-1} \zeta_k'$ tends to $-\infty$ almost surely. Therefore, v_t tends to $-\infty$ and e^{v_t} tends to 0, almost surely. By definition of v_t, we have $\mu_t \le e^{-\gamma t} e^{v_t}.$ $\qquad\qquad\qquad\qquad\qquad\qquad\qquad\qquad\qquad\qquad\qquad\qquad\qquad\qquad$ ■

4.8.2 A Model of Learning with Two Types of Agents

In each period, agent t receives his signal s_t in a sequence of two independent steps. First, the precision q_t of his private signal takes either the value $\overline{q}$ with probability

---

15

$$1 + y_{k+1} = 1 + \frac{1}{k} - \frac{1}{k} - \frac{1}{k^2} + y_k + \frac{y_k}{k} - 2y_k\frac{k+1}{k^2} - y_k^2\frac{k+1}{k^2} < 1 + y_k.$$

π, or the value $\underline{q}$ with probability $1 - \pi$. By convention, $\overline{q} > \underline{q}$. Second, the value of the signal is realized randomly and such that $P(s_t = j \mid \theta = j) = q_t$. Each agent t observes the realization (q_t, s_t), which is not observable by others. The parameters $\underline{q}$, $\overline{q}$, and π and the signaling process are known by all agents. In order to facilitate the discussion, the fraction π of the agents endowed with a signal of high precision is assumed to be small. In any period, the model is in one of three possible regimes which depend on the public belief λ.

A. In the first regime, regime A, no agent herds. Define the values λ_A^* and λ_A^{**} such that

$$
\left. \begin{aligned}
\lambda_A^* &= \gamma - \log\left(\frac{\underline{q}}{1 - \underline{q}}\right) \\
\lambda_A^{**} &= \gamma + \log\left(\frac{\underline{q}}{1 - \underline{q}}\right)
\end{aligned} \right\} \quad \text{with} \quad \gamma = \log\left(\frac{c}{1 - c}\right).
$$

If $\lambda_A^* < \lambda_t \leq \lambda_A^{**}$, any agent with low precision invests if and only if the signal is good. An agent with high precision follows the same strategy *a fortiori*. Because no one herds, the observation of x_t is equivalent to the observation of an agent who does not herd and has a signal with precision equal to the average precision of signals in the population. The updating of the public belief is therefore[16]

$$
\lambda_{t+1} = \begin{cases} \lambda_t + \alpha & \text{if } x_t = 1, \\ \lambda_t - \alpha & \text{if } x_t = 0 \end{cases}
$$

$$
\text{with} \quad \alpha = \log\left(\frac{(1 - \pi)\underline{q} + \pi\overline{q}}{(1 - \pi)(1 - \underline{q}) + \pi(1 - \overline{q})}\right).
$$

B. In the second regime, regime B, only the agents with a higher precision do not herd. The regime is bounded by the critical values λ_B^* and λ_B^{**} with

$$
\lambda_B^* = \gamma - \log\left(\frac{\overline{q}}{1 - \overline{q}}\right),
$$

$$
\lambda_B^{**} = \gamma + \log\left(\frac{\overline{q}}{1 - \overline{q}}\right).
$$

Because $\underline{q} < \overline{q}$, one verifies that

$$
\lambda_B^* < \lambda^*{}_A < \gamma < \lambda_A^{**} < \lambda_B^{**}.
$$

This regime is divided into two subcases.

1. If $\lambda_A^{**} < d_t \leq \lambda_B^{**}$, the agents with lower precision herd and invest. Agents with high precision do not herd and reveal their signal only if that signal is bad.

---

[16] To find these expressions, note that $\dfrac{P(\theta = 1 | x = 1)}{P(\theta = 0 | x = 1)} = \dfrac{P(\theta = 1)}{P(\theta = 0)} \dfrac{P(x = 1 | \theta = 1)}{P(x = 1 | \theta = 0)}.$

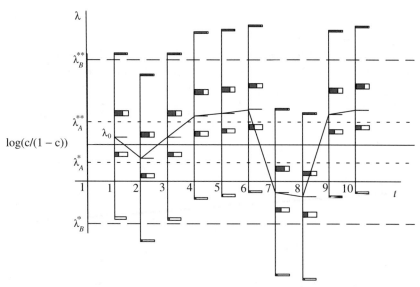

Figure 4.7 The evolution of the public belief with two types of agents. There are two precisions of the binary signals. If the public LLR is outside the band $[\lambda_A^*, \lambda_A^{**}]$, the agents with the lower precision herd. Because there are fewer agents with higher precision, who do not herd, the evolution of the belief in the herd is slow. If the herd is broken by a black sheep, the public belief jumps.

Bayes's rule takes the form

$$\lambda_{t+1} = \begin{cases} \lambda_t + \beta \quad \text{with} \quad \beta = \log\left(\dfrac{1 - \pi + \pi\overline{q}}{1 - \pi + \pi(1 - \overline{q})}\right) & \text{if } x_t = 1, \\[2ex] \lambda_t - \log\left(\dfrac{\overline{q}}{1 - \overline{q}}\right), & \text{if } x_t = 0. \end{cases}$$

The LLR changes by a larger amount when the action $x = 0$ is taken.

2. If $\lambda_B^* < \lambda_t \le \lambda_A^*$, the low-precision agents do not invest, and Bayes's rule is the mirror image of subcase 1:

$$\lambda_{t+1} = \begin{cases} \lambda_t + \log\left(\dfrac{\overline{q}}{1 - \overline{q}}\right) & \text{if } x_t = 1, \\[2ex] \lambda_t - \beta & \text{if } x_t = 0. \end{cases}$$

One verifies that the change of the belief is much stronger when the action against the herd is taken.

C. In the third regime, regime C, all agents herd. Either $\lambda \le \lambda_B^*$ or $\lambda > \lambda_B^{**}$.

An example of evolution of the public belief is represented in Figure 4.7, which is a special case of Figure 4.3. It illustrates some properties of the social learning with heterogeneous agents.

In the regime with moderate optimism where $\lambda_t \in (\lambda_A^{**}, \lambda_B^{**}]$, investment generates a relatively small increase of the belief. On the other hand, a zero investment generates a significant jump down of the belief. No matter how high λ_t may be, after an observation of no investment ($x_t = 0$), λ_{t+1} must be smaller than $\log(c/(1 - c))$. Following such bad news, the new regime may be of type A or B. Note also that the continuation of the learning phase does not depend on alternating private signals as in the simple model with identical agents.

5 Limited Memories

To learn one needs to forget.

When agents observe a sample of past actions or different sets of neighbors, they do not share a common public history. The diversity of observations may facilitate social learning because there is no common public history that dominates all individual beliefs. Social learning may be faster if agents observe a smaller sample of past actions. As the social learning cannot be summarized by the martingale of the public belief, the analysis of the convergence of beliefs and actions requires new tools: the average social welfare function, which operates like a Lyapunov function, and the welfare-improving principle.

In all models so far, agents know the entire history of actions. This assumption may be too strong when the number of periods is large. (Note, however, that the entire history is summarized by one number, the public belief.) It is now relaxed: each agent observes only part of the past. We have seen in the previous chapter how the commonly known history of actions can dominate private beliefs and prevent agents from revealing their private information through their actions. If the common memory prevents the diffusion of private information, a restriction on the observation of past actions may be efficient.

Two settings are considered. In the main one, agents are put in an exogenous sequence, as in all models of social learning in previous chapters, but they observe a small random sample from the set of past observations. The sampling is done over all past observations and not just over the most recent ones. The second setting departs from the sequential structure: agents act like farm managers who observe in each period a random sample of crop choices in other farms.

Partial Recall and Sampling

Section 5.1 is derived from Smith and Sørensen (1997): agents are put in an exogenous sequence as in the BHW model with two states and two actions. A first phase, the *seed phase*, is introduced to build an initial population for sampling: in that phase, which may be short, each agent acts according to his private information. In the second and main phase, each agent samples a fixed number N of agents in the history of actions. The properties of the social learning depend on the size of the sample and the distribution of private beliefs. A numerical simulation shows that a *smaller* sample size N improves the efficiency of social learning after some period. This property validates the intuition in the first paragraph.

The sampling restriction does not prevent the occurrence of cascades when private beliefs are bounded, because a sufficiently long string of identical actions is possible and such a string generates observations of identical actions that initiate a cascade. However, if private beliefs are unbounded, beliefs converge to the truth.

The Average Welfare Function and the Welfare-Improving Principle

When agents do not observe the complete history, there is no common memory of the past, and the fundamental process of social learning in Figure 3.1 does not apply. Because the observation set of each agent is idiosyncratic, the learning from others cannot be summarized by a public belief that is a converging martingale. When an agent observes only a subset of past actions, the sample of his observations is specific to him. Others have therefore a more complex inference task when they observe his action. The technical analysis of the convergence of beliefs and actions becomes more difficult. In order to derive general results, Banerjee and Fudenberg (1995) introduced a new and elegant tool, the *average welfare function*. This tool has been also used by Smith and Sørensen to analyze the convergence properties of the present model (Section 5.1.2).

The average welfare function (AWF), not to be confused with the social welfare function, is the expected payoff of an outsider with the same payoff function as the agents of the model but who has a fixed belief about the state of nature and who copies the action of a randomly selected agent. Without loss of generality, this belief can be chosen with equal probabilities for all states. The outsider's payoff is thus the average payoff of the copied actions for all possible states. Suppose now that agents gradually learn from others. Learning means that the agents do strictly better than just imitating the action of another random agent. As long as agents learn in this sense, the AWF is strictly increasing between consecutive periods: this is the welfare-improving principle (WIP). It provides a criterion to prove that learning takes place. Because the AWF is bounded, it converges. By analyzing the value of the AWF at the limit point, we will be able to assess how agents behave and what they learn when time goes to infinity.

Adequate and Complete Learning

Adequate learning has been defined by Smith and Sørensen (1997) as the situation where at the limit ($t \rightarrow \infty$) all agents take the action that is optimal for the true state. *Complete learning* is the situation where the belief of an agent who makes a decision in period t tends to the true state $\theta \in \{0, 1\}$. Complete learning implies adequate learning, but in general the reverse is not true. However, in models with sampling, adequate and complete learning are equivalent: if there is adequate learning, the likelihood ratio from the observation of one investment tends to infinity. Hence, for any value of the private belief, the belief of the agent tends to the truth: there is complete learning.

Convergence

Smith and Sørensen (1997) use the WIP to show that learning is adequate in the sequential model with sampling if private beliefs are unbounded. Their work addresses a number of other issues, which cannot be considered here. One issue has not been investigated, however. The previous chapter has emphasized that the importance of the convergence to the truth may be exaggerated. What really matters is the speed of the convergence. We have seen that this convergence is slow, even when private beliefs are unbounded. It remains to be seen how the restriction to an observation sample of size two, for example, would accelerate the convergence in a model with unbounded private beliefs.

Sampling in a Very Large Population

Section 5.3, taken from Banerjee and Fudenberg (1995), departs from the sequential model for the first time in this book. In each period, there is a large number of new agents (a continuum) who take some action. Each of these agents samples N other agents. A large diversity of information is thus imbedded in the new population with different fractions of investing agents in the two states of nature. The model is actually more a model of *chain sampling* than a model of social learning. The properties of the model are sharply different from those in Section 5.1. If $N \geq 3$, beliefs converge to the truth even if agents do not have any private information.

5.1 The Sequential Model with Sampling

Consider the 2-by-2-by-2 model of Section 4.1.1: there are two states $\theta \in \{0, 1\}$ and two actions $x \in \{0, 1\}$, and agent t maximizes his payoff in period t, $(E_t[\theta] - c)x_t$ with $0 < c < \frac{1}{2}$. Private beliefs (probability of state 1) have in state θ a c.d.f., which is defined by F^θ. Both states have the same probability *ex ante*. Following Smith and Sørensen (1997), we depart from that model by assuming that for any $t \geq T + 1$, agent t observes N randomly selected actions in the history $h_t = \{x_1, \ldots, x_{t-1}\}$. The values of N and T are fixed such that $N \leq T$, and the random selection is as from an urn with replacement. (The case without replacement would be very similar[1].) In the periods $t \leq T$, which form the *seed phase* of the model, each agent acts according to his private belief.

---

[1] Smith and Sørensen (1997) analyze more general sampling methods.

The Process of Social Learning

Consider the agent in period t. Let Z_t be the number of investments in the history h_t (the number of actions $x_\tau = 1$ for $1 \leq \tau \leq t - 1$). For each draw from the past, the probability of observing an investment is $Z_t/(t - 1)$. The probability of observing k investments, in a sample of N observations, is identical to the probability of obtaining k black balls after N drawings from an urn containing Z_t black balls and $t - 1 - Z_t$ white balls. The distribution of the number of investments y_t is given by

$$(5.1) \qquad P(y_t = k | Z_t) = \frac{N!}{k!(N-k)!} \left(\frac{Z_t}{t-1} \right)^k \left(1 - \frac{Z_t}{t-1} \right)^{N-k}.$$

The distribution of Z_t in the history h_t depends on the state θ. Assume that the two distributions $P(Z_t|\theta)$ for $\theta = 0, 1$, are common knowledge. We will show how they are computed in the common knowledge for period $t = 1$.

The number of observed investments y_t has a distribution that depends on θ according to

$$(5.2) \qquad P(y_t = k | \theta) = \sum_{Z_t=0}^{t-1} P(y_t = k | Z_t) P(Z_t | \theta).$$

The value of y_t is therefore a signal on θ. After the observation of k investments in his N-sample, the agent computes his LLR, $\lambda_t(k)$. Because both states have the same probability *ex ante*,

$$(5.3) \qquad \lambda_t(k) = \log \left(\frac{P(y_t = k | \theta = 1)}{P(y_t = k | \theta = 0)} \right).$$

Agent t invests if and only if his LLR is greater than $\gamma = \log(c/(1 - c))$. Because his LLR is the sum of the LLR from the observation of N other agents, $\lambda_t(k)$, and of his private LLR, λ_t, he invests if and only if his private LLR is such that

$$\lambda_t > \gamma - \lambda_t(k).$$

Let F^θ be the c.d.f. of the private beliefs measured as LLR when the state is θ. For each k, there is a probability $\zeta_t(k; \theta)$ that the agent who observes k investments invests:

$$\zeta_t(k; \theta) = 1 - F^\theta \left(\gamma - \lambda_t(k) \right).$$

Hence, the probability of an investment in period t depends on the actual number of investments Z_t and on the state according to

$$(5.4) \qquad P(x_t = 1 | Z_t, \theta) = \sum_{k=0}^{N} P(y_t = k | Z_t) \zeta_t(k; \theta).$$

This expression determines the transition probabilities between Z_t and $Z_{t+1} = n$. The distributions of Z_{t+1} in the two states are computed from the distributions of Z_t and the transition probabilities:

$$(5.5) \qquad P(Z_{t+1} = n|\theta) = P(Z_t = n|\theta)(1 - P(x_t = 1|Z_t = n, \theta))$$
$$+ P(Z_t = n - 1|\theta) \, P(x_t = 1|Z_t = n, \theta).$$

The evolution of investment is completely defined by equations (5.1) to (5.5).

The Information Requirement in the Common Knowledge

When agents observe the entire history of actions h_t, the common knowledge is summarized by one number, the public belief (probability of the good state). When agents observe only a sample of past actions, the common knowledge is about the distributions of Z_t in the two states. This information requires $2(t - 2)$ numbers in period t. In this sense, the setting without common history is more complex. The additional complexity arises because the observation by each agent of others' actions is private information.

5.1.1 The Case of One Observation ($N = 1$): Asymptotic Herding

Assume that agent t observes only the action of one agent in the past. For simplicity, assume also that the private information is derived from a SBS with precision $q > \frac{1}{2}$ and that $c = \frac{1}{2}$. The important property is that the SBS generates a bounded distribution of private beliefs. Let R_t^θ be the public expected value of the fraction of investing agents in the history h_t, $X_t^\theta = Z_t^\theta/(t - 1)$ (over all possible histories h_t). Agent t can only observe one investment or no investment. In the first case, the likelihood ratio between states 1 and 0 is updated to R_t^1/R_t^0; in the second case, it is equal to $(1 - R_t^1)/(1 - R_t^0)$. The agent then compares this likelihood ratio with his private likelihood ratio: $q/(1 - q)$ if he has a good signal, $(1 - q)/q$ if he has a bad one.

If, in some period τ,

$$(5.6) \qquad \frac{R_\tau^1}{R_\tau^0} > \frac{q}{1 - q} > 1,$$

then the observation of an investment dominates any bad private signal and agent t invests. Likewise, if

$$(5.7) \qquad \frac{1 - R_t^1}{1 - R_t^0} < \frac{1 - q}{q} < 1,$$

then agent t does not invest even if he has a good signal. Assume both inequalities hold: agent t herds and copies his observation. The probability that an agent invests

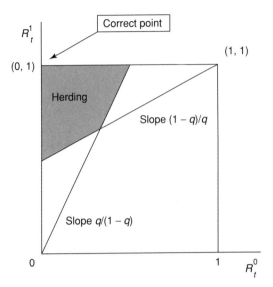

Figure 5.1 Herding with one observation ($N = 1$). The expected fractions of investing agents in the history h_t are R_t^0 in state 0 and R_t^1 in state 1. The correct point where agents take on average the correct action has coordinates (0, 1). In the shaded area, all agents copy their first observation regardless of their private signal (which is a SBS), and the representing point is stationary. The shaded area shrinks if the precision of private signals, q, increases. In the shaded area, the expected values of $X_t^\theta /(t - 1)$ are constant; the actual fractions evolve randomly and converge to their expected value.

in period t, π_t^θ, is the same as the probability of observing one investment, R_t^θ. The expected value of X_{t+1}^θ is therefore also R_t^θ. The strategies in period $t + 1$ are the same as in period t, and so on. A cascade takes place in which each agent copies one observation (investment or no investment). In each state θ, the actual fraction of investing agents in the history h_t, X_t^θ, converges to R_t^θ.

The region of values (R_t^0, R_t^1) in which conditions (5.6) and (5.7) are satisfied is represented by the shaded area in Figure 5.1. It is apparent that learning cannot be adequate in this case. Let π_t^θ be the probability of investment in period t when the state is θ. If learning is adequate, π_t^θ should tend to $\theta \in \{0, 1\}$. However, because the private signal is bounded, these probabilities must be driven by the observation of others, asymptotically. The value R_t^θ must tend to θ, and the representing point of coordinates (R_t^0, R_t^1) must converge to the *correct point* of coordinate (0, 1) in Figure 5.1. This is impossible, because the representing point is stationary in the shaded region which contains the correct point.

When the representing point (R_t^0, R_t^1) is not in the shaded area of the figure, it is not stationary. The analysis of its stochastic evolution requires special tools and will be considered again in Section 5.2.3. At this stage, one can argue intuitively that the representing point converges to a point in the shaded area, which is the cascade set. That set contains the correct point and therefore prevents convergence to that point. When the precision q of the private signals is higher, the cascade set is smaller, and asymptotically, when $t \to \infty$, more agents take the correct action.

5.1.2 The Case of More than One Observation ($N \geq 2$)

We begin by considering the simplest case, with two observations: $N = 2$.

Weak Evidence from Others and the Role of Private Information

Suppose that agent t observes one investment: $y_t = 1$. From (5.1) and (5.2) with $N = 2$, his likelihood ratio is

$$\frac{P(y_t = 1|\theta = 1)}{P(y_t = 1|\theta = 0)} = \frac{\sum_{n=1}^{t-2} n(t - 1 - n)P(Z_t = n|\theta = 1)}{\sum_{n=1}^{t-2} n(t - 1 - n)P(Z_t = n|\theta = 1)}.$$

Suppose that the distribution of Z_t is increasing in Z_t if the state is $\theta = 1$ and decreasing if the state is $\theta = 0$, and that the two distributions are symmetric around the midpoint $(t - 1)/2$. Such a case may be compatible with sharply different distributions in the two states. However, the likelihood ratio in the previous expression is equal to 1: the agent does not update his belief after the observation of the sample. In this case, *the observation of others provide no evidence.*

In general, the two distributions may not be perfectly symmetric and the statement needs to be modified accordingly. The main property, however, is that the observation of one investment in a sample of size two provides weak evidence on the state. When an agent faces weak evidence from the observation of others, he relies more on his private information. The occurrence of weak evidence is the key channel through which private information is fed into the process of social learning. Weak evidence could not occur if all agents received strong information from the entire history. Social learning may be more efficient with limited observations because of the occurrence of weak evidence, which enables some agents to add their private information to the pool of social information.

Cascades

The reception of weak information from others cannot take place if all agents in the history h_t invest, or if they do not invest. Suppose for example that agents derive their private belief from a SBS with precision q and that the seed phase lasts for the first two periods. Suppose further that in each period of the seed phase, the agent invests (an event with positive probability). The third agent can observe only two investments. Exercise 5.1 shows that he herds. A cascade begins.

The seed phase generates with strictly positive probability a sequence of identical decisions. In general, if the private beliefs are bounded, it is intuitive that if the seed phase is sufficiently long, a cascade is induced by the seed phase, with positive probability.[2] However, if the length of the seed phase increases, the probability of a cascade induced by the seed phase decreases. This issue is considered again at the end of the section.

---

[2] Smith and Sørensen (1997) show that if private beliefs are unbounded, learning is adequate.

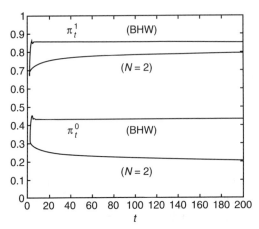

Figure 5.2 The probabilities of investment. The mean probability of investment in period t, conditional on the state θ and over all possible histories h_t, is measured by π_t^θ. In the BHW case, agent t observes the complete history of actions h_t. In the case $N = 2$, each agent t ($t \geq 5$) observes two randomly selected actions in the history h_t. Parameters: $c = 0.49$; precision of the SBS, $q = 0.6$; the two states are equally likely. The seed phase takes three periods.

AN EXAMPLE

A numerical simulation of the model is illustrated by Figure 5.2, which presents the probabilities of investment in each period, π_t^θ, conditional on the state. The BHW case where each agent t observes the entire history h_t is also presented for comparison. Because the investment cost c is chosen to be less than $\frac{1}{2}$, the probability of a cascade with investment is high. In the BHW model, the probability of investment is high in each of the two states.

When agents make only two observations,[3] the limit probability of investment in the bad state appears to be much smaller. The limit probability of investment in the good state also appears to be smaller than in the BHW model. In the figure, the sampling model generates a superior outcome overall: the asymptotic probability of investment in the bad state is reduced from about 40 to 20 percent; the probability of investment in the good state is reduced from about 85 to 80 percent.

THE EFFECT OF A LARGER SAMPLE SIZE

With a larger size N of the sample of observations, one may think that agents will learn more. This apparently obvious conclusion is false. A higher value of N implies that history has a greater weight on individual choices and prevents the private information from being conveyed through these actions. The evolution of the probability of investment in period t is represented in Figure 5.3 for the cases $N = 2$ and $N = 4$. The other parameters are the same as in Figure 5.2. (The case $N = 2$ is therefore identical.) A larger sample size improves noticeably the efficiency of learning at the

---

[3] Under sampling with replacement, in period 3 the set of observations from two past actions is different from the knowledge of the history: an agent may sample the same agent twice.

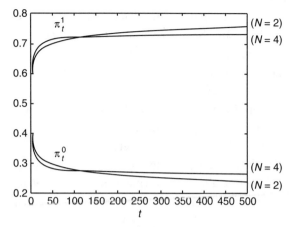

Figure 5.3 The probabilities of investment. The parameters are the same as in Figure 5.2. For $t \geq 5$, agent t observes the actions of N independent drawings from the history h_t. For t sufficiently large, a *smaller* sample size generates more social learning.

beginning of the learning phase. This was to be expected: agents sample more informative actions in the seed phase, which lasts six periods if $N = 4$.

It is remarkable that the effect of the sample size is reversed in the long run (after period 134 here). When N is smaller, the occurrence of weak evidence is more likely, and this weak evidence enables agents to release their private information through their action. *A reduction of the information provided by history may improve the efficiency of social learning.*

The convergence of the beliefs and actions cannot be analyzed with the MCT, because there is no martingale of public beliefs. We need new tools, which are presented in the next section.

5.2 The Welfare-Improving Principle

5.2.1 The Average Welfare Function

Consider the model of the previous section with two equally probable states and with uniform sampling of past agents. Consider an outsider who ignores the state and the choice of agents. This outsider knows the decision process of all agents. He can compute for each t the fractions[4] X_t^θ of agents who have invested up to t, conditional on each state θ. By assumption, the outsider assigns equal probabilities to the two states. Under this veil of ignorance, the level of social welfare at time t is proportional to the AWF[5], W_t, defined by

$$(5.8) \qquad 2 W_t = (1 - c) R_t^1 - c R_t^0,$$

---

[4] For the model of Section 5.1, X_t^θ is to be replaced by its expected value R_t^θ (Smith and Sørensen, 1997).

[5] The AWF was introduced by Banerjee and Fudenberg (1995). (See Section 5.3.)

where R_t^θ is the public expected value of X_t^θ. Recall that R_t^θ is a deterministic sequence. The AWF has a nice interpretation: suppose that an agent has identical probabilities for the two states and observes one randomly selected agent in the history h_t, with uniform probabilities, and copies the action of that agent; then his expected welfare is W_t.

The evolution of the AWF depends on the average welfare of new agents. We will see that if new agents learn, they have an average welfare that is superior to the AWF, and therefore the AWF is increasing. With the monotone property, the AWF can be used as a Lyapunov function for the analysis of the evolution of R_t^θ.

Let π_t^θ be the expected value of the probability of investment of agent t in state θ. This probability depends on the particular history h_t from which the agent is sampling. We have

$$(5.9) \qquad R_{t+1}^\theta - R_t^\theta = \frac{\pi_t^\theta - R_t^\theta}{t}.$$

Let U_t be the average utility of agent t, as measured by the outsider who assigns equal probabilities to the two states. By definition,

$$2U_t = (1 - c)\pi_t^1 - c\pi_t^0.$$

Using (5.9), we have

$$(5.10) \qquad W_{t+1} - W_t = \frac{U_t - W_t}{t}.$$

If agent t copies one action in his sample of observations, this action can always be assumed to be the first that is observed. If he copies an observation, his probability of making an investment is R_t^θ (as measured before making the observation). If $\pi_t^\theta = R_t^\theta$, his average utility U_t is identical to the AWF W_t. Hence, $W_{t+1} = W_t$. When the agent can do better than copying, his utility is higher than the AWF.

5.2.2 The Welfare-Improving Principle

We can always write the information of agent t as $(\hat{x}, s)$, where $\hat{x}$ is his first observation and s is a signal that contains all other information (other observations and private information, if available). The time subscript is not necessary and is omitted in this argument. If the agent uses only his observation $\hat{x}$, the copying strategy $x = \hat{x}$ is optimal. In that case, the AWF is constant. The next result states the WIP.

PROPOSITION 5.1 (Welfare-Improving Principle) *The average welfare function W_t is monotonically increasing over time. If U_t is the average utility of agent t, then for any t, $W_{t+1} - W_t = (U_t - W_t)/t \geq 0$. The inequality is strict if copying the first observation in the sample of size N is a strictly dominated decision rule at time t.*

To prove the result, assume that the copying decision is strictly suboptimal. We can assume that there are two sets of signal values $\underline{S}$ and $\bar{S}$ such that if the agent observes an investment, $\hat{x} = 1$, and $s \in \underline{S}$, he does not invest; if $\hat{x} = 0$ and $s \in \bar{S}$, he does invest. At least one of the two sets $\underline{S}$ and $\bar{S}$ has strictly positive probability. The signal s is independent of the observation $\hat{x}$. Let π^θ be the probability of investment in state θ when the agent follows the noncopying strategy.

The *ex ante* welfare level of the agent who follows the noncopying strategy is $2U = (1 - c)\pi^1 - c\pi^0$. We distinguish four possible types of information:

$$(5.11) \quad 2U = (1 - c)R^1\Big(1 - P(s \in \underline{S}|\theta = 1)\Big) - cR^0\Big(1 - P(s \in \underline{S}|\theta = 0)\Big)$$
$$+ (1 - c)(1 - R^1)P(s \in \bar{S}|\theta = 1) - c(1 - R^0)P(s \in \bar{S}|\theta = 0).$$

In the first line, the agent observes one investment (with probability R^θ in state θ) and invests if his signal is not in the set $\underline{S}$. In the second line, the agent observes no investment and invests if his signal is in the set $\bar{S}$. Taking the difference between U and the payoff of the copying strategy $W = (1 - c)R^1 - cR^0$, we have

$$2(U - W) = -\Big((1 - c)R^1 - cR^0\Big)P(s \in \underline{S})$$
$$+ \Big((1 - c)(1 - R^1) - c(1 - R^0)\Big)P(s \in \bar{S}).$$

Now the sets $\underline{S}$ and $\bar{S}$, if not empty, are defined so that

$$\frac{R^1}{R^0}\frac{P(s \in \underline{S}|\theta = 1)}{P(s \in \underline{S}|\theta = 0)} < \frac{c}{1 - c} \quad \text{and} \quad \frac{1 - R^1}{1 - R^0}\frac{P(s \in \bar{S}|\theta = 1)}{P(s \in \bar{S}|\theta = 0)} > \frac{c}{1 - c}.$$

Inasmuch as at least one of the sets $\underline{S}$ and $\bar{S}$ is not empty, $U > W$. If the copying of the first observation is an optimal decision rule, then the sets $\underline{S}$ and $\bar{S}$ are empty, $\pi^\theta = X^\theta$, and $U = W$. The result follows[6] from (5.10).

5.2.3 Convergence

Learning is *complete* if the mean belief of agent t (which depends on the history h_t) tends to the truth. Learning is *adequate* if the expected probability of investment for an outsider in period t, π_t^θ, tends to 1 if $\theta = 1$, and to 0 if $\theta = 0$. Complete learning implies adequate learning, and here the reverse is also true: if learning is adequate, the proportion of investing agents in the history h_t tends to 1 (the good state) or 0 (the bad state). The observation of one agent provides asymptotically a signal of arbitrarily large precision.

The AWF, which is monotone increasing, converges to some value W^*. The upper bound of the AWF is by definition $(1 - c)/2$ and is reached if $R^\theta = \theta$. If the AWF

---

[6] Smith and Sørensen (1997) show that the WIP applies for some sampling mechanisms that are not uniform. It does not apply, however, when each agent observes the actions of the agents in the two previous periods (Çelen and Kariv, 2002a).

tends to its upper bound, then we must have $R_t^\theta \to \theta$ and learning is complete. The reverse is also true. The AWF provides therefore a criterion to assess whether learning is complete or not. Smith and Sørensen use the AWF and the WIP to prove the following result (which holds for more general "recursive samplings" and is adapted here).

PROPOSITION 5.2 (Smith and Sørensen, 1997, Proposition 1)

(i) *If private beliefs are unbounded, learning is complete: $\pi_t^\theta \to \theta$.*

(ii) *If private beliefs are bounded, then learning is incomplete. A cascade occurs in finite time with strictly positive probability.*

The proof of the first part uses the WIP repeatedly. If learning is incomplete, (π_t^0, π_t^1) does not converge to $(0, 1)$. Because $(\pi_t^0, \pi_t^1) \in [0, 1] \times [0, 1]$ and the average utility is such that $2U_t = (1 - c)\pi_t^1 - c\pi_t^0$, we have $\liminf U_t = v < (1 - c)/2$. There is an infinite sequence $\tau = t_k$ such that the average utility of agent τ satisfies $U_\tau \to v$. Because $W_\tau \leq U_\tau$ (by the WIP) and W_t is increasing (by the WIP), W_t is bounded by v. Because $v = \liminf U_t$ and $W_{t+1} - W_t = (U_t - W_t)/t$, we have $W_t \to v$.

Recall that W_t is the average utility of an agent who copies his first observation and ignores his private belief. Using the assumption of unbounded private beliefs, we can adapt the proof of the WIP (Proposition 5.2.2) to show that the probability of the union of the sets $\underline{S}$ and $\overline{S}$ is bounded below by some number $\beta > 0$. From expression (5.11) in the proof of the WIP, it follows that there exist T and $\eta > 0$ such that for $t > T$ we have $U_t > W_t + \eta$. Because $W_t \to v$, this contradicts the definition $v = \liminf U_t$.

The proof of the second part provides an interesting insight. Suppose by contradiction that learning is complete: $\pi_t^1 \to 1$. As mentioned previously, there is a date T such that for $t \geq T$, if agent t observes only investments in his sample, that signal dominates his private signal (which is bounded), and he herds. The probability of the history $h_T = (1, \ldots, 1)$ is strictly positive. If agent T is herding and invests, the history h_{T+1} contains only investments. The same argument applies in that period and any subsequent period. If all agents herd, however, we cannot have $\pi_t^0 \to 0$, which brings the contradiction.

The previous argument shows how a cascade may arise in which all agents take the same action. There can also be cascades in which agents take different actions (e.g., when copying one observation is an optimal strategy).

Proposition 5.2 proves the convergence of the expected probability of investment, π_t^θ. The convergence almost surely of the action is analyzed by Smith and Sørensen (1997), who use the urn function.[7]

---

[7] Arthur and Lane (1994) analyze a model where agents observe a sample of past outputs and use the urn function (Hill, Lane, and Sudderth, 1980; Arthur, Ermoliev, and Kaniovski, 1983, 1986).

5.3 Sampling in a Very Large Population

The previous model is extended as follows. In each period, there is a continuum of new agents with a fixed mass. Each of these agents chooses his action $x \in \{0, 1\}$ to maximize his payoff $(E[\theta] - c)x$, given his information. Each agent has a private SBS with precision q. The sampling of past actions is not uniform but imbeds a *fading effect*: the probability of sampling earlier actions is smaller; more specifically, in each draw at time t the probability of observing an action taken in period $t - \tau$ is proportional to $(1 - \alpha)^{\tau-1}$, where α is a parameter, $0 < \alpha < 1$. As before, the period in which the action is taken is not observable. The model is operationally equivalent to a model where an agent born in period t is observable in period $t + \tau$ with probability $(1 - \alpha)^{\tau-1}$. We may therefore assume that he makes a permanent exit with probability α at the end of each period.[8] The population of observable agents is maintained at a constant level by assuming that the mass of observable agents is normalized to one and that the mass of new agents in each period is α. This introduction links the previous model with that of Banerjee and Fudenberg (1995), hereafter BF.

The BF model may be interpreted as follows: there is an economy with a continuum of firms, which operate one of two technologies. In each period, a constant fraction of the firms disappears by attrition. It is replaced by a continuum of new firms with the same mass. Each new firm chooses irreversibly one of the two technologies. It receives information by the observation of the choices in N existing firms, and possibly some private signal. The N firms are selected randomly in the entire population. We do not have neigborhood effects, which will be introduced in Chapter 9. This spatial interpretation of the BF model is obviously equivalent to the first interpretation. As discussed below, the first interpretation (and therefore the BF model) departs significantly from the standard model of social learning.

In order to simplify the presentation and without loss of generality, the action $x = 1$ is called investment and the cost of investment is $c = \frac{1}{2}$. An agent invests if and only if state 1 is more likely than state 0, given his information. The period is vanishingly short, and time is continuous. (The analysis in discrete time is formally equivalent.) At the beginning of time, the masses of firms that have invested are X_0^0 and X_0^1 for the two states 0 and 1, and these values are common knowledge.

The assumption of the continuum of agents introduces a key simplification into the technical arguments. We do not need to distinguish between the expected fraction of agents who have invested in the history h_t and the actual fraction. This fraction in state θ is denoted by X_t^θ.

The decision process at time t determines the variation of $X_t = (X_t^0, X_t^1)$ per unit of time, i.e., the value of $\dot{X}_t = G(X_t)$, where the function G depends on the

---

[8] One could also assume that the exit is physical.

process of social learning. We need to determine if the solution of the differential equation

$$(5.12) \qquad \dot{X}_t = G(X_t)$$

converges to the *correct point* $(0, 1)$ where all agents take action 1 if $\theta = 1$ and action 0 if $\theta = 0$. The evolution of the representing point with coordinates (X_t^0, X_t^1) is illustrated in Figure 5.4. The arrows indicate the directions of evolution in the cases where each new agent observes two other agents (left panel) or one other agent (right panel). We begin with the case of one observation.

5.3.1 Two Examples

ONE OBSERVATION: *N* = 1

Assume first that no agent has private information about the state. The evolution of the point X_t is found in the left panel of Figure 5.4. The important region is the one above the 45° line. Because $X_t^1 > X_t^0$, the observation of an investment yields a probability estimate greater than $\frac{1}{2}$, and the observation of no investment a probability smaller than $\frac{1}{2}$: agents copy the action of the firm they observe and the point X_t is invariant over time. Any point above the 45° line (shaded area) is invariant.

The analysis of the dynamics in the other regions of the figure is left as an exercise. The observation of one other action is sufficient to eliminate limit points with the error that $X^1 < X^0$ (more agents use action 1 in state 0 than in state 1).

Assume now that each new agent has private information. The shaded area in the right-hand panel of Figure 5.4 is reduced to that of Figure 5.1. The discussion related to that figure applies.

TWO OBSERVATIONS: *N* = 2

No Private Information

Assume first that each agent observes only the actions of two other agents and has no private information about the state. Omitting the time subscript, an agent who observes k investments in his sample infers a likelihood ratio $\ell(k)$ between states 1 and 0, with

$$\ell(2) = \left(\frac{X^1}{X^0}\right)^2, \qquad \ell(1) = \left(\frac{X^1}{X^0}\right)\left(\frac{1 - X^1}{1 - X^0}\right), \qquad \ell(0) = \left(\frac{1 - X^1}{1 - X^0}\right)^2.$$

Suppose for example that $X^1 > X^0$ and that $X^1 + X^0 < 1$. We have $\ell(2) > \ell(1) > 1 > \ell(0)$. Because the cost of investment is $\frac{1}{2}$, an agent chooses action 1 if and only if he observes at least one investment. The proportion of new agents who see at least one investment is $1 - (1 - X^\theta)^2$. Because the masses of new agents and of exiting

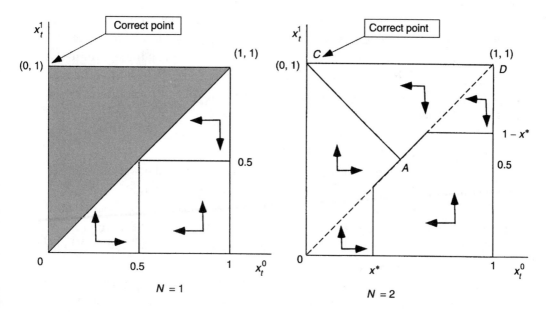

Any point in the shaded area is invariant. Any position below the diagonal generates a convergence to the diagonal.

The value of x^* is equal to $(3 - \sqrt{5})/2$, solution of $x^2 - 3x + 1 = 0$. The limit points are on the segment AC. There is no convergence to the correct point.

Figure 5.4 Observing N choices without private information.

agents are α, the time derivative of X^θ is

$$\dot{X}^\theta = \alpha\left(-X^\theta + 1 - (1 - X^\theta)^2\right) = \alpha X^\theta (1 - X^\theta).$$

The evolution of the point X_t is illustrated in the right panel of Figure 5.4. In the region where $X_t^1 > X_t^0$ and $X_t^1 + X_t^0 < 1$, the point X_t moves northeast. The point X_t converges to some limit on the segment AC. The limit depends on the initial position $X_0 = (X_0^0, X_0^1)$.

The segments OD and AC are special. Consider first a point $X = (X^0, X^1)$ on the segment OD with $X^1 = X^0$. The observation of others is not informative. Any decision rule is optimal. If the agent copies one observation selected randomly, or the first one, the point X is stationary. Under a different rule the point may move on the line OD or move off the line.

Any point on the segment AC is a limit point because of the following argument: assume $X^1 + X^0 = 1$ with $0 < X^0 < X^1 < 1$. An agent who observes two investments invests, whereas an agent who observes zero investment does not invest. An agent who observes one investment has a likelihood ratio $(X^1/X^0)\left((1 - X^1)/(1 - X^0)\right) = 1$. He is indifferent. Let us assume the tie-breaking rule according to which he chooses one of the two actions with equal probability. The evolution of X is given by $\dot{X} = \alpha(-X + X^2 + X(1 - X)) = 0$. The representing point is invariant.

This property is interesting in the context of the discussion on social learning versus diffusion of available information (Section 5.4). In the present model, the information about the actions of all existing agents would reveal the state of nature perfectly. The learning from a small sample of agents is not sufficient to generate a convergence to the truth. Complete learning can be achieved only if agents have some private information about the state of nature.

Private Information

Without loss of generality, assume now that each new agent has a private information in the form of a SBS with precision q. Consider the region where $X^1 > X^0$, $X^0 + X^1 < 1$. The observation of the actions in two other firms moves the representing point northeast. When new agents receive a private signal, this effect is reinforced: the reader may work out the details, but this argument will be reconsidered in the next section with a new tool.

Suppose now that the representing point is on the segment AC. We have seen that if agents observe only the actions of two firms, the point is stationary. If agents receive an additional private signal about the state, the agents who have no information from the observation of others (i.e., one investment for two observations) are more likely to invest when the state is good than when the state is bad. *The private information determines the agent's action when the observation of others yields weak evidence.* On the segment AC, the representing point moves toward the correct point. In state 1, the evolution of X is given by

$$\dot{X}^1 = \alpha\left(-X^1 + (X^1)^2 + 2q\,X^1(1 - X^1)\right) = \alpha(2q - 1)X^1(1 - X^1) > 0,$$

and $X^0 = -\dot{X}^1$. The sum $X^1 + X^0$ is invariant and the representing point stays on the segment AC and converges to the correct point.

The Absence of Cascades

It is intuitive (and will be proven in the next section) that the representing point converges to the correct point even if the private beliefs are bounded (as is the case with a SBS). There is no cascade, because the underlying information in the pool of actions taken is sufficiently different in the good and the bad states. (It would reveal that state if it were observable.) Recall that with a finite set of actions in a seed phase, the two states may generate identical (or nearly identical) histories with positive probability. This property makes a cascade possible.

5.3.2 Convergence

Banerjee and Fudenberg (1995) invented the AWF and the WIP for the general analysis of the convergence in the model in Section 5.3 with N observations. These concepts are equivalent to the ones presented in the previous section with the quantities R_t^θ replaced by X_t^θ. Without loss of generality, we assume that the private information of an agent is a SBS with precision $q > \frac{1}{2}$ and $c = \frac{1}{2}$. The point (X_t^0, X_t^1) belongs to the compact set $[0, 1] \times [0, 1]$; hence the solution of the differential equation (5.12) converges to a limit $\overline{X} = (\overline{X}^0, \overline{X}^1)$.

NO COMPLETE LEARNING: $N = 1$

Define the region Δ of the points $X = (X^0, X^1)$ such that $X^1 / X^0 \geq q/(1 - q)$ and $(1 - X^1)/(1 - X^0) \leq (1 - q)/q$. (It is the shaded area of Figure 5.1.)

If the limit point $\overline{X}$ is not in Δ, an exercise shows that copying is strictly suboptimal. (It is strictly superior to take the decision $1 - \hat{x}$ if $X^1 < X^0$ and to use the private signal if $X^1 > X^0$.) Hence the AWF is strictly increasing at the limit point $\overline{X}$, and there exists $\beta > 0$ and a neighborhood $\mathcal{B}$ of $\overline{X}$ such that if $X \in \mathcal{B}$, then $\dot{W}_t > \beta$, which contradicts the convergence to $\overline{X}$. The limit point $\overline{X}$ must be in the set Δ.

Note that in the set Δ, the WIP cannot be used: herding is optimal, and it is identical to copying the observation.

COMPLETE LEARNING WITH BOUNDED PRIVATE BELIEFS: $N = 2$

Suppose first $N = 2$. At any point that is not on the segment AC (left panel of Figure 5.4) the use of both observations by an agent strictly dominates the copying of the first observation. On the segment AC, the use of both observations does not strictly dominate the copying rule. The agent can ignore his second observation. (Recall that he is indifferent between investing and not investing.) However, the use of the private signal generates a strictly superior rule. From the WIP and an argument about the limit point as in the case $N = 1$, it follows that the limit point cannot be different from the correct point with coordinates $(0, 1)$.

PROPOSITION 5.3 *In the model of Section 5.3, if $N = 2$ and new agents have informative private signals, learning is complete and $X_t^\theta \to \theta$.*

NO PRIVATE INFORMATION NEEDED: $N \geq 3$

We assume first that $N = 3$ and that agents have no private information: their only information is derived from the observation of N other agents. Suppose the first observation of an agent is investment. Copying that action is optimal only if $X^1 / X^0 \geq 1$, and for any string of other observations, not investing is not strictly preferred. We must have

$$\frac{X^1}{X^0} \frac{X^1}{X^0} \frac{1 - X^1}{1 - X^0} \geq 1 \quad \text{and} \quad \frac{X^1}{X^0} \left(\frac{1 - X^1}{1 - X^0} \right)^2 \geq 1.$$

Because $X^1 \geq X^0$, the second inequality implies the first.

Likewise, if the copying of noninvestment is optimal for any observation, we must have

$$\frac{1 - X^1}{1 - X^0} \left(\frac{X^1}{X^0} \right)^2 \leq 1.$$

The combination of these inequalities implies that $X^1 \leq X^0$. If copying the first observation is optimal at a point X that is different from the correct point, we must have $X^0 = X^1$: the observation of others generates no information. Any decision rule is optimal, and the point X stays on the line OD in Figure 5.4.

If the initial point X_0 is not on the line OD, then X_t converges to the correct point and learning is perfect asymptotically. The initial value of the AWF is $(X_0^1 - X_0^0)/2$, which is strictly positive. Because the AWF is strictly increasing off the line OD, the point X_t cannot converge to a point on the line OD where the AWF is nil. From the same argument as in the previous case $N = 2$, the limit point must be the correct point.

The argument for the case $N = 3$ applies to any case $N > 3$.

PROPOSITION 5.4 *Assume that in the model of Section 5.3, $N \geq 3$ and agents do not have private information. If, at time 0, $X_0^1 \neq X_0^0$, then learning is complete and $X_t^\theta \to \theta$.*

If agents have private information, then learning is complete because of the WIP for all cases, including $X^1 = X^0$. However, the case $X^1 = X^0$ is trivial and can be ruled out, almost surely. The previous result is remarkable in that it shows that a sample of size larger than two improves the asymptotic properties of social learning. For $N \geq 3$, private information is not necessary. The information imbedded in the actions already taken is sufficient to generate complete information at the limit.

5.4 Social Learning or Sampling in a Large Population?

Smith and Sørensen (1997) argue, rightly, that the model of BF, though "more tractable, is not an appropriate approximation of the right sequential entry learning model." The main messages of the sequential entry model (Section 5.1) and of the BF model with a very large population (Section 5.3) are indeed opposite.

In the BF model, a larger number N of observations improves the efficiency of learning in the limit (Propositions 5.3 and 5.4): private information (which may be bounded) is required for complete learning when $N = 2$. It can be dispensed with entirely, however, if $N \geq 3$. If agents could sample the whole population, they would know the truth. Each agent samples only N other agents, and then he is sampled by other agents, and so on. In this respect, the model is about the gradual sampling of the population with sampling of the samplers. It seems clear that in this case a larger sample size would make learning from sampling more efficient.[9]

In the sequential model that is analyzed by Smith and Sørensen (1997), social learning does not converge to the truth if private beliefs are bounded. In Figure 5.3, social learning is more efficient when the sample size is smaller. These properties are supported by the intuition about social learning in sequential models that was developed in the previous chapter.

When agents enter in a sequence, some histories may develop in which a string of choices overwhelm individual choices. As private informations are not channeled through actions in these histories, the mix between individual choices is not sharply different between the two states and the observation of others does not convey much information, if any. In the BF model, it is assumed that at the beginning of time there is a strong diversity of actions, for there is a continuum with different fractions of investing agents in the two states, $X_0^1 \neq X_0^0$. This assumption is not that important, however. (A similar assumption could be introduced in the sequential model.) The key feature of the BF model is that a continuum of agents is introduced in each period. The diversity of their samplings ensures distributions of actions that will be informative about the true state when they are themselves observed by others. The model is actually not a model of social learning but a model of chain sampling in a very large population.

EXERCISES

EXERCISE 5.1 Cascades
In the model of Section 5.1, assume that the signals of the first two agents are equal to 1. Determine the public belief at the beginning of period 3. Show that a cascade begins in period 3.

EXERCISE 5.2
Consider the model of Section 5.3 where new agents observe N other agents and have a private SBS with precision q.

1. Assume $N = 1$. Determine the set of invariant points that corresponds to the shaded area in the left panel of Figure 5.4.
2. Show that any path in the noninvariant set converges to the frontier of the invariant set. (Do not use the AWF.)
3. Assume $N = 2$. Determine the evolution of $X = (X^0, X^1)$ on the left panel in Figure 5.4. (Do not use the AWF.)

---

[9] One may conjecture that the rate of convergence in the model of Banerjee and Fudenberg increases with the sample size N. No analysis has been provided yet.

EXERCISE 5.3 Learning from the previous action (Çelen and Kariv, 2002a)
There are N agents. Each agent has a signal s_i from a uniform distribution on $[-1, 1]$. The state of nature is $\theta = \sum_1^N s_i$. Agent t chooses $x_t \in \{0, 1\}$ to maximize $x_t E_t[\theta]$ in round t. Each agent t observes only the action of the previous agent, x_{t-1}: $E_t[\theta] = E[\theta | s_t, x_{t-1}]$.

1. Show that if $x_{t-1} = j \in \{0, 1\}$, agent t invests ($x_t = 1$) if and only if his signal is greater than $\bar{S}_t^j = -E[\sum_{k=1}^{t-1} s_k | x_{t-1} = j]$.

2. Show that $\bar{S}_t^1$ satisfies the relation

$$\bar{S}_t^1 = P(x_{t-2} = 1 | x_{t-1} = 1)\left(\bar{S}_{t-1}^1 - E[s_{t-1} | x_{t-2} = 1]\right)$$

$$= P(x_{t-2} = 0 | x_{t-1} = 1)\left(\bar{S}_{t-1}^0 - E[s_{t-1} | x_{t-2} = 0]\right).$$

3. Using the symmetry of the model, note that $\bar{S}_t^1 = -\bar{S}_t^0$, and show that

$$\bar{S}_t^0 = \frac{1 + (\bar{S}_{t-1}^0)^2}{2}.$$

4. Analyze the limit properties of the model if $N \to \infty$ and $t \to \infty$.

6 Delays

Does the waiting game end with a bang or a whimper?

Each agent chooses when to invest (if at all) and observes the number of investments by others in each period. That number provides a signal on the private information of other agents about the state of nature. The waiting game has in general multiple equilibria. An equilibrium depends on the intertemporal arbitrage between the opportunity cost of delay and the value of the information that is gained from more observations. The informational externality generates strategic substitutabilities and complementarities. Multiple equilibria appear, which exhibit a rush of activity or delays and generate a small or large amount of information. The convergence of beliefs and the occurrence of herds are analyzed under a variety of assumptions about the boundedness of the distribution of private beliefs, the number of agents, the existence of an observation noise, the length of the periods, and the discreteness of investment decisions.

In 1993, the U.S. economy was in a shaky recovery from the previous recession. The optimism after some good news was dampened by a few pieces of bad news, raised again by other news, and so on. In the trough of the business cycle, each agent is waiting for some good news about an upswing. What kind of news? Some count occupancy rates in the first-class sections of airplanes. Others weigh the newspapers to evaluate the volume of ads. Housing starts and expenditures on durables are standard indicators to watch. The news is the actions of other agents. Everyone could be waiting because everyone is waiting in an "economics of wait and see" (Nasar, 1993).

In order to focus on the problem of how a recession may be protracted by the game of waiting for more information, we have to take a step back from the intricacies of the real world and the numerous channels of information. In this chapter, agents learn from the observation of the choices of action taken by others, but not from the payoffs of these actions. This assumption is made to simplify the analysis. It is also justified in the context of the business cycle, where lags between the initiation of an investment process and its payoff can be long (at least a year or two). The structure of the model is thus the same as in Chapter 3, but each agent can make his investment in any period: he has one option, to make a fixed-size investment. The central issue is when to exercise the option, if at all.

When the value of the investment is strictly positive, delay is costly because the present value of the payoff is reduced by the discount factor. The *opportunity cost of delay* for one period is the product of the net payoff of investment and the discount rate. Delay enables an agent to observe others' actions and infer some information on the state of nature. These observations may generate good or bad news. Define the bad news as an event such that the agent regrets *ex post* an irreversible investment he has made, and would pay a price to undo it (if that were possible). The expected value of this payment in the next period, after observation of the current period's aggregate investment, is the option value of delay. The key issue that underlines all results in this chapter is the trade-off, in equilibrium, between the opportunity cost and the option value of delay.

Consider the model of Chapter 4 with two states of nature, and assume that agents can choose the timing of their investment. If all beliefs (probabilities of the good state) are below the cost of investment, then the only equilibrium is with no investment, and there is a herd as in the BHW model. If all beliefs are higher than the cost of investment, there is an equilibrium in which all agents invest with no delay. This behavior is like a herd with investment in the BHW model, and it is an equilibrium, for nothing is learned by delaying. The herds in the BHW model with exogenous timing are equilibria in the model with endogenous timing.

However, the model with endogenous timing may have other equilibria with an arbitrage between the option value and the opportunity cost of delay. For a general distribution of private beliefs, the margin of arbitrage may occur at different points of the distribution. Generically, there are at least two equilibrium points, one in the upper tail of the distribution and another in the lower tail. In the first equilibrium, only the most optimistic agents invest; in the second, only the most pessimistic delay. The two equilibria in which most agents delay or rush, respectively, are not symmetric, because of the arbitrage mechanism. In the first, the information conveyed by the aggregate activity must be large in order to keep the agents at the high margin of beliefs (with a high opportunity cost) from investing. In the second, both the opportunity cost of relatively pessimistic agents and the information conveyed by the aggregate activity are low. In the particular case of a bounded distribution, the rush where few agents delay may be replaced by the corner solution where no agent delays.

Multiple equilibria are evidence of strategic complementarities (Cooper and John, 1988). These complementarities arise here only because of informational externalities. There is no payoff externality. As in other models with strategic complementarities, multiple equilibria may provide support for sudden switches of regime with large fluctuations of economic activity (Chamley, 1999).

The main ideas of the chapter are presented in Section 6.1 with a simple two-agent model based on Chamley and Gale (1994). The unique equilibrium is computed explicitly.

The general model with heterogeneous beliefs is presented in Section 6.2. It is the full extension of the BHW model to endogenous timing. The model of heterogeneous beliefs is a plausible assumption *per se*, and it generates nonrandom strategies. The model has a number of players independent of the state of nature and generalizes that of Chamley and Gale (1994), who assume identical beliefs. In the model with identical beliefs, the endowment of an option is the private signal, and the number of players thus depends on the state of nature. This case is particularly relevant when the number of players is large.

When private beliefs are not identical, the analysis of the symmetric subgame perfect Bayesian equilibria (PBE) turns out to be simple because of an intuitive property that is related to the arbitrage condition: an agent never invests before another who is more optimistic. Therefore, the agent with the highest belief among those who delay must be the first to invest in the next period if there is any investment in that period (because he has the highest belief then). All equilibria where the arbitrage condition applies can be described as sequences of two-period equilibria.

Some properties of the model are presented in Section 6.3. Extensions will be discussed in the next chapter. When the public belief is in a range (μ^*, μ^{**}), the level of investment in each period is a random variable, and the probability of no investment is strictly positive. If there is no investment, the game stops with a herd, and no investment takes place in any subsequent period. Hence the game lasts a number of periods that is at most equal to the number of players in the game. If the period length tends to zero, the game ends in a vanishingly short time. Because an agent can always delay until the end of the game, and the cost of delay tends to zero with the length of the period, the information generated by the game also tends to zero with the period length: another effect of arbitrage.

The game is illustrated in Section 6.3.4 by an example with two agents with normally distributed private signals (unbounded), which highlights the mechanism of strategic complementarity. When the time period is sufficiently short, there cannot be multiple equilibria, under some specific conditions. The presence of time lags between observation and action is thus necessary for the existence of multiple equilibria.

The case of a large number of agents (Section 6.3.7) is interesting and illustrates the power of the arbitrage argument. When the number of agents tends to infinity, the distribution of the levels of investment tends to a Poisson distribution with a parameter that depends on the public belief and on the discount rate. This implies that as long as the public belief μ is in the interval (μ^*, μ^{**}), the level of investment is a random variable that is small compared with the number of agents. The public belief evolves randomly until it exits the interval: if $\mu < \mu^*$, investment goes from a small random amount to nil forever; if $\mu > \mu^{**}$, all remaining agents invest with no further delay. The game ends with a whimper or with a bang.

The appendix (Section 6.4) presents two extensions of the model, which show the robustness of the results: (i) with a very large number of agents (a continuum) and an observation noise, there are multiple equilibria as in the model with two agents; the equilibrium with high aggregate activity generates an amount of information significantly smaller than the equilibrium with low activity and delays; (ii) multiple equilibria also appear when individual investments are nondiscrete.

6.1 The Simplest Model

There are two agents, and time is divided into periods. There are two states of nature, $\theta \in \{0, 1\}$. In state 0, only one of two players (chosen randomly with equal probability) has one option to make an investment of a fixed size in any period. In state 1, both players have one option. To have an option is private information and is not observable by the other agent; the private signal of the agent is the option. The number of players in the game depends on the state of nature.[1] As an illustration, the opportunities for productive investment may be more numerous when the state of the economy is good.

For an agent with an option, the payoff of investment in period t is

$$U = \delta^{t-1}(E[\theta] - c) \qquad \text{with} \quad 0 < c < 1,$$

where E is the expectation conditional on the information of the agent and δ is the discount factor, $0 < \delta < 1$.

All agents in the game have the same private information (their own option), and observe the same history. They have the same belief (probability of state $\theta = 1$). Let μ_t be the belief of an agent at the beginning of period t. The belief in the first period, μ, is given[2] and satisfies the next assumption in order to avoid trivialities.

ASSUMPTION 6.1 $0 < \mu - c < \delta\mu(1 - c)$.

Agents play a game in each period, and the strategy of an agent is his probability of investment. We look for a symmetric PBE: each agent knows the strategy of the other agent (it is the same as his own); he rationally anticipates receiving a random amount of information at the end of each period and that the subgame that begins next period with a belief updated by Bayes's rule has an equilibrium.

---

[1] One could also suppose that the cost of investment is very high for one or neither agent, thus preventing the investment. Recall that in the BHW model, the number of players does not depend on the state of nature.

[2] One could assume that agents know that nature chooses state $\theta = 1$ with probability μ_0. In this case, by Bayes's rule, $\mu = 2\mu_0/(1 + \mu_0)$.

Let z be the probability of investment in the first period by an agent with an option. Such an agent will be called a *player*. We prove that there is a unique symmetric equilibrium with $0 < z < 1$.

- $z = 1$ cannot be an equilibrium. If $z = 1$, both agents "come out" with probability one; the number of players and therefore the state is revealed perfectly at the end of the period. If an agent deviates from the strategy $z = 1$ and delays (with $z = 0$), he can invest in the second period if and only if the true state is good. The expected payoff of this delay strategy is $\delta\mu(1 - c)$: in the first period, the good state is revealed with probability μ, in which case he earns $1 - c$. The discount factor is applied because the investment is made in the second period. The payoff of no delay is $\mu - c$, and it is smaller by Assumption 6.1. The strategy $z = 1$ cannot define a PBE. Note that the interpretation of the inequality on the right is now clear: the payoff of investment, $\mu - c$, should be smaller than the payoff of delay with perfect information in the next period.

- $z = 0$ cannot be an equilibrium either. The argument is a bit more involved and proceeds by contradiction. If $z = 0$, there is no investment in the first period for any state, there is no information, and therefore the same game holds at the beginning of period 2, with the same belief μ. Indefinite delay cannot be an equilibrium strategy, because it would generate a zero payoff, which is strictly smaller than the payoff of no delay, $\mu - c > 0$ (Assumption 6.1). Let T be the first period in which there is some investment with positive probability. Because $z = 0$, we have $T \geq 2$. In period T, the current value of the payoff of investment is $\mu - c > 0$, because nothing has been learned before. The present value of this payoff is strictly smaller than the payoff of immediate investment, $\mu - c$. Hence, $T \geq 2$ is impossible and $z = 0$ cannot be an equilibrium strategy.

THE NECESSITY OF INVESTMENT IN EVERY PERIOD

We have shown that in an equilibrium, agents randomize with $0 < z < 1$. The level of total investment is a random variable. We will see that the higher the level of investment, the higher the updated belief after the observation of the investment. In this simple model, one investment is sufficient to reveal to the other player (if there is one) that the state is good. No investment in the first period is bad news. Would anyone invest in the second period after this bad news? The answer is no, and the argument is interesting.

If anyone delays in the first period and expects to invest in the second period after the worst possible news (zero investment), his payoff in the subgame of period 2 is the same as that of investing for sure in period 2. (He invests if he observes one investment.) That payoff, $\delta(\mu - c)$, is inferior to the payoff of immediate investment because of the discount. The player cannot invest after observing no investment. Hence, *if there is no investment in the first period, there is no investment in any period after.* We will see in this chapter that this phenomenon occurs in more general models.

The argument shows that (i) if there is no investment, the *ex post* belief of any agent must be smaller than the cost of investment, c; (ii) because agents randomize in the first period, the event of no investment has a positive probability. There is a positive probability of an incorrect herd.

Using the previous argument, we can compute the payoff of delay. If an agent delays, he invests in period 2 if and only if he sees an investment (by the other agent) in period 1, in which case he is sure that the state is good and his second-period payoff is $1 - c$. The probability of observing an investment in the first period is μz (the product of the probabilities that there is another agent and that he invests). The payoff of delay (computed at the time of the decision) is therefore $\delta \mu z(1 - c)$.

ARBITRAGE AND THE EXISTENCE OF A UNIQUE PBE

Because $0 < z < 1$, agents randomize their investment in the first period and are indifferent between no delay and delay. This arbitrage condition between the value of investment and the value of the option to invest is essential in this chapter and is defined by

$$(6.1) \qquad \mu - c = \delta \mu z(1 - c).$$

By Assumption 6.1, this equation in z has a unique solution in the interval $(0, 1)$. The analysis of the solution may be summarized as follows: first, the arbitrage condition is necessary if a PBE exists; second, the existence of a unique PBE follows from the arbitrage condition by construction of the equilibrium strategy. This method will be used in the general model.

INTERPRETATION OF THE ARBITRAGE CONDITION

A simple manipulation shows that the arbitrage equation can be restated as

$$(6.2) \qquad \frac{1 - \delta}{\delta}(\mu - c) = \mu z(1 - c) - (\mu - c)$$
$$= P(x = 0|\mu)\Big(c - P(\theta_1|x = 0, \mu)\Big),$$

where $P(x = 0|\mu)$ is the probability for an agent with belief μ that the other agent does not invest in period 1, i.e., the probability of bad news. The term $\mu - c$ has the dimension of a stock, as the net present value of an investment. The left-hand side is the *opportunity cost of delay*: it is the value of investment multiplied by the interest rate between consecutive periods. (If $\delta = 1/(1 + r)$, then $(1 - \delta)/\delta = r$.) The right-hand side will be called the *option value of delay*. It provides the measurement of the value of the information obtained from a delay. To interpret it, note that the term $P(\theta_1|x = 0, \mu)$ is the value of an investment after the bad news in the first period. If an agent could reverse his decision to invest in the first period (and get the cost back), the associated value of this action would be $c - P(\theta_1|x = 0, \mu)$. The option value of delay is the expected "regret value" of undoing the investment when the agent wishes he could do so. The next properties follow from the arbitrage condition.

INFORMATION AND TIME DISCOUNT

The power of the signal that is obtained by delay increases with the probability of investment z. If $z = 0$, there is no information. If $z = 1$, there is perfect information.

The discount factor is related to the length of the period, τ, by $\delta = e^{-\rho\tau}$, with ρ the discount rate per unit of time. If δ varies, the arbitrage equation (6.1) shows that the product δz is constant. A shorter period (higher δ) means that the equilibrium must generate less information at the end of the first period: the opportunity cost of delay is smaller, and by arbitrage, the information value of delay decreases. Because this information varies with z, the value of z decreases. From Assumption 6.1, $0 < z < 1$ only if δ is in the interval $[\delta^*, 1)$, with $\delta^* = (\mu - c)/(\mu(1 - c))$.

If $\delta \to \delta^*$, then $z \to 1$. If $\delta \leq \delta^*$, then $z = 1$ and the state is revealed at the end of the first period. Because this information comes late (with a low δ), agents do not wait for it.

If $\delta \to 1$ and the period length is vanishingly short, information comes in quickly but there is a positive probability that it is wrong. The equilibrium strategy z tends to δ^*. If the state is good, with probability $(1 - \delta^*)^2 > 0$ both agents delay and end up thinking that the probability of the good state is smaller than c and that investment is not profitable. There is a trade-off between the period length and the quality of the information that is revealed by the observation of others. This trade-off is generated by the arbitrage condition. The opportunity cost of delay is smaller if the period length is smaller. Hence the value of the information gained by delay must also be smaller.

A remarkable property is that the waiting game lasts one period, independently of the discount factor. If the period is vanishingly short, the game ends in a vanishingly short time, but the amount of information that is released is also vanishingly short. In this simple model with identical players, the value of the game does not depend on the endogenous information that is generated in the game, because it is equal to the payoff of immediate investment. However, when agents have different types of private information, the length of the period affects welfare (as shown in the next chapter).

INVESTMENT LEVEL AND OPTIMISM

In the arbitrage equation (6.1), the probability of investment and the expected value of investment are increasing functions of the belief μ: a higher μ entails a higher opportunity cost and, by arbitrage, a higher option value of delay. The higher information requires that players "come out of the wood" with a higher probability z. This mechanism is different from the arbitrage mechanism in the q-theory of Tobin, which operates on the margin between the financial value μ and an adjustment cost.

OBSERVATION NOISE AND INVESTMENT

Suppose that the investment of an agent is observed with a noise: if an investment is made, the other agent sees it with probability $1 - \gamma$ and sees nothing with probability

γ (γ small). The arbitrage operates beautifully: the information for a delaying agent is unaffected by the noise, because it must be equal to the opportunity cost, which is independent of the noise. Agents compensate for the noise in the equilibrium by increasing the probability of investment (Exercise 6.2).

LARGE NUMBER OF AGENTS

Suppose that in the good state there are N agents with an option to invest and that in the bad state there is only one agent with such an option. These values are chosen to simplify the game: one investment reveals that the state is good, and no investment stops the game. For any N, which can be arbitrarily large, the game lasts only one period, in equilibrium, and the probability of investment of each agent in the first period tends to zero if $N \to \infty$. Furthermore, the probability of no investment, conditional on the good state, tends to a positive number. The intuition is simple. If the probability of investment by a player remains higher than some value $\alpha > 0$, his action (investment or no investment) is a signal on the state with a nonvanishing precision. If $N \to \infty$, delay provides a sample of observations of arbitrarily large size and perfect information asymptotically. This is impossible, because it would contradict the arbitrage with the opportunity cost of delay, which is independent of N. The equilibrium is analyzed in Exercise 6.4.

STRATEGIC SUBSTITUTABILITY

Suppose an agent increases his probability of investment from an equilibrium value z. The option value (in the right-hand side of (6.1) or (6.2)) increases. Delay becomes strictly better, and the optimal response is to reduce the probability of investment to zero: there is strategic substitutability between agents. In a more general model (next section), this property is not satisfied and multiple equilibria may arise.

NONSYMMETRIC EQUILIBRIUM

Assume there are two agents, A and B, who can see each other but neither of whom can see whether the other has an option to invest. It is common knowledge that agent B always delays in the first period and does not invest ever if he sees no investment in the first period.

Agent A does not get any information by delaying: his optimal strategy is to invest with no delay, if he has an option. Given this strategy of agent A, agent B gets perfect information at the end of period 1, and his strategy is optimal. The equilibrium generates perfect information after one period. Furthermore, if the state is good, both agents invest. If the period length is vanishingly short, the value of the game is $\mu - c$ for agent A and $\mu(1 - c)$ for agent B, which is strictly higher than in the symmetric equilibrium. If agents could "allocate the asymmetry" randomly before knowing whether they have an option, they would be better off *ex ante*.

6.2 A General Model with Heterogeneous Beliefs

The structure of the model extends the canonical model in Section 4.2 by allowing each agent to make his fixed-size investment in any period of his choice. There are N agents, each with one option to make one irreversible investment of a fixed size. Time is divided into periods, and the payoff of exercising an option in period t is $\delta^{t-1}(\theta - c)$ with δ the discount factor, $0 < \delta < 1$, and c the cost of investment, $0 < c < 1$. The payoff from never investing is zero. Investment can be interpreted as an irreversible switch from one activity to another.[3]

The rest of the model is the same as in the beginning of Section 4.2. The productivity parameter θ, which is not observable, is set randomly by nature once and for all before the first period and takes one of two values: $\theta_0 < \theta_1$. Without loss of generality, these values are normalized at $\theta_1 = 1$ for the good state and $\theta_0 = 0$ for the bad state. As in Section 2.2.1, each agent is endowed at the beginning of time with a private belief which is drawn from a distribution with c.d.f. $F_1^\theta(\mu)$ depending on the state of nature θ. For simplicity and without loss of generality, it will be assumed that the cumulative distribution functions have derivatives.[4] The support of the distribution of beliefs is an interval $(\underline{\mu}_1, \overline{\mu}_1)$, where the bounds may be infinite and are independent of θ. The densities of private beliefs satisfy the proportional property (2.12). Hence, the cumulative distribution functions satisfy the property of first-order stochastic dominance: for any $\mu \in (\underline{\mu}_1, \overline{\mu}_1)$, $F_1^1(\mu) < F_1^0(\mu)$.

After the beginning of time, learning is endogenous. In period t, an agent knows his private belief and the history $h_t = (x_1, \ldots, x_{t-1})$, where x_k is the number of investments in period k.

The only decision variable of an agent is the period in which he invests. (This period is postponed to infinity if he never invests.) We will consider only symmetric equilibria. A strategy in period t is defined by the *investment set* $I_t(h_t)$ of beliefs of all investing agents: an agent with belief μ_t in period t invests in that period (assuming he still has an option) if and only if $\mu_t \in I_t(h_t)$. In an equilibrium, the set of agents who are indifferent between investment and delay will be of measure zero and is ignored. Agents will not use random strategies.

As in the previous chapters, Bayesian agents use the observation of the number of investments, x_t, to update the distribution of beliefs, F_t^θ, to the distribution in the next period, F_{t+1}^θ. Each agent (who has an option) chooses a strategy that maximizes his expected payoff, given his information and the equilibrium strategy of all agents for any future date and future history. For any period t and history h_t, each agent computes the value of his option if he delays and plays in the subgame that begins in

---

[3] The case where the switch involves the termination of an investment process (as in Caplin and Leahy, 1994) is isomorphic.

[4] The characterization of equilibria with atomistic distributions is more technical in that equilibrium strategies may be random (e.g., Chamley and Gale, 1994).

the next period $t + 1$. Delaying is optimal if and only if that value is at least equal[5] to the payoff of investing in period t. All equilibria analyzed here are symmetric subgame PBEs.

As in the model with exogenous timing (Section 4.2.1), a belief can be expressed by the LLR between the two states, $\lambda = \log(\mu/(1 - \mu))$. With n_t remaining players, the LLR is updated between periods t and $t + 1$ by Bayes's rule:

$$\lambda_{t+1} = \lambda_t + \zeta_t, \qquad \text{where} \quad \zeta_t = \log\left(\frac{P(x_t \mid I_t, \theta_1)}{P(x_t \mid I_t, \theta_0)}\right),$$

(6.3)

$$P(x_t \mid I_t, \theta) = \frac{n_t!}{x_t!(n_t - x_t)!}\pi_\theta^{x_t}(1 - \pi_\theta)^{n_t - x_t}, \qquad \pi_\theta = P(\lambda_t \in I_t \mid \theta).$$

All agents update their individual LLR by adding the same value ζ_t. Given a state θ, the distribution of beliefs measured as LLRs in period t is generated by a translation of the initial distribution by a random variable ζ_t.

6.2.1 Characterization and Existence of Equilibria

The incentive for delay is to get more information from the observation of others. Agents who are more optimistic have more to lose and less to gain from delaying: the discount factor applies to a high expected payoff, whereas the probability of bad news to be learned after a delay is relatively small. This fundamental property of the model restricts the equilibrium strategies to the class of *monotone strategies*. By definition, an agent with a monotone strategy in period t invests if and only if his belief μ_t is greater than some value μ_t^*. The next result, which is proven in the appendix (Section 6.4), shows that equilibrium strategies must be monotone.

LEMMA 6.1 (Monotone strategies) *In any arbitrary period t of a PBE, if the payoff of delay for an agent with belief μ_t is at least equal to the payoff of no delay, any agent with belief $\mu_t' < \mu_t$ strictly prefers to delay. Equilibrium strategies are monotone and defined by a value μ_t^*: agents who delay in period t have a belief $\mu_t \leq \mu_t^*$.*

Until the end of the chapter, a strategy will be defined by the minimum belief for investment, μ_t^*. Because no agent would invest with a negative payoff, $\mu_t^* \geq c$. The support of the distribution of μ in period t is denoted by $(\underline{\mu}_t, \overline{\mu}_t)$. If all agents delay in period t, one can define the equilibrium strategy as $\mu_t^* = \overline{\mu}_t$.

The existence of a nontrivial equilibrium in the subgame that begins in period t depends on the payoff of the most optimistic agent,[6] $\overline{\mu}_t - c$. First, if $\overline{\mu}_t \leq c$, no agent has a positive payoff and there is no investment whatever the state θ. Nothing

---

[5] By assumption, an indifferent agent delays. This tie-breaking rule applies with probability zero and is inconsequential.

[6] Recall that such an agent may not actually exist in the realized distribution of beliefs.

is learned in period t (with probability one), or in any period after. The game stops. Second, if $\overline{\mu}_t > c$, the next result (which parallels a property for identical beliefs in Chamley and Gale, 1994) shows that in a PBE, the probability of some investment is strictly positive. The intuition of the proof, which is given in the appendix (Section 6.4), begins with the remark that a permanent delay is not optimal for agents with beliefs strictly greater than c (because it would yield a payoff of zero). Let T be the first period after t in which some agents invest with positive probability. If $T > t$, the current value of their payoff would be the same as in period t (nothing is learned between t and T). Because of the discount factor $\delta < 1$, the present value of delay would be strictly smaller than immediate investment, which is a contradiction.

LEMMA 6.2 (Condition for positive investment) *In any period t of a PBE*

  (i) *if $c < \overline{\mu}_t$ (the cost of investment is below the upper bound of beliefs), then any equilibrium strategy μ_t^* is such that $c \le \mu_t^* < \overline{\mu}_t$; if there is at least one remaining player, the probability of at least one investment in period t is strictly positive;*
 (ii) *if $\overline{\mu}_t \le c$ (the cost of investment is above the upper bound of beliefs), then with probability one there is no investment for any period $\tau \ge t$.*

The decision to invest is a decision whether to delay or not. In evaluating the payoff of delay, an agent should take into account the strategies of the other agents in all future periods. This could be in general a very difficult exercise. Fortunately, the property of monotone strategies simplifies greatly the structure of equilibria. A key step is the next result, which shows that any equilibrium is a sequence of two-period equilibria, each of which can be determined separately.

LEMMA 6.3 (One-step property) *If the equilibrium strategy μ_t^* of a PBE in period t is an interior solution ($\underline{\mu}_t < \mu_t^* < \overline{\mu}_t$), then an agent with belief μ_t^* is indifferent between investing in period t and delaying to make a final decision (investing or not) in period $t + 1$.*

Proof

Because the Bayesian updating rules are continuous in μ, the payoffs of immediate investment and of delay for any agent are continuous functions of his belief μ. Therefore, an agent with belief μ_t^* in period t is indifferent between investment and delay. By definition of μ_t^*, if he delays, he has the highest level of belief among all players remaining in the game in period $t + 1$, i.e., his belief is $\overline{\mu}_{t+1}$. In period $t + 1$ there are two possibilities: (i) if $\overline{\mu}_{t+1} > c$, then from Lemma 6.2, $\mu_{t+1}^* < \overline{\mu}_{t+1}$ and a player with belief $\overline{\mu}_{t+1}$ invests in period $t + 1$; (ii) if $\overline{\mu}_{t+1} \le c$, then from Lemma 6.2 again, nothing is learned after period t; a player with belief $\overline{\mu}_{t+1}$ may invest (if $\overline{\mu}_{t+1} = c$), but his payoff is the same as that of delaying forever. ∎

In an equilibrium, an agent with belief μ compares the payoff of immediate investment, $\mu - c$, with that of delay for exactly one period, $W(\mu, \mu^*)$, where μ^* is the strategy of others. (For simplicity we omit the time subscript and other arguments such as the number of players and the c.d.f. F^θ). From Lemma 6.3 and the Bayesian formulae (6.3) with $\pi^\theta = 1 - F^\theta(\mu^*)$, the function W is well defined. An interior equilibrium strategy must be solution of the arbitrage equation between the payoff of immediate investment and of delay:

$$\mu^* - c = W(\mu^*, \mu^*).$$

The next result shows that this equation has a solution if the cost c is interior to the support of the distribution of beliefs.

LEMMA 6.4 *In any period, if the cost c is in the support of the distribution of beliefs, i.e., $\underline{\mu} < c < \overline{\mu}$, then there exists $\mu^* > c$ such that $\mu^* - c = W(\mu^*, \mu^*)$: an agent with belief μ^* is indifferent between investment and delay.*

Proof
Choose $\mu^* = \overline{\mu}$: there is no investment and therefore no learning during the period. Hence, $W(\overline{\mu}, \overline{\mu}) = (1 - \delta)(\overline{\mu} - c) < \overline{\mu} - c$. Choose now $\mu^* = c$. With strictly positive probability, an agent with belief c observes $n - 1$ investments, in which case his belief is higher (n is the number of remaining players). Hence, $W(c, c) > 0$. Because the function W is continuous, the equation $\mu^* - c = W(\mu^*, \mu^*)$ has at least one solution in the interval $(c, \overline{\mu})$.   ∎

The previous lemmata provide characterizations of equilibria (PBE). These characterizations enable us to construct all PBE by forward induction and to show existence.

THEOREM 6.1 *In any period t where the support of private beliefs is the interval $(\underline{\mu}_t, \overline{\mu}_t)$,*

  (i) *if $\overline{\mu}_t \leq c$, then there is a unique PBE with no agent investing in period t or after;*
 (ii) *if $\underline{\mu}_t < c < \overline{\mu}_t$, then there is at least one PBE with strategy $\mu_t^* \in (c, \overline{\mu}_t)$;*
(iii) *if $c \leq \underline{\mu}_t$, then there is a PBE with $\mu_t^* = \underline{\mu}_t$ in which all remaining players invest in period t.*

In cases (ii) and (iii) there may be multiple equilibria. The equilibrium strategies $\mu_t^* \in (\underline{\mu}_t, \overline{\mu}_t)$ are identical to the solutions of the arbitrage equation

(6.4) $\mu^* - c = W(\mu^*, \mu^*),$

where $W(\mu, \mu^*)$ is the payoff of an agent with belief μ who delays for exactly one period while other agents use the strategy μ^*.

The only part that needs a comment is (ii). From Lemma 6.4, there exists μ_t^* such that $c < \mu_t^*$ and $\mu^* - c = W(\mu^*, \mu^*)$. From Lemma 6.1, any agent with belief $\mu_t > \mu_t^*$ strictly prefers not to delay, and any agent with belief $\mu_t < \mu_t^*$ strictly prefers to delay. (Otherwise, by Lemma 6.1 an agent with belief μ_t^* would strictly prefer to delay, which contradicts the definition of μ_t^*.) The strategy μ_t^* determines the random outcome x_t in period t and the distributions F_{t+1}^θ for the next period, and so on.

6.3 **Properties**

6.3.1 Arbitrage

Let us reconsider the trade-off between investment and delay. For the sake of simplicity, we omit the time subscript whenever there is no ambiguity. If an agent with belief μ delays for one period, he forgoes the implicit one-period rent on his investment, which is the difference between investing for sure now and investing for sure next period, $(1 - \delta)(\mu - c)$; he gains the possibility of undoing the investment after bad news at the end of the current period (the possibility of not investing). The expected value of this possibility is the option value of delay. The following result, proven in the appendix (Section 6.4), shows that the belief μ^* of a marginal agent is defined by the equality between the opportunity cost and the option value of delay.

PROPOSITION 6.1 (Arbitrage) *Let μ^* be an equilibrium strategy in a game with $n \geq 2$ remaining players, $\underline{\mu} < \mu^* < \overline{\mu}$. Then μ^* is solution of the arbitrage equation between the opportunity cost and the option value of delay,*

(6.5) $\qquad (1 - \delta)(\mu^* - c) = \delta Q(\mu^*, \mu^*),$

with

$$Q(\mu, \mu^*) = \sum_{k=0}^{n-1} P(x = k \mid \mu, \mu^*, F^\theta, n)$$

$$\times \max\left(c - P(\theta = \theta_1 \mid x = k; \mu, \mu^*, F^\theta, n), 0\right),$$

where x is the number of investments by other agents in the period.

The function $Q(\mu, \mu^*)$ is a *regret function* that applies to an agent with belief μ. It depends on the strategy μ^* of the other agents and on the c.d.f.'s F^θ at the beginning of the period. The gain of undoing an investment is c minus the value of the investment after the bad news, so the regret function $Q(\mu, \mu^*)$ is the expected value of the amount the agent would be prepared to pay to undo his investment at the beginning of next period.

At the end of that period, each agent updates his LLR according to the Bayesian formula (6.3) with $\pi_\theta = 1 - F^\theta(\mu_t^*)$. A simple exercise shows that the updated LLR is an increasing function of the level of investment in period t and that the lowest value of investment $x_t = 0$ generates the lowest level of belief at the end of the period. Can the game go on after the worst news of no investment? From Proposition 6.1, we can deduce immediately that the answer is no. If the agent invested after the worst news, the value of $Q(\mu^*, \mu^*)$ would be equal to zero and would therefore be strictly smaller than $\mu^* - c$, which contradicts the arbitrage equation (6.5).

PROPOSITION 6.2 (The case of worst news) *In any period t of a PBE for which the equilibrium strategy μ_t^* is interior to the support $(\underline{\mu}_t, \overline{\mu}_t)$, if $x_t = 0$, then $\overline{\mu}_{t+1} \leq c$ and the game stops at the end of period t with no further investment in any subsequent period.*

The result shows that a game with N players lasts at most N periods. If the period length τ is vanishingly short, the game ends in a vanishingly short time. This case is analyzed in Section 6.3.6.

6.3.2 Representation of Beliefs

An example of the evolution of beliefs is illustrated in Figure 6.1. The reader may compare it with the equivalent Figure 4.3 in the case of exogenous timing. Beliefs are measured by the LLR and are bounded, by assumption. The support of their distribution at the beginning of a period is represented by a segment. Suppose that the state is good: $\theta = 1$. At the beginning of period 1, the private beliefs of the N players are the realizations of N independent drawings from a distribution with density $f^1(\cdot)$, which is represented by a continuous curve. (The density in state $\theta = 0$ is represented by a dashed curve.)

In period 1, agents with a belief above λ_1^* exercise their option to invest. The number of investments, x_1, is the number of agents with belief above λ_1^*, which is random according to the process described in the previous paragraph.

Each agent who delays knows that x_1 is generated by the sum of $N - 1$ independent binary variables equal to 1 with a probability π^θ that depends on θ: $\pi^\theta = 1 - F^\theta(\lambda_1^*)$. The probability is represented in Figure 6.1 by the lightly shaded area if $\theta = 0$ and the darker area if $\theta = 1$.

From the updating rule (6.3), the distribution of LLRs in period 2 is a translation of the distribution of the LLRs in period 1, truncated at λ_1^* and rescaled (to have a total measure of one): $\lambda_1^* - \underline{\lambda}_1 = \overline{\lambda}_2 - \underline{\lambda}_2$. An agent with LLR equal to λ_1^* in period 1 and who delays has the highest belief in period 2. The news at the end of period 1 depends on the random number of agents with beliefs above λ_1. In Figure 6.1, the

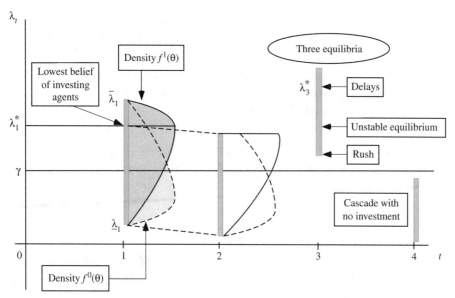

Figure 6.1 An example of evolution of beliefs. Here $\gamma = \log(c/(1-c))$. The number of investments in a period t depends on the number of agents with a belief higher than λ_t^*. At the end of a period, the updated distributions in the two states are truncated, translated, and rescaled. Period 3 (in which the representation of the densities is omitted) corresponds to a case with three equilibria. In period 4, there is no investment, because all beliefs are smaller than the cost of investment.

observation of the number of investments in period 1 is bad news: the agent with highest belief has a lower belief in period 2 than in period 1.

There are two critical values for the LLR in each period: (i) an agent who has a LLR below the breakeven value $\gamma = \log(c/(1-c))$ does not invest; (ii) no agent who has an LLR above some value λ^{**} delays. The value λ^{**} is defined so that if $\lambda > \lambda^{**}$, the payoff of no delay is higher than that of delay with perfect information one period later. Because the latter yields $\delta\mu(1-c)$ to an agent with belief μ, we have

$$(6.6) \qquad \lambda^{**} = \log\left(\frac{\mu^{**}}{1-\mu^{**}}\right) \qquad \text{with} \quad \mu^{**} - c = \delta\mu^{**}(1-c).$$

Note that λ^{**} (or μ^{**}) depends essentially on the discount rate. If the discount rate is vanishingly small, then the opportunity cost of delay is vanishingly small, and only the superoptimists should invest: if $\delta \to 1$, then $\lambda^{**} \to \infty$.

6.3.3 Herds: A Comparison with Exogenous Sequences

Case (iii) in Theorem 6.1 is represented in period 3 of Figure 6.1. The lower bound of the distribution of beliefs is higher than the cost of investment, with $\underline{\lambda}_3 > \gamma = \log(c/(1-c))$. There is an equilibrium called a *rush*, in which no agent delays. In that equilibrium, nothing is learned by delay, because the number of investments is equal to the number of remaining players, whatever the state of nature. This outcome occurs here with endogenous delay under the same condition as the cascade of BHW, in which all agents invest, regardless of their private signal.[7]

For the distribution of beliefs in period 3, there may be another equilibrium with an interior solution λ_3^* to the arbitrage equation (6.4). Because agents with the lowest LLR $\underline{\lambda}_3$ strictly prefer to invest if all others do, there may be multiple equilibria with arbitrage, some of them unstable. This issue is reexamined in the next subsection.

For the case of period 4, all beliefs are below the breakeven point: $\overline{\lambda}_4 < \gamma$. No investment takes place in period 4 or after. This equilibrium appears also in the BHW model with exogenous timing, as a cascade with no investment. From Proposition 6.2, this equilibrium occurs with positive probability if agents coordinate on the equilibrium λ_3^* in period 3.

The present model integrates the findings of the BHW model in the setting with endogenous timing. We could anticipate that the herds of the BHW model with exogenous timing are also equilibria when timing is endogenous, because they generate no information and therefore no incentive for delay.

A rush where all agents invest with no delay can take place only if the distribution of beliefs (LLR) is bounded below. However, if beliefs are unbounded, the structure of equilibria is very similar to that in Figure 6.1. In a generic sense, there are multiple equilibria and one of them may be similar to a rush. This issue is examined in an example with two agents and Gaussian signals. The Gaussian property is a standard representation of unbounded beliefs.

6.3.4 Two Agents

Assume there are two agents: agent i $(i = 1, 2)$ receives a signal s_i that is normally distributed with mean θ and variance σ^2; s_1 and s_2 are independent, conditional on θ. From Proposition 6.2, there are at most two periods in which investment takes place, and the first period is the only active period in which the decision problem is not trivial. Each agent i forms his belief $\mu(s_i) = P(\theta = \theta_1 | \mu, s_i)$ in the first period according to Bayes's rule from the public belief μ of state θ_1 and his signal s_i. The support of the distribution of beliefs is the entire set of real numbers. Individual strategies can be defined with respect to the private signal (to invest if $s > s^*$) or with respect to the individual belief (to invest if $\mu(s) > \mu^*$). In this subsection we use the formulation in terms of private signals. Likewise, the value of investment is expressed as a function of the private signal $\mu(s) - c$, and the option value of an agent is a function of the private signal s and the strategy s^* of the other agent. By an abuse of notation, $Q(s, s^*) = Q(\mu(s), \mu(s^*))$. A symmetric PBE is characterized by

$$(6.7) \qquad \frac{1 - \delta}{\delta}\left(\mu(s^*) - c\right) = Q(s^*, s^*).$$

---

[7] In the BHW model, distributions are atomistic, but the argument is identical.

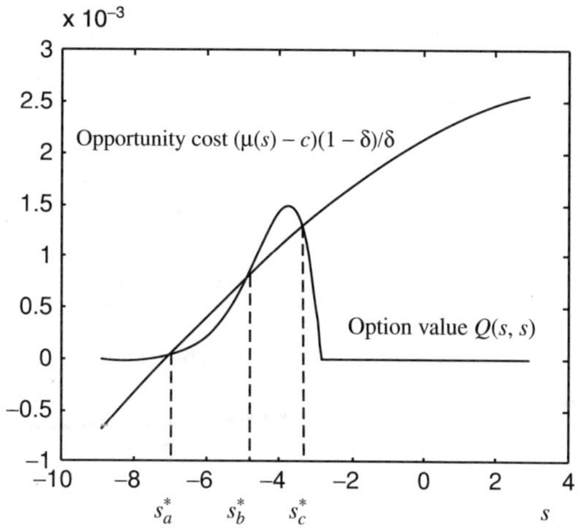

Figure 6.2 Multiple equilibria with two agents. Parameter values: $\sigma = 2$, $\theta_0 = 0$, $\theta_1 = 1$, $c = 0.5$, $P(\theta = \theta_1) = 0.87$, $\delta = 1 - 0.06$.

The decision problem is illustrated in Figure 6.2 with the graphs of the option value of delay $Q(s, s)$ and of the opportunity cost $((1 - \delta)/\delta)(\mu(s) - c)$ (measured in the second period). The main feature of the figure is the hump shape of the option value $Q(s, s)$ as a function of s. This feature does not depend on the specifics of the example and has a general interpretation. Suppose first that the equilibrium strategy s^* is very low. The probability of an investment is high in both states. It is higher in the good state, but the difference from the bad state is small. The observation of investment by the other agent is not very informative, as it is expected to occur most of the time.[8] The expected information gained by delay as measured by the option value is therefore small. The same property holds when s^* is sufficiently high, in which case an agent does not invest, most of the time. Finally, when s^* is in the intermediate range, the observation of the actions of other agents is informative and the option value is higher than in either tail of the distribution.

By (6.5), the option value of delay is equal to

$$Q(s, s^*) = c(1 - \mu(s))F(s^* - \theta_0) - (1 - c)\mu(s)F(s^* - \theta_1).$$

The partial derivative of the option value of delay for an agent with signal s is decreasing in s, given the strategy s^* of the other agent:

$$Q_1(s, s^*) = -(cF(s^* - \theta_0) + (1 - c)F(s^* - \theta_1))\mu'(s) < 0.$$

The intuition is straightforward: an agent with a higher signal s is more optimistic and has a lower expected regret after the first period.

The partial derivative of the option value of delay with respect to the other agent's strategy, s^*, is equal to

$$Q_2(s, s^*) = \left(\frac{c}{1 - c} \frac{1 - \mu(s)}{\mu(s)} \frac{f(s^* - \theta_0)}{f(s^* - \theta_1)} - 1 \right)(1 - c)\mu(s) f(s^* - \theta_1).$$

---

[8] In the simple model of Section 6.1, this equilibrium could occur because the number of players depended on the state.

For simplicity, assume $c = \frac{1}{2}$. Using Bayes's rule for $\mu(s)$,

(6.8) $Q_2(s^*, s^*)$

$$= \left(\frac{1 - \mu}{\mu} \exp\left(\frac{\theta_1 - \theta_0}{\sigma^2} \left(s - \frac{\theta_1 + \theta_0}{2} \right) \right) - 1 \right) \frac{\mu(s)}{2} f(s^* - \theta_1).$$

We have the following property[9]:

(6.9)   There exists $\hat{s}$ such that $Q_2(s, s) < 0$ if and only if $s > \hat{s}$.

The variation of the function $Q(s, s)$ is $Q'(s, s) = Q_1(s, s) + Q_2(s, s)$. A straight-forward exercise shows that if s is sufficiently small, the effect of the second component (the strategy of the other agent) dominates that of the first (the private signal): $Q_1(s, s) + Q_2(s, s) > 0$. The option value $Q(s, s)$ is increasing in s.

6.3.5 Strategic Complementarity and Substitutability

The reaction $R(s^*)$ to the strategy s^* of the other agent is defined by

$$\frac{1 - \delta}{\delta} \left(\mu(R(s^*)) - c \right) = Q(R(s^*), s^*).$$

The model generates regions of strategic complementarity (with $R' > 0$) and strategic substitutability (with $R' < 0$). When s^* is relatively small and delay does not generate much information, an increase in s^*, i.e., a reduction in the propensity to invest, raises the option value of delay and thus the opportunity cost $(1 - \delta)(\mu - c)$ of the optimal response in s. In this case, the reaction function is increasing in s^* and there is strategic complementarity. When s^* is large, an increase in s^* reduces the option value of delay and thus lowers the marginal belief between investment and delay. There is strategic substitutability. These properties can be verified formally by differentiation of the previous equation:

(6.10) $\left(\frac{1 - \delta}{\delta} \mu'(s) - Q_1 \right) R' = Q_2.$

From the previous discussion, the multiplier of R' is positive and the sign of R' is the same as that of Q_2. From (6.9), the sign of $Q_2(s^*, s^*)$ is positive if $s^* < \hat{s}$ for some value $\hat{s}$ and negative if $s^* > \hat{s}$. This occurrence of strategic complementarity and substitutability is robust, as shown in Chamley (2003a).

Strategic complementarity is necessary for the existence of multiple equilibria (Cooper and John, 1988). Strategic complementarity occurs here only because of

---

[9] If $\mu = \frac{1}{2}$, then $\hat{s} = (\theta_0 + \theta_1)/2$.

information externalities. There is no payoff externality. In Figure 6.2 there are three equilibrium strategies, $s_a^* < s_b^* < s_c^*$, and the middle one is unstable.[10]

The strategy s_a^* generates a rush with a high probability of investment by any agent, whereas with the strategy s_c^*, the probability of investment in the first period is small. The s_c^*-equilibrium is more informative than the s_a^*-equilibrium in the sense that if an agent receives a signal in the range (s_a^*, s_c^*), he prefers to delay and to incur an opportunity cost. He invests immediately in the s_a^*-equilibrium. Any agent who takes different actions in the two equilibria strictly prefers the one with more delay. It can be verified numerically that the loss of information under the strategy s_a^* as compared with that under s_c^* cannot be interpreted as a loss of information due to some noise, à la Blackwell.[11]

6.3.6 Period Length

Suppose that in the two-agent model of the previous section, the period length decreases toward zero, with a constant discount rate per unit of time, or equivalently that the discount factor δ tends to one. In Figure 6.2, the graph of the option value of delay (in current terms) stays invariant but the graph of the opportunity cost rotates clockwise around its intersection with the 0-line. In that example, there is a value δ^* such that if $\delta > \delta^*$, the rush equilibrium vanishes and there remains a unique equilibrium where each agent delays unless his signal is high.

This property is general and has an intuitive explanation. When the discount rate becomes vanishingly small, the opportunity cost of delay, for any given belief μ, becomes smaller than the option value of delay. Such a belief cannot be the belief of a marginal agent. An equilibrium with arbitrage must occur in the range of relatively high beliefs. However, (6.9) shows that for $s > \hat{s}$ that is independent of δ, there is strategic substitutability and there cannot be multiple equilibria. The uniqueness of the equilibrium with a low discount rate is formalized in the next proposition (which is generalized in Chamley, 2003a).

PROPOSITION 6.3 *Assume that in the two-agent game of Section 6.3.4, the parameters of the model (except δ) are given. Then there exists δ^* such that if $\delta \in (\delta^*, 1)$, there is a unique equilibrium.*

Proposition 6.3 highlights the fact that some delay in the observation of others is important for the existence of multiple equilibria and rushes. A delay in the

---

[10] The middle strategy s_b^* is unstable in the following sense: at that point, a small change in the strategy s_2^*, say of agent 2, induces a reaction in s_1^* by agent 1, with the same sign and with a greater magnitude.

[11] Because of the absence of the Blackwell property, it is doubtful that the equilibria can be Pareto-ranked for general distributions of beliefs. Such a Pareto ranking is easy to establish, however, when the distribution of agents is atomistic with two classes, optimists and pessimists.

observation of others is a plausible assumption. Periods are a measure of the lag between the observation of others and the possibility of action in response to the information provided by the observation. Proposition 6.3 shows that multiple equilibria may arise only if this lag is not too short. We will see in the next chapter that the case of continuous time is not the limit of a model with vanishingly short periods.[12]

6.3.7 Large Number of Agents

We have seen in Theorem 6.1 that the game can be reduced to a sequence of independent two-period games, each of which is completely specified by the densities of beliefs f^θ in the two states. The time subscripts will therefore be omitted until the end of this subsection. The densities f^θ are taken as given. The only parameter that varies is the number of players n, which is arbitrarily large. This case is relevant for large economies and for the comparison of social learning with endogenous and exogenous timing.[13] We will see that the limit properties of the model depend only on the upper bound of the beliefs, $\overline{\mu}$, and not on the distributions of beliefs.

In order to focus on the main issues, assume $\underline{\mu} < c < \overline{\mu}$ (case (ii) in Theorem 6.1). The analysis of the other cases is left to the reader. By Theorem 6.1, all equilibria have a strategy $\mu^* \in (c, \overline{\mu})$, and there is at least one such equilibrium. How does an equilibrium strategy change when the number of players $n \to \infty$, *ceteris paribus*?

The key mechanism is the arbitrage between the opportunity cost and the option value of delay for an agent with marginal belief μ^*. To develop the intuition, suppose first that μ^* stays constant. Because the probability that any player invests is equal to $1 - F^\theta(\mu^*)$ in state θ, the level of investment in the period, x, operates like a sampling of size n with probability $1 - F^\theta(\mu^*)$, and is more informative on state θ when n increases. The prospect of a piece of information of high value generates a higher incentive for delay. Therefore, the equilibrium value μ^* cannot stay constant: it must increase when $n \to \infty$.

Recall that an agent with belief above μ^{**} (defined in (6.6)) does not delay. The next two results characterize the asymptotic properties of equilibria as $n \to \infty$ and are shown in the appendix (Section 6.4). These properties depend on whether the upper bound of the distribution $\overline{\mu}$ is greater or smaller than μ^{**}: (i) when $\overline{\mu} < \mu^{**}$, a large number of players has no effect on the information generated in an equilibrium; (ii) when $\overline{\mu} > \mu^{**}$, a large number of players solve the information problem asymptotically. We begin with $\overline{\mu} < \mu^{**}$.

---

[12] If $c \leq \underline{\mu}$, a rush in which no agent delays is an equilibrium (Theorem 6.1, case (iii)). In such an equilibrium, there is no information gained in a delay, and the equilibrium holds for any value of the discount rate or the opportunity cost. In the model of Section 6.3.4, however, the rush equilibrium at s_a^* disappears if the period is sufficiently short. This issue is discussed in the next chapter.

[13] The convergence with exogenous learning makes little sense if the number of players is not arbitrarily large.

PROPOSITION 6.4 *Assume that in some arbitrary period the cumulative distribution functions F^θ are given, with support such that $\underline{\mu} < c < \overline{\mu} < \mu^{**}$, where μ^{**} is defined by $\mu^{**} - c = \delta\mu^{**}(1 - c)$. Then any equilibrium strategy $\mu^*(n)$ depends on the number of players n. If $n \to \infty$, then*

$$\mu^*(n) \to \overline{\mu} \quad and \quad F^\theta(\mu^*(n)) = 1 - \frac{\beta_n^\theta}{n} \quad with \quad \lim_{n\to\infty} \beta_n^\theta = \beta^\theta > 0.$$

The result shows that under the stated assumptions, if $n \to \infty$, the game is played by agents whose beliefs are vanishingly close to the upper bound of the beliefs $\overline{\mu}$. Because of the arbitrage property, the value of the information revealed by investment is bounded by the opportunity cost of an agent with belief $\overline{\mu}$, which is independent of the number of players. The number of investments has a Poisson distribution, and the game is the same as in the model of Chamley and Gale (1994) with identical agents and n arbitrarily large. The upper bound of the support $\overline{\mu}$ summarizes completely the effect of the distribution of beliefs on the equilibrium.[14]

The condition $\underline{\mu} < c < \overline{\mu}$ in Proposition 6.4 ensures the existence of an equilibrium with delay and learning. If this condition is lifted, that equilibrium could be maintained or could disappear, and there could also be an equilibrium with a rush. These various possibilities can easily be seen by the reader at this point.[15] The important condition in Proposition 6.4 is that $\overline{\mu} < \mu^{**}$. The next result focuses on the reverse case $\overline{\mu} > \mu^{**}$.

PROPOSITION 6.5 *Assume that in some arbitrary period, $\overline{\mu} > \mu^{**}$ and $\underline{\mu} < c < \overline{\mu}$. Then if $n \to \infty$, there is a unique equilibrium strategy $\mu^*(n)$ with*

$$\lim_{n\to\infty} \mu^*(n) = \mu^{**},$$

and information is asymptotically perfect at the end of the period. For any $\mu \in [\underline{\mu}, \overline{\mu}]$, the payoff of delay converges to $\delta\mu(1 - c)$.

If the distribution of beliefs is bounded ($\overline{\mu} < 1$) and the period is sufficiently short, then $\overline{\mu} < \mu^{**}$ and Proposition 6.4 applies. If the distribution is unbounded, then $\overline{\mu} = 1$ and Proposition 6.5 applies for any discount factor. When the period

[14] The analysis of that model, using the standard tools of dynamic programming, is also available on the web site of this book (see page 16).

[15] One could show that if the density of private beliefs is strictly positive on $[\underline{\mu}, \overline{\mu}]$ and n is sufficiently large, there are at most three equilibria, two of which are stable in a standard sense. The first of these two is the equilibrium with an interior solution to the arbitrage equation, and the second is a rush. In the third equilibrium, the investment set is an interval $(\underline{\mu}, \mu^*)$ where $\mu^* \to \underline{\mu}$ if $n \to \infty$. In that equilibrium, the Poisson parameter is such that asymptotically, an agent with belief $\underline{\mu}$ is indifferent between investment and delay.

is vanishingly short, the information problem is solved. An agent with belief μ gets perfect information in a vanishingly short time,[16] and his payoff is equal to $\mu(1 - c)$.

This result is obviously different from that of Chamley and Gale (1994), where the support of the distribution of beliefs is restricted to a point and is therefore bounded. Recall that in the model with exogenous timing, beliefs converge to the truth if the distribution of beliefs is unbounded (Proposition 4.8). In Proposition 6.5, agents are not restricted in the timing of their investment and convergence to the truth occurs after one period if $n \to \infty$.

EXERCISES

EXERCISE 6.1
Consider the model of Section 6.1. Determine the belief (probability of the good state) after the bad news of no investment. Determine the limit of this value when $\delta \to 1$.

EXERCISE 6.2 Observation noise
Consider the model of Section 6.1 with observation noise. Assume that if an agent invests, he is seen as investing with probability $1 - \gamma$ and not investing with probability γ, where γ is small. Determine the equilibrium strategy. Show that for some interval $\gamma \in [0, \gamma^*)$ with $\gamma^* > 0$, the probability of the revelation of the good state and the probability of an incorrect herd are independent of γ.

EXERCISE 6.3
Consider the simple model of delay in Section 6.1 where there are two possible states 1 and 0. In state 1, there are two agents, each with an option to make an investment equal to 1 at the cost $c < 1$. In state 0, there is only one such agent. The gross payoff of investment is θ. The discount factor is $\delta < 1$, and the initial probability of state 1 is μ such that $0 < \mu - c < \mu\delta(1 - c)$.

1. A government proposes a policy that lowers the cost of investment through a subsidy τ, which is assumed to be small. Unfortunately, because of lags, the policy lowers the cost of investment by a small amount in the *second* period, and only in the second period. This policy is fully anticipated in the first period. Analyze the effect of this policy on the equilibrium and the welfare of agents.
2. Suppose in addition (in each state) one more agent with an option to invest (and discount factor δ), and a belief (probability of the good state) $\underline{\mu} < c$. How is your previous answer modified?

---

[16] For simplicity, one may assume that $n \to \infty$ faster than $\delta \to 1$.

EXERCISE 6.4

Consider the model of Section 6.1 with N players in the good state and one player in the bad state. Solve for the symmetric equilibrium. Show that the probability of a herd with no investment converges to $\pi^* > 0$ if $N \to \infty$. Analyze the probability of investment by any agent as $N \to \infty$.

EXERCISE 6.5

In the model of Section 6.3.7, assume $n \to \infty$ and the period length converges to zero $(\delta \to 1)$ at a rate slower than n. Assume that not all agents invest in the equilibrium (there is no rush).

1. Determine the payoff of an agent with private belief μ as a function of μ, $\overline{\mu}$, and c.
2. Is there a measure of the externality of information that an agent with private belief μ receives from the agents in the upper tail of the distribution of beliefs?

6.4 Appendix

6.4.1 A Continuum of Agents with Observation Noise

In macroeconomics, aggregate data are reported at discrete intervals, quarterly or monthly. These data (e.g., GDP growth, housing starts, durable expenditures) pertain to a large number of agents. They are also affected by noise and imperfection, and may be subject to revisions. The theoretical model of this section should be viewed in that context.

By assumption, there is a continuum of agents of total mass equal to one. As in the two-agent model, each rational player gets his private information in the form of a signal $s = \theta + \epsilon$ where the noise ϵ is independent of any other private noise or other variables in the economy and is normally distributed $\mathcal{N}(0, \sigma_\epsilon^2)$. This process of private information generates in the first period an unbounded support of the distribution of private beliefs. At the end of each period, each agent observes the level of aggregate activity

$$Y_t = y_t + \eta_t,$$

where y_t is the integral of the investments by the rational agents, and η_t is a random term which is exogenous, independent from all the other variables in the economy and normally distributed $\mathcal{N}(0, \sigma_\eta^2)$. The history h_t is now defined by $h_t = (Y_1, \ldots, Y_{t-1})$.

The analytical method of Section 6.2 applies. In any period t of a PBE, the strategy is monotone. It is defined by the marginal value of the signal s_t^*, which depends on

h_t: an agent delays if and only if his signal[17] is smaller than s_t^*. The value of s_t^* is determined by the arbitrage between the payoff of immediate investment and that of delay for one period only. The equilibrium with an infinite number of periods is thus reduced to a sequence of two-period equilibria. As long as the learning phase proceeds, agents in the interval of beliefs $(s_t^*, \bar{s}_t)$ invest in period t and are taken away from the game at the end of period t. If an agent with signal s_t^* delays in period t, he has the highest belief in period $t+1$. Note that *the distribution of beliefs is bounded above in each period after the first.*

Let F be the cumulative distribution function of the normal distribution $\mathcal{N}(0, \sigma_\epsilon^2)$. Because the mass of agents is equal to one, the observation in period t is equal to

$$Y_t = \underbrace{\max\Big(F(s_{t-1}^* - \theta) - F(s_t^* - \theta), 0 \Big)}_{\text{endogenous activity } y_{\theta,t} \,=\, y(\theta, s^*)} + \underbrace{\eta_t}_{\text{noise}},$$

with $s_1^* = \infty$ by convention.

The variable Y_t is a signal on θ through the arguments of the cumulative distribution functions. If s_t^* is either large or small, the endogenous level y_t is near zero or near the mass of remaining players, for any value of θ. In this case, the signal of the endogenous activity y_t is dwarfed by the noise η_t, and the information content of Y_t becomes vanishingly small.

Consider an agent with LLR equal to λ_t at the beginning of period t. Conditional on the observation Y_t, his LLR at the end of the period is equal to λ_{t+1} with

$$\lambda_{t+1} = -\frac{(Y_t - y_{1,t})^2 - (Y_t - y_{0,t})^2}{2\sigma_\epsilon^2} + \lambda_t,$$

$$= \frac{y_{1,t} - y_{0,t}}{\sigma_\epsilon^2}\Big(Y_t - \frac{y_{1,t} + y_{0,t}}{2} \Big) + \lambda_t.$$

An agent with a marginal belief for investment who delays in period t has the highest belief in period $t+1$. He does not invest in the next period $t+1$ if and only if his *ex post* observation LLR is smaller than $\log(c/(1-c))$. We have the following result, which is analogous to Proposition 6.2.

PROPOSITION 6.6 *In any period t of a PBE, if the observation Y_t is such that*

$$\frac{y_{1,t} - y_{0,t}}{\sigma_\epsilon^2}\Big(Y_t - \frac{y_{1,t} + y_{0,t}}{2} \Big) < \log\Big(\frac{c(1 - \mu_t^*)}{\mu_t^*(1 - c)} \Big),$$

where μ_t^* is the belief associated to s_t^*, then there is no endogenous investment after period t. All activity is identical to the noise and provides no information.

---

[17] It is simpler to work here with signals than with beliefs.

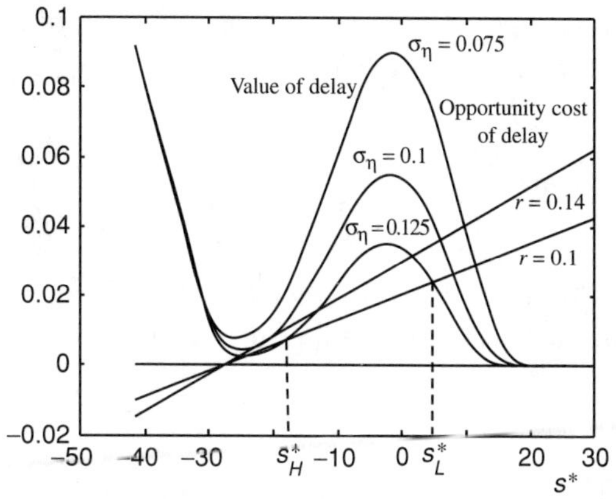

Figure 6.3 Equilibria with a continuum of agents. Other parameters: $\mu = 0.6$, $\theta_0 = 0$, $\theta_1 = 2$, $\sigma_\epsilon = 12$, $\delta = 1 - r$.

A NUMERICAL EXAMPLE

Figure 6.3 represents the option value $Q(s, s)$ and the opportunity cost of delay, $((1 - \delta)/\delta)(\mu(s) - c)$, as functions of the signal value s in the first period. Three graphs are represented for different standard errors of the observational noise. The diagram is very similar to Figure 6.2 for the case with two agents.[18] There are multiple equilibria if the discount rate and the variance of the observation noise are not small. These properties are intuitive.

THE SPEED OF LEARNING

Recall that in the model of Section 6.2 with a bounded distribution of beliefs, there may be multiple equilibria with delay or no delay, respectively. An equilibrium with delay generates significant information when the marginal belief for investment is high (because of the opportunity cost), whereas a rush generates no information. We will now see that the rush is a stylized representation of an equilibrium in the model with a continuum of agents and observation noise in which few agents delay.

Consider in the first period an agent with a belief measured by a LLR equal to λ_1. Denote by $f(\cdot; \sigma)$ the density of the distribution $\mathcal{N}(0, \sigma^2)$, and by s^* the equilibrium strategy in the first period. Following the observation of aggregate investment in the period, $Y = 1 - F(s^* - \theta; \sigma_\epsilon) + \eta$, the agent updates his LLR from λ_1 to $\lambda_2(\theta, \eta, s^*)$ defined by

$$\lambda_2(\eta, \theta; s^*) = \lambda_1 + \log\left(\frac{f(Y - 1 + F(s^* - \theta_1, \sigma_\epsilon); \sigma_\eta)}{f(Y - 1 + F(s^* - \theta_0, \sigma_\epsilon); \sigma_\eta)}\right).$$

If the true state is good ($\theta = \theta_1$), this equation becomes

$$(6.11) \quad \lambda_2(\eta, \theta; s^*) - \lambda_1 = \frac{\left(F(s^* - \theta_0, \sigma_\epsilon) - F(s^* - \theta_1, \sigma_\epsilon) + \eta\right)^2}{2\sigma_\eta^2} - \frac{\eta^2}{2\sigma_\eta^2}.$$

---

[18] The values are functions of μ in Figure 6.2 and functions of s in Figure 6.3.

The expectation, or the *ex post* average, of this updating over all realizations of the observation noise η is

$$(6.12) \quad \Delta(\theta_1; s^*) = E[\lambda_2(\eta, \theta; s^*) - \lambda_1] = \frac{\left(F(s^* - \theta_0, \sigma_\epsilon) - F(s^* - \theta_1, \sigma_\epsilon)\right)^2}{2\sigma_\eta^2}.$$

Let $\Delta(s^*) = \Delta(\theta_1; s^*)$ be the certainty equivalent of the updating expression (6.11). If the true state is bad, using the same notation one finds

$$\Delta(\theta_0; s^*) = -\Delta(\theta_1; s^*) = -\Delta(s^*).$$

The two expected values of the updates of the LLR conditional on the good and the bad states are opposite of each other. The positive value $\Delta(s^*)$ provides an indicator of the learning process in the period and depends on the equilibrium strategy s^*.

In the example of Figure 6.3, for $\sigma_\eta = 0.125$ and $r = 0.10$, there are two stable equilibria with strategies $s_H^* < s_L^*$. Investment is higher in the s_H^*-equilibrium than in the s_L^*-equilibrium. The respective mean values of the changes of beliefs are

$$\Delta(s_H^*) = 0.0015, \qquad \Delta(s_L^*) = 0.129.$$

The difference in information between the two equilibria is significant. In the equilibrium with low investment in the first period (s_L^*), the variation of the LLR is 80 times[19] higher than in the H-equilibrium.

In the equilibrium with high investment (s_H^*), a large fraction of agents invest with no delay. In that period and the periods after, agents do not learn much. The equilibrium is remarkably similar to the rush equilibrium of the model with bounded beliefs of Section 6.2 (in which they learned nothing). The rush is a stylized property of the s_H^*-equilibrium.

Learning in Multiple Periods

After the first period, the support of private beliefs has a finite upper bound. This is important: it means that agents never learn with certainty whether the state is good. Furthermore, in each period after the first, with a strictly positive probability investment stops completely in a cascade with no investment: assuming a marginal value s_τ^* in the support of beliefs[20] for each $\tau \le t$, then $s_{t+1}^* \ge \bar{s}_{t+1}$ with some strictly positive probability. The game and the evolution of beliefs proceed as in the model of Section 6.2 with a finite number of agents. In each period, the possible equilibria are of the types described in Theorem 6.1.

---

[19] Other simulations have shown similar results.

[20] The marginal value is not close to the upper bound of the support as in Section 6.3.7, because the mass of endogenous investment would be dwarfed by the observation noise and would not convey significant information.

6.4.2 Investments of Variable Size

The previous setting is now extended to include a variable investment size and an observation noise. Each agent has one option to invest, and the investment, which is made only once (if ever), is chosen in the set of real numbers. For example, agents decide both the period in which to purchase a new car and the amount spent on the car (number of accessories, etc.). Each agent has therefore two choice variables: the time of the investment and its scale. As before, investment is irreversible. Following the previous results, one can assume without loss of generality that there are two periods. Because the scale of investment is taken in a continuum, we redefine the payoff function.

Any agent who has not yet exercised his option to invest receives a payoff equal to $(1 - \delta)b$ per period where δ is the discount factor. An agent who never invests receives a payoff equal to b. The difference $1 - \delta$ corresponds to the rate of return between two periods.

For tractability, the payoff of investment is a quadratic function.[21] If the agent invests in period t, he forgoes in that period the payoff of never investing and gets a payoff with a current value equal to $E[2az - (\theta - z)^2]$, where the expectation operator E depends on the information of the agent, and a is a constant parameter. The scale of investment z is chosen in the set of real numbers, and θ is the productivity parameter, which is determined as in the previous sections.

The payoff of investing in period 1 is

$$U_1 = 2az - E\left[(\theta - z)^2\right] - b,$$

and the payoff of investing in the second period is

$$U_2 = (1 - \delta)b + \delta E\left[2az - (\theta - z)^2 - b\right].$$

By assumption, nature's distribution of θ is $\mathcal{N}(\bar{\theta}, \omega_0)$. Here θ is not directly observable, but each agent receives once, before the first period, a signal

$$s = \theta + \epsilon \qquad \text{with} \quad \epsilon \sim \mathcal{N}(0, \sigma_\epsilon).$$

In this section the symbol s denotes the private signal of an agent (not his belief). The private noise ϵ is normally distributed and independent of any other random variable in the model.

As in Section 6.4.1, each agent is infinitesimal and the total mass of agents is equal to one. At the end of period 1, the observed level of aggregate investment is equal to

$$Y = y + \eta \qquad \text{with} \quad \eta \sim \mathcal{N}(0, \sigma_\eta),$$

---

[21] The model presented here is inspired by Bar-Ilan and Blinder (1992).

where y is the integral of the individual investments z. The variable η is an exogenous random term, which is independent of the other variables in the economy.

It can be shown that for some parameter values, there are multiple PBEs with monotone strategies such that agents delay if and only if they have a private signal smaller than some value s^*. The signal at the end of the first period is the aggregate investment

$$Y = z_1(\theta; s^*) + z_2(\theta; s^*) + \eta.$$

Each of the two terms $z_1(\theta; s^*)$ and $z_2(\theta; s^*)$ is an increasing function of θ, for given s^*, and thus contributes to the information on θ. The two terms represent two separate effects. The first is proportional to the mass of agents who invest in period 1. It is identical to the endogenous investment in a model where each investment has a fixed scale. This is the *timing effect*. The second term depends on the mean scale of investment by investing agents and is called the *level effect*.

Because of the observation noise η, the information that is conveyed through each of the two effects depends on the effect of θ on z_1 and z_2. If that effect is small, it is drowned in the noise. It can be shown that the magnitude of the level effect in $z_2(\theta; s^*)$ becomes vanishingly small if the precision of the individual signal, $1/\sigma_\epsilon^2$, tends to zero. There is a simple interpretation: if an individual has a signal of small precision, the scale of his investment does not depend much on his signal. The timing effect, however, remains of the same order of magnitude as the (given) mass of agents, and does not become vanishingly small when $1/\sigma_\epsilon^2$ tends to zero. The information property of Y is similar to that in a model with fixed investment scale.

A NUMERICAL EXAMPLE

There is no algebraic solution to the model, so we consider a numerical example. From the previous discussion, we know that the important parameter is the precision of the private signals. The ratio σ_ϵ/ω_0 is taken to be equal to 5. That implies that if an agent could observe directly the signals of others, in order to double the precision of his estimate (as measured by the reciprocal of the variance), he would have to observe roughly 25 other private signals.

The option value $Q(s, s^*) = \omega_1^2 - E_{\{s, s^*\}}[\omega_2^2(Y, s, s^*)]$ and the opportunity cost $c(s)$ of delay for the marginal agent $s = s^*$ are represented in Figure 6.4, which is remarkably similar to Figures 6.2 and 6.3. In particular, there are two stable equilibria, with a large and a small mass of delaying agents, respectively.

AN ANALYSIS

Individual Decisions

An agent with a signal s updates the public information distribution on θ with his own signal s. His subjective distribution is therefore $\mathcal{N}(m_1(s), \omega_1)$, with

$$(6.13) \quad m_1(s) = \bar{\theta} + \gamma(s - \bar{\theta}), \qquad \gamma = \frac{\omega_0^2}{\omega_0^2 + \sigma_\epsilon^2}, \quad \text{and} \quad \frac{1}{\omega_1^2} = \frac{1}{\omega_0^2} + \frac{1}{\sigma_\epsilon^2}.$$

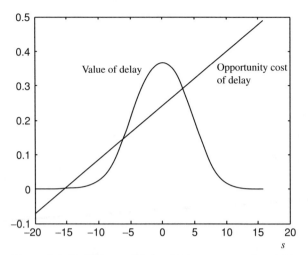

Figure 6.4 Multiple equilibria with investment of variable scale. Parameters: $\sigma_\theta = 1, \sigma_\epsilon = 5\sigma_\theta,$ $\sigma_\eta = 1, 1 - \delta = 0.02, a = 5, b = 44.$

If he invests in the first period, he chooses a level $z(s)$ that depends on his information:

$$(6.14) \qquad z(s) = a + m_1(s) = a + (1 - \gamma)\overline{\theta} + \gamma s,$$

and the payoff of investing in the first period is

$$U_1(s) = -\omega_1^2 + 2am_1(s) + a^2 - b.$$

An agent with signal s who delays while others use the strategy s^* invests in period 2 and has a payoff

$$U_2(s, s^*)$$
$$= (1 - \delta)b + \delta E_s\left[-\omega_2^2(Y, s, s^*) + 2am_2(Y, s, s^*) + a^2 - b\right],$$

where the expectation is computed over $\omega_2^2(Y, s, s^*)$ and $m_2(Y, s, s^*)$, which are the mean and the standard error of θ, respectively, after the observation of Y.

Because $m_2(Y, s, s^*)$ is an updating of $m_1(s)$, we have $E_s[m_2(Y, s, s^*)] = m(s)$, and the difference between the payoffs of delay and investment in the first period is

$$U_2(s, s^*) - U_1(s) = \delta\left(\omega_1^2 - E_s[\omega_2^2(Y, s, s^*)]\right)$$
$$- \left(1 - \delta\right)\left(-\omega_1^2 + a^2 + 2am_1(s) - 2b\right).$$

This difference can be rewritten as the difference between the option value $Q(s, s^*)$ and the opportunity cost $c(s)$ of delay:

$$(6.15) \qquad U_2(s, s^*) - U_1(s) = \delta\left(Q(s, s^*) - c(s)\right),$$

with

$$Q(s, s^*) = \omega_1^2 - E_s[\omega_2^2(Y, s, s^*)],$$

$$c(s) = \frac{1 - \delta}{\delta}\left(-\omega_1^2 + a^2 + 2am_1(s) - 2b\right).$$

In models with normal distributions and linear decision rules, the learning rules are linear and the *ex post* variance ω_2 is independent of the observation and can be computed *ex ante*. This very nice property does not hold in the present model, because the endogenous investment y is not a linear function of the random variables.

Equilibrium and Information

A symmetric equilibrium in monotone strategies is defined by a value s^* that satisfies the arbitrage equation between the option value and the opportunity cost:

$$Q(s^*, s^*) = c(s^*).$$

By use of the updating rule (6.13) and the expression of the individual level of investment $z(s)$ in (6.14), the level of endogenous aggregate activity is equal to

$$y(\theta; s^*) = \int_{s^*-\theta} \left(a + (1 - \gamma)\bar{\theta} + \gamma(\theta + \epsilon)\right) f(\epsilon; \sigma_\epsilon)\, d\epsilon$$

$$= \left(a + (1 - \gamma)\bar{\theta} + \gamma\theta\right)\left(1 - F(s^* - \theta; \sigma_\epsilon)\right)$$

$$+ \gamma \int_{s^*-\theta} \epsilon f(\epsilon; \sigma_\epsilon)\, d\epsilon.$$

We can normalize $\bar{\theta} = 0$ (or incorporate $(1 - \gamma)\bar{\theta}$ in the definition of a).

Because $\int_{s^*-\theta} \epsilon f(\epsilon; \sigma_\epsilon)\, d\epsilon = \sigma_\epsilon^2 f(s^* - \theta; \sigma_\epsilon)$ and $1 - F(z; \sigma) = F(-z; \sigma)$, we have

(6.16) $\quad y(\theta; s^*) = \left(a + \dfrac{\omega_0^2 \theta}{\omega_0^2 + \sigma_\epsilon^2}\right) F\left(\dfrac{\theta - s^*}{\sigma_\epsilon}; 1\right) + \dfrac{\omega_0^2 \sigma_\epsilon^2}{\omega_0^2 + \sigma_\epsilon^2} f\left(\dfrac{\theta - s^*}{\sigma_\epsilon}; 1\right)$

$$= z_1(\theta; s^*) + z_2(\theta, s^*).$$

The aggregate activity that is observed is

$$Y = z_1(\theta; s^*) + z_2(\theta; s^*) + \eta.$$

Suppose that $\sigma_\epsilon \to \infty$. Because

$$\sigma_\epsilon^2 f\left(\frac{\theta - s^*}{\sigma_\epsilon}; 1\right) = \frac{\sigma_\epsilon}{\sqrt{2\pi}} \exp\left(-\frac{(\theta - s^*)^2}{2\sigma_\epsilon^2}\right),$$

one can see in equation (6.16) that the magnitude of the level effect in $z_2(\theta; s^*)$ becomes vanishingly small.

6.4.3 Proofs

Proof of Lemma 6.1

We first prove the following: in any arbitrary period t of a PBE, if an agent with belief μ_t delays, then any agent with belief $\mu'_t < \mu_t$ strictly prefers to delay. Let the arbitrary period be the first one. Consider an agent with belief μ who has a strategy with delay: this is a rule to invest in period t (with $t \geq 2$) if and only if the history h_t in period t belongs to some set H_t. For this agent the difference between the payoff of the strategy of delay and the payoff of immediate investment is

$$W(\mu) = \sum_{t \geq 2,\, h_t \in H_t} \delta^{t-1} P(h_t \mid \mu)\Big(P(\theta = \theta_1 \mid \mu, h_t) - c\Big) - (\mu - c)$$

$$= \sum_{t \geq 2,\, h_t \in H_t} \delta^{t-1} P(h_t \mid \mu)\left(\frac{P(h_t \mid \theta = \theta_1)}{P(h_t \mid \mu)}\mu - c\right) - (\mu - c)$$

$$= \sum_{t \geq 2,\, h_t \in H_t} \delta^{t-1}\Big(\mu(1 - c)P(h_t \mid \theta = \theta_1)$$

$$- c(1 - \mu)P(h_t \mid \theta = \theta_0)\Big) - (\mu - c)$$

$$= as - b - (\mu - c),$$

where a and b are independent of μ:

$$a = \sum_{t \geq 2,\, h_t \in H_t} \delta^{t-1}\Big((1 - c)P(h_t \mid \theta = \theta_1) + c P(h_t \mid \theta = \theta_0)\Big),$$

$$b = c \sum_{t \geq 2,\, h_t \in H_t} \delta^{t-1} P(h_t \mid \theta = \theta_0).$$

For $\mu = 0$, because $t \geq 2$, $\delta < 1$, and $\sum_{t \geq 2,\, h_t \in H_t} P(h_t \mid \theta = \theta_0) \leq 1$, we have

$$W(0) = c\left(1 - \sum_{t \geq 2,\, h_t \in H_t} \delta^{t-1} P(h_t \mid \theta = \theta_0)\right) > 0.$$

Because an agent with belief μ delays, $W(\mu) \geq 0$. Because W is linear in s, $W(\mu') > \mu - c$ for any $\mu' < \mu$.

Consider now an agent with belief μ' who mimics an agent with belief μ: he invests at the same time as the agent with belief μ (i.e., in period t if and only if $h_t \in H_t$). For such an agent, the difference between the payoff of this strategy and that of investing with no delay is $W(\mu')$, which by the previous argument is strictly positive if $\mu' < \mu$. The agent with belief μ' strictly prefers to delay.

The set of beliefs for delay is not empty, for it includes all values below c. The value of μ_t^* in the lemma is the upper bound of the set of beliefs of delaying agents. The previous result in this proof shows that any agent with $\mu_t < \mu_t^*$ delays. ∎

Proof of Proposition 6.1

Denote by $W(\mu, \mu^*)$ the payoff of an agent with belief μ who delays for one period while other agents follow the strategy μ^*. By (6.4), μ^* is solution of

$$\mu^* - c = W(\mu^*, \mu^*).$$

Denote by $P(x_t = k \mid \mu, \mu^*, f^j, n)$ the probability that $x_t = k$ for an agent with belief μ when all other agents use the strategy μ^*; the density functions are f^j, and the number of remaining players is n. By use of Bayes's rule and the sum of probabilities equal to one,

$$\mu^* - c = \sum_k P(x_t = k \mid \mu^*, \mu^*, f^j, n)$$

$$\times \left(P(\theta = \theta_1 \mid x = k; \mu^*, \mu^*, f^j, n) - c \right)$$

$$= \sum_k P(x_t = k \mid \mu^*, \mu^*, f^j, n)$$

$$\times \max\left(P(\theta = \theta_1 \mid x = k; \mu^*, \mu^*, f^j, n) - c, 0 \right)$$

$$- \sum_k P(x_t = k \mid \mu^*, \mu^*, f^j, n)$$

$$\times \max\left(c - P(\theta = \theta_1 \mid x = k; \mu^*, \mu^*, f^j, n), 0 \right).$$

An agent who delays invests in the next period only if his payoff is positive. Therefore, the payoff of delay is

$$W(\mu^*, \mu^*) = \delta \sum_k P(x = k \mid \mu^*, \mu^*, f^j, n)$$

$$\times \max\left(P(\theta = \theta_1 \mid x = k; \mu^*, \mu^*, f^j, n) - c, 0 \right).$$

We conclude the proof by comparing the two previous equations and using the decomposition $\mu^* - c = (1 - \delta)(\mu^* - c) + \delta(\mu^* - c)$. ∎

Proof of Proposition 6.4

From case (ii) of Theorem 6.1, there is at least one value $\mu^*(n)$ that defines an equilibrium strategy for the density f with n players. Because $\mu^*(n) \in [0, 1]$, there is a subsequence of $\mu^*(n)$ that tends to a limit in $[c, \overline{\mu}]$. We now show by contradiction that $\mu^*(n) \to \overline{\mu}$.

Suppose that $\mu^*(n) \to \hat{\mu} < \overline{\mu}$. Denote by π_n^θ the probability that in the equilibrium with strategy $\mu^*(n)$ any given agent does not delay if the true state is $\theta \in \{0, 1\}$: $\pi_n^\theta = 1 - F^\theta(\mu^*(n))$. When $\mu^*(n) \to \hat{\mu}$, then $\pi_n^\theta \to 1 - F^\theta(\hat{\mu}) = \pi^\theta$.

Because $\hat{\mu} \in (\underline{\mu}, \overline{\mu})$, then $0 < \pi^\theta < 1$. The number of investments generated by this strategy is a random variable, which is denoted by x_n. Consider $y_n = x_n/n\pi_n^0$, which is observed at the end of the period:

$$E[y_n \mid \theta = 0] = 1, \qquad E[y_n \mid \theta = 1] = \frac{\pi_n^1}{\pi_n^0} \rightarrow \frac{\pi^1}{\pi^0},$$

$$\mathrm{Var}(y_n \mid \theta) = \frac{1 - \pi_n^\theta}{n\pi_n^\theta} \leq \frac{1}{n\pi_n^\theta} \rightarrow 0, \qquad \text{as} \quad n \rightarrow \infty.$$

By use of a standard argument with the law of large numbers, asymptotically (for $n \rightarrow \infty$), y_n reveals perfectly the state of nature at the end of the period. Because $\mu^*(n) \leq \overline{\mu} < \mu^{**}$, an agent with belief $\mu^*(n)$ would strictly prefer to delay, which contradicts the definition of $\mu^*(n)$. Therefore, $\mu^*(n) \rightarrow \overline{\mu}$.

The previous argument implies also that the sequence $n\pi_n^\theta$ is bounded. From any subsequence one can extract a subsequence such that $n\pi_n^\theta$ converges to some value β^θ. With Bayes's rule,

$$\frac{\beta^1}{\beta^0} = \lim \frac{n\pi_n^1}{n\pi_n^0} = \lim \frac{\int_{s(n)}^{\overline{\mu}} f^1(s)\,ds}{\int_{s(n)}^{\overline{\mu}} f^0(s)\,ds} = \frac{\overline{\mu}}{1 - \overline{\mu}}.$$

We can define β such that

(6.17) $\beta^1 = \overline{\mu}\beta$ and $\beta^0 = (1 - \overline{\mu})\beta.$

The distribution of x_n tends to the Poisson distribution with parameter β^θ in state θ.[22] Let $\pi_k(\beta^\theta, \overline{\mu})$ be the probability for an agent with belief $\overline{\mu}$ that there are k investments generated by a Poisson distribution β^θ as defined in equation (6.17). Let $\mu(x \mid \beta^\theta)$ be his *ex post* probability of the good state. Asymptotically, the arbitrage equation (6.5) becomes

$$(1 - \delta)(\overline{\mu} - c) = \delta \sum_{k \geq 0} \pi_k(\beta, \overline{\mu}) \max\Big(c - \mu(x \mid \beta), 0\Big).$$

The value of β is strictly positive; otherwise the option value on the right-hand side of this equation would be equal to zero, which is impossible because $c < \overline{\mu}$.

An exercise similar to that in Chamley and Gale (1994) shows that the right-hand side of the previous equation, which is the option value of delay, is strictly increasing in β.[23] The solution is therefore unique.   ∎

---

[22] $P(x_n = k \mid \theta) \rightarrow \dfrac{(\beta^\theta)^k}{k!} e^{-\beta^\theta}.$

[23] Suppose that there are two values $\beta' < \beta$. The Poisson distribution with parameter β is identical to that of a variable that is obtained from a Poisson distribution with parameter β in which each investment is observed with probability $\lambda = \beta'/\beta < 1$. The observation noise reduces the option value of delay.

Proof of Proposition 6.5

Any agent with $\mu > \mu^{**}$ does not delay. Following the argument in the proof of Proposition 6.4, the observation of x_n is asymptotically perfectly informative. For any agent with belief $\mu < \mu^{**}$, there exists $\hat{n}$ such that if $n > \hat{n}$, the agent delays and therefore $\mu^*(n) > \mu$. ∎

7 More Delays

Wait and see.

An equilibrium with delays of the game with periods does not converge, in general, to an equilibrium of the game with the same payoff and information structures but where time is continuous. In important cases, there is no equilibrium with continuous time. A waiting game takes place when the information is generated by the payoffs of actions, as when penguins watch for killer whales, oil drillers observe the results of exploration in neighboring patches, or agents receive gradually private information.

A model of economic growth or business cycles can be specified in periods or in continuous time. Its properties do not depend on that choice. In discrete time, quantities like consumption or output in a period have the same dimension as the length of the period, and if that length is vanishingly small, their ratios to the length are asymptotically equal to the flows of consumption and output in the continuous-time specification. This equivalence fails, generically, in models of social learning.

The essence of the equilibria with delay is the arbitrage between the opportunity cost of delay and the option value of delay, which is the expected value of undoing an investment after bad news. If the period shrinks, by arbitrage, the amount of information is smaller. However, this reduced information comes earlier. The overall effect is ambiguous, as shown in Section 7.1.1

When the period length is vanishingly short, the option value of delay shrinks to zero. However, the variance of the change of beliefs remains bounded below by a strictly positive number (Section 7.1.2). The homogeneity of the dimension with respect to time that applies in models of capital accumulation, for example, does not apply in the model of social learning.

Section 7.2 shows that the equilibrium properties of a model with continuous time are not the asymptotic properties of a model with vanishingly short periods. When an agent holds an option to invest (to choose an action x in a set Ξ), the benefit of delaying for an infinitesimal amount of time is the difference between the expected value of the capital gain of the option if some good news occurs during the infinitesimal time interval and the capital loss if there is no good news. This difference must be positive to compensate for the cost of delaying (which is the value of the option multiplied by the rate of discount). The difference between the two terms depends on the distribution of the state of nature and the private information. In general, its sign is ambiguous. If it is negative, there cannot be an equilibrium with delay, and it is possible that there is no symmetric equilibrium.

Two cases are considered. The first is the simplest model with delay of Section 6.1 with discrete actions. In continuous time, this model has no equilibrium.

In the second case, the structure is similar to the one in Chapter 3: agents maximize a quadratic payoff with an action taken in the set of real numbers. Their private information is derived from a SBS with a uniform distribution of precisions. This model has no equilibrium if there are agents who are sufficiently optimistic (with a belief greater than $\frac{1}{2}$).

The interpretation of the property is intuitive. The essential mechanism for the existence of an equilibrium with delay in continuous time is the expected capital gain on the value of the option, which arrives by a Poisson process. If the expected value of the capital gain is low, there is no sufficient incentive to hold the option, and the arbitrage fails. If there is no arbitrage, a positive mass of agents invests without delay, thus providing instantly a discrete amount of information on the state, which is incompatible with immediate investment. In the model considered here, for agents with sufficiently high beliefs, the expected value of good news is relatively small because they are already optimistic and the highest value of θ is 1. When the upper bound of the distribution of beliefs is not too large (less than $\frac{1}{2}$ here), the capital gain induced by the investment of the other agents is higher and arbitrage can sustain an equilibrium with delay.

Gul and Lundholm (1995) present a model with delay in continuous time. The previous analysis shows that they obtain an equilibrium only because of their particular assumption on the private signals.

In the remaining sections of the chapter, time is divided into periods. In Section 7.3, each agent receives a sequence of private signals as in Caplin and Leahy (1994). The model turns out to be very similar to the one in the previous chapter.

In Section 7.4, agents observe the results of actions. For example, penguins are waiting on a cliff for the first fellow to plunge and find out whether a killer whale is roaming around. The same issue arises for oil drillers who may pay the cost of exploration or wait to see the results of others.

Another example of delays with the observation of the payoff of actions has been analyzed by Caplin and Leahy (1998): at the southern end of Sixth Avenue, a number of buildings were vacant for a long time. Then Bed Bath & Beyond (BB&B) opened a retail store, which turned out to be very successful. It was followed by a rapid increase of other stores in the same neighborhood. The rents of the new leases were higher than that of the first lease.

7.1 The Length of a Period

7.1.1 Are Longer Periods More Efficient?

A longer period raises the cost of waiting for information, which is available only at the beginning of the next period. It induces more activity and more information. Because this information is discounted from the next period, the overall effect is ambiguous.

Consider the following example: there are three agents and a distribution of private information such that

- in the good state ($\theta = 1$), two agents (optimists) have a belief equal to $\mu^+ = \frac{2}{3}$, and one agent (a pessimist) has a belief equal to $\mu^- = \frac{1}{3}$;
- in the bad state ($\theta = 0$), one agent has a belief equal to $\mu^+ = \frac{2}{3}$, and two agents have a belief equal to $\mu^- = \frac{1}{3}$.

The cost of investment is $c = \frac{4}{7}$, and the payoff of investment is $\theta - c$. This example is analyzed in Exercise 7.2. In an equilibrium, no pessimist invests before an optimist, and the game is actually played by the optimists. Because they arbitrage between investment and delay, the value of the game for an optimist is the value of investment in the first period and does not depend on the period length. The issue is the value of the game for a pessimistic agent.

Exercise 7.2 shows that the value of the game for the pessimists is a nonmonotone function of the discount factor.[1]

7.1.2 Vanishingly Short Periods

Consider the simplest model of delay, presented at the beginning of the previous chapter (Section 6.1): there are two players with an option to invest in the good state ($\theta = 1$), and only one player in the bad state ($\theta = 0$). The unique symmetric equilibrium in the first period is defined by the probability of investment ζ and is solution of

$$\mu - c = \delta\zeta(1 - c),$$

where μ is the belief of a player. The discount factor δ is related to the period length τ and to the discount rate per unit of time, ρ, with $\delta = e^{-\rho\tau}$. If the period length tends to zero, for fixed ρ, we have $\delta \to 1$, and the strategy ζ converges to $\hat{\zeta}$ defined by $\mu - c = \hat{\zeta}(1 - c)$. The limit value $\hat{\zeta}$ is strictly between 0 and 1. For any period length, even small, there is a symmetric PBE.

Recall that at the end of the first period, either one agent has invested, in which case the belief (the probability that $\theta = 1$) jumps to 1, or there is no investment, in

---

[1] If $\delta < \frac{1}{3}$, optimists do not delay, because of the low discount factor. Pessimists would prefer to have that information earlier. The value of the game increases with δ (decreases with an increasing discount rate). There is an equilibrium with delay if $\delta \in (\frac{1}{3}, 1)$. In that interval, the value of the game for the pessimists is first decreasing, then increasing.

which case the belief jumps to a value smaller than c and there is no investment any more. If the period is vanishingly short, the value of these jumps remains bounded away from 0 and their probabilities are also bounded away from 0: for an outside observer, the probability of a jump down is $(1 - \zeta)^2$ in the good state, and it converges to $(1 - \hat{\zeta})^2 > 0$ when $\tau \to 0$. Hence, the variance of the change of belief does not become vanishingly small when the period is vanishingly short, but remains bounded away from 0. Per unit of time, the variance of the change of the public belief between the beginning and the end of the first period tends to infinity.

This nonhomogeneity of the variation of beliefs with respect to time stands in stark contrast with some other economic models: in an intertemporal general equilibrium model of capital accumulation, the quantities of consumption and output are proportional to the length of the period. The quantity of information in a model of social learning with discrete periods does not have the dimension of a flow. The settings with vanishingly short periods and continuous time are essentially different.

The properties of this simple model are analyzed formally in Exercise 7.1. They are generalized to a setting with N players and arbitrary distributions of private beliefs in Chamley (2003a). It is shown that when $\delta \to 1$, (i) the probability of a permanent collapse of investment tends to a strictly positive value; (ii) the game stops with no investment only after the observation of no investment ($x = 0$), and goes on after any positive amount of investment (if there is a remaining player); (iii) the expected value of bad news must converge to 0. A good exercise is to derive the intuition for these properties from the arbitrage between the opportunity cost and the option value of delay.

7.2 Continuous Time

7.2.1 The Nonexistence of an Equilibrium with Discrete Actions

We continue with the simple model of the previous section with one or two players and assume that time is continuous: a player can take the action $x = 1$ at any point in time and observe the action of the other (if there is any) immediately after it is taken. Let μ_t be the belief of a player at time t with $\mu_0 > c$ given. We consider only symmetric PBEs.

Immediate investment at time 0 cannot be an equilibrium strategy, because it is dominated by a small delay. Suppose now that the player delays for a time interval $(t, t + dt)$, $t \geq 0$, conditional on no investment before time t. If he does not see any investment by the other agent during that interval, and he is still willing to invest at time $t + dt$, then he is willing to invest at time $t + dt$ whatever the news during the time interval $(t, t + dt)$. The present value of that strategy is the value of immediate investment, discounted by the rate ρdt. This argument, which was presented in the previous chapter, shows that there cannot be an equilibrium with delay. There is no equilibrium.

Exercise 7.3 shows that the right-hand side of the arbitrage equation is equal to 0. The delay cannot yield a return that compensates for the cost of delay per unit of time, $\rho(\mu_t - c)$.

The same argument applies in the central model of the previous chapter with N agents if the cost of investment, c, is in the interior of the support of beliefs. In this case, any agent with belief smaller than c does not invest at time 0. If all agents with a belief greater than $\mu^* \geq c$ invest at time 0, the aggregate investment at time 0 provides information about the state θ, and a small delay dominates immediate investment. When the previous argument is used, there cannot be an equilibrium with delay. There is no symmetric equilibrium.

If all agents have a belief at least equal to c, then a rush in which all agents invest immediately is an equilibrium. In such a rush the total investment is independent of the state of nature and conveys no information. As in the setting with periods, there is no incentive to delay, and immediate investment is an equilibrium strategy.[2]

When the period length is vanishingly short, the cost of delay is vanishingly small, and there is always an equilibrium strategy with delay, even if all agents have a belief higher than c. The next result follows.

PROPOSITION 7.1

(i) *The standard model with discrete actions has no symmetric equilibrium if time is continuous and the cost of investment c is strictly between the lower bound $\underline{\mu}$ and the upper bound $\overline{\mu}$ of the distribution of beliefs.*

(ii) *If $c \leq \underline{\mu}$, the rush is the unique equilibrium of the standard model with continuous time; if $\overline{\mu} \leq c$, no investment is the unique equilibrium of the standard model with continuous time.*

(iii) *For any period length that is sufficiently short, the standard model with discrete time has at least one equilibrium with delays.*

The result highlights that the properties of the model in continuous time are not the limit properties of the discrete model with vanishingly short periods.

7.2.2 Nondiscrete Actions

When the level of an action is taken in the set of real numbers, it conveys more information than when it is taken in a discrete set. How does this additional information affect the existence of an equilibrium in continuous time? For simplicity, assume two agents. The state of nature has a value in the set Θ and the agents have private signals

---

[2] Zhang (1997) considers a model of investment in continuous time that is equivalent to the case where the lower bound of the distribution of beliefs is equal to the cost of investment. Zhang claims rightly that there is only one equilibrium with a herd (which is called a rush here). From the present discussion, it should be clear that this property depends on the assumption that time is continuous and that it is not robust when time is discrete.

s and s', respectively. When the option is exercised, the agent chooses the scale of the investment $x \in \mathbb{R}$ to maximize the payoff $e^{-\rho t} U\left(E_t[u(x, \theta)]\right)$, where E_t is the expectation given the information available to the agent at time t, and ρ is the discount rate.

We focus on a symmetric equilibrium. In such an equilibrium, immediate investment at time 0 cannot be an equilibrium strategy, because it would be dominated by a small delay. If an agent has invested, there is no gain from further delay and the other agent invests immediately. A symmetric equilibrium strategy should therefore be a function from the signal s to the time $t(s)$, possibly infinite, such that if no agent has invested before time t, the agent with signal s invests at time t. Let $s(t)$ be the inverse of this function. If the agent invests at time t, he must be indifferent between investment and a small delay. The opportunity cost of delay has the dimension of the length dt. Therefore the probability that the other agent invests in the time interval $(t, t + dt)$ must also have the dimensions of dt. This event is equivalent to having the signal s' in the interval between $s(t)$ and $s(t + dt)$. Therefore, the difference $s(t + dt) - s(t)$ must have the dimension of dt, and $s(t)$ must be differentiable.

Following the intuition we have developed so far, a more optimistic agent does not delay as much as a less optimistic agent, and one can show that $s(t)$ should be a decreasing function of time. The expected value of θ for an agent with signal s who knows that the other signal is less than $\tilde{s}$ is $E[\theta | s, s' < \tilde{s}]$. Let $\pi_t \, dt$ be the probability that at time t, conditional on no prior investment, the other agent has a signal in the interval $(s(t + dt), s(t))$. We have

$$\pi_t = -\phi(s)\dot{s},$$

where $\phi(s)$ is the density of the distribution of the event "the other player has the signal $s' = s$," conditional on $s' \leq s$. The computation of ϕ depends on the specification of the model.

The function $s(t)$ must be such that the following arbitrage[3] equation is satisfied:

(7.1) $$\rho U(E[\theta | s(t), s' < s(t)])$$
$$= \pi_t \Big(U(E[\theta | s(t), s' = s(t)]) - U(E[\theta | s(t), s' < s(t)]) \Big)$$
$$+ U' \frac{d(E[\theta | s(t), s' < \tilde{s}])}{d\tilde{s}} \dot{s}(t).$$

The first term on the right-hand side is the capital gain from the good news that the other agent invests in the time interval of length dt. The second term is the depreciation of the value of the option if the other agent does not invest in the short time interval.

---

[3] A heuristic derivation, using a discrete approximation of time, is presented in the appendix (Section 7.5). However, students should train themselves to write such arbitrage equations, which are intuitive, without the discrete approximation of time.

This equation can be rewritten

$$(7.2) \qquad \rho U(E[\theta|s(t), s' < s(t)]) = -H(s)\dot{s}$$

with

$$(7.3) \qquad H(s) = \phi(s)\Big(U(E[\theta|s(t), s' = s(t)]) - U(E[\theta|s(t), s' < s(t)])\Big)$$
$$+ U'\frac{d(E[\theta|s(t), s' < \tilde{s}])}{d\tilde{s}}.$$

An admissible solution exists only if $\dot{s} < 0$. Hence $H(s) > 0$ is a necessary condition for an admissible solution. The sign of H is clearly ambiguous. The first term is the capital gain when the other agent invests. It is positive, because this event raises the support of the distribution of the signal s' from the interval $s' < s(t)$ to the point $\{s(t)\}$. The second term is negative: if the other agent does not invest, his signal s' is not in the interval $(s(t + dt), s(t))$, the estimate of his signal is lowered, and the expected value of θ is lowered accordingly.

We consider now two examples with a quadratic payoff function where the scale of the investment is a real number. The first model, which has a "standard" information structure as in previous chapters, may have no equilibrium. The second example is due to Gul and Lundholm (1995). It has a different information structure and generates an equilibrium.

THE STANDARD MODEL WITH NONDISCRETE ACTIONS

Assume two states of nature, $\theta \in \{0, 1\}$, and two agents, each with an option to invest and to maximize the payoff $2E_t[\theta]x - x^2$, where the expectation is conditional on the available information at time t. Each agent is endowed with a private belief (probability of the good state) taken from a distribution with support $[0, 1]$. Let $f^\theta(\mu)$ be the density of the distribution. It is defined by[4] $f^1(\mu) = 2\mu$, $f^0(\mu) = 2(1 - \mu)$.

Consider an agent with private belief μ who knows that the other agent has a private belief not higher than μ'. Let m be the probability that the state is good for this agent. By Bayes's rule,

$$\frac{m(\mu, \mu')}{1 - m(\mu, \mu')} = \frac{\mu}{1 - \mu}\frac{F^1(\mu')}{F^0(\mu')},$$

where F^θ is the c.d.f. of the distribution of private beliefs. An exercise shows that $F^1(\mu)/F^0(\mu) = \mu/(2 - \mu)$. Hence,

$$(7.4) \qquad m(\mu, \mu') = \frac{\mu\mu'}{\mu\mu' + (1 - \mu)(2 - \mu')}.$$

---

[4] Such a distribution is equivalent to a two-step process for private information: first, the agent draws a precision q with a uniform density on the interval $[\frac{1}{2}, 1]$; second, he obtains a SBS on θ with precision q.

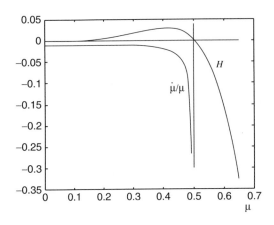

Figure 7.1 Values of $H(\mu)$ in the arbitrage equation (7.5). There is an equilibrium with delay only if $H(\mu) \geq 0$, which holds only if $\mu \leq 0.5$.

In an equilibrium, an agent invests at time t, conditional on no investment before, if he has a belief $\mu(t)$. In this case, by definition of the function m, his expected value of θ is $m(\mu, \mu)$, his action is $x = m(\mu, \mu)$, and his payoff is $m^2(\mu, \mu)$.

At time t, the agent with belief $\mu(t)$ estimates that the probability that the other agent invests, per unit of time, is $-\phi(\mu)\dot{\mu}$ (as in the model of the previous section, where the signal s is replaced by the belief μ). The event is decomposed according to the good and the bad states:

$$\phi(\mu) = m(\mu, \mu)\frac{f^1(\mu)}{F^1(\mu)} + (1 - m(\mu, \mu))\frac{f^0(\mu)}{F^0(\mu)}.$$

The arbitrage equation is similar to that in (7.2)–(7.3):

(7.5) $\rho m^2(\mu, \mu) = -H(\mu)\dot{\mu},$

with

$$H(\mu) = \phi(\mu)\left(\left(\frac{\mu^2}{\mu^2 + (1-\mu)^2}\right)^2 - m^2\right) - 2m\frac{\partial m(\mu, \mu)}{\partial \mu'}.$$

A solution is admissible only if $\dot{\mu} < 0$ and therefore $H(\mu) > 0$. For $\mu \approx 1$, we have $m \approx 1$, $\phi \approx 2$, $\partial m/\partial \mu' \approx 1$, and $H \approx -2$. There cannot be an equilibrium with delay if the support of the private beliefs has an upper bound close to one.

The values of H and $\dot{\mu}$ are represented in Figure 7.1 when the distribution is truncated to the interval $[0, \mu]$. The computation indicates that there is an equilibrium with delay only if the upper bound of the distribution is smaller than $\frac{1}{2}$. In this case, the value of $\dot{\mu}$ tends to 0 when t tends to infinity. The differential equation (7.5) can be approximated near $\mu = 0$ by

$$\dot{\mu} = -\rho\mu.$$

Asymptotically, the rate of convergence of μ toward 0 is constant and equal to ρ.

The essential mechanism for the existence of an equilibrium with delay in continuous time is the expected capital gain on the value of the option, which arrives by a Poisson process. If the expected value of the capital gain is low, there is no sufficient incentive to hold the option and the arbitrage fails. If there is no arbitrage, a positive mass of agents invests without delay, thus providing instantly a discrete amount of information on the state, which is incompatible with immediate investment. In the model considered here, for agents with high beliefs, the expected value of good news is relatively small because they are already optimistic and the highest value of θ is 1. When the upper bound of the distribution of beliefs is not too large (less than $\frac{1}{2}$ here), the capital gain induced by the investment of the other agent is higher, and arbitrage can sustain an equilibrium with delay.

A MODEL WITH AN EQUILIBRIUM

This example[5] is due to Gul and Lundholm (1995). The state and the private signals s and s' are such that $\theta = s + s'$, where s and s' are independent and have a uniform distribution on $[0, 1]$. The action set and the payoff function are the same as in the previous example.

The model uses the convenient property that if $s' < s$, its conditional distribution is uniform on the interval $[0, s]$. Hence, in the expression (7.3) for H, we have $\phi(s) = 1/s$. The same property of the density function is used to establish that

$$E[\theta|s, s' = s] = 2s, \qquad E[\theta|s, s' < s] = \frac{3s}{2}.$$

If the other agent does not invest in the interval of time $(t, t + dt)$, the expected value of s' is lowered by $-\dot{s}\,dt/2$. Therefore,

$$\frac{d(E[\theta|s, s' < \tilde{s}])}{d\tilde{s}} = \frac{1}{2} \quad \text{at } \tilde{s} = s, \quad \text{and} \quad U'(m) = 2m.$$

By substitution in (7.3), $H = (1/s)(4s^2 - \frac{9}{4}s^2) - \frac{3}{2}s = (\frac{7}{4} - \frac{6}{4})s = s/4$. The difference between the two terms in H is positive. Replacing the left-hand side in equation (7.2), we have $\dot{s}/s = -9\rho$ and $s(t) = s(0)e^{-9\rho t}$.

An arbitrage argument for $t = 0$ shows[6] that $s(0) = 1$. The solution of the differential equation defines a necessary condition for the equilibrium strategy:

(7.6) $s(t) = e^{-9\rho t}.$

The symmetric equilibrium is defined by the following strategy: an agent with signal s invests at time $T(s)$, conditional on no other investment before, where

$$T(s) = \frac{1}{9\rho} \log \frac{1}{s}.$$

The proof that the condition (7.6) is sufficient is left to the reader.

---

[5] Gul and Lundholm emphasize that the purpose of their paper is to show that when agents can choose the timing of their investment, "their decisions become clustered together, giving the appearance of a cascade even if information is actually being used efficiently." The reader may be puzzled, because this clustering property is obviously a property of all models of social learning where the information in history grows over time, as shown from the very first model in Section 3.2, where information is used efficiently.

[6] If $s(0) < 1$, agents with a signal greater than $s(0)$ should wait at least an infinitesimal amount of time.

7.3 Buildup of Private Information

In the model we have considered so far, all private information is set at the beginning of time. Caplin and Leahy (1994) propose a model in which agents receive private signals over time. The population of agents is fixed and forms a continuum of mass normalized to 1. Each agent has one option to make an investment[7] of a fixed size in any period $t \geq 1$, with payoff $E[\theta] - c$, at the time of the investment ($\theta \in \{0, 1\}$ and $0 < c < 1$). The payoff at time t is discounted to the first period by δ^{t-1}. Each agent receives a new SBS about θ in *every* period with precision q that is independent of other variables.

EQUILIBRIUM WITH DETERMINISTIC STRATEGIES

We look for a symmetric subgame PBE with deterministic strategies. (If necessary, the parameters of the model will be adjusted to obtain deterministic strategies.) We will show later that the players who move first are the superoptimists (they have an unbroken string of good signals). We can focus on these players. From Bayes's rule, their LLR between the good and the bad states, λ_t, increases linearly with the number of periods:

$$\lambda_t = \lambda_0 + at \qquad \text{with} \qquad a = \log \frac{q}{1-q}.$$

Let λ^* be the minimum belief (measured by the LLR) for a positive payoff of investment: $\lambda^* = \gamma$, which is defined by $\gamma = \log(c/(1-c))$. Define by λ_1^{**} the belief of an agent who is indifferent between investing and waiting for the revelation of the true state one period later. An exercise shows that

$$\lambda_1^{**} = \lambda^* + \log \frac{1}{1-\delta},$$

which is strictly higher than λ^* because of the information obtained after one period.

A necessary condition for investment by a superoptimist in period t is $\lambda_t \geq \lambda^*$. This condition is not sufficient, however: if all the superoptimists invest in period t, they reveal the state perfectly (there is a continuum of them). If the state is revealed at the end of period t, they prefer not to delay only if $\lambda_t \geq \lambda_1^{**}$. The evolution of the belief of the superoptimists is represented in Figure 7.2.

Let T be the smallest t such that $\lambda_t > \lambda_1^{**}$. If no agent has invested prior to period T, superoptimists all invest in period T. They know that their action reveals the state one period later, but by definition of T, this incentive is not sufficient to make them

---

[7] Caplin and Leahy consider the symmetric problem of agents who have an option to stop an investment process. The two models are isomorphic. The model with options to invest generates a boom, with positive probability; the model with options to stop the flow of investment expenditures generates a crash. The model with a crash was chosen for its effect on the reader, but it is technically more complicated. The model with an option to invest enables us to make a direct comparison with the model of Chamley and Gale (1994).

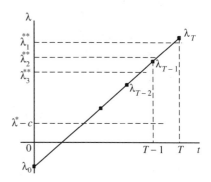

Figure 7.2 The evolution of beliefs. The LLR of the superoptimists increases linearly with time. In period T (smallest t such that $\lambda_t > \lambda_1^{**}$), investment dominates delay with perfect information one period later. In period $T - k$, investment is dominated by delay with perfect information $k + 1$ periods later.

wait. In period $T + 1$, all the other agents either invest (if $\theta = 1$) or don't (if $\theta = 0$). If the equilibrium strategy is to delay until period T, all agents know perfectly that full information is revealed at the end of period T. The value of T is determined by all agents in the first period.

It remains to show that the superoptimists delay until period T. Let λ_k^{**} be the value of the likelihood ratio for an agent who is indifferent between not delaying and delaying for k periods exactly and then making a decision with perfect information.

Begin with period $T - 1$. Assume that the parameters of the model are such that for the superoptimists, investment in period $T - 1$ is dominated by delay until period $T + 1$ with perfect information in period $T + 1$:

$$(7.7) \qquad \lambda_{T-1} < \lambda_2^{**}.$$

In that case, delay for two periods is not the optimal strategy: a superoptimist who will receive one more positive signal in period $T - 1$ invests in that period. The geometry of Figure 7.2 shows that such parameters can be found.[8]

In the same way, a sufficient condition for the optimality of delay in any period $T - k$ with $k \geq 1$ is $\lambda_{T-k} < \lambda_{k+1}^{**}$. The following result shows that the only condition required for getting optimality is (7.7).[9]

LEMMA 7.1 *If $\lambda_{T-1} < \lambda_2^{**}$, then $\lambda_{T-k} < \lambda_{k+1}^{**}$ for any $k \leq T - 1$.*

We have focused so far on the superoptimists. The optimal strategies of the other agents are simple: any agent who is not a superoptimist has at least one fewer positive signal than the superoptimists. Therefore his LLR in period t is not greater than $\lambda_t - a = \lambda_{t-1}$. The argument for the delay of a superoptimist in period $T - k$, with $k \geq 1$, applies *a fortiori* to any other agent.

---

[8] Noting that λ_1^{**} and λ_2^{**} do not depend on a, choose $a > \lambda_1^{**} - \lambda_2^{**} + \eta$, and λ_0 such that $\lambda_1^{**} < \lambda_T < \lambda_1^{**} + \eta/2$.

[9] In Figure 7.2, the interval between λ_k^{**} and λ_{k+1}^{**} shrinks if k increases, whereas the interval between consecutive values of λ_t is constant and equal to a.

From the previous discussion, inequality (7.7) is sufficient for the symmetric PBE where the superoptimists invest in period T. This condition is restated in terms of structural parameters in the following proposition.

PROPOSITION 7.2 *There is a unique symmetric PBE if the parameters of the model satisfy the following conditions (represented in Figure 7.2):*

$$\lambda_0 + Ta > \gamma - \log(1 - \delta), \qquad \lambda_0 + (T - 1)a < \gamma - \log(1 - \delta^2).$$

In this PBE, all superoptimists invest in period T. All other agents invest in period $T + 1$ if and only if the good state is revealed (by the mass of superoptimists) at the end of period T.

COMPARISON WITH THE MODEL OF CHAMLEY AND GALE (1994)

The conditions of Proposition 7.2 were introduced to simplify the analysis of the equilibrium.[10] Under those conditions, superoptimists do not delay in period T. How come agents delayed in the previous chapter? The conditions of Proposition 7.2 rule out the type of equilibrium with random strategies of the model in Chapter 6. Recall that random strategies are used when the period length is sufficiently short (or δ is near 1), and agents strictly prefer to delay if they get perfect information. In the present model, the period is sufficiently long to prevent this outcome.

In the model of the previous chapter, there is a regime where aggregate investment is small and random during a learning phase. This phase ends with all remaining agents suddenly investing if the level of belief is sufficiently high that perfect information is not sufficient to lure agents to delay. Note also that all private informations are given at the beginning of time.

The present model introduces an additional phase in which agents have low beliefs and do not invest at all. The learning phase in the model is very short and lasts only one period, with the superoptimists investing while others delay (exactly as agents with lower beliefs delay in the previous chapter). At the end of that period, beliefs are sufficiently high or low (as at the end of the learning phase in the previous chapter) so that all remaining agents invest immediately or do not invest.

When the conditions of Proposition 7.2 do not hold, the learning phase in the model of Caplin and Leahy lasts for more than one period and the analysis is more complicated. The model is actually not suited for such an analysis. (The right model for this is the one in Chapter 6.) The following remarks suggest how the learning phase may be extended.

Assume the second condition of Proposition 7.2 is not met and $\lambda_{T-1} > \lambda_2^{**}$: in period $T - 1$ a superoptimist would prefer to invest right away rather than delay for two periods and get perfect information. To simplify the discussion, assume further

---

[10] Caplin and Leahy (1994) have similar conditions.

that $\lambda_T = \lambda_1^{**} + \epsilon$, where ϵ is vanishingly small. In period T, the payoff of investment for a superoptimist is almost the same as that of delay until period $T + 1$.

Consider a superoptimist in period $T - 1$. If he does not invest in that period, he invests in period T if he gets another positive signal, and delays until period $T + 1$ otherwise. Because ϵ is vanishingly small, the payoff of delay is almost the same as that of a sure delay for two periods. Because $\lambda_{T-1} > \lambda_2^{**}$, a probability of investment $\zeta_{T-1} = 0$ cannot be an equilibrium strategy.

The strategy $\zeta_{T-1} = 1$ cannot be an equilibrium strategy, because it would generate perfect information at the beginning of period T and agents would strictly prefer to wait ($\lambda_{T-1} < \lambda_1^{**}$).

In an equilibrium, superoptimists in period $T - 1$ arbitrage between investing in period $T - 1$ and delay for some information in period T, with a probability of investment ζ_{T-1} strictly between 0 and 1. This is the situation in the model of the previous chapter. The analysis of the equilibrium is more complex because the private information is not invariant over time.

7.4 Observation of Payoffs

So far in this book, social learning has operated through the observation of actions. Actions are informative because they depend on informative private beliefs. In a variety of contexts, the results of the actions also convey important information. Penguins on an Antarctic cliff wait for someone to jump and reveal whether a killer whale is roaming around. Oil drillers learn from the success or failure of neighboring wells. Academic researchers follow successful colleagues into new areas of investigation. We consider now a simple model, which has been motivated by the example of oil exploration. The main property of the model, which is due to Hendricks and Kovenock (1989), rests on the arbitrage between the payoff of immediate investment and delay, as in the model of Chamley and Gale (1994).

DRILLING FOR OIL (HENDRICKS AND KOVENOCK, 1989)

There are N companies, which own adjacent tracts for exploration. All the tracts contain the same amount of oil, and there is no flow from one tract to another (for simplicity). Drilling entails a fixed cost. The first company that drills will find out if there is oil in its tract. If oil spurts from the well, it can be seen by all. There is an informational externality in the observation of the drilling's payoff. Companies have an incentive not to delay drilling, because of the discount rate; but they have also an incentive to delay and find out whether the other company has struck oil.

There are two states of nature, $\theta = 0$ or 1, with prior probability μ for state 1. There are N agents $i = 1, \ldots, N$, who all have the same belief. Until now, information has been obtained from the observation of actions that were function of the private beliefs. In that context, it was essential for the distribution of beliefs (and therefore of actions) to depend on the state θ. In the present context, the introduction of different private beliefs would distract us from the main issue. We assume therefore that all agents have the same belief μ_1 in the first period. This belief satisfies the following assumption.

ASSUMPTION 7.1 $0 < \mu_1 - c < \delta\mu_1(1 - c)$.

Time is discrete, and the payoff of investment in period t is

$$U = \delta^{t-1}(E_t[\theta] - c), \qquad \text{where } c \text{ is the investment cost,} \quad 0 < c < 1.$$

The value of θ is revealed at the end of the first period in which an investment takes place. We focus on a symmetric PBE.

Under Assumption 7.1, agents cannot invest for sure in the first period in a symmetric PBE: delaying would yield perfect information. There cannot be an equilibrium in which all agents delay for sure, according to an argument similar to that in Chamley and Gale (1994). Note that there is strategic substitutability. If all agents increase their probability of investment, delaying yields more information and the option value increases. This induces each agent to reduce its (probability of) investment. There is a unique symmetric PBE.

Let ζ be the probability of investment of each agent. By the previous arguments, $0 < \zeta < 1$. If there is an equilibrium, agents are indifferent between investment with no delay and delay. Hence, the value of the game is the value of investment in the first period, $\mu - c$. If an agent delays, the probability that at least one of the $N - 1$ other agents invests in the first period and thus conveys perfect information to others is $\pi = 1 - (1 - \zeta)^{N-1}$. If no agent invests in the first period, nothing is learned.[11] The value of the game in period 2 after no investment in period 1 is therefore the *same* as in period 1, $\mu - c$, and the arbitrage equation for delay is

$$\mu - c = \delta\Big(\pi\mu(1 - c) + (1 - \pi)(\mu - c)\Big).$$

The right-hand side is equal to $\delta(\mu - c)$ if $\pi = 0$ and to $\delta\mu(1 - c)$ if $\pi = 1$, and it is linear in π. From Assumption 7.1, the arbitrage equation has a unique solution in π and therefore a unique solution in the strategy ζ with $\pi = 1 - (1 - \zeta)^{N-1}$.

DEVELOPMENT OF URBAN AREAS

The introduction described how the opening of a successful store by Bed Bath & Beyond was followed by other stores in the same neighborhood and higher rents. Caplin and Leahy (1998) present a model of social learning with search and matching:

---

[11] If agents had private information on θ, the event of no investment would carry more information. Because we want to focus on *one* channel of information (the observation of output), we should not include heterogeneous beliefs at this first stage. Hendricks and Kovenock (1989) assume a distribution of beliefs. In a PBE, agents have nonrandom strategies in which the most optimistic agents do not delay.

landlords own vacant lots, which can be used for residential purpose or for retail activities, and they receive applications from agents of different qualities for commercial use. For simplicity, the conversion of a vacancy to a residence or to a retail store is taken to be irreversible. A vacancy can be turned into a residence at any time.

The value of turning a vacancy into a residence is assumed to be known, but the value of the commercial use is not known. It depends on the intrinsic quality of the retail store and on the "potential" of the neighborhood. The second factor affects in the same way all vacancies in the neighborhood. As long as no retail store has opened, no one knows that common factor. As soon as one store opens, by assumption, the common factor becomes public information. In the same way, the state of nature is known after the first penguin's jump or the first oil drilling.

Owners have an incentive to search for the best applicants. They also have an incentive to delay because the value of the retail activities in the neighborhood may become known. If the value is revealed, they may avoid the downside risk that the space is less valuable for retail (with a search for a reservation quality) than for immediate conversion into a residence of known value. The analysis of the model is presented in Exercise 7.5.

EXERCISES

EXERCISE 7.1
Consider the simple model in Section 7.1.2, and assume $\delta \to 1$.

1. Determine the limit of the belief (as $\delta \to 1$) after no investment in the first period.
2. Could the previous result be anticipated by an intuitive argument?
3. Determine a lower bound for the limit value of the variance of the change of belief between periods 1 and 2.
4. Assume that there are two players in the bad state and three players in the good state. Analyze the equilibrium when $\delta \to 1$.

EXERCISE 7.2
Consider the model of Section 7.1.1 with the specified parameter values and $\delta \geq \frac{1}{3}$.

1. Show that in an equilibrium, no pessimist invests in the first period.
2. Let ζ be the strategy of an optimist in the first period (the probability of investment). Using an arbitrage argument, show that ζ is determined by

$$\mu^+ - c = \delta P(x = 1|\mu^+)(1 - c) = \delta \zeta \mu^+(1 - c).$$

Determine the value of ζ if $\delta = \frac{1}{3}$.
3. Show that if a pessimist observes one investment at the end of the first period, he does not invest in the second period.
4. Using the previous results, determine the unique symmetric PBE.

5. Show that the value of the game for a pessimist at the beginning of the first period is

$$V(\delta) = \mu^- \delta \zeta (1 - c)\left(\zeta + 2\delta(1 - \zeta)\right).$$

   Show that for the values of the parameters of the model, $V(\delta)$ is not a monotone
   function of δ if $\delta \geq \frac{1}{3}$.
6. Show that for the values of the parameters of the model, $V(\delta)$ is an increasing
   function of δ if $\delta \leq \frac{1}{3}$.

EXERCISE 7.3 No equilibrium in the simple model of Section 7.2.1

Let ζ_t be the probability of investment per unit of time in a symmetric equilibrium.

1. Show that the arbitrage equation is $\rho(\mu_t - c) = \zeta_t \mu_t (1 - \mu_t) + \dot{\mu}_t$. Use two
   methods: (i) the intuitive argument of the pricing of the option to invest; (ii)
   the decomposion of time into periods of length dt and the arbitrage between
   investment and delay.
2. Using Bayes's rule in discrete time with periods of length dt, express μ_{t+dt} as
   a function of μ_t and ζ_t. Taking $dt \to 0$, show that $\dot{\mu}_t = -\zeta_t \mu_t (1 - \mu_t)$, and
   conclude that the arbitrage equation cannot be satisfied for $\rho > 0$.

EXERCISE 7.4

There are two states of nature, $\theta \in \{-1, 1\}$, and two investment projects, denoted
by -1 and 1. Project i has a gross payoff equal to 1 if $i = \theta$ and equal to 0 if $i \neq \theta$.
The cost of the investment is equal to c. There are two agents, each with one option
to make one investment in one of the two projects. The probability of state 1 is equal
to $\mu > \frac{1}{2}$. Each agent has a binary signal $s \in \{-1, 1\}$ such that $P(s = \theta \mid \theta) = q$,
where q is drawn from a distribution with support $[\frac{1}{2}, \mu]$. Time is continuous, and
the options can be exercised at any time. Assume that $\frac{1}{2} < c < \mu$. Show that there is
no symmetric PBE.

EXERCISE 7.5 The BB&B model of Caplin and Leahy (1998)

There are N landlords, who each own one vacancy. In each period, a landlord who
still owns a vacancy can either commit to residential use or receive one application by
a retail store. The conversion to a residence yields a value W and is irreversible. If the
landlord searches and receives an application, he has to decide whether to commit to
a permanent lease or to turn the application down and carry the vacant space to the
next period. There is no recall of past applications.

Each applicant has a private type α, which is drawn from a uniform distribution
on $(0, 1)$ and is independent of other types and variables. If the lease is signed, the
landlord captures the entire value of the space (with a take-it-or-leave-it offer). This
value is equal to $\alpha\theta$, where θ is the value of the neighborhood and is drawn from a
uniform distribution on $(0, 2)$. Once a lease has been signed, the store opens within
the period, and the value of θ is publicly known in the next period. The discount

factor of the landlords is δ. If no lease has been signed yet, the value of signing with an applicant of type α is $\alpha E[\theta] = \alpha$.

1. Consider first the second phase of the game after the first lease has been signed and θ has been observed by all agents.
   (a) Assume first that $W = 0$. (There is no residential use.) Using a Bellman equation, show that landlords accept applications above the reservation value α_I given by $\alpha_I = \delta(1 + \alpha_I^2)/2$.
   (b) Assume now $0 < W < 2$. Let $V(\theta)$ be the value of continuing the search at the end of a period. Show that there is a value $\underline{\theta}$ such that $\theta < \underline{\theta} \Leftrightarrow V(\theta) < W$. Determine the strategy of a landlord when θ is known.
2. Assume now that the value of θ is not known (in the first phase of the game, when no lease has been signed yet).
   (a) Determine the expected value of learning the value of θ, V_I, as a function of W, α_I, and $\underline{\theta}$.
   (b) Show that the reservation value of a landlord is now

   $$\underline{\alpha} = \delta\left(\pi V_U + (1 - \pi)V_I\right),$$

   where π is the probability that a waiting landlord remains uninformed at the beginning of next period and V_U is the expected value of being uninformed.
   (c) Show that $\pi = \underline{\alpha}^{N-1}$, and solve the model. Compare the rents before and after the first lease is signed.

7.5 Appendix

HEURISTIC DERIVATION OF THE ARBITRAGE EQUATION (7.1)

The arbitrage for agent A is between investing at time t and investing at time $t + dt$. Writing this equality, we have

$$U(E[\theta|s(t), s' < s(t)]) = \frac{1}{1 + \rho \, dt}\left((\pi_t \, dt)U\left(E[\theta|s(t), s' = s(t)]\right)\right.$$

$$\left. + (1 - \pi_t \, dt)U\left(E[\theta|s(t), s' < s(t + dt)]\right)\right).$$

On the right-hand side, the first term describes the event that occurs when the other agent, agent B, invests. This event occurs when $s(t + dt) < s' < s(t)$ and has a probability $\pi_t \, dt$. If agent B invests, agent A knows that B has a signal $s' = s(t)$ by approximation of the interval $(s(t + dt), s(t))$. (The approximation error is of the order of dt, which is multiplied by $\pi_t \, dt$ and therefore of the order of dt^2.)

The second term is the value of investment at time $t + dt$ when no investment is made by agent B in the time interval $(t, t + dt)$. Agent A knows now that the signal of agent B is below $s(t + dt)$, which is smaller than $s(t)$. We have the approximation

$$U\Big(E[\theta|s(t), s' < s(t + dt)]\Big) = U\Big(E[\theta|s(t), s' < s(t)]\Big)$$

$$+ U' \frac{d(E[\theta|s(t), s' < \tilde{s}])}{d\tilde{s}} \dot{s}(t)dt.$$

This expression is substituted in the top equation.

We now proceed in a standard way: in the top equation, we multiply both sides by $1 + \rho\, dt$. The constant terms on both sides are identical and are canceled. The terms of the order of dt must be identical. (Divide both sides by dt and take $dt \to 0$.) This identity is the same as equation (7.1).

Proof of Lemma 7.1

If an agent knows that he will get perfect information k periods later ($k \geq 1$), he delays only if $\mu - c < \delta^k \mu(1 - c)$, which is equivalent to

$$\lambda_t < \lambda_k^{**} = \lambda^* + \log \frac{1}{1 - \delta^k}.$$

Because $1 + \delta + \cdots + \delta^{k-1} = \dfrac{1 - \delta^k}{1 - \delta}$, then

(7.9) $\qquad \lambda_k^{**} = \lambda_1^{**} - \log(1 + \delta + \cdots + \delta^{k-1}).$

Suppose that $\lambda_{T-1} < \lambda_2^{**}$. We now show that for $k \geq 2$, $\lambda_{T-k} < \lambda_{k+1}^{**}$.

From (7.9), using $\delta < 1$ and the concavity of the log function, we find that the difference $\lambda_k^{**} - \lambda_{k+1}^{**}$, which is positive, is decreasing in k. For $k = 1$, this difference is smaller than $\lambda_T - \lambda_{T-1} = a$, by assumption. Because the difference $\lambda_{T-k} - \lambda_{T-k-1} = a$ is constant, the inequality $\lambda_{T-k} < \lambda_{k+1}^{**}$ holds for $k \geq 2$. ∎

8 Outcomes

The triumph of hope over experience.

Social learning occurs through the observation of the outcomes of others' actions. Beliefs may fail to converge to the truth when these outcomes fail to be sufficiently informative. Various examples are analyzed: (i) a monopoly faces intersecting demand curves; (ii) the probability of economic success depends on effort through an unknown relation; (iii) the probability of success depends on more than one factor; (iv) private beliefs are bounded. There may be some relation between fiscal policies and the evolution of beliefs (which in turn may affect the policies). New agents with beliefs arbitrarily close to the truth can sway people away from an incorrect herd into an optimal action.

In the previous chapters, the information about the true state of nature came from private *ex ante* beliefs. This information was brought, imperfectly, into the social knowledge through the filter of the action choices by individuals pursuing their own interest. The implicit assumption was that the outcomes of actions would occur after all decisions were made. In some settings, however, actions bear lessons for future decisions. Firms may adjust their prices after the market response. Unemployed agents observe the results of their search. Farmers observe some results at the end of a crop cycle before making choices for the next one. Evidence on the risks of cousin marriages eventually becomes known. These settings share the common feature that actions send a random signal: chance plays a role in the finding of a new job; agricultural outputs are famously uncertain; the outcomes of medical treatments depend to a large extent on personal characteristics that cannot be observed.

In this chapter, the probabilities of the actions' outcomes depend on the state of nature. The signal issued by an action may be an output, a payoff, or some other variable. This new channel of information introduces a specific property: if one wants to learn whether an action is profitable for the given state of nature, one has to try it. Discouraged unemployed do not learn much about their ability to fit with the evolving conditions of the job market; if no farmer plants a new hybrid corn, no one will learn whether the crop is suitable for the conditions of the land. The information is not generated by private beliefs *ex ante*, but is fed in by nature over time when actions are taken.

The Armed-Bandit Problem

An agent who can repeatedly choose an action takes into account the immediate pay-off of his action and his learning for better decisions. He is like a player who pulls one of the two arms of a slot machine to generate a random output of money. One of them, unknown to the player, generates on average a higher output. The *armed-bandit problem* is to choose which arm to pull. Berry (1972) and Rothschild (1974) have analyzed this well-known problem for a finite number of actions.[1] Eventually, the agent settles for one arm, which he believes to be more productive than the other. Because he stops using the other arm, his belief is invariant; but it may be incorrect. The nonconvergence to the truth may be optimal even though the agent fully internalizes the benefit of learning, when deviation from the myopic maximization is more costly than the potential benefit from experimentation.

Social Learning from the Outcomes of Others' Actions

In the standard framework of social learning, the nonconvergence to the truth may be suboptimal because agents do not take into account the informational benefits of their actions for others. In this chapter, following the current state of the literature, we study whether the agents' beliefs converge to the truth or not, as the number of observations becomes arbitrarily large. We will not analyze the rate of convergence or the cost of the failure to take the information benefits into account.

Learning the Demand Curve of a Monopoly

Finding the demand curve and adjusting the price to the demand are basic problems in economics. We begin in Section 8.1.1 with a model of McLennan (1984), who assumes a zero–one demand where the probability of a sale in a period depends on the price quoted by a monopoly during the period. The monopoly is run by a sequence of one-period managers, who choose a price to maximize the period's expected payoff without experimenting for the benefit of future managers. There are two possible schedules for the demand, and by assumption, they intersect at a price that separates the optimal prices for the two schedules. The sequence of prices chosen by the managers converges with strictly positive probability to the intersection point between the demand curves, where there is no learning. In such a case there is no convergence to the truth. The model is remarkably tractable and yields useful insights. A related model by Kiefer (1989) assumes that the monopoly chooses the quantity and that the equilibrium price is subject to an additive shock. The model has

---

[1] See Berry and Fristedt (1985).

to be simulated and generates similar properties (Section 8.1.2). The limited ability of agents to learn in this context may have some implications for the rigidity of prices or individuals' behavior.

The Determinants of Economic Success: Luck or Effort?

The model of McLennan can be applied to the case of an agent who searches for a new job or plans for a new career. His effort depends on his belief about the relative contributions of effort and luck to the probability of success. This belief is affected by his past successes and failures. The model of Section 8.2.1 explains how a low initial belief in the value of effort may set the agent on a path where he never learns that effort actually pays off. This property has obvious policy implications.

Multidimensional Reality and Unidimensional Outcomes

The factors that determine economic success obviously have more than one dimension, and yet the experience from an average of successes or failures is one-dimensional. It is not surprising that such restricted experience does not enable agents to learn the true state. An extension of the model of McLennan leads to a model of Piketty (1995), which exhibits interesting properties of the limit distributions of beliefs (Section 8.2.2). For example, successful children of poor parents are more likely to believe that effort has a large effect than those who remain poor. Such properties are not based on self-serving psychological mechanisms, but depend on the interaction between belief and effort.

Complete Learning with Diverse Private Beliefs

In the previous models, the agents share a common history, and the weight of that history may prevent them from learning the truth. One way out of the trap of history is to have new agents with strong beliefs who reject the lesson of history. These agents choose different actions, the outcomes of which generate new information, which may bring everyone out of the trap. Bala and Goyal (1995) analyze social learning from the outcomes of actions chosen in a finite set (Section 8.3.1). This framework can be applied to an agricultural setting where farmers choose one crop in a small menu and observe the output at the end of a cycle. A finite number of actions may also be an approximation of an action in a continuum (e.g., a monopoly's price). The technique of analysis relies on the finite number of actions: it implies that some actions are taken an infinite number of times and thus reveal their true payoff by the law of large numbers. This revelation of information is obviously not sufficient for learning the truth, for the agents (e.g., farmers) could herd on a suboptimal action. However, no incorrect herd can take place if some agents have beliefs that are arbitrarily close to the truth. This assumption is reminiscent of the unbounded beliefs assumption in Chapter 3. The operating mechanism is different, however. Agents never learn from others' choices (by an assumption of bounded rationality). They learn only from the outputs. The agents with beliefs close to the truth choose an optimal action, and the repeated observations of these correct actions eventually convince everyone to adopt them.

8.1 Incomplete Learning

Following McLennan (1984), we consider a seller who learns about the demand for his good by selling the good.[2] This is a standard problem of learning about the state of nature from the outcomes of the actions. As usual, the model is simplified as much as possible.

8.1.1 A Monopoly Facing a Zero–One Demand

The seller (the agent) produces in each period one unit of a good that cannot be stored for the next period. Without loss of generality, the cost of production is zero. The seller faces in each period a customer who has an unknown reservation price. The seller quotes a price, once, and the customer either buys the good or leaves forever. The demand curve for the good is defined by the probability that the customer buys the good. We will make two essential assumptions. The first one is minimal: there are two possible demand curves, and these two curves intersect at some price a. They have different elasticities, and we define the more elastic as the demand in state 1. Without loss of generality, the demands in the two states are linear. The probability of a sale is assumed to be[3]

$$(8.1) \qquad \pi_\theta(p) = \max\{0, \min\{1, b - m_\theta(p - a)\}\}$$

$$\text{with} \quad a > 0, \quad 0 < b < 1.$$

The parameter m_θ depends on the state of nature θ, which is fixed at 0 or 1, with equal probabilities, before the first period. The two possible demand curves are represented in Figure 8.1.

Because the demand is more elastic in state 1 than in state 0, the optimal price in state 1 is lower than in state 0. We now make a second essential assumption: the price a (at which the demands intersect) is between the optimal prices in state 1 and state 0. This assumption will drive all the results.

We can understand immediately, without any algebra, the fundamental mechanism at work. Let μ be the belief of the agent (seller), i.e., the probability of state 1. If $\mu = 1$, his optimal price is below a; if $\mu = 0$, his optimal price is above a. Hence there is some intermediate belief between 0 and 1 under which the optimal price is a. For that price, however, the probabilities of a sale are the same in the two states.

---

[2] The exposition by McLennan is not an easy read. The presentation here will be simpler and include new results. The problem of learning a demand curve was already mentioned by Drèze (1972).

[3] The linear probability of a sale is equivalent to a uniform density for the reservation prices of the buyer.

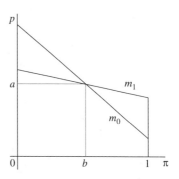

Figure 8.1 Demand curves. The demand is more elastic in state 1 than in state 0. The schedules intersect at some price a. The parameters are such that the optimal price in state 1 (0) is below (above) a. Hence, for some intermediate belief $\mu^* \in (0, 1)$, the optimal price is a. For that price, the demands are the same in the two states and the seller learns nothing. The belief μ^* is invariant.

The agent learns nothing from the demand. If he does not experiment (say, he is in charge of the monopoly for one period only), his belief is the same in the next period and all periods after. We will see that even if the agent can manipulate the demand in order to learn, he may reject that experimentation as too costly in comparison with the potential benefit.

SOCIAL LEARNING BY MYOPIC MANAGERS

Assume that the good is supplied by a firm that is run by a different manager in each period. The manager chooses the price to maximize the expected profit (equal to the value of the sale) in his period, without taking into account the benefit from learning for better decisions in the future. The manager knows the history of prices and sales of the monopoly. He learns as a Bayesian from the history of sales. This is an example of the standard framework of social learning. There may be an inefficiency in that the manager does not experiment for the benefit of better decisions by future managers. We will consider the problem of optimal experimentation later.

Let μ be the belief of the manager in some period. A standard exercise shows that the profit-maximizing price is

$$(8.2) \qquad p(\mu) = \frac{b}{2E[m]} + \frac{a}{2} \quad \text{with} \quad E[m] = m_0 + \mu(m_1 - m_0).$$

As announced previously, we assume that the intersection price a is between the optimal prices in the two states.

ASSUMPTION 8.1 $\quad p(0) > a > p(1), \quad$ *or equivalently,* $\quad \dfrac{b}{m_1} < a < \dfrac{b}{m_0}.$

Because the optimal price function $p(\mu)$ in (8.2) is strictly decreasing, Assumption 8.1 implies that there is a unique belief μ^* such that $p(\mu^*) = a$. A manager with belief μ^* chooses the price a for which the probabilities of a sale are identical in the two states. The next manager learns nothing from the outcome in the period and has the same belief. The belief μ^* is *invariant*.

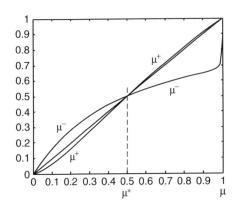

Figure 8.2 The evolution of the belief. Parameters: $m_0 = 0.67$, $m_1 = 2$, $b = 0.8$, $a = 2/(m_0 + m_1)$. The curve represents the *ex post* belief after a no-sale event, given the belief μ and an optimal price. When μ is greater than the fixed point, the no-sale event is more likely if the state is θ_0.

The Stability of the Invariant Belief

Let $\mu^+(\mu)$ and $\mu^-(\mu)$ be the end-of-period beliefs following a sale and no sale respectively, when the beginning-of-period belief is μ and the pricing is optimal given that belief. By Bayes's rule and the equations (8.1) and (8.2), we have

$$(8.3) \qquad \frac{\mu^+}{1 - \mu^+} = \frac{\pi_1(p(\mu))}{\pi_0(p(\mu))} \frac{\mu}{1 - \mu} \quad \text{and} \quad \frac{\mu^-}{1 - \mu^-} = \frac{1 - \pi_1(p(\mu))}{1 - \pi_0(p(\mu))} \frac{\mu}{1 - \mu}.$$

The graphs of $\mu^-(\mu)$ and $\mu^+(\mu)$ are represented in the left panel of Figure 8.2. Suppose for example that in some period, the manager has a belief μ below μ^*. He prices the good above a (Figure 8.1). A no-sale outcome is a signal favoring state 1, because the probability of a sale is lower in state 1 (Figure 8.1): $\mu^-(\mu) > \mu$ (Figure 8.2). Likewise, if a sale occurs, the belief is lowered: $\mu^+(\mu) < \mu$.

Both functions μ^- and μ^+ have a fixed point μ^* by Assumption 8.1. What is remarkable is that both functions are increasing (Exercise 8.1). Because μ^+ and μ^- are increasing and have a unique fixed point at the invariant belief $\mu^* \in (0, 1)$, the next result follows.

PROPOSITION 8.1 *The value μ^* partitions the set of beliefs in two stable regions:*

If $\mu_t < \mu^*$, then for any $k \geq 1$, $\mu_{t+k} < \mu^*$.
If $\mu_t > \mu^*$, then for any $k \geq 1$, $\mu_{t+k} > \mu^*$.

If the manager at date t has a belief below (above) μ^*, all the subsequent managers will have a belief below (above) μ^*. Obviously, there cannot be complete learning.

Suppose the initial belief is below μ^* ($\mu_1 < \mu^*$) and the true state is 1. The belief μ_t is a martingale and therefore converges. From the previous paragraph, it must converge to a limit $\hat{\mu}$ in the interval $[0, \mu^*]$. From Proposition 2.9, it cannot be totally wrong, and $\hat{\mu} > 0$. The limit $\hat{\mu}$ cannot be in the open interval $(0, \mu^*)$, because then the outcomes (sale or no sale) would remain informative near $\hat{\mu}$, thus contradicting the convergence. Hence, $\hat{\mu} = \mu^*$. Likewise, if $\mu_1 > \mu^*$ and the true state is 0, then μ_t converges to μ^*.

In summary, if the initial belief is *seriously incorrect* (below μ^* while the true state is 1, or above μ^* while the state is 0), then μ_t converges to the intermediate value μ^* and learning is incomplete and inadequate. This property is remarkable, but the case of *fairly correct* initial beliefs is even more remarkable.

Assume that $\mu_1 < \mu^*$ and that the true state is 0. One might think that μ_t converges to the truth – to zero – but it does not. The belief μ_t is a martingale and therefore converges. The limit cannot be in the open interval $(0, \mu^*)$ by the standard argument that the outputs would be informative. However, μ_t is bounded, and by Proposition 2.6, it cannot converge to 0 in probability. More specifically, let ℓ_t be the likelihood ratio $\ell_t = \mu_t/(1 - \mu_t)$. By Proposition 2.5, ℓ_t is a martingale[4] (because $\theta = 0$). It converges to 0 or $\ell^* = \mu^*/(1 - \mu^*)$, and the expected value at the limit is equal to the initial value: $\ell_1 = \pi \ell^*$, where π is the probability of the convergence of ℓ_t to ℓ^* (of μ_t to μ^*). There are two cases for the convergence of the belief μ_t, as shown in the following result.

PROPOSITION 8.2

(i) *If the initial belief is seriously incorrect ($\mu_1 < \mu^*$ while $\theta = 1$, or $\mu_1 > \mu^*$ while $\theta = 0$), then $\mu_t \to \mu^*$.*

(ii) *If the initial belief does not satisfy the previous condition, then $\mu_t \to \mu^*$ with probability π and μ_t approaches the true θ with probability $1 - \pi$, where*

$$\pi = \frac{\mu_1}{1 - \mu_1} \frac{\mu^*}{1 - \mu^*}.$$

The proposition shows that myopic and selfish managers have some difficulties in learning the truth.

NONMYOPIC OPTIMIZATION

Assume now that the agent maximizes, in each period, the discounted sum of all future payoffs using a discount factor $\delta < 1$. Suppose that his belief is μ^*. When he chooses the price p, he maximizes the sum of the current period's payoff and of the discounted future payoffs. The latter depends on the belief at the end of the period, and therefore on the learning in the period. The agent could deviate from the myopic optimization solution $p = a$ to learn about θ and increase his future payoff with better informed decisions. However, by deviating from $p = a$ he faces a loss, which is measured by the concavity of the payoff function $u(p, \mu^*) = (1 - E[m|\mu^*](p - a))p$. Its second derivative at the optimum $p = a$ is $u_{11} = -2E[m|\mu^*] = -2(\mu^* m_1 + (1 - \mu^*)m_0) < 0$. If the discount factor δ is below some value δ^*, the loss in the

---

[4] Recall that μ_t is not a martingale conditional on $\theta = 0$. One can verify – at least numerically – that $E[\mu_{t+1} - \mu_t|\theta = 0] < 0$ if $\mu_t < \mu^*$. Although the expected value of the change of μ_t is strictly negative for any value of μ_t on any path, μ_t converges to the upper bound of its range with a strictly positive probability.

current period dominates the gain from learning, in which case the myopic rule $p = a$ is also optimal for a nonmyopic agent. (Note that the discount factor δ^* is not zero.) If $\delta < \delta^*$, the belief μ^* is invariant for the nonmyopic agent.

8.1.2 A Linear Demand

The previous model is modified to allow for a demand q_t that is a real number and depends linearly on the price p_t:

$$(8.4) \qquad p_t = a_\theta - b_\theta q_t + \epsilon_t.$$

The parameters (a_θ, b_θ) depend on the state of nature $\theta \in \{0, 1\}$ and are invariant over time. The noises ϵ_t have a normal distribution $\mathcal{N}(0, \sigma_\epsilon^2)$ and are independent. The good is produced costlessly by a monopoly.[5]

Suppose that $b_1 < b_0$. (As in the previous model, state 1 is the one with a more elastic demand.) The parameters are such that the deterministic parts of the two demand schedules intersect for some quantity

$$q^* = \frac{a_0 - a_1}{b_0 - b_1}.$$

The manager of the monopoly chooses the quantity (and not the price as in the previous section) to maximize the period's profit. Given a belief μ, the optimal quantity is

$$q(\mu) = \frac{E[a_\theta]}{2 E[b_\theta]},$$

where the expectation depends on the belief. The supply is related to the expected elasticity and is therefore increasing in μ. As in the previous model, the parameters are such that $q(0) < q^* < q(1)$. There is a belief μ^* such that $q(\mu^*) = q^*$. For that belief, all price variations are due to ϵ and none are due to the difference between the deterministic components (because they are identical). There is no learning, and the belief is invariant.

Contrary to the previous model, the invariant belief μ^* cannot separate all the beliefs in two stable intervals, because of the random term ϵ. There is always a possibility that a large shock pushes the public belief to the other side[6] of μ^*. This is especially true if the optimal prices are far from the price at which the deterministic parts of the demand are equal. Suppose for example that if μ is small, the optimal price is very low, and that $\theta = 1$. Because of the very low price, the difference between the deterministic parts in the two states is large, and one observation may push the belief above μ^* near 1.

---

[5] This model may be more appropriate than the binary model in some contexts, but it has not generated specific analytical results in the literature.

[6] See Exercise 8.4.

Despite these variations of the properties, the simulations of Kiefer (1989) show that the belief μ_t converges to the invariant value μ^* with strictly positive probability.

RIGID PRICES

In macroeconomics, the issue of price rigidities is central for the discussion of equilibrium and monetary policy. When prices are determined by the agents, we have to assume that each of them is facing a demand curve in a setting of imperfect competition.[7] The previous models indicate that agents may have little incentive to change their prices. Even if the beliefs of agents converge to the truth, the convergence may be slow. More work is needed on this issue.[8]

8.2 The Determinant of Economic Success: Luck or Effort?

What determines economic success? Luck, family background, personal effort? The beliefs on these determinants are translated into political opinions. Individuals who believe that luck is the main factor may support legislation with a high income tax rate. This tax may reduce the labor supply and the level of economic success and comfort people in their beliefs. The issue needs further research. As an introduction, two models are presented in this section. In the first, effort has either a strong or a weak effect on success, and beliefs are one-dimensional between these two states. In general, a simple outcome like economic success may be affected by a large set of causes. It is not easy to infer the true state of nature from such a simple outcome even when there are many observations. To illustrate the difficulties of learning, the second model assumes that the state of nature belongs to a set of dimension two.

8.2.1 One-Dimensional Beliefs

The first model is an application of the model of McLennan. Assume that an agent supplies in each period a level of effort x. His income at the end of the period (which can be a lifetime) is either 1 or 0 (a normalized value). The probability of economic success with an income of 1 is assumed to be

$$(8.5) \qquad \pi_\theta(x) = \max\{0, \min\{1, a_\theta + m_\theta x\}\},$$

where x represents the effort of the agent. The function is a stylized representation of the decreasing marginal productivity of effort for the probability of success. The agent maximizes the net payoff $E[\pi_\theta(x)] - x^2/(2\alpha)$, where the second term is the cost of effort and α is a parameter. The probabilities in the two states are represented

---

[7] See for example Benassy (1982), Blanchard and Kiyotaki (1987).

[8] Each of the two models may apply to a different setting. (One of them is considered in the next section.) It would be useful to combine the two models with a model where firms determine the price and the demand is random.

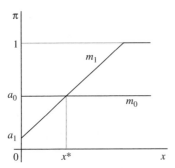

Figure 8.3 Probability of success as a function of effort. Effort has a large effect on the probability of success in state 1, and a small effect in state 0. The parameter values for the example are the same as in Figure 8.1.

in Figure 8.3, which is similar to Figure 8.1. In state 1, effort has a large impact on the probability of success. In state 0, it has a vanishingly small impact.

The optimal level of effort is $x(\mu) = \alpha E[m_\theta]$. The parameters are such that $x(0) < x^* < x(1)$. There is a belief μ^* such that $x(\mu^*) = x^*$, and that belief μ^* is invariant. If $\mu < \mu^*$, the level of effort is smaller than x^*. The probability of success is smaller in state 1. An unsuccessful outcome raises the belief. The updated beliefs after good and bad news are functions $\mu^+(\mu)$ and $\mu^-(\mu)$ that can be represented in a figure similar to Figure 8.2. The same arguments apply to the convergence of beliefs.

THE IMPACT OF REDISTRIBUTIVE POLICIES

The existence of an invariant belief in the interval $(0, 1)$ has striking implications. Assume the true state is 1 and effort has a large effect on the probability of success. An agent who does not believe that effort is rewarded provides a low level of effort, below x^*. He then gradually increases his belief up to μ^*, but he never gets to know the truth, and his effort is below the level that is optimal for the true state.

An agent whose belief is sufficiently optimistic eventually learns the truth: effort has a large effect on success.

Consider now the design of a redistributive tax, and assume that the net payoff of the agent is $(1 - \tau) E[\pi_\theta(x)] - x^2/(2\alpha) + \tau_0$, where τ is the tax rate on income and τ_0 is a lump-sum payment. If agents believe that effort has little effect on success, they favor a high tax rate. If the tax rate lowers the level of effort below x^*, then agents may never get to learn that effort pays off.

The analysis of the interaction between beliefs and policy would benefit from further investigation.

8.2.2 Two-Dimensional Beliefs

The previous model is now extended to allow for a set of states of dimension two. Following Piketty (1995), the definition of the probability of success in (8.5) is replaced by a function that depends on two parameters (γ, θ):

$$(8.6) \qquad \pi_{(\gamma,\theta)}(x) = \max\{0, \min\{1, \gamma + \theta x\}\}.$$

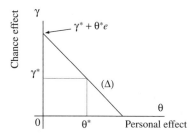

Figure 8.4 Asymptotic beliefs with fixed effort.

Agent t belongs to a dynasty. (He represents generation t.) He observes the history of efforts and of successes (and failures). Incomes in different periods are independent, conditional on effort. The agent has in period 1 an initial subjective distribution on (γ, θ) with density $f_1(\gamma, \theta)$ such that (γ, θ) is bounded. The density of the subjective distribution in period t is denoted by $f_t(\gamma, \theta)$.

Let y_t be the outcome (the income) in period t: $y_t = 0$ or 1. Given the observation of y_t, the belief of the dynasty is updated by Bayes's rule. The density in period t, f_t, is updated at the end of the period so that

$$f_{t+1}(\gamma, \theta) = AP(y_t|(\gamma, \theta), x_t) f_t(\gamma, \theta),$$

where the coefficient A is such that the integral of f_{t+1} is equal to 1, and

$$P(y_t|(\gamma, \theta), x_t) = \begin{cases} \gamma + \theta x_t & \text{if } y_t = 1, \\ 1 - (\gamma + \theta x_t) & \text{if } y_t = 0. \end{cases}$$

We begin by analyzing learning from history and assume as a first step that the level of effort is fixed at $\hat{x}$.

Learning with Fixed Effort

As the initial distribution of (γ, θ) is bounded, $E_t[\theta]$ converges (it is a martingale). When $t \to \infty$ and the number of observations tends to infinity, the estimated probability of success $\gamma + \theta \hat{x}$ converges to its true value by the law of large numbers. The support of the asymptotic distribution on (γ, θ) must therefore be in the locus such that

(8.7) $\gamma + \theta \hat{x} = \gamma^* + \theta^* \hat{x}$,

where γ^* and θ^* denote the true values of the parameters. The asymptotic probability distribution on the structural parameters belongs to the line (Δ) in Figure 8.4. Asymptotically, some agents believe that success is mainly due to chance whereas others believe that effort has a predominant role.

There is no complete learning, because the parameter is of higher dimension than the observations. By the law of large numbers, an arbitrarily large number of observations generates a number in the interval $[0, 1]$, which is of dimension one. This number is not sufficient to estimate the correct value of (γ, θ), which is in a set of dimension two. So far these different beliefs have had no effect on effort, because effort is exogenous.

Endogenous Effort

Suppose now that each agent chooses his effort x to maximize the payoff function

$$u(x) = \frac{E\left[\pi_{(\gamma,\theta)}(x)\right] - x^2}{2a} \quad \text{with} \quad a > 0.$$

Assume there is no corner solution and that beliefs are such that the probability π is between 0 and 1. (The extension is trivial.) Given the specification of the probability where the multiplier of effort is θ, the level of labor supply is $x = a E[\theta]$: it increases, quite naturally, with the belief that effort pays off. From (8.7), the limit distribution of beliefs is on the line described by the equation

(8.8) $\gamma = \gamma^* + a E[\theta](\theta^* - \theta).$

Asymptotic beliefs are represented in Figure 8.5. The higher the expected value $E[\theta]$, the steeper the slope of the line. The region where the distribution of beliefs has a higher density is represented in Figure 8.5 by a contour.

In order to understand the boomeranglike contour, consider agent 1 in the figure, who has a low estimate $E_1[\theta]$. His distribution is on the line (Δ_1), which has a small slope in absolute value (equal to $a E[\theta]$). His density is higher toward the left part of the line, because his estimate $E_1[\theta]$ is small. The agent makes little effort, because he believes that effort is not rewarded.

Agent 2 has by assumption a higher belief $E[\theta]$. The support of his distribution (Δ_2) is steeper, and the main mass of his distribution is to the right of agent 1 because of the higher estimate $E_2[\theta]$. (The mean of the first coordinate of the points on the thick segment is higher.) Agent 2 works more. He is more successful on average than agent 1 because the true value θ^* is positive and effort does pay. However, he still underestimates θ (because $E_2[\theta] < \theta^*$). He knows the probability of success by the law of large numbers. Because he underestimates the value of θ, he must "explain" the higher probability of success (compared with that of agent 1) by a higher value of γ: his mean value of γ is higher than the mean value for agent 1.

The reader can complete the argument for agent 3, who believes $E_3[\theta] > \theta^*$. The model explains why rationally learning agents may end up with labor supplies consistent with their beliefs: the hardworking agents believe that effort pays, whereas the "lazy" ones believe rationally that it has little effect on the outcome.

DYNASTIC BELIEFS

In the previous model, the chance factor operated independently of past realizations of income. Most people would agree that if chance has an impact, it depends on the

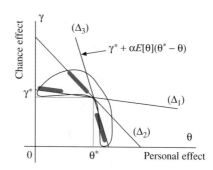

Figure 8.5 Asymptotic beliefs with endogenous effort. The distribution of beliefs in the population is an average of all individual beliefs. The thick segments represent the supports of the asymptotic distributions of three particular agents, in increasing order of expected values $E_1[\theta] < E_2[\theta] < E_3[\theta]$. The population's distribution is represented by a contour.

status or income of one's parents.[9] In the model of Piketty (1995), there is a dynasty of individuals living one period. The economic success of each individual depends on his effort and the income of his parents. Income takes one of two values, y^L or y^H, $y^L < y^H$, and the transition between the two values is a Markov process with transition probabilities

(8.9)
$$P(y_t = y^H | x, y_{t-1} = y^L) = \gamma_0 + \theta x,$$
$$P(y_t = y^H | x, y_{t-1} = y^H) = \gamma_1 + \theta x,$$

where γ_0, γ_1, θ are the structural parameters. Agents learn rationally, from the experience in their own family and the law of large numbers, the correct values of the left-hand side of the previous equations. They also know their labor supply, x. To simplify the model, we assume they do not learn from the experience of other families. (Suppose that they cannot observe the efforts in other families.) The structure of the model is such that the two equations in (8.9) do not enable a family to learn the three parameters γ_0, γ_1, and θ.

In analyzing the asymptotic belief of a family, one can focus on the first equation. The analysis is the same as in the previous model. The asymptotic distribution of (γ_0, θ) has support on the line

$$\gamma_0 = \gamma_0^* + a E[\theta](\theta^* - \theta),$$

where γ_0^* and θ^* are the true values of the parameters. Figure 8.5 applies.

Each family can be indexed by its asymptotic value $E[\theta]$ and moves stochastically among the binary values HH, HL, LH, and LL, with rich parents and high income, rich parents and low income, etc. Assume that all distributions are stationary and that there are a large number of families with a given $E[\theta] = \bar{\theta}$. Within this group, denote by α_H the fraction of agents with high income and by π_{ij} the fraction of people moving from state i to state j ($i, j \in \{L, H\}$). The equality between the flows into

---

[9] We ignore potentially interesting effects such as cognitive dissonance (Festinger, 1957), in which beliefs are chosen such that the interpretation of experience generates a higher belief in one's personal skill.

and out of high income implies

$$(1 - \alpha_H)\pi_{LH} = \alpha_H(1 - \pi_{HH})$$
$$\text{with} \quad \pi_{LH} = \gamma_0 + \bar{\theta}x(\bar{\theta}), \quad \pi_{HH} = \gamma_1 + \bar{\theta}x(\bar{\theta}).$$

Let $\sigma_{HH}(\bar{\theta})$ and $\sigma_{HL}(\bar{\theta})$ be the fractions of agents[10] in states HH and HL in a stationary state. Let $f(\bar{\theta}|HH)$ and $f(\bar{\theta}|HL)$ be the distributions of $\bar{\theta}$ for all agents with experience HH and HL, respectively. By Bayes's rule,

$$\frac{f(\bar{\theta}|HL)}{f(\bar{\theta}|HH)} = \frac{\sigma_{HL}(\bar{\theta})}{\sigma_{HH}(\bar{\theta})} A = h(\bar{\theta})A, \qquad \text{with} \quad h(\bar{\theta}) = \frac{1 - \gamma_1 - a\bar{\theta}^2}{\gamma_1 + a\bar{\theta}^2},$$

and where A is a constant. The function $h(\bar{\theta})$ is strictly decreasing if and only if $a > 0$. We now need a result on distributions.[11]

LEMMA 8.1 *Consider two distributions with densities $f(\theta)$ and $g(\theta)$ such that $f(\theta) = h(\theta)g(\theta)$, where h is strictly decreasing. Then the densities have cumulative distribution functions F and G, respectively, such that for each θ one has $F(\theta) > G(\theta)$: G dominates F in first order.*

From the previous lemma, the median of F is lower than the median of G. Within the population of agents who are in state HL, there is a distribution of expected values $\bar{\theta}$. (Recall that each agent has a distribution on θ.) The median of the distribution in the cell HL is lower than the median of the population, which is in the cell HH.[12]

Let us make the crude simplification that agents who believe that success is due to chance or family background tend to vote on the left for more redistribution.[13] More people vote for the left in cell HL than in cell HH. The same argument can be

---

[10] We have

$$\sigma_{HH}(\bar{\theta}) = \pi_{HH}\alpha_H = \frac{\pi_{HH}\pi_{LH}}{1 - \pi_{HH} + \pi_{LH}} = \frac{(\gamma_1 + a\bar{\theta}^2)(\gamma_0 + a\bar{\theta}^2)}{1 - \gamma_1 + \gamma_0},$$

and

$$\sigma_{HL}(\bar{\theta}) = \frac{(1 - \pi_{HH})\pi_{LH}}{1 - \pi_{HH} + \pi_{LH}} = \frac{(1 - \gamma_1 - a\bar{\theta}^2)(\gamma_0 + a\bar{\theta}^2)}{1 - \gamma_1 + \gamma_0},$$

or

$$\sigma_{HL}(\bar{\theta}) = h(\bar{\theta})\sigma_{HH}(\bar{\theta}) \qquad \text{with} \quad h(\bar{\theta}) = \frac{1 - \gamma_1 - a\bar{\theta}^2}{\gamma_1 + a\bar{\theta}^2}.$$

[11] For the proof, $\dfrac{F(\theta)}{1 - F(\theta)} = \dfrac{\int^\theta h(x)g(x)dx}{\int_\theta h(x)g(x)dx} < \dfrac{h(\theta)\int^\theta g(x)dx}{h(\theta)\int_\theta g(x)dx} = \dfrac{G(\theta)}{1 - G(\theta)}.$

[12] Likewise, the median of the level of effort is lower in the population HL than in the population HH.

[13] To derive this property, Piketty (1995) incorporates in the present model a vote on a linear income tax.

TABLE 8.1 Percentage of votes for the left as a function of experience

	Low-Income Agent	High-Income Agent
Low-income parents	72%	38%
High-income parents	49%	24%

verified as an exercise for the pairwise comparisons of the cells LL and LH and of HL and LL.

Empirical Evidence

Table 8.1 presents data from Cherkaou (1992) on the votes for the left (as opposed to the right) in a population that is partitioned in four groups, according to the income of the agents and the income of their parents.

The pattern in Table 8.1 is intuitive and fits the properties of the model. Note, however, that the argument of Piketty (1995) is subtle: it operates through the endogenous labor supply. If $a = 0$, then the labor supply is fixed, $h(\bar{\theta})$ is constant, and the relation between the probabilities of the four states and the point estimate θ disappears.

8.3 Complete Learning with a Diversity of Private Beliefs

In the previous sections, no agent had any private information and all the learning occurred from the output of actions. We have learned that agents can be trapped in some combination of action and belief. In the monopoly model of McLennan, the action may converge to an incorrect belief that supports that action. If the managers of the monopoly came into their jobs with a variety of private beliefs, the monopoly could experiment on a wider set of actions and learning could converge to the truth. This is one application of an argument by Bala and Goyal (1995), who show that when the distribution of private beliefs is unbounded, learning is adequate: agents choose asymptotically an action that is optimal for the realization of the state of nature. Smith and Sørensen (2001) show a similar result when agents learn from the actions (Chapter 3). The mechanism of learning is different when agents learn from the output of actions. The essential effect of the unboundedness of beliefs is to generate a sequence of correct actions. The observation of the outputs from the correct action generates adequate learning.

8.3.1 The Framework

Following Bala and Goyal (1995), the set of states of nature, Θ, is finite with $|\Theta|$ elements: $\Theta = \{\theta_0, \theta_1, \ldots, \theta_{|\Theta|-1}\}$. The true state is not directly observable, and by convention it is θ_0. The set of actions, Ξ, is finite. This assumption will be discussed below. As in Easley and Kiefer (1988) (see Section 8.5), an action x called the *input* generates a random outcome y called the *output* with a density $f(y|x, \theta)$ that depends on the input and the true state. The yield of the action depends on the input and the output through a function $r(x, y)$. The output will convey information about the state (to some agents or to all agents, depending on the particular model), at least for one action in Ξ. This two-step formulation adds some generality. In a special case, the output and the yield are identical: $r(x, y) = y$.

Let μ be the belief of an agent. This belief is an element of the $|\Theta|$-simplex: $\mu = (\mu(\theta_0), \ldots, \mu(\theta_{|\Theta|-1}))$. The payoff of action x is

$$(8.10) \qquad u(x, \mu) = \sum_{\theta \in \Theta} \mu(\theta) \int_Y r(x, y) f(y|x, \theta) dy.$$

Let $\omega(\theta)$ be the point distribution on θ that assigns probability 1 to θ and 0 to other states. By an abuse of notation, we define

$$u(x, \theta) = u(x, \omega(\theta)) = \int_Y r(x, y) f(y|x, \theta) dy.$$

Hence,

$$(8.11) \qquad u(x, \mu) = \sum_{\theta \in \Theta} \mu(\theta) u(x, \theta).$$

Each agent who takes an action maximizes his payoff $u(x, \mu)$. As in all previous models of social learning, no agent takes into account the impact of his action on the learning by others.

PRIVATE BELIEFS AND BOUNDED RATIONALITY

Each agent is endowed with a private belief $\hat{\mu}$, which is an element of the $|\Theta|$-simplex. Following Bala and Goyal (1995), the distribution of private beliefs is fixed and independent of the state. A distribution of private beliefs that is independent of the state cannot be constructed from the Bayesian framework with a public belief on the state of nature and private signals. The assumption of a fixed distribution is made to focus on the information channel through the observation of outputs.

Over time, agents observe the input–output combinations (x, y) of a subset of the other agents (which may include all agents). Agents have *bounded rationality*: they use input–output observations to infer information about θ, knowing the density function $f(y|x, \theta)$. However, they do not infer any information from the choice of the actions by other agents. The very mechanism of learning in the previous chapters is ignored here. This assumption of bounded rationality is not plausible if the distribution of initial beliefs depends on the state of nature.[14]

---

[14] Some issues have not been explored. If the distribution of private beliefs does not depend on the state, to ignore the message provided by the choice of an agent may be rational if all agents observe the common history h_t, as assumed here. If agents do not share a common history, then the choice of an agent provides some information on his private observations of others. This issue will be examined briefly in the next chapter.

8.3.2 Some General Properties of the Learning Mechanism

Because agents are Bayesian rational, they update their private belief on the state of nature with the history of outputs they observe. An agent's belief is a martingale and thus converges to a *limit belief*, which is in the $|\Theta|$-simplex. Whether individual actions converge to an action that is optimal for the true state is the main issue here. Whether beliefs converge to the truth is less important. Let μ^* be the limit belief of an agent, and x^* an action that is optimal under that belief. If $u(x^*, \theta_0) = u(x^*, \mu^*)$, the agent achieves the optimal payoff asymptotically. We will say in this case that the limit belief is *adequate*. We will also say that the learning is adequate (Aghion et al., 1991).

The key mechanism will be the observation of an infinite sequence of outputs from the same action. Such an action in the sequence of histories for an agent will be called an *infinitely repeated action* (IRA). Because the number of actions is finite, any sequence of histories has at least one such action.

DEFINITION 8.1 (IRA) *An action is an infinitely repeated action for an agent if he observes the output of that action an infinite number of times.*

In the previous chapters, where agents learned from the choice of actions, social learning could stop when the same action was chosen by all agents. Here the repeated choice of an action does not necessarily stop the flow of information, because the output generates a sequence of signals. Those signals may or may not be informative. For example, the output of a crop may reveal little information or nothing about the potential for another crop. We therefore define a discriminating action.

DEFINITION 8.2 (Discriminating action) *An action x discriminates between states θ and θ' if it generates two different distributions of output in the two states: $f(y|x, \theta)$ is not almost surely equal to $f(y|x, \theta')$.*

We will identify conditions under which agents' beliefs converge to the truth or their actions converge to an optimal choice. For this task, the only actions that will matter are those which are the IRAs. Because the set of actions is finite, after some finite time T, any action is an IRA. The observation of the outputs of an IRA will enable agents to use the law of large numbers. This is the meaning of the next result.

LEMMA 8.2 *If an action is an IRA observed by an agent and this action discriminates between the true state θ_0 and some other state θ_j, then the limit belief of the agent is such that $\mu^*(\theta_j) = 0$.*

If an action generates different payoffs in states θ_j and θ_0 where $j \neq 0$ and θ_0 is the true state, it must generate two different distributions of output. Hence, this action discriminates between the true state θ_0 and state θ_j. Using Lemma 8.2, we have the following result.

LEMMA 8.3 *If an action is an IRA, and for some state $\theta_j \neq \theta_0$ one has $u(x, \theta_j) \neq u(x, \theta_0)$ (where θ_0 is the true state), then the limit belief (of any observing agent) is such that $\mu^*(\theta_j) = 0$.*

An *optimal action* $\bar{x}$ is such that $u(\bar{x}, \theta_0) \geq u(x, \theta_0)$ for any $x \in \Xi$. Let $\overline{X}(\theta_0)$ be the set of optimal actions if $\theta = \theta_0$. If an agent is certain that state θ_j is the true state, i.e., if he has the point belief $\mu(\theta_j) = 1$, then he chooses an action that is optimal for state θ_j. Recall that the set of actions is discrete. Hence if $\theta = \theta_j$, any action will generate either the optimal payoff or a strictly smaller payoff. It follows immediately that if the belief $\mu(\theta_j)$ is sufficiently close to 1, the agent chooses an action that is optimal for the state θ_j.

LEMMA 8.4 *There exists $\overline{\mu}$ such that if an agent has a belief $\mu(\theta_j) > \overline{\mu}$, he chooses an action in the optimal set $\overline{X}(\theta_j)$.*

The previous lemma shows that a strong belief in some state induces an agent to choose an action that is optimal for that state. If there is an infinite sequence of observed agents with such strong beliefs, the set of IRAs will contain an optimal action from which one can learn asymptotically sufficient information to make a correct decision. In this chapter, we consider the case of a sequential history that is publicly known by all agents. In the next chapter, each agent will learn from a set of neighbors.

8.3.3 Learning from the Whole History and Sequential Actions

Following Bala and Goyal (1995), the set of agents is countable. Each agent is as described in the previous section. The history at the beginning of period t, $h_t = \{(x_1, y_1), (x_2, y_2), \ldots, (x_{t-1}, y_{t-1})\}$, is the sequence of input–output pairs in the past, and it is public information.

After some finite time, the only actions that are taken are IRAs (because the set of actions is finite). The next result, which is proven in the appendix (Section 8.6), shows that if the set of IRAs contains an optimal action, then learning is adequate for any agent with a positive private belief about the true state.

THEOREM 8.1 *Assume that an optimal action is an IRA. Then for any $\alpha > 0$, there exists T such that if $t > T$, any agent t with private belief about the true state that is not smaller than α ($\hat{\mu}(\theta_0) \geq \alpha$) takes an optimal action.*

In general, one may encounter a situation where some IRAs fail to discriminate between the true state and some other state, and generate a payoff strictly smaller than the payoff of an optimal action. In such a case, learning is not adequate (and therefore not complete). In Chapter 3, herds on a wrong action do not occur if the distribution of private beliefs is unbounded. A similar property has been shown by Bala and Goyal (1995) in the context of the present model. From Lemma 8.4, one can guess that if some agents have a private belief about the true state with $\hat{\mu}(\theta_0) > \alpha$ for α arbitrarily close to one, they choose an optimal action independently of the history. In that case, the set of IRAs will contain an optimal action, and Theorem 8.1 shows that learning will be adequate. The next assumption characterizes unbounded private beliefs about the true state.

ASSUMPTION 8.2 (Unbounded private beliefs) *For any state θ_j and any $\alpha > 0$, the probability that a randomly chosen agent has a belief $\mu(\theta_j) > 1 - \alpha$ is strictly positive.*

Let μ_t be the *public belief* in period t, which is the belief of an agent with uniform private belief who observes the history h_t. (Until the end of this section, $\hat{\mu}_t$ will denote an agent's private belief and $\tilde{\mu}_t$ will denote his belief). By the MCT and Proposition 2.9 (the limit belief cannot be absolutely wrong), μ_t converges almost surely to μ^* with $\mu^*(\theta_0) > 0$. For any path of histories $\{h_t\}$, there exist $\gamma > 0$ and T such that if $t > T$, then $\mu_t(\theta_0) = P(\theta_0 | h_t) > \gamma$.

Let $\overline{\mu}$ be a value such that an agent with belief $\tilde{\mu}(\theta_0) > \overline{\mu}$ chooses an action in $\overline{X}(\theta_0)$ (according to Lemma 8.4). There exists γ' such that if an agent has a private belief $\hat{\mu}$ such that $\hat{\mu}(\theta_0) > \gamma'$, and the public belief in period t is such that $\mu_t(\theta_0) > \gamma$, then his belief $\tilde{\mu}_t$ is such that $\tilde{\mu}_t(\theta_0) > \overline{\mu}$. If he has to choose an action in period t, by Lemma 8.4, he chooses an optimal action.

From Assumption 8.2, it follows that for any path of histories $\{h_t\}$, there exist T and $\alpha > 0$ such that if $t > T$, the probability that an optimal action is taken in period t is at least equal to α. We have the following result.

LEMMA 8.5 *Under Assumption 8.2 of unbounded private beliefs, any path of histories contains almost surely an IRA that is an optimal action.*

From this lemma and Theorem 8.1, we have the next result, which shows that learning is adequate if the distribution of private beliefs is unbounded.

THEOREM 8.2 *Under Assumption 8.2 of unbounded private beliefs, for any $\alpha > 0$ and (almost) any path of histories, there exists T such that if $t > T$, any agent t with private belief about the true state that is not smaller than α ($\hat{\mu}(\theta_0) \geq \alpha$) takes an optimal action.*

As an exercise, the reader may show the following corollary.

COROLLARY 8.1 *Under Assumption 8.2 of unbounded private beliefs, for any $\epsilon > 0$ and any path, there is T such that if $t > T$, the probability that agent t does not take an optimal action is smaller than ϵ.*

Consider the model of McLennan of the monopoly manager facing a zero–one demand (Section 8.1.1). When all agents have the same private belief, the monopoly may not learn the true state: there is with positive probability a set of histories such that agents choose a sequence of actions that converges to the intersection of the two demands and such that beliefs do not converge to the truth. If agents have private beliefs from an unbounded distribution, there cannot be any such history: if there were a path with a public belief converging to μ^* between 0 and 1, there would be agents with sufficiently strong beliefs who would choose actions far away from the intersection point. For these actions, the demands would be very different in the two states, and an infinite string of such observations would reveal the true state.

8.3.4 Extensions

A CONTINUUM OF ACTIONS: THE MANAGERS OF A MONOPOLY

The property of incomplete learning is not restricted to models with a finite set of actions. In the second model of Section 8.1.1, Kiefer (1989) shows numerically that if the myopic managers choose an output level in a continuum, the public belief may converge to the confounding value μ^*. Bala and Goyal (1995) introduce managers with an unbounded distribution of beliefs in such a model. With a diversity of beliefs, the public learning converges to the truth.

Suppose now that the output decision is taken in each period t by a manager with an initial private belief $\hat{\mu}_t$ from a distribution of unbounded private beliefs satisfying Assumption 8.2. The manager combines this belief with the public belief μ_t that is inferred from the history h_t of outputs and profits. Bala and Goyal (1995) simulate numerically the learning process of such a manager when the distribution of $\hat{\mu}$ is bounded and when it is not bounded.

DISCRETE ACTIONS, A CONTINUUM OF STATES, AND RISK AVERSION

As a variation on the framework of Easley and Kiefer (1988), assume there are two actions $x \in \{0, 1\}$ and that the *outputs* of actions 0 and 1 are the realizations of two independent random variables θ_0 and θ_1 that are normal $\mathcal{N}(\mu_x, 1/\rho_x)$. The state of nature is thus defined by the realization (θ_0, θ_1). Agents have a constant absolute risk aversion and have the same information on the state of nature at the beginning of time. Because they observe the same history, they have the same belief in any period. Agent t takes one of the two actions to maximize his *payoff*

$$u = -E[e^{-2\gamma\theta_x}],$$

where $\gamma > 0$. If $\gamma = 0$, the utility function is linear and $u = E[\theta_x]$. At the end of each period, the history, which is public knowledge, is augmented by the variable y_t, which is the observation of the output of the action of agent t, with a noise:

$$y_t = \theta_{x_t} + \epsilon_t \qquad \text{with} \quad \epsilon_t \sim \mathcal{N}(0, \sigma_\epsilon^2).$$

This model has been proposed by Arthur and Lane (1994). It shows how risk aversion may facilitate the onset of an informational cascade. When agents take the same action repeatedly, the uncertainty on the output of the action decreases. Hence, even if the mean does not change, the payoff of the action rises, and agents have more incentive to keep choosing that action. If they do so, the output of the other action may keep a high uncertainty and that action may never be chosen.

Let $\mu_x(t)$ and $\rho_x(t)$ be the mean and the precision of the belief of an agent in period t about the action x. (The beliefs are normal distributions.) The payoff of action x for agent t is

$$U = \mu_x(t) - \frac{\gamma}{\rho_x(t)}$$

with

$$\mu_x(t) = \frac{\rho_x}{\rho_x + n_x \rho_\epsilon} \mu_x + \frac{n_x \rho_\epsilon}{\rho_x + n_x \rho_\epsilon} y_x, \qquad \rho_x(t) = \rho_x + n_x \rho_\epsilon,$$

where n_x is the number of observations of action x in periods before t, and y_x is the average observation of the outputs of these actions.

Herds without Informational Cascades

In this model, informational cascades never occur, but a herd begins at some finite date almost surely. The probability of an incorrect herd is strictly positive. The proof of the next result is left as an exercise.

PROPOSITION 8.3 *All agents herd and take the same action after some finite date, almost surely. The probability that agents switch to another action remains strictly positive in any period.*

When more agents choose the same action, there is more information on its value. There are two effects: The first is on the estimated mean, which may go up or down. The second is a positive effect on the precision of the estimate and thus on the payoff. This higher-precision effect is similar to increasing returns and stimulates herding: Suppose that at some date $\mu_1(t) > \mu_0(t)$, and that the payoff of 1 is also higher than that of 0. Agent t chooses action 1. Unless its output at the end of period t is low, the next agent chooses the same action. Each time this action is chosen, it gets an additional advantage over the other one because of the reduced variance.

8.3.5 Observation of Outputs May Reduce Welfare

Cao and Hirshleifer (2000) consider an example where there are two actions 0 and 1. The payoff of action 0 is random and equal to $1 - b$ or $1 + b$, with equal probabilities. The payoff of 1 is equal to 0 or $2 - a$ with equal probabilities. As in the BHW model, agents, in an exogenous sequence, have the choice between two actions. The parameters a and b are small positive numbers. Agents have a symmetric binary signal of precision q on the payoff of action 1. There is no signal on action 0. The model is equivalent to that of BHW. Because action 1 has an *ex ante* payoff greater than that of action 0, a herd does not occur as long as the sequence of signals is alternating $(0, 1, 0, 1, \ldots)$.

Suppose now that the first agent has a signal that induces him to choose action 0, that the payoff of the action is revealed at the end of the period, and that it is revealed to be $1 + b$. Let $v = 1 + a/2$, and assume $1 + b < v$. If agent 2 has a good signal, he takes action 1 with an expected payoff of v. One sees that the model has the same properties as before, and the *ex ante* value of the welfare level in the long run is unchanged. Suppose now that b increases to such a value that $1 + b$ is greater than v and vanishingly close to v. If the payoff of 0 is revealed to be $1 + b$ (which occurs with probability $\frac{1}{2}$), then a herd on action 0 begins if it is chosen. After period 1, the expected value of the long-term payoff is $1 + b$. However, if $1 + b$ were slightly smaller than v, there would be a strictly positive probability of a herd on action 1, and the expected value of the long-term payoff would be strictly greater. This indicates that the observation of the output of action 0 reduces the expected payoff in the long term. The steps of the formal analysis are outlined in Exercise 8.5.

8.4 Bibliographical Notes

THE FRAMEWORK OF EASLEY AND KIEFER (1988)

Easley and Kiefer (herafter EK) develop and analyze a canonical model of the behavior of an agent who lives an infinite number of periods, optimizes, and learns. In each period, the agent chooses an action that optimizes his payoff and his learning about the state of nature. He learns from the output of his action, which depends on the state of nature. This paper is a must for the reader who wants to study some of the technical aspects of learning. Here, the presentation is limited to a description of its main results.

In each period t, the agent chooses an action $x_t \in \Xi$ and observes a random variable y_t, which depends on the state $\theta \in \Theta$ and on his action. To simplify, the variable y_t is called the output, but it might as well be a cost or a signal. The reward of the agent is a function $r(x_t, y_t)$. His payoff in period t is the expected value of his reward[15]:

$$(8.12) \quad u(x_t, \mu_t) = \int_\Theta \int_Y r(x_t, y_t) f(y_t | x_t, \theta) dy_t \, d\mu_t.$$

By assumption, all variables belong to subsets of $\mathbb{R}^n$. (EK consider more general sets and make suitable assumptions on the continuity of the functions r and f.) The agent

---

[15] The formulation of Easley and Kiefer seems fairly general, but there are other similar specifications that do not fit exactly in their framework. For an example, see Section 8.3.4.

maximizes the expected value of the discounted sum of $u(x_t, \mu_t)$, where the discount factor is $\delta < 1$. He takes into account the impact of his action x_t on his information in period $t + 1$. His welfare in period t is a function $V(\mu_t)$ of his belief, which is similar to a "state variable" in dynamic programming. The optimal welfare level satisfies the dynamic programming equation

$$(8.13) \qquad V(\mu) = \max_{x \in \Xi} \left\{ u(x, \mu) + \delta \int V(\mu') dF(\mu'; \mu, x) \right\}.$$

Under suitable and standard conditions (i) there exists a function V that satisfies this equation; (ii) in any period and for any belief μ, there is a set of optimal actions $A(\mu)$ that is an upper hemicontinuous correspondence (Theorem 3 in EK).

Even though the beliefs μ_t are endogenous to actions, they still form a martingale. The MCT applies, and there is a random value μ_∞ such that $\mu_t \to \mu_\infty$. Asymptotically, there is no learning (EK, Lemma 3), and the optimal action maximizes the instantaneous utility function $u(x, \mu_\infty)$ (Lemma 4). When there is no learning, the optimal action maximizes the current expected payoff $u(x, \mu)$, because there is no capital accumulation. The optimal value of $u(x, \mu)$ in the one-period optimization problem is called the *one-period value function* $V^1(\mu)$.

EK introduce useful definitions: an *invariant belief* μ is a belief such that if x maximizes $u(x, \mu)$, then the *ex post* belief is identical with μ. An *optimal invariant belief* μ is a belief that is invariant when the agent takes an optimal action for the discounted sum of payoffs, $V(\mu)$. A *potentially confounding action* is an action that is optimal for an invariant belief that is different from the correct belief (the atomistic distribution on the true state of nature).

EK show that if there are no potentially confounding actions, then beliefs must converge to the correct belief (Theorem 8). If Θ is finite, the one-period value function is convex, and the discount factor is greater than some δ^*, then beliefs must converge to the correct belief (Theorem 9). If the space of actions Ξ is finite and there is an invariant belief μ^* such that the optimal action for μ^* strictly dominates other actions, then μ^* is optimal invariant for a sufficiently small discount factor (Theorem 10).

EXERCISES

EXERCISE 8.1
Show that the functions $\mu^+(\mu)$ and $\mu^-(\mu)$ defined in (8.3) are increasing.

EXERCISE 8.2 Local stability of the true belief in the model of McLennan
Show that if $\theta = 1$ and $\mu_1 < \mu^*$, then μ_t converges to 0. (Assume that $H(\mu) < \mu$ on $(0, \mu^*)$. You may prove that $H(\mu) < \mu$ if $\mu \in (0, \mu^*)$ and the parameters of the model have appropriate values.)

EXERCISE 8.3 The monopoly model of Easley and Kiefer (1988)

Consider the problem of the monopoly with the demand curve in (8.4). Assume that the manager is myopic and optimizes the profit in the current period, while learning from the history of prices.

1. Show that if μ is the belief (probability of state 1), then the optimal output is

$$\hat{q}(\mu) = \frac{\mu a_1 + (1 - \mu)a_0}{2(\mu b_1 + (1 - \mu)b_0)}.$$

2. Show that the belief in LLR is updated from λ to λ' with

$$\lambda' = \lambda + \frac{1}{\sigma^2}\left(p - \frac{a_0 + a_1 - (b_0 + b_1)\hat{q}(\mu)}{2}\right)$$
$$\times (a_1 - a_0 - (b_1 - b_0)\hat{q}(\mu)).$$

3. Show that under suitable conditions on the parameters of the model, there is an invariant belief in $(0, 1)$ with value

$$\mu^* = \frac{a_0(b_1 - b_0) - 2b_0(a_1 - a_0)}{(b_1 - b_0)(a_1 - a_0)}.$$

EXERCISE 8.4

Consider the model of Easley and Kiefer (1988) in equation (8.4). Assume that the belief of the manager, μ, is different from the stationary belief μ^* (but can be arbitrarily close). Show that for any $\alpha > 0$ there exists $\bar{\epsilon}$ such that if $\epsilon > \bar{\epsilon}$, the belief at the end of the period is at least equal to $1 - \alpha$. Show a similar result for an *ex post* belief smaller than α.

EXERCISE 8.5 Cao and Hirshleifer (2000)

Consider the BHW model where agents have the choice between two projects $\mathcal{A}$ and $\mathcal{B}$. The payoff of $\mathcal{A}$ is 0 or $2 + \epsilon$ with equal probability, and the payoff of $\mathcal{B}$ is $1 + \epsilon$ or $1 - \epsilon$ with equal probability, where ϵ is a small number. Agents have a symmetric binary signal of precision q that $\mathcal{A}$ yields a high payoff. There is no signal on whether $\mathcal{B}$ yields a high payoff. By assumption, $\epsilon < (2q - 1)/(2 - q)$.

1. Show that the standard BHW property of herding occurs. Compute the expected value W_1 of utility of an agent who makes a decision in period T where $T \to \infty$.
2. Assume now that any agent can observe the decisions of past agents and the payoff of project $\mathcal{B}$ if a past agent adopts $\mathcal{B}$. Show that if individual t adopts $\mathcal{B}$ and $\mathcal{B}$ yields a high payoff, all agents k with $k > t$ herd and adopt $\mathcal{B}$. Compute the expected value W_2 of the utility of an agent who makes a decision in period T where $T \to \infty$. Show that $W_1 > W_2$ (Result 1 in Cao and Hirshleifer). Provide an intuitive interpretation.
3. The setting of question 2 is modified in that the payoff of project $\mathcal{B}$ is observed with a delay of T periods. Show by an intuitive argument that if T is sufficiently

large, the setting generates an expected payoff in the long term that is higher than W_1.

4. Assume now that the delay is only one period ($T = 1$ in the previous question). Compute the expected value W_3 of the utility of an agent who makes a decision in period T where $T \to \infty$. Show that $W_3 > W_1$ (Result 2 in Cao and Hirshleifer).

8.5 Appendix

Proof of Lemma 8.4

Let $\bar{u}$ be the maximum yield under state θ_0: $\bar{u} = u(\bar{x}, \theta_0)$ for any $\bar{x} \in \overline{X}(\theta_0)$. Because the set of actions is finite, there exists $\alpha > 0$ such that for any $x \notin \overline{X}(\theta_0)$ we have $u(x, \theta_0) < \bar{u} - \alpha$. We have then

$$u(x, \mu) - u(\bar{x}, \mu) = \mu(\theta_0)\left(u(x, \theta_0) - u(\bar{x}, \theta_0)\right)$$

$$+ \sum_{j \geq 1} \mu(\theta_j)\Big(u(x, \theta_j) - u(\bar{x}, \theta_j)\Big)$$

$$< -\mu(\theta_0)\alpha + (1 - \mu(\theta_0))\,A$$

for some finite number A (because $\sum_{j \geq 1} \mu(\theta_j) = 1 - \mu(\theta_0)$). The result follows with $\bar{\mu} > A/(A + \alpha)$. ∎

Proof of Theorem 8.1

Assume that the set of IRAs contains an optimal action $\bar{x}$ (for the true state θ_0) and an action x such that $u(x, \theta_0) < \bar{u} = u(\bar{x}, \theta_0)$. Fix a number $\alpha > 0$, which can be arbitrarily small, and consider an agent with a private belief $\hat{\mu}$ such that $\hat{\mu}(\theta_0) > \alpha$: such an agent has a positive belief about the true state. In period t, the belief of this agent is $\tilde{\mu}_t$ (which is computed from $\hat{\mu}$ and the public belief μ_t). His payoffs from action x and action $\bar{x}$ are

$$u(x, \tilde{\mu}_t) = \sum_{u(x,\theta_j) \neq u(x,\theta_0)} \tilde{\mu}_t(\theta_j)u(x, \theta_j)$$

$$+ u(x, \theta_0)\left(1 - \sum_{u(x,\theta_j) \neq u(x,\theta_0)} \tilde{\mu}_t(\theta_j)\right),$$

$$u(\bar{x}, \tilde{\mu}_t) = \sum_{u(\bar{x},\theta_j) \neq u(\bar{x},\theta_0)} \tilde{\mu}_t(\theta_j)u(\bar{x}, \theta_j)$$

$$+ u(\bar{x}, \theta_0)\left(1 - \sum_{u(\bar{x},\theta_j) \neq u(\bar{x},\theta_0)} \tilde{\mu}_t(\theta_j)\right).$$

For all the states such that $u(x, \theta_j) \neq u(x, \theta_0)$, we have $\mu_t(\theta_j) \to 0$ (Lemma 8.3). Likewise for the optimal action $\bar{x}$. Because $\hat{\mu}(\theta_0) > \alpha$, the same property holds for $\tilde{\mu}_t(\theta_j)$. From the previous expressions of the payoffs, for any $\epsilon > 0$, there exists T such that if $t > T$,

$$u(x, \bar{\mu}_t) < \epsilon + u(x, \theta_0) \quad \text{and} \quad u(\bar{x}, \theta_0)(1 - \epsilon) < u(\bar{x}, \bar{\mu}_t).$$

Because $u(x, \theta_0) < u(\bar{x}, \theta_0)$, we can choose ϵ such that $\epsilon + u(x, \theta) < u(\bar{x}, \theta_0)(1 - \epsilon)$. For $t > T$, the agent does not choose x. We can repeat the argument for any suboptimal action. Because the number of actions is finite, the upper bound of the values of T is finite and equal to $\overline{T}$. The theorem applies to $\overline{T}$. ∎

9 Networks and Diffusion

It is not what you know, but whom you know.

In the diffusion of a new technology, agents learn from the output of others new techniques or how to use the techniques. Some applications in the adoption of high-yield variety crops are discussed. The theoretical analysis of learning in networks is introduced.

Sociologists were the first to publish empirical studies on the spatial or intertemporal diffusion of innovations, and they began early. In 1897, Durkheim presented maps of suicide frequencies by district in France and Germany to refute the contagion hypothesis of Tarde (Chapter 1). Sociologists are interested in the diffusions of innovations as "social changes."

The agricultural context offers many examples of learning from others with the gradual adoption of new crops and new techniques. The short study by Ryan and Gross (1943) has been pathbreaking in *rural sociology*, which has become a field of investigation in itself. Ryan and Gross interviewed 259 farmers in Iowa where hybrid corn was first introduced in the thirties, and focused on the *time profile* of diffusion. Their results are descriptive: (i) the time profile of the share of hybrid corn in the total corn acreage follows a curve that is similar to the cumulative distribution function of a normal distribution (with some skewness toward the first year of introduction); this profile of adoption has therefore an S-shape (as illustrated in Figure 9.1, from another study by Griliches (1957)); (ii) farmers learned about hybrid corn from salespeople; (iii) during a first phase of the diffusion (three years), 50 percent of the farmers were convinced by salesmen and about 20 percent by neighbors; after this phase, the proportions are reversed. These claims are based on recollections.

The *spatial pattern* of diffusion has been studied by geographers. Hägerstrand (1953) presented maps of the locations in which new techniques were used at

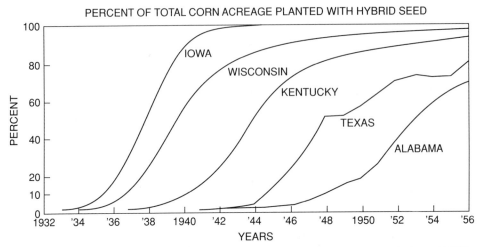

Figure 9.1 **Percentage of total corn planted with hybrid seed.** Reprinted from Griliches (1957).

different points of time in the same region.[1] These include grazing,[2] tests for bovine tuberculosis, soil mapping, postal checking services, and the automobile. One should expect geographers to produce maps. However, it is hard to draw any conclusion from them beyond the examples of diffusion patterns.

Since Ryan and Gross (1943), hundreds of studies on the diffusion of innovations in agriculture, medicine, and other fields have been undertaken by sociologists. They are summarized in the works of Rogers (1995).[3] These studies may elicit three reactions:

1. The wealth of facts and empirical details is extraordinary.
2. Sociologists seem to have an urge to build numerous *ad hoc* concepts. By construction, these concepts cannot be very stable, nor lead to a useful organization of the data, much less have predictive power. (The strength and weakness of economics is to keep parsimonious concepts.)

[1] Hägerstrand lists numerous studies in Swedish by others (e.g., on the dissemination of wheat cultivation in Sweden, on the introduction of steam-powered saws in Norrland between 1850 and 1900, on the glassworks region of southeastern Småland, and on the small-plant industrial region in the western part of that same province).

[2] "It was once a deeply rooted custom among forest district farmers to put their livestock out for grazing in the forest and to allow them to nourish themselves on natural grasses. A shift toward more rational practices – the rotation of crops with pasturing and the improvement of natural grazing areas – began during the first decade of the 20th century" (Hägerstrand, 1953, Chapter 3).

[3] Coleman et al. (1957) analyze the introduction of a new drug – called "gammanym" – in four urban areas. As sociologists, they devote their attention to a portrait of an innovator – an early adopter – (Chapter 4), the adoption lags (Chapter 5), and the networks (Chapter 6). They distinguish two types of doctors, those who are integrated in a hospital network and those who are more isolated. For the first type, the rate of adoption obviously increases faster, with a profile that seems to be concave; for the second type the profile seems to be S-shaped. Wennberg and Gittelsohn (1973) report that the chance of a child having a tonsillectomy varied from 7 percent to 70 percent, depending on his village in Vermont. Phelps (1992), like the Swedish geographers, presents a map of the average length of hospital stays, by state.

3. In quite a few instances, agents seem to be irrational in their behavior toward adoption or rejection of a new technique. However, this is only the case when the learning process is restricted to a very limited set of parameters, as in most theoretical models in this book. Seemingly irrational behavior may be rational when the set of the states of nature is extended beyond the payoff of a particular technique.

THE DIFFUSION CURVE OF HYBRID CORN

The econometric study of Griliches (1957), which was the first of its kind in economics, offers an emblematic contrast with the methods in sociology. Griliches observes the S-shaped patterns of adoption of hybrid corn in different states, as illustrated in Figure 9.1. Using this observation, he first organizes the data with a parsimonious set of parameters. He assumes that the share P_t at time t of acreages planted with hybrid evolves according to a logistic curve with $\log(P_t/(K - P_t)) = a + bt$, where K, a, and b are parameters.[4] The fraction P_t is thus equal to $P_t = K/(1 + e^{-(a+bt)})$ and tends to $K \leq 1$ when t tends to infinity. Each district generates a profile of adoption, or *growth curve*, and a set of estimated parameters (K, a, b). The evolution of the share P_t is presented by states in Figure 9.1.

Griliches has "little doubt that the development of hybrid corn was largely guided by expected pay-off, 'better' areas being entered first, even though it may be difficult to measure very well the variables entering into these calculations" (p. 515). The introduction of hybrid corn in an area depends on the installation of a center that supplies hybrids suitable to the area. The introduction of such a center depends on its future expected profits. According to Griliches, the introduction date of hybrids depends on the potential of an area and is strongly determined by profit-maximizing suppliers.

Consider the *date of origin* of an area, which is the date at which 10 percent (an arbitrary ratio) of the area is seeded in hybrids. This date is computed with the logistic curve fitted in the area. The date of origin in an area is positively correlated with the date of origin in the nearest area. The date is regressed on an index of density of corn acreage in the area and the date of origin in the most immediate area. For Griliches, the new variety is introduced first in the areas where corn has a higher density in the land, because this is where the supply is more profitable.[5] Likewise, there is a "contagion" between adjacent areas because supply centers can provide seeds to neighboring areas.

The adjustment coefficient b (which determines the slope of the logistic curve) is determined by the *acceptance* of farmers and thus by demand factors. "Differences in the rate of acceptance of hybrid corn, the differences in b, are due at least in part to differences in the profitability of the changeover." Griliches finds that the variable

---

[4] Griliches does not provide an economic model to support the logistic curve.
[5] He finds $Y = -17.8X_1(2.5) + 1.02X_{10}(0.07)$, with the standard errors in parenthesis ($R^2 = 0.982$), where X_1 is the index of density and X_{10} the date in the adjacent area.

bK is positively related to the average number of corn acres per farm reporting corn and the average difference between hybrid and traditional yields (or the prehybrid average yield).[6] In the models of learning that will be considered below, the differential yield plays an important role. Variables emphasized by rural sociologists, such as the socioeconomic status or the level of living, are not significant.

9.1 Optimization and Diffusion of Innovations

The standard example of innovation is the introduction of a new variety of crop in agriculture (e.g., maize, wheat, rice). We can distinguish two types of learning. Agents may learn whether a new variety is suitable for the region and is profitable, or they may learn how to produce efficiently the new variety. The two issues are analyzed in separate models in the next two sections.

9.1.1 Learning about the Profitability of an Innovation

The value of the new activity defines the state of nature. It is a realization of the normal distribution $\mathcal{N}(\mu_1, 1/\rho_1)$. The output of any agent i is the sum $\theta + \epsilon_i$, where ϵ_i is an agent-specific component that is normally distributed $\mathcal{N}(0, 1/\rho_\epsilon)$. This output is observed at the end of the period in which the agent enters the new activity. Suppose there are n entrants in a period. Their idiosyncratic components are independent, and the observation of their outputs is informationally equivalent to the variable $\theta + (\sum_1^n \epsilon_i)/n$, which is a Gaussian signal on θ with precision $n\rho_\epsilon$. The precision of the period's signal increases linearly with the number of entrants. In equilibrium, there will be an arbitrage between immediate "investment" and delay with strategic substitutability: the flow of information increases with the number of adopters of the new technology; the value of delay for the observation of this information is therefore higher, so that there is more incentive to delay adoption.

Following Persons and Warthers (1995), assume a continuum of agents, in order to simplify the analytics. Each agent has one option, which can be exercised in any period to enter the new activity. An agent is characterized by his (fixed) cost of entry c, which is the realization of a distribution on the support $(0, \infty)$ with c.d.f. $F(c)$. Let X_t be the mass of agents entering the new activity in period t. We generalize the linear relation between the precision of the period's output and the number of agents: at the end of period t, all agents observe

$$y_t = \theta + \frac{\epsilon_t}{\sqrt{X_t}} \qquad \text{with} \quad \epsilon_t \sim \mathcal{N}(0, 1/\rho_\epsilon).$$

The precision of the signal y_t is $\rho_\epsilon X_t$; it is linear in the mass of entrants.

---

[6] He finds $bK = c_0 + 0.0073 X_3 (0.0008) + 0.079 X_7 (0.009)$ ($R^2 = 0.57$), where X_3 and X_7 are the number of acres per farm and the yield difference.

Equilibrium

The equilibrium is defined by a sequence of consecutive intervals $I_t = [c_{t-1}, c_t)$ ($c_0 = 0$), which are increasing and randomly determined by the history. In period t, investing agents are defined by a cost in the interval I_t. The highest cost of investing agents, c_t, is determined by arbitrage, as in Section 6.2.1, as an application of the *one-step property*: an agent with cost c_t is indifferent between (i) investing right away and (ii) delaying for one period only and then investing if and only if in the next period the payoff of investment is positive. There is a positive level of investment if and only if the expected value of θ given the history is higher than the lowest cost among the remaining agents.

Because the output in each period is normally distributed, the belief about θ at the beginning of period t is normal $\mathcal{N}(\mu_t, 1/\rho_t)$. At the beginning of period t, the costs of the remaining agents, who have not invested yet, are higher than c_{t-1}.

If $\mu_t < c_{t-1}$, no remaining agent has a positive payoff of investment. There is no investment and therefore no information. The belief is identical in the next period, and so on. A cascade begins with no investment in any period.

If $\mu_t > c_{t-1}$, the value of the highest cost of investment in the period, c_t, is computed by arbitrage. The payoff of immediate investment is $\mu_t - c_t$. If the agent delays, he observes

$$y_t = \theta + \frac{\epsilon_t}{\sqrt{X_t}} \qquad \text{with} \quad X_t = F(c_t) - F(c_{t-1}),$$

and he updates his belief to $\mathcal{N}(\mu_{t+1}, 1/\rho_{t+1})$ with $\rho_{t+1} = \rho_t + X_t\rho_\epsilon$ and

$$(9.1) \qquad \mu_{t+1} = \frac{\rho_t}{\rho_t + X_t\rho_\epsilon}\mu_t + \frac{X_t\rho_\epsilon}{\rho_t + X_t\rho_\epsilon}\left(\theta + \frac{\epsilon_t}{\sqrt{X_t}}\right).$$

If the agent delays, he invests in the next period if there is any investment in that period by the one-step property: he has the lowest cost in the next period. The payoff of delay that is the value of holding the option to invest is

$$(9.2) \qquad V = \delta E_t[\max(\mu_{t+1} - c_t, 0)].$$

The agent can compute at the beginning of period t the strategy of other agents and therefore the mass of investment in the period, X_t. He knows *ex ante* the precision of the information that will be revealed about θ in the period. (This is a nice property of Gaussian random variables, which is exploited a few times in this book.) At the beginning of period t, the agent anticipates that μ_{t+1} has a normal distribution $\mathcal{N}(m_t, \hat{\sigma}_t^2)$, because $m_t = E[\mu_{t+1}]$ is a martingale. The variance of the change of the mean belief, $\mu_{t+1} - \mu_t$, is obtained from (9.1):

$$\hat{\sigma}_t^2 = \left(\frac{X_t\rho_\epsilon}{\rho_t + X_t\rho_\epsilon}\right)^2\left(\frac{1}{\rho_t} + \frac{1}{X_t\rho_\epsilon}\right) = \frac{X_t\rho_\epsilon}{\rho_t(\rho_t + X_t\rho_\epsilon)}.$$

A higher level of aggregate entry X_t generates more information and therefore a higher expected value of the change of the mean belief. The variance $\hat{\sigma}^2$ is an increasing function of X_t.

The value of delay in (9.2) is increasing in the variance of μ_{t+1} (Exercise 9.1). There is strategic substitutability: a higher level of aggregate activity increases the value of the option to invest V. The equilibrium is characterized by the following result.

PROPOSITION 9.1 *In any period t: if $\mu_t \leq c_{t-1}$, there is no investment in period t, or after; if $\mu_t > c_{t-1}$, all agents with cost $c \in (c_{t-1}, c_t)$ invest in period t, where c_t is the unique solution of*

$$\mu_t - c_t = \delta E_t[\max(\mu_{t+1} - c_t, 0)],$$

where the variable μ_{t+1} is defined in (9.1).

Because the distribution of costs is unbounded, intuition implies that the game ends almost surely in a finite number of periods.

Properties

1. Let T be the last period in which there are some entrants. By definition, $\mu_{T+1} \leq c_T$. There are some last entrants with cost near c_T who regret they have invested. They have *ex post* a negative payoff. This property is found in other models such as that of Caplin and Leahy (1993).
2. The level of investment is below the optimum: assume for example that in some period t, $\mu_t = c_{t-1}$. Agents with a cost slightly above c_{t-1} have a negative payoff, but the value of the loss would be negligible compared with the information gain provided by the observation of the output of their investment.
3. One may conjecture that for some parameters, the model exhibits on average a diffusion curve with an S-shape (Exercise 9.2).

GROWING WHEAT AND RICE IN INDIA

Munshi (2002) studies the introduction and diffusion of high-yield variety (HYV) wheat and rice in India during the 1960s. In his model, farmers learn about the yield of the new crop. Let x_{it} be the total acreage allocated by farmer i in period t to the new variety. Assume that the yield of the traditional crop is known but the yield of the new crop is subject to uncertainty. Farmers learn from the payoffs of past plantings in their own farm and in other farms of the same village. A structural model of decision is not specified, but one could find one such that the acreage x_{it} is approximated by a linear function

(9.3) $x_{it} = \alpha_0 + \alpha_1 x_{it-1} + \alpha_2 X_{t-1} + \alpha_3 y_{t-1}.$

The acreage in the previous period is a proxy for the agent's learning from the outputs in his own farm. The total acreage planted by other farmers in period $t-1$, X_{t-1}, is learned at the end of period $t-1$; it embodies the average belief by others at the beginning of period $t-1$. The average yield y_{t-1} at the end of period $t-1$ provides a signal on the yield of the new crop. The learning from doing is measured by α_1, and the learning from others is measured by $\alpha_2 > 0$ and $\alpha_3 > 0$.

The Two Pitfalls of Estimation in Models of Learning

Equation (9.3) is standard in econometric models of learning. These models attempt to measure effects of *endogenous learning*. In the model of Munshi, agents learn from their own farm or from the choices and the actions' results of other agents. All these models face two problems:

1. There may be a *diffusion of exogenous information* that is not observable by the econometrician. This information may affect the coefficients of the equation, which should measure only the endogenous learning.
2. Agents may *mimic* others, i.e., imitate others in a mechanical way.

Consider now the model of Munshi, and suppose that exogenous information on the yield of the new variety is available to half the agents at the beginning of period $t-1$ and to all agents at the beginning of period t: the diffusion of this information is exogenous. The information is positively correlated with the acreage in period $t-1$ (because of the planting by half the farmers), and in period t for the farmers who are informed with a one-period delay. Such a variable may increase the estimated value of the coefficient α_2, which depends on the correlation between the acreage in periods $t-1$ and t. If there is a mimicking effect, it increases the value of α_2 as well.

In order to avoid the two pitfalls mentioned above, Munshi analyzes the diffusion of HYV for two different crops, wheat and rice. The difference between the two crops is that the output of a particular plot seeded in HYV rice is more dependent on idiosyncratic factors than a plot seeded in HYV wheat. The diffusion of exogenous information and mimicking are probably similar for the two crops. A stronger effect for wheat than rice indicates stronger social learning for HYV wheat than for HYV rice. The exogenous diffusion of information and mimicking should not have much of an impact on α_3, which measures the learning from the observation of the average output in the village.[7]

The data were collected from villages in three consecutive years, 1968 to 1970. Because there is one lag, there are two sets of regressions, for 1969 and 1970. The results, which are stronger for the second of these two years, show that α_2 is significant for

---

[7] Munshi notes that the acreage x_{it} depends also on the variance of the estimated yield by the farmer. This variance is not observable, but it should be a decreasing function of past experience. Because past experience is increasing in the acreage in the past, the variance effect increases the coefficients α_1 and α_2.

wheat and rice, but higher for wheat. Symmetrically, the coefficient of the previous period's acreage in the farm, α_1, is significant for rice but not for wheat. The yield coefficient, α_3, is significant for wheat but not for rice.[8] These results are confirmed by the statistical analysis on different data collected at the district level.

A Critique of the Diffusion Models with Learning about Yields

In the models of learning from yields, agents delay because they are not sure whether the yield of the new crop is positive or not. If the delay is rational, however, the distribution of adoptions *ex post* should exhibit this uncertainty. One should observe *ex post* successes, but also failures and patterns where the adoption stopped at a low level. This does not seem to be the case in the econometric studies. Of course, one may argue that econometricians have focused on success stories, but in this case there may be a selection bias. One may suspect that when farmers delay the introduction of new crops, they wait for new information about the inputs of the new crops. We now turn to this type of model.

9.1.2 Learning How to Use a New Technology

The yield of HYVs is highly sensitive to the proper use of inputs such as fertilizers and pesticides, and farmers have an incentive to delay in order to learn how to adjust these inputs.

THE TARGET MODEL

In order to simplify the exposition, assume that all agents are identical. The payoff of an agent from the new crop depends on the acreage x in the new crop and the average use y of fertilizer per acreage. To simplify (and without loss of generality), the price of fertilizer is assumed to be negligible. The payoff function in a period (a crop cycle) is

$$u(x, y) = ax - \frac{x^2}{2} - \alpha x E[(\theta - y)^2].$$

The first two terms exhibit the decreasing marginal returns, and the last term embodies the uncertainty about the use of the fertilizer. If the agent has a belief $\mathcal{N}(m, \sigma^2)$ about θ, he chooses $y = m$, and the last term depends only on the variance σ^2.

---

[8] Table 3 in Munshi (2002) shows two typical regressions with standard errors in parenthesis (year 1970):

$$\begin{array}{ll}
\text{wheat (417 observations):} & x_{it} = 0.089 + 0.228x_{it-1} + 1.738X_{t-1} + 0.056y_{t-1} + \cdots; \\
R^2 = 0.298 & \qquad\quad (0.038) \quad (0.189) \qquad (0.352) \qquad (0.009) \\
\text{rice (608 observations):} & x_{it} = 0.090 + 0.846x_{it-1} + 1.299X_{t-1} - 0.0001y_{t-1} + \cdots. \\
R^2 = 0.365 & \qquad\quad (0.016) \quad (0.224) \qquad (0.312) \qquad (0.005)
\end{array}$$

In each period, the agent gets two independent signals about θ, one from his own farm and one from the observation of his neighbors:

$$s_t = \theta + \frac{\epsilon_t}{\sqrt{\beta x_t}},$$

$$s_t' = \theta + \frac{\epsilon_t'}{\sqrt{\beta' \bar{x}_t}}, \qquad \text{with} \quad \epsilon_t \text{ and } \epsilon_t' \text{ independent } \mathcal{N}(0, 1),$$

where $\bar{x}_t$ is the average acreage in his neighborhood, and β, β' are parameters. The parameter θ has an initial distribution that is $\mathcal{N}(\mu_1, 1/\rho_1)$. The precision of each signal is a linear function of the acreage in his own farm and of the average acreage in other farms. If the agent has a precision ρ_t about θ at the beginning of period t, his precision in the next period is

$$\rho_{t+1} = \rho_t + \beta x_t + \beta' \bar{x}_t.$$

Define the *experience* of the agent as the cumulative acreage for all previous periods, and the *average experience* as the cumulative average acreage of others:

$$z_t = \sum_{k=1}^{t-1} x_k, \qquad \bar{z}_t = \sum_{k=1}^{t-1} \bar{x}_k.$$

The profit in period t is

(9.4) $\qquad u(x_t, z_t, \bar{z}_t) = a x_t - \frac{x_t^2}{2} - \frac{\alpha x_t}{\rho_0 + \beta z_t + \beta' \bar{z}_t},$

where ρ_0 is the precision of the estimate about θ before the first crop cycle.

The farmer chooses a program $\{x_t\}$ to maximize the discounted sum of the payoffs

(9.5) $\qquad J = \sum_{t \geq 0} \delta^t E[u(x_t, z_t, \bar{z}_t)]$

with

$$u(x, z, \bar{z}) = a x - \frac{x^2}{2} - \frac{\alpha x}{\rho_0 + \beta z + \beta' \bar{z}},$$

$$z_{t+1} = z_t + x_t, \qquad \bar{z}_{t+1} = \bar{z}_t + \bar{x}_t.$$

He takes the average acreage of other agents $\bar{x}_t$ as given. By symmetry, $\bar{x}_t = x_t$.

Let $k_t = \rho_0 + \beta z_t + \beta' \bar{z}_t$. Hence, $k_{t+1} - k_t = \beta x_t + \beta' \bar{x}_t$. The model is similar to a growth model where x_t is consumption and the experience variable k_t is capital.

Let λ be the shadow price of k. The first-order conditions can be written

(9.6)
$$a - x_t - \frac{\alpha}{k_t} + \zeta \beta \lambda_t = 0,$$

$$\lambda_t = \delta \left(\lambda_{t+1} + \alpha \frac{x_{t+1}}{k_{t+1}^2} \right).$$

The parameter ζ is introduced to compute simultaneously the solutions of two problems: if $\zeta = 1$, the agent optimizes the function J and takes into account the learning by doing in his own farm for future benefits; if $\zeta = 0$, the agent maximizes his current-period payoff without taking the information gain into account. However, when making a decision about fertilizer in period t, he still takes into account the learning from the observation in his own farm and in the farms of others.

One can see immediately that learning operates through two channels. The first channel is an *experimentation effect*: because a farmer learns from his own output, the larger the number of plots in the new crop (the acreage), the larger the number of independent signals he receives and hence the more he learns toward an efficient use of input in the future. The mechanism gives an incentive to seed more plots in order to learn more.

The second channel is the learning from others. There is an information externality between farmers, but none of them takes into account the externality in his decisions. The more others seed, the lower the variance of θ in the next period, and therefore the lower the information gain from one's own experience. This effect induces a strategic substitution by different farmers.

The Optimal Solution

The solution is found by taking $\zeta = 1$ in equation (9.6). The analysis of the problem is similar in discrete and in continuous time. To simplify the exposition, we use first the continuous-time formulation. Let r be the (fixed) rate of discount. The first-order conditions take the form

$$a - x - \frac{\alpha}{k} + \beta\lambda = 0,$$

(9.7)
$$\alpha\frac{x}{k^2} = r\lambda - \dot{\lambda},$$

$$\dot{k} = (\beta + \beta')x.$$

In the first equation, the agent takes into account the information benefit accruing from his own acreage: the value of λ is multiplied by β. (A social planner would multiply by $\beta + \beta'$.) In the last equation, the accumulation of knowledge is due to the agent's experience and to the average experience from others: both β and β' appear.

Differentiating the first equation with respect to time and using all equations (9.7) for substitutions, we find that the dynamic path is characterized by the evolution of the variables (k, x) given by

$$\dot{k} = (\beta + \beta')x,$$

(9.8)
$$\dot{x} = \left(\frac{\alpha\beta'}{k^2} + r\right)x + r\left(\frac{\alpha}{k} - a\right).$$

On a phase diagram (Exercise 9.4) the locus (k, x) such that $\dot{x} = 0$ is an increasing graph with an asymptote $x = a$. The variable x is increasing in time above the curve

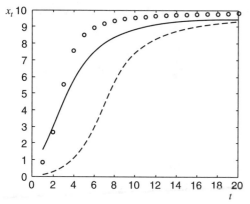

Figure 9.2 Time profiles of adoption of the new technique. The lower curve is the profile over time of the acreage when farmers choose the amount of acreage to maximize the current payoff without taking into account the gain of information. The higher curve is the profile when agents take into account the additional learning obtained by more intensive use of the new technique and more experimentation. (Parameters: $a = 10, \alpha = 0.99, \beta = 0.002, \gamma = 0.01, \delta = 0.98, \rho_0 = 0.1$). For the dotted curve, the parameter γ, which measures the information externality, is increased from 0.01 to 0.03. The acreage is smaller in the first two periods because agents rely more on the externality and invest less in information. It is larger after period 3 because more has been learned in the first two periods.

$\dot{x} = 0$, and decreasing below the curve. It follows that in the solution of the optimization problem, x must be above the curve and converge to a as $t \to \infty$. However, the property of an increasing profile conveys, in general, no information on the concavity of the profile. The solution with dynamic optimization must be solved numerically. An example of simulation (using the discrete formulation) is presented in Figure 9.2.

On the dynamic path, the acreage is an increasing function of time. The model does not exhibit an S-profile. We now compare this solution with that when agents do not optimize over time.

The Myopic Solution

Assume now that the agent does not experiment in a rational way, but takes into account the experience of the past: $\zeta = 0$. The previous computation yields the dynamic equation

$$\dot{x} = \gamma x(a - x)^2 \quad \text{with} \quad \gamma = \frac{\beta + \beta'}{\alpha}.$$

The time derivative of the slope $\dot{x}$ is equal to

$$\ddot{x} = \gamma(a - x)(a - 3x).$$

The time derivative increases with time if $x < a/3$ and decreases if $x > a/3$. The acreage x exhibits an S-shaped time profile. The simulation of the previous example with ζ replaced by 0 is represented in Figure 9.2.

The difference between the optimal dynamic and the myopic solutions is intuitive. At the beginning of the introduction of a HYV crop, the uncertainty is large and the payoff of the crop adjusted for the uncertainty is small. The acreage is small and does not increase much. This phase corresponds to the convex part of the S-shaped time profile. When agents take into account the effect of learning by doing and the higher payoffs in the future, they raise their input x during the initial phase. This effect abolishes the convex part of the profile, which becomes a concave function of time for the entire horizon.

EMPIRICAL STUDY

Any empirical analysis of the imitation of others is about the changes of agents who are neighbors either in time or in space. The previous model is the theoretical model behind the econometric study of Foster and Rosenzweig (1995), hereafter FR. They take the neighborhood unit as the village. The issue is whether farmers in the same village learn from each other. As mentioned previously, we should be aware of the two problems raised by exogenous information and by mimicking.

The data are from a panel that provides longitudinal information for 4,118 households in 250 villages for three consecutive crop years from 1968 to 1970. The innovation is HYV rice seeds. The fraction of farmers using HYV seeds grew from 19 to 42 percent during the three years. Because of lagged terms, the years 1969 and 1970 can be used. FR use two types of tests.

First, they estimate the profit function $u(x, z, \bar{z})$ in (9.4). Recall that the argument z measures the effect of learning by doing (from one's own experience), whereas $\bar{z}$ measures the effect of learning from others. The profit function is linearized with the addition of agent-specific features like education as explanatory variables, and the estimation is on first differences in order to omit farm-specific effects. Some attention is devoted to the removal of spurious effects that relate the profitability of a farm and its rate of expansion.

Second, FR estimate the decision rule as in equation (9.7), which is repeated here:

$$(9.9) \qquad x_t = a - \frac{\alpha}{k_t} + \beta \zeta \lambda_t,$$

where $\zeta = 1$ for rationally planning farmers and $\zeta = 0$ for myopic farmers, and $\beta \lambda_t$ is the value of information from an additional unit of acreage. However, FR do not solve the optimization problem, and they do not have a measurement of the marginal value of experience, λ_t. They are content with estimating a linear equation that is the same as the profit function, where the dependent variable is now the acreage increment, $x_t = z_t - z_{t-1}$ (in discrete time). It is hard to interpret the results of such an equation. It is even harder to relate its coefficients with the results of the estimation of the payoff function in the first step. In fact, the only consistent method is to estimate a structural model. Such an estimation could be done if the behavioral equation is obtained as a solution of the optimization problem, which depends on the structural parameters of the model, and the estimation of these parameters through the comparison of the behavioral equation (or the payoff function) with the data. FR do not pursue this method. They simulate the evolution of adoption for the estimated decision function, and they obtain an S-shape. The previous theoretical model has shown that the adoption profile is more likely to be the S-shape when agents do not optimize the current acreage as a function of the anticipated learning.

9.2 Learning in Networks

Conley and Udry (2000a, 2000b) study how families learn from each other about the quantity of fertilizer to be used with pineapple trees in Ghana. Pineapple trees are sensitive to fertilizer. The model is similar to the previous target model, with a quadratic term $U = -(y - \theta)^2$, where y is the amount of fertilizer and θ is a random variable.[9] One of the interesting features of the study is the construction of *information neighborhoods* from survey data. By definition, agents i and j are informationally linked if i is observed by j or j is observed by i. The neighborhood of i is the set of agents informationally linked to i. The information links are obtained from direct interviews.[10] Neighborhood relations are represented by Conly and Udry in a map, which is reproduced here in Figure 9.3. The figure shows that for pineapple growers in Ghana, the village is not the appropriate definition of a neighborhood in which agents learn from each other. One can see that informational neighbors are not identical to geographical neighbors.

Conley and Udry show that if an agent is informationally linked to an agent who increased fertilizer use over the survey period *and* had profit higher than the median, then he was more likely to use fertilizer.

9.2.1 Neighbors

Following Bala and Goyal (1998), there are N agents indexed by $i \in N = \{1, \ldots, N\}$. Each agent i observes at the end of each period the actions and the payoffs of the agents j who are in a subset $N(i) \subset N$. The set $N(i)$ is defined as the *neighborhood* of i. This framework may be compared with that of Banerjee and Fudenberg (1995), discussed in Section 5.3.2. In that model, agents observe the actions – not the outputs – of a sample of randomly selected agents in the population. The sampling in the whole population is important for the pooling of all the agents' information. In this section, the neighborhoods are fixed and do not depend on time. As in the

[9] A regression of profit per plant, y, on fertilizer input, x, produces the estimated equation $y = ax - bx^2 + \cdots$, with $a > 0, b < 0$, which shows that the productivity of fertilizer is not monotonic in its argument.

[10] The interviewer asks specific questions like "Have you asked . . . for advice about your farm? How often?" Other methods were used to minimize underestimates of the neighborhoods.

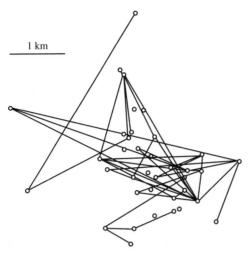

1 km

Figure 9.3 Information neighborhoods. A link represents a relation in which an agent at one end receives information from the agent at the other end. There is no privileged direction for the information flow. (Reproduced with the permission of Conley and Udry.)

examples of the previous section, agents observe both the actions and the outcomes of the actions of their neighbors. Recall that the use of the term neighbor does not necessarily imply geographical proximity. (See for example Figure 9.3.)

The framework is related to that of Section 8.3.1, with which the reader should be familiar. There is a finite set Θ of states of nature, and each agent is endowed in the first period with a private belief on the $|\Theta|$ states of nature $\{\theta_0, \ldots, \theta_{|\Theta|-1}\}$. In each period, each agent chooses the action $x \in \mathbb{R}$ to maximize the payoff,

$$(9.10) \qquad u(x, \mu) = \sum_{\theta \in \Theta} \mu(\theta) \int_Y r(x, y) f(y|x, \theta) dy,$$

which is the same as in (8.10). The variable y may be any variable that affects the return $r(x, y)$. It could be the output, the return itself, or some other variable. Although agents act repeatedly, it is assumed that they behave myopically: they do not experiment for better decisions in the future. This assumption is made in order to focus on the main issue: the diffusion of information in networks.

Let us highlight the difference from the "linear" framework of Section 8.3.3: (i) in each period, each agent takes a decision; (ii) there is no common history; each agent learns from the history of his own neighbors.

The belief (probability on the set Θ) of any agent j tends to a limit value by the MCT. Hence, after some finite date, the action of an agent is fixed, say, to x_j. Suppose that this agent is a neighbor of agent i. Action x_j is an IRA for agent i, who gets asymptotically perfect information on the payoff of action x_j. His limit payoff cannot be less than the payoff of x_j. We have the following result.

LEMMA 9.1 *An agent has asymptotically a payoff at least as high as that of any of his neighbors.*

Bala and Goyal (1998) introduce the notion of connectivity.

CONNECTED SOCIETY

Agent i is connected to agent j if there is a finite sequence of agents $\{i_l\}_{1 \leq l \leq L}$ such that $i_1 = i$, $i_L = j$, and i_l is a neighbor of i_{l-1}. A *connected society* is a society in which any two agents are connected. The next result of Bala and Goyal (1998) follows from Lemma 9.1.

PROPOSITION 9.2 *In a connected society, the payoff of any agent tends to the same value u^*.*

The limit payoff u^* may be suboptimal if agents herd on a wrong action, namely an action that does not discriminate between the true state and another state. As in the previous section, we consider the case of unbounded private beliefs in the sense of Assumption 8.2. The next result is similar to Theorem 8.1. Its proof is an application of the previous results and techniques (Exercise 9.3).

THEOREM 9.1 *In a connected society and under the assumption 8.2 of unbounded private beliefs, after finite time, the actions of all the agents are optimal.*

9.2.2 The Curse of Information

One of the important themes in the preceding chapters is that more information can slow down the process of social learning, or can actually prevent any learning. We find this principle at work again when agents learn from the outcomes of actions.

THE ROYAL FAMILY AND INFORMATIONAL CASCADES

Bala and Goyal (1998) show that more observations can reduce welfare. If a group of a few individuals is observable by all agents, they may initiate an informational cascade. Bala and Goyal call this group the "royal family." This analogy was anticipated by Tarde and his "water tower" of the aristocracy. Take away this group, and the power of the masses will establish the truth: if each agent observes only relatively small and disjoint neighborhoods and the number of agents tends to infinity, the probability of adequate learning tends to 1. The property is shown in an example by Bala and Goyal.[11]

---

[11] For the general result, the reader is referred to their study. Bala and Goyal also consider the case where the outputs of actions generate unbounded signals. From the previous analyses in this book, one can see that such signals will substitute for unbounded private signals and induce adequate learning, asymptotically.

Assume two states of nature, θ_0 and θ_1 with equal probabilities *ex ante*, and two actions 0 and 1. Action 0 yields 0 or 1 randomly with equal probabilities. If $\theta = \theta_1$, action 1 yields 1 with probability π and 0 otherwise, with $\pi > \frac{1}{2}$. If $\theta = \theta_0$, the probabilities are switched; the probability of success with a yield of 1 is $1 - \pi$. State θ_1 is the good state, in which action 1 has a higher expected yield. There are N agents, each with a SBS of precision q. An agent chooses action 1 if and only if he believes state θ_1 to be more likely. Agents are located on a circle, and the neighbors of agent i are agents $i - 1$ and $i + 1$.

In addition to his two surrounding neighbors, each agent observes the agents $\{1, 2, 3, 4\}$. This group of four individuals is observed by all and is called the *royal family*.

In the first period, each agent follows his own signal, because he has not observed anyone yet. Suppose that the binary signals of agents are such that each individual in the royal family chooses action 1 in the first period, and that the output of each action in the royal family in the first period is 0. The probability of this event is strictly positive.

At the end of the first period, each agent has two types of information: his private signal (which he received at the beginning of time), and the outputs of the individuals he observes. We assume that the power of the first signal is weak with respect to the second, i.e., $q - \frac{1}{2}$ is small with respect to $\pi - \frac{1}{2}$.

Consider an individual who is not in the royal family and observes four bad outcomes from action 1 in the royal family. He observes at most three good outcomes from his two immediate neighbors and his own action. His observation from the outputs generates a belief (probability of state θ_1) that cannot be higher than after the observation of a single failure (output equal to 0). The power of that information increases with the value of π. When the precision of his SBS, q, is sufficiently small with respect to π, his belief at the end of the first period is smaller than $\frac{1}{2}$, whatever his private signal. In period 2, he chooses action 0.

The same argument is even stronger for any member of the royal family. In period 2, all agents choose action 0. Because that action provides no information on the state, beliefs are unchanged at the end of period 2. The choices are the same in period 3, and so on: an informational cascade begins in period 2. From that period on, all agents are herding.

The probability that the royal family induces all agents to herd on a wrong action has a lower bound that is strictly positive and independent of the number of agents.

SANS FAMILLE ROYALE

Assume that each individual observes only his two immediate neighbors and that the state is good ($\theta = \theta_1$). Let $h_t(i)$ be the history of observations of individual i in period t from his neighbors and his own outputs. Let $\mu_t(i)$ be his belief from that history: $\mu_t(i) = P(\theta = \theta_1 | h_t(i))$. Individual i computes his belief in period t by updating $\mu_t(i)$ with his private signal.

Because the individual is Bayesian, $\mu_t(i)$ tends to a limit $\mu_i^* > 0$, almost surely. Because the initial value of $\mu_t(i)$ is $\frac{1}{2}$ (nature's probability of choosing state θ_1), the expected value of μ_i^* is $\frac{1}{2}$. In the good state, that expected value is greater than $\frac{1}{2}$. Hence the probability that $\mu_i^* > \frac{1}{2}$ is strictly positive. The signal of individual i is equal to 1 with a positive probability. Hence, individual i chooses action 1 after some finite date and gets the optimal payoff after that date, with a strictly positive probability $\alpha > 0$.

The reader can check that the society is connected. If individual i gets the optimal payoff asymptotically, all agents do so (Theorem 9.1). The interesting part of the argument is the reverse property. The probability that all individuals do not get the optimal payoff asymptotically is smaller than $1 - \alpha$.

Consider now individual $i + 3$. He observes the outputs of the actions of individuals $\{i + 2, i + 3, i + 4\}$. These are not observed by individual i. The outputs in the history $h_{i+3}(t)$ are independent of those in the history $h_i(t)$. The event $\mu_{i+3}^* > \frac{1}{2}$ is independent of the event $\mu_i^* > \frac{1}{2}$, and obviously the private signal of $i + 3$ is independent of the private signal of i (conditional on the state). The previous argument can be repeated. All individuals get the same payoff asymptotically by Theorem 9.1. This payoff is not optimal if it is not optimal for both individuals i and $i + 3$. Because the two events are independent, the probability is smaller than $(1 - \alpha)^2$.

The repetition of the argument for a larger number of agents shows that the probability of no optimal payoff, asymptotically, has an upper bound that tends to 0 exponentially when the number of individuals in the society tends to infinity.[12] If there is an infinite number of agents, there is no failure of social learning, asymptotically.

9.3 Bibliographical Notes

Neighbors were introduced in models of learning from others' actions by Allen (1982a). An agent chooses $x \in \{0, 1\}$ in each period and "adopts an innovation" if $x = 1$. The adoption is reversible. The decision rule is the specification of a probability of adoption, which depends on the choices of actions of the neighbors of the agent. The only assumption is one of *nonstubbornness*: the probability of adoption is strictly positive for any choice of the neighborhood. One defines a *global phase*, the long-run distribution of the probabilities that $x = 1$ on the set of agents. The analysis focuses exclusively on that distribution. The main result is the existence of a unique distribution under the assumption of nonstubbornness. It is a straightforward consequence of the results in the literature on Markov random fields, to which Allen refers for a proof.

The paper assumes a probabilistic decision rule, but this rule need not be *ad hoc*: it may use Bayesian inference from the payoffs of the neighbor's actions. The model can take into account payoff externalities, positive or negative. Its main shortcoming

---

[12] Bala and Goyal provide some numerical simulations in which the convergence of the probability is indeed exponential.

in comparison with the literature on learning is the absence of memory from history. (An agent does not learn from his own action, but this restriction could probably be lifted.) The flavor of the model is similar to that of automata with neighbors (as in the game of life). The results of the paper may be a bit too general for interesting applications.

In Allen (1982b), $x = 1$ is defined as the state of an *informed* agent. (Agents can learn and forget.) Most of the paper is isomorphic to the previous one, except for a section on dynamics where the global phase is not constant. A special case of the model in continuous time generates the logistic curve of the diffusion.[13]

EXERCISES

EXERCISE 9.1

1. Assume that $x \sim \mathcal{N}(m, \sigma^2)$. Show that for $c < m$,

$$V = E[\max(x - c, 0)]$$
$$= \frac{1}{\sqrt{2\pi}\sigma} \int_{-a} (x + a)e^{-x^2/2\sigma^2} dx \qquad \text{with} \quad a = m - c > 0.$$

2. Show that the function $G(\sigma) = \frac{1}{\sigma} \int_{-a} (x + a)e^{-x^2/2\sigma^2} dx$ is increasing in σ when $a > 0$.

EXERCISE 9.2

Simulate numerically the model of Section 9.1.1 with all the noise terms $\epsilon_t \equiv 0$. Determine whether the time profile of adoption has an S-shape.

EXERCISE 9.3

Prove Theorem 9.1.

EXERCISE 9.4

Determine the phase diagram for the dynamic equations (9.8).

---

[13] Let y_t be the fraction of informed agents: then $\dot{y}_t = ay_t(1 - y_t)$, where $a > 0$ is a constant. This equation is found in other models of diffusion (Gersho and Mitra, 1975).

10 Words

If we all think alike, it means we do not think anymore.

Trust but verify.

In this chapter, the actions of agents (experts) are words (messages). The payoff depends on the message and some independent information of the receiver of the message. The condition for no herding and telling the truth is the same as in the BHW model of Chapter 4. In some cases, the payoff depends on a reputation for being informed or for being nonmanipulative. An expanded set of messages may not improve the transmission of information (contrary to Chapter 4). If the expert has information on the independent information of the receiver, the receiver should try to increase his information. The order in which experts should speak in a panel (trial jury) is analyzed: the antiseniority rule does not seem to be superior to other rules.

Communication with words is the subject of a vast literature. This chapter will be selective and focus on the relations between models of communication through words (models of "cheap talk") and the issues of social learning that are addressed in other parts of this book. For example, herding may arise in financial markets because of the observation of others' actions or because of the behavior of financial advisors who are influenced by others' predictions. We will see that herding on actions and herding on words occur under similar conditions.

In the generic setting, an agent is an expert with private information on the state of nature, and his action takes the form of a message that is sent to a receiver. How can he transmit his information credibly by mere words? The key is that the receiver has some independent information on the true state – information that may be gotten before or after the time the expert gives his advice. The receiver thus can *verify* the expert's message against his independent information. (The precision of the independent information of the receiver does not matter.) The payoff of the expert depends on his message (his advice) and on the independent information of the receiver.

Section 10.1 presents the basic model with two states and a binary private signal of the expert. For simplicity, the receiver verifies exactly the true state *ex post* (as an investor who experiences the fluctuations of the stock market after receiving an advice). Three types of payoff functions are considered.

(i) The least restrictive case is that of an arbitrary function with two arguments: the expert's message and the state as verified by the receiver. The goal of the expert is to conform as much as possible to the verified state. His belief is formed from the public belief and his private signal. If the public belief in one of the two states is high, the probability of that state is high even with a private signal favoring the other state. In that case, the expert predicts the same state as the public belief. The expert tells the truth (sends a prediction according to his private signal) only if the public belief is not too strong on one of the two states. The condition for truthtelling by the expert turns out to be identical to the condition for no herding in the BHW model of Chapter 4.

(ii) The payoff is based on reputation. This reputation may be valuable because of future business for the expert, or his ability to have influence in the future. The reputation is about the high precision of the private information. There are two types of private signals for the expert, one more informed than the other; and, in a first case, the expert does not know the quality of his signal. A key difference from (i) is that the value of reputation, and therefore the payoff of the expert, depends on an equilibrium. If the expert sends an irrelevant message (he *babbles*), then the receiver may ignore his message. If the receiver ignores his message, however, the expert has no incentive to tell the truth. There is always a *babbling equilibrium*. We focus on the condition for the existence of a *truthtelling equilibrium*. It is similar to the condition in case (i): the public belief, as expressed by the probability of one of the two states, must be neither too high nor too low. When the expert knows the quality of his private information, the expert with low precision herds for a wider set of public beliefs than the highly informed expert.

(iii) The payoff is derived from a reputation for not being a manipulative expert. All experts have private information of the same precision, but some experts would like the agent to take a specific action. As an example, some people would like to systematically increase welfare programs. An unbiased expert may be in a position to support a particular program, but he does not want to be identified with those people. In order to enhance his reputation, he may advise against the program.

In Section 10.2, the set of messages is expanded while keeping two states. An expert may give a strong or a weak recommendation that the market will go up or down, and the receiver can perceive only that the market goes up or down (not the amount of the change). Why would the expert give a weak recommendation, thus revealing that his information has low precision? The analysis confirms the intuition. There is no truthtelling equilibrium. An expert has an incentive to give the strongest possible advice (in the direction most likely to occur). The problem is that the receiver can verify the advice only against one of two states. If the state takes values in a richer set, for example the evolution of the market is in the set of positive numbers, then the expert may have an incentive to tell the truth.

In all the models considered so far, the expert does not know the independent information used by the receiver for the verification and the reward of the expert. This assumption is relaxed in Section 10.2.3. For example, the expert may know the financial literature read by the receiver, or the consultant may know the prejudice of the boss. It is essential that the receiver does not know what the expert knows about him, or how the expert uses that information. If the receiver knows what the expert knows about him, he can simply "factor out" the expert's information on him from the advice and still get at the expert's true knowledge.

In Section 10.3, there is a collection of "experts." How does the opinion issued by the first have an impact on the saying of the second, and so on? People influence each other in jury trials (e.g., the motion picture *Twelve Angry Men*); financial advisors or economic forecasters are suspected of herding.

When experts are put in an exogenous order, the basic model of Section 10.1 is repeated in a sequence. The public belief evolves after each expert's messsage, and there is a herd by all remaining experts if the public belief favors one of the two states sufficiently strongly. The model is isomorphic to the BHW model. The isomorphism is not affected if the private signals of the experts are correlated.

In the Talmud, the elder speaks after the young. Presumably the elder is wiser, and his advice could intimidate the young into assenting instead of conveying the information truthfully. This issue is examined in Section 10.3.2.

10.1 Advice by One Expert

There are two states of nature $\theta \in \{0, 1\}$. The agent is an *expert* with private information on θ. Without loss of generality, this information takes the form of a signal s, which is a SBS with a precision that may or may not be random. If the precision of the signal is random, unobserved by the expert and of mean ρ, the information of the signal is equivalent to that of a binary symmetric signal with known precision equal to ρ.

The expert sends to a receiver a message m that is a (possibly random) function of his signal, $m(s)$. The expert cannot communicate more than his information, which is in the set of values $\{0, 1\}$. We can therefore assume that his message takes values in the set $\{0, 1\}$. The truthtelling strategy will be defined[1] by $m(s) = s$.

---

[1] My son Sebastian frequently reminds me that $m(s) = 1 - s$ is also a truthtelling strategy.

10.1.1 Evaluation Payoff after Verification

Assume the receiver observes the state after receiving the message from the expert. For example, the receiver asks for financial advice, takes some action – to buy or to sell – and rewards the expert a few weeks later after observing the evolution of the market. The receiver rewards the expert according to an *evaluation function*, which is a function of the message and of the state and is defined by four values: $v_{m\theta}$ for $(m, \theta) \in \{0, 1\} \times \{0, 1\}$. Exercise 10.1 extends the model by allowing the receiver to have some imperfect information on the state in the form of a symmetric binary signal z with precision $q \in (\frac{1}{2}, 1]$. When $q < 1$, one may assume that the receiver gets his private signal at the same time or before the message of the expert. It is essential that the private signal z of the receiver is not known by the expert. (Otherwise the expert would just send a message equal to z in an attempt to please the receiver.) Exercise 10.1 shows that the results of this section apply to the extension.

The expert computes his payoff by assessing the probabilities of the receiver's independent verifications. This payoff is a function $V(s, m)$ of his private signal s and of his message m:

$$(10.1) \qquad V(s, m) = P(\theta = 1|s, \mu)v_{m1} + P(\theta = 0|s, \mu)v_{m0},$$

where his belief $P(\theta = 1|s, \mu)$ depends on his private signal and on the public belief μ according to Bayes's rule.

The truthtelling strategy is optimal if it yields to the expert a payoff that is not strictly smaller than that obtained from deviating. We have two incentive compatibility constraints, one for each signal value of the expert:

$$(10.2) \qquad V(s_1, s_1) \geq V(s_1, s_0) \quad \text{and} \quad V(s_0, s_0) \geq V(s_0, s_1).$$

From the expression of $V(s, m)$ in (10.1), these constraints are equivalent to

$$(10.3) \qquad P(\theta = 1|s_0, \mu) \leq c \leq P(\theta = 1|s_1, \mu)$$

$$\text{with} \quad c = \frac{v_{00} - v_{10}}{v_{11} + v_{00} - v_{01} - v_{10}}.$$

Because the probabilities $P(\theta|s, \mu)$ are the beliefs of the expert, the incentive compatibility constraints are identical to the condition for no herding in the BHW model where agents have a cost of investment c. The previous condition is equivalent to a condition on the *public* belief in the BHW model:

$$(10.4) \qquad \mu^* \leq \mu \leq \mu^{**},$$

as in Proposition 4.1. This condition is intuitive. The goal of the expert is to predict the state in order to conform to the information of the receiver. Suppose that the public belief about $\theta = 1$ is strong with $\mu > \mu^{**}$. The expert takes into account his private signal and the public belief to predict the state. His belief about $\theta = 1$ is strong even if he has a signal 0. Because he is rewarded for conforming his message to the true state, he predicts $\theta = 1$ whatever his private signal. He *is herding,* exactly as in the BHW model where the action maximizes the payoff of a real investment.

Consider the important case of a symmetric evaluation function where the receiver gives a fixed reward for a "correct" message $m = \theta$, and a smaller reward for an "incorrect" message with $m \neq \theta$:

$$(10.5) \qquad v_{00} = v_{11} > v_{10} = v_{01}.$$

The value of the parameter c in (10.3) is equal to $\frac{1}{2}$. The truthtelling condition becomes

$$1 - \rho < \mu < \rho,$$

where ρ is the precision of the expert's signal. The range of values of the public belief with truthtelling by the expert increases with the precision of his information.

If the receiver can choose the reward function, he may always get the private information of the expert by choosing $v_{m\theta}$ such that the value of c in (10.3) falls between the beliefs of an optimistic and a pessimistic expert (with signals 1 and 0). In some cases, however, rewards cannot be implemented by the receiver. A number of studies have assumed that the evaluation function is generated by the reputation of the expert.

10.1.2 Equilibrium with an Evaluation Based on Reputation

In the previous section, the precision of the expert's signal is known. Assume now there are good and bad experts with high and low precisions of their private information. A message that is observed to be correct after the receiver gets to know the true state raises the reputation of the expert. Reputation may be a powerful incentive to send a message that gives the best possible prediction.

The expert has a SBS that has precision ρ_H with probability α, and precision $\rho_L < \rho_H$ otherwise ($\rho_L \geq \frac{1}{2}$). Suppose, as a first step, that the expert does not know the precision of his signal. The implicit assumption is that he has more than one signal with the same precision and cares about his *reputation*, i.e., the probability that he is endowed with high-precision signals. His *ex ante* reputation is α, and $v_{m\theta}$ is his *ex post* reputation as perceived by the receiver who compares[2] the message m with the state θ. The value $v_{m\theta}$ could also be an increasing function of the reputation. An example of a reputation function is given in Exercise 10.2.

The evaluation by the receiver depends on the strategy of the expert, and the strategy of the expert depends on the evaluation function, which can be regarded as the strategy of the receiver. Both strategies have to be determined simultaneously in a game. The situation is thus different from the previous case with an exogenous function $v_{m\theta}$.

---

[2] As in the previous case, the independent information of the receiver could also be imperfect.

THE BABBLING EQUILIBRIUM

The endogenous property of the reward function is highlighted by the existence of the babbling equilibrium. If the agent sends a message that is independent of his signal, he cannot be evaluated. His message is ignored by the receiver, and his reputation stays constant at α. If the receiver does not listen, however, the expert has no incentive to speak the truth. No strategy can strictly improve his reputation. He sends an irrelevant message: he babbles. For example, he can send $m = 1$ for any private signal s, or a random value. For any value of the public belief, there is a babbling equilibrium. This property did not appear in the previous section, where the receiver could choose the reward function.

THE TRUTHTELLING EQUILIBRIUM

Suppose the agent tells the truth with $m = s$. Let $\mathcal{H}$ and $\mathcal{L}$ be the events that his signal has high or low precision. By Bayes's rule, the *ex post* reputation is

$$(10.6) \qquad v_{s\theta} = P(\mathcal{H}|s, \theta) = \frac{P(s|\mathcal{H}, \theta)\alpha}{P(s|\mathcal{H}, \theta)\alpha + P(s|\mathcal{L}, \theta)(1 - \alpha)}.$$

The quantities $P(s|\mathcal{H}, \theta)$ and $P(s|\mathcal{L}, \theta)$ are the probabilities of the realization of the expert's signal given the type of the signal and the state of nature. They depend only on the structure of the expert's signals. Because the signal is symmetric,

$$(10.7) \qquad v_{11} = v_{00} > v_{10} = v_{01}.$$

A truthtelling equilibrium exists if the public belief μ satisfies the constraint (10.4). Comparing with the previous section, if $\mu \in [\mu^*, \mu^{**}]$, there are now two equilibria: in the first, the agent tells the truth; in the second, he babbles. If μ is outside of the interval $[\mu^*, \mu^{**}]$, babbling defines the unique equilibrium, as in the previous section. The comparison between cascades in the BHW model and the babbling equilibrium applies. Proposition 10.1 summarizes the previous discussion and introduces an additional result.

PROPOSITION 10.1 *Let ρ be the average precision of the expert. For any value of the public belief $\mu = P(\theta = 1)$, there is a babbling equilibrium that is stable.*

Let $\rho = \alpha\rho_H + (1 - \alpha)\rho_L$ be the average precision of the expert's signal. If $1 - \rho < \mu < \rho$, there is a truthtelling equilibrium that is stable. If $\frac{1}{2} < \mu < \rho$ $(1 - \rho < \mu < \frac{1}{2})$, there is an equilibrium in which the expert tells the truth if he has a good (bad) signal and lies with some probability if he has a bad (good) signal. This equilibrium is unstable.

The concept of stability in the proposition is elementary: if the expert increases by a small amount his probability of lying, the receiver adjusts the evaluation function, to which the response of the expert is to reduce his probability of lying. In the case of the unstable equilibrium of the proposition, a small increase of the probability of lying induces a variation of the evaluation function to which the best response is to lie for sure.

Although the partially revealing equilibrium is unstable and should be dismissed as an implausible outcome, its intuition may be useful. Assume the expert sends the message 1 if he has signal 1, and the message 1 with probability ζ if his signal is 0. The evaluations v_{00} and v_{01} do not depend on ζ, because the probability of lying reduces the probability of the message $m = 0$ for both types of experts. The evaluation v_{11} is decreasing in ζ, because the probability of lying reduces the power of the message $m = 1$. The evaluation v_{10} is smaller than α, because of the incorrect prediction, but if ζ tends to 1, the message 1 is uninformative with an *ex post* evaluation near α. v_{10} is increasing in ζ. The payoff difference between lying and telling the truth is

$$V(0, 1) - V(0, 0) = P(\theta = 1 | s = 0, \mu)(v_{11} - v_{01})$$
$$+ P(\theta = 0 | s = 0, \mu)(v_{10} - v_{00}).$$

In this expression, the probability that multiplies v_{10} is higher than the probability that multiplies v_{11}. If initially the expert randomizes and is indifferent between the messages $m = 0$ and $m = 1$, an increase in his probability of lying ζ has a positive impact on the above payoff difference: the expert has a strict incentive to lie (Exercise 10.4).

When the prior μ is sufficiently strong and $\mu \notin [\mu^*, \mu^{**}]$, babbling is the only equilibrium. Is this bad for the receiver? Not necessarily: he would ignore the advice of the expert anyway if he were to assess the more likely state. A truthful message by the expert would not change this assessment.

THE TYPE OF THE EXPERT IS (ALMOST) PUBLICLY KNOWN

Assume $\rho_H > \frac{1}{2}$ and $\rho_L = \frac{1}{2}$. From the analysis in the previous section, the expert tells the truth if the public belief is in the interval $(1 - \rho, \rho)$ with $\rho = \rho_H \alpha + 0.5(1 - \alpha)$. Suppose that the value of α is infinitesimally close to one: the probability that the expert is not informed is vanishingly small. Asymptotically, the expert gives his best possible advice given his precision ρ_H. The case $\alpha \rightarrow 1$ generates the following result.

PROPOSITION 10.2 *If the type of the expert is known with a probability infinitesimally close to one, there is a truthtelling equilibrium in which the expert speaks against the public belief if and only if he believes his advice is more likely to be true.*

THE EXPERT KNOWS HIS TYPE (ASYMMETRIC INFORMATION)

Suppose now that the expert receives with probability α a SBS with precision ρ_H and with probability $1 - \alpha$ a SBS with precision $\rho_L < \rho_H$. The expert knows the precision of his private signal, whereas the receiver knows only α. The evaluation function is computed as in the previous case: it rewards conformity with the true state. Each expert behaves as in the previous model and computes his belief using the public belief and his private signal. Assuming a symmetric evaluation function as in (10.5), each expert with precision ρ sends a message identical to his signal if and only if the public belief μ is such that $1 - \rho \leq \mu \leq \rho$. This range is $[1 - \rho_L, \rho_L]$ for the expert with low precision. It is narrower than the range in the case where the experts cannot observe the precision of their signal. In general, the model applies whether experts know their precision or not. The important assumption is that there are at least two levels of precision and the receiver cannot observe the precision of the expert's information.

10.1.3 Reputation for Nonmanipulation: PC Behavior?

A person may say what is "politically correct" instead of what she truly thinks in order to identify herself with some group of people. There is more than one possible motive for this identification. The need to associate oneself with a cause is probably important. During times of polical oppression, formal or informal, it is a good idea to say the "right thing."

Morris (2001) takes the opposite view: a person may say what is politically correct because she wants to show that she is objective against a backdrop of biased people. She opposes an aid program that she knows to be good because she does not want to be identified with some "liberals" who systematically promote welfare programs.[3]

The model of Morris is a variation on the model in the previous section. The bad expert has now the same information as the good expert, but he is biased: he provides advice to manipulate the receiver's action in some direction. As in the previous section, there are two states of nature, $\theta \in \{0, 1\}$, with equal probabilities *ex ante*. The receiver faces an expert of an unknown type, honest or dishonest, i.e., good (with probability α) or bad. After receiving the message, the receiver chooses an action $x \in \mathbb{R}$ that maximizes $-E[(x - \theta)^2]$.

In order to focus on the issue of manipulation, assume the good and the bad experts have a SBS on θ with the same precision q. The good expert wants the receiver to maximize his payoff, and the bad expert wants the receiver to choose a level of action as high as possible. We consider here a one-period model in which the payoff of the good expert is

$$(10.8) \qquad U(s, m) = -E[(x - \theta)^2] + \beta E[v_{m\theta}],$$

where β is a positive parameter and x is the action taken by the receiver following the expert's message. The expectations are made by the expert. They depend on his information from his private signal s. The first term is the payoff of the receiver. The determinants of his action x are omitted for simplicity. The second term is the

---

[3] The argument is usually illustrated with a conservative manipulator (Morris, 2001). This is further indication that the model has little to do with PC behavior, but may explain politically *incorrect* behavior.

expected value of the reputation, which is updated by the receiver after comparing the message m with the true state θ. The person who advises in favor of a welfare program knows that her reputation to be objective will be modified only once the comparison between the advice and the observation of whether the social program is good or not is made.

The first term in the expression for the payoff $U(s, m)$ is new. It reflects the property that the good expert cares about the payoff of the receiver. In the second term, the value of the reputation is taken to be linear, but it could be endogenized (Exercise 10.2). The main assumption is that the payoff of reputation should be an increasing function.

The payoff of the bad expert is

$$(10.9) \qquad \hat{U}(s, m) = x + \gamma\, E\,[v_{m\theta}].$$

The first term embodies the bias. The bad expert cares about reputation because a higher reputation enhances his manipulative power.

The model will show that in an equilibrium (i) under some conditions, the bad expert lies and says 1 whatever his message; (ii) there may be multiple equilibrium strategies for the good expert; in any equilibrium, he either tells the truth, or says 0 whatever his signal in order to enhance his reputation.

THE GOOD EXPERT

The main issue is the behavior of the good expert, so we assume that the bad expert has a given strategy: if his signal is 1, then his message is 1; if his signal is 0, his message is 1 with probability $z \in (0, 1]$, because he wants to manipulate the advisee into taking action 1. The optimization of the strategy z will be analyzed later. Because $z > 0$, a message 1 is more likely to come from the bad expert, and the message 0 increases the reputation of the expert.[4]

If the good expert sends the message 0, he gets an improvement of his reputation. He therefore always sends the message 0 if he has a private signal $s = 0$. The problem arises when his private signal is 1. He may want to send the message 0 in order to enhance his reputation. The cost of doing so is the error committed by the receiver in the period. We consider therefore the following strategies: the good expert tells the truth if his signal is 0, and sends the message $m = 0$ with probability $\zeta \in [0, 1]$ if his signal is 1. We look for an equilibrium value of ζ (given the strategy z of the bad expert). In an equilibrium, the receiver knows the values of ζ and z. If he receives the message m, he computes his expected value of θ as a function of the probability of facing a good expert and the strategies of the good and the bad experts. Let $x(m, \zeta)$ be this expected value, which is also his level of action. (The strategy z is omitted from the

---

[4] The message 0 with a verified state 1 is not indicative of a poorly informed expert, because all experts have the same precision.

arguments because it is given.) It is computed through Bayes's rule.[5] We can verify –
or, better, derive from intuition – that for any $\zeta \in (0, 1)$, the action is higher after the
message 1, $x(0, \zeta) < x(1, \zeta)$, and for $\zeta \in [0, 1]$,

(10.10) $\quad$ $x(1, \zeta)$ is decreasing in ζ and $x(1, 0) < q$,
$\quad\quad\quad\quad$ $x(0, \zeta)$ is increasing in ζ and $x(0, 1) < q$.

The evaluation of the reputation at the end of the period is given by the four values
$v_{m\theta}$ as in Section 10.1.1. One shows[6] that

$$v_{01}(\zeta) \geq v_{00}(\zeta) \geq \alpha \geq v_{11}(\zeta) \geq v_{10}(\zeta).$$

Moreover,

(10.11) $\quad$ $v_{00}(\zeta)$ and $v_{01}(\zeta)$ are increasing,
$\quad\quad\quad\quad$ $v_{10}(\zeta)$ and $v_{11}(\zeta)$ are decreasing.

The payoff of the good expert in (10.8) takes the form

$$U(s, m) = -\pi(s) + x(m, \zeta)(2\pi(s) - x(m, \zeta))$$
$$+ \beta\Big(\pi(s)v_{m1} + (1 - \pi(s))v_{m0}\Big),$$

where $\pi(s)$ is his probability of state $\theta = 1$ (which is equal to q if $s = 1$ and to $1 - q$
otherwise).

$\quad$ One verifies that if the expert has a signal $s = 0$, he is strictly better off by sending
the truth $m = 0$ than by sending the message $m = 1$. Truthtelling is the only optimal
strategy in this case. Assume now that the expert has a private signal $s = 1$. Let $\Delta(\zeta)$
be the difference between the payoffs of sending $m = 0$ (lying) and sending $m = 1$

---

[5] Namely,

$$\frac{x(1, \zeta)}{1 - x(1, \zeta)} = \frac{P(m = 1|\theta = 1)}{P(m = 1|\theta = 0)} = \frac{\alpha q(1 - \zeta) + (1 - \alpha)(q + (1 - q)z)}{\alpha(1 - q)(1 - \zeta) + (1 - \alpha)(1 - q + qz)},$$

$$\frac{x(0, \zeta)}{1 - x(0, \zeta)} = \frac{P(m = 0|\theta = 1)}{P(m = 0|\theta = 0)} = \frac{\alpha(1 - q + q\zeta) + (1 - \alpha)(1 - q)(1 - z)}{\alpha(q + (1 - q)\zeta) + (1 - \alpha)q(1 - z)}.$$

[6] Indeed,

$$v_{00} = \frac{\alpha(q + (1 - q)\zeta)}{\alpha(q + (1 - q)\zeta) + (1 - \alpha)q(1 - z)},$$

$$v_{11} = \frac{\alpha q(1 - \zeta)}{\alpha q(1 - \zeta) + (1 - \alpha)(q + (1 - q)z)},$$

$$v_{10} = \frac{\alpha(1 - q)(1 - \zeta)}{\alpha(1 - q)(1 - \zeta) + (1 - \alpha)(1 - q + qz)},$$

$$v_{01} = \frac{\alpha((1 - q) + q\zeta)}{\alpha((1 - q) + q\zeta) + (1 - \alpha)(1 - q)(1 - z)}.$$

(telling the truth):

$$\Delta(\zeta) = U(1, 0) - U(1, 1) = A(\zeta) + \beta B(\zeta)$$

with

$$A(\zeta) = x(0, \zeta)(2q - x(0, \zeta)) - x(1, \zeta)(2q - x(1, \zeta)),$$
$$B(\zeta) = q(v_{01}(\zeta) - v_{11}(\zeta)) + (1 - q)(v_{00}(\zeta) - v_{10}(\zeta)).$$

From (10.10), $A(\zeta)$ is an increasing function in ζ. The property is intuitive: $A(\zeta)$ is negative because it is the loss from a piece of bad advice in the period. When $\zeta \to 1$, the advisee pays less attention to the advice (and chooses an action closer to $\frac{1}{2}$). Hence, the loss measured by $A(\zeta)$ is smaller in absolute value (it tends to zero), and the term $A(\zeta)$ increases.

From (10.11), the reputation effect $B(\zeta)$ is an increasing function in ζ. When ζ is 1, the good expert never sends the message 1 and the reputation effect is the strongest.

The monotone properties of $A(\zeta)$ and of $B(\zeta)$ imply that, in an equilibrium, the differential payoff of lying, $\Delta(\zeta)$, is increasing in the probability of lying, ζ. Depending on the parameters of the model, one of the following cases takes place:

- If $\Delta(1) < 0$, there is a unique equilibrium strategy $\zeta = 0$: the good expert tells the truth.
- If $\Delta(0) > 0$, there is a unique equilibrium strategy $\zeta = 1$: the good expert always sends the message $m = 0$, independently of his signal.
- If $\Delta(0) \leq 0 \leq \Delta(1)$, there are two stable equilibrium strategies, $\zeta = 0$ and $\zeta = 1$. There is an equilibrium strategy $\zeta \in (0, 1)$, but this strategy is *unstable*: if ζ increases slightly from the equilibrium value (more accurately, if the perception of ζ by the receiver increases slightly), then the good expert should use the strategy $\zeta = 1$. Likewise, *mutatis mutandis*, if ζ is reduced from its equilibrium value.[7]

THE BAD EXPERT

Assume now that the stragegy of the good expert, ζ, is taken as given. The payoff function of the bad expert is

$$\hat{U}(s, m) = x(m, z) + \gamma\left(\pi(s)v_{m1} + (1 - \pi(s))v_{m0}\right),$$

where $\gamma > 0$ is a fixed parameter. The functions $v_{m\theta}$ are obviously the same as in the payoff of the good expert. Suppose that the bad expert has the signal $s = 0$. We have

$$\hat{\Delta}(z) = \hat{U}(0, 1) - \hat{U}(0, 0)$$
$$= x(1, z) - x(0, z)$$
$$+ \gamma\left((1 - q)(v_{11}(\zeta) - v_{01}(\zeta)) + q(v_{10}(\zeta) - v_{01}(\zeta))\right).$$

---

[7] Morris (2001) emphasizes the equilibrium in which the good expert randomizes but does not verify the stability of the equilibrium.

Using footnote 6, this function is *decreasing* in ζ. The optimum strategy of the bad expert is unique. If $\hat{\Delta}(0) < 0 < \hat{\Delta}(1)$, the optimal strategy is random with z strictly between 0 and 1. In a Nash equilibrium, the strategies ζ and z of the good and the bad experts are determined simultaneously.

10.2 Larger Sets of States and Messages

How robust are the previous results when the set of states, Θ, and the set of signal values, S, are expanded (with identical sets of messages and private signals)? A critical issue is the dimensions of the two sets. The expert reveals the truth only because of the evaluation, and the evaluation is based on the message and the state. If S has a higher dimension than Θ, the comparison between the message, which is in a rich set, and the state, which is in a poor set, may not allow for truthtelling incentives.

10.2.1 A Set of Signals Richer Than the Set of States

There are two states of nature, and the set of values of the expert's private signal is expanded to an arbitrary number of elements. Can the message be reliably equal to the expert's signal? As in the previous sections, we distinguish the case where the receiver can implement a reward function of his choice from the case where the reward is constrained to depend on the *ex post* reputation of the agent.

AN ARBITRARY REWARD FUNCTION

We have seen in Chapter 3 that the expert's signal can be replaced by his belief μ (the probability of state $\theta = 1$ after receiving his private signal). The message sent by the expert is a function from μ to a (possibly random) number in $[0, 1]$. Without loss of generality, the receiver observes the state θ *ex post*. The payoff of the expert with belief μ who sends the message m is the same as in (10.1), where $v(m, \theta)$ extends the notation for the discrete values $v_{m\theta}$:

$$V(\mu, m) = \mu v(m, 1) + (1 - \mu) v(m, 0).$$

The receiver determines two functions $v(m, 1)$ and $v(m, 0)$ such that the expert has an incentive to tell the truth with $V(\mu, \mu) \geq V(\mu, m)$ for all possible values of μ and all $m \in [0, 1]$. The payoff $V(\mu, m)$ is represented in Figure 10.1 as a function of the expert's belief μ for three different values of m. The receiver sets the values $v(m, 0)$ and $v(m, 1)$ on the two vertical axes. One can see immediately that it is possible to devise functions $v(m, 0)$ and $v(m, 1)$ such that for any μ, the highest schedule is the one with $m = \mu$. In this case, the expert sends a message identical to his belief. The case of a continuum of beliefs is analyzed in Exercise 10.5.

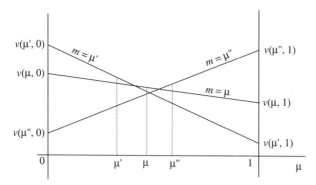

Figure 10.1 Self-selection of messages. The reward schedules depend on the message m of the expert. The message m determines the schedule $V(\mu, m) = \mu v(m, 1) + (1 - \mu)v(m, 0)$. The expert with belief μ chooses the schedule with the highest reward and thus reveals his belief.

REWARD BASED ON REPUTATION

To simplify the discussion, assume only four possible values for the expert's signal: $S = \{-2, -1, 1, 2\}$. The message set has therefore four elements (as in the possible financial recommendations "strong sell," "sell," "buy," and "strong buy," which are made by *Value Line*). The prior probabilities of the two states are equal. If the expert receives an uninformative signal (with probability $1 - \alpha$), the signal can take any value with probability $\frac{1}{4}$, in any state. If the signal is informative, it has the monotone likelihood-ratio property (MLRP): the likelihood ratio $P(s|\theta = 1)/P(s|\theta = 0)$ is strictly increasing[8] in the signal value s. To simplify further and with no loss of generality, we can assume that the beliefs after receiving the signals -2, -1, 1, and 2 are $1 - \rho_H$, $1 - \rho_L$, ρ_L, and ρ_H with $\frac{1}{2} < \rho_L < \rho_H$. For example, the reception of the signal $s = 1$ is equivalent to the reception of good news with low precision ρ_L. The information structure is equivalent to a model where an expert receives a SBS with low or high precision and knows the precision of this signal. The message sent by the expert is an element of S, or equivalently a message of the form (m, ρ) where m is equal to 0 or 1 and ρ is ρ_L or ρ_H.

When an expert has a good and weak signal on θ (i.e., a signal 1), it is clear that he predicts that the more likely state is $\theta = 1$. The realization of the state will be seen by the receiver before the evaluation, but the receiver will never get a message on the precision. In the previous section, the receiver could devise an evaluation function that penalizes heavily the expert who claims to be highly informed (with ρ_H) and makes a wrong prediction on θ. When, however, the evaluation is constrained to be a function of the reputation, if experts tell the truth, then an expert with a signal $s = 1$

---

[8] Because

$$\frac{P(\theta = 1|s)}{P(\theta = 0|s)} = \frac{P(s|\theta = 1)}{P(s|\theta = 0)} \frac{P(\theta = 1)}{P(\theta = 0)},$$

the property is equivalent to a likelihood ratio between $\theta = 1$ and $\theta = 0$ that is increasing in s.

(with a precision ρ_L) has an incentive to lie and claim that his precision is higher. This is now analyzed formally.

Let $v_{m\theta}$ be the evaluation function as defined in Section 10.1.1, i.e., the probability that the expert has an informative signal. Assume that the expert tells the truth. Sending the message 1 or -1 shows that the expert has a signal of precision ρ_L. Likewise, sending the message 2 or -2 shows the precision to be ρ_H. Accordingly, the payoff of sending the message $m = 1$ is

$$V(1, 1) = P(\theta = 1|s = 1)v_{11} + P(\theta = 0|s = 1)v_{10},$$

and the payoff of sending the message 2 is

$$V(1, 2) = P(\theta = 1|s = 1)v_{21} + P(\theta = 0|s = 1)v_{20}.$$

The agent has an incentive to lie and send the message $m = 2$ if $V(1, 2) > V(1, 1)$, which is equivalent to

$$(10.12) \qquad \frac{P(\theta = 1|s = 1)}{P(\theta = 0|s = 1)} = \frac{\rho_L}{1 - \rho_L} > \frac{v_{10} - v_{20}}{v_{21} - v_{11}}.$$

An exercise shows that for given $\rho_L < \rho_H$, if α is sufficiently close to 0, the inequality holds.[9] For some parameters, there cannot be a truthtelling equilibrium.

PROPOSITION 10.3 *If there are two states of nature and experts know the precision of their signal (when that signal is informative), there cannot be a truthtelling equilibrium if the probability of an informative signal is sufficiently small: if experts told the truth, a low-precision expert would have an incentive to overstate his precision.*

10.2.2 A Continuum of States and Messages

Let us expand both the set Θ of states of nature and the set S of the expert's signal values so that there is a bijection between them. The expert can choose a message in the same set S. We can anticipate that for a suitable reward function, the expert will tell the truth and reveal his private signal s.

Assume that both Θ and S are the sets of real numbers, $\mathbb{R}$, that $\theta \sim \mathcal{N}(0, 1/\rho_\theta)$, and that the signal of the expert is $s = \theta + \epsilon_s$ with $\epsilon_s \sim \mathcal{N}(0, 1/\rho_s)$. The receiver does

---

[9] We have

$$v_{21} = \frac{\rho_H \alpha}{\rho_H \alpha + \frac{1-\alpha}{2}},$$

$$v_{11} = \frac{\rho_L \alpha}{\rho_L \alpha + \frac{1-\alpha}{2}}, \qquad v_{10} = \frac{(1 - \rho_L)\alpha}{(1 - \rho_L)\alpha + \frac{1-\alpha}{2}}, \qquad v_{20} = \frac{(1 - \rho_H)\alpha}{(1 - \rho_H)\alpha + \frac{1-\alpha}{2}}.$$

The reader may want to explore whether the inequality (10.12) holds for any $\alpha \in (0, 1)$.

not observe the state, but gets private information (not observed by the expert) in the form of a signal $z = \theta + \epsilon_z$ with $\epsilon_z \sim \mathcal{N}(0, 1/\rho_z)$. After the receiver gets the message $m \in \mathbb{R}$ from the expert, he applies to the expert a reward function $a - (m - z)^2$, where the constant $a \geq 0$ may be introduced to ensure a positive payment on average.

The expert sends a message to minimize his expected penalty $C = E[(m - z)^2|s]$, which is computed over the possible values of z. Because both the signal of the expert and that of the receiver are driven by the true state of nature θ, the penalty is equal to

$$C = E[(m - \theta - \epsilon_z)^2|s] = E[(m - \theta)^2|s] + E[\epsilon_z^2].$$

The optimal value of the message m satisfies the first-order condition

$$m = E[\theta|s].$$

The expert gives his unbiased estimate of θ. The receiver who gets the message updates the distribution of θ from $\mathcal{N}(0, 1/\rho_\theta)$ to $\mathcal{N}(m, 1/(\rho_\theta + \rho_s))$. He then updates the distribution of θ using his own signal z.

10.2.3 "Yes Men" for a Partially Informed Receiver

In all the models considered so far, the expert does not know the private information of the receiver about the state. This is critical, because that information is used by the receiver for the reward function. If the expert knew this information, he could change his message to manipulate the reward. Of course, the expert could do this only if the receiver did not know what the expert knows about him.

Following Prendergast (1993), the model of the previous section is extended by assuming that the expert has an additional signal on the information of the receiver, the "boss" for Prendergast. The expert is rewarded for a message conforming to the information of the boss (as in the previous sections), but he has some information on the information (opinion) of the boss. It is important that the expert's information on the boss is private. Otherwise, the boss could "factor out" that information in his evaluation of the expert: (i) the expert knows something about the receiver, (ii) the receiver does not know what the expert knows about him. There are two private signals for the expert: a signal s_θ on the true state and a signal s_z on the signal z of the receiver:

$$s = \theta + \epsilon_s,$$
$$s_z = z + \eta \quad \text{with} \quad \eta \sim \mathcal{N}(0, 1/\rho_\eta).$$

The signal s_z provides no information to the expert that the receiver does not have. Any impact of s_z on the message of the expert cannot add to the information content of the message (for the receiver). Because it perturbs the message of the expert without being observed by the receiver, it adds a noise to that message.

The signal of the receiver is the same as in Section 10.2.2, $z = \theta + \epsilon_z$. As in the previous sections, given a reward function, the expert attempts to predict z and sends the message

$$m = E[z|s, s_z].$$

The expectation can be computed in two steps. First, one uses the signal s on θ to update the distribution of θ from $\mathcal{N}(0, 1/\rho_\theta)$ to $\mathcal{N}\big(E[\theta|s], 1/(\rho_\theta + \rho_s)\big)$ with

$$(10.13) \quad E[\theta|s] = \frac{\rho_s}{\rho_\theta + \rho_s} s.$$

Given this expectation, the expert has a prior on the receiver's signal z, which is normal with mean $E[\theta|s]$ and precision ρ_1 such that

$$(10.14) \quad \frac{1}{\rho_1} = \frac{1}{\rho_z} + \frac{1}{\rho_\theta + \rho_s}.$$

In the second step, the expert updates this prior with his signal $s_z = z + \epsilon_z$, where ϵ_z is independent of the other variables. For the expert, the expected value of the receiver's signal z is

$$E[z|s, s_z] = \frac{\rho_1}{\rho_1 + \rho_\eta} E[\theta|s] + \frac{\rho_\eta}{\rho_1 + \rho_\eta} s_z.$$

The message sent by the expert is equal to this expected value. Using (10.13) for $E[\theta|s]$, we have an expression of the form

$$(10.15) \quad m = \alpha s + \beta s_z,$$

where the weights α and β are publicly known. Replacing s and s_z by their expressions, and using a standard normalization, we see that the message m is informationally equivalent to the signal

$$y = \frac{m - \beta z}{\alpha} = \theta + \epsilon_s + \frac{\beta}{\alpha}\eta.$$

The noise of the message has two components: the first is the noise of the expert's signal on θ; the second is the noise of the expert's signal on the opinion z of the receiver. If the receiver could observe the expert's information on him, s_z, he could "factor out" the impact of s_z on the message.

The noise η reduces the information content of the message. The variance of the noise is

$$(10.16) \quad \sigma^2 = \frac{1}{\rho_\eta}\left(\frac{\beta}{\alpha}\right)^2 = \rho_\eta \left(\frac{\rho_\theta}{\rho_s \rho_z} + \frac{1}{\rho_s} + \frac{1}{\rho_z}\right)^2.$$

The variance of the message's noise increases with the precision ρ_η of the information that the expert has on his boss.

Suppose now that the receiver is more informed on θ: the precision ρ_z increases; then the variance σ^2 of the expert's message decreases in (10.16). The mechanism is the following: the expert's signal s on θ generates more information about the receiver's signal z, because the receiver's signal has a higher correlation with θ. Hence, the expert relies more on his signal s about the state and less on his direct information s_z about the receiver's signal. The message of the expert is more informative about the true state. A receiver who is better informed about θ gets better advice.

ENDOGENOUS INFORMATION

If the receiver can improve, at some cost, the precision of his private signal $z = \theta + \epsilon_z$, he should take two benefits into account in the cost–benefit analysis: first, the higher precision of his private signal z; second, the higher precision of the message he gets from the expert. The computation of the optimal solution for a given cost function is left as an exercise.

10.3 Panel of Experts

When the advice is given by a panel of experts (a committee, a jury in a trial), members of the panel hear the advice given by other members and influence each other. Financial or medical advisors, economic forecasters, discussants of papers, are aware of the predictions of others and do take them into account. We first analyze a simple model in which each expert "speaks" once in a preestablished order. We then compare the quality of the panel's advice for different sequences in which members speak.

The model is the same as in Section 10.1.2. We add a sequence of experts with independent types and signals on the state $\theta \in \{0, 1\}$. Each expert is described as in the previous section and has a symmetric binary signal of precision ρ_H with probability α and of precision ρ_L otherwise, $\rho_H > \rho_L$. The precision is not observable directly. The value of α is infinitesimally close to 1.

Each expert speaks once and knows the messages of the experts who have spoken before him. Once all the experts have spoken, the receiver learns the true state and updates his estimate of the precision of each expert. Because the evaluation of each expert depends only on his message and the true state, each expert has no incentive to manipulate the messages of other experts. Each expert in the panel is exactly in the same situation as the unique expert in Section 10.1. An expert who speaks in round t formulates his message according to the public belief μ_t (which depends on the history of messages $h_t = \{m_1, \ldots, m_{t-1}\}$) and his own signal s_t. Recall that in any round, babbling is an equilibrium. We will assume that whenever there is another equilibrium with no babbling (herding), both the expert and the receiver (through the evaluation function) coordinate on this equilibrium. Following the analysis in the previous section, an expert herds if and only if the public belief is outside the band $(1 - \rho, \rho)$, where $\rho = \alpha\rho_H + (1 - \alpha)\rho_L$ is the average precision. We assume of course that the public belief in the first period, μ_1, is in the interval $(1 - \rho, \rho)$.

10.3.1 Reputational Herding

Given the condition $1 - \rho < \mu_1 < \rho$, the first expert reveals his signal. Because of the equivalence with the BHW model with a cost of investment c equal to $\frac{1}{2}$, the analysis of Chapter 4 applies. Suppose that $\mu_1 > \frac{1}{2}$ (state θ_1 is more likely) and that the signal of the first expert is bad: $s(1) = 0$. He tells the truth and sends the message $m(1) = s(1) = 0$. His information is incorporated into the public belief μ_2. When two consecutive experts in the sequence have the same signal, the truthtelling condition is not met. At that point, the babbling equilibrium is the only equilibrium. Inasmuch as nothing is learned, the truthtelling condition is not met in the following period, and so on. The babbling equilibrium is the only equilibrium for all subsequent periods. Learning from experts stops. One might as well assume that all experts give the same advice. The expression "herding" is appropriate here. Given the equivalence between herding and babbling, the model is isomorphic to the BHW model of Chapter 4. The probability that a herd has not occurred by round T converges to zero at an exponential rate. Note that the behavior of the agents does not depend on the probability α of a signal with high precision.

Scharfstein and Stein (1990), in the first analysis of herding by experts, assume that the signals of experts are correlated in the following sense: if the signals of both experts are informative, they are identical. Scharfstein and Stein seem to support the following story: the first expert has no incentive to lie, and he tells the truth. The second expert, who learns the signal of the first expert, could say, if I have a signal of high precision, it is more likely that my signal is the same as that of the first expert because signals of high precision are more likely to be identical. As emphasized by Ottaviani and Sørensen (2000), such an argument is irrelevant and confuses the issue. This case is left as an exercise for the reader. The condition for babbling is modified when the experts' signals are correlated. This modification is the same as in the BHW model where agents' actions are observed.

10.3.2 Who Should Speak First: The Strongly or the Weakly Informed?

In a deliberating group, the order in which people voice their opinion may be critical for the outcome. The less experienced expert often speaks first, and the old and wise[10] waits and speaks last. Presumably, this rule of *antiseniority* (to use an expression of Ottaviani and Sørensen, 2001)[11] enables the less experienced to express their opinion free of the influence by the more experienced. Can the antiseniority rule be validated by the analysis of this chapter? The answer will be negative.

---

[10] This expression is used as a picturesque convenience for the analysis.
[11] The presentation in this section is complementary to that of Ottaviani and Sørensen (2001).

Figure 10.2 Possible cases with a panel of two experts.

Assume N experts, indexed by $i \in \{1, \ldots, N\}$, each with a SBS of precision almost equal to q_i. (Each private signal is uninformative with arbitrarily small probability.) By convention, q_i is strictly increasing in i. (Expert N is the most informed, or the senior.) The values of q_i are publicly known, and the receiver, before receiving any message, can choose the order in which experts speak. Each expert knows which experts have spoken before him and their messages.

The goal of the receiver is to choose the state that is most likely once he has listened to each expert. This objective is equivalent to the maximization of the payoff $E[\theta]x - c$ with $c = \frac{1}{2}$, where the action x is taken in the set $\{0, 1\}$. Once all the experts on the panel have spoken, the state is revealed, and each expert is evaluated by comparing his message with the true state, as shown in Section 10.1. In round t, expert t "speaks": he sends a message that maximizes his expected evaluation as in the model of Section 10.1. His message depends on the evaluation function and his belief, which in turn depends, in a Bayesian fashion, on the public belief μ_t in round t and on his private message s_t. We begin with the case of two experts.

THE TWO-EXPERT PANEL ($N = 2$)
The two experts are called Junior (with a signal of precision q_1) and Senior (with a signal of precision $q_2 > q_1$). The *ex ante* public belief as expressed by the LLR between the good and the bad states is denoted by λ. Let $\gamma_i = \log(q_i/(1 - q_i))$.

Without loss of generality, it is assumed that $\lambda \geq 0$ and that $\gamma_2 - \gamma_1 > \gamma_1$. (The case $\gamma_2 - \gamma_1 < \gamma_1$ is similar, and it is left as an exercise.) There are four possible cases, which depend on the value of λ, as represented in Figure 10.2:

1. Suppose first that λ is in the interval $\mathcal{A}$: $0 \leq \lambda < \gamma_1$. If Junior speaks first, his signal is stronger than the public belief ($\gamma_1 > \lambda$) and he speaks the truth.[12] However, because $\lambda + \gamma_1 < \gamma_2$, the public belief once he has spoken is smaller ("weaker") than the strength of the signal of Senior. For any signal of Senior, Junior is overruled and has no influence on the decision of the receiver. If Junior speaks after Senior, the only equilibrium is the babbling equilibrium. Whatever his message, he is not listened to.

2. Suppose that λ is in the interval $\mathcal{B}$: $\gamma_1 < \lambda < \gamma_2$.[13] If Junior speaks first, he babbles. (His signal is weaker than the public belief.) If Junior speaks second, he also babbles

---

[12] Recall that if there is a truthtelling equilibrium, this equilibrium is chosen by the expert and the receiver.

[13] The case of $\lambda = \gamma_1$ can be ignored because its *ex ante* probability is zero.

(as can be verified). Junior is irrelevant. In region $\mathcal{B}$, the receiver never gets to observe Junior's signal, whatever the rule.

3. Suppose that λ is in the interval $\mathcal{C}$. If Junior speaks first, he babbles, as in region $\mathcal{B}$. Suppose that Senior (who does not babble) speaks first a message $s_2 = 0$. The public belief LLR for Junior is $\lambda - \gamma_2 < 0$. Because $\lambda - \gamma_2 - \gamma_1 < 0 < \lambda - \gamma_2 + \gamma_1$, Junior reveals his signal. Junior has an influence on the decision of the receiver. The seniority rule strictly dominates the antiseniority rule.

4. In region $\mathcal{D}$, all experts babble, whatever the order in which they speak, and the panel can be ignored.

We have proven the following result.

PROPOSITION 10.4 (Dominance of the seniority rule) *Assume that a receiver chooses $x \in \{0, 1\}$ to maximize the payoff function $E[\theta]x - \frac{1}{2}$, with $\theta \in \{0, 1\}$, and gets advice from a junior and a senior expert who have private signals with precision q_1 and $q_2 > q_1$, respectively. For any prior μ on state $\theta = 1$, the seniority rule (where the senior agent with higher precision speaks first) dominates the antiseniority rule. For some values of $\mu \in (\beta_1, \beta_2)$, where $\frac{1}{2} < \beta_1 < \beta_2 < 1$, the payoff with the seniority rule is strictly higher than that with the antiseniority rule. For other values of μ, both rules generate the same outcome.*

THE THREE-EXPERT PANEL ($N = 3$)

The three experts have each a SBS, and they are ranked in increasing order of precision $q_1 < q_2 < q_3$. The receiver, after listening to the panel, chooses $x \in \{0, 1\}$ to maximize $E[\theta]x - \frac{1}{2}$. From Proposition 10.4, once an expert has spoken, the other two should speak according to the seniority rule, in decreasing order of precision. There are only three orders (among the possible six) to consider: seniority $(3, 2, 1)$, and $(1, 3, 2)$, $(2, 3, 1)$. The payoffs of the three rules are represented[14] in Figure 10.3.

The lowest straight line is the payoff when the panel is not consulted. The highest line is the *ex ante* payoff when the receiver gets perfect information and observes the true state. We can make the following remarks:

1. No rule dominates the other two for all values of the prior μ.
2. The choice of the rule does not affect the payoff by a significant amount.
3. The addition of the experts with lower precision to the panel yields a higher payoff than that from consulting the most informed expert (with $q = 0.75$), but the improvement is not very significant.
4. The reader may compare the two rules. One may conjecture that when the two states are equally likely *ex ante* ($\mu = \frac{1}{2}$), the seniority rule $(3, 2, 1)$ is dominated by the other two rules.

---

[14] Other numerical values generate similar figures.

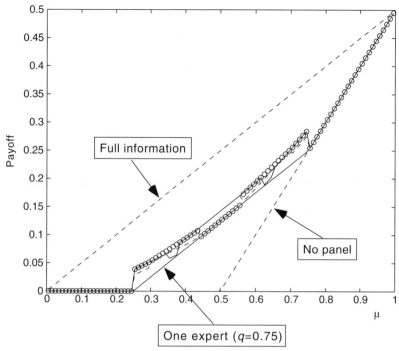

Figure 10.3 Payoff with a three-member panel. Experts' precisions: $q_1 = 0.65$, $q_2 = 0.7$, $q_3 = 0.75$. Among the three graphs that are close to each other, the solid graph corresponds to the experts' order $(1, 3, 2)$; the dashed graph to the order $(2, 3, 1)$; and the graph with circles to the order $(3, 2, 1)$. The cost of the investment is 0.5. The public belief μ is represented on the horizontal axis.

10.3.3 The Receiver Does Not Make the Evaluation

An expert cares about his reputation for future consultations. In general, the receiver of the expert's advice does not have the means to control the evaluation of the expert and to tailor a reward that mimics his own payoff. It is assumed that the valuation by others is such that an expert tells the truth if and only if his signal is stronger than the public belief, and that the receiver's objective function is $E[\theta]x - 0.75$.

A numerical example with a panel of two experts is represented in Figure 10.4. Consider the case where the public belief μ is equal to 0.6. Under the antiseniority rule $(1, 2)$, the payoff of the receiver is equal to 0, so it is strictly smaller than under the seniority rule: the receiver does not invest, whatever the advice from the two experts. Under the antiseniority rule, Junior does not babble. If he has a good signal, he advises to invest. Once the advice is given, the public belief increases from 0.6 to 0.7358 (by use of Bayes's rule). With that public belief, Senior babbles (his precision is only 0.7). The public belief is unchanged and stays lower than the cost of the investment, 0.75. The investment is not undertaken. Any other combinations of private signals (with the same antiseniority order) yield the same outcome.

The interesting part of the story is that if Junior does not speak, the receiver is better off. In that case, Senior does not babble, and if he has a good signal, the

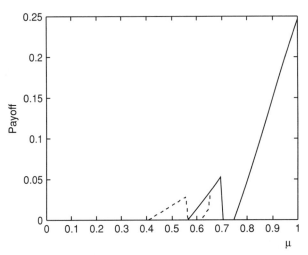

Figure 10.4 Payoff with a high cost of investment. The dashed graph represents the antiseniority rule $(1, 2)$; the solid graph represents the seniority rule $(2, 1)$. Precisions of the experts:
$q_1 = 0.65$, $q_2 = 0.7$. The cost of the investment is 0.75.

receiver's belief increases to 0.777 and the investment takes place. The investment can
be undertaken only with the credible approval of Senior, but that credibility is ruined
whenever Junior speaks.

The numerical results in this section indicate that the learning from others in a
panel of experts can reduce significantly the effectiveness of the consultation. This
property is recurrent in the models of learning from others in Chapters 4 and 5.

10.4 Bibliographical Notes

In Section 10.1.2, the case where experts know their precision corresponds to the
model of Trueman (1994). This model is presented in Exercise 10.6. Proposition 10.2
applies.

In Section 10.1.3, the fundamental paper on manipulative experts is by Crawford
and Sobel (1982). They assume that θ is in an interval of real numbers and that
the expert has a systematic bias toward a higher (or lower) level of action by the
receiver. They show that the message of the expert takes discrete values: the expert
lies, but not too much. Very nice papers about the transmission of information, which
unfortunately cannot be discussed here, have been written by Benabou and Laroque
(1992) and Brandenburger and Polak (1996). Zwiebel (1995) analyzes how agents
choose similar actions in order to be able to be evaluated by a manager.

In Section 10.2, Ottaviani and Sørensen (1999) analyze an extension of the model
in which the sets of values for θ, s, and m are the interval $[-1, 1]$. An expert is endowed
with a type t and a signal s with a density $f(s, t, \theta) = (1 + st\theta)/2$. (A higher type
t means a higher precision of the signal s.) They show that there is no truthtelling

equilibrium. Glazer and Rubinstein (1996) propose a mechanism to prevent herding between referees.

In a remarkable study, Welch (2000) develops an econometric methodology to estimate imitation when choices are discrete.[15] He analyzes how the probabilities of analysts' revisions of the recommendations (which take place in a set of five values from "strong buy" to "strong sell") depend on the established consensus. His results indicate that some herding takes place, especially in a bull market. A next step in this research could be the construction of a structural model with both an exogenous process of information diffusion and learning from others, and the analysis of its empirical properties. (See also Grinblatt, Titman, and Wermers, 1995.)

EXERCISES

EXERCISE 10.1 Imperfect verification of the expert's message
Consider the model of Section 10.1.1. The receiver does not observe the state *ex post*, but has a private symmetric binary signal y with precision $q \in (\frac{1}{2}, 1]$. The timing of that signal is not important if its value is not observed by the expert.

1. Using the notation of Section 10.1.1 for the reward function v_{my}, determine the payoff function $V(s, m)$.
2. Establish the condition for truthtelling by the expert.
3. Show that if the reward function is such that $v_{00} = v_{11}$ and $v_{10} = v_{01}$, the condition for truthtelling is independent of $q \in (\frac{1}{2}, 1]$. Provide an intuitive interpretation.

EXERCISE 10.2 The value of reputation
Following Morris (2001), assume that an expert gives advice in a second period (with a new signal of the same precision) to a receiver who has a payoff function $-E[(x - \theta)^2]$ and that the expert's payoff is the same as that of the receiver. Both states are equally likely.

1. Determine the action taken by the receiver in the next period as a function of the *ex post* reputation of the expert, β.
2. Determine the value of β for the expert.

EXERCISE 10.3 Computation of the reputation function
In the model of Section 10.1.2, assume that with probability α, the agent has a binary signal of precision $\rho > \frac{1}{2}$, and with probability $1 - \alpha$ a binary signal of precision $\frac{1}{2}$ (which is not informative). Determine the algebraic expression of $v_{s\theta}$ in (10.6). Show (10.7).

---

[15] The estimation software is downloadable from his web site. The data come from Zacks's Historical Recommendations Database (which is used by the *Wall Street Journal* to review the major brokerage houses).

EXERCISE 10.4 The equilibrium with partial truth revelation of Proposition 10.1
Determine the evaluation function $v_{m\theta}$ in the equilibrium with a random strategy of
Proposition 10.1. Show that the equilibrium in unstable in the sense defined in the
text.

EXERCISE 10.5 A continuum of beliefs (Section 10.2.1)
Assume that the private belief of the agent takes a value in the bounded interval $[\underline{\mu}, \overline{\mu}]$,
$0 < \underline{\mu} < \overline{\mu} < 1$. Set $v(m, 0) = 1 - m$, and replace $v(m, 1)$ by $v(m)$.

1. Determine a necessary condition on the derivative $v'(m)$ such that the expert
   reveals his belief μ (and sends the message μ for any $\mu \in [\underline{\mu}, \overline{\mu}]$).
2. Determine the family of admissible functions.
3. Is the condition in question 1 sufficient?

EXERCISE 10.6 The model of Trueman (1994)
Assume there are four states of nature $\{\theta_{-2}, \theta_{-1}, \theta_1, \theta_2\}$ and that an expert has a
signal s with values in $\{-2, -1, 1, 2\}$ with the probabilities reported in the table
below. k is nature's probability that $\theta = 1$, or that $\theta = -1$. The precision of the signal
is determined by q, which is equal to ρ_H with probability α and to ρ_L otherwise,
$\rho_L < \rho_H$. The expert knows his type. Show that the model is isomorphic to the one
in Section 10.1.2 where the expert knows his type.

Nature's Prob.	State\Signal	Expert's Probability			
		$s = 2$	$s = 1$	$s = -1$	$s = -2$
$1 - k$	$\theta = 2$	q	$1 - q$	0	0
k	$\theta = 1$	$1 - q$	q	0	0
k	$\theta = -1$	0	0	q	$1 - q$
$1 - k$	$\theta = -2$	0	0	$1 - q$	q

EXERCISE 10.7 The value of reputation (Section 10.1.3)
Let α be the reputation of the expert (probability of being of the good type). Suppose
there is only one period and the expert does not care about his reputation at the end
of the period; he gives advice such that the receiver takes an action that maximizes
the expert's payoff.

1. Determine the action of the receiver as a function of the message m and the
   reputation α.
2. Compute the *ex ante* expected payoff of the good expert, $V_G(\alpha)$, and of the bad expert, $V_B(\alpha)$, at the beginning of the period, before he gets his private information.
   Show that both functions are strictly increasing in α.

Coordination

11 Guessing to Coordinate

Shall we dance?

Actions bear externalities, which may generate strategic substitutability (e.g., entering a new competitive market) or strategic complementarity (e.g., speculating against a currency with a fixed exchange rate). Each agent has to choose his strategy and guess what others do at the same time.

Under some conditions, some strategies are strictly dominated and thus ruled out. The iterated elimination of dominated strategies may converge to a unique strategy that defines a strongly rational expectations equilibrium (SREE). When the process is applied under strategic substitutabilities, it strengthens the Nash equilibrium. When there are strategic complementarities and multiple Nash equilibria under perfect information, the game is extended to include imperfect information, and there may be a unique equilibrium in the extended game. Applications to speculative attacks against a fixed exchange rate are discussed.

In the previous chapters, actions generate an externality because they convey valuable information about a state of nature that affects the actions and the payoff of each agent. In this and the following two chapters, actions generate externalities *per se*. An externality may affect the level of payoff, and this may be important for social welfare, but such an effect is not the issue here. Our focus is on the incentive of agents to act together or not. This incentive depends on the marginal payoff of the activity or the differential payoffs between discrete choices. Theory considers any type of externalities, but in practice, most of them fall in two broad categories: the incentive of an agent to act is either dampened or stimulated by the average level of activity of other agents.

For example, the profitability of the entry into a new market depends on the entry decisions of others. More entries reduce the incentive of any agent to enter:

there is strategic substitutability. In a speculative attack against a currency with a fixed exchange rate, more entry raises the probability of a devaluation and thus the incentive to speculate and earn a capital gain: there is strategic complementarity.

Learning about the actions of others is a critical issue when these actions affect one's payoff. The interaction between actions and learning in a multiperiod setting will be the focus of the next two chapters. We begin with the one-period setting. There will be no learning but a lot of guessing.

In the guessing game, agents guess what others guess what others guess, and so on. This seemingly intractable problem has been analyzed indirectly in the literature by the reverse approach: agents rule out some strategies, hence can rule out the responses to these strategies, and so on. The two cases of strategic substitutability and complementarity have been treated separately. However, they have a similar structure in that in both cases the reaction to the actions of others is monotone: it is decreasing in strategic substitutability or increasing in strategic complementarity. Both cases are analyzed in this chapter.

An overview of the method of iterated elimination of dominated strategies is presented in the next section. In the case of strategic substitutability, the method enables agents to guess that they all play the Nash equilibrium strategy, under some condition. The condition is identical to the stability of the cobweb in the example of hog cycle with myopic agents. In that example, prices and quantities are realized in real time. In the present framework, they take place in *notional* time, in a process that has been called *eductive*.

The eductive method can be applied to strategic complementarities when there is a unique Nash equilibrium, but it fails in a situation of multiple equilibria, which is the most interesting one. Fortunately, it is rescued by the introduction of some uncertainty and the removal of the assumption of common knowledge, a plausible assumption. Agents with a low cost of action (or a high signal about the productivity of investment) invest anyway. Furthermore, because agents are fairly similar, they guess that others should invest also. This guess is an incentive for agents with a higher cost to invest, and so on. A process of contagion – in notional time but not in real time – takes place, which induces agents with a relatively low cost to invest. Likewise, agents at the top range of the spectrum of costs do not invest, and by contagion the same applies for agents next to the top range, and so on. Under some conditions, this iterative method reduces the set of strategies to one threshold value: agents with a cost below this value do not invest; above the value they invest. This remarkable approach, which is due to Carlsson and van Damme (1993a, 1993b), solves the problem of multiple equilibria with strategic uncertainty by introducing some structural uncertainty (which can be very small). Section 11.4 presents an application to the case of speculative attacks against a currency with a fixed exchange rate.

11.1 Overview

11.1.1 The Coordination of Simultaneous Actions

To simplify the analysis, the externality is modeled by assuming that each agent has the same payoff function[1] $u(x, X)$, where the agent's action x is taken in a set Ξ that is a subset of the real numbers,[2] and the second argument, X, is the average of the actions of others. "Others" may be a finite number of agents or a continuum. The second argument generates the payoff externality. We will distinguish *strategic substitutability* ($u_{12} < 0$) from *strategic complementarity* ($u_{12} > 0$). In the first case, a higher level of activity by others reduces the marginal payoff of action and therefore the level of the action; in the second case, a higher level of activity by others stimulates the incentive to act. Strategic substitutability arises in the market for an agricultural product: a higher aggregate supply X lowers the price of the output and the individual's payoff, as in the model of Muth (1961). Strategic complementarity occurs when the level of aggregate investment increases the marginal return of investment for any individual firm, as in the structural model of Kiyotaki (1988). Other examples of strategic complementarities are found in speculative attacks against currencies with fixed exchange rates, bank runs, and the adoption of standards.[3]

Throughout this chapter, there is only one period, and agents can choose an action once. Suppose first that when each agent chooses his action, he knows the strategies of others. The optimal choice of an agent is a response to the average level of activity X, which, by an abuse of notation, will be identified with the aggregate level of activity. This optimal response defines the *reaction function* $R(X)$, which is determined by the first-order condition $u_1(R(X), X) = 0$. The slope of the reaction function is $u_{12}/(-u_{11})$. Because $u_{11} < 0$ by the second-order condition, the reaction function is decreasing (increasing) when the payoff function u exhibits strategic substitutability (complementarity). Following Cooper and John (1988), the two cases are illustrated in Figure 11.1.

NASH EQUILIBRIA AND RATIONAL-EXPECTATIONS EQUILIBRIA

In a one-period game with interactions between agents, the Nash equilibrium is the natural equilibrium concept. Because X is the average of the agents' actions, in a

---

[1] The function u has continuous derivatives up to the second order and $u_{11} < 0$.

[2] The effect of externalities is related to some ordering: if others act "more," the payoff of an agent is affected (positively or negatively). In many cases, the level of activity can be represented by a real number, with a natural ordering. A generalization of the theory requires the use of lattices. An excellent introduction is given by Cooper (1999). See also Milgrom and Roberts (1990), Vives (1990).

[3] Many examples from day-to-day life are described in the delightful book by Schelling (1978), Chapter 3.

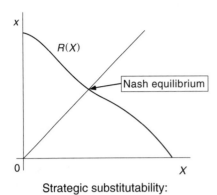

Strategic substitutability: Strategic complementarity:

The reaction function is decreasing;   The reaction function is increasing;
there is a unique Nash equilibrium.   there may be multiple Nash equilibria.

Figure 11.1 Reaction functions.

symmetric Nash equilibrium, $x = X = R(X)$. Such an equilibrium is represented
by the intersection of the graph of $R(X)$ with the first diagonal. In Figure 11.1, one
can see that (i) if there is strategic substitutability, a Nash equilibrium is unique;
(ii) if there is strong strategic complementarity (i.e., the slope of the reaction function, $-u_{12}/u_{11}$, is sufficiently large over some domain), there are multiple equilibria
(Cooper, 1999).

Those diagrams are convenient for exposition, and they apply when agents are sure
about each others' choices. However, because agents make choices simultaneously,
they cannot actually be sure about each others' choices, and each needs to have
expectations about the behavior of the others. The expectations are not about the
structure of the game and the payoff functions of other agents. These features are
common knowledge. The expectations are about the strategies of others. There is no
structural uncertainty, but there is strategic uncertainty.

In a Nash equilibrium, each agent *assumes* that others play the equilibrium strategy
(which may be random). Agents have point expectations on the strategies of others,
and these expectations are correct. The Nash equilibrium is equivalent to a rational-
expectations equilibrium (REE). Following Guesnerie (1992), we identify rational
expectations and Nash equilibria.[4]

DEFINITION 11.1 (Rational-expectations equilibrium) *A REE is defined by a level
of activity x^* for all agents such that*

$$u_1(x^*, x^*) = 0.$$

RATIONALIZABILITY AND THE COORDINATION OF ACTIONS

The problem of the coordination of strategies is about how to think about how others
think about how others think, and so on. This Gordian knot has been cut by Bernheim

---

[4] The REE here is a perfect foresight equilibrium in Guesnerie (1992).

(1984) and Pearce (1984), who follow a different path of thoughts: Some strategies are ruled out by every agent because they are strictly dominated, i.e., they generate a strictly lower payoff under any strategies of all agents. All agents know that these strategies are strictly dominated, and it is therefore common knowlege that they are not played. The set of admissible strategies is thus reduced in the common knowledge. We can now iterate the procedure to rule out some other strategies in this reduced set. At each step k of the process, it is common knowledge that the set of strategies that is used by all players is reduced to the set J_k. Each set J_k contains the next one like a Russian doll. The limit of the nested sequence of sets (which is the intersection of all the J_k), will be called the set of *rationalizable* strategies. When that limit is reduced to a unique strategy, following Guesnerie (1992), that strategy defines a *strongly rational-expectations equilibrium* (SREE).

11.1.2 Rationalizable Strategies and Iterative Elimination

Assume the action set is the set of positive real numbers as represented in Figure 11.2, and the reaction function is $R(X)$. Consider first the case of strategic substitutability. Any $x > R(X)$ is too high, and a reduction of x yields a higher payoff. The gradient of the payoff is represented by an arrow in the figure.

Suppose that because of some yet unspecified argument, $X \geq a$ for some number a. The region $\{X < a\}$ is thus eliminated. One sees immediately that any strategy $x > R(a)$ yields a payoff that is lower than that of $R(a)$. It is dominated by $R(a)$.

LEMMA 11.1 *Assume strategic substitutability ($u_{12} < 0$). If $X \geq a$ for some number a, then any strategy $x > R(a)$ is strictly dominated. If $X \leq b$ for some number b, then any strategy $x < R(b)$ is strictly dominated.*

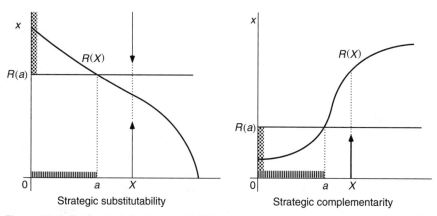

Figure 11.2 Regions of dominance. A thick horizontal segment represents values of X that are eliminated. As a consequence, a region of x is strictly dominated, as represented by a thick vertical segment.

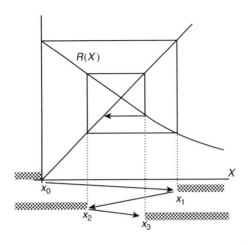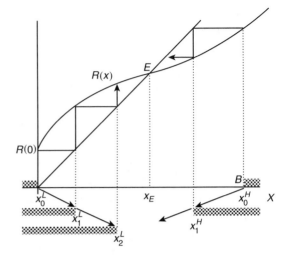

The elimination of the low values in the interval $X < x_0 = 0$ entails the elimination of the high values $X > x_1 = R(x_0)$, which entails the elimination of the low values $X < x_2 = R(x_1)$, and so on, back and forth.

The elimination of strategies in the interval $X < x_0^L = 0$ entails the elimination of strategies $X < x_1^L = R(x_0^L)$, and so on in an increasing sequence of intervals to the left of the Nash equilibrium x_E. Likewise on the right of x_E.

Figure 11.3 Iterative elimination of dominated strategies.

Under strategic substitutability, a low level of aggregate activity elicits a high response and vice versa. Therefore, if a low level of aggregate activity X is ruled out, then any strategy that is above some level is dominated and ruled out.

The case with strategic complementarities is represented in the right panel of Figure 11.2. The optimal response to a low (high) level of aggregate activity is a low (high) response. The elimination of low values for X induces the elimination of low values for x. An exercise proves the next result.

LEMMA 11.2 *Assume strategic complementarity* $(u_{12} > 0)$. *If* $X \geq a$ *for some number* a, *then any strategy* $x < R(a)$ *is strictly dominated. If* $X \leq b$ *for some number* b, *then any strategy* $x > R(b)$ *is strictly dominated.*

ITERATED ELIMINATION OF DOMINATED STRATEGIES

The previous lemmata are now applied iteratively. Consider the case of strategic substitutability (on the left of Figure 11.3). Assume $R(0)$ exists and is finite. The procedure does not work if $R(0)$ does not exist. Let $x_0 = 0$. Because no agent chooses $x < x_0 = 0$, the average activity X is also nonnegative. By Lemma 11.2, any strategy $x > R(x_0) = x_1$ is strictly dominated. We eliminate the interval $x > x_1$ on the vertical axis. Then we use the symmetry with respect to the first diagonal in order to eliminate the region $X > x_1$ on the horizontal axis. Likewise, we can eliminate the region

$X < x_2 = R(x_1)$. The procedure is iterated an arbitrary number of times, as illustrated in the left panel of Figure 11.3.

The sequence of points $x_k = R(x_{k-1})$ defines a cobweb pattern. If the cobweb converges, it converges to the Nash equilibrium strategy x_E. Any strategy different from x_E is eliminated at some finite stage of the procedure. This motivates the following definition.

DEFINITION 11.2 (Iterative dominance and rationalizability) *Assume all agents have the same set of strategies $J \subset \mathbb{R}$. A strategy $x \in J$ is iteratively dominated if there is a finite sequence of increasing sets $I_0 = \emptyset, \ldots, I_N, x \in I_N$, such that strategies in I_k are strictly dominated when all agents play in the subset of strategies $J - I_{k-1}$. A strategy is rationalizable if it is not iteratively dominated.*

The sets I_k of the eliminated strategies are defined in the left panel of Figure 11.3 by $I_0 = \emptyset$, $I_1 = (x_1, \infty)$, $I_{2k} = [0, x_{2k}) \cup (x_{2k-1}, \infty)$, and $I_{2k+1} = I_{2k} \cup (x_{2k+1}, x_{2k-1}]$.

The case of mild strategic complementarity is represented in the right panel of Figure 11.3. By assumption, the set of feasible actions is the finite interval $[0, B]$, and the payoff function u is such that the reaction function is the one depicted in the figure. The procedure of iterated elimination is in two steps: first, a sequence of sets of iteratively dominated strategies is constructed on the left of the Nash equilibrium; second, the same procedure is applied on the right. In both steps, the iterations are determined by a staircase, which is the equivalent of the cobweb. The sets I_k of Definition 11.2 are defined by $I_k = [0, x_k^L) \cup (x_k^H, B]$.

STRONGLY RATIONALIZABLE EQUILIBRIUM

DEFINITION 11.3 (Strongly rational-expectations equilibrium) *The strategy x^* defines a SREE if and only if any strategy $x \neq x^*$ is iteratively dominated.*

From the previous analysis, one has immediately the following property.

THEOREM 11.1 *Assume the set of actions is the interval $[0, B]$, $R(0) > 0$ is finite, and $R(B) < B$. A sufficient condition for the existence of a SREE is that $-1 < R'(x) < 1$ for $0 < x < B$. A necessary condition for the existence of a SREE is that $-1 < R'(x^*) < 1$ at the Nash equilibrium x^*.*

The sufficiency condition states that the reaction of any agent to the actions of others should not be too large. One can see in Figure 11.3 that the sufficient condition can be weakened in some special cases.

EDUCTIVE STABILITY

When the iterated elimination converges to a single strategy, the SREE, it is sufficient to keep track of the sequence of reactions $x_{k+1} = R(x_k)$. The convergence of the process is isomorphic to the convergence of myopic agents who at each stage react to the strategy in the previous stage. There is an essential difference, however. In the context of myopic agents, the process takes place in real time with one stage per period and a "real" action in each period. In the context of the one-period model where agents think about others who think about others, . . . , the process takes place simultaneously in the heads of all agents, in notional time. All actions are notional before the real ones take place.

The method of thinking about others presented above has been called *eductive* by Guesnerie (1992), following Binmore (1987); learning from the observation of others has been called *deductive*. The stability of the process (i.e., of the sequence $x_{k+1} = R(x_k)$ in notional time) is called *eductive stability*. A REE that is eductively stable is a SREE.

11.2 Eductive Stability in a Standard Market

THE EQUIVALENCE BETWEEN STRATEGIES AND PRICE EXPECTATIONS

Consider a large number of small independent farmers[5] who seed wheat in the spring and sell their crop in a competitive market in the summer (Muth, 1961). The market price P is determined by the equality between the total supply Q and the demand $D(P)$. Each farmer (agent) i is a pricetaker. His cost of production is quadratic and equal to $x_i^2/(2\alpha)$, where α is a parameter. The critical property is that an agent commits to a production x_i without observing the actions of others. He relies on his expectation about the market price in the summer.

The farmer's supply maximizes his expected profit: it is such that his marginal cost, x_i/α, is equal to his marginal revenue, which is his price expectation $E_i[P]$. Because $x_i = \alpha E_i[P]$, there is an equivalence between the strategies x_i and the price expectations $E_i[P]$. The coordination of the supplies is equivalent to the coordination of the expectations.[6] This setting is a well-known example of strategic substitutability: the marginal return of production to a farmer is inversely related to the level of activities of others; if others raise their production, the price drops and the marginal return falls.

11.2.1 The Model and Its Equilibrium

Following Muth (1961), there is a continuum[7] of farmers indexed by i, with total mass M, uniformly distributed on $[0, M]$. The quadratic cost of production generates a linear supply function. Let X be the supply per farmer. The total supply is given by $\int x_i \, di = MX$.

---

[5] The same structure applies for other markets (for hogs, lawyers, etc.).

[6] These points were highlighted in the context of the agricultural model of Muth by Evans (1983) in his first of numerous papers on the topic, and by Bernheim in his dissertation (published in his 1984 article).

[7] The continuum is the limit case for N agents, each with a mass normalized to $1/N$.

The demand for wheat is given by a function $D(P)$, which is known to all agents, with $D' < 0$. The equilibrium price is

$$P = D^{-1}\left(\int x_i \, di\right) = D^{-1}(MX).$$

Each agent makes his decision as a function of his expected price. However, because the price depends on the average of all actions, we formulate the game in terms of strategies defined by production levels. Substituting for the expected price, we find that the payoff of farmer i is

$$(11.1) \qquad U^i = E_i\left[u^i(x_i, X)\right] \qquad \text{with} \qquad u^i(x_i, X) = D^{-1}(MX)x_i - \frac{x_i^2}{2\alpha}.$$

The strategic substitutability between the supply x_i of agent i and the average supply X of others follows from

$$\frac{\partial^2 u^i}{\partial x_i \, \partial X} = \frac{1}{D'\left(D^{-1}(X)\right)} < 0.$$

The marginal return of x_i is inversely related to the total supply X. The model of an agricultural market is a special case of the canonical form in Section 11.1.1. To simplify further, assume the demand function is linear: $D = a - \beta P$. The reaction function is

$$(11.2) \qquad R(X) = \alpha \frac{a - MX}{\beta}.$$

The analysis of Section 11.1.1 may be applied in terms of quantities and prices, because of the equivalence between the price expectations and the quantities supplied by the agents. Such a representation is given in Figure 11.4.

The total quantity supplied is represented on the horizontal axis. This quantity is also the supply per agent. The price cannot be greater than P_1^H (for which the demand is zero). For any agent, a supply strictly greater than αP_1^H would entail a marginal cost above the highest possible price and is therefore strictly dominated. By integration, the total supply must be smaller than $x_1^H = \alpha P_1^H$. The price is therefore at least equal to its value for that maximum, $P_1^L = D^{-1}(x_1^H)$. In the next step, the "minimum price" P_1^L determines a minimum supply αP_1^L, and so on.

The boundaries of the regions that are eliminated are determined by the cobweb, and the condition for convergence corresponds to the stability of the cobweb, which holds if the supply schedule has a smaller price derivative than the demand. As an application of Theorem 11.1 to equation (11.2), the REE is a SREE if and only if $\alpha M < \beta$. Because strong rationalizability and eductive stability of the Nash equilibrium are equivalent, we can state the next result.

PROPOSITION 11.1 *The necessary and sufficient condition for the eductive stability of the Nash equilibrium (the existence of the SREE) in the linear model of supply and demand is $\alpha M < \beta$.*

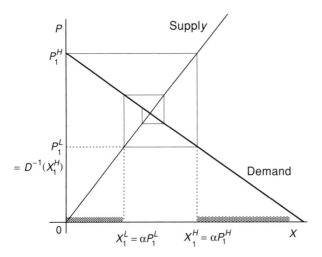

The mass of agents is normalized: $M = 1$.

Figure 11.4 The SREE in an agricultural market.

As in the cobweb model in real time, eductive stability holds if the supply is not too elastic with respect to the demand. If the mass of farmers is larger, the reaction to expectations is amplified: given a fixed technology for each farm, the supply is more elastic and the condition for eductive stability is less likely to be met.

Let us review again the main features of the method in the context of a standard market where the supply is determined before the opening of the market. Each agent knows that the activity of others is not below some minimal value. Because of the inverse relation between the activity of others and one's own activity, an agent does not supply more than his optimal response to that minimal value. Hence there is an upper bound on the activity of each agent and therefore on the total activity. This upper bound in turn generates a lower bound on the level of activity, and so on. The procedure bounces between the ranges of low and high activities. Each upward extension of the range of the low activity leads to a downward extension of the range of the high activity and reciprocally. The boundaries of the eliminated regions follow the sequence $x_t = R(x_{t-1})$. The success of the method depends on the convergence of the sequence to the fixed point of the reaction function. Convergence requires agents not to react too much to the actions of others.

The eductive stability is more likely to hold if the farmers are put in a sequence where each farmer takes an irreversible action once and observes the actions of the previous farmers in the sequence. In that case, the supply elasticity at each stage is small and the stability is reinforced. This setting is analyzed now.

11.2.2 Supply Decisions in a Sequence

Assume the good is supplied in two periods. In the first, there is a mass $1 - \gamma$ of identical agents, each with the same cost function $x^2/(2\alpha_1)$, as in the previous section. These agents make a final and simultaneous decision about their production levels.

They know the structure of the subgame that begins at the end of the first period. In the second period, a mass γ of identical agents with the same individual cost function $x^2/(2\alpha_2)$ make a supply decision. These agents know the total supply of the first period, but they do not know the supplies of others. The total supply of all agents is brought to the market after the second period and sold at the equilibrium price P with $D(P) = a - \beta P$. For example, the first type of agents seeds wheat in the winter, and the second in the spring. Agents in the second period observe the actions of the first period, and agents in the first period know the payoff structure of the second-period agents.

Let x_1 and x_2 be the supplies of the good per agent in the first and the second period. In dynamic programming fashion, we begin with second-period agents. They know the total supply at the end of the first period, $(1 - \gamma)x_1$, and face the net demand $D(P) = a - (1 - \gamma)x_1 - \beta P$. This demand has the same slope as in the one-period model of the previous section. Because the second-period total supply has a price derivative equal to $\gamma\alpha_2$, the condition for a SREE in the subgame for the second period is $\gamma\alpha_2 < \beta$ (Proposition 11.1). If this condition is not met, there is no point in analyzing the game in the first period. We therefore assume that $\alpha_2 < \beta/\gamma$. Under this condition, the second-period subgame has a SREE, and the total supply function in the second period is $\gamma\alpha_2 P$.

Consider now the agents in the first period, where the structure of the second-period subgame is common knowledge. This knowledge is equivalent to the demand $D(P) = a - (\beta + \gamma\alpha_2)P$. From Proposition 11.1, the game in the first period has a SREE if and only if $(1 - \gamma)\alpha_1 < \beta + \gamma\alpha_2$. Combining the conditions in the two periods, the game has a SREE if and only if

$$(1 - \gamma)\alpha_1 < \beta + \gamma\alpha_2 \quad \text{and} \quad \alpha_2 < \beta/\gamma.$$

To simplify the exposition, assume that all agents have the same cost function and $\alpha_1 = \alpha_2 = \alpha$. If the mass of the second period agents γ is at least equal to $\frac{1}{2}$, the first condition (for the first period) is not binding. The condition for a SREE reduces to $\alpha < \beta/\gamma$. It is obviously weaker than the condition in the one-period setting. When agents are divided into two groups and the second group observes the decision of the first group, the equilibrium is more stable in the eductive sense. (The SREE condition on the supply parameter α is weaker.)

We can generalize to any number T of periods. Assume all agents have the same individual cost function $x^2/(2\alpha)$, a mass $1/T$ of agents make their supply decision simultaneously in period t ($t = 1, \ldots, T$), and agents in period t know the supply of agents in the previous periods and anticipate the subgames in periods after t. The condition for the SREE in the last period is $\alpha < \beta T$. Assuming this condition to hold, the condition for the SREE in period $T - 1$ is $\alpha/T < \beta + \alpha/T$. It is not binding. Agents in period $T - 2$ face a net demand $a - \beta P - 2\alpha P/T$. The condition for the SREE in that period's subgame is $\alpha/T < \beta + 2\alpha/T$, which is weaker than the previous one and therefore not binding. Likewise, the condition for any period $t < T - 2$ is not binding. Therefore the condition for the SREE is

$$\alpha < \beta T.$$

For any parameters (α, β), there is a number T such that if the number of periods in the sequential model is greater than T, the SREE exists.

When agents are divided into a sequence of groups,[8] the elasticity of supply of each group becomes smaller than the elasticity of demand of the market, which is the condition for eductive stability.

11.2.3 Discussion

Eductive stability has been considered by Guesnerie and others as a criterion of stability of a market. Such an association between eductive stability and stability fails to characterize the behavior of a market when the condition for eductive stability is not met. It is probably more accurate to state that under some conditions, the eductive method provides a strong rationale for expectations to coordinate on a Nash equilibrium.

The condition for eductive stability of a market can be reduced to a simple criterion, which should be highlighted: the Nash equilibrium is a SREE if the supply is inelastic compared with the demand. Any effect that reduces or increases the elasticity of the supply expands or shrinks the set of parameters for which the eductive process is stable. Three such effects are discussed now.

1. We saw in Section 11.2.2 that the market is more stable in the eductive sense if suppliers are divided into groups where group k observes the (irreversible) decisions by all preceding groups $i < k$. Agents in each group make a simultaneous decision, but the supply elasticity of a given group is smaller than the elasticity of all suppliers. Hence, it is not too surprising that eductive stability holds for larger sets of parameters of the demand and of the individual costs.
2. Suppose that suppliers are risk-averse (and keep the same cost function $x^2/(2\alpha)$). Their supply elasticity is smaller than when they are risk-neutral. Again, eductive stability holds for a larger set of the parameters (α, β).
3. Consider now the introduction of a futures market. Guesnerie and Rochet (1993) argue that such a market is destabilizing. This statement is surprising in that the additional market should convey more information and facilitate the coordination of expectations between suppliers. Again, if we want to understand the meaning of the statement, we have to disentangle the mechanism. To simplify the exposition, Guesnerie and Rochet replace the previous farmers by agents who store a good between two periods. There are exogenous and random supplies of the good in the two periods.

---

[8] One could take a unique agent at each stage, but the assumption of a group of agents simplifies the computation of the solution, because agents are pricetakers.

At first, there are agents who can store the good. The storage decision is made before the opening of the market in the first period (like the supply decision of the farmers). The agents are risk-averse and thus affected by the uncertain supply in the second period.

In the second step, a futures market is added, with new agents who can trade only in it. These agents have no storage facility and have the same payoff function as the agents of the first type who can store the good, with the same risk aversion. The agents with a storage facility can also trade in the futures market. The critical mechanism is that the additional agents are able to provide some insurance to the agents of the first type. It is not surprising then that the storage is more elastic with respect to the anticipated price and that the market is less stable.

11.3 Strategic Complementarities

When there are strategic complementarities, the method of iterated elimination of dominated strategies is effective if there is a unique Nash equilibrium, as in the right panel of Figure 11.3. The most interesting situation may be that of multiple equilibria. They arise if the strategic complementarities are strong, i.e., the reaction function is sufficiently steep to generate multiple intersections[9] with the 45° line. In the example of Figure 11.5, the set of rationalizable strategies is an interval.[10] There is no SREE.

The argument in this section can be summarized in terms of Figures 11.5 and 11.3. Assume that when agents have perfect information on the parameters of the model, there are multiple equilibria as in Figure 11.5. The assumption of perfect information is an expository device and is not plausible. In most conceivable situations, agents have imperfect private information on the parameters of the model. Under suitable assumptions, the introduction of imperfect information (even with a vanishingly small noise) generates a function, called the cumulative value function, which is similar to the reaction function in the right panel of Figure 11.3. Imperfect information generates a SREE.

In order to simplify the exposition, we assume in the rest of the chapter that agents take a zero–one action. For example, the investment size may be fixed, or if the agent invests, he chooses the highest possible level against a constraint (e.g., the withdrawal of the entire balance in a bank run, the speculation against a currency up to a liquidity constraint). The set of actions is reduced to two elements: $\Xi = \{0, 1\}$. We begin with a simple case where the investment costs of agents are distributed according to a Gaussian distribution.

---

[9] For a given concavity of the individual payoff, measured by u_{11}, the slope $R' = -u_{12}/u_{11}$ increases with the degree of strategic complementarity as measured by the cross derivative u_{12}.

[10] The pattern of Figure 11.5 is general. Milgrom and Roberts (1990) show in a more general setting (where strategies are taken in a lattice) that the set of rationalizable strategies has a lower and an upper bound that are Nash equilibria (Theorem 5). A lattice is a set where each pair of elements has a lower and an upper bound in the set.

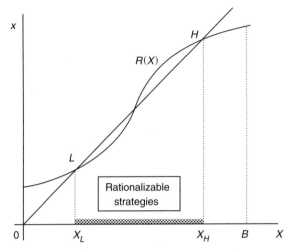

Figure 11.5 Multiple equilibria with strategic complementarities. When there are multiple Nash equilibria, the rationalizable strategies form an interval. There is no SREE.

11.3.1 The Gaussian Distribution of Investment Costs

As in all models of coordination with strategic complementarities, we first assume common knowledge on the structure of the model. This step is required to present the problem.

There is a continuum of agents with total mass equal to one. Each agent has a cost of investment, c, which is drawn from a Gaussian distribution $\mathcal{N}(\theta, \sigma_c^2)$ with $\theta = 0.5$. The payoff of an agent is equal to $AX - c$, where X is the mass of investing agents (with action $x = 1$), and A is a parameter.

PERFECT INFORMATION ON THE STRUCTURE

Agents know that the distribution of costs is Gaussian $\mathcal{N}(\theta, \sigma_c^2)$, and they know the parameters θ and σ_c^2. Let $V(c)$ be the *gross* payoff of investment for an agent with cost c when the acting set, the set of costs with $x = 1$, is $(-\infty, c)$. We have

$$V(c) = AF(c - \theta; 0, \sigma_c^2),$$

where $F(\cdot; 0, \sigma_c)$ is the c.d.f. of $\mathcal{N}(0, \sigma_c^2)$. An exercise shows that Nash equilibria are defined by a monotone strategy x (to invest if the cost is smaller than x), which is a solution of

(11.3) $x = V(x)$.

The graph of $V(c)$ (which is proportional to the c.d.f. of the costs) is represented in Figure 11.6, and a Nash equilibrium is characterized by the intersection of the 45° line and the graph of $V(c)$. Three cases with different variances of the costs are represented in the figure: when the variance is large ($\sigma_c \geq 0.4$), there is a unique Nash equilibrium; when the variance is small and agents are less heterogeneous ($\sigma = 0.1$), there are three equilibria, one of which can be eliminated by a crude stability argument.

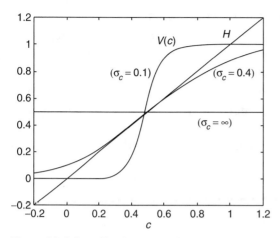

Figure 11.6 Payoffs with strategic complementarities. $V(c)$ is the mass of agents with cost lower than c and is identical with the c.d.f. of $\mathcal{N}(0.5, \sigma_c^2)$. When the variance is sufficiently small, there are multiple equilibria.

The figure illustrates a simple property: multiple equilibria arise only if the heterogeneity of agents is not too large. When the variance of individual costs is large, the c.d.f. is smoother and the intersection with the 45° line is unique: there is a single equilibrium. This property is general and important for the evaluation of the possibility of multiple equilibria with a large number of agents and strategic complementarity.

IMPERFECT INFORMATION

Assume agents do not know the value of θ (the mean of the cost distribution), but they do know the variance σ^2. It is common knowledge that θ is the realization of a random variable with normal distribution $\mathcal{N}(\bar{\theta}, 1/\rho_\theta)$ with known parameters $\bar{\theta}$ and ρ_θ, and that each agent observes only his own cost.

Each agent computes his subjective distribution on θ, using the information provided by his own cost. An agent with a higher cost has a higher belief about the mean of θ and the average cost in the economy. This effect, which will occur in this chapter and in the next, is called the *cluster effect* on individuals' beliefs: agents know that the individuals' costs are clustered around some mean value. Each agent believes rationally that his cost is not too far from the mean, with a high probability. Hence, each agent has a biased belief on the mean cost of others toward his own cost.

Using Bayes's rule with normal distributions (2.6), an agent with cost c has a subjective distribution on θ that is normal $\mathcal{N}(E[\theta|c], 1/(\rho_\theta + \rho_c))$ where $E[\theta|c]$ is an average of the *ex ante* value $\bar{\theta}$, which is common to all agents, and the individual cost c:

$$E[\theta|c] = (1 - \alpha)\bar{\theta} + \alpha c \qquad \text{with} \quad \alpha = \frac{\rho_c}{\rho_\theta + \rho_c}.$$

The cluster effect operates through the weight α of the cost c. It is stronger when the variance of the cost distribution is smaller.

A UNIQUE EQUILIBRIUM WITH MONOTONE STRATEGIES

Extending the case with common knowledge, we consider monotone strategies and suppose that all agents with cost less than x invest (strategy x). The purpose of this section is to show how imperfect information may generate a unique Nash equilibrium with monotone strategies. In the next section, the method of iterative dominance will be extended to the case of imperfect information to show that the unique Nash equilibrium is a SREE.

For an agent with cost x, the gross payoff of investment is $E[F_\theta(x)|x]$, where the expectation is on θ and depends on the information of the agent. Let

$$V(x) = E[F_\theta(x)|x].$$

One can prove (Exercise 11.2) that

$$(11.4) \qquad V(x) = F\left(x; (1-\alpha)\overline{\theta} + \alpha x, \frac{2\rho_c + \rho_\theta}{\rho_c(\rho_c + \rho_\theta)}\right),$$

which is equivalent to

$$(11.5) \qquad V(x) = F(x - \overline{\theta}; 0, \sigma^2) \quad \text{with} \quad \sigma^2 = \sigma_c^2\left(1 + 2\frac{\sigma_\theta^2}{\sigma_c^2}\right)\left(1 + \frac{\sigma_\theta^2}{\sigma_c^2}\right).$$

The right-hand side of this expression has the same form as in the case of perfect information, expression (11.3). Under imperfect information, the model is formally equivalent to that of perfect information with a higher variance of the individual costs. *Ceteris paribus*, one of the following two conditions is sufficient for a unique Nash equilibrium:

(i) the uncertainty about the state θ as measured by the variance σ_θ^2 is sufficiently large;

(ii) the heterogeneity of agents as measured by the variance σ_c^2 is sufficiently small.

Vanishingly Small Heterogeneity

The case of a vanishingly small σ_c is particularly interesting. If $\sigma_c \to 0$, the variance σ^2 in (11.5) tends to infinity. For any c in a bounded interval $[a, b]$, the value of $F(c - \overline{\theta}; 0, \sigma^2)$ tends to $\frac{1}{2}$. Given some uncertainty on the state θ, the absence of common knowledge has a larger effect when agents are vanishingly close! When $\sigma_c^2 \to 0$, there are multiple equilibria if agents observe θ, and there is a SREE if agents do not observe θ.

This property is general and does not depend on the use of a normal distribution. The intuition is important: when all agents have nearly identical costs (but not identical costs), the precision of the private signal c on θ dwarfs the prior distribution $\mathcal{N}(\overline{\theta}, \sigma_\theta^2)$, whatever this distribution.[11] Each agent believes that about one-half of the other agents have a cost lower than his, and about one-half a higher cost. (These fractions tend to

---

[11] The case of vanishingly small heterogeneity of agents (σ_c^2 vanishingly small) is the one analyzed by Carlsson and van Damme (1993a).

$\frac{1}{2}$ when $\sigma_c^2 \to 0$.) Hence, the gross payoff of any agent tends to $\frac{1}{2}$, independently of his own cost.

11.3.2 The Cumulative Value Function and the SREE

In this section, we show how a coordination game with multiple Nash equilibria under perfect information may have a SREE when agents do not have common knowledge on the parameters of the model. Our main goal is to develop a simple tool of analysis, which will be applied later in this chapter and in the next. The method is a generalization of the method of global games that was formulated by Carlsson and van Damme (1993a).

Agents form a continuum, but the presentation would be the same with a finite number N of agents ($N \geq 2$). Each agent takes action 0 or 1. The payoff of action 0 is nil, and the payoff of action 1, investment, is $E[u(s, X)]$, where X is the average over all others' levels of action, and s is a parameter, specific to the agent, that is drawn from a distribution with support $[b, B]$. The boundaries of the support may be positive or negative. At this stage, it may be convenient to think of the parameter s as the cost of investment, but s may also be an information signal and not be related to any cost.

The state of nature θ is drawn from a distribution on the set of real numbers. We do not admit parameters with a dimension higher than one. The value of θ is not observable by the agents, and it determines the distribution of individuals' costs. Each agent knows that his parameter s is drawn from the distribution. The value s is a private information about the state θ.

A strategy is defined by the *acting set* $\mathcal{A}$ of the values s for which an agent invests. Given a realization θ that defines a particular distribution of agents, the aggregate activity is equal to the mass X of agents in $\mathcal{A}$: $X = \mu_\theta(\mathcal{A})$, where $\mu_\theta(\mathcal{A})$ is the measure of $\mathcal{A}$ for the population distribution associated to the realization θ (using the Lebesgue measure for a continuum and the number of agents for a finite population). For an agent with parameter s, the payoff of investment is

(11.6) $U(s, \mathcal{A}) = E[u(s, \mu_\theta(\mathcal{A}))|s]$,

where the expectation is taken on θ, conditional on the information, s. An *equilibrium acting set* $\mathcal{A}$ is defined such that

$$s \in \mathcal{A} \quad \text{if and only if} \quad U(s, \mathcal{A}) \geq 0.$$

Each agent can compute the payoff and the strategy of any other agent. Hence, all agents agree on the same acting set which is common knowledge. Recall that different agents have different expectations about the mass of agents in the acting set.

In general, an equilibrium acting set may have any shape. However, let us focus on the intervals where investing agents have a parameter less than some value s. Define the interval $I(s) = [b, s]$. The analysis will use the following tool, which is called the *cumulative value function* (CVF).

DEFINITION 11.4 *Assume the payoff of investment depends on an agent's parameter $s \in \mathbb{R}$ and on the aggregate investment X. The cumulative value function $V(s)$ is the sum of s and the payoff of an agent with parameter s when agents have a monotone strategy and invest if their parameter s' is smaller than s:*

$$V(s) = E\left[u\left(s, \mu_\theta(\{s' \leq s\})\right) + s \mid s \right].$$

When the parameter s is a cost of investment, the CVF is like a gross payoff function. When the individual parameter s is an information signal, the CVF cannot be interpreted as a gross payoff function and it may be more intuitive to use the *net CVF*:

$$V_N(s) = E\left[u\left(s, \mu_\theta(\{s' \leq s\})\right) \mid s \right].$$

ITERATIVE DOMINANCE

Without loss of generality, we can define the parameter s as the cost of a fixed-size action and denote it by c until the end of the section. The CVF corresponds to the gross payoff of investment.[12] Its graph is represented in Figure 11.7, which is similar to Figure 11.3 (with perfect information). We make the important assumption that the graph intersects the first diagonal once and from above.

ASSUMPTION 11.1 *The support of the agents' types is a closed subset of $\mathbb{R}$ with finite bounds b and B. There exists $c^* \in (b, B)$ such that $V(c) > c$ if $c < c^*$ and $V(c) < c$ if $c > c^*$, where $V(c)$ is the CVF.*

Let $c_1 = b$. From the previous assumption, $V(c_1) > c_1$. Define the function $W(z, c)$ as the payoff of investment for an agent with cost c when it is common knowledge that agents invest if their cost is less than z:

$$W(z, c) = E\left[u\left(c, \mu_\theta(\{y \leq z\})\right) + c \mid c\right].$$

We assume that $W(z, c)$ is continuous. By definition of the CVF, $V(c) = W(c, c)$ and $W(c_1, c_1) > c_1$. Because $W(c_1, c)$ is continuous in c, we can extend the region of investment: there exists $c_2 > c_1$ such that $W(c_1, c') > c'$ for any c' in the interval $[c_1, c_2)$. The critical step is the following: the common knowledge that all agents with cost lower than c_1 invest implies that for all agents in the interval $[c_1, c_2)$, not to invest is strictly dominated, and this property is common knowledge. The value of c_2 is taken as the highest possible one. It is characterized by $W(c_1, c_2) = c_2$. The function $W(c_1, c)$ is smaller than $V(c)$, because $c_1 < c$.[13] Its graph is presented in Figure 11.7.

---

[12] The gross payoff may include c as an argument.
[13] Usually the function $W(c_1, c)$ is decreasing in its first argument, but it could be an increasing function.

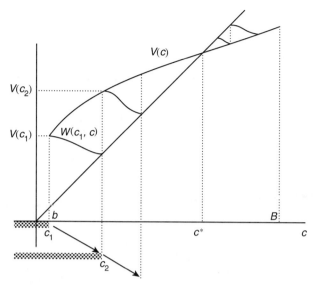

Figure 11.7 Iterative dominance with imperfect information. At each step, the region of dominance of investment is extended under the common-knowledge assumption that all agents in the previously defined region invest. The difference from Figure 11.3 (right panel) is due to the imperfect information.

If $V(c_2) > c_2$, we repeat the procedure. The method is similar to the staircase method in Figure 11.3 (right panel). The steps are twisted because of imperfect information. The sequence c_t is increasing and bounded by c^* (because of Assumption 11.1); it converges. It cannot converge to $\underline{c} < c^*$, because then $V(\underline{c}) = \underline{c}$ (using a continuity argument), which would contradict Assumption 11.1. A similar argument shows that there is a decreasing sequence $\{\hat{c}_t\}$ with $\hat{c}_1 = B$ that converges to c^* such that investment is strictly dominated at step t for all agents with parameter $c > \hat{c}_t$. We have shown that the strategy to invest if and only if $c < c^*$ defines a SREE.

THEOREM 11.2 *If the function* $W(z, c) = E\left[u\left(c, \mu_\theta(\{y \le z\})\right) + c \mid c\right]$ *is continuous and Assumption 11.1 holds, then the fixed point of the CVF, $c^* = V(c^*)$, defines a SREE.*

DISCUSSION

In Assumption 11.1, the condition $V(b) > b$ implies that an agent at the low end of the support will invest even if no other agent invests. Agents do not need the externality of each others' actions for a positive payoff of investment. Likewise, at the high end of the support, an agent will not invest even if all other agents do. For these agents, investment never has a positive payoff. If one of these conditions, $V(b) > b$ or $V(B) < B$, fails, the elimination procedure behind the result cannot start.

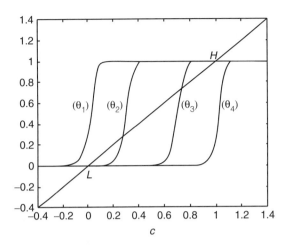

Figure 11.8 Cost distributions and multiple equilibria with perfect information. $\theta_1 < \theta_2 < \theta_3 < \theta_4$. There is a unique equilibrium with high activity in case 1, and a unique equilibrium with low activity in case 4. In cases 2 and 3, there are multiple equilibria.

Consider again the case of the Gaussian cost distribution with mean θ, as represented in Figure 11.8 for different values $\theta_1 < \theta_2 < \theta_3 < \theta_4$ (with the same variance). If it is common knowledge that θ is in the interval (θ_2, θ_3), then the CVF cuts the diagonal from above at the points L and H, and there is no SREE.

In this example, under *imperfect* information, the CVF has a unique intersection with the 45° line only if, with sufficient positive probability, we have realizations as θ_1 and θ_4 in Figure 11.8 for which there is a unique equilibrium under *perfect* information. This remark motivates a standard method in the analysis of coordination with imperfect information: First, consider the cases with perfect information and show that if a unidimensional parameter takes a value at either end of its support, there is a unique equilibrium with high or low level of activity; second, remove the assumption of common knowledge. Under imperfect information, the CVF function is smoother and there is a SREE. This method is followed in a number of studies, including the model of Morris and Shin (1998a) presented later.

However, these examples do not show that the existence of a unique equilibrium at each end of the support of θ is a necessary condition for the existence of a SREE when there is no common knowledge. Theorem 11.2 may be applicable for some families of distributions such that under perfect information there are always multiple equilibria. This issue is pursued in Exercise 11.3.

Models with strategic complementarities, zero–one actions, and multiple equilibria are stylized descriptions that omit the important feature of uncertainty. Under uncertainty, if the conditions of Theorem 11.2 are met, agents choose the same strategy. Because agents are similar in the actual structure of the economy, in a cluster, most of them turn out to take the same action. The level of aggregate activity is in most cases either high or low, as for the equilibria with perfect information.

The analysis with normal distributions shows that uncertainty may be more effective in generating a SREE when agents are nearly alike, but not exactly identical. Because a vanishingly small amount of heterogeneity has such a drastic impact on the equilibrium, the assumption of common knowledge may not generate robust results in models with strategic complementarities.

The arguments presented here originate in the pioneering work of Carlsson and van Damme (1993a, 1993b). As a motivation, they emphasize the justification of the criterion of risk dominance in one-period coordination games. They argue that the payoff structure of games with no uncertainty should be viewed as the realization of a random variable that is not perfectly observable by agents. The agents thus play in a *global game* (their terminology) with imperfect information on the payoffs of other players. Because the authors are interested in the criterion of risk dominance in a game with no uncertainty, they are especially interested in a global game with vanishingly small heterogeneity. Their main result shows that because of the absence of common knowledge, the set of rationalizable strategies is vanishingly small when the degree of heterogeneity is vanishingly small. This result is shown and discussed in Exercise 11.7.

11.3.3 Stag Hunts

Stag hunts may occur against currencies with a fixed exchange rate, banks, firms, or political regimes. A central bank that manages a fixed exchange rate for its currency must fill any gap between the supply and the demand by trading. If its reserves do not match the supply of domestic currency, a devaluation must take place, which benefits the agents who have bought the foreign currency before the change of regime.

A speculative attack is like a stag-hunt game (Rousseau, 1762). Each speculator does not have sufficient reserves to topple the regime of fixed exchange rate (hunt the stag), but the combined attacks of many agents can be successful. A critical mass of acting agents is necessary for a successful attack.

We consider a canonical game that can actually apply to many stag hunts. There is a continuum of agents of mass one. Each agent either invests (participates in the hunt) or does not invest. The cost of investment, γ, is the same for all agents. The hunt pays off if and only if the mass of total investment, X, is greater than some level θ. For simplicity, the gross payoff A is independent of θ and X.

The net payoff of investment is therefore

$$u(\theta, X) = \begin{cases} A - \gamma & \text{if } X \geq \theta, \\ -\gamma & \text{if } X < \theta. \end{cases}$$

THE GAME WITH COMMON KNOWLEDGE

Assume first that θ is common knowledge. There are multiple equilibria if θ is between 0 and 1, and there is a unique equilibrium if θ is below 0 or above 1:

(i) If $0 < \theta < 1$, there are two (stable) equilibria: either all agents invest or none of them does.

(ii) If $\theta \leq 0$, there is a unique equilibrium with investment by all agents: $X = 1$.
(iii) If $\theta > 1$, there is a unique equilibrium with no investment: $X = 0$.

THE GLOBAL GAME WITH IMPERFECT INFORMATION

We now remove the assumption of common knowledge by imbedding the game in a global game with imperfect information. The application of the global game to any coordination problem proceeds in two steps:

(i) The state θ is randomly drawn according to a distribution with density $h(\theta)$. For simplicity, we assume here that the distribution is uniform on $[-a, 1 + a]$. It is important that the interior of the support $(-a, 1 + a)$ contains the interval $[0, 1]$.
(ii) Each agent has a private signal $s = \theta + \epsilon$, where ϵ is an idiosyncratic noise that is independent of other variables in the economy. Let F be the c.d.f. of ϵ. For simplicity, ϵ has a uniform distribution on $[-\sigma, \sigma]$ with $\sigma < a$.

From the discussion in the previous section, we consider the monotone strategy $\hat{s}$: an agent invests if and only if his signal s is lower than $\hat{s}$: $s < \hat{s}$. Because $s = \theta + \epsilon$, this condition is equivalent to $\epsilon < \hat{s} - \theta$. (Of course, the agent does not know ϵ or θ.)

The application of the global-game method to determine the SREE proceeds in four steps:

1. The payoff of investment by the marginal agent is a function of the state: the state θ determines the distribution of private signals and therefore the mass of agents with a signal lower than $\hat{s}$. Therefore the payoff of investment is a function $u(\theta, \hat{s})$.
2. The payoff of the marginal agent is the expected value of $u(\theta, \hat{s})$ over the possible states and depends on his subjective probability distribution about θ. Let $\phi(\theta|s)$ be the density of that distribution that depends on his private information s. His payoff of investment is

$$(11.7) \quad U(\hat{s}, s) = \int u(\theta, \hat{s}) \phi(\theta|s) d\theta.$$

3. The *net* CVF is defined by $V_N(s) = U(s, s)$. Under suitable parameter assumptions, $V(s)$ is decreasing and there is a unique value s^* such that $V_N(s^*) = 0$, which by Theorem 11.2 defines the SREE.
4. Given the equilibrium strategy s^*, one determines the outcome of the game, which depends on θ. In the present case, the speculative attack is successful if $\theta < \theta^*$ for some value θ^* such that the mass of investments given the strategy s^* and the state θ^* reaches the critical mass.

Having summarized the global-game method in this model, we now provide the technical details.

1. The Payoff of Investment by the Marginal Agent as a Function of the State

Because a hunt is successful only if the mass of investment is greater than θ,

$$u(\theta, \hat{s}) = \begin{cases} A - \gamma & \text{if } \theta < F(\hat{s} - \theta), \\ -\gamma & \text{if } \theta \geq F(\hat{s} - \theta). \end{cases}$$

Given the special case of a uniform distribution of ϵ, if $|\hat{s} - \theta| \leq \sigma$, then $F(\hat{s} - \theta) = (\hat{s} - \theta + \sigma)/2\sigma$. Therefore,

$$(11.8) \qquad u(\theta, \hat{s}) = \begin{cases} A - \gamma & \text{if } \theta < \dfrac{\hat{s} + \sigma}{1 + 2\sigma}, \\ -\gamma & \text{if } \theta \geq \dfrac{\hat{s} + \sigma}{1 + 2\sigma}. \end{cases}$$

2. The Subjective Distribution of the Marginal Agent about the State

$\phi(\theta|s) > 0$ only if $|\theta - s| \leq \sigma$. For any two values θ and θ' within σ of s, we use Bayes's rule in likelihood ratios:

$$\frac{\phi(\theta|s)}{\phi(\theta'|s)} = \frac{\psi(s|\theta)}{\psi(s|\theta')} \frac{h(\theta)}{h(\theta')},$$

where ψ is the density of s conditional on θ, and $h(\theta)$ is the density of θ. In this canonical model, both ψ and h are densities of a uniform distribution. Hence, the posterior is also uniform and

$$(11.9) \qquad \phi(\theta|s) = \frac{1}{2\sigma} \qquad \text{if } |\theta - s| \leq \sigma.$$

3. The Net CVF and the SREE

Using the previous two steps, we find that the net CVF is[14]

$$(11.10) \qquad V_N(s) = \int u(\theta, s)\phi(\theta|s)d\theta$$

$$= \begin{cases} A - \gamma & \text{if } s \leq -\sigma, \\ A\dfrac{1 + \sigma - s}{1 + 2\sigma} - \gamma & \text{if } -\sigma \leq s \leq 1 + \sigma, \\ -\gamma & \text{if } s \geq 1 + \sigma. \end{cases}$$

The graph of this function is represented in Figure 11.9.

From Theorem 11.2, a SREE is defined by s^* with $V_N(s^*) = 0$. Therefore,

$$(11.11) \qquad s^* = 1 - \frac{\gamma}{A} + \sigma\left(1 - 2\frac{\gamma}{A}\right).$$

---

[14] The only nontrivial case is the middle one: from (11.8), $V_N(s) = (A/2\sigma)\int_{s-\sigma}^{(s+\sigma)/(1+2\sigma)} d\theta - \gamma$.

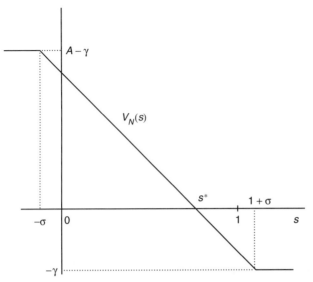

Figure 11.9 The net CVF of the canonical stag-hunt game.

4. The Outcome of the Game

The value of θ determines the distribution of the private costs and therefore the mass of agents with a cost smaller than s^*, who invest. This mass is

$$X = \text{Min}\left\{\text{Max}\left\{\frac{s^* - (\theta - \sigma)}{2\sigma}, 0\right\}, 1\right\}.$$

The condition for a successful stag hunt, $\theta \leq X$, is equivalent to

$$\theta \leq \theta^* = 1 - \frac{\gamma}{A}.$$

A stag hunt takes place if there are some agents with signal below s^*. Because the lowest private signal is $\theta - \sigma$, this condition is equivalent to $\theta - \sigma < s^*$ or $\theta < (1 + 2\sigma)\theta^*$. We have therefore the following outcomes:

- if $\theta < \theta^* = 1 - \gamma/A$, a stag hunt takes place and it succeeds;
- if $\theta^* < \theta < (1 + 2\sigma)\theta^*$, a stag hunt takes place and it fails: the mass of investment is smaller than θ;
- if $(1 + 2\sigma)\theta^* < \theta$, no stag hunt takes place.

In this model, the critical value for a successful stag hunt, $\theta^* = 1 - \gamma/A$, is independent of the heterogeneity of private information, as measured by σ. It depends only on the cost–benefit ratio γ/A. If that ratio tends to 0, then θ^* converges to 1. A successful stag hunt takes place most of the time. This remarkable property may be due to the simplicity of the model. However, choosing a density on θ that is not uniform will not affect the value of θ^* if σ is vanishingly small. An agent with signal s knows that θ is in $[s - \sigma, s + \sigma]$. When $\sigma \to 0$, the variations of the density of θ in the interval $(s - \sigma, s + \sigma)$ are vanishingly small. The density can be approximated by a uniform density.[15] An essential property of the density of θ is that its support is connected and contains 0 and 1 in its interior.

In the same model, one could assume that the state θ and the private signals have Gaussian distributions. This case is proposed as Exercise 11.4.

11.4 Speculative Attacks against a Fixed Exchange Rate

A regime of fixed exchange rates is for speculators an open invitation to a stag hunt. Because the central bank is prepared to trade the currency at some fixed price, it must have some reserves, either directly or through loans from other central banks. When the purchase orders for the foreign currency exceed the reserves, the fixed price of the exchange rate is not sustainable and a devaluation must take place. This devaluation brings a capital gain to the agents who have purchased the foreign currency. If they act in coordination, their combined reserves dwarf those of the central bank, thus forcing a devaluation and a distribution of good profits to the hunters. The game has been formalized by Obstfeld (1996), who also provides some empirical justification: under perfect information on the strategies and the payoffs of individuals, there are two equilibria in pure strategies, as in any standard stag-hunt game: either speculators cooperate and gain, or they don't, in which case there is neither gain nor loss.

This problem is analyzed here with a one-period model. The information of the speculators and the timing of the attack are two essential issues in a speculative attack. They cannot be addressed in a one-period framework, which is only a first step. They will be considered in Chapter 16.

If agents have imperfect information, what information is important for their choices? Two parameters may play a role: the amount of reserves of the central bank relative to the reserves of the speculators, and the level of the devaluation. In the first model below, the state of the world, θ, defines the amount of reserves of the central bank; in the second model, θ defines the exchange rate after the devaluation.

IMPERFECT INFORMATION ON THE CRITICAL MASS FOR A DEVALUATION

The reserves of the central bank amount to θ, which is not observable by agents, who form a continuum of mass one. Each agent can purchase foreign currency up to some maximum level that is determined by a liquidity constraint. Because they are risk-neutral, they will either place an order equal to the maximum or place no order. As in the previous model, we may assume that the decision of agents is about a fixed-size order, which is normalized to one (per individual). The cost of placing an order is γ. This cost can be due to transaction costs or to an interest rate when agents borrow the balance of their order. The gross payoff of the order is the capital gain that is incurred if the currency is devalued after the order is placed. The rate

---

[15] This property is used by Carlsson and van Damme (1993a) for their analysis. (See Lemma 11.3 in Exercise 11.7.)

of the devaluation is assumed to be independent of the amount of orders and of the reserves of the central bank. The payoff is $A - \gamma > 0$ if there is a devaluation, and $-\gamma$ otherwise. This model is simplified to fit the canonical model. The distributions of θ and of the private signals are the same as in the previous canonical model. Let X be the total mass of orders. A devaluation takes place if and only if $\theta \leq X$. For $\theta \leq 0$, we adopt the convention that the reserves of the central bank are exhausted and a devaluation takes place for any amount of orders.

In the analysis of the canonical model in Section 11.3.3, the central bank can fend off a speculative attack only if the level of reserves θ is greater than θ^*. If the cost of transaction, γ, is small (with respect to the rate of the devaluation, A), that minimum θ^* is close to the total reserves of the speculators.

IMPERFECT INFORMATION ON THE MARKET EXCHANGE RATE

Assume the fixed exchange rate is equal to 1 and that if a devaluation takes place, the exchange rate is equal to the *market exchange rate* $\theta < 1$. The value of θ reflects the state of the economy: the economy is in a better state if θ is higher. A devaluation takes place if the total purchases X of the foreign currency are at least equal to a fixed value $\alpha \in (0, 1)$. In order to apply the argument of iterative dominance, we need to have a region of θ such that an investment (purchase of the foreign currency) yields a positive payoff even if no agent places an order. Accordingly, we assume that a devaluation takes place if θ is smaller than a fixed value $\underline{\theta} \in (0, 1)$.

Any devaluation in the model generates an exchange rate θ that is lower than 1. We assume that θ has a uniform distribution on the interval $[\theta_0, 1]$ where $0 \leq \theta_0 < \underline{\theta}$. When θ is near 1, the gain from the devaluation, $1 - \theta$, is smaller than the cost γ. The speculators can trigger a devaluation in the current model (contrary to the previous one), but the gain from the devaluation is negative if the market exchange rate is not much different from the fixed exchange rate. For sufficiently large values of the private signal, investment is dominated.

As in the previous model, for suitable parameters, there is a SREE (Exercise 11.5). For parameters such that the optimal strategy is not close to $\underline{\theta}$, the SREE is defined by the strategy

$$(11.12) \quad s^* = 1 - \frac{\gamma}{1 - \alpha} + \alpha\sigma.$$

A speculative attack is successful if the mass of orders, X, is greater than α. The value of θ determines the distribution of the private signals and therefore the mass of agents with a signal smaller than s^*, who place an order. Because for $0 \leq X \leq 1$,

$$X = \frac{s^* - (\theta - \sigma)}{2\sigma},$$

the condition for a devaluation, $X \geq \alpha$, is equivalent to

$$(11.13) \quad \theta < \theta^* = 1 - \frac{\gamma}{1 - \alpha} + (1 - \alpha)\sigma.$$

A lower precision of private information (higher σ) induces a higher probability of a successful stag hunt. When the precision of the private information is arbitrarily large (vanishingly small σ), the fixed exchange rate is sustainable as long as it does not differ from the market rate by more than $\gamma/(1 - \alpha)$. This gap is small if the transaction cost is small with respect to the exchange rate and the reserves of speculators are not just above the reserves of the central bank (α not close to 1).

THE MODEL OF MORRIS AND SHIN

The previous model is a reduced form of the model of Morris and Shin (1998a). They assume that the market exchange rate is an increasing function $a(\theta)$ where the distribution of θ is uniform. (Recall that if the variance of the private information is small, the density of θ near the equilibrium strategy has little impact.) Private signals are uniform with bounded support, as in the previous model.

The assumption of a fixed level of reserves α at the central bank no longer holds: the central bank may now defend the currency at some cost that depends on the total investment (the total purchase of the foreign currency) and on the state θ. A critical assumption is that the central bank has perfect information about θ. It can therefore compute from the value of θ the distribution of private signals. Because it knows the strategy of the agents, it knows the total "amount of the attack" X as a function of the state. The central bank makes a zero–one decision whether to defend the currency, by comparing the value of preserving the fixed exchange rate with the cost of defense (which is an increasing function of X). The central bank, given its information, has a decision rule that is a deterministic function from (θ, s^*) to 1 (devaluation) or 0 (no devaluation). This rule is not essentially different from the previous one under which a devaluation occurs if the mass of agents' investments, X, which depends on θ and s^*, is greater than α. When σ is vanishingly small, the gap between the sustainable exchange rate and the market exchange rate in the model of Morris and Shin with a central bank is also given by equation (11.13). The level of reserves α is determined endogenously by the cost function of the central bank.

Morris and Shin (1998a) show that there is a unique Nash equilibrium in monotone strategies. However, the present analysis shows that, following Carlsson and van Damme (1993a), one can prove more easily a stronger property: under the assumptions of Morris and Shin, there is a SREE.

A COMMENT

The one-period models of speculative attacks resolve the issue of multiple equilibria and provide some indication about the effects of the parameters on the likelihood of an attack. However, they seem to generate implausibly high probabilities of an attack. More important, they miss essential elements. A speculative attack does not take place in one period.[16] Agents observe each other in a multiperiod setting. When

---

[16] The model of Morris and Shin (1998b) has many periods with a state of nature that follows a stochastic process. Agents learn exogenously, in each period, the state of nature in the previous

an agent delays, he faces the risk of placing an order too late, after the devaluation has occurred. The analysis of a speculative attack in a dynamic context will be presented in Chapter 16.

11.5 Bibliographical Notes

The literature on the topics of this chapter is very large. There is room to indicate here only a few items that could not be given sufficient treatment in the text.

The analysis of Guesnerie that is presented in Section 11.2 is extended in Guesnerie (2002). Cooper (1999) provides a very useful introduction to one-period games with strategic complementarities in macroeconomics.

Vives (1990) analyzes games with strategic complementarities when strategies are taken in a lattice (which is a set where any two elements have an upper and a lower bound in the set). The concept of stability of a Nash equilibrium, which is considered by Vives, applies to the tâtonnement process $x_{t+1} = R(x_t)$. One can verify in Figure 11.5 that this process converges monotonically to a Nash equilibrium and does not generate any complex behavior as it does for strategic substitutability. However, this process does not address the issue of the selection between multiple equilibria.

Milgrom and Roberts (1990) analyze an adaptive dynamic process in a general setting, but their focus is different from the global-game method. Numerous applications of the global-game method are presented in the highly informative paper of Morris and Shin (2000).

EXERCISES

EXERCISE 11.1

Consider the game in T periods of Section 11.2.2.

1. Assume $T = 2$ and $\alpha_1 = \alpha_2 = \alpha$. Determine the largest value γ^* of γ such that there is a SREE.
2. Provide an intuitive interpretation for $\gamma^* > \frac{1}{2}$.

EXERCISE 11.2

Using the properties of the Gaussian distribution, prove (11.4) and (11.5).

EXERCISE 11.3

Consider the model of Section 11.3.2 with a zero–one action, a distribution of the private costs of investment, and a payoff $E[X] - c$. Construct two distributions of costs with c.d.f.'s F_0 and F_1 with the following properties:

(i) each distribution has multiple intersections with the first diagonal, and thus generates multiple Nash equilibria under perfect information;

period. There is no learning from others and no intertemporal choice. The model is effectively a sequence of one-period models.

(ii) under imperfect information with a probability μ for F_1 and when each agent knows only μ and his own cost, the CVF satisfies the conditions of Theorem 11.2 and there is a SREE.

(One may use piecewise linear functions for F_0 and F_1).

EXERCISE 11.4 Coordination with Gaussian signals

Consider the coordination model of Section 11.3.3 where a stag hunt is successful if and only if the mass of investment X is at least equal to θ, which specifies the state of nature. Assume that θ is distributed $\mathcal{N}(\bar{\theta}, \sigma_\theta^2)$, and that each agent has a private signal $s = \theta + \epsilon$, with a noise $\epsilon \sim \mathcal{N}(0, \sigma_\epsilon^2)$. Let $\rho_\theta = 1/\sigma_\theta^2$ and $\rho_\epsilon = 1/\sigma_\epsilon^2$.

1. Given the strategy $\hat{s}$, show that the hunt is successful if and only if $\theta \leq \phi(\hat{s})$, with

$$F\left(\frac{\hat{s} - \phi(\hat{s})}{\sigma_\epsilon}\right) = \phi(\hat{s}),$$

where F is the c.d.f. of the normal distribution $\mathcal{N}(0, 1)$. Show that $\phi(\frac{1}{2}) = \frac{1}{2}$ and that

$$0 < \phi'(s) < \frac{f(0)}{f(0) + \sigma_\epsilon},$$

where f is the density function associated to F.

2. Show that an agent with signal s has an estimate on θ which is $\mathcal{N}(m(s), \rho)$, with

$$m(s) = \frac{\rho_\theta}{\rho}\bar{\theta} + \frac{\rho_\epsilon}{\rho}s \quad \text{with} \quad \rho = \rho_\theta + \rho_\epsilon.$$

3. Show that the net CVF is defined by

$$V(s) = AF\left((\phi(s) - m(s))\sqrt{\rho}\right) - \gamma.$$

4. Assume that agents have vanishingly close beliefs with $\sigma_\epsilon \to 0$. Using questions 1 and 2, show that for any $A > 0$ there exists σ^* such that if $\sigma_\epsilon < \sigma^*$, then $\phi(s) - m(s) < A$. Show that $V(s)$ is a decreasing function if $\sigma_\epsilon < \sigma^*$ and that there is a SREE. Show that if $\sigma_\epsilon \to 0$, then the equilibrium strategy s^* converges to $\frac{1}{2}$. (Note that the limit is independent of A and γ.)

EXERCISE 11.5 A speculative attack with uncertainty about the market exchange rate

Solve the model of speculative attack with uncertainty about the exchange rate θ with the assumptions leading to the SREE in (11.12).

EXERCISE 11.6 Should the policy maker reveal information?

Consider an economy with a fixed exchange rate and a continuum of agents (speculators) of mass one. In this regime, the value of the foreign currency is 1. If a devaluation occurs, the value of the foreign currency is $D > 1$. There is only one period. Each agent can either buy a fixed amount of foreign currency at the fixed cost γ, or not buy. Let X be the mass of speculators who buy the foreign currency. A devaluation takes place if and only if $\theta \leq X$. The value of θ is a realization of the Gaussian random variable $\mathcal{N}(\overline{\theta}, \sigma_\theta^2)$. Each agent has a private signal on θ, which is the sum of θ and an idiosyncratic noise ϵ with a normal distribution $\mathcal{N}(0, \sigma_\epsilon^2)$. The parameters are such that $\sigma_\theta^2 = 1$, $D = 2c$.

1. Assume that the parameters are such that there is a SREE in which all agents follow the strategy to buy if and only if their signal is smaller than some value s^*. Show that in this case, a devaluation takes place if and only if $\theta < \theta^*$, where θ^* is a linear function of s^* that you will determine.
2. Show that if $\sigma_\epsilon < \sigma^*$ for some value σ^*, the model has a SREE.
3. Assume the central bank can credibly commit to issue a Gaussian signal about θ after θ is realized and before agents play the game. Analyze the effect of the policy on the equilibrium. Should the central bank release information? (You will distinguish between the cases of low $\overline{\theta}$ and high $\overline{\theta}$.)

EXERCISE 11.7 The model of Carlsson and van Damme

Consider the standard coordination game for two agents that is specified in the following table:

	Actions	Agent β	
		0	1
Agent α	0	0, 0	$0, -c_\beta$
	1	$-c_\alpha, 0$	$1 - c_\alpha, 1 - c_\beta$

1. Show that if $0 < c < 1$ and γ is common knowledge, there are multiple equilibria.

We make the following assumption:

ASSUMPTION 11.2 *The state θ has a density $h(\theta) > 0$ for $\theta \in [-a, 1 + a]$ with $a > 0$. Agent α has a signal $s = \theta + \sigma\epsilon_\alpha$, and agent β a signal $s = \theta + \sigma\epsilon_\beta$, where σ is a parameter and $(\epsilon_\alpha, \epsilon_\beta)$ has a density $\phi(\epsilon_\alpha, \epsilon_\beta)$ that is symmetric on the bounded support $(-1, 1) \times (-1, 1)$.*

2. Show the next lemma, and provide an intuitive interpretation.

LEMMA 11.3 *For any $\eta > 0$, there exists $\hat{\sigma} > 0$ such that if $\sigma < \hat{\sigma}$, then for any $c \in [0, 1]$, $P(c' < c|c) > \frac{1}{2} - \eta$.*

3. Use the previous lemma and Theorem 11.2 to prove

THEOREM 11.3 (Carlsson and van Damme) *Under Assumption 11.2, for any $\eta > 0$ there exist $\hat{\sigma}$ such that if $\sigma < \hat{\sigma}$, then there exist $\underline{s}$ and $\overline{s}$ with*

$$\frac{1}{2} - \eta < \underline{s} < \overline{s} < \frac{1}{2} + \eta,$$

and for any agent with cost $c < \underline{s}$ ($c > \overline{s}$), acting (not acting) is iteratively dominant.

4. What is the important assumption about the distribution of θ?
5. Compare the set of equilibria with $\sigma = 0$ (under perfect information) and the one with σ arbitrarily small. Comment.
6. *The absence of common knowledge.* Consider the global game where the densities h and ϕ are uniform and $\sigma = 0.01$. Suppose that agent α has a cost $c = 0.75$. He is sure that the other agent has a cost $c' \leq 0.77$. The other agent, whatever his cost, is sure that agent α has a cost less than 0.79. Show that no agent invests, although both agents are sure that both costs are less than 1 and that coordination (investment by both) is feasible (i.e., profitable to both). Explain.

12 Learning to Coordinate

— C'est une révolte?

— Non Sire, une révolution.

In an economy with strategic complementarities, the structure of individual payoffs evolves randomly and slowly. When agents have perfect information on the payoffs' structure, multiple equilibria may occur in some phases. Under imperfect information, the existence of a SREE is shown in which a strong hysteresis effect takes place: the level of aggregate activity hovers near its value in the previous period most of the time and jumps to a different level with a small probability. Applications may be found in macroeconomics and revolutions.

In the previous chapter, the coordination game with strategic complementarities took place in one period. All individuals were thinking simultaneously without learning from the past. The process of equilibrium selection between a high and a low level of aggregate activity rested on the agents' imperfect information about others' payoffs and the possibility that the fundamentals of the economy took "extreme values" where one action (e.g., investment or no investment) was optimal independently of others' actions. In the one-period setting, there is no possibility of learning.

In this chapter, agents learn from the actions taken in the past by others. Social learning may affect critically the assumptions that were made in the one-period context. For example, the observation that few agents invest in some period rules out the extreme event that investment is a dominant strategy for a large fraction of the population. We will see that when agents learn from history, a strongly rational-expectations equilibrium (SREE) exists if the degree of heterogeneity between agents is neither too large nor too small, an assumption that fits the macroeconomic context.

In the SREE, the level of aggregate activity in period t exerts a strong influence on individual choices in period $t + 1$ because of imperfect information. Most of the time, agents choose a strategy close to the one in the previous period, and the profile of aggregate activity exhibits hysteresis with random switches between protracted regimes at high and low levels. During a regime, information about the mass of agents willing to take a contrary action is poor. A switch releases a large amount of information about that mass.

THE GENERAL FRAMEWORK

When agents are heterogeneous, the structure of the economy may be fairly complex. Complexity and imperfect information are closely related. In constructing a model, we will have to keep the essence of the complexity while simplifying the structure as much as possible to keep the analysis tractable.

In all models of this chapter, there is a continuum of agents in each period, who live only for one period. Each agent makes a zero–one decision: he can make a fixed-size investment at the cost c or do nothing. If he invests, he gets the payoff $E[X_t|c] - c$, where X_t is the aggregate investment in period t. If he does not invest, his payoff is zero. Each agent's cost c is drawn randomly from a distribution.

The distribution has a cluster, a property that is required for multiple equilibria under perfect information or for large changes of aggregate activity under imperfect information. Each Bayesian agent observes only his own cost and the history of aggregate activities, and has a different belief about the *position* of the cluster.

HYSTERESIS FOR EQUILIBRIUM SELECTION

Suppose that in some period, the actual distribution of costs is represented by the c.d.f. F_1 as in Figure 12.1. Under perfect information about F_1, there are two equilibria L_1 and H_1: in the equilibrium L_1, the acting set is the interval to the left of c_1. Under imperfect information, agents observe in any period t the history of the aggregate activities $h_t = \{X_1, \ldots, X_{t-1}\}$. We will see that whenever for any period the level of aggregate activity has been low in the previous periods, there is a SREE in which agents choose a strategy x_1 near the fixed point c_1. They do not coordinate on a strategy near the high equilibrium H_1, because they do not have perfect information about the c.d.f. F_1.

Suppose now that the true c.d.f. moves randomly from F_1 to F_2. Agents still observe only the total level of investment. The strategy x_1 near c_1 generates the observation $F_2(x_1)$, after which agents revise their belief. We will see that in the SREE, the strategy x_2 is near L_2 (Figure 12.1), which is the fixed point of F_2 closest to L_1. That property of hysteresis holds as long as there exists a low fixed point of the c.d.f., that is, an equilibrium under perfect information with a low level of activity. In the figure, the low fixed point disappears in period 3. In the SREE under imperfect information, the level of activity jumps to a value near the high point H_3.

The process is summarized by an approximation rule. Take the actual c.d.f., F, that is not observed by the agents. Suppose that the agents coordinate on one of the equilibria, say at the low fixed point of F. If F evolves randomly by a small amount and the low fixed point still exists, agents *coordinate* on this point: there is a SREE near this point. Agents jump to the high point only if the low point disappears. This rule

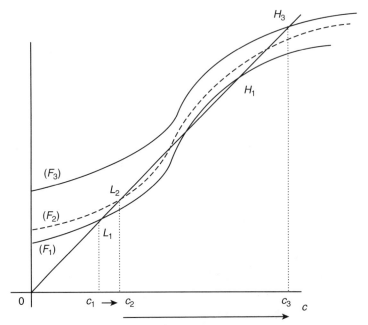

Figure 12.1 Learning about an evolving distribution. F_1, F_2, and F_3 are the realizations of the c.d.f. F for t_1, t_2, and t_3. The c.d.f. evolves slowly between consecutive periods, and the equilibrium strategy is near a fixed point of the CVF. Between t_2 and t_3, the strategy jumps to a higher equilibrium level.

is equivalent to the following *ad hoc* selection rule: in any period, agents coordinate on the fixed point of F that is closest to the equilibrium in the previous period.[1] The SREE is summarized by a rule of inertia: agents move from the neighborhood of one fixed point (of the c.d.f.) to the neighborhood of another fixed point only if the first fixed point vanishes.

SOCIAL CHANGES AND REVOLUTIONS

Why do sudden changes of opinion or revolutions that were not anticipated with high probability seem anything but surprising in hindsight? This question was asked by Kuran (1995). The gap between the *ex ante* and the *ex post* views is especially striking when no important exogenous event occurs (e.g., the fall of the communist regimes).[2] These social changes depend essentially on the distribution of individuals' payoffs, on which each agent has only partial information. According to Kuran, "historians have systematically overestimated what revolutionary actors could have known." If a revolution were to be fully anticipated, it would probably run a different course. The July 14th entry in the diary of Louis XVI was "today, nothing."[3] Before a social change,

---

[1] Such a rule is posited by Cooper (1994) in a model of coordination where the structure is determined by a production technology and a utility for consumption, and evolves over time.

[2] For a common view before the fall, read the speeches of H. Kissinger in Halberstam (1991).

[3] However, the entry may mean "no hunting." The quotation at the beginning of this chapter is from a conversation between Louis XVI and the duke of La Rochefoucault-Liancourt. In the numerous stages of the French revolution, the actors did not seem to have anticipated well the subsequent stages, especially when they manipulated the crowds.

individuals who favor the change do not have perfect information on the preferences of others, but they are surprised to find themselves in agreement with so many *ex post*, and this common view in hindsight creates a sense of determinism.

The models of Kuran (1987, 1995) fall into the class of models considered in this chapter. Suppose that individuals have to decide in each period between two actions or expressed opinions as revealed by some behavior: action 1 supports a given political regime, whereas action 0 does not (or supports a revolution). Each individual is characterized by a preference variable c, which is distributed on the interval $[0, 1]$ with a cumulative distribution function $F(c)$. The preference for the regime increases with c. There is a continuum of individuals with a total mass equal to one. For an individual with parameter c, the payoff of his action x (which is either 0 or 1) is a function that is (i) decreasing in the distance between his action and his preference, (ii) increasing in the mass of individuals who choose the same action. Kuran interprets the externality effect as an individual's taste for *conformism*. Strategic complementarities may also arise because the probability of the change of regime depends on the number of individuals expressing an opinion, or taking an active part in a revolution.

Let X be the mass of individuals who choose action 0 (the revolution) in a given period. (The mass of individuals who choose action 1 is $1 - X$.) Following the previous discussion, the payoff function of an individual who takes action x is defined by

$$w(x, X, c) = \begin{cases} X - c & \text{if } x = 0, \\ 1 - X - (1 - c) & \text{if } x = 1. \end{cases}$$

The difference $w(0, X, c) - w(1, X, c)$ is the function u given by

$$u(c) = 2(X - c) \qquad \text{with} \quad c \in [0, 1],$$

which is a multiple of the payoff function $X - c$. The model of Kuran is thus a special case of the canonical model with strategic complementarities. For a suitable distribution of individual preferences, the model has multiple equilibria under perfect information. Kuran follows the *ad hoc* rule of selection and assumes that a regime stays in power as long as the structure of preferences allows it. This structure may evolve in such a way that the regime is no longer a feasible equilibrium and society jumps to the other equilibrium regime. The changes and surprises cannot be analyzed with the *ad hoc* rule in a static model. They require a dynamic approach with imperfect information about the structure of payoffs and an explicit formulation of expectations. These features have a central place in the dynamic models of this chapter.

We will see that until the very end of the old regime, the public information is that a large fraction of the population supports the old regime, whereas the actual distribution could support a revolution. When the regime changes, beliefs change in two ways: first, the perceived distribution of preferences shifts abruptly toward the new regime; second, the precision of this perception is much more accurate. The high confidence in the information immediately after the revolution may provide all individuals with the impression that the revolution was deterministic.

Further work may apply the Bayesian approach to an analysis of a policy undertaken by an authority who attempts to stay in power. Removal of a penalty for action 0 may increase the probability of a switch to another equilibrium: as noted by Tocqueville (1856), regimes do not crumble when they are at their most repressive, but when this state of repression is partially lifted.[4]

12.1 A Distribution with a Cluster

Following the introduction, we build a model that (i) incorporates heterogeneous expectations about the structure of the economy and a random evolution of that structure, (ii) remains simple, (iii) has generic features that indicate the robustness of the main properties. The main modeling issue is the *tail property.*

THE TAIL PROPERTY

Distributions of costs are represented in Figure 12.2 by their c.d.f. in the upper part of the figure, and by the associated density in the lower part. Strategic complementarity implies that if there are multiple equilibria, the mass of active agents is either small or large, and the cutoff value c^* is not in the middle range of costs where the density of agents is high. If agents have perfect information on the c.d.f. F, there are two equilibria L and H with low and high activity. Assume that the actual distribution of individual costs is a random realization in a class of possible distributions, and that agents observe only the level of aggregate activity. Three examples of distributions are represented in the top part of the figure.

Assume that agents choose a strategy near c_L (identified with c_L here). The level of aggregate activity $X = F(c_L)$ measures the mass of agents in the left tail of the distribution (represented in the lower part of the figure). A generic property of an inference problem is that the observation of the tail does not provide a precise signal about the entire distribution. This property is the *tail property.* As illustrated in the lower part of Figure 12.2, the mass of agents to the left of c_L should not enable agents to discriminate clearly between the density f (under which high activity is an equilibrium) and the density f_1 (under which there is no equilibrium with high activity).

We build a representation of the tail property[5] which is sufficiently simple for analysis. We cannot restrict the distributions to belong to the family of normal

---

[4] The Tocqueville effect is *not* driven by imperfect information on the power of the king. In a state with partially lifted repression, "le mal est devenu moindre il est vrai, mais la sensibilité est plus vive" (Chapter 4).

[5] The tail property is obviously the same for a right tail. In Figure 12.2, the observation of $F(c_H)$ does not enable agents to discriminate between the distributions F and F_2.

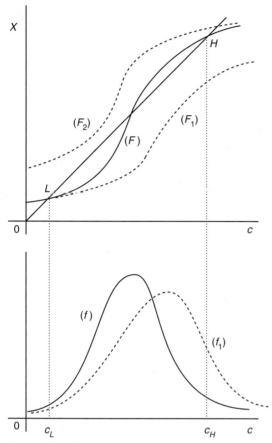

Figure 12.2 The tail property. Cumulative distribution functions are represented in the upper part, and associated density functions in the lower part.

distributions $\mathcal{N}(\theta, \sigma^2)$ where agents do not observe θ, as one observation of $F(c)$ would reveal θ and the entire distribution. (A finite number of parameters would not help either.)

We will consider two models, which are special but have nevertheless some generic features. In the first, the distribution with a cluster is stylized by a rectangular density: the graph of the density function has the shape of a hat, and the top of the hat corresponds to the cluster. This model is analyzed in Chamley (1999) and is presented less formally here. In the second model, the distribution is Gaussian and aggregate activity is observed with a noise.

If the total level of investment is observed with a noise, the information at the end of a period is $Y = F_\theta(c^*) + \epsilon$, where θ is a parameter and ϵ is a noise (which can be normally distributed $\mathcal{N}(0, \sigma_\epsilon^2)$). When c^* is low or high, the power of the signal Y on θ is small[6] because $F(c^*)$ is near 0 or 1. The model incorporates the tail

---

[6] A similar property appears in other parts in this book (Chapters 3, 15, 16).

property and has a plausible "look and feel." However, it cannot be solved analytically. Numerical simulations will show that switches between regimes occur and confirm the robustness of the stylized model.

12.1.1 An Analytical Model

In each period, there is a continuum of agents parameterized by the private cost of a fixed-size investment c. The payoff of investment is $E_c[X] - c$, where E_c is the expectation of the agent. The distribution of individual costs is defined by the density function

$$(12.1) \qquad f(c) = \begin{cases} \beta & \text{for } -b \leq c < \theta \text{ and } \theta + \sigma < c \leq B, \\ \alpha + \beta & \text{for } \theta < c < \theta + \sigma, \quad \text{with} \quad 0 < 1 - \beta < \alpha. \end{cases}$$

This function and its c.d.f. are represented in Figure 12.3. The distribution can be decomposed as the sum of two distributions: first, the *spread* has a uniform density β; second, the *cluster* has a uniform density α on the interval $(\theta, \theta + \sigma)$. The cluster has a mass $\alpha\sigma$ and a width σ. The support of the distribution is $[-b, B]$. For reasons that will be clear later, we assume the following inequalities:

$$(12.2) \qquad b > 0, \qquad B > \frac{\beta b + \alpha \sigma}{1 - \beta}.$$

All parameters are constant except for the state θ, which determines the position of the cluster. When θ is high (low), costs are on average high (low).

PERFECT INFORMATION

Suppose first that θ is observable. The CVF is the same as the c.d.f. There are two stable Nash equilibria: active agents have a cost lower than $c^* \in \{X_L, X_H\}$ defined by

$$(12.3) \qquad X_L = \frac{\beta b}{1 - \beta}, \qquad X_H = \frac{\beta b + \alpha \sigma}{1 - \beta}.$$

By (12.2), $0 < X_L < X_H < B$. The equilibria are represented by the points L and H in Figure 12.3, which are the intersections of the c.d.f. with the 45° line. Depending on the value of θ, there are three possible cases, denoted (1), (2), and (3) in the figure:

$$(12.4) \qquad \begin{cases} (1) \text{ if } \theta < X_L, \text{ then } X_H \text{ is the only equilibrium;} \\ (2) \text{ if } \theta > X_H - \sigma, \text{ then } X_L \text{ is the only equilibrium;} \\ (3) \text{ if } \theta \in (X_L, X_H - \sigma), \text{ then both } X_L \text{ and } X_H \text{ are equilibria.} \end{cases}$$

At the point H, all agents in the cluster are acting. At the point L, no agent in the cluster is acting. We will see below that the model exhibits the tail property.

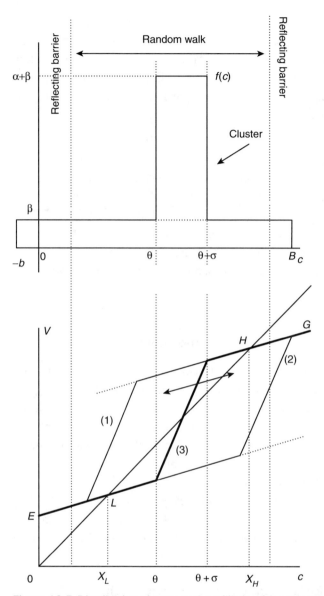

Figure 12.3 Distribution of costs and equilibria with perfect information. The density function exhibits a cluster in the interval $(\theta, \theta + \sigma)$. The width σ is fixed, but θ moves randomly one step at a time between two reflecting barriers. When θ moves randomly, the c.d.f. "slides" between the lines EL and HG. The point L is a fixed point of the c.d.f. for any value $\theta > X_L$. The point H is a fixed point of the c.d.f. for $\theta < X_H - \sigma$. When agents observe only the activity, the point L (H) reveals only that $\theta > X_L$ ($\theta < X_H - \sigma$).

The Evolution of the Structure of the Economy

By assumption, the variable θ that defines the structure of the economy evolves over time according to a random process. An important element of the model here is that the structure of the economy does not jump between periods, but evolves gradually. (Quoting Leibniz, "Natura non facit saltus.") In order to obtain analytical results, let the set Θ be a grid, $\Theta = \{\omega_1, \ldots, \omega_K\}$, with $\omega_1 = \gamma$, $\omega_K = \Gamma$ ($-b < \gamma < \Gamma < B - \sigma$). The distance between consecutive values is equal to ϵ, which can be small. Between consecutive periods, the value of θ evolves according to a symmetric random walk: it may stay constant or move to one of the two adjacent grid points with the same probability p. If θ is on a reflecting barrier (γ or Γ), it moves away from that barrier with some probability. [7]

IMPERFECT INFORMATION

Assume θ is not observable and agents observe the aggregate activity at the end of each period. We will see that an equilibrium must be monotone: an agent invests if and only if his cost is smaller than c^*. If $c^* < \theta$, the aggregate activity is $\beta(c^* + b)$, and it is independent of $\theta > c^*$. The observation of the left tail of the distribution of costs is a poor signal about the values of θ on the right of c^*.

The model exhibits the tail property. The same property is verified when the strategy c^* is such that $c^* > \theta + \sigma$.

12.1.2 The Equilibrium under Imperfect Information

We present the properties of the model in an informal way. A technical description is sketched in the Appendix (Section 12.3), and a complete presentation is given in Chamley (1999). In each period t, the history $h_t = \{X_1, \ldots, X_{t-1}\}$ of the levels of aggregate activity determines the public information about θ_t. Each agent uses his private information (his own cost c) to update this public information and to compute his subjective distribution on the set Θ. By an abuse of notation, the strategy to invest for a cost lower than c^* will be called the strategy c^*.

The range of the states for which there are multiple equilibria under perfect information is the range of the grid points $\{\theta_L + \epsilon, \ldots, \theta_H - \epsilon\}$, where θ_L is the highest grid point to the left of X_L, and θ_H the lowest grid point to the right of $X_H - \sigma$. From (12.4), and given the c.d.f. F,

(12.5) $$\begin{cases} (1) \text{ if } \theta \leq \theta_L, \text{ then } X_{\bar{H}} \text{ is the only fixed point of } F(X); \\ (2) \text{ if } \theta \geq \theta_H, \text{ then } X_L \text{ is the only fixed point of } F(X); \\ (3) \text{ if } \theta_L < \theta < \theta_H, \text{ then } X_L \text{ and } X_H \text{ are fixed points of } F(X). \end{cases}$$

The First Period

Assume that in period 0 the value of θ is $\theta_0 = \theta_H$ and that it is observable by all agents. This assumption will be justified later. By the definition of θ_H, there is a

---

[7] The generalization to an arbitrary number of moves between periods is considered in numerical simulations. The random walk is fully specified in the appendix (Section 12.3).

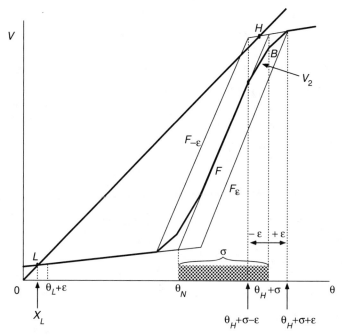

Figure 12.4 The beginning of the low regime. In period 1, the CVF is the same as the c.d.f. F. (Compare with Figure 12.3.) In period 2, some smoothing takes place. The cumulative value function V_2 is strictly below the 45° line for all $c > X_L$.

unique equilibrium with strategy $c^* = X_L$. The c.d.f. in period 0 is represented by its graph F in Figure 12.4. It is identical with the CVF in that period.

For any period $t > 1$, agents observe only the history h_t and know the structure of the random process of θ. At the end of period 1, the level of aggregate investment is $X_1 = \beta(c^* + b)$, and it is perfectly anticipated. Nothing is learned from that observation. At the beginning of period 2, agents know that θ may have moved with equal probability to the left or to the right of $\theta_1 = \theta_H$. The cumulative value function CVF$_2$ is an average of three cumulative distribution functions: F for $\theta = \theta_H$, and the ones for the grid points on the right and on the left. Because the c.d.f. is concave near the point X_H, the function CVF$_2$ is smaller than F. It has a unique intersection with the 45° line at the point X_L. Theorem 11.2 applies, and the strategy $c_2^* = X_L$ defines a SREE.

THE LOW REGIME

Because θ changes by at most one grid point in any period during the first few periods, we can use the same argument as in period 2: in period k (k small), it is common knowledge that $\theta_H - k\epsilon \leq \theta_k \leq \theta_H + k\epsilon$, and the argument of period 1 applies: the strategy in period k is $c_k^* = X_L$, and the observation of the aggregate activity $X = \beta(X_L + b)$ conveys no information on θ. The level of the aggregate activity is low in this regime.

Let n be the number of grid points between θ_H and θ_L ($\theta_L = \theta_H - n\epsilon$). The argument in the previous paragraph applies in any period $k < n$. In period n there is a strictly positive probability that $\theta = \theta_L < X_L$, i.e., that a fraction of the cluster has a cost lower than X_L. The payoff of investment of an agent with cost X_L is strictly positive. Therefore, the equilibrium strategy c^* is strictly higher than X_L. It is shown in the appendix (Section 12.3) and in Chamley (1999) that under some conditions the CVF has a unique intersection with the 45° line and that this intersection is very near X_L. More specifically, this intersection at c^* satisfies

$$(12.6) \qquad \theta_L < X_L \le c^* < \theta_L + \epsilon.$$

When the equilibrium strategy satisfies this condition (the strategy lies between X_L and the nearest grid point on the right), we will say that the economy is in a *low regime*.

Assume the low-regime property holds for all periods $1, \dots, t$, and consider period t. The equilibrium strategy c_t^* satisfies (12.6.) There are two possible cases: either $\theta_t > \theta_L$ or $\theta_t = \theta_L$. (Recall that θ_t is on a grid.) Let us show that in the first case the low regime goes on, whereas in the second case there is a switch to a high regime.

Assume $\theta_t > \theta_L$. At the end of period t, the observed level of activity is $X_t = \beta(c_t^* + b)$. From this observation, one learns only that $\theta_t > \theta_L$. (The tail property is operative here.) At the beginning of period $t + 1$, agents know that θ may have decreased and crossed X_L. However, the probability of that event is small. This is an important step, which needs some comment. We will see that after the state crosses the value X_L, a switch to a high regime is triggered. The state θ_{t+1} can cross X_L and reach θ_L only if $\theta_t = X_L + \epsilon$ in period t. The probability of the latter event in period t is small, because the low regime has held since period 1. In all previous periods, agents inferred from the observation of the aggregate activity that $\theta_t > X_L$. The information about the low regime in the history h_t is equivalent to the information that $\theta_k > X_L$ for all $k \le t$. The evolution of the public belief in a low regime is illustrated by an example in Figure 12.5.

To summarize, in a low regime, the equilibrium strategy c^* is near X_L. As long as the level of aggregate investment is equal to $\beta(c^* + b)$, agents infer that $\theta > \theta_L$ and use a low-regime strategy in the following period.

The CVF in a Low Regime

Each agent forms his own belief by combining the public belief in Figure 12.5 with the information about his own cost c. The evolution of the CVF, $V(c) = E[F_\theta(c)|c]$, in the low regime is illustrated in Figure 12.6. One verifies in the figure that the CVF satisfies the conditions of Theorem 11.2 for the existence of a SREE. Two assumptions play an important role in generating a CVF, as shown in Figure 12.6.

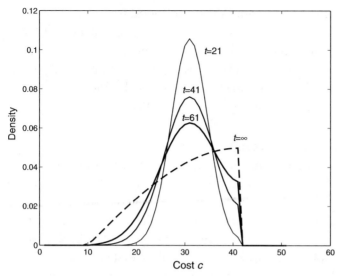

Figure 12.5 The public belief in a low regime. The graph represents the density of θ in a low regime. The strategy c^* is near X_L, and $\theta > X_L$. The level of aggregate activity is $X = \beta(b + c^*)$ and reveals only that $\theta > X_L$. Parameters: $\epsilon = 1$, $\theta_L = 10 = X_L - 0.5$, $\theta_H = 31 = X_H - \sigma + 0.5$, $\gamma = 1$, $\Gamma = 41$, $\sigma = 10$, $\beta = 0.3$, $\alpha = 2.1$, $p = \frac{1}{3}$.

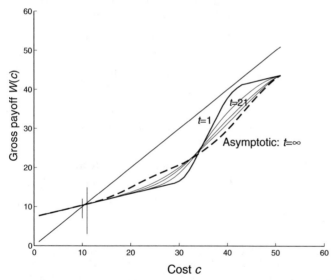

Figure 12.6 The evolution of the CVF in a low regime. Immediately after the switch to the low regime ($t = 1$), the CVF is identical to the cumulative distribution function. Over time, the CVF is gradually smoothed because the public belief is gradually spread (as shown in Figure 12.5). The CVF has a unique fixed point. The two vertical lines on each side of the fixed point mark the nearest two grid points for θ. The fixed point is not the same for all periods but its variations are too small to be represented. The parameters are the same as in Figure 12.5.

The Power of the Possibility of Extreme Values of the State

According to the first assumption, there is an interval[8] of high values of the state θ with unique equilibrium at a low level of activity X_L under perfect information. Likewise, there is an interval of low values of θ for which X_H is the only fixed point of $F_\theta(c)$. As in the model of Carlsson and van Damme (1993a), the positive probability of *extreme values of the state* is essential in generating a SREE.[9]

Heterogeneity, History, and Hysteresis

The second important assumption is that the degree of heterogeneity must be neither too large nor too small.[10] If it is too large, there are no multiple equilibria under perfect information (as shown in Section 11.3), and the same is true *a fortiori* when agents do not observe others' costs. More interestingly, if the degree of heterogeneity is very small as in Carlsson and van Damme (1993a), there is no SREE, because the information of history is not sufficiently powerful to induce hysteresis.

The case with a highly concentrated distribution of costs is illustrated in Figure 12.7. In a first phase after a switch to a low regime,[11] there is a SREE. After some interval of time, the CVF has multiple fixed points. Both stable fixed points define Nash equilibria. There is no SREE.

There is a fixed point close to X_L as in Figure 12.5, but there is also a new fixed point at A. Its existence is due to the small degree of heterogeneity, as in Carlsson and van Damme. Suppose that the degree of heterogeneity is vanishingly small, and consider an agent with a cost in the middle range of the interval (X_L, X_H). For such an agent, the weight of history is vanishingly small compared with the weight of the information of his own cost. He believes that about half of the other agents have a cost lower than his (see the previous chapter). In this case, the CVF converges to half the mass of agents and has an intersection with the 45° line near the midpoint of (θ_L, θ_H).

For the agents with a cost c near X_L, history dominates the private information of c no matter how small the heterogeneity. The argument of iterative dominance does not apply to these agents.[12] To summarize, the agents think: if there were (a significant

---

[8] In the analytical appendix (Section 12.3.1), this region is fairly large with $\Gamma - \theta_H \geq \theta_H - \theta_L$, but numerical simulations show that this restriction can be weakened considerably.

[9] *A contrario*, a small perturbation that excludes the possibility of a strong event may have a critical impact on the level of activity. If the region with $\theta > X_H - \sigma$ vanishes, the economy stays in a low equilibrium even if it could jump to a high equilibrium under perfect information [as in case (3) of Figure 12.3].

[10] For tractability, in the appendix (Section 12.3.1), $\alpha < 2(1 - \beta)$. Numerical simulations show that this assumption can be weakened considerably.

[11] Note that the region with extremely high values of θ does not need to be large: it is reduced here to one grid point.

[12] Given any heterogeneity parameter σ, for an agent with c sufficiently close to X_L ($c > X_L$), history shows that the lower end of the cluster, θ, cannot be significantly below c. The CVF, $V(c)$, is below the 45° line if $c \in (X_L, \bar{c})$ for some $\bar{c} > X_L$. Hence, there is an equilibrium point between X_L and $\bar{c}$.

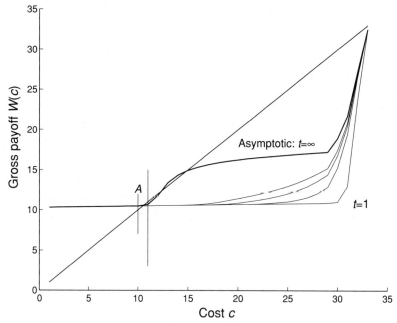

Figure 12.7 The CVF with a highly concentrated cluster. The population is highly concentrated with $\alpha/\beta > 40$. After a switch to a low regime, a SREE exists for $t < T$ where T is some finite number. For $t \geq T$, the CVF has an additional fixed point A where history is dominated by private beliefs. There are multiple Nash equilibria and no SREE. Parameters: $\gamma = 1$, $\theta_L = 10 = X_L - 0.5$, $\theta_H = \Gamma = 31 = X_H - \sigma + 0.5$, $\sigma = 2$, $\beta = 0.05$, $\alpha = 10.45$. The probability of a change of θ is small ($p = 0.1$).

mass of) agents with a lower cost, we would have seen some action in the previous period. Agents in the lower bound of the cluster would have taken action because investment would have been dominant. We have seen nothing of the sort and thus we still think that with high probability, agents in the cluster have a high cost.

THE SWITCH TO A HIGH REGIME AND THE INFORMATION BANG
As long as $\theta > X_L$, the low regime goes on. Let t be the first period in which $\theta = \theta_L$, the first grid point on the left of X_L. In the equilibrium strategy, all agents with cost smaller than c_t^* invest, and $c_t^* \geq X_L > \theta_L$. Thus the aggregate investment at the end of the period, $X_t = \beta(c_t^* + b) + \alpha(c_t^* - \theta_L)$, reveals that $\theta = \theta_L$. We are now back to the beginning of our story, in a symmetric position. Agents have perfect information about θ at the end of period t, as at the end of period 1. For this value, there is a unique equilibrium under perfect information, at the high level X_H. In period $t + 1$, the story is symmetric to that in period 2 (Figure 12.4 and the associated discussion). The CVF is an average of three c.d.f.'s, which are convex near θ_L. Therefore, it is higher than the CVF under perfect information at the end of period t. The strategy X_H still defines a SREE, and so on.

The economy evolves randomly between regimes of high and low activity. Once a regime has been established for some time, individuals have imperfect information on the state of nature. The probability of a switch is low, but when a switch occurs, there is a bang of information, which becomes perfect for a short while.

12.1.3 Application to Policy

When the economy is in a low regime, a fiscal policy that subsidizes investment reduces the net cost of acting agents and thus increases the probability of a transition to a high regime. In the present model, the effect is equivalent to a shift of the cluster to the left. The subsidy has minor effects if individuals believe that the average cost in the cluster is high. Hence, in a business cycle, the policy is not very effective after the downturn, when agents believe that the average cost is still high. For a given amount of subsidy, it may be advisable to wait until the public belief in a switch of regime reaches a higher level. A policy of subsidies is more effective when the public belief is that a significant mass of agents are near the point of investment.

However, if the policy is applied and it fails to trigger a recovery to a high regime, then people have learned that costs are higher than previously thought and the continuation of the subsidy does not have much chance of success.

12.1.4 Observation Lags and Random Walks with Drift

So far, we have assumed that the aggregate activity is observed after each move of θ, and that the grid on which θ moves is sufficiently fine. It can be viewed as an approximation of a model with continuous time. However, observations of macroeconomic data are often made with significant lags. Such lags can be introduced here by assuming a finite number of steps for the random moves of θ, between periods. Numerical simulations provide some support for the robustness of a unique equilibrium with random switches. The equality of the probabilities for increases and decreases of θ can also be somewhat relaxed. If appropriate values for these probabilities and for γ, X_L, X_H, and Γ are chosen, it is possible to reproduce a large set of transition probabilities between the two regimes.[13]

12.2 Observation Noise

The rectangular density function is now replaced with a smooth function: the population is divided in two groups as in the previous sections; the first has a uniform density of costs β on the interval $[-b, B]$; the second is the cluster and is distributed normally $\mathcal{N}(\theta_t, \sigma_\theta^2)$, where σ_θ is a publicly known constant, and θ_t follows the random walk defined by (12.8). The mass of active agents is X_t, as in the standard model, and

---

[13] As an indication, or a curiosity, one can reproduce the transition probabilities of the model of Hamilton (1989), which fits the U.S. business cycle to a model with two growth rates.

agents observe at the end of period t the variable Y_t defined by

$$Y_t = X_t + \eta_t,$$

where the noise η_t is normally distributed $\mathcal{N}(0, \sigma_\eta^2)$, and σ_η is publicly known.[14] The noise may arise from imperfect data collection or from the activity of "noise agents" who act independently of the level of the aggregate activity. Given the strategy c^* and omitting the period's index, the level of aggregate activity is

$$(12.7) \qquad Y = \beta(b + c^*) + F(c^*; \theta) + \eta,$$

where $F(c^*; \theta)$ is the c.d.f. at the point c^* of the normal distribution $\mathcal{N}(\theta, \sigma_\theta^2)$. Agents extract some information about θ from Y, which depends on θ through the function $F(c^*; \theta)$. When $|c^* - \theta|$ is large, $F(c^*; \theta)$ does not depend much on θ and is near 0 or 1. In that case, the noise η dwarfs the effect of θ on $F(c^*; \theta)$, and the observation of Y conveys little information on θ. Learning is significant only if $|c^* - \theta|$ is sufficiently small, i.e., if the associated density function $f(c^*; \theta)$ is sufficiently high. However, the strength of the strategic complementarity is positively related to $f(c^*; \theta)$ (which is identical to the slope of the reaction function under perfect information). *Learning and strategic complementarity are positively related.* As in the previous model with rectangular densities, agents only learn a significant amount of information when the density of agents near a critical point is sufficiently large to push the economy to the other regime.

The model cannot be solved analytically, and its properties are examined through numerical simulations. In an arbitrary period t, each agent uses his cost c and his subjective distribution on the set Θ to determine his probability assessment of Y_t. From this computation, one can deduce the CVF. If the model is useful, there should be a unique value c^* such that $V_t(c_t^*) = c_t^*$, and the condition of Theorem 11.2 should hold, at least for most periods. In this case, the acting sets are intervals $[-b, c_t^*]$.

The model cannot exhibit a unique equilibrium for *all* values of the random noise. Suppose for example that the economy is in a low state and that the distribution of costs is such that there are two equilibria under perfect information. A very high value of the noise in some period may induce a large mass of agents to act in the next period. This could reveal a large amount of information and generate two equilibria for the next period.

The main purpose of the model in this section is not to show that there is a unique equilibrium for all realizations of (θ_t, η_t). It is to show that the properties of the analytical model apply for most of these realizations: under the types of uncertainty and heterogeneity that are relevant in macroeconomics or in other contexts of social

---

[14] Negative values of Y_t have a very small probability and are neglected, as in all linear econometric models with normal distributions.

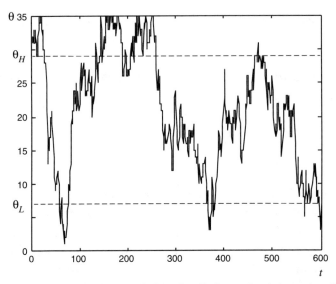

Figure 12.8 A random evolution of θ. Under perfect information, if $\theta > \theta_H$ ($\theta < \theta_H$), the equilibrium is unique with a low (high) level of activity. In the middle band there are two equilibria with high and low activity.

behavior, the model generates a SREE for most periods. In the numerical model below, there is a SREE in each of the 600 periods that are considered.

THE NUMERICAL EXAMPLE

The parameters of the model are chosen such that the random walk is symmetric with $p = \frac{1}{3}$ and has five independent steps within each period (which is defined by the observation of the aggregate activity). There is a mass of agents equal to 2 who have negative private costs. The first subpopulation has a uniform density equal to $\beta = 0.5$. The other parameters are $\sigma_\theta = 1.5$, $\sigma_\eta = 1$, and $K = 35$. The mass of the cluster is equal to 14.

The particular realization of the random walk of θ (the mean of the cluster) is represented in Figure 12.8. In the region $\theta \leq 7$, there is only one equilibrium under perfect information, with high activity. In the region $\theta \geq 29$, there is only one equilibrium under perfect information, with low activity. The sum of the stationary probabilities of these two events is less than $\frac{1}{2}$. The values of η_t are set to zero. This last information is unknown to the agents. One observes that in the first period of the simulation in Figure 12.8, θ is so high that the economy is in a regime of low activity. The public beliefs and the CVF are represented in Figure 12.9 for some of the 600 periods. A vertical line represents the true value of θ_t. The right side of each panel represents the graph of the CVF $V_t(c)$.

In Figure 12.9, the evolution of beliefs and of the level of activity are similar to the ones in the previous section. A switch from low to high activity occurs in period 60. The sudden change of beliefs between two consecutive periods is striking. After the transition, the mean of the public belief is altered drastically, and its

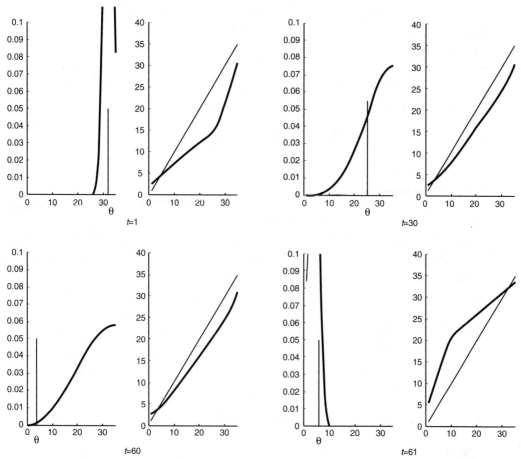

Figure 12.9 The evolution of learning. The values of the state θ are the same as in Figure 12.8. In each period, the left panel illustrates the public belief about θ as in Figure 12.5, and the right panel illustrates the CVF as in Figure 12.6. The vertical segment indicates the actual value of θ in the period. A regime switch occurs in period 61. Note (i) the difference between the actual value of θ and the public belief in period 30 before the switch; (ii) the difference between the public beliefs and the CVF after and before the switch.

precision is increased no less significantly. A similar switch to low activity occurs in period 133. These transitions occur a number of times given the path of θ in Figure 12.8.

12.3 Appendix

12.3.1 An Analytical Model of Regime Switches

At the beginning of the initial period (period 0), nature chooses an initial θ_0, according to a probability distribution $\pi_0 = (\pi_{1,0}, \ldots, \pi_{K,0})$ on the set $\Theta = \{\omega_1, \ldots, \omega_K\}$. This initial distribution, which will satisfy some specific assumptions later, is known to all agents.

The value of θ in period t is denoted by θ_t. It belongs to the discrete set $\Theta = \{\omega_k\}_{1 \leq k \leq K}$, with $\omega_k = \gamma + (k-1)\epsilon$, $\gamma > 0$, $\epsilon > 0$. For convenience, the ratio between the width of the cluster, σ, and the width of the grid, ϵ, is an integer. The value of ϵ will be small in a sense specified later, but it will not have to be infinitesimal.

Let p be a positive parameter, $0 < p \leq \frac{1}{3}$. With a probability denoted by P, the random evolution of θ_t is defined by the following equations:

$$(12.8) \quad \begin{cases} \text{if } \omega_1 < \theta_t < \omega_K, & P(\theta_{t+1} = \theta_t + \epsilon) = P(\theta_{t+1} = \theta_t - \epsilon) = p, \\ & P(\theta_{t+1} = \theta_t) = 1 - 2p; \\ \text{if } \theta_t = \omega_1, & P(\theta_{t+1} = \theta_t + \epsilon) = p, \quad P(\theta_{t+1} = \theta_t) = 1 - p; \\ \text{if } \theta_t = \omega_K, & P(\theta_{t+1} = \theta_t - \epsilon) = p, \quad P(\theta_{t+1} = \theta_t) = 1 - p. \end{cases}$$

The assumption that $p \leq \frac{1}{3}$ is reasonable: the random evolution of θ_t in the previous equations can be viewed as the discrete specification of a smooth diffusion process in continuous time. In such a process, the distribution of θ_t that evolves from an initial value θ_0 is hump-shaped. The discrete formulation of the random process generates a hump-shaped distribution only when $p \leq \frac{1}{3}$. The asymptotic distribution of θ_t does not depend on the value of p, and numerical simulations show that the properties of the model may hold when $p > \frac{1}{3}$. Agents know the law of evolution of θ in (12.8) but do not observe the state θ directly.

The values of X_L and X_H that are defined in (12.3) are separated by the grid points ω_M and ω_N satisfying

$$(12.9) \quad \omega_M < X_L < \omega_{M+1} \quad \text{and} \quad \omega_{N-1} < X_H - \sigma < \omega_N.$$

Assume the economy is in a low regime as defined in (12.6). Each agent updates the public belief with the information of his private cost c. Given the rectangular shape of the distribution in Figure 12.3, the Bayesian agent computes his density of θ by multiplying the density in Figure 12.5, call it $\phi(\theta)$, by a factor $\lambda > 1$ for the values of θ such that $|\theta - c| < c$ and by the factor $(\beta/(\alpha + \beta))\lambda < 1$ for the other values. This effect tends to increase the CVF when c is large. Indeed, an argument similar to that of Carlsson and van Damme shows that if agents are nearly identical, the CVF is asymptotically equal to $(X_L + X_H)/2$. In this case, there cannot be a SREE near X_L. Therefore, we must assume that the degree of heterogeneity is sufficiently large. Chamley (1999) proves that there is a SREE under the following assumptions.

ASSUMPTION 12.1 $\alpha < 2(1 - \beta)$.

ASSUMPTION 12.2 $\omega_M - \omega_1 \geq \omega_N - \omega_M$ and $\omega_K - \omega_N \geq \omega_N - \omega_M$.

The first assumption implies that the distribution of costs is not too concentrated. The second assumption requires that the *extreme ranges* of values for θ – where there is only one equilibrium under perfect information (case 1 or 2 in Figure 12.3) – be sufficiently wide. This assumption ensures that in a low (high) regime, the distribution is sufficiently skewed to the right (left), as shown in Figure 12.5.

PROPOSITION 12.1 *Under Assumptions 12.1 and 12.2, there exists a SREE. In period t, the equilibrium strategy is defined by $c_t^* \in [X_L, X_H]$. Either $c_t^* < X_L + \epsilon$ (in a low regime), or $c_t^* > X_H - \epsilon$ (in a high regime). The low regime is maintained as long as $\theta > X_L$, and ends as soon as $\theta < X_L$. The same applies mutatis mutandis for the high regime.*

The proof of the result is technical and is found in Chamley (1999). It is an application of Theorem 11.2.

12.3.2 The Model with Noise

Let $\pi_{\theta,t}$ be the probability of a value θ in period t in the public belief. This belief is updated from period t to period $t+1$ in two steps: first, at the end of period t following the observation of Y_t; second, at the beginning of period $t+1$ with the knowledge of the random process of evolution (12.8). Let $G(c_t^*, \theta)$ be the mass of acting agents with the strategy c_t^* and a given θ. The random variable Y_t is distributed according to $\mathcal{N}\big(G(c_t^*, \theta), \sigma_\eta\big)$. Define the public belief at the end of period t by $\hat{\pi}_{\theta,t}$. Following the observation of Y_t,

$$\log \hat{\pi}_{\theta,t} = \gamma - \frac{\big(Y_t - G(c_t^*, \theta)\big)^2}{2\sigma_\eta^2} + \log \pi_{\theta,t},$$

where γ is a constant such that $\sum_{\theta \in \Theta} \hat{\pi}_{\theta,t} = 1$. Note that within the model, agents could use the fact that θ_t takes discrete values in order to obtain more information from the observation of Y_t. However, this feature is spurious. The random changes of θ_t could be such that the distribution of θ_t has a piecewise linear density function in every period. The previous updating formula should therefore be understood as the relevant formula for the nodes of the density function of θ_t (at integer values of θ_t). The entire distribution of θ_t could be recovered through a linear interpolation.

A straightforward application of the rule (12.8) of the random walk of θ_t gives $\hat{\pi}_{\theta,t+1}$ from $\hat{\pi}_{\theta,t}$.

13 Delays and Payoff Externalities

It takes two to tango.

Agents optimize their decisions over time with externalities of information and in payoffs. Examples of strategic substitutability include learning about the capacity of demand in a market, the marginal cost of production of a new technology, or the potential capacity of supply. When there are strategic complementarities, coordination may be easier to achieve in the multiperiod setting if the number of agents is finite, but it may be impossible if the number of agents is large. An example of strategic complementarity is the diffusion of contraceptives in some countries.

When agents can choose the timing of their actions, they have an incentive to delay in order to gain information. We have seen in Chapter 6 that the information externalities can generate strategic substitutabilities or complementarities. In this chapter, we reconsider the issue of delays with the introduction of payoff externalities. Given the current state of the literature, the problem of coordination, which was the main one in the previous two chapters, is assumed away here. Agents coordinate on a Nash equilibrium. If such an equilibrium is not unique, some *ad hoc* rule will be followed for its choice.

STRATEGIC SUBSTITUTABILITY

Payoff externalities have been shown to be a source of delays in the abundant literature on wars of attrition. An example is the private provision of a public good. Harris and Nalebuff (1982) describe a hot room with people who each would like the window to be opened. The open window is a public good that benefits all, but each person shuns the embarrassment of standing up in front of others and going to open the window. Everyone is waiting for someone else to go. After an interval of time where nothing apparently happens, one person stands up and opens the window.

During the waiting game,[1] all agents observe what others do. They know that each agent has a private cost of opening the window and that the private costs (unobservable) are randomly distributed. Each person has a "reservation time," which increases with his own private cost. When she decides to stand up, she knows that no one else has a cost higher than her cost. She waits in the hope that someone else had a higher cost. The model exhibits strategic substitutability: more efforts by others to provide the public good reduce the effort of each agent.

The models in Section 13.1 have payoff externalities, and their equilibria have features of wars of attrition. The analysis will put a special emphasis on the interactions between the information externalities in learning about the state of nature and the payoff externalities.

The supply of a good and the entry into a new market provide standard examples of strategic substitutability. For a given demand curve, the profits of a firm are inversely related to the number of competitors or to their supply. The profitability of each entry decreases as the number of entrants rises. Entry requires a commitment, a fixed cost. The uncertainty may be about the size of the demand or about the supply (the cost of production or the number and the sizes of potential competitors). The parameters of the market are learned once the cost is paid and other agents take action. In Chapter 5, a higher rate of entry by others increased the flow of social learning and thus increased the incentive for delay. The same effect is at work here, but it is enhanced by the negative effect of the rate of entry on the profitability of investment.

Behind the models of Section 13.1, there is a simple and general idea. The public information expands only when agents take new actions: they "push the envelope." Each agent who takes an action does so at the risk of finding some bad news after which others stop taking any action.

Uncertainty about the Size of the Demand
In the model of Zeira (1994), suppliers learn about the size of the demand for a good, the *capacity* of the market. This can be learned only when the number of suppliers exceeds the capacity. As long as the capacity exceeds the supply, we know only that it exceeds the supply. Once the suppliers reach the capacity, the price collapses and suppliers cannot recoup the cost of their investment. Eventually, such a collapse must occur.

Uncertainty about the Number of Potential Entrants
Section 13.1.2 presents a new model of agents entering a market with uncertainty about the investment costs of other potential entrants. The model is the simplest one, with two agents. It is very similar to the simple model in Section 6.1 on delays. Here,

---

[1] The model of Harris and Nalebuff is presented in Exercise 13.1.

there is only one agent in the good state: he can capture the whole market. In the bad state, there are two agents, who reduce profits to zero through competition if they have entered the market (by assumption). In the symmetric perfect Bayesian equilibrium, there is delay. The number of periods during which agents delay (on average) increases if the period is shorter, but the mean time of delay is reduced. When time is continuous, there is no equilibrium. Other types of models are presented and related to models where firms learn the demand.

Uncertainty about the Cost of Production

In Caplin and Leahy (1993), the suppliers know the demand for the good, but they are uncertain about the marginal cost of producing it. This cost is the same for all suppliers, for simplicity, and is fixed at the beginning of time. An agent learns the marginal cost after incurring the fixed cost of putting the production process in place. The outsiders, who are potential entrants, know that no insider would produce at a marginal cost above the price. They observe the price of the good. As long as entry goes on and the price is falling, outsiders know that the marginal cost is strictly below the price. Because of the positive gap between the price and the expected marginal cost, there is an inflow of new suppliers and the price falls gradually. In some cases, the price reaches the marginal cost, and the supply cannot be expanded: that would drive the price below marginal cost. In that event, the supply does not increase, the price stops falling, and outsiders realize that the price has hit the marginal cost. They do not enter the market anymore.[2]

STRATEGIC COMPLEMENTARITY

In a standard stag-hunt game that takes place in one period, there are two equilibria: the first, with no investment, is Pareto-dominated by the second, where agents invest; we saw how agents under imperfect information "choose" one of the equilibria (Chapter 11). Can the inefficient equilibrium be ruled out when the game has many periods? Gale (1995) provides, remarkably, a positive answer when the investment is irreversible and the number of agents is not too large (Section 13.2.1). The argument is simple and powerful. Suppose there are two agents and investment yields a positive dividend in each period once both agents have made their irreversible investment. In an equilibrium, agents cannot delay their investment a long time if the period is short. If one agent, A, invests immediately, he is sure that the other, B, if he has not invested also in the first period, will do so in the second: at that stage, B is the only agent it takes for a positive payoff. When the period is vanishingly short, any agent can guarantee himself a payoff that is arbitrarily close to the first-best where

---

[2] Actually, some agents who entered before that event realized, after their entry, that the marginal cost was near the price and that their profits would not cover the fixed cost of investment. Unfortunately, they cannot call their former colleagues outside the market to warn them not to enter. It remains to be investigated whether this anecdotal property is idiosyncratic to the model and would be eliminated in another setting.

both agents coordinated their investment in the first period. The argument can be extended to any finite number of agents. The key to the argument is that each agent recognizes his pivotal role: he knows that if he invests, he induces a game with at least one fewer player; the properties of the equilibrium are derived by induction. The main conclusion from the analysis of Gale is that when agents are pivotal (and have some kind of "market power"), the decision setting with multiple periods may facilitate the coordination between agents.

In Section 13.2.2, an opposite property is found when the number of agents is large and uncertain (as in many macroeconomic models): if agents can delay their investment, coordination may be impossible. If agents do not invest in a period, there is no incentive to invest in that period; if a sufficiently large fraction of them invest, there is an incentive to delay to see whether the mass of players is sufficient to achieve a positive payoff when they all invest.

The problem of finding whether the mass of players is sufficient to achieve a positive payoff already appeared in the previous chapter in a context where agents could not delay. Munshi and Myaux (2002) show that the issue arises in connection with the adoption of contraceptives in Bangladesh (Section 13.2.3). There are, to simplify, two types of agents: those who are prepared to adopt the new technology and those who are not. The payoff of an adopter increases with the probability of being matched with another adopter. A government program can induce individuals to "come out of the woods" in a seed phase and raise the expectation of any potential adopter to find a similar mate. After a phase of subsidization, agents may coordinate on an equilibrium where all agents who are willing to switch indeed adopt the new technology.

13.1 Strategic Substitutability

Learning about the conditions in a market has two sides: learning the demand and learning the supply by competitors.

13.1.1 Learning the Demand

In Chapter 8, a monopoly was managed by a sequence of one-period agents who each maximized the profit in their period. By assumption, they could not delay their decision. The arbitrage between different periods will be an important feature of the equilibria in this section.

AN UNCERTAIN CAPACITY OF DEMAND

Zeira (1994) models the capacity of the market by a rectangular demand function. The demand price p is a function of the quantity Q as defined by

$$p = \begin{cases} 1 & \text{if } Q < \theta, \\ 0 & \text{if } Q \geq \theta. \end{cases}$$

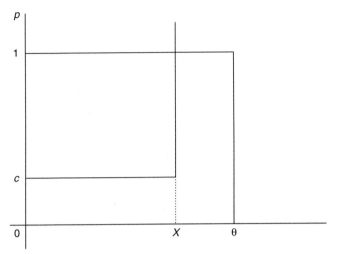

Figure 13.1 An uncertain demand capacity. The demand price p is constant for a quantity smaller than θ, which is random. The marginal value of the good falls to zero for quantities above θ. The supply is equal to X.

The variable θ is the state of nature that characterizes the capacity of the market. The distribution of θ has a c.d.f. $F(\theta)$ on the support $[a, b]$ with $a \geq 0$. The demand evidently has a very special form, which will be discussed later. Its schedule is represented in Figure 13.1. We begin with a one-period game.

A One-Period Setting

There is a continuum of agents who are potential entrants into the market. Each player who has entered the market can produce at the constant marginal cost c a maximum quantity h of the good, where h is the size of a firm, which is infinitesimal with respect to the size of the market. The assumption of a continuum is the limit case of a finite number of players, n, as $n \to \infty$, with a firm size $h = 1/n$. The production capacity when all agents enter the market – the mass of the continuum – is normalized to 1. An agent can set up a firm if he pays the fixed investment cost kh. (The parameter k is the value of the cost measured per unit of production capacity.) In this one-period game, the investment depreciates completely at the end of the period. In order to have a nontrivial equilibrium, the parameters satisfy the following assumption.

ASSUMPTION 13.1 $k < 1 - c$ *and* $\theta \leq b < 1$.

The first inequality ensures that entry is profitable for a single agent; the second ensures that not all agents can enter with a positive profit.

We consider only symmetric equilibria. In such an equilibrium, each player enters the market (and pays the fixed cost of investment) with probability ζ. If every agent plays ζ, the supply is determined by the law of large numbers and is equal[3] to $X = \zeta$.

---

[3] When the number n of players is large, each with production capacity $h = 1/n$, the mean and the variance of the supply are $\zeta h n = \lambda$ and $\zeta(1 - \zeta)/n$, respectively. When $n \to \infty$ with ζ constant, the mean stays constant and the variance tends to zero.

Two outcomes are possible. If the supply X is smaller than the capacity of the market θ, the price is 1. The probability of that event is $1 - F(X)$. If $X > \theta$, the price is equal to the marginal cost of production and there are no profits.[4]

By arbitrage, the expected profit from entering the market is zero, and the equilibrium strategy ζ must be solution of

(13.1) $\quad k = (1 - c)\Big(1 - F(\zeta)\Big).$

By Assumption 13.1, the solution in ζ exists and is unique. In the equilibrium, either the supply falls short of the capacity of the market, θ, and the price is equal to 1, or the supply exceeds θ and investors make zero profit and do not recoup the investment cost. One should emphasize that if the strategy of agents is an equilibrium strategy, both events have a strictly positive probability. (The situation is the same as in an optimal inventory where the probability of a stockout must be strictly positive.) Here, if the probability of a price collapse is zero, perfect competition implies that the supply should increase.

The equilibrium is a constrained Pareto optimum: a social planner (with no private information about θ) who can choose the strategy of the agents chooses the equilibrium strategy (Exercise 13.2).

Multiple Periods: Learning the Demand Curve
Suppose now that there are multiple periods and that agents know the history of past prices. Let ζ_1 be the equilibrium strategy in the first period, which is determined by the arbitrage equation (13.1). If the supply in the first period is smaller than the market size θ ($\zeta_1 < \theta$), agents use this information to update the distribution of θ at the end of period 1. Let $F_t(\theta)$ be the c.d.f. of θ at the beginning of period t. Conditional on $\zeta_{t-1} < \theta$, the game goes on to period t, where the equilibrium strategy ζ_t is such that

(13.2) $\quad k = (1 - c)\Big(1 - F_t(\zeta_t)\Big).$

An Example
Assume the initial distribution of θ to be uniform on $[0, b]$. Conditional on $\zeta_{t-1} < \theta$, the distribution of θ is uniform on $[\zeta_{t-1}, b]$, and equation (13.2) becomes

$$b - \zeta_t = \beta(b - \zeta_{t-1}) \quad \text{with} \quad \beta = \frac{k}{1-c} < 1.$$

Conditional on not having hit the capacity of the market ($\zeta < \theta$), the supply tends to the maximum size of the market, b, at an exponential rate. Therefore, the supply ζ_t reaches the capacity of the market θ in a finite number of periods. The value of θ and the demand curve are learned perfectly in a finite (random) number of periods.

---

[4] By assumption, producers can modify the output in the period to adjust supply and demand, and because of perfect competition, the price is equal to the marginal cost.

The model can be extended by assuming that investment does not depreciate within a period. In that case, each agent computes the probability that the price falls below c in the future periods. This computation has to be done numerically.

The model presented here is a reduced version of that of Zeira (1994), who assumes that θ follows a random walk $\theta_{t+1} = \theta_t + \epsilon_t$ and that the production capacity depreciates fully at the end of each period. The random term ϵ_t is an increase of the demand with $\epsilon_t \geq 0$. It is not observable, but agents know its distribution. In each period the production capacity is determined by the no-profit condition. In random periods, the capacity of the market is reached (as in the optimal-inventory problem). In that case, agents learn the exact value of θ for that period (assuming that they can observe the supply, to simplify the problem). In the period following a "capacity crisis," the increment of θ is random again and the supply increases. The model thus exhibits phases with a gradually growing supply, separated by crises with oversupply.

CRISES OF OVERACCUMULATION OF CAPITAL IN MACROECONOMICS

The issue of excessive capital accumulation is an old one in macroeconomics and goes back at least to Marx (1867). According to Marx, "crises" of capitalism occur when the rate of profit falls because of excessive accumulation. The argument is subject to an obvious critique: Marx's investors seem to be myopic. Investment takes place because of future expected profits. Because investors have a forward look, the anticipation of the future decrease of profits should prevent the excessive accumulation. The model of Zeira shows that crises of overaccumulation may occur regularly, at random intervals, when rational forward-looking investors have imperfect information on the demand. In the model, the actual demand θ is learned only when a crisis occurs.

Zeira presents a numerical simulation in which crises are rather short, and after a crisis the rate of accumulation returns rapidly to a stationary value. Perhaps additional investigations will produce a richer set of results. The analysis of cycles of excessive supply in a tractable model that embodies the main features of the business cycle remains a topic for further research.

ON MODELING THE UNCERTAINTY OF DEMAND

The distinctive feature of the demand curve in Figure 13.1 is the abrupt drop of the price at the unknown quantity θ. Often in this book, a good model is one sufficiently simple for tractable analysis and sufficiently rich to represent the complexity of the environment in which agents make decisions under imperfect information. The rectangular representation of Figure 13.1 is elegant in that all the uncertainty is captured by a single variable θ and this value is not trivially revealed by agents' actions.[5] The specification of a linear demand curve $p = a - \theta Q$, where a is known and

---

[5] The simplicity of the rectangular shape is particularly useful when θ grows randomly over time, which was an important feature in the model of Zeira.

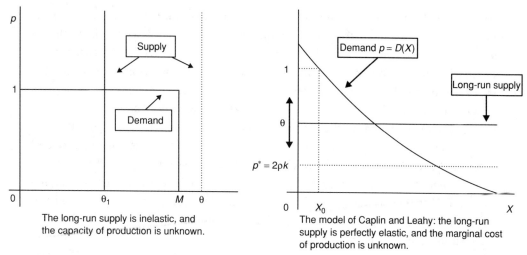

Figure 13.2 Uncertain supply.

$\theta > 0$ is unobservable, seems more general but is in fact less so, because one market equilibrium would reveal the demand curve entirely.

There are two possible extensions with generic properties: the first is to parameterize the demand curve with a small set of parameters and introduce an observation noise; the second is to introduce a rich set of demand schedules. The second approach will be pursued in the next section to model supply schedules. We will see that it is symmetric to the modelization of the demand.

13.1.2 Learning the Supply

Uncertainty about the supply can take two polar forms: it can be about the number of potential entrants in the market or about the cost of production.

In the first, the supply is perfectly inelastic at some value of θ, which defines the state of nature and is not observable. Each firm has a fixed capacity to produce at some known marginal cost, which can be assumed to be zero, and the uncertainty is about the number of firms that can produce. Entrants pay the cost of investment and bet that the number of other entrants will be sufficiently low for a positive profit. This case is represented in the left panel of Figure 13.2. The state θ determines the total capacity of potential entrants.

If θ is greater than the size of the market, M, and all potential entrants set up firms, the price falls to 0. In an equilibrium, the risk of excess capacity of production provides an incentive for delay.

In the second polar form, the supply of the good is perfectly elastic at the price θ and there is a fixed entry cost per firm. The mass of potential entrants is known, but a firm learns the cost of producing the good only after it makes an initial investment to begin the production process. This "hands-on" learning is certainly plausible. An active firm can produce the good at a constant marginal cost θ up to some capacity, which is small with respect to the size of the market (to ensure pricetaking). The state of nature θ defines the marginal cost, which is the same for all agents. The value of θ is not observed by outsiders who have not entered the market yet. An agent enters the market by paying a fixed investment cost to set up a new firm. For a given θ the supply of the good is therefore perfectly elastic.

Outsiders who have not entered yet can get indirect information by observing the firms already in the market. If they do not produce much, it is a sign that the production costs are high. If production is high, production costs must be low, and entering the market should be profitable. Each entrant pays an irreversible fixed cost of investment to bet on finding a low production cost. If the market indicates that the cost is low, however, other competitors will enter later, and the price of the good and the profits of the early entrants will be reduced. Caplin and Leahy (1993) analyze this interesting issue in an elegant model.

AN UNCERTAIN CAPACITY OF SUPPLY

The Simplest Model

The simplest model for the left panel in Figure 13.2 is that of two states and one or two agents. Let the state be $\theta = \{0, 1\}$, and the number of potential entrants be $2 - \theta$. Time is divided into periods, and each agent has an option to enter the market at the fixed cost c. If both agents have entered the market, the gross payoff for each agent is 0. If a single agent has entered the market, the gross payoff per period is $1 - \delta$, where δ is the discount factor. No agent will enter once the other agent has entered. Therefore, if an agent enters in period t and the other agent does not enter in the same period, the payoff in period t is

$$(13.3) \qquad U = -c + \sum_{k \geq 0} \delta^k (1 - \delta) = 1 - c.$$

The Symmetric Equilibrium

Let μ_t be the probability of $\theta = 0$ in period t. The payoff of investment in period t is

$$U(\mu_t, \zeta_t) = \mu_t + (1 - \mu_t)(1 - \zeta_t) - c = 1 - c - (1 - \mu_t)\zeta_t.$$

It is (obviously) a decreasing function of the probability of investment, ζ_t. Because the payoff is strictly positive when $\zeta_t = 0$, not to invest for sure is not a strategy in the symmetric equilibrium. The agent either invests for sure or is indifferent between investment and delay. If $\zeta_t < 1$, the payoff of the continuation of the game in period $t + 1$ is the same as the payoff of an investment for sure in period $t + 1$ knowing that the other agent uses the strategy ζ_{t+1}. Therefore, if $0 < \zeta_t < 1$,

$$(13.4) \qquad U(\mu_t, \zeta_t) = \delta(\mu_t + (1 - \mu_t)(1 - \zeta_t))U(\mu_{t+1}, \zeta_{t+1}),$$

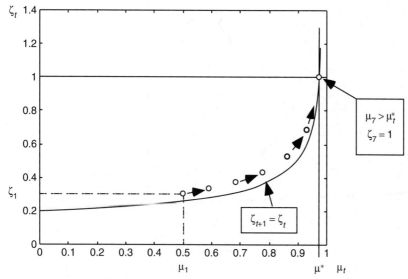

Figure 13.3 Evolution of beliefs and strategies. Parameters: $\delta = 0.9, c = 0.8, \mu_1 = 0.5$. In this example, there are $T = 7$ periods in which the game is actively played (conditional on no termination before date 5). The dynamic path fits the number of periods, T, in such a way that the boundary conditions are satisfied: μ_1 is the initial belief, and $\zeta_T = 1$ because there is no incentive for delay in the last period.

where μ_{t+1} is the probability of the good state in period $t = 1$, following the observation of no investment in period t, and ζ_{t+1} is the equilibrium strategy in period $t + 1$.

From Bayes's rule, the expression for U in the arbitrage equation (13.4), and some algebraic manipulations, the evolution of the variable (μ_t, ζ_t) is characterized by the dynamic equations

(13.5)
$$\mu_{t+1} = G(\mu_t, \zeta_t) = \frac{\mu_t}{1 - (1 - \mu_t)\zeta_t} > \mu_t,$$

$$\zeta_{t+1} = H(\mu_t, \zeta_t) = \frac{\zeta_t(1 - \mu_t)(1 - \delta(1 - c)) - (1 - \delta)(1 - c)}{\delta(1 - \mu_t)(1 - \zeta_t)},$$

with the condition that the solution satisfies $0 \leq \zeta_t \leq 1$. One can verify that this condition is

$$\mu_t < \mu^* \quad \text{with} \quad \mu^* - c < \mu^*\delta(1 - c).$$

This condition is the same as in the simple model with delays and information externalities.

The evolution of (μ_t, ζ_t) is determined by the functions G and H in the previous system. It is represented in the phase diagram of Figure 13.3.

In each period during the waiting regime, each agent randomizes his probability of investment, ζ_t. When there is no investment, the belief μ_t increases. The probability of investment, ζ_t, also increases with time. In some period T the belief μ_T is sufficiently

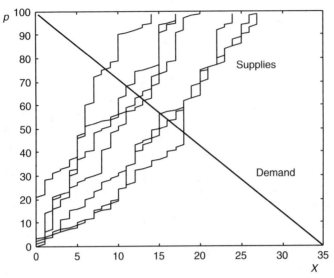

Figure 13.4 Supply schedules. There are six realizations of the random supply schedule. In the least elastic realization, there are 9 firms in the long-term equilibrium with a price equal to 78; in the most elastic realization, there are 18, with a price equal to 58.

high and $\mu_T - c \geq \mu_T \delta(1 - c)$. The game ends in that period with a bang or a whimper.

Extension with a Random Supply Schedule

Each agent is characterized by an idiosyncratic parameter c, which is his fixed cost for setting up a firm with a capacity of production normalized to 1 (which is small with respect to the market size). The marginal cost of production is assumed to be zero, without loss of generality. We consider a distribution where an agent cannot infer from his own cost any information about the costs of others. The sole information he will obtain will be derived from the observation of others.

The agent's costs are realized on a grid of *cost points* $z_i = a_i$, $i = 1, \ldots, N$. Each value z_i is a potential production cost. The value of a is fairly small with respect to the equilibrium price, and N is fairly large. (In the numerical example below, $a = 1$ and the market price is about 50.) For each i, there is an actual firm with a production cost z_i with a probability α. The existence of a firm at a cost point is independent of the existence of other firms. Hence, the cost to one agent provides no information on the costs to others. A realization of the random variables for all the cost points generates a supply function. Some examples are presented in Figure 13.4. (The probability that a firm exists at a cost point is $\frac{1}{4}$.)

The demand of the market is known as in the previous model, and without loss of generality, it is linear: $p = a - bX$. Time is divided into periods. At the beginning of time, the distribution of costs is realized. Let $F(c)$ be the c.d.f. of this distribution: $F(c)$ is the number of agents with a cost not strictly higher than c.

In each period any agent can make an investment with the fixed cost c specific to him. If he invests, he produces a fixed quantity normalized to one. All the supplies are brought to the market, and the price is established by perfect competition. At the end of the period, all agents observe the price and the quantity of the good. The capital of the firms that have invested depreciates completely. In period 2 and in any subsequent period, the same game takes place with the same agents (with the public information about the prices and the total supplies in the previous periods).

In the competitive equilibrium, a process of tâtonnement, in real time, takes place. Consider the first period. The equilibrium strategy is to invest if and only if the cost c is smaller than c_1 defined by

$$c_1 = a - bE[X_1] \quad \text{with} \quad E[X_1|c_1] = E[F(c_1)].$$

For the exposition, we can make the approximation that each firm is small and $E[X_1] = \alpha c_1$. The equilibrium strategy in the first period is such that

$$c_1 = a/(1 + b\alpha).$$

The supply X_1 is a random variable, which is realized at the end of the period: $X_1 = F(c_1)$. If $p_1 = a - bX_1 > c_1$, the game continues in period 2, in which all agents with cost smaller than c_2 invest. An exercise shows that $c_2 > c_1$. As long as $p_t > c_t$, the supply increases by random increments with an increasing sequence c_t.

Suppose now that t is the first period in which $p_t < c_t$, and there is an oversupply. (All goods are sold in the market, but the investors with highest cost incur a loss.) Agents know the distribution of costs at the two points c_{t-1} and c_t. The equilibrium c_{t+1} is between these two points. Eventually the sequence c_t converges to the point c^* defined by $c^* = a - bF(c^*)$.

The Model with Uncertain Demand Revisited

The previous model with an uncertain capacity of supply can be applied to a setting where agents know the supply but learn the demand schedule. By assumption the price is in the interval $[0, A]$. Define the values $z_i = iA/N, i = 1, \ldots, N$. For each i, with probability α, there is a mass 1 of buyers with reservation price z_i: these agents buy at most one unit of the good at a price not strictly higher than z_i. The supply schedule is known and linear in the price. There is a continuum of suppliers who can produce a quantity h (which is very small) at the cost hc. The cost c is drawn from a uniform distribution: the supply schedule is linear.

This model is an extension of the first model in Section 13.1.1. It does not generate the large jumps that were a bit too stylized in that first model. Note the symmetry with the model of an uncertain supply in Figure 13.4.

AN UNCERTAIN MARGINAL COST OF PRODUCTION (CAPLIN AND LEAHY, 1993)

The state is defined by the marginal cost of production, θ, which is fixed at the beginning of time and drawn from a uniform distribution on $[0, \bar{\theta}]$. There is a continuum of mass K of agents who can enter the market at any time. Time is continuous. Each agent can enter the sector and set up a new firm by paying a fixed investment cost c.

Once the agent has entered, he learns θ and can produce the good at each instant at the marginal cost θ up to a maximum capacity, which is normalized to 1 and is small with respect to the total supply. Production is instantaneous, and the flow of the total supply, X, is sold to a market with a demand curve $p = D(X)$, which is common knowledge. Agents who have not paid the entry cost observe only the price p of the market. Each agent maximizes the expected discounted present value of his profit. In order to avoid trivial equilibria, the structure of the model satisfies the following inequalities.

ASSUMPTION 13.2 $D(0) > 1$ *and* $D(K) < 2\rho c < 1$.

Let X_t be the mass of agents who have entered at time t. The equilibrium has two phases:

(i) During the first phase, the price of the good is higher than the marginal cost: $p_t > \theta$. All firms produce at maximum capacity $p_t = D(X_t)$, and the flow of entry is positive. The supply X_t grows, and the price p_t falls along the demand schedule $p_t = D(X_t)$. Agents who have not entered yet observe through the market price p_t that the new entrants produce up to their capacity. Therefore the price must be strictly above the marginal cost of production, θ. For the potential entrants, the updated belief about θ is the uniform distribution on $[0, p_t]$. Because of perfect competition, the level of entry is such that the expected profit of entry is nil.

(ii) The first phase ends if the price p_t reaches θ with the supply X_t such that $\theta = D(X_t)$: the price cannot fall further, because the marginal return to production would be negative; the "last" entrant does not produce. At that instant, the level of production stops increasing, and the price stays constant. This event signals immediately to the remaining potential entrants that the marginal cost equals the price and that entry cannot be profitable. There is no further entry.

The evolution of X_t as a function of time is determined by arbitrage. Let v_t be the value of an option to enter at time t. Agents who have not entered can buy such an option at any time at the price c. In a perfect competition equilibrium, the value of the option will be equal to its purchase cost c. The value of the option satisfies the arbitrage equation[6]

$$\rho v_t = p_t - E_t[\theta | p_t] + \frac{\dot{p}_t}{p_t} v_t.$$

---

[6] The equation can also be obtained through the standard dynamic programming technique with vanishingly short periods: Decompose time into periods of length dt. The value of the option in period t is $v_t = (1/(1+\rho dt))((1 - \pi dt)(p - E_t[\theta]) + \pi dt \cdot 0)$, where $\pi dt = (\dot{p}/p)dt$ because $1/p$ is the density of θ at time t. Take $dt \to 0$.

On the right-hand side, the first term is the expected profit per unit of time. Because the updated distribution of θ is uniform on $[0, p_t]$, we have $E_t[\theta \mid p_t] = p_t/2$. The second term measures the expected capital loss per unit of time, which occurs when the price reaches the marginal cost θ.

Because there is perfect competition for entry, we have $c = v_t$ and the previous equation becomes

(13.6) $$\frac{\dot{p}_t}{p_t} = \frac{1}{2c}(2\rho c - p_t).$$

Let X_0 be the supply such that $1 = D(X_0)$. From Assumption 13.2, $X_0 > 0$. There cannot be an interval of time $(0, \tau)$ in which the supply is strictly below X_0: profits would be strictly positive in that interval (because the price would be strictly above the upper bound of the marginal cost of production); any entry strategy would be dominated by an earlier entry. Hence, at the beginning of time the supply jumps to X_0 because of perfect competition, and the price is $p_0 = 1$.

For $t > 0$ and conditional on $p_t > \theta$, the time path of the price is determined by the initial value $p_0 = 1$ and the differential equation (13.6). From that equation one can see immediately that the price cannot fall below the limit value

$$p^* = 2\rho c.$$

If the price reaches p^*, the expected flow of profit is $p^* - E[\theta \mid \theta < p^*] = p^*/2$ and has a discounted value $p^*/2\rho = c$. The profit of entry is nil, and there cannot be any further entry, which would lower the price. Given the limit value p^*, the solution of the differential equation (13.6) is

(13.7) $$p_t = \frac{p^*}{1 - (1 - p^*)e^{-\rho t}}.$$

The game has two possible outcomes, which depend on the actual value of θ that is realized before the beginning of the game:

- If $\theta > p^*$, the price falls according to (13.7), reaches θ in a finite time T such that $\theta = D(X_T)$, and stays constant after. Entry takes place during the interval of time $[0, T]$. Agents who enter shortly before time T have the bad surprise that the cost of production θ is higher than their expectation before paying the investment to create a new firm.
- If $\theta \leq p^*$, the price falls forever according to (13.7) and tends to p^*. The flow of entry is always positive but tends to zero as $t \to \infty$. The level of production increases and converges to X^*, which is defined by $p^* = D(X^*)$. Agents are never disappointed, in the sense that their observation of θ after entering the market is always lower than their expectation before entering.

Social Inefficiency

Following the previous description of the outcomes, the price eventually reaches θ or converges to p^*. This convergence takes time because the suppliers act competitively and a higher rate of entry would generate private losses. A social planner maximizes the social surplus. In a constrained Pareto optimum, the social planner has no information superior to that of the market, and he can choose the rate of entry (say, through some suitable incentive).

The social planner compares the present value of the social surplus of one more entry, $(p - E[\theta|\theta < p])/\rho$, with the cost of entry, c. If $p > p^*$, the first is strictly greater than the second (by definition of p^*), and any delay of entry is socially inefficient. In the competitive equilibrium, an agent compares his expected discounted profits $(V_t(p) - E[\theta|\theta < p])/\rho$ with the cost c, where $V_t(p) = \int_0^\infty e^{-\rho\tau} p_\tau \, d\tau$ is the present value of the gross revenues after time t. Because the path of prices after time t is declining, that present value is strictly smaller than the quantity p_t/ρ that is considered by the social planner. In the competitive equilibrium, the private-value entry is smaller than the social value. In the constrained optimum, any delay is socially inefficient as long as $p_t > \max(\theta, p^*)$. The social planner should provide an incentive such that the rate of entry is as high as possible as long as p_t is higher than the maximum of θ and p^*.

A Remark

The model of Caplin and Leahy is very elegant, but it rests on the sharp dichotomy between insiders who know the value of θ and outsiders whose information is the declining price of the good. An information gap about production costs between insiders and outsiders is very plausible, but the model is so stylized that it may be useful to explore other modeling directions.

13.2 Strategic Complementarities

How can an agent's action induce others to act? This "leader's effect" can operate only when agents are not negligible and they are in finite number. This issue needs to be addressed first in a context of perfect information on the parameters of the model. Gale (1995) has shown that in an economy without uncertainty, with a finite number of agents, and where the actions are irreversible investments, a very short period "solves" the coordination problem. A simplified version of his model is presented in the next section.

13.2.1 Pivotal Effects: Learning through Time May Foster Coordination

THE MODEL OF GALE (1995) WITH TWO AGENTS

In order to simplify, assume first two agents, each with one option to make one irreversible investment at a cost c. Investment in period t generates a return in each period $k \geq t$ that is an increasing function of the total investment in period k. This function is written $(1 - \delta)v(X_k)$,[7] where v is an increasing function of the number of investments in period k, $X_k \in \{0, 1, 2\}$, and δ is a discount factor. The total return of investment is the present value of the return for all periods: investment in period t generates a net payoff

$$(13.8) \qquad U = \sum_{k \geq t} \delta^{k-1}(1 - \delta)v(X_k) - \delta^{t-1}c \qquad \text{with} \quad t \geq 1.$$

Without loss of generality, $v(X)$ is such that $v(X) = 0$ if $X \leq 1$, $v(2) = 1$, and $0 < c < 1$: the investment is profitable only if both agents invest. The discount factor δ is related to the length of a period by $\delta = e^{-\rho\tau}$, where ρ is the rate of discount and τ is the length of a period.

The Static Game

The static game takes place when the period length is infinite and $\delta = 0$. The payoff function becomes $U = v(X) - c$. There are two Nash equilibria: in the first, no agent invests; in the second, both agents invest.[8] The second equilibrium, with high activity, Pareto-dominates the first one, because it yields $v(2) - c$, which is higher than the zero payoff of the first equilibrium. These simple properties are summarized in a lemma to highlight the contrast with the main results.

LEMMA 13.1 *When $\delta = 0$ (and there is actually only one period), there are two equilibria, in which no agent and all agents invest, respectively. The equilibrium with investment Pareto-dominates the other one.*

The Dynamic Game

Assume now that the period length is finite and $0 < \delta < 1$. We consider only subgame PBE. Suppose that a player $\mathcal{A}$ invests in period 1. If the other player $\mathcal{B}$ invests in period 1, the game is over with coordination achieved immediately. If player $\mathcal{B}$ does not invest in period 1, he is the only player in the subgame that begins in period 2, and he reaps the benefit of investment as soon as he invests. His dominating strategy in period 2 is to invest without delay. Player $\mathcal{A}$ knows that if he invests in period 1, he can guarantee that player $\mathcal{B}$ invests no later than period 2 and that the critical mass necessary for $v(X) = 1$ is reached no later than in period 2.

The previous argument does *not* support immediate investment, but it provides a lower bound $\underline{U}$ for the payoff that any equilibrium must meet:

$$\underline{U} = -c + \delta.$$

---

[7] In this form, the function v has the dimension of a present value, and $(1 - \delta)v(X_k)$ has the dimension of a dividend on this present value.

[8] There is also an equilibrium with randomization, which is neglected here because it is unstable with respect to some dynamic process.

Any strategy that does not generate a payoff at least equal to $\underline{U}$ is dominated by investment with no delay, in period 1. When the period is vanishingly short, $\delta \to 1$ and the payoff of any symmetric PBE tends to $1 - c$, which is the payoff in the first best. The argument does not rule out a PBE with delays; but all equilibria with delays have a payoff that tends to the first best if $\delta \to 1$. An agent can induce the other not to delay more than one period, but no agent can induce the other agent to invest immediately. If A knows that B invests for sure in period 2, then the optimal strategy is to delay for one period.

From the previous discussion, investment in period 1 generates a payoff no less than $-c + \delta v(2)$. Investment by both agents in period t generates a payoff $\delta^{t-1}(v(2) - c)$. This can be a Nash equilibrium only if

$$\delta^{t-1}(v(2) - c) \geq -c + \delta v(2) > 0,$$

which is equivalent to $t \leq T$, with

$$T = 1 + \frac{1}{-\log \delta} \log \left(\frac{v(2) - c}{-c + \delta v(2)} \right).$$

If $\delta \to 1$, the number of admissible periods with delay in a Nash equilibrium tends to infinity. However, for a fixed discount rate, the time length of the longest delay in equilibrium tends to zero.

The two main lessons are that a vanishingly short period enables agents to achieve the first best payoff (asymptotically) in any PBE, and that there can be a delay of at least one period. Any investment induces a subgame with at least one fewer player. Gale generalizes the argument to any game with a finite number N of players.

THE MODEL WITH N PLAYERS

Suppose that there are N agents, $N > 2$, and $v(X)$ is increasing with $v(1) < c < v(N)$. Denote by n^* the minimum number that is required for profitable investment: $n^* = \min\{n \mid v(n) > c\}$.

The argument used in the two-agent model applies by induction for any n^*.

LEMMA 13.2 *In any PBE, the value of the game is at least equal to*

$$\underline{U} = -c + \delta^{n^*-1} v(N).$$

If N is given and the period becomes arbitrarily short ($\delta \to 1$), the payoff in any PBE tends to the first-best value $v(N) - c$.

There are many PBEs, as in the case of two agents. The previous result shows, however, that they must achieve coordination in a vanishingly short time as the length of a period tends to zero.[9] This time span can of course include many periods. The important result, however, is on the payoff. A vanishingly small length of a period induces near-perfect coordination.

The property of near-perfect coordination is another illustration of the importance of the period length in models where information is conveyed through actions.

A Large Number of Agents

In the previous result, N is fixed and the period length tends to zero. This order is critical. Take the reverse: fix the period length and take $N \to \infty$. In that case, coordination may fail.

The essential mechanism in the argument is that any agent knows that he is not negligible and that his investment precipitates a subgame with at least one fewer player. However, this subgame begins one period later. The player knows that he can guarantee himself a payoff equal to the one that is generated by all agents investing not later than $n^* - 1$ periods from now (in period n^*). If the number n^* of players of the critical mass increases, then the chain of triggers by each players is longer and the period in which the critical mass is reached recedes into the future. In this sense, when the critical number of agents, n^*, rises, coordination becomes more difficult. When n^* is sufficiently large, the present value of the payoff that can be guaranteed by triggers may decrease and become lower than the cost of investment: coordination may fail completely. There exists a value $\bar{n}$ such that if $n^* > \bar{n}$, the coordination failure in which no agent ever invests is a PBE.

To summarize the results[10]: (i) each agent recognizes that he is pivotal and his investment induces a subgame with fewer players; (ii) if the number of players required for coordination, n^*, is fixed whereas the period length tends to zero, the payoffs of all PBEs (there are many of them) are bounded below by a value that tends to the value of the first best; (iii) if the period length is fixed, there is $\bar{n}$ such that if $n^* > \bar{n}$, then there is a PBE in which no one ever invests.

The two main assumptions of the model are (i) the irreversibility of investment, which ensures the commitment of an agent who has invested; (ii) the finite number of agents, which enables any one of them to play a pivotal role.[11] The fact that there can be multiple equilibria is not important when the period length tends to zero, for they all generate the same payoff asymptotically.

---

[9] Theorem 1 in Gale (1995) shows that if $\delta \to 1$, all agents invest within a time span less than ϵ that tends to zero, provided that agents have nonrandom strategies. If they have random strategies, the statement holds in a probabilistic sense.

[10] There are more results in Gale (1995), to which the reader is referred.

[11] Admati and Perry (1991) consider a different model of coordination, which can be illustrated by two people writing a joint paper. They alternate in each period and make a contribution (a real positive number). The paper is finished when the cumulative sum of the inputs of the team reaches a level that is fixed. The value of the paper is greater than that cost. It is shared equally by the two agents and discounted from the time of completion of the paper. Once the paper is done, it is worth more than the total contribution of the two people. However, in equilibrium, the *ex ante* value is dissipated by delays.

13.2.2 Large Number of Agents: Learning May Prevent Coordination

A lesson from the model of Gale is that with finite agents and perfect information on the payoffs of other agents, a short period *facilitates* coordination (in the precise sense that was given). We will see now that when the information on the structure of other agents is imperfect, a short period may make coordination impossible.

A MODEL WITH NONATOMISTIC AGENTS

The model presented here is similar to the one in Matsumura and Ueda (1996). There is a continuum of agents, each with one option to make one irreversible investment at a fixed cost c. The state of nature θ is in $\{0, 1\}$, and the mass of agents in state θ is M_θ.

ASSUMPTION 13.3 $M_0 < c < M_1$.

Time is discrete, and the payoff function is the same as in the previous model of Gale. Investing in period t yields

$$U = E\left[\sum_{k \geq t} \delta^{k-1}(1-\delta)X_k - \delta^{t-1}c\right],$$

where X_k is the mass of agents who have invested no later than in period k, and δ is a discount factor that is smaller than one. The investment in period t entails a cost c in that period. The flow of the investment's payoffs begins in the same period, and for each period $k \geq t$, it is an increasing function of the number of agents who have invested by the end of period k. Without loss of generality, this function is linear.

The Multiple Equilibria with Perfect Information

Assume first that the state is known to all agents. By Assumption 13.3, if the state is low ($M = M_0$), there is only one equilibrium: no agent ever invests. If the state is high ($M = M_1$), there are many equilibria. One of them involves perfect coordination with all agents investing in period 1. Another one entails complete coordination failure where no one invests. For any $k \geq 0$ there is a PBE in which all agents delay for k periods and invest in period $k + 1$.

Imperfect Information

Assume now that the state is not observable and that in period 1 all agents with an option to invest assign to the high state a probability[12] μ_1 that satisfies the following condition.

---

[12] We have seen in previous chapters how μ_1 may depend on the structure of information. We can posit here a value for the subjective probability of all agents.

ASSUMPTION 13.4 $c < \mu_1 M_1 + (1 - \mu_1) M_0$.

Let us consider a symmetric equilibrium where each agent invests with probability ζ in period 1. Suppose that $\zeta > 0$. Because the strategy ζ is known to all, the mass of investment in the first period is ζM: it reveals perfectly the value of M and therefore the state. A delaying agent can make a decision in period 2 under perfect information: he will never invest if the low state is revealed. Given any strategy of the other agents, the payoff difference between investing in period 2 if and only if the state is revealed to be high by then (no matter what other agents do) and investing in period 1 is at least equal to

$$B(\delta) = -(1 - \delta)(\mu_1 M_1 + (1 - \mu_1) M_0 - c) + \delta(1 - \mu_1)(c - M_0).$$

From Assumption 13.4, there is a unique value δ^* such that $B(\delta^*) = 0$. The proof of the next result is left to the reader.

PROPOSITION 13.1 *For any parameters of the model* (μ_1, M_0, M_1, c) *with* $M_0 < c < M_1$, *there is a value* δ^* *such that*

if $\delta > \delta^*$, *the only equilibrium is that where no agent ever invests;*
if $\delta < \delta^*$, *there is an equilibrium in which all agents invest in the first period.*

The previous result is different from those in Chamley and Gale (1994), Chapter 6, where the only externality is on the information about the exogenous payoff. In those models, a short period does not alter the essential property of the equilibrium: the amount of information per unit of time is (asymptotically) independent of the length of the period. Here a short period makes a critical difference. When the period is short, the option value of delay always dominates the opportunity cost. All agents delay forever.

The result is also different from those in Gale (1995), where short periods facilitated coordination. In the present model, agents are nonatomic. There is no possibility of playing a pivotal role. Furthermore, agents have imperfect information on each other.

13.2.3 Interactions with Complementarities and Learning

There is a continuum of infinitely lived agents of two types. Active agents choose in each period a zero–one action. Inactive agents can choose only the action 0 in each period. The mass of all agents in the continuum is normalized to one, and the fraction of the active agents is M_θ, where the state of nature $\theta \in \{0, 1\}$ is set randomly at the beginning of time: $M_1 > M_0$. In each period, an active agent first makes a zero–one decision. Then he meets another agent, who is drawn randomly from the whole population. From this meeting, the agent receives a payoff, which depends on the action of the other agent, and also on the information about the state of nature:

TABLE 13.1 Social interaction.

		Other's Action	
		$y = 1$	$y = 0$
Action of	$x = 1$	α	$-\beta$
Individual i	$x = 0$	$-\gamma$	0

because inactive agents choose $x = 0$ and there are more inactive agents in the state $\theta = 0$, the observation of an action 0 raises the probability of that state. We focus on the active agents, and the term "active" will be omitted if there is no ambiguity. In a period, an agent's payoff depends on the action of the other agent he meets during the period as specified in Table13.1, with $\alpha > 0$, $\beta > 0$, $\gamma \geq 0$. For simplicity and without loss of generality, it is assumed that $\gamma = 0$.

The agent chooses the action that maximizes his expected payoff. That expected value depends on the mass of active agents. If the mass M_θ is small, the probability of meeting another active agent is small and the expected payoff is small. There is a unique equilibrium with $x = 0$. If the mass M_θ is sufficiently large and all active agents choose the action $x = 1$, then the strategy $x = 1$ may become an equilibrium strategy. We choose the values of M_0 and M_1 such that under perfect information (i) if the state is bad ($\theta = 0$), the only equilibrium is with no action by any agent; (ii) if the state is good, there is an equilibrium in which each agent takes action 1; in this case, there is also another equilibrium in which agents take action 0. These properties are embodied in Assumption 13.5.

ASSUMPTION 13.5 $\alpha M_0 - \beta(1 - M_0) < 0 < \alpha M_1 - \beta(1 - M_1)$.

We now assume imperfect information. The state is not observable. Each agent has a belief (a probability of the state $\theta = 1$) at the beginning of time. This belief μ is drawn from a distribution with c.d.f. $F_1^\theta(\mu)$, which may depend on the state θ. In each period, agents observe only the action of the other agent, but not the type of the other agent.

In each period, the strategy of an agent is a function from his belief to the set of actions $\{0, 1\}$. We consider only symmetric equilibria. The equilibrium strategy is common knowledge. From the observation of the interaction and the knowledge of the stategies of others, the agent updates his belief at the end of the period.[13] The distribution of beliefs evolves between periods. The distributions of beliefs in the two states are in general different. In period t, they are represented by the c.d.f.'s $F_t^\theta(\mu)$.

It is reasonable to consider the monotone strategies in which the most optimistic agents invest. Assume that all agents with belief greater than μ choose action 1. The payoff of action $x = 1$ for an agent with the marginal belief μ is a function $V(\mu)$,

---

[13] It would be possible to separate these two functions of a match in a generalization of the model. One could assume for example that the observation of the action generates a weak signal on the state because of idiosyncratic effects, or that each agent observes the actions of more than one other agent.

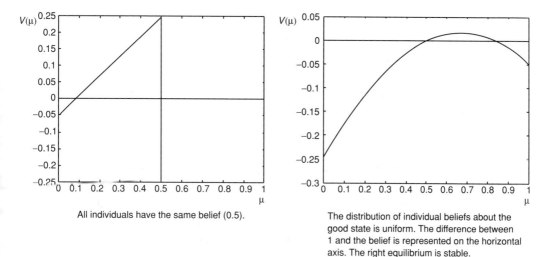

Figure 13.5 Net cumulative value functions.

Below the left panel: All individuals have the same belief (0.5).

Below the right panel: The distribution of individual beliefs about the good state is uniform. The difference between 1 and the belief is represented on the horizontal axis. The right equilibrium is stable.

which is represented in Figure 13.5 for two different distributions of beliefs. On the left all agents have the same belief equal to 0.5. If the cutoff value μ is above 0.5, no agent takes action 1, which has the negative payoff $-\beta$. If the marginal belief is below 0.5, all active agents take action 1. The parameters are such that the expected payoff of action 1 is positive. When the cutoff μ decreases from 0.5, the mass of agents taking action 1 does not change, but the belief of the marginal agent (that the mass of active agents is high) decreases and the payoff decreases. For $\mu = 0$, the payoff is equal to $\alpha M_0 - \beta(1 - M_0) < 0$ because of Assumption 13.5.

In the right panel of Figure 13.5, the distribution of beliefs is uniform in the interval $[0, 1]$. The overall shape of the graph is a smoothing of the graph in the left panel.

A Nash equilibrium monotone strategy is defined by $V(\mu) = 0$. In both cases, there are two interior solutions. However, the higher value of μ is unstable: suppose that μ increases from the higher equilibrium position where $V(\mu)$ is decreasing; the payoff $V(\mu)$ is negative, which induces the marginal agent to switch to the action 0; the marginal value μ is raised, and so on. The equilibrium is unstable in the sense of this discussion.

Recall that in all cases, the strategy in which no agent invests is another stable equilibrium.

SOCIAL CHANGE AND CONTRACEPTION IN BANGLADESH

Munshi and Myaux (2002), hereafter MM, study the adoption of contraceptive methods in rural Bangladesh during a period in which policies promoted these methods.[14] The data show that individuals of the same village tend to act in similar ways and

[14] The overall rate of contraceptive prevalence increased from about 43 percent in 1983 to 63 percent in 1993. The profile of adoption shows a mild convexity before 1990 and a strong concavity after 1990 (Figure 1 in MM, 2002).

that different villages seem to converge to different long-run levels of adoption. The evidence of the data and of the observation of "social pressure" indicate that an individual's regulation of fertility has a strong component of complementarity. Innovators face a social cost, which is reduced when the fraction of adopting individuals is higher.

There are two types of individuals: for *traditional* individuals, the "cost" of contraception is so high as to prevent their use; for *innovators* the use of a contraceptive ($x = 1$) or a traditional method ($x = 0$) generates the payoffs[15] in Table 13.1. In the actual experiment, a government program induced agents to adopt the innovation through some incentive in a first "seed" phase. Because of the incentive, a fraction of the innovators adopted the new technology, but traditional agents did not switch. Because the matching with an agent provides a signal on the state of nature, agents learn about the state during the seed phase. At the end of that phase, the distribution of beliefs is such that an equilibrium with endogenous innovation is possible without government incentive.

A Numerical Simulation

The model is simulated numerically and the results are presented in Figures 13.6 and 13.7. The left panels in Figure 13.6 represent the distribution of beliefs in different periods, and the right panels represent the function $V(\mu)$, which is the payoff of an agent with belief μ under the condition that all agents with belief higher than μ choose the same action $x = 1$.

In the first period, all agents (innovators) have the same belief $\mu_1 = 0.25$. The payoff of innovation $V(\mu)$ is negative for all values of μ. The fraction of agents choosing action $x = 1$ is set at $\frac{1}{2}$. At the beginning of period 2, agents who have met an agent with action $x = 1$ in the first period increase their belief while the others reduce their belief. In the state $\theta = 1$ there are more adopting agents; hence the population with higher beliefs is greater than when the state is $\theta = 0$. The distributions of beliefs in the two states $\theta = 0$ and $\theta = 1$ are represented in the left panel of the second row ($t = 2$). The graph of the payoff function $V(\mu)$ on the right shows that if there were no incentive, there would not be any innovation.

During the seed phase, agents learn, and the distribution of beliefs evolves accordingly. The distribution moves to the right in state $\theta = 1$ and to the left in the other state. Because the initial distribution was concentrated on a point, all distributions are atomistic. The seed phase lasts until the end of period 7. For $t \leq 7$, $V(\mu) < 0$ for all values of μ and there is no equilibrium with innovation in the absence of government incentives. These incentives are terminated at the end of period 7.

In period 8, the distribution of beliefs is such that in the good state there is a relatively high mass of agents with high beliefs. Hence, the mass of agents with belief higher than some intermediate value μ is large in state $\theta = 1$, and the function $V(\mu)$ is sufficiently large for these values of μ. The right panel shows that there is an

---

[15] The payoffs of Munshi and Myaux are simplified here.

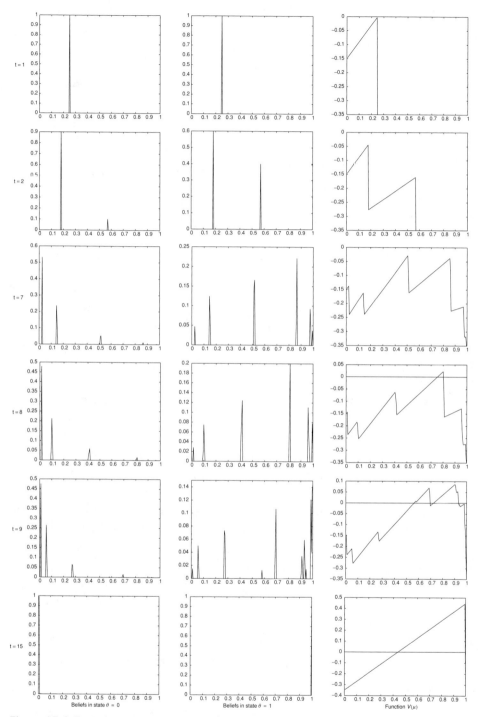

Figure 13.6 Evolution of beliefs and payoff. Parameters: $\alpha = 1 - u_0$ where $u_0 = 0.35$ is the payoff of no innovation ($x = 0$). $\beta = -u_0$. The masses of innovators in the high and low state are $M_1 = 0.8$ and $M_0 = 0.2$. All initial beliefs (probability that $M = M_1$) are identical and equal to 0.25. During the first 7 periods (see phase), half the active agents innovate (choose the action 1) because of some incentives.

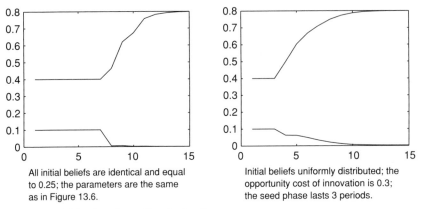

All initial beliefs are identical and equal
to 0.25; the parameters are the same
as in Figure 13.6.

Initial beliefs uniformly distributed; the
opportunity cost of innovation is 0.3;
the seed phase lasts 3 periods.

Figure 13.7 Simulated profile of adoption.

equilibrium value μ^* such that all agents with belief higher than μ^* choose the action $x = 1$.

Because there are more optimistic agents in state $\theta = 1$ and there are more active agents in state $\theta = 1$, the observation of others is a signal about the state that is more powerful than in the seed phase. Learning is faster after the seed phase.

In period $t = 9$ there are two (stable) equilibria with a solution interior to the interval $(0, 1)$: the graph of $V(\mu)$ intersects the line $V = 0$ twice while it is increasing. The multiple equilibria are generated by the atomistic distribution. In general, we should not be surprised by the occurrence of multiple equilibria with strategic complementarities.

The asymptotic distribution of beliefs and of the function $V(\mu)$ are well approximated in period $t = 15$. In that period, the beliefs are near the truth, and the function $V(\mu)$ is approximated by a linear function on the open interval $(0, 1)$ with the values $V(0) = V(1) = 0$.

The profile of the fraction of agents adopting the innovation is represented in the left panel of Figure 13.7 with the same parameters as in Figure 13.6. The upper curve represents the profile when the mass M of agents who can innovate is large and equal to M_1. The lower curve represents the profile when M is small and equal to M_0. In the right panel, initial beliefs have a uniform distribution, the seed phase lasts only for three periods, and the payoff of innovation is equal to 0.3. In both panels, if M is large, all potential innovators adopt the new technology after no more than ten periods. The profile is S-shaped in the left panel and concave after the seed phase in the right. If M is small, the fraction of adopting agents tends rapidly to zero after the seed phase.

EXERCISES

EXERCISE 13.1 The war of attrition for the provision of a public good (Harris and Nalebuff, 1982)

There are two agents, each with an individual parameter c that is independently drawn from a uniform distribution on $[0, 1]$. There is a public good of value 1 for each of the agents. The good has to be supplied by one of the agents at the private cost c. Time is continuous. If the good is supplied at time t, the payoff for the agent who supplies the good is $e^{\rho t} - c$, where ρ is a discount rate, and the payoff for the other agent is $e^{\rho t}$. In equilibrium, there is a one-to-one relation between the cost of an agent and the time he supplies the good, $c(t)$, conditional on no supply from the other agent before time t.

1. Write the arbitrage condition for the optimal time.
2. Determine the function $c(t)$.

EXERCISE 13.2

In the one-period model of Section 13.1.1, assume that θ has a density function $f(\theta)$.

1. Show that the equilibrium is the constrained social optimum.
2. Answer the same question when capital does not depreciate after one period. (Present an informal argument without solving the model.)

EXERCISE 13.3

Analyze the nonsymmetric equilibria in Section 13.2.3.

EXERCISE 13.4 "Hot Money" (Chari and Kehoe, 1998)

This exercise shows how the BHW model can be applied to a case where the payoff of investment depends on the actions of others and on the state of nature.

Consider a small open economy in which a government borrows from foreign lenders to fund a project. There are M risk-neutral agents, who are ordered in an exogenous sequence. Agent i can make a loan of size 1 in period i. The project is funded if there are N agents who make the investment. There are two states for the developing country, $\theta = 0$ or 1. Each loan pays a return R if the project is funded, after M periods, *and* the state of the economy is good ($\theta = 1$). Each agent has a symmetric binary signal with precision q about θ. If an agent does not make a loan, he earns the market return r. Each agent i observes the actions of agents j with $j < i$. Define $\mu^* = r/R$. Nature's probability of state 1 is μ_0. By assumption,

$$\frac{1-q}{q} \frac{\mu_0}{1-\mu_0} < \frac{\mu^*}{1-\mu^*} < \frac{\mu_0}{1-\mu_0}.$$

Assume $N = 3$ and $M = 5$. Analyze the equilibrium. (Show that if there is no herding, agents with a good signal invest and agents with a bad signal do not invest. Note that the sequence $(0, 1, 0, 1, 0)$ does not lead to funding.)

EXERCISE 13.5 Experience and recessions (Jeitschko and Taylor, 1999)

Consider an economy with a continuum of agents of mass 1. In each period, each agent chooses the action $x = 1$ (investment) or $x = 0$ (no investment). The action $x = 1$ entails a fixed cost $c > 0$. In each period, an agent is matched with another agent. If both agents are investing, the gross payoff of the project is 1 with probability

θ, and 0 with probability $1 - \theta$. If one of the agents does not invest, the project yields 0. No agent can observe θ or the action of the match. Matches last only for one period. By assumption, $\theta \in \{\theta_0, \theta_1\}$ with $\theta_0 < c < \theta_1$. At the beginning of period 1, all agents have a belief such that μ_1 is the probability of state θ_1. It is assumed that $\mu_1 \theta_1 + (1 - \mu_1)\theta_0 > c$.

1. Show that in the first period there are two stable equilibria. (State a concept of stability that is not very sophisticated, yet rigorous.) Does the model exhibit strategic complementarity or substitutability? Is there an unstable equilibrium?

2. At the end of each period, agents revise their beliefs from the observation of the payoff of their investment (if they have invested in the previous period). Assume that in the first period, all agents invest. Determine the belief at the beginning of the second period of the agents who have a zero payoff in the first period.

3. Assume the following parameter values: $\theta_0 = \frac{1}{4}$, $\theta_1 = \frac{3}{4}$, $c = \frac{1}{3}$, $\mu_1 = \frac{1}{2}$. Show that in the second period, there is a unique equilibrium in which no agent invests. Explain the intuition of the mechanism.

4. Fix any parameter of the model (with the assumption $\mu_1 \theta_1 + (1 - \mu_1)\theta_0 > c$). Does all activity in the economy stop after some finite time? Explain intuitively. Is this model a plausible description of the "inevitability" of pessimism and recessions?

PART THREE

Financial Herding

14 Sequences of Financial Trades

Can exuberance be rational?

In this chapter, the actions that reveal private informations about the value of an asset are the agents' trades. In a model where agents are placed in an exogenous sequence, have different private information, and trade with the market (Glosten and Milgrom, 1985), the trading price provides a sufficiently detailed signal to prevent the occurrence of cascades. However, the price may be subject to large and sudden variations and to extended regimes with an incorrect valuation. Transaction costs may keep a large amount of private information hidden. Cascades may occur when agents act strategically in an auction.

Learning and herding have fascinated people at least since the tulip mania in the seventeenth century and the experiment of John Law. The standard line is that financial markets are wonderful pools in which information is shared efficiently between people. For Keynes, however, they were little more than casinos or "beauty contests" in which the main goal is not to learn intrinsic values but to guess what people think that other people think (and so on) has the greatest value.

Literary descriptions such as Keynes's have great allure. They arouse emotions, but they only titillate the rational mind. A proper assessment of the mechanism of learning and herding in financial markets requires the modelization of some rational behavior. The modeling task that is required is difficult because it must incorporate sufficient complexity to analyze how agents deal with this complexity, and yet at the same time be simple enough for analysis.

We have seen that the space of actions of the individuals defines the "vocabulary" used by the agents in their communication, and plays a critical role in the learning mechanisms. In Chapter 3, when an agent takes an action in a continuum, this action reveals perfectly his private signal (which takes also values in a continuum of dimension one). Herding depends critically on the restricted set of possible actions (Chapter 4).

In financial markets, the price of an asset is a fine instrument and should therefore convey efficiently private information on the intrinsic value of the asset. We have seen in previous chapters how profit-motivated actions convey private information. The payoffs of these actions are granted by nature. In financial markets, however, agents act by trading with others, and the gains of some are often the losses of others. If trading partners are learning rationally, the incentive to communicate through trading may be reduced drastically. An offer to sell conveys the seller's private information that the asset has a low value. Hence, there is no incentive to buy. A potential seller knows this before proposing to sell and does not bother to trade. This *no-trading* result (Milgrom and Stokey, 1982) shows that if the meaning of a price is sufficiently well defined, it cannot be used to convey information between rational agents.

Yet people do trade. That must be because of some other motive, which is not conveyed perfectly by the prices of the assets. Some agents need to sell to meet an emergency, others need to buy to insure against uncertain income in the future, and so on. If these motives were observable by all trading parties, the no-trading result would still apply. It is therefore critical that the non-information-related motives are not perfectly observable to all the trading agents. A convenient method to incorporate idiosyncratic motives for trading is the introduction of *noise traders*, whose trades are not based on the intrinsic value of the asset. These noise traders will appear in most of the models of financial markets we will consider. Because the observation of noise traders is equivalent to the observation of idiosyncratic motives, their trade will be indistinguishable from that of other informed traders, by assumption.

Models with noise traders have been very successful because they imbed some of the complexity of transactions within a tractable framework. They come in two main varieties. The first considers a sequence of transactions between two agents with asymmetric informations; each transaction releases some information. The main model in this line is that of Glosten and Milgrom (1985). The other line of models assumes that agents meet as a group in a market where the equilibrium price conveys a signal about the agents' informations. Competition in the market may be perfect or imperfect. The solution of the equilibrium is analytically simple when agents have a CARA utility function with constant absolute risk aversion and the random variables have normal distributions. Emblematic models with a CARA–Gauss structure have been presented by Grossman (1976), Grossman and Stiglitz (1980), and Kyle (1985, 1989).

A sequential model à la Glosten and Milgrom provides a fine microstructure of actions, which is close to that of the BHW model of Chapter 4. It is a natural first step for the analysis of herding in financial markets. The CARA–Gauss model will be the subject of the next chapter.

The model of Glosten and Milgrom generates an endogenous bid–ask spread that is not due to transaction costs. We will see that in this model the convergence is as fast as if private signals were observable. This model will be the basis for a model of herding by Avery and Zemsky (1998) presented in Section 14.2. The results of Avery and

Zemsky are essentially negative. We have seen in Chapter 4 that herds may occur when the action space is limited (for example, discrete). In a financial market with one asset of uncertain value, the price is a pretty fine signal, which prevents mimetic chains from taking place. We will also examine an argument of Avery and Zemsky for temporary herds and sudden price changes.

Auctions are one form of financial markets. The possibility of herding with auctions has been analyzed by Neeman and Orosell (1999) in a model that is presented in Section 14.4.

14.1 Learning in the Model of Glosten and Milgrom

A financial asset is a claim on a random variable to be realized after the actions have taken place (as in all models in this book, where learning operates through actions). This asset is traded as follows. The market is represented by a broker who runs a trading desk and is perfectly competitive with other brokers (the sole purpose of the *background brokers* is to enforce perfect competition, which simplifies the model). The broker, called the *marketmaker*, is risk-neutral and maximizes his expected profit in each transaction. In each period, he is visited by one agent. The agent is either an informed trader who has private information on the fundamental value of the asset, or a noise trader who is determined to buy or to sell with equal probabilities (to simplify). The agent who comes to the market proposes to buy or sell exactly one unit of the asset. (There is no choice of the quantity of the asset.) The best the marketmaker can do is to post two prices, a bid price to buy and an ask price to sell. (The marketmaker can sell short.) Suppose that the visitor is willing to sell at the bid price. The marketmaker is taking a chance: he could take a loss if the visitor is an informed agent who is willing to sell because he knows that the asset is not worth its price; but he could also make a gain if the visitor has to sell for personal reasons, no matter what the value of the asset. Because the marketmaker may face a loss with the informed agent, his bid price, i.e., his price contingent on facing an agent who is willing to sell, is below the expected value of the asset in the common knowledge, i.e., before he meets a visitor who could be of either of the possible types. Likewise, the ask price will be above the expected value before he meets a potential partner for trading. I present here a special case of Glosten and Milgrom's (1985) model, which will suffice for the analysis of herding.

THE MODEL

The financial asset is a claim on a random variable $\theta \in \{\theta_0, \theta_1\}$. Without loss of generality, $\theta_0 = 0$ and $\theta_1 = 1$. Nature's probability of the good state $\theta = 1$ is μ_0. There are two types of agents, informed agents and noise traders. Each informed agent has one private signal s with a distribution which depends on θ. The definition of this signal could be quite general. Let us assume here that the signal is a SBS with precision $q > \frac{1}{2}$.

In each period, one agent meets the marketmaker. With probability π, he is of the informed type and trades to maximize his expected profit.[1] With probability $1 - \pi$, he is uninformed and buys, sells, or does nothing with equal probabilities $\frac{1}{3}$. The type of an agent is private information to that agent: it is not observed by anyone but himself. However, the probability that the agent is informed is common knowledge. In any period, the history of transactions (quantities and prices) is public information. As in the standard model of Chapters 3 and 4, history will be summarized by the exhaustive statistic of the public belief, i.e., the probability of the good state given the history.

EQUILIBRIUM

Denote the public belief at the beginning of an arbitrary period by μ. (The time subscript can be omitted temporarily.) The marketmaker posts a selling price p_A and a buying price p_B such that his expected profit is equal to zero (by perfect competition). The only informed agents who buy are the optimists with signal $s = 1$.

The zero-profit conditions for a sale and a purchase are rewritten

$$(14.1) \quad \begin{aligned} \frac{1-\pi}{3}(p_A - \mu) + \pi\Big(\mu q(p_A - 1) + (1 - \mu)(1 - q)p_A\Big) &= 0, \\ \frac{1-\pi}{3}(p_B - \mu) + \pi\Big(\mu(1 - q)(p_B - 1) + (1 - \mu)q p_B\Big) &= 0. \end{aligned}$$

Consider the zero-profit condition for a sale. In the first term of the left-hand side, $(1 - \pi)/3$ is the probability of meeting a noise trader who buys. The quantity $p_A - \mu$ is the expected profit from the sale. It can also be written as $p_A - \mu = \mu(p_A - 1) + (1 - \mu)p_A$ to highlight the outcomes in the good and the bad states, each with the probability assessment of the marketmaker, who has the public belief. The expected profit from selling to a noise trader is positive. It is balanced by the negative expected profit of selling to an informed trader, which is the second term of the expression.

Simple intuition dictates that the ask price of a sale must be between μ and the belief $\bar{\mu}(1)$ of an optimist who is an informed agent with a good signal,[2] whereas the bid price is between μ and the belief of a pessimist. In this example the market never breaks down.[3] The equilibrium in period t is determined by (p_B, p_A), the solution of (14.1).

---

[1] The assumption of a fixed π ensures that the trade is "reasonably balanced" in the sense of Glosten and Milgrom.

[2] One has

$$\mu < p_A = \frac{\mu\dfrac{1-\pi}{3\pi} + \mu q}{\dfrac{1-\pi}{3\pi} + \mu q + (1 - \mu)(1 - q)} < \frac{\mu q}{\mu q + (1 - \mu)(1 - q)} = \bar{\mu}(1).$$

[3] Glosten and Milgrom show that the market may break down as a market for lemons à la Akerlof (1970).

LEARNING

The information is transmitted from the private information of an agent by the action "sell" or "buy." This action is informative because its probability depends on the state of the world. From the results of Chapter 2, the public belief μ_t is a martingale, which converges. In the special case of a binary signal, the bid and ask prices p_B and p_A are set so that informed traders buy if and only if they are optimists and sell if and only if they are pessimists. In each period the observation of the action (sale or purchase) is equivalent to the observation of the signal of the informed agent with some noise. When $t \to \infty$, the public belief μ_t tends to the true value $\theta \subset \{0, 1\}$. The noise reduces learning in a period, but it has no effect on the *rate* of learning when $t \to \infty$.

The probability of a sale by a marketmaker is the same as the probability of meeting an optimist or a noise trader who buys. Denote by $\beta_S(\theta)$ and $\beta_B(\theta)$ the probabilities of a sale and a purchase by the marketmaker:

$$\beta_S(\theta) = \frac{1 - \pi}{3} + \pi(q\theta + (1 - q)(1 - \theta)),$$

$$\beta_B(\theta) = \frac{1 - \pi}{3} + \pi((1 - q)\theta + q(1 - \theta)).$$

These expressions are independent of the public belief. After a sale with public belief μ_t, the public belief μ_{t+1} is given by Bayes's rule:

$$\frac{\mu_{t+1}}{1 - \mu_{t+1}} = \frac{\mu_t}{1 - \mu_t} \frac{\beta_S(1)}{\beta_S(0)}.$$

Let us reflect once more on the mechanism of the model if private signals have a very general structure. Suppose that the sale price of the marketmaker, p_A, is equal to the public belief μ. He makes no profit on sales to noise traders, and a sure loss when he sells to informed agents with a relatively good signal. Hence his sale price p_A must be above the public belief to generate a profit on the noise traders. However, this margin (which depends on the public belief) raises the minimum value of the signal for informed agents who buy at some value $\bar{s}$. Because the probability that $s > \bar{s}$ is higher when $\theta = 1$ than $\theta = 0$, the sale carries a powerful message on the state.

As long as the equilibrium does not break down, there cannot be a cascade. In a cascade, there would be no learning from buying or selling. (Recall that some buying and selling take place because of the noise traders.) Both prices p_A and p_B would be identical to μ by the zero-profit condition. In this case, however, some informed agents would buy whereas some others would sell (because private signals do convey some information), and the equilibrium would convey some information. The nonexistence of a cascade is very much related to the fine structure of the market price. The bid–ask spread is endogenous in the model. When learning takes place, the bid–ask spread shrinks to zero asymptotically (Proposition 4 in Glosten and Milgrom, 1985), but it is sufficient to discriminate between some informed agents, and trade conveys some information. The situation would be very different, of course, if the bid–ask spread were generated by a fixed cost of trading. In that case, cascades could occur.

14.2 Herds

We know from Chapters 2 and 3 that the properties of a model with social learning depend critically on the structure of private information and actions. The previous section showed that with binary signals, the model cannot generate cascades and beliefs do converge to the truth. The prices, which can take values in a continuum, prevent the occurrence of a cascade: if all informed agents ignored their private signals, the price would not reveal information and it would have to be identical to the public belief, by arbitrage. In that case, however, informed agents would take into account their private information, which would contradict the initial assumption. Avery and Zemsky (1995) generalize this property to the case where private signals satisfy the MLRP, introduced in Section 2.3.1.[4]

Convergence results are often overstated. It is certainly more relevant to study how people may be wrong over an extended length of time and how a sudden price change may occur. This issue is, in my view, the main one in the study of Avery and Zemsky. They extend the model of the previous section with a special structure of private information, which they call *nonmonotone*.

NONMONOTONE PRIVATE SIGNALS

Assume that θ takes a value in the set $\{0, \frac{1}{2}, 1\}$. The *normal* state is defined by $\theta = \frac{1}{2}$. If a *shock* occurs,[5] θ is equal to 1 or 0. Informed agents know perfectly whether a shock occurs, i.e., they know whether $\theta = \frac{1}{2}$ or $\theta \in \{0, 1\}$; but they have imperfect information on the type of the shock.

If a shock occurs and $\theta \in \{0, 1\}$, each informed agent receives a SBS about θ. This signal has two possible precisions: with probability α it is of precision q, and with probability $1 - \alpha$ of precision q' with $0.5 < q' < q$. Each agent knows the precision of his signal, but does not know the value of α. This value is the same for all agents. The value of α defines the *precision* of the economy, i.e., the proportion of agents with a high precision. It is set randomly at the same time as θ in the set of two values $\{\alpha_L, \alpha_H\}$ with $0 < \alpha_L < \alpha_H$.

The aggregate state of the economy is defined by the realization of the two random variables θ and α, which are independent. The probability that a shock occurs is μ, and conditional on a shock, the states $\theta = 1$ and $\theta = 0$ have the same probability. The probability of a high-precision economy ($\alpha = \alpha_H$) is equal to λ. These probabilities are common knowledge. In each period, the probability that the marketmaker meets

---

[4] Avery and Zemsky assume that $\theta \in [0, 1]$, but the assumption of two values $\{0, 1\}$ does not restrict the generality of the results.

[5] As usual, θ is realized and set before any action is taken.

an informed trader is equal to π and is independent of the aggregate state of the economy.

BOOM AND CRASH

Avery and Zemsky produce a numerical example with the precision parameters $q = 1$, $q' = 0.51$, and proportions of low- and high-information agents $\alpha_L = 0$ and $\alpha_H = 0.5$. The fraction of informed traders in the whole population is $\pi = 0.25$, and noise traders buy or sell with probability 0.25 and do not trade with probability 0.5. The true state is chosen such that $\theta \in \{0, 1\}$ and $\alpha = \alpha_L$. The probability μ that $\theta \in \{0, 1\}$ is very small and the probability that the economy is poorly informed ($\alpha = \alpha_L$) is also very small. Hence, the public belief is $\theta = \frac{1}{2}$ and agents are well informed. In Avery and Zemsky, $\mu = 0.0001$, and the probability of the low precision is $\lambda = 0.01$.

The true state is the combination of two realizations: θ is not the normal state, $\theta \in \{0, 1\}$, and all informed agents have a low precision $q' = 0.51$. The path of beliefs is generated by a specific sequence of agents. The example exhibits the following regimes:

1. A few buys take place initially. They are generated either by informed traders or by noise traders. These buys increase the probability of the good state for the informed traders. These traders are poorly informed, but they believe with probability near one ($1 - \lambda = 0.99$) that half the traders are perfectly informed. Their belief about θ increases significantly. At the same time, the belief of the marketmaker does not change very much. (His *ex ante* probability of a shock is only 10^{-4}.) Hence, after a few periods, an informed agent with a high belief buys from the marketmaker, independently of his private signal. He herds according to the definition in Chapter 4 (which is also the definition of Avery and Zemsky here), believing that the market is driven by highly informed agents.

2. There is a string of purchase orders in this herding phase. During the first part of the phase, the marketmaker thinks that he is just lucky to sell to hapless noise traders. (Remember that he thinks a shock occurs with probability 10^{-4}.) The marketmaker is sufficiently convinced that he does not revise his expectation that there is no shock, and the price stays around $\frac{1}{2}$. (A standard feature of binary models – which appears in other parts of this book – is that revisions of beliefs are vanishingly small when beliefs are near certainty.)

3. At some point (after about 50 periods in the example), the marketmaker realizes that something is wrong, and that all these purchases are very unlikely if there is no shock. He increases his probability that a shock has taken place. This revision can only be an upward revision: his belief that the economy is well informed was equal to 0.99 *ex ante*, and there is not much evidence to revise that belief. Given the long string of previous purchases, the price shoots up to near 1.

4. When the price is near 1, the bid–ask spread reflects the belief by the marketmarker that, conditional on meeting an informed agent, that agent has perfect information

with probability near $\frac{1}{2}$. It is intuitive in the model of Glosten and Milgrom that the bid–ask spread is large if the fraction of informed agents *anticipated by the marketmaker* is large. Here, the marketmaker anticipates a large fraction of informed agents, whereas the true fraction is small. As a consequence, the spread is so large that it prevents the informed agents from trading, because they all have a signal with poor precision ($q' = 0.51$), and the difference in information with the marketmarker is smaller than the spread. They do not trade. The only trades are made by the noise traders. Because the public belief that $\theta = 0$ is low (around 0.01), the observation of a lower frequency of trade has little impact on the public belief for a while. (The phase lasts about 50 periods in the example.)

5. After a while, the marketmaker realizes that the low volume is not compatible with the high precision of informed traders: if $\alpha = \alpha_H$, half of the informed traders have perfect knowledge on θ and buy or sell regardless of the bid and ask prices. "But if the informed traders have low precision," thinks the marketmaker, "then I have been completely wrong all along: informed agents have a low precision, and the history tells us that a shock has occurred, most likely, but does not say much about the value of θ." Because the *ex ante* probability of the high state, conditional on a shock, is equal to $\frac{1}{2}$, the price reverts to $\frac{1}{2}$. In the example, the transition from a price of 1 to a price of $\frac{1}{2}$ (the crash) is rapid, but less so than the sudden boom from $\frac{1}{2}$ to 1 that occurred in step 3.

DISCUSSION

The sequence of price changes produced in the example of Avery and Zemsky is certainly spectacular. What do they show? In my view, the description of the inferences made by agents is fascinating, but the empirical relevance of the example is not convincing. These events require an improbable state of nature and sequence of traders. The probability of the state of nature is 10^{-6} (with a shock and an economy with low precision). The special sequence of trading agents further reduces the probability of the described event. Indeed, the wild price changes occur because such events were rationally deemed by the agents to have a negligible likelihood, near the point of irrelevance.

14.3 Avalanches

Following Lee (1998), consider a financial asset that is a claim on $\theta \in \{0, 1\}$. There are N agents and $N + 1$ periods. The value of θ is equal to 1 with probability μ_1. It may be realized randomly before period N as follows. During each period $t \leq N$, once trades are made, if θ has not been realized previously, it is realized and observed with probability β and the game ends. If it is not realized before period $N + 1$, its realization occurs at the end of the last period, $N + 1$.

Each agent has a private signal s on the future realization of θ. The signal is independent of other variables, contingent on θ, and is received before the first period. It takes one of K possible values, $s_1 < \cdots < s_K$, with the MLRP: $P(\theta = 1|s) = \tilde{\mu}(s, \mu_1)$ is an increasing function of s. The model is built on the following assumptions:

- A fixed transaction cost is incurred by any agent for his first trade.
- Each agent i can make a transaction in any period $t \geq i$: agents are put in an exogenous sequence, and the first period in which agent i can trade is period i. He can delay his first transaction after period i.
- The agents trade with a marketmaker who is risk-neutral. The information of the marketmaker is the history h_t of all transactions by the agents up to period $t - 1$. The marketmaker does not take into account the information given in period t. He *ignores* the information provided by the very fact that an agent is willing to trade with him in period t. The model thus omits a step that is critical in most models of trade between rational agents. The price of the asset in period t is equal to the public belief:

(14.2) $\qquad p_t = E[\theta|h_t] = P(\theta = 1|h_t) = \mu_t.$

If an agent does not trade, his payoff is $u(W_0)$, where W_0 is his initial wealth and u is strictly concave. For simplicity, the agent has an absolute risk aversion equal to one: $u(x) = -e^{-x}$.

If the agent makes one or more trades, his payoff is the expected value of $u(W_{N+1}) - c$, where W_{N+1} is his wealth at the end of period $N + 1$ and c is the transaction cost.

The transaction cost is the essential element that may induce agents not to trade when they receive their signal, and thus may generate the buildup of a large amount of hidden information. In order to simplify the model, significantly, it is assumed that the transaction cost is incurred only on the first transaction. As in the models of Chapters 4 and 6, we study how endogenous information can generate sudden changes of beliefs. All the private informations are distributed at the beginning of time. There is no new information coming from an exogenous source as time goes on. Agents do not reveal their private information as long as they do not trade. The first trade reveals the information of the agent: once the fixed transaction cost is paid, the agent adjusts the level of the trade according to his private signal.

EQUILIBRIUM

We proceed in standard fashion by backward induction and consider the last trade of an agent. This last trade will turn out to be his second one.

Suppose that in some period a risk-averse agent holds a nonzero position in the asset. He has therefore traded in the past and faces no further transaction cost. Suppose further that the agent has exactly the same information as the marketmaker. Because the latter is risk-neutral, the risk-averse agent can get perfect insurance by unloading his position with him. The insurance increases his welfare because of the concavity of $u(x)$. An agent with a position in the asset and the same information as the public information of the marketmaker undoes his position immediately. Delay would only expose him to the risk of the observation of θ in the next period.

Consider now the case of an agent with a private signal s who has an expectation different from that of the marketmaker in period t. Suppose that if he trades, his net demand for the asset is a strictly increasing function of his signal. His trade reveals perfectly his private information, which is included in the information of the marketmaker in the next period. From the previous argument, the agent knows that he will undo in period $t+1$ his trade of period t.

The equilibrium strategy is twofold: (i) in some period t to be determined, the agent trades at the price p_t with the marketmaker to take advantage of his private information; (ii) in period $t+1$, when the marketmaker and the agent have the same information (from the observation of all trades in period t), the agent returns to the marketmaker to trade for a riskless position. The period t is chosen such that the payoff difference between this strategy and doing nothing is greater than the transaction cost c. This description is not a rigorous proof of the equilibrium, but it explains the following result of Lee, which characterizes an equilibrium.

PROPOSITION 14.1 (Lee) *There is an equilibrium in which the agent trades at most twice, first based on the difference between his private information and the common knowledge, second to undo that transaction in the following period.*

The amount of trading x in the first nonzero trade is the solution to the following problem, contingent on the maximand's being positive:

(i) for $t = N + 1$, maximize $E_{N+1}\left[-e^{(\theta - p_{N+1})x}\right] - c;$

(ii) for $1 \leq t \leq N$, maximize $\beta E_t\left[-e^{(\theta - p_t)x}\right] + (1 - \beta) E_t\left[-e^{-(p_{t+1} - p_t)x}\right] - c.$

Condition (i) for the last period is straightforward. Condition (ii) applies for all the periods before the last one. If the agent trades in period t, with probability β the value of θ is realized and perfectly known at the end of the period, and the payoff of the trade is the coefficient of β in the expression. With probability $1 - \beta$, the game goes on to the next period, in which case the agent undoes the trade in period t and gets a payoff that is the coefficient of β in the expression. The computation of the expectation $E_t\left[-e^{-(p_{t+1} - p_t)x}\right]$ is not an obvious exercise. The agent has to take into account that other agents may also trade in period t (as will be the case below in the description of the crash), and these trades affect the variation of the public belief $p_{t+1} - p_t$.

AVALANCHE AND CRASH (OR BOOM)
Assume that each agent receives a SBS of precision q with probability $1 - \alpha$ and of precision q' with probability α. The values are such that q' is much larger than q and α is very small. This structure is such that the agent can receive four possible signal values[6]: strongly negative (-2), negative (-1), positive (1), strongly positive (2).

---

[6] Lee considers only three signal values, but the present example may fit better with previous presentations in this book. The reader may use as a reference the extension of the BHW model with two precisions in Section 4.8.2 of the appendix in Chapter 4.

The true state is assumed to be $\theta = 0$. The sequence of the realizations of the private signals is constructed as follows.

For $t \in I_B = \{1, \ldots, K\}$, $s_t = 1$. The transaction cost c is sufficiently low that all these agents trade. The public belief μ_t increases to a value $\overline{\mu}$ that is sufficiently close to 1 that any agent with a signal -1 or 1 (with a low precision q) is herding. This phase is called by Lee the "boom."

For $t \in I_E = \{K + 1, K + M - 1\}$ with M large, agent t has a signal with low-precision q. All agents in I_E are herding and do not trade. This phase is called "euphoria." The public belief is constant in that phase, because the appearance of an agent with a strong belief (positive or negative) does not depend on the state. The length M of that phase is sufficiently long to build a large amount of hidden private information with good and bad signals. We assume that because $\theta = 0$, the fraction of agents with bad signals is much higher than $\frac{1}{2}$.

In period $K + M$, the agent has a strong negative signal. He trades, his information is revealed in the next period, and μ_{K+M+1} decreases to a value such that agents with low precision and a bad signal do not herd anymore. Note that the drop of the public belief in period $K + M$ does not need to be large. This period is the "trigger."

In period $K + M - 1$, a large number of agents who had been herding in the regime of euphoria trade *at the fixed price* $p_t = \mu_{K+M+1}$. (These may be all agents or just the ones with a bad signal.) There is an *avalanche* of information. Given the construction of the signals in the regime of "euphoria," the trades give a strong information that the state is bad, and μ_{K+M+2} drops to a very low value. This is the crash.

DISCUSSION

The model has no particular bias for a crash. The same mechanism can generate a boom. In the publishing business, a crash is a better "sell." (The same remark applies to Avery and Zemsky, 1995, and Caplin and Leahy, 1994.)

The model nicely imbeds the gradual buildup of private information that is released suddenly after some contrarian event. It has some similarity with the model of Caplin and Leahy (1993). The serious weakness of the model is that the marketmaker ignores the implication of current trades for the information. This assumption is not very plausible in financial markets and is certainly contrary to the whole discussion on the relation between trade and information introduced at the beginning of the chapter. However, it is essential for the main property of the model, the avalanche of information. The large quantity of trades in some period is possible only because the marketmaker is willing to trade any quantity at a fixed price. If the marketmaker were to adjust his price after observing each trade, the frenzy of trades would probably not occur.[7]

---

[7] Other models of trade frenzies have been presented for auctions. The model of Bulow and Klemperer (1994) is important. An excellent and succinct presentation is given by Brunnermeier (2001).

14.4 Herding in Auctions

In an auction, a buyer faces the well-known problem of the *winner's curse*: he is more likely to buy when his estimate is too high. His expected payoff must be negative if he places a bid at his expected value. The setting has some analogy with a model of sequential trades à la Glosten and Milgrom. An important difference is that a bid made by a buyer is not followed immediately by a transaction. The bid gives the seller an option to postpone trading so as to gather more information from other bids.

A buyer should bid below his expected value. The spread between his estimated valuation and his bid is similar to the spread found in the model of Glosten and Milgrom. We will see here that this spread may induce agents to stop bidding early, thus withholding private information. Contrary to the model of Glosten and Milgrom, the auction mechanism may prevent effective social learning.

Neeman and Orosel (1999) present the following model. A seller faces N agents (buyers) to sell an object through an auction. The value of the object to the seller is $\bar{a}$. The value of the object is the same for all potential buyers and is a realization $\theta \in \{\theta_0, 1\}$, which is not observable. Each agent has a standard binary symmetric private signal $s \in \{0, 1\}$ on θ with precision q.

In any period, the seller can ask for a bid by any agent (new or from whom he has already asked a bid). The agent replies with a bid. If the bid is 0, we will say that the buyer does not bid. The seller may (i) stop the game with no sale, (ii) accept any past or present bid, or (iii) solicit another bid from a new buyer or from a buyer whom he has already solicited in the past. The history in period t is denoted by h_t and is defined by the identities of solicited buyers and their bids in periods before t. It is common knowledge. Seller and buyer maximize their expected payoff: for the seller it is $\max(E[p - \theta_0], 0)$, and for the buyer $E[\theta - p]$.

AN EQUILIBRIUM WITH IMPERFECT LEARNING

Denote by p_t the highest bid in the history h_t. Suppose that the number of buyers is infinite and countable. In any period t, a buyer who is asked for a bid (new or old) has the following strategy:

- If the signal is $s_t = 0$ or if $E[\theta|h_t, s_t] \leq p_t$, do not bid: $b_t = 0$.
- If $s_t = 1$ and if $E[\theta|h_t] > p_t$, then bid $b_t = E[\theta|h_t]$. Because the signal is symmetric, we have $E[\theta|h_t] = E[\theta|h_t, s_t = 1, s = 0]$, and the agent's bid is the expectation of θ given the history h_t, the private signal s_t, and an additional private signal, which is zero.

The previous strategy reveals the private signal if $E[\theta|h_t] > p_t$. An agent does not make a higher bid, given the strategies of other agents, for the following reason. He does not bid above his expected value $E[\theta|h_t, s_t = 1]$. Suppose his bid is in the interval $(E[\theta|h_t], E[\theta|h_t, s_t = 1])$. If there is a bid in the next round, that bid is

$b_{t+1} = E[\theta|h_{t+1}] = E[\theta|h_t, s_t = 1]$, and he does not make a net gain. Note that $E[\theta|h_{t+1}] > p_{t+1}$: agent $t + 1$, if called, will reveal his signal.

Suppose that $T + 1$ is the first period (the smallest t) such that $s_t = 0$. For $t \leq T$, we have $s_t = 1$, and according to the previous strategy, the bid $b_t = E[\theta|h_t]$ reveals the signal s_t and is determined by

$$\frac{b_t}{1 - b_t} = \frac{\mu_1}{1 - \mu_1} \left(\frac{q}{1 - q}\right)^{t-1}.$$

Proposition 3 in Neeman and Orosell shows that, under some conditions, the game stops in period $T + 1$. The action of the buyer in round $T + 1$ (i.e., no bid) reveals his signal. If there is a round $T + 2$, then $E[\theta|h_{T+2}] = E[\theta|h_T, s_T = 1, s_{T+1} = 0] = E[\theta|h_T]$. The buyer in round $T + 2$ is in the same position as the buyer in round T. He cannot outbid the player at time T, and he does not bid, whatever his private signal. The game stops with herding: agents take the same action whatever their private signal.

In this equilibrium, the game goes on as long as there is an unbroken string of positive signals. At the first negative signal, the game stops. Neeman and Orosell make an analogy with a herding situation. The equilibrium is a remarkable example of an information failure in a financial market where the structure of trade is determined by an auction.

AN EQUILIBRIUM WITH ASYMPTOTICALLY PERFECT LEARNING
Assume that the number N of buyers is finite and that they are called in a sequence to make a bid. Consider the "very prudent" strategy for an agent:

- If he is called when other players have not been called yet, he bids the best he could offer if he could observe the private signals of all players who have not been called yet and these signals turned out to be negative.
- If he is the last player to be asked, there are two cases: (i) if there is at least one other player with a positive signal, the last player bids like the others; (ii) if all previous players have a zero signal, then he bids as if he had a zero signal.

This strategy is an equilibrium strategy and reveals the private signals of all agents, whatever the number N (Proposition 1 in Neeman and Orosell, 1999).

The contrast between the two equilibrium outcomes is quite remarkable. In the first, the seller gets information as long as he asks players who are optimists. With high probability the game ends with a high variance on the value of the object. In the second case the seller gets to observe the private signals of all buyers. By the law of large numbers, the game ends with high probability and with a low variance on the object's value.

The difference between the outcomes is a striking example of the importance of strategic interactions. An agent plays one of the two equilibrium strategies because other agents play that strategy.

15 Gaussian Financial Markets

Buy low or when the price is rising?

In a CARA–Gauss setting, the demand for the asset is similar to the demand for investment in a quadratic model, with the important difference that the cost is endogenous to the information revealed by others. Two models of trade are considered: (i) limit orders are net demand schedules, which are contingent on the information revealed by the price; social learning does not slow down when more agents trade; (ii) market orders specify fixed quantities (rationally determined); social learning slows down by the same mechanism as in the model of Vives (1993) in Chapter 3.

In this chapter, a financial market is modeled according to a standard structure: a large number of agents, each with a net demand curve, meet the market, and an auctioneer clears the market with an equilibrium price. The structure of the CARA–Gauss model is based on a utility with constant absolute risk aversion of agents and Gaussian random variables. It is presented here from first principles. This model has been studied extensively because of its nice properties.[1] The purpose of this chapter is to relate some of the properties of the CARA–Gauss model to other models of social learning in this book.

INDIVIDUAL ACTIONS

In previous chapters, actions conveyed private informations to others. In a financial market, these actions are the trades. Section 15.1 emphasizes how the information of an agent about the value of an asset (the unobservable state of the world) affects his demand for the asset.

We saw in Chapter 3 that if the precision of the public information increases (for example through history), an agent's action depends less on his private signal and

---

[1] A few references in the abundant literature: Admati (1985), Kyle (1985, 1989).

more on the public information. This is an important mechanism in the slowing down of social learning when the action is subject to a noise. Such a reduction does not operate when the action is the demand by a CARA agent: as it is highlighted here, the reduction of the impact on the expected value of the asset operates as before; but the better precision of the public information reduces the risk of the agent, and his demand is more sensitive to changes in the expected value of the asset. One of the beauties of the CARA–Gauss model is that the two effects cancel each other exactly.

MARKETS AND INFORMATION

All models in this chapter describe a market for a single risky asset where individuals allocate their portfolio between the risky asset and a riskless asset. The risky asset has a value θ, which is drawn from a normal distribution $\mathcal{N}(\bar{\theta}, \sigma_\theta)$ and is not directly observable. In all models, there are three types of traders:

- *Informed agents* have private information on θ (as in the previous chapters). The type of the private information will vary from model to model. The informed agents maximize a utility function. It turns out that when the random asset has a normal distribution, the maximization of the expected utility with CARA generates a simple demand function. This demand function will be linear in the private signal of an agent and thus be very similar to the actions of agents in Chapter 2. We have seen that Bayesian learning from others is linear when the distributions are normal and the decision functions of others are linear. Such nice properties are just too tempting. Although the assumption of absolute risk aversion is debatable (the assumption of normality of the returns has also been questioned), we will use it shamelessly in this chapter, which presents standard results. Later, we will see that some of these results are robust to utility functions that are not CARA.
- *Uninformed agents* do not have any private signal and rely only on the public information generated by the market. They trade because they have a degree of risk aversion different from that of the informed agents. (A smaller degree of risk aversion is plausible but not necessary.)
- *Noise traders* simply buy or sell a fixed quantity, say for a private motive that is not related to the return θ of the asset. Their net demand is random.

Following the standard procedure, we assume that agents place *limit orders*: each agent brings to the market his entire *demand schedule*. Let $X_I(p)$ be the total net demand of the asset by all informed traders (who may have different private information). The uninformed agents bring their demand schedule, $X_U(p)$, which depends only on p, and the noise traders bring their exogenous demand, Q. The total demand schedule is the sum of the three: $X_I(p) + X_U(p) + Q$. An auctioneer takes the total net demand and determines the price p that clears the market, i.e., the solution of the equilibrium equation

$$(15.1) \qquad X_I(p) + X_U(p) + Q = 0.$$

The price conveys a signal on the information of the informed traders. The signal is noisy because of the noise traders. When an agent specifies a demand $x(p)$, he formulates his demand conditional on p being an equilibrium price and conveying some information (on the value of the asset). Hence, after trade actually takes place at the price p, no rational agent would want to revise his order.

The extraction of the agents' information through the market equilibrium price is presented in two steps (Section 15.2). First, it is assumed that all agents with private information have the same information. In this way, one concentrates on the transmission of this information to uninformed agents through the market. In the second step, informed agents have heterogeneous private information. Their actions are therefore determined both by their private information and by the equilibrium price, which depends on their actions. Fortunately, the learning rules in a Gaussian model are linear (Chapter 3), and the solution of the model is similar to that of standard models of rational expectations.

Special attention is devoted to the elasticity of the demand, which may affect the stability of the market and the existence of multiple equilibria. If the price rises, the first effect is a smaller demand, as in any market. However, the higher price is also interpreted by uninformed agents as an indication that informed agents may be buying because of good news. The second effect dampens the first one: the demand is less elastic.

In the next two sections, we focus on two issues: the convergence of beliefs and the fluctuations of the prices and demand.

LIMIT AND MARKET ORDERS, AND CONVERGENCE OF BELIEFS

In the standard situation, the market has a unique equilibrium and a sequence of market equilibria induces a process of learning, which converges to the truth – but how fast? This issue is addressed in Section 15.3, and the answer depends on the type of the orders for trade.

As stated above, a higher precision of public information has no effect on the multiplier of the agent's signal in his demand. Because of this neutrality, there is no slowing down of social learning in the CARA–Gauss model if agents place limit orders: the precision of the public information increases linearly with the number of observations.

Market orders are placed by informed agents before the opening of the market and are specified as fixed quantities of net purchases. An order depends on the expectations of the informed traders about the equilibrium price. It does not, however, depend on the realization of this price, and it has to be executed at some equilibrium price. Someone has to clear the market, however: the uninformed traders and the noise traders are assumed to post a demand schedule, as in the previous case, and the equilibrium price is such that the total net demand is equal to zero.

Because the orders of informed traders are fixed quantities instead of demand schedules, they may convey less information. In addition, the agents face the uncertainty of the actual trading price. It turns out that the first issue does not matter, but the second one is critical. Vives (1995) has shown that there is no reduction of the rate of convergence if the uninformed agents are risk-neutral. In this case, they are able to absorb completely the price fluctuations induced by the noise traders, and the informed agents do not face a trading risk. When the number of observations increases, the reduction of the risk associated with higher public information operates as in the case of limit orders, and the growth of the public information's precision is linear.

If uninformed agents are risk-averse, then the informed agents face an uncertainty about the trading price because of the variance induced by the noise traders. The trading price does not vanish when the precision of the public information increases. The reduction of the multiplier of private information in the private demand (with the higher public information) operates fully now. The situation is isormorphic to that of Vives (1993). The convergence to the truth is slow: the variance of the public estimate tends to zero like $1/n^{1/3}$, where n is the number of observations.

MULTIPLE EQUILIBRIA

Large and sudden variations of the price without any strong news are sometimes interpreted as manifestations of "herds" or irrationality. However, they may be mere examples of multiple equilibria and jumps between these equilibria. The crash of October 1987 has led to many postmortems that are beyond the scope of this chapter. As an introduction, the model of Genotte and Leland (1990) is presented in Section 15.4. The model adds to the standard agents, who trade with respect to their expectations about the fundamental, another type of agents, the "price traders," with a net demand that is an increasing function of the price. This demand is justified by a trading strategy of portfolio insurance. If the standard agents know the strategy of the price traders, they are able to factor it out and there is a unique equilibrium, as in the standard model. However, if the standard agents have *ex ante* a low assessment of the probability that price traders intervene in the market, whereas their mass is actually large, then there can be multiple equilibria and sudden price jumps between these equilibria.

15.1 Actions in the CARA–Gauss Model

In this section, we begin with the demand by one "standard" agent and then aggregate over a number of individuals.

15.1.1 The Individual

An agent is endowed with a fixed wealth w, which he allocates between an asset with a fixed return r at a unit price and the financial asset, which yields a random return θ per unit and has a price p. The random variable θ has a normal distribution $\mathcal{N}(E[\theta], \mathrm{Var}(\theta))$.

Let x be the amount of asset that is demanded (a short sale, $x < 0$, is allowed). The consumption is

$$(15.2) \qquad C = r(w - xp) + x\theta.$$

The agent evaluates this random consumption by a *CARA utility function* (with constant absolute risk aversion). The *ex ante* value of the random variable C before its realization is equal to

(15.3) $U = -E[e^{-\gamma C}]$,

where γ is the coefficient of absolute risk aversion. Because C has a normal distribution, an exercise shows that the payoff takes the form

(15.4) $U = -\exp\left(-\gamma\left(\overline{C} - \dfrac{\gamma V}{2}\right)\right)$,

where $\overline{C}$ and V are the mean and the variance of C, respectively.[2] Using the expression of the consumption in (15.2), we find that the maximization of U is equivalent to the maximization of the certainty equivalent

$$\overline{C} - \frac{\gamma V}{2} = rw + \left(E[\theta] - rp\right)x - \frac{\gamma}{2}\text{Var}(\theta)\,x^2.$$

The term rw is constant and can be ignored. The agent therefore maximizes the objective function

(15.5) $V = E[\theta]x - \left(rpx + \gamma\dfrac{x^2}{2}\text{Var}(\theta)\right)$.

This function is similar to the standard payoff of an investment of size x with a purchase cost rp and a quadratic adjustment cost $(\gamma\,\text{Var}(\theta)/2)x^2$. The quadratic term is due solely to the variance of the return and the associated risk. It increases with the coefficient of absolute risk aversion, γ. This term is the cost of risk. The adjustment cost is exogenous in a standard model of investment, but it will be endogenous to the equilibrium in financial markets, because the variance of the distribution of θ will be endogenous to the equilibrium. This difference will play an important role for the properties of social learning. The demand for the asset is similar to the optimal level

---

[2] One has

$$U = -E[e^{-\gamma C}] = -\frac{1}{\sqrt{2\pi V}}\int \exp\left(-\gamma C - \frac{(C - \overline{C})^2}{2V}\right) dC.$$

The exponent of the integrand can be rewritten

$$-\gamma C - \frac{(C - \overline{C})^2}{2V} = -\frac{(C - \overline{C} + \gamma V)^2}{2V} + \frac{\gamma^2 V}{2} - \gamma\overline{C}.$$

Substituting in the expression for U, we have

$$U = -\exp\left(-\gamma\overline{C} + \frac{\gamma^2 V}{2}\right)\frac{1}{\sqrt{2\pi V}}\int \exp\left(-\frac{(C - \overline{C} + \gamma V)^2}{2V}\right) dC.$$

The integrand is a density function, and the integral is equal to 1.

of investment in the standard model:

$$(15.6) \qquad x = \frac{E[\theta] - rp}{\gamma \, \text{Var}(\theta)}.$$

The associated optimal payoff is

$$(15.7) \qquad U^* = -\exp(-\gamma rw) \exp\left(-\frac{(E[\theta] - rp)^2}{2\,\text{Var}(\theta)}\right).$$

Equation (15.6) is the basic tool in the CARA–Gauss model, and the reader should become familiar with it. The demand function x depends in a simple way on the mean and the variance of θ.

THE EFFECT OF PRIVATE INFORMATION ON THE DEMAND

The mean and the variance of θ, which determine the demand in (15.6), depend on the entire information of the agent, which is the combination of the *public* and the *private information.* The effect of the private information on the demand will be essential for the diffusion of the private information through the individual's demand. The standard features of the Gaussian model include the following:

- the public information is that θ is drawn from the normal distribution $\mathcal{N}(\bar{\theta}, 1/\rho_\theta)$, where $\bar{\theta}$ and ρ_θ are publicly known;
- the private information comes from a signal $s = \theta + \epsilon$, where ϵ is a noise $\mathcal{N}(0, 1/\rho_\epsilon)$, which is independent of θ.

By use of the Bayes–Gauss formulae (2.5), the agent's belief is $\mathcal{N}(E[\theta], 1/\rho)$, where

$$(15.8) \qquad \rho = \rho_\theta + \rho_\epsilon = \frac{1}{\text{Var}(\theta)}, \qquad E[\theta] = \frac{\rho_\epsilon}{\rho}s + \frac{\rho_\theta}{\rho}\bar{\theta}.$$

Substituting in the expression for the demand (15.6), we find that this demand becomes

$$x = \frac{1}{\gamma}\left(\rho_\epsilon(s - rp) + \rho_\theta(\bar{\theta} - rp)\right)$$

$$= \frac{1}{\gamma}\left(\rho_\epsilon(s - \bar{\theta}) + (\rho_\theta + \rho_\epsilon)(\bar{\theta} - rp)\right).$$

This expression has wonderful properties: (i) all the coefficients can be computed *ex ante*, before the realization of the signal s; (ii) the multiplier of the private signal s in x is equal to the precision of this private signal; (iii) this multiplier is independent of the precision of the public information ρ_θ.

PROPOSITION 15.1 *In the simple CARA–Gauss model with CARA equal to γ, the demand of an informed agent is of the form*

$$(15.9) \qquad x = \frac{1}{\gamma}\left(\rho_\epsilon(s - \bar{\theta}) + (\rho_\theta + \rho_\epsilon)(\bar{\theta} - rp)\right).$$

The multiplier of an agent's private signal in his demand for the financial asset is independent of the common-knowledge distribution.

The relation between an agent's private signal and his action is different from the one we found in Chapter 3. In Chapter 3, when the cost of investment is quadratic, the agent chooses a level of action that is a fixed multiple of his expected value of θ. The private signal s operates on the expected value of θ through the multiplier $\alpha = \rho_\epsilon/(\rho_\epsilon + \rho_\theta)$. The multiplier in the level of action is therefore proportional to α (equation (3.4)). It becomes vanishingly small if the precision of the public information, ρ_θ, becomes arbitrarily large. This property is critical for the slow convergence of social learning in that chapter (Vives, 1993). Remarkably, this effect does not take place here, and its absence is obviously important for the learning properties of the CARA–Gauss model.

The demand for the financial asset in (15.6) is proportional to the expected value $E[\theta]$, but the multiplier is endogenous and is proportional to the precision of the estimate. If the precision ρ_θ increases, then (i) the multiplier of the private information is reduced (as in the model of real investment), and (ii) the cost of risk is also reduced, and this effect exactly cancels the first one. The two mechanisms imply that the contribution to the public information made by an agent's trading does not slow down as social learning progresses.

Proposition 15.1 can be generalized to the case where the agent receives any finite set of private signals.

COROLLARY 15.1 *In the CARA–Gauss model, the demand by an agent with CARA equal to γ who receives n signals $s_k = \theta + \epsilon_k$ with independent noises ϵ_k of precision ρ_k has a net demand equal to*

$$x = \frac{1}{\gamma}\left(\sum_{k=1}^{n}\rho_k(s_k - \bar\theta) + (\rho_\theta + \rho_k)(\bar\theta - rp)\right).$$

When the signals are not independent, a standard transformation has to be used before the formula is applied.[3]

15.1.2 The Demand of a Large Number of Agents with Independent Information

Suppose there are N agents with the same information on θ. From the previous results (equation (15.6)), their total demand for the risky asset, denoted by X, is

---

[3] If Ω is the covariance matrix of the signals s_i, then $J\Omega J' = D$, where $JJ' = I$, I is the identity matrix, and D is a diagonal matrix with positive elements. Denoting by s the (column) vector of the signals, by e the vector of ones, and by $\hat s$ the vector of independent signals $\hat s = Js$, with $r = \gamma = 1$,

$$x - \rho_\theta(\bar\theta - p) = e'D^{-1}(\hat s - pe) = e'D^{-1}(Js - pe) = (J'e)'J'D^{-1}J(s - pJ'e),$$

which is equal to $(J'e)'J'D^{-1}J(s - pJ'e) = (J'e)'\Omega^{-1}(s - pJ'e)$.

equal to

$$(15.10) \quad X = \frac{N}{\gamma} \frac{E[\theta] - p}{\mathrm{Var}(\theta)}.$$

All the models in this section assume that N is sufficiently large for the competitive assumption to hold.[4] Note that the demand of an agent is independent of his wealth w, and the total demand increases linearly with the number of agents, for a given γ. In order to relate the coefficient of absolute risk aversion to that of relative risk aversion around the level of wealth w, let us introduce the parameter Γ defined by $\Gamma = \gamma w$: Γ is the coefficient of relative risk aversion when the agent does not invest in the risky asset. By assumption, this coefficient is not constant for a CARA utility function. We take the total wealth of all agents to be fixed at W and divided equally among agents. (The equal division is not necessary.) The coefficient N/γ in the demand equation (15.10) is equal to $N/\gamma = Nw/\Gamma = W/\Gamma$.

The total demand is therefore

$$(15.11) \quad X = \frac{W}{\Gamma} \frac{E[\theta] - p}{\mathrm{Var}(\theta)}.$$

This formula is useful for the calibration of a model. (Recall that the agent does not have constant relative risk aversion.) The previous formula applies for any N, and by extension to a continuum of agents.

Suppose now that there is a continuum of agents, each indexed by $i \in (0, 1)$. The public belief on θ is normally distributed $\mathcal{N}(\bar{\theta}, 1/\rho_\theta)$. Two examples of informed agents will be particularly useful.

(i) If all agents have the same signal $s = \theta + \epsilon$, the aggregate demand is

$$(15.12) \quad X = \frac{W}{\Gamma} \left(\rho_\epsilon (\theta - p) + \rho_\epsilon \epsilon + (\rho_\epsilon + \rho_\theta)(\bar{\theta} - p) \right).$$

(ii) If each agent i has a private signal $s_i = \theta + \epsilon_i$, where ϵ_i are independent of any other variables and have the same precision ρ_ϵ, the individual noises ϵ_i average out[5] and the aggregate demand is

$$(15.13) \quad X = \frac{W}{\Gamma} \left(\rho_\epsilon (\theta - p) + (\rho_\epsilon + \rho_\theta)(\bar{\theta} - p) \right).$$

---

[4] The market power of an agent with superior information is obviously an important issue; it has been analyzed by Kyle (1985, 1989) and Bénabou and Laroque (1992), among others.

[5] One has

$$X = \frac{W}{\Gamma} \left(\lim_{N \to \infty} \left(\frac{1}{N} \sum_{i=1}^{N} \epsilon_i \right) + \rho_\epsilon (\theta - p) + (\rho_\epsilon + \rho_\theta)(\bar{\theta} - p) \right).$$

The expression $(1/N) \sum \epsilon_i$ is a random variable of variance $1/(\rho_\epsilon N)$, which becomes vanishingly small as $N \to \infty$. It converges to zero in probability, and we assume that it is zero for a continuum.

In the rest of the chapter, we assume without loss of generality that the risk-free rate of return is equal to one: $r = 1$.

15.2 Markets

As described in the introduction, a Gaussian market has three types of agents: informed (with private information), uninformed (without private information), and noise traders. The equilibrium equation is

$$(15.14) \quad X_I(p) + X_U(p) + Q = 0,$$

where $X_I(p)$ and $X_U(p)$ are the total demands by the informed and uninformed, and the noise Q is an exogenous term with distribution $\mathcal{N}(0, 1/\rho_Q)$. The supply of the asset is normalized to 0 without loss of generality.

Uninformed Agents

The uninformed agents are standard agents with no private signal. Their mass and risk aversion are such that their demand (15.11) is given by

$$(15.15) \quad X_U(p) = M\frac{E_U[\theta] - p}{\mathrm{Var}_U(\theta)},$$

where the expectation $E_U[\theta]$ and the variance $\mathrm{Var}_U(\theta)$ are conditional on the agents' information. This information includes the structure of the model and the market price p. The demand of uninformed agents takes into account the information revealed by the price p, which depends on their demand. The simultaneous determination is possible because the agents place *limit orders*, i.e., schedules that take into account the information conveyed by the price. We can write

$$(15.16) \quad E_U[\theta] = E[\theta|p] \quad \text{and} \quad \mathrm{Var}_U(\theta) = \mathrm{Var}(\theta|p).$$

Informed Agents

Informed agents are standard agents who form a continuum. Let s_i be the private signal of agent i (which may be a vector). Given the proper mass for the continuum and the coefficient of risk aversion, the total demand of informed agents is

$$(15.17) \quad X_I(p) = \int \frac{E[\theta|p, s_i] - p}{\mathrm{Var}(\theta|p, s_i)}\,di.$$

Putting together all the demands, the market equilibrium condition is

$$(15.18) \quad \int \frac{E[\theta|p, s_i] - p}{\mathrm{Var}(\theta|p, s_i)}\,di + M\frac{E_U[\theta] - p}{\mathrm{Var}_U(\theta)} + Q = 0.$$

This is the fundamental equation that determines the asset price p in the CARA–Gauss market. We begin with a simple case where all informed agents have the same private information.

15.2.1 The Transmission of the Information through the Market

In this first model, we focus on the transmission of private information from informed to uninformed agents through the market. We simplify the model and assume that all informed agents have the *same* information, which is a signal $s = \theta + \epsilon$ of precision ρ_ϵ (the noise is normal $\mathcal{N}(0, 1/\rho_\epsilon)$). Because they are the only agents who feed information to the market (by their actions), they do not have anything to learn from the market. This makes for a simple computation of the equilibrium. The case with heterogeneous private informations is introduced in Section 15.2.4.

The equilibrium equation $X_I(p) + X_U(p) + Q = 0$ can be rewritten as

$$X_I(p) + Q = -X_U(p).$$

The key mechanism of the CARA–Gauss model can now be presented. On the right-hand side of the equation, the net supply of the uninformed agents depends only on the information available to all. Uninformed agents know the right-hand side of the equation. By the equilibrium equation, they know the left-hand side: the uninformed observe through the market equilibrium the *order flow* from the informed agents and the noise traders. That order flow is informative on θ, because it depends on θ.

Informed agents do not get any additional information from the market equilibrium, because the market price p is a function of θ only through their private signal. Because this signal is the same for all private agents, the market price brings no new information to them. (In all the other models of this chapter, things will not be that simple.) By use of (15.9) in Proposition 15.1, the demand of the informed traders is

$$(15.19) \quad X_I(p) = \rho_\epsilon(s - \bar\theta) + (\rho_\theta + \rho_\epsilon)(\bar\theta - p).$$

Substituting in the market equilibrium equation (15.14), we obtain

$$(15.20) \quad \underbrace{\rho_\epsilon(s - \bar\theta) + (\rho_\theta + \rho_\epsilon)(\bar\theta - p)}_{\text{informed traders}} + \underbrace{Q}_{\text{noise}} + \underbrace{\frac{M}{\mathrm{Var}(\theta|p)}\left(E[\theta|p] - p\right)}_{\text{uninformed traders}} = 0.$$

$$\underbrace{}_{\text{observed order flow}}$$

The Information of the Market

In the order flow, the term $(\rho_\theta + \rho_\epsilon)(\bar\theta - p)$ is public information. The order flow is therefore informationally equivalent to the variable $\rho_\epsilon(s - \bar\theta) + Q$. Because $s = \theta + \epsilon$, when a standard normalization is used, the market is informationally equivalent to the variable y defined by

$$(15.21) \quad y = s + \frac{Q}{\rho_\epsilon} = \theta + \epsilon + \frac{Q}{\rho_\epsilon}.$$

The method we have followed is general for CARA–Gauss models: the market generates information through a variable, which is here the order flow. This variable is transformed into a simple expression of θ plus a noise.

From (15.21) the market conveys a signal on θ with precision

$$(15.22) \quad \rho_y = \frac{\rho_\epsilon^2 \rho_Q}{1 + \rho_\epsilon \rho_Q}.$$

The uninformed agents use the market signal y to update their information on θ. From Proposition 15.1, their demand is

$$(15.23) \quad X_U(p) = M\Big(\rho_y(y - \bar{\theta}) + (\rho_\theta + \rho_y)(\bar{\theta} - p)\Big).$$

Substituting in the equilibrium equation (15.20), we find that the price is given by

$$\rho_\epsilon(y - \bar{\theta}) + (\rho_\theta + \rho_\epsilon)(\bar{\theta} - p)$$
$$+ M\Big(\rho_y(y - \bar{\theta}) + (\rho_\theta + \rho_y)(\bar{\theta} - p)\Big) = 0,$$

or

$$(15.24) \quad p - \bar{\theta} = \alpha(y - \bar{\theta}) = \alpha\Big(\theta - \bar{\theta} + \epsilon + \frac{Q}{\rho_\epsilon}\Big)$$

$$\text{with} \quad \alpha = \frac{\rho_\epsilon + M\rho_y}{\rho_\theta + \rho_\epsilon + M(\rho_\theta + \rho_y)}.$$

The price deviates from the *ex ante* expected value $\bar{\theta}$ when the order flow deviates from its mean because of a shock on either the fundamental θ, the noise of the private signal ϵ, or the demand of the noise traders Q.

By substitution in (15.23), the demand of the uninformed is

$$(15.25) \quad X_U(p) = \frac{M\rho_\theta}{1 + (M + 1)\rho_\epsilon \rho_Q}(\bar{\theta} - p).$$

THE CASE OF RISK-NEUTRAL ARBITRAGEURS

Suppose that uninformed agents have an absolute risk aversion that tends to zero whereas their mass is constant.[6] The parameter M tends to infinity. The price equation (15.24) becomes

$$(15.26) \quad p - \bar{\theta} = \frac{\rho_y}{\rho_\theta + \rho_y}(y - \bar{\theta}) = \frac{\rho_y}{\rho_\theta + \rho_y}\Big(\theta - \bar{\theta} + \epsilon + \frac{Q}{\rho_\epsilon}\Big).$$

This equation shows that $p = E[\theta|y]$. This is not surprising, for the uninformed agents are risk-neutral and have a perfectly elastic demand at the price $E[\theta|y]$. We can divide equation[7] (15.20) by M. When $M \to \infty$, $p \to E[\theta|p] = p$.

---

[6] It is equivalent to assume that the mass of uninformed agents tends to infinity with a fixed CARA: each risk-averse arbitrageur has a position that tends to zero and is risk-neutral at the limit.

[7] The market equilibrium equation (15.20) seems strange if M is infinite: we still have a market equilibrium, because M is multiplied by $E[\theta|p] - p$, which is equal to 0. Note that the same issue arises with perfect competition in standard markets: if all agents are pricetakers, who determines the equilibrium price? Perfect competition is an approximation of a market with a finite but arbitrarily large elasticity. We do the same here. The case of arbitrageurs is the limit case of uninformed agents with a vanishingly low risk aversion.

The variance of the equilibrium price depends on the risk aversion of the uninformed agents. When they are less risk-averse, they average the shocks to the demand more, and the variance of p is smaller. For a fixed amount of information, the demand of risk-neutral arbitrageurs is perfectly elastic. However, because the price conveys information, the demand of risk-neutral uninformed agents is not perfectly elastic in p. We now analyze the relation between the information content of the price and the elasticity of the demand.

15.2.2 Elasticities of Demand

The *stability* of the market is often associated with the amplitude of the price fluctuations. Because the price is driven by shocks to the demand, its fluctuations depend on the elasticities of the demand of the different types of agents. The elasticity is related to the *liquidity* of the market: a highly elastic demand absorbs large shocks with little price variations in the same way as a liquid market. The elasticity of the demand, or the liquidity of the market, will play a critical role when agents follow a trade strategy based on prices (e.g., a sell when the price falls), as shown in the next section (Genotte and Leland, 1990).

Suppose that informed and uninformed agents have a CARA equal to 1. The demand of an informed agent and that of an uninformed agent are given by

$$
\begin{aligned}
x_I &= \rho_\epsilon(s - \bar\theta) + (\rho_\theta + \rho_\epsilon)(\bar\theta - p), \\
x_U &= \rho_y(y - \bar\theta) + (\rho_\theta + \rho_y)(\bar\theta - p).
\end{aligned}
$$

(15.27)

These demands have similar forms. The informed agents have a signal s with precision ρ_ϵ; the uninformed have a signal y (from the market) with precision ρ_y, lower than ρ_ϵ. A price change has two effects:

- First, it alters the expected rate of return of the asset.[8] This effect operates in the second term in each of the previous expressions. The response is higher for the informed agents, because they face less uncertainty: $\rho_\epsilon > \rho_y$.
- The second effect operates only on the demand of the uninformed agents, through the first term. Because the market signal y is positively related to p, a higher price is a signal of a possibly higher demand by the informed, and hence a higher θ. This effect shifts the demand x_U upwards.

The two effects are illustrated in Figure 15.1. For the uninformed, the first effect is represented by the schedule (D). The shift that is due to the second effect is represented by the vertical arrow. The demand of uninformed agents, $X_U = M x_U$, is less elastic than that of informed agents, $X_I = x_I$.

---

[8] Recall that the multiplier of the expected rate of return is the reciprocal of the variance (because the risk aversion is 1), which is the precision $\rho_\theta + \rho_\epsilon$ for informed traders.

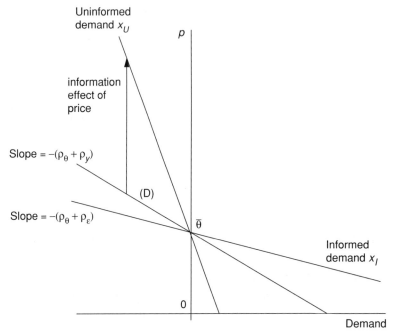

Figure 15.1 Demand for the financial asset. The demand of the uninformed agents has a smaller price elasticity than the demand of informed agents because (i) the asset is more risky for them; (ii) when the price p goes up, the good news boosts their demand.

PRIVATE INFORMATION AND THE ELASTICITY OF THE MARKET

Consider now the impact of a higher precision ρ_ϵ of the informed agents on the price elasticity of their demand. When the precision ρ_ϵ increases, the demand by the informed X_I is more elastic, because the asset is less risky; the slope $\rho_\theta + \rho_\epsilon$ in Figure 15.1 is smaller. The demand by the uninformed, X_U in (15.25), is less elastic. There are two opposite effects: First, the market is less risky, hence the elasticity is higher. (The line with slope $-(\rho_\theta + \rho_y)$ in Figure 15.1 rotates counterclockwise.) Second, the market is more informative, which decreases the elasticity. This second effect dominates.

The overall effect on the elasticity of the total demand (by both the informed and the uninformed) is ambiguous: if uninformed agents dominate (with a high M that is due to their mass or their low risk aversion), the total demand is less elastic when the precision of the informed agents increases.

15.2.3 The Variance of the Price

Fluctuations of the price p are driven by fluctuations of the noise Q and of the signal s of the informed agents. Using the expression for the market price in (15.24), we find that the variance of p is

$$(15.28) \quad \sigma_p^2 = \alpha^2 \left(\frac{1}{\rho_\theta} + \frac{1}{\rho_\epsilon} + \frac{1}{\rho_\epsilon^2 \rho_Q} \right),$$

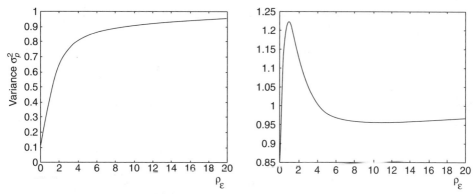

Figure 15.2 The variance of the market price. On the left, the mass of uninformed agents is $M = 1$, and $\rho_\theta = 1$. On the right, $M = 0.25$ and $\rho_\theta = 1$. (A similar graph is found for $M = 1$ and $\rho_\theta = 0.1$.) In both graphs, $\rho_Q = 9$.

with

$$\alpha = \frac{\rho_\epsilon + M\rho_y}{\rho_\theta + \rho_\epsilon + M(\rho_\theta + \rho_y)} \quad \text{and} \quad \rho_y = \frac{\rho_\epsilon^2 \rho_Q}{1 + \rho_\epsilon \rho_Q}.$$

The effect of the precision ρ_ϵ of the informed agents on the variance of the price is ambiguous. This ambiguity can be explained intuitively. The shock Q has an impact on the price that is inversely related to the price elasticity of the demand. We have seen that the precision ρ_ϵ has an ambiguous effect on this elasticity. The same argument applies to the noise of the signal s. Figure 15.2 represents the variance of the price, σ_p^2, as a function of the precision ρ_ϵ for different parameter values.

When the mass M of the uninformed agents is small (or their CARA is high), the variance σ_p^2 is not a monotone function of ρ_ϵ. In the expression (15.28) for the variance σ_p^2, a high variance σ_θ^2 has an effect like that of a low mass M. One verifies that the pattern on the right in Figure 15.2 for $M = 0.25$ can be obtained with $M = 1$ (as in the left graph) and $\sigma_\theta^2 = 10$.

15.2.4 The Aggregation of Independent Private Information

In the main formulation of the CARA–Gauss model, informed agents have heterogeneous private information and the market aggregates that information. The actions of informed agents reflect both their private information and the information of the market, which is itself generated by the informed agents' actions. There is a continuum of informed agents indexed by i, which is uniformly distributed on $[0, 1]$. Each informed agent i receives a private signal $s_i = \theta + \epsilon_i$ with an idiosyncratic noise ϵ_i, which is normally distributed $\mathcal{N}(0, 1/\rho_\epsilon)$.

The noise ϵ_i is independent of the noise of the market (which originates in Q). We posit that the demand of each informed agent is a linear function of his signal and therefore a linear function of the true θ. We therefore postulate that the observation of the market is equivalent to the observation of a signal $z = \theta + \epsilon_z$, where ϵ_z is a noise of variance $1/\rho_z$ independent of the other variables. (The variable z will play the same role as the variable y in Section 15.2.1.) Let us find the variable z and its precision ρ_z.

From Corollary 15.1, the demand of agent i is

$$x_i = \rho_\epsilon(s_i - \bar{\theta}) + \rho_z(z - \bar{\theta}) + (\rho_\theta + \rho_\epsilon + \rho_z)(\bar{\theta} - p).$$

By integration over i and using the law of large numbers, we find that the demand by the informed is

$$(15.29) \quad X_I(p) = \rho_\epsilon(\theta - \bar{\theta}) + \rho_z(z - \bar{\theta}) + (\rho_\theta + \rho_\epsilon + \rho_z)(\bar{\theta} - p).$$

From the method of informational equivalence, the market equilibrium is informationally equivalent to the observation of $X_I(p) + Q$. When the publicly observable terms in z and p are taken out, the equilibrium is informationally equivalent to the variable $\rho_\epsilon\theta + Q$. This variable therefore summarizes the information generated by the market, and we can state that, with a normalization, it is identical to the variable z that was postulated initially:

$$(15.30) \quad z = \theta + \frac{Q}{\rho_\epsilon} \quad \text{with the precision} \quad \rho_z = \rho_\epsilon^2\rho_Q.$$

This precision is higher than in the previous model with identical private information (equation (15.22)) because the market pools independent private signals on θ. The demand of the uninformed agents is as in the previous model (15.23), with a new definition of y, and the equilibrium equation is

$$\rho_\epsilon(\theta - \bar{\theta}) + \rho_z(1 + M)(z - \bar{\theta})$$
$$+ (\rho_\theta + \rho_z)(1 + M)(\bar{\theta} - p) + \rho_\epsilon(\bar{\theta} - p) + Q = 0,$$

which can be written

$$(15.31) \quad p - \bar{\theta} = \beta\left(\theta - \bar{\theta} + \frac{Q}{\rho_\epsilon}\right) = \beta(z - \bar{\theta})$$

$$\text{with} \quad \beta = \frac{\rho_\epsilon + (M + 1)\rho_z}{\rho_\epsilon + (M + 1)(\rho_\theta + \rho_z)} > \alpha.$$

This price function is similar to (15.24) in the previous model with identically informed agents. The demand schedule is less elastic now because the market pools independent signals from the informed traders and it is more informative. If uninformed agents are risk-neutral, $M \approx \infty$, and the price is given by

$$p - \bar{\theta} = \frac{\rho_\epsilon^2\rho_Q}{\rho_\theta + \rho_\epsilon^2\rho_Q}\left(\theta - \bar{\theta} + \frac{Q}{\rho_\epsilon}\right).$$

15.3 The Convergence of Beliefs

The equilibrium price provides a signal on the fundamental value of the financial asset. A sequence of equilibria, given a constant fundamental, provides an increasing precision on the fundamental. The rate of convergence of the variance of the subjective distribution is analyzed here in a model of tâtonnement. There are two main results: when agents receive costless private information and place limit orders, the convergence of beliefs is "fast"; when agents place market orders, the convergence is "slow."

These results apply to a wide class of utility functions: if the belief converges to the truth, the uncertainty converges to zero, and for vanishingly small uncertainty the decision problem for any von Neumann–Morgenstern utility is approximated by the problem with a CARA utility function (see the appendix, Section 15.5).

By assumption, the value of θ is drawn from the distribution $\mathcal{N}(\bar{\theta}, 1/\rho_\theta)$ and stays constant over time. There is a continuum of informed traders, each of whom receives one unique private signal $s_i = \theta + \epsilon_i$ at the beginning of time. In each period, or *round*, the informed agents place bids in a market identical to that of the previous section. The equilibrium price is determined likewise. However, the market actually opens according to a Poisson process with probability π in each period. If the market opens, all transactions take place as in the one-period model. No further transaction is conducted, and the process stops. If the market does not open (with probability $1 - \pi$), the equilibrium price in round t, p_t, is added to the public information, and the process goes on: agents place bids for the next round $t + 1$. The value of θ is realized after all rounds have taken place.

The tâtonnement process described here is due to Vives (1995) and is technically very convenient: in each round, the demand of an agent is the same as in the one-period model. If all bids are executed in each round, the process is more complex. To see this, assume that in each round t an informed agent has a demand of the form

$$x = \frac{E[p_{t+1}] - p_t}{\text{Var}(p_{t+1})},$$

where the expectation and the variance are conditional on the information of the agent. The agent knows that p_{t+1} is determined by the equilibrium in the next round. For example, if round $t + 1$ is the last round, p_{t+1} is determined by an equation similar to (15.31), which is of the form

$$p_{t+1} - E[\theta|h_t] = \beta_{t+1}(\theta - E[\theta|h_t] + \eta_{t+1}),$$

where h_t is the history of prices before round $t + 1$, β_{t+1} is a coefficient that depends on various precisions in round $t + 1$ (as in (15.31)), and η_{t+1} is a noise term that also depends on precisions in round $t + 1$. The expressions for β_t and η_t have to be derived recursively. The process is obviously more complex than the tâtonnement.[9]

---

[9] Vives observes that the mechanism shares some features with the tâtonnement that takes place in some markets (e.g., Tokyo, Toronto, Paris, and Madrid), where agents submit orders for one hour before the opening, equilibrium prices are quoted, and orders may be revised. The tâtonnement process proposed by Vives is somewhat different from the one used here.

15.3.1 Limit Orders and Fast Learning

When agents can place limit orders under the tâtonnement process, the model in each period is the same as the one-period model of the previous section. In each round, the market is informationally equivalent to the variable defined in equation (15.30), $z = \theta + Q/\rho_\epsilon$. It follows that if ρ_t is the precision on θ at the end of round t, then

$$(15.32) \quad \rho_t = \rho_\theta + t\rho_\epsilon^2 \rho_Q.$$

The precision increases linearly with the number of rounds. We will see later that when agents place market orders, the precision increments in each round converge to 0 as $t \to \infty$.

15.3.2 Market Orders and Slow Learning

So far in this chapter, informed agents have placed bids in the financial market in the form of limit orders, which are demand schedules. This section presents the work of Vives (1995), which analyzes the effect of market orders on the convergence of the beliefs. An order with a fixed quantity to trade seems *a priori* a coarser signal to others than a limit order, which conveys a demand schedule. More importantly, informed agents will face an additional uncertainty on their return due to the uncertain transaction price. This uncertainty might reduce their trade in the market and therefore the amount of information they convey by their trading. Whether this uncertainty matters and slows down social learning depends on the existence of risk-neutral arbitrageurs. The argument is first presented informally.

An Informal Presentation

The tâtonnement is the same as above. We will see that the market order by an informed agent is of the form

$$(15.33) \quad x = \frac{E[\theta|s] - E[p|s]}{\text{Var}(\theta - p|s)},$$

where the expectation and the variance are conditional on the information of the agent, but cannot depend on the market price p, which is not observed at the time the order is placed. There are two cases.

(i) Assume first that the uninformed traders are risk-neutral. As the number of rounds increases, the fundamental uncertainty converges to zero and the arbitrageurs assign most of the variations of the order flow (informed agents plus noise traders) to the noise traders. Because they smooth out the variations attributed to the noise, the variation of the price converges to zero over time. The demand for limit orders by the informed agents is asymptotically the same as for market orders, and the convergence properties of the beliefs are asymptotically the same for the two types of trades.

(ii) Assume now that uninformed agents are risk-averse. They do not insure completely against the uncertainty that is due to the noise traders. Asymptotically, the variance of the return on investment remains above a strictly positive number. The demand of the informed agents is then driven by the numerator in (15.33), i.e., by their expectation of the fundamental θ. This demand is mixed with that of the noise traders with constant variance. We are in the same situation as in the model of Vives (1993) described in Chapter 2. Social learning converges to the truth, but the variance of the estimator tends to zero like $n^{1/3}$, where n is the number of market observations.

In the case of limit orders, the precision of the market does not slow down social learning, because the reduction of the effect of private information on the numerator of the demand is exactly compensated by the reduction of the variance in the denominator (Section 15.1.1). When the uninformed are risk-neutral in a market with market orders, the variance of an order's return does not converge to zero, and no offsetting effect takes place.

THE MODEL OF VIVES (1995)

When an agent places an order of quantity x (independent of the realization of the market price), he faces two types of risk: the first (as in Section 15.2) is a risk on the intrinsic value of the asset θ; the second is a risk on the transaction price p. A straightforward variation on the argument presented in Section 15.1 shows that any trader with CARA equal to 1 has a demand

$$(15.34) \quad x = \frac{E[\theta|s] - E[p|s]}{\text{Var}(\theta - p|s)}.$$

The other agents in the economy are as in the previous model:

- The uninformed and rational agents are also called *marketmakers*; their demand is equal to $A(E[\theta|p] - p)$. The coefficient A can be fixed without loss of generality. (It depends on the mass of the uninformed and on their risk aversion.) The marketmakers have one advantage over the informed traders: they can base their demand on the equilibrium price p. (For market clearing, *someone* must have a demand depending on the price.) In this way, they are identical to risk-neutral uninformed agents in the model with limit orders.
- The net demand of the noise traders is the realization Q of a variable with a normal distribution $\mathcal{N}(0, 1/\rho_Q)$.

The equilibrium price is such that the total net demand is equal to zero:

$$(15.35) \quad \underbrace{\int \frac{E[\theta - p|s_i]}{\text{Var}(\theta - p|s_i)} \, di}_{\substack{x = \int x_i \, di \\ \text{informed agents}}} + \underbrace{Q}_{\text{noise traders}} + \underbrace{A(E[\theta|p] - p)}_{\text{marketmakers}} = 0.$$

Two remarks are in order before computing the equilibrium.

1. Informed agents do not know p, by definition of the market orders, but the variance of p matters for their payoff (in the denominator of x_i). They compute this variance from their information.
2. An informed agent i computes his expectation of p according to his information s_i; in the numerator of x_i, the term $E[p|s_i]$ is new with respect to the model with limit orders.

Denote by ρ_θ the precision of the public information on θ before orders are placed. For an informed agent i with signal $s_i = \theta + \epsilon_i$, θ is normally distributed with precision ρ_i and mean $E[\theta|s_i]$ with

$$\rho_i = \rho = \rho_\theta + \rho_\epsilon,$$

(15.36)
$$E[\theta|s_i] - \bar{\theta} = \frac{\rho_\epsilon}{\rho}(s_i - \bar{\theta}) = \frac{\rho_\epsilon}{\rho}(\theta - \bar{\theta} + \epsilon_i).$$

From equation (15.35), we look for a demand by the informed agent i of the form

(15.37) $x_i = a(s_i - \bar{\theta}),$

where a is a coefficient to be determined. By integration of individual demands and use of $\int s_i \, di = \theta$, the market equilibrium equation is

(15.38) $a(\theta - \bar{\theta}) + Q + A(E[\theta|p] - p) = 0.$

The market is informationally equivalent to the variable

(15.39) $y = a(\theta - \bar{\theta}) + Q.$

The market signal y is not observed by the informed traders, who place their orders before the realization of y. The market signal is, however, observed by the marketmakers; it affects their expectation $E[\theta|p]$, and thus the equilibrium price. The variance of the equilibrium price affects the orders placed by the informed traders. The next result shows that there is a unique value of the coefficient a such that the demand functions in (15.37) generate an equilibrium. The proof is given in the appendix (Section 15.5).

PROPOSITION 15.2 *There is an equilibrium in which the demand of each informed agent i with signal s_i is of the form $x_i = a(s_i - \bar{\theta})$, where a is solution of the equation*

(15.40) $a = \dfrac{\rho_\epsilon(\rho_\theta - Ba)(\rho_\theta + a^2\rho_Q)}{(\rho_\theta - Ba)^2 + (a\rho_Q + B)^2\left(\dfrac{\rho_\theta + \rho_\epsilon}{\rho_Q}\right)}$ *with* $B = \dfrac{\rho_\theta + a^2\rho_Q}{A}.$

When marketmakers are risk-neutral arbitrageurs, $B = 0$ and the previous equation

reduces to

$$(15.41) \quad a = \rho_\epsilon \rho_\theta \frac{\rho_\theta + a^2 \rho_Q}{\rho_\theta^2 + a^2 \rho_Q (\rho_\theta + \rho_\epsilon)}.$$

RISK-AVERSE MARKETMAKERS

Suppose now that marketmakers are risk-averse and that $A = 1/B$ is finite. From Proposition 15.2, the value of a is solution of equation (15.40). One can show easily that learning takes place and $\rho_t \to \infty$. Equation (15.40) is asymptotically equivalent to

$$(15.42) \quad a \approx \frac{\rho_\epsilon \rho_Q}{(1 + B^2)\rho_t} = \frac{\beta}{\rho_t}, \qquad \text{where } \beta \text{ is a constant.}$$

The power of the market signal converges to zero if the precision of the public information tends to infinity. What is more remarkable is the form of the coefficient a. The observation of the market is equivalent to the observation of the variable

$$y_t = a_t(\theta - \bar\theta) + Q \qquad \text{with} \qquad a_t \approx \frac{\beta}{\rho_t}.$$

Recall that in the model of Vives (1993) with investment and observational noise, agents observe in each period the signal $x_t = \alpha_t(\theta + \epsilon_t) + \eta_t$ with $\alpha_t = \rho_\epsilon/(\rho_t + \rho_\epsilon)$ (equation (3.7)). Asymptotically, this signal is informationally equivalent to $\hat{x}_t = (\rho_\epsilon/\rho_t)\theta + \eta_t$. When $\rho_t \to \infty$, the signals $\hat{x}_t$ and y_t above have the same power. The results of Vives (1993) apply immediately. By use of equation (15.40), where ρ_ϵ is replaced by β, $\sigma_t^2 = 1/\rho_t$ converges to zero as $t \to \infty$, and

$$(15.43) \quad \frac{\sigma_t^2}{\left(\sigma_\eta^2/3t\beta^2\right)^{1/3}} \to 1.$$

RISK-NEUTRAL MARKETMAKERS

Assume now that marketmakers are risk-neutral and $B = 0$. Let ρ_t be the precision of the public information on θ at the beginning of period t. From Proposition 15.2, the coefficient a takes the value a_t in period t, which is the solution of the equation

$$(15.44) \quad a_t = \rho_\epsilon \frac{\rho_t^2 + a^2 \rho_Q \rho_t}{\rho_t^2 + a^2 \rho_Q \rho_t + a^2 \rho_Q \rho_\epsilon} < \rho_\epsilon.$$

We have seen that the market price in period t is informationally equivalent to $y_t = a_t(\theta - \bar\theta) + Q_t$. The market with market orders was informationally equivalent to a signal $\rho_\epsilon \theta + Q$ (expression (15.30)). Because $a_t < \rho_\epsilon$, the setting with limit orders provides in each round a weaker signal on θ than the setting with market orders.

Consider now the rate of convergence of learning. In equation (15.44), the right-hand side is an increasing function of ρ_t. Because $\rho_t \geq \rho_1$, the solution in a_t is bounded below by a_1: for all $t \geq 2$, $a_t \geq a_1$. (In fact, a_t is increasing over time, as we will see below.) From one round to the next, the precision ρ_t increases according to

$$\rho_{t+1} \approx \rho_t + a_t^2 \rho_Q.$$

Because $a_t \geq a_1$, we have $\rho_t \to \infty$, and from equation (15.44), $a_t \to \rho_\epsilon$. Asymptotically, the precision on θ increases linearly and the information of the market with market orders is the same as with limit orders. The striking property is that the demand of informed agents is such that the reduction of the variance in the denominator cancels (for t large) the reduction of the multiplier of the private signal in the numerator, as in the model with limit orders. This can be worked out as a separate exercise and is left to the reader.

15.4 Multiple Equilibria, Crashes, and Booms

Theories of "portfolio insurance" became popular in the eighties. They recommend to sell a fraction of the portfolio of financial assets when its value declines, thus limiting the loss, and to buy when the price rises. In the previous sections, the strategies of rational agents were also based on the price of the asset. For a rational trader, a high price is a signal of higher intrinsic value (because the price is boosted by some informed agents), and it shifts the demand up. *Ceteris paribus*, however, a price rise has a negative impact on the demand. In Figure 15.1, the demand of the uninformed was less elastic than that of the informed, but this demand still had a negative slope.

Some of the trading strategies that have been recommended for portfolio insurance may not have a negative slope. When the price falls, for example, agents sell and sell so much that there may be a crash. The same strategies may also generate a boom, *mutatis mutandis*. The main purpose of the study of Genotte and Leland (1990) is to investigate this mechanism.

The method of analysis involves the addition of some agents with a price-based strategy to the CARA–Gauss model of the market for a financial asset. This strategy is represented by a demand $D(p)$. When this demand is added to the demands of the other agents, the total net demand, which is a function of the price (and other variables), may have a positive slope for some price range. This property may generate multiple equilibria. When the fundamentals shift the total net demand, one of these equilibria may disappear, thus generating a jump (up or down) of the price, triggering a boom or a crash.

The story needs the following ingredients: (i) the demand $D(p)$ should have a positive slope in some price range; (ii) the demand curve of the "rational" agents should be already sufficiently inelastic (otherwise the total net demand may not have a positive slope); (iii) whether the demand $D(p)$ is observable or not by other agents is an important issue. Suppose that rational agents are *mistaken* and believe that there is no such demand whereas in fact there is. A price fall is amplified by the price traders, and the large change is interpreted (wrongly) by uninformed traders as poor fundamentals. They sell more. The market is more unstable and may generate a crash.

Genotte and Leland (1990) use the CARA–Gauss model where informed agents have independent signals (Section 15.2.4), and add agents with some information on the noise traders (Exercise 15.2). This assumption is used to generate a sufficiently inelastic demand of the rational traders with some plausible parameters. It is made for empirical plausibility and is not important for the theoretical argument. Their argument is presented here with a simpler model where all informed agents have the same signal on the fundamental value of the asset.

THE MODEL OF GENOTTE AND LELAND

The standard model is extended with price traders who have a demand $D(p)$. The equilibrium equation is

(15.45) $\dfrac{E_I[\theta] - p}{\mathrm{Var}_I(\theta)} + Q + A\left(E[\theta|p] - p\right) + D(p) = 0.$

OBSERVABLE PRICE TRADERS

Suppose first that the quantity demanded by the price traders, $D(p)$, is observable by all traders. All agents know the form of the equilibrium equation (15.45). In order to look for some information equivalence, the equation is rewritten

(15.46) $s - \bar{\theta} + \dfrac{1}{\rho_\epsilon} Q = \psi(p),$

$$\text{with}\quad \psi(p) = -\frac{\rho_\theta + \rho_\epsilon}{\rho_\epsilon}(\bar{\theta} - p) - \frac{1}{\rho_\epsilon}\left(A\left(E[\theta|p] - p\right) - \frac{D(p)}{\rho_\epsilon}\right).$$

Declining Demand Curve of the Price Traders

Assume that the function D is decreasing (like a standard demand curve). Let us show that there is an equilibrium solution. Suppose first that there is a function $\psi(p)$, strictly increasing and continuous. From the first line in equation (15.46), there is a bijection between the left-hand side and p. Hence p reveals perfectly

(15.47) $z = s - \bar{\theta} + \dfrac{1}{\rho_\epsilon} Q.$

The uninformed traders can then build their expectation $E[\theta|p]$ from this observation. We have seen in the previous chapter that this expectation is an increasing function of p with a slope less than one ($E[\theta|p] - p$ is decreasing in p). One then substitutes in the right-hand side of the second line of (15.46) to obtain the function $\psi(p)$ that satisfies the initial assumption of a decreasing function. When the price

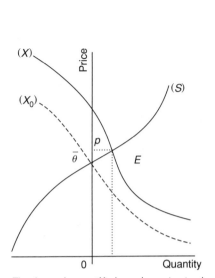

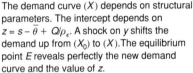

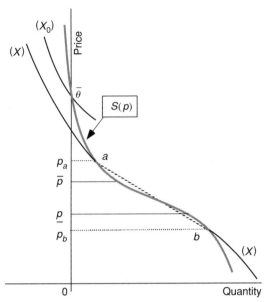

The demand curve (X) depends on structural parameters. The intercept depends on $z = s - \bar{\theta} + Q/\rho_\epsilon$. A shock on y shifts the demand up from (X_0) to (X). The equilibrium point E reveals perfectly the new demand curve and the value of z.

The demand schedule (X) depends on the supply $S(p)$ and is separated into two branches by the segment ab. The slope of the segment ab is $-1/\text{Var}_I(\theta) - A$. A shock on y shifts the demand down from (X_0) to (X). The equilibrium point (a or b) reveals perfectly the new demand curve and the value of z.

Figure 15.3 Demand with insurance trading.

traders have a demand that is declining and observable, the standard equilibrium takes place.

Let us rewrite the equilibrium equation as the equality between the supply of the price traders, $S(p) = -D(p)$, and the net demand of all other agents, denoted $X(s, Q, p)$, where $s = \theta + \epsilon$ is the signal of the informed agents:

$$(15.48) \qquad \frac{E_I[\theta] - p}{\text{Var}_I(\theta)} + Q + A\Big(E[\theta|p] - p\Big) = X(\theta + \epsilon, Q, p) = S(p).$$

When the demand D is decreasing in p, the supply $S(p)$ is increasing. The equilibrium in the previous equation is represented in Figure 15.3.[10]

The demand schedule (X) depends on the supply function of the price traders, because that function affects the signaling property of the price. Uninformed agents interpret a price increase as good news for the informed agents. An upward supply dampens the price fluctuations. Hence an increase in the price is more indicative of good news and should induce a larger upward shift of the demand of the uninformed.[11]

---

[10] Figure 15.1 is a special case of Figure 15.3 when there are no price traders ($S(p) \equiv 0$).

[11] The mechanism is the same as in Figure 15.1.

The demand schedule (X) should be less elastic. Accordingly, in Figure 15.3, the demand schedule is less elastic for the region around the mean where the supply schedule is more elastic. For large variations of the price, the supply is less elastic, and the demand is accordingly represented as more elastic.

The Case of Increasing Demand by the Price Traders

Assume now that the demand is increasing in the price because of the insurance motive that was described in the introduction. The supply $S(p) = -D(p)$ is declining in p. When the supply is very inelastic (with a negative slope), the equilibrium mechanism is the same as in the previous case. The negative supply amplifies the price variations, and therefore the demand of the uninformed agents is more elastic.

Assume now that the supply curve has for some range a negative elasticity with a large absolute value. Such a case is represented in the right panel of Figure 15.3. The schedule (X) has two intersections a and b with the supply curve (the middle point is excluded as unstable). The information contents of the prices p_a and p_b are *identical*. Both prices reveal the same shift of the demand curve, i.e., the same market variable z, as defined in (15.47). The slope of the segment ab is defined by the price effect on the demand of the rational agents for the given information. From equation (15.48), this slope is $-1/\text{Var}_I(\theta) - A$.

Because the supply is monotonic, the price reveals the market variable z perfectly. (When $S(p)$ is nonmonotonic, an equilibrium price may correspond to different demand curves. In order to discriminate between them, the rational traders have to observe the effective supply of the price traders.)

Each price is determined by the intersection of the demand schedule (X) (which is shifted by z) with the supply schedule (S). These intersections must be on one of the two branches along the supply schedule with prices $p \geq \overline{p}$ and $p \leq \underline{p}$ (see Figure 15.3). There is no equilibrium point between the two branches.[12] Suppose that a shock shifts the demand curve (X) gradually downward. The price responds first by a gradual reduction. For some value of z, however, the equilibrium point necessarily jumps to the lower branch, and a crash occurs at that moment. As usual with multiple equilibria, the crash may occur before the gradual shift forces the equilibrium point to jump to the lower branch. The selection of the equilibrium is obviously beyond the scope of the present model.

NONPERCEIVED PRICE TRADERS

Suppose that with probability π there is a supply $S(p)$ by price traders, and with probability $1 - \pi$ there is no price trader ($S(p) \equiv 0$). The other agents know the

---

[12] The end points of the branches are determined by the slope of the tangent to (X), which is $-1/\text{Var}_I(\theta) - A$.

probability of the event (and the supply $S(p)$), but cannot observe its realization. To simplify the problem, assume that the probability π is vanishingly small. The rational expectations equilibrium with $\pi > 0$ is not very different from that with $\pi = 0$. We therefore assume that rational agents ignore the possible existence of price traders (assume $\pi = 0$) but that such price traders happen to exist and their supply is defined by $S(p)$, as in the previous case.

The demand schedule (X) is less elastic than in the previous case, and multiple equilibria may occur, whereas they would not if $S(p)$ were observable. This is intuitive. Suppose a negative shock affects z. The price falls. Because of insurance trading, price traders sell, and this amplifies the shock. Uninformed traders attribute the large fall to bad news about the fundamentals (they do not think about insurance selling). They reduce the demand more. For some shock, the market clearing may require a large jump of the price. (Note again that the crash is attributed to really bad news.) The same argument applies for booms.

We close this section with a final note on the model of Genotte and Leland. Their structure of informed agents is more elaborate than the one used here. Their purpose is to generate a very inelastic demand schedule (X) (with more possibilities for multiple equilibria). Informed agents are of two types: θ-agents have a private signal on θ, and each private signal is independent of that of others. The demand of the noise traders is the sum of two independent variables, $Q + \eta$; and Q is observed by the Q-agents (who have all the same signal). As in the other models, there is a third type of rational agents, the uninformed. Such a model can produce a fairly inelastic demand because of the Q-agents. For these agents, the market can be very informative. (If η is nil, the market is perfectly informative for them.) A price increase shifts their demand significantly. These agents do not receive any signal on θ, but they may be much better informed than the θ-agents, who have no information on the noise in the market. The analysis of the model is presented as Exercise 15.2.

EXERCISES

EXERCISE 15.1

Analyze whether an increase of the parameter A in equation (15.48) makes the financial market more or less likely to experience a crash when a negative shock occurs.

EXERCISE 15.2 A model with partial information on real shocks (Genotte and Leland, 1990)

Consider the model of Section 15.2.4, and assume that the noise demand is the sum of Q and η, which are independent of any other variables and distributed $\mathcal{N}(0, 1/\rho_Q)$ and $\mathcal{N}(0, 1/\rho_\eta)$, respectively. Agents with a signal on θ are called the θ-agents. There is an additional type of informed traders, who observe Q. To simplify, assume that the demand of these Q-agents is $B(E_Q[\theta | Q, p] - p)$, and that of the uninformed agents is $A(E[\theta | p] - p)$.

1. Show that the market generates different information variables z and z' for the θ- and the Q-agents, respectively, with

$$z = \theta - \bar{\theta} + \alpha Q + \beta \eta,$$

where α and β are coefficients that are publicly known. The precision of this signal (the reciprocal of the variance of $\alpha Q + \beta \eta$) is ρ_z. We will not need to compute it. The general method to solve for the equilibrium is to determine the demand functions of the various types of agents who receive private signals and observe z. These demands depend on the coefficients α and β, and these coefficients are identified by substitution of the demand functions of all the agents in the equilibrium equation.

2. Show that the demand of all θ-agents is of the form

$$X_\theta(p) = \rho_\epsilon(\theta - \bar{\theta}) + \rho_z z + (\rho_\epsilon + \rho_z + \rho_\theta)(\bar{\theta} - p).$$

3. Find an analogous expression for the demand by the Q-agents.
4. Using the market equation, determine α and β.
5. Show that the equilibrium price p is a linear combination of the three independent variables θ, Q, and η:

$$p - \bar{\theta} = a_\theta(\theta - \bar{\theta}) + a_Q Q + a_\eta \eta.$$

6. Solve the model. (You may experiment with numerical values of the parameters to find the price elasticity of the demand.)

15.5 Appendix

A GENERAL PROPERTY OF CONVERGENCE

The analysis of the convergence of beliefs is set by definition in a context where the variance of the estimate of θ is vanishingly small. In this context, we can use approximations for a large class of decision models. We see that social learning has an efficient rate of convergence for a general class of financial markets. We give only a heuristic presentation.

We keep the basic structure of the previous model with three types of agents – informed, uninformed, and noise traders – who act in a tâtonnement process, and where the market opens in each period (conditional on no previous opening) with probability $\pi > 0$. The informed have a general von Neumann–Morgenstern utility function. The uninformed are risk-neutral and maximize their expected return, and the noise traders generate an exogenous and independent shock as before.

An informed trader has a wealth w. He has a subjective distribution on θ, which is characterized by the density function $f(s)$ on $s = (\theta - \bar{\theta})/\sigma$, where $\bar{\theta}$ and σ denote the mean and the standard error of θ, respectively. (Note that the mean of s is equal to 0.) The density function is arbitrary and does not have to be normal. The expected utility of an agent who buys an amount x of the risky asset is

$$U(x) = \int u(w + (\bar{\theta} - p + \sigma s)x) f(s)\, ds.$$

His optimal decision is the solution of the first-order condition

$$\int (\bar{\theta} - p + \sigma s) u'(w + (\bar{\theta} - p + \sigma s)x) f(s)\, ds = 0.$$

If σ and $\bar{\theta} - p$ are small, we can use a Taylor expansion:

$$\int (\bar{\theta} - p + \sigma s)\Big(1 - \gamma x(\bar{\theta} - p + \sigma s)\Big) f(s)\, ds \approx 0,$$

where $\gamma = -u''(w)/u'(w)$ is the coefficient of absolute risk aversion at w. When $\int f(s)\, ds = 1$, $\int s f(s)\, ds = 0$, and $\int s^2 f(s)\, ds = 1$, the previous expression is equivalent to

$$(\bar{\theta} - p)(1 - \gamma(\bar{\theta} - p)x) - \gamma \sigma^2 x \approx 0.$$

When beliefs converge to the truth, the term $\gamma(\bar{\theta} - p)x$ can be neglected, provided that x is bounded (which can be shown in a more formal analysis). We have therefore a first-order approximation of x:

$$x \approx \frac{\bar{\theta} - p}{\gamma \sigma^2}.$$

This demand has the same form as that of the CARA–Gauss model. As in the previous section, the precision of the market information increases linearly (asymptotically here).

Proof of Proposition 15.2
One proceeds by informational equivalents. For marketmakers, the equilibrium is informationally equivalent to the variable $y = a(\theta - \bar{\theta}) + Q$: $E[\theta|p] = E[\theta|y]$. Conditional on the market information, θ is normally distributed with precision

$$\rho = \rho_\theta + a^2 \rho_Q$$

and mean

$$E[\theta|p] = \bar{\theta} + \frac{a^2 \rho_Q}{\rho}\left(\frac{y}{a}\right) = \bar{\theta} + b(a(\theta - \bar{\theta}) + Q) \qquad \text{with} \quad b = \frac{a\rho_Q}{\rho}.$$

The price in (15.38) is therefore determined by

$$p - \bar{\theta} = \left(b + \frac{1}{A}\right)(a(\theta - \bar{\theta}) + Q);$$

hence

$$(15.49) \qquad \theta - p = (1 - (b + B)a)(\theta - \bar{\theta}) - (b + B)Q \qquad \text{with} \quad B = \frac{1}{A}.$$

An informed agent knows that when the market opens, $\theta - p$ is determined by the previous equation. Conditional on his signal s_i, $\theta - \bar{\theta}$ is normal with mean and variance given by

$$E[\theta - \bar{\theta}|s_i] = \frac{\rho_\epsilon}{\rho_i}(s_i - \bar{\theta}), \qquad \text{Var}(\theta|s_i) = \frac{1}{\rho_i}, \quad \text{and} \quad \rho_i = \rho_\theta + \rho_\epsilon.$$

Substituting in (15.49), we obtain

$$E[\theta - p|s_i] = (1 - (b + B)a)\frac{\rho_\epsilon}{\rho_\epsilon + \rho_\theta}(s_i - \bar{\theta}),$$

$$\text{Var}(\theta - p|s_i) = \frac{(1 - (b + B)a)^2}{\rho_i} + \frac{(b + B)^2}{\rho_Q}.$$

Because the demand by any informed agent is of the form

$$\frac{E[\theta - p|s_i]}{\text{Var}(\theta - p|s_i)} = a(s_i - \bar{\theta}),$$

the coefficient a must satisfy the equation

$$a = \frac{(1 - (b + B)a)\rho_\epsilon}{(1 - (b + B)a)^2 + (b + B)^2\left(\frac{\rho_\theta + \rho_\epsilon}{\rho_Q}\right)}.$$

Using the definition of b and ρ, a is solution of

$$a = \frac{\rho_\epsilon(\rho_\theta - B'a)(\rho_\theta + a^2\rho_Q)}{(\rho_\theta - B'a)^2 + (a\rho_Q + B'(\rho_\theta + a^2\rho_Q))^2\left(\frac{\rho_\theta + \rho_\epsilon}{\rho_Q}\right)},$$

$$\text{with} \quad B' = B(\rho_\theta + a^2\rho_Q).$$

In the special case where marketmakers are risk-neutral, $B = 0$. The previous equation simplifies to

$$(15.50) \quad a = \rho_\epsilon\rho_\theta\frac{\rho_\theta + a^2\rho_Q}{\rho_\theta^2 + a^2\rho_Q(\rho_\theta + \rho_\epsilon)}.$$

This equation has a unique positive solution in a: the right-hand side is a decreasing function that is hyperbolic in a^2; the left-hand side is increasing from 0 to ∞ in $\sqrt{a^2}$. ∎

16 Financial Frenzies

Dow 30,000

This chapter is devoted to three current research issues: (i) the integration of learning and coordination in a model of speculative attacks that is based on a Gaussian financial market with market orders; (ii) the self-fulfilling equilibrium with large endogenous uncertainty and low level of trade in a financial market; (iii) the absence of common knowledge in a bubble ending with a crash.

Three issues of current research are introduced in this chapter. The first is the analysis of speculative attacks, or stag hunts in general, in a multiperiod context. The one-period framework of Chapter 11 does not allow for any learning from the actions of others. It seems that in a speculative attack, against a currency or in a bank run, agents observe the actions of others and optimize the timing of their actions. In Chapter 12, agents observed the actions of others, but they could not, by assumption, optimize when to invest. The optimization of timing is one of the main issues in the model of dynamic speculative attacks, which is presented in Section 16.1.

In Section 16.2, the permanent value of an asset is increasing in the number of buyers, and the uncertainty is about the number of the potential buyers, i.e., the number of agents. This positive relation between the value of the asset and the number of agents is similar to that in previous chapters when there are information or payoff externalities. In equilibrium, a higher level of purchases generates more information about a large number of agents, as in Chapter 6. There may be multiple equilibria; in one of them, a high level of demand may generate a strong signal that the number of agents is indeed large; in another, the demand may be low and the uncertainty about the number of agents remains high, which will keep the demand low.

Section 16.3 is devoted to a model by Abreu and Brunnermeier (2003), who analyze how a bubble crashes. An examination of famous bubbles in the past shows that they always originated in some genuine good news. The spectacular rise of the price of John Law's company in 1719 was supported by real events. The critical issue is the transition from an extraordinary growth to a bubble. Here, Abreu and Brunnermeier (2003) introduce a lack of common knowledge about the time when the extraordinary growth stops: at that time, the mass of agents who are aware that the price is above the fundamentals grows gradually over time. Agents ride the bubble for a while, because they think (rationally) that the mass of informed agents is still low and that the bubble will go on a little longer.

16.1 Speculative Attacks against a Fixed Exchange Rate

Regimes of fixed exchange rates are opportunities for speculative attacks, which are similar to stag-hunt games. In a one-period setting, the global-game method resolves the problem of selection between multiple equilibria (Section 11.4). However, it fails to embody some important features of currency markets.

(i) An essential property of the one-period model is that all agents have to make a decision once and simultaneously. There is no interaction between the learning from others' actions and strategic decisions (i.e., to speculate now or delay after some observation of others' actions). Actual currency attacks may be short, but during an attack, agents intensively observe the actions taken by others and react quickly to their perceptions of these actions.

(ii) The global-game method requires the distribution to have a tail of agents on each side for whom the dominant strategy is to attack or not to attack the currency. In a multiperiod context, one tail may disappear (e.g., the tail of agents with high expectations who exercise their option to attack the currency), and the method is not applicable in the following period unless a new shock regenerates the tail.[1] If the period is short (as it should be in speculative attacks), such a new shock is asymptotically equivalent to a discontinuous jump of the parameters and may not be plausible.

(iii) A fixed transaction cost plays a critical role in the one-period model. When that cost is vanishingly small, the difference between the sustainable exchange rate and the fundamental exchange rate is also vanishingly small. A realistic value of this cost as a fraction of the transaction is very small for positions that last just a few days.

(iv) The model assumes that the exchange rate is fixed with absolutely no room for variations. Unless the currency belongs to a monetary zone (as did the euro between January 1, 1999 and January 1, 2002), some fluctuations (as in the

---

[1] Morris and Shin (1998b) consider a sequence of one-period models with no strategic decisions. The state of nature θ_t evolves randomly from period to period. The assumption that θ_t is learned exogenously in period $t + 1$ rules out social learning. In any case, the exogenous learning seems a bit slow compared to the time frame of a speculative attack. Corsetti *et al.* (2000) consider the strategic behavior of a large player and infinitesimal players. Given the assumption of the model, the outcome is trivial with the large player moving first.

regime before 1999) are allowed. These fluctuations have two opposite effects. The first is to provide a channel of communication. A speculative attack typically induces a depreciation of the exchange rate within the allowed band before any devaluation. This communication increases the risk of an attack. The second effect reduces this risk by introducing a penalty if the attack fails: after a failed attack, the price of the foreign currency falls, thus generating a loss for the holders of the foreign currency. This penalty is incurred without any *ad hoc* transaction cost.

(v) The payoff after the abandonment of the fixed rate is independent of the actions of the players if the attack is successful. All the bids are carried out at the old exchange rate, and the speculators gain from the devaluation. However, actual players in a dynamic game face the risk of arriving at the window too late. This is obviously why they may want to rush, as in a bank run. The model should incorporate the trade-off between going early at a smaller cost (with a favorable exchange rate) and little information, and delaying for more information with the risk of coming too late.

(vi) In most models of speculative attacks, the central bank has perfect information on the state of the world. However, a critical factor for the success of a speculative attack is the distribution of characteristics of the speculators about which the central bank may not have superior information. The one-period approach does not leave much room for the role of the central bank during a speculative attack.

These issues are addressed in Section 16.1 with a model where agents act strategically in a multiperiod context. The equilibrium exchange rate is allowed to fluctuate within a band, and a devaluation takes place only if the ceiling of the band is reached. The mass of these speculators is the uncertain parameter in the economy. For simplicity, there are two states of nature. In one of the two states, the *high* state, the mass of speculators is sufficiently large to induce a devaluation if all speculators buy the foreign currency; in the other, *low* state, that mass is subcritical.

The emphasis is not on the resolution of multiple equilibria as in the global-game approach, but on the opportunities offered by the dynamic setting for speculative attacks when agents have heterogeneous expectations on the mass of potential speculators. In all the cases considered here, there will be an equilibrium with no speculative attack. Under some conditions, there will also be an equilibrium with a speculative attack. The role of policy, if any, will be to abolish this second equilibrium. The strategic aspect is critical: the interesting cases occur when the parameters of the model are such that if there is one-period (and thus no opportunity to learn from others), there is a unique equilibrium with no attack.

Payoff externalities have a particular property here. When speculators face a coordination problem (e.g., attack a currency), there is some incentive to delay in order to obtain more information on others. There is also a premium, though, for the agents who invest earlier when the asset price is still relatively low. If the agent delays too long, he may come too late for the gain of the attack and may not get anything.

The present model is built on a standard structure of a financial market with noise traders. The main feature of the model is that speculators observe the exchange rate at the end of each period and place market orders for the next period. Following Hellwig (1982) and Blume, Easley, and O'Hara (1994), these orders depend on all the information available at the time they are placed and the rational expectations about the price in the next period. Speculators may delay the timing of their attack. An equilibrium is constructed analytically for any finite number of periods by backward induction.

In all periods, the subgame has an equilibrium in which there is no speculation for all remaining periods. Under some conditions on the beliefs of the agents, there are other equilibria with speculative attacks, as analyzed[2] in Section 16.1.2. The purpose of the analysis is not to construct a model with a unique equilibrium in which there may be a speculative attack, but to analyze how a speculative attack may be facilitated by the learning from prices in markets, and how such equilibria with a speculative attack can be prevented by policy. Some properties of the model are illustrated by a numerical example with Gaussian noise.

Policies are analyzed in the last section. The central bank can prevent a speculative attack by widening the band of fluctuations or through trading. If the central bank intervenes by stabilizing the exchange rate (i.e., selling when the exchange rate increases) and this policy is anticipated by rational speculators, a speculative attack is more likely. Speculative attacks may be prevented either by a rationally anticipated intervention that amplifies the fluctuations of the exchange rate or by a random intervention that cannot be anticipated.

16.1.1 The Model

There are a finite number of periods, $T + 1$, and a continuum[3] of speculators, called agents, of mass $\theta \in \{\theta_0, \theta_1\}$. The value of θ determines the state that is selected by nature before the first period. In each period, an agent can hold at most one unit of foreign currency, also called the *asset*. This constraint embodies a credit constraint. At the beginning of the first period, all agents hold only the domestic currency, also called simply the *currency*. In period $T + 1$, all agents undo their position: by assumption, all agents must hold only the currency at the end of period $T + 1$; if an agent holds the asset at the beginning of period $T + 1$, he sells it in period $T + 1$. The game is actually played during T periods.

---

[2] More results are shown in Chamley (2003b): a larger number of periods extend the set of beliefs for which a speculative attack is an equilibrium (Proposition 1); the equilibrium strategy that is analyzed here tends to a stationary solution when the number of periods tends to infinity (Proposition 2).

[3] Dynamic speculative attacks with pivotal agents are analyzed in Rodionova and Surti (1999).

MARKET ORDERS

At the beginning of any period, an agent who holds the currency can place a *buy* order for the asset, and an agent who holds the asset can place a *sell* order. The orders are market orders, i.e., they specify a quantity to be traded (conditional on no devaluation) for any market price in the period. An order depends on the information available at the beginning of the period and on the rational expectations, given that information, about the transaction price.[4] Market orders embody the sequential nature of trades. Another assumption that is used in the microstructure of financial markets is that of limit orders. When agents can place limit orders, they submit their entire demand schedule contingent on the information revealed by the equilibrium price. Orders are executed only at the equilibrium price, and agents would not change their orders after the closing of the market even if they had an opportunity to do so. No rationing can occur. Such a setting is not appropriate for modeling a bank run or a situation where agents would change their trade after the equilibrium price is known.

We will consider only symmetric equilibria. Because agents are risk-neutral, the payoff for placing an order of amount $\ell < 1$ for the asset will be equivalent to that for an order of 1 placed with probability ℓ. We will assume the second formulation to facilitate the presentation. In this way, an agent either holds one unit of the asset (and is an asset holder) or holds no amount of the asset (and is a currency holder).

THE MARKET FOR THE ASSET

There is a game in period t if no devaluation (a process described below) has taken place before period t. Let λ_{t-1} be the fraction of agents who hold the asset at the beginning of period t. The mass of agents who hold the asset at the beginning of period t is therefore $\lambda_{t-1}\theta$. By assumption, no agent holds the asset at the beginning of the first period: $\lambda_0 = 0$.

We will consider only symmetric strategies: there is one strategy (possibly random) for the asset holders and one for the currency holders. Let ζ_t be the fraction of agents who place a buy order for the asset in period t. By an abuse of notation, ζ_t will also denote the strategy of currency holders who place a buy order with probability $\zeta_t/(1 - \lambda_{t-1})$. The strategy of the asset holders will be simpler, as we will see later: if some agents buy in an equilibrium, no asset holder sells, and if some asset holders sell, they all sell. Because there will thus be no ambiguity, "order" will mean a buy order. Suppose $\zeta_t > 0$. Given the quantity of orders $\zeta_t\theta$, the demand for the asset by the agents in period t (a stock) is $(\lambda_{t-1} + \zeta_t)\theta$. The total demand for the asset in period t is the sum of the agents' endogenous demands and of an exogenous noise η_t. The introduction of noise traders is standard in financial markets and facilitates trading

---

[4] Market orders are analyzed in the model of Vives (1995), Section 15.3.2. The informational properties of a financial market with market orders have been analyzed by Hellwig (1982) and by Blume, Easley, and O'Hara (1994).

between agents with asymmetric information (Chapter 15). The noise traders in period t undo their position at the beginning of the next period. The distribution of η_t is stationary. The terms η_t are serially independent, and the mean of η_t is equal to zero.

The supply of the asset is a linear function of its price p: $S(p) = (p-1)/a$, where a is a fixed parameter. The value of S represents the net supply when the price departs from the middle of the band of exchange rate fluctuations, which can be interpreted as a long-run value as determined by real trade and policy. This long-run price is an equilibrium value when there is no speculative attack, and it is normalized to 1. The supply schedule $S(p)$ can be defined as minus the net demand of risk-averse marketmakers who place price-contingent orders that may take into account the information revealed by the transaction price. Their net demand is of the form $\kappa(E[p_{t+1}|p_t] - p_t)/\mathrm{Var}(p_{t+1}|p_t)$, where p_t and p_{t+1} are the prices of the asset in periods t and $t+1$, and $\kappa > 0$ is a parameter. Because marketmakers attach a lower *ex ante* subjective probability to state θ_1 than speculators, they interpret the market data differently. (The speculators are more optimistic about their high mass.) For simplicity, we assume that the marketmakers assign *ex ante* a vanishingly low probability to there being a high mass of speculators and that a devaluation will take place. Hence, contingent on the observation of the equilibrium price, the revised probability of a devaluation is still vanishingly low: $E[p_{t+1}|p_t] = 1$, and the variance of p_{t+1} in the subjective distribution is constant. In this case, their net demand is of the form $(1-p)/a$ with $a = \mathrm{Var}(p_{t+1}|p_t)/\kappa$. If the current price p_t has a significant effect on the expected value $E[p_{t+1}|p_t]$, a higher price p_t shifts the demand curve up, and the effect is equivalent to that of a less elastic demand curve. We will consider below the effect of such a lower elasticity on the properties of the model.

The schedule $S(p)$ may also incorporate the strategy of other agents whose trades depend only on p_t. The central bank is assumed to perform the function of a clearinghouse by matching the trade orders. The central bank may also use its reserves for trading. In that case, its net supply is incorporated in the schedule $S(p)$. Policies of the central bank will be discussed in Section 16.1.5. Before that subsection, the central bank is assumed not to trade.

The regime of the exchange rate within a band of fluctuations stipulates that the price of the asset is allowed to fluctuate in a band below a threshold value $1 + \gamma$, with $\gamma > 0$. If the equilibrium price (to be defined later) is above $1 + \gamma$, a devaluation takes place according to a specification that will be given later. The event of a price below $1 - \gamma$ will have a negligible probability and will be ignored.

Assuming no devaluation before period t, let p_t be the price determined by the equation

(16.1) $\qquad p_t = 1 + a\left((\lambda_{t-1} + \zeta_t)\theta + \eta_t\right).$

If $p_t \leq 1 + \gamma$, the price that clears the demand and the supply is within the band and is equal to p_t in (16.1). There is no devaluation in period t. All buy orders are satisfied. The fraction of agents who hold the asset at the beginning of the next period is $\lambda_t = \lambda_{t-1} + \zeta_t$.

If $p_t > 1 + \gamma$, the price at which supply and demand are equal is greater than that allowed by the band of fluctuations. Let $\overline{X}$ be the critical mass of the demand (speculators and noise traders), i.e., the highest value of the demand that can be accommodated by an equilibrium in the band. From equation (16.1), $\overline{X}$ is defined so that

$$\gamma = a\overline{X}.$$

A devaluation takes place when the demand is higher than the critical mass. All orders cannot be executed. To simplify the process, it is assumed that first, noise traders of period $t - 1$ undo their positions; second, noise traders of period t place their orders. All these orders are executed (even if the total amount exceeds the critical mass).[5] The amount of the asset that is available for new orders without devaluation is therefore $\max(\overline{X} - \lambda_{t-1}\theta - \eta_t, 0)$. (We will see later that if new orders come in, no asset holder sells.)

Suppose that the mass of new orders in period t is strictly positive: $\zeta_t > 0$. (The case $\zeta_t = 0$ will be described below.) By assumption, all the agents' new orders are executed with the same probability, which is the highest probability. The transaction price is the highest possible in the band, $1 + \gamma$, and the probability of execution of a buy order is

$$\pi = \frac{\max(\overline{X} - \lambda_{t-1}\theta - \eta_t, 0)}{\zeta_t\theta}.$$

By construction, $0 \leq \pi \leq 1$. If a devaluation takes place, the price of the foreign asset is set at $1 + A$, where $A > \gamma$ is a fixed parameter.[6]

INFORMATION

The true state θ is not observable. At the beginning of the first period, all agents have a subjective probability μ_0 of the high state θ_1. At the end of each period t, if a devaluation takes place, the game ends. If no devaluation takes place, a subgame begins in period $t + 1$. Agents observe the price p_t in period t. They use this observation to update their belief in a Bayesian fashion from μ_{t-1} to μ_t. Because the strategies are common knowledge, agents know the fraction of agents who place orders in period t. Hence, the fraction of agents who hold the asset at the beginning of the next period, λ_t, is known. We will show that the subgame that begins in period t depends only on t and on $(\lambda_{t-1}, \mu_{t-1})$.

---

[5] This assumption is made to simplify the process. The probability of a demand greater than the critical mass at that stage is very small.

[6] One could consider the case where the amount of the devaluation is determined by the intensity of the attack or by an equilibrium mechanism. Such an effect would enhance the strategic complementarity but would not alter the properties of the model.

PAYOFFS

The payoff of an agent is the sum of the discounted values of the trades in all periods, valued in the (domestic) currency. The discount factor δ, $0 < \delta < 1$, embodies a positive difference between the rate of return in the domestic currency and that of the foreign asset, for a fixed exchange rate. Such a positive difference ensures that in the context of the model, the band of the asset price is *sustainable*: if there is no speculative attack, speculators prefer to hold the currency (or to sell the foreign asset, which they may own), in an equilibrium. If the difference between interest rates were not strictly positive (or $\delta = 1$), the band might not be sustainable.[7] In the next section, we will introduce a mild sufficient condition on the discount rate for the sustainability of the exchange rate band.

16.1.2 Equilibria

THE EVOLUTION OF BELIEFS

If there is no devaluation in period t, the equilibrium price is $p_t = 1 + a y_t$. By use of this equation, the observation of p_t is equivalent to the observation of the total demand

$$(16.2) \qquad y_t = (\lambda_{t-1} + \zeta_t)\theta + \eta_t,$$

which conveys a signal on the state θ. Because agents know the strategies and $\lambda_{t-1} + \zeta_t$, the observation of y_t is equivalent to the observation of the variable

$$(16.3) \qquad z_t = \theta + \frac{\eta_t}{\lambda_{t-1} + \zeta_t}.$$

The variance of the noise term is reduced when more agents place an order. The information conveyed by the market (conditional on no devaluation) increases with the fraction of agents who place orders. Recall that the belief at the beginning of period t (probability that $\theta = \theta_1$) is denoted by μ_{t-1}. Let $f(\eta)$ be the density of η (which is independent of t). If there is no devaluation in period t, the belief on θ_t in the next period is determined by the Bayesian updating formula

$$(16.4) \qquad \frac{\mu_t(y_t; \lambda_{t-1} + \zeta_t, \mu_{t-1})}{1 - \mu_t(y_t; \lambda_{t-1} + \zeta_t, \mu_{t-1})} = \frac{\mu_{t-1} f(y_t - (\lambda_{t-1} + \zeta_t)\theta_1)}{(1 - \mu_{t-1}) f(y_t - (\lambda_{t-1} + \zeta_t)\theta_0)}.$$

PAYOFF OF AN ORDER

From the description of the trades, a devaluation takes place in period t if $y_t > \overline{X}$, in which case the *ex post* payoff of an order is $(A - \gamma) \max(\overline{X} - \lambda_{t-1}\theta - \eta, 0)/\zeta_t\theta$.

If no devaluation takes place in period t, the *ex post* payoff is the value of holding the asset in the continuation of the game minus the purchase price, $1 + a y_t$, i.e., $\underline{u}(\theta, \eta) = \delta V_{t+1}(\lambda_{t-1} + \zeta_t, \mu_t) - (1 + a y_t)$. In this expression, the continuation value V_{t+1}

---

[7] For example, if the support of the distribution of noise traders extends beyond γ/a, holders of the foreign asset never sell, and if the number of periods is sufficiently large, all agents with an option to buy the asset exercise it with no delay.

depends on the fraction of speculators holding the asset $\lambda_t = \lambda_{t-1} + \zeta_t$, and on the belief μ_t at the end of period t, which has been expressed in (16.4).

The payoff of an order is the expected value of all *ex post* payoffs for all possible values of θ and η. If the c.d.f.[8] of (θ, η), is denoted by $F(\theta, \eta; \mu_{t-1})$, this payoff is

$$(16.5) \quad u_t(\zeta_t; \lambda_{t-1}, \mu_{t-1})$$

$$= \int_{y_t > \overline{X}} (A - \gamma) \frac{\max(\overline{X} - \lambda_{t-1}\theta - \eta, 0)}{\zeta_t \theta} dF(\theta, \eta; \mu_{t-1})$$

$$+ \int_{y_t < \overline{X}} \left(\delta\, V_{t+1}(\lambda_{t-1} + \zeta_t, \mu_t) - (1 + a y_t) \right) dF(\theta, \eta; \mu_{t-1}).$$

The method of backward induction can characterize all equilibria of all subgames, but such a complete characterization is beyond the scope of this chapter. We will assume that if in period t there is no equilibrium strategy with $\zeta_t > 0$ (no new order comes in), then the speculative attack stops completely.[9] One can show that such an outcome is an equilibrium in this model (Chamley, 2003b). In the subgame that begins in period t, there may be multiple equilibrium values for $\zeta_t > 0$. (An example will be given below.) When there are such multiple equilibrium strategies, we assume that agents coordinate on the highest equilibrium value of ζ_t.

ASSUMPTION 16.1 *In any period t, if there is no strictly positive equilibrium value of ζ_t for buy orders, then agents coordinate on the zero equilibrium, and the game ends at the end of the period. If there are multiple equilibrium strategies with strictly positive ζ_t, agents coordinate on the highest such value. This coordination rule is common knowledge.*

ARBITRAGE AND THE PAYOFF OF DELAY

By Assumption 16.1, the game ends in period $t + 1$ if the payoff of an order in that period is negative. Hence, in equilibrium, the payoff of delay is equal to that of making a final decision in the following period, either to place a buy order in period $t + 1$ or to never place a buy order. This *one-step* property is the same as in Chamley and Gale (1994) and is a consequence of Assumption 16.1. The payoff of delay is therefore equal to

$$(16.6) \quad w_t(\zeta_t; \lambda_{t-1}, \mu_{t-1})$$

$$= \delta \int_{y_t < \overline{X}} \max \left(U_{t+1}(\lambda_{t-1} + \zeta_t, \mu_t), 0 \right) dF(\theta, \eta; \mu_{t-1}),$$

where U_t is the value of holding the currency.

---

[8] Here θ and η are independent; the distribution of θ depends on the belief μ_{t-1}, and the distribution of η_t is independent of the period.

[9] Because the incentive to hold is stronger than the incentive to buy, there may be a level of belief such that no speculator buys but asset holders do not sell. The price in period t may convey sufficient information to induce a resumption of new orders in period $t + 1$ and eventually a successful attack. Although such an equilibrium is theoretically possible, we assume that agents do not coordinate on it.

Because the mass of asset holders is no greater than one, we have $\zeta \in [0, 1 - \lambda_{t-1}]$. A necessary condition for ζ to be an equilibrium value in period t is that the payoff of a buy order is at least equal to that of delay:

$$(16.7) \qquad u_t(\zeta; \lambda_{t-1}, \mu_{t-1}) \geq w_t(\zeta; \lambda_{t-1}, \mu_{t-1}).$$

Case a: If there is no $\zeta > 0$ that satisfies (16.7), then the equilibrium value is $\zeta_t = 0$, and by Assumption 16.1, the game ends in period t with the zero equilibrium. All speculators hold only the currency for all remaining periods.

Case b: If there is a value $\zeta > 0$ such that (16.7) is satisfied, by Assumption 16.1 the equilibrium value ζ_t is

$$\zeta_t = \max\left\{\zeta \in (0, 1 - \lambda_{t-1}] \,|\, u_t(\zeta; \lambda_{t-1}, \mu_{t-1}) \geq w_t(\zeta; \lambda_{t-1}, \mu_{t-1})\right\}.$$

In general, the strategy in period t is a function $\zeta_t = \phi_t(\lambda_{t-1}, \mu_{t-1})$ with

$$(16.8) \qquad \phi_t(\lambda_{t-1}, \mu_{t-1})$$

$$= \max\left\{0, \left\{\zeta \in (0, 1 - \lambda_{t-1}] \,|\, u_t(\zeta; \lambda_{t-1}, \mu_{t-1}) \geq w_t(\zeta; \lambda_{t-1}, \mu_{t-1})\right\}\right\}.$$

When $\zeta_t = \phi_t > 0$, a speculative attack takes place. It is of one of the following two types:

(i) If $\zeta_t = 1 - \lambda_{t-1}$, all agents who have an option place an order. Because there cannot be new orders in period $t+1$, the attack either succeeds in period t or fails with all agents selling the foreign asset in period $t+1$.

(ii) If $0 < \zeta_t < 1 - \lambda_{t-1}$, by continuity of u_t and w_t, (16.7) must be an equality, $u_t(\zeta_t; \lambda_{t-1}, \mu_{t-1}) = w_t(\zeta_t; \lambda_{t-1}, \mu_{t-1})$. In such an equilibrium, there is an *arbitrage* between buying in period t at a relatively low price with less information, and delaying until period $t+1$ to get more information while facing the risk of missing the benefit from a devaluation in period t.

The strategy $\phi_t(\lambda_{t-1}, \mu_{t-1})$ determines the payoff of an order, in equilibrium:

$$(16.9) \qquad U_t(\lambda_{t-1}, \mu_{t-1}) = u_t(\phi_t(\lambda_{t-1}, \mu_{t-1}), \lambda_{t-1}, \mu_{t-1}).$$

VALUE OF HOLDING THE ASSET

Suppose that the belief μ is such that some agents place a buy order. These agents buy after the agents who already own the asset and face a higher price. In this situation, if some agents find it profitable to place a new order, then the agents who already own the asset and have the same information strictly prefer to hold rather than to sell. This property is formalized in Lemma 16.1.

LEMMA 16.1 *In an equilibrium, if some agents place a buy order in period t (and $\phi_t(\lambda_t, \mu_t) > 0$), then no asset holder sells in period t.*

The value of holding the asset at the beginning of period t depends on whether the speculative attack continues in the period. By use of Lemma 16.1, this value satisfies the following recursive equations:

- If $\phi_t(\lambda_{t-1}, \mu_{t-1}) > 0$,

$$(16.10) \quad V_t(\lambda_{t-1}, \mu_{t-1}) = \int_{y_t > \overline{X}} (1 + A) \, dF(\theta, \eta; \mu_{t-1})$$

$$+ \delta \int_{y_t < \overline{X}} V_{t+1}(\lambda_{t-1} + \phi_t, \mu_t) \, dF(\theta, \eta; \mu_{t-1}).$$

- If $\phi_t(\lambda_{t-1}, \mu_{t-1}) = 0$, by Assumption 16.1 the equilibrium is the zero equilibrium and

$$V_t(\lambda_{t-1}, \mu_{t-1}) = \overline{V}.$$

BACKWARD DETERMINATION OF THE EQUILIBRIUM

In the last period $T + 1$, we have $U_{T+1} \equiv 0$ and $V_{T+1} \equiv \overline{V} = 1 - \beta$. Assume that for $t \leq T$, U_{t+1} and V_{t+1} are given. The payoff of a buy order in period t is determined by (16.5), and that of delay by (16.6). The policy function $\phi_t(\lambda_t, \mu_t)$ is then determined by (16.8). This function determines U_t by (16.9) and V_t by (16.10). The equilibrium is determined for all periods by backward induction.

The previous definition of the policy function generates an equilibrium that is stable in the sense that a small deviation of all currency holders from the equilibrium strategy induces a reaction toward the equilibrium strategy. Consider first the corner solution, and assume that $\zeta_t = 1 - \lambda_t > 0$. Ruling out an event with probability zero, we have $u_t(\zeta_t; \lambda_{t-1}, \mu_{t-1}) > 0 = w_t(\zeta_t; \lambda_{t-1}, \mu_{t-1})$. Assume that a perturbation occurs in the form of a small reduction of ζ_t to $\zeta_t' < \zeta_t$ (or that a small fraction of the currency holders do not speculate). By continuity, it is still true that exercising the option and speculating carries a higher payoff, $u_t(\zeta_t'; \lambda_{t-1}, \mu_{t-1})$, than holding the option, which has the value $w_t(\zeta_t'; \lambda_{t-1}, \mu_{t-1})$. The optimal response is still to place an order with probability 1.

Suppose now that there is arbitrage with $0 < \phi_t(\lambda_{t-1}, \mu_{t-1}) < 1 - \lambda_t$, and consider the difference between the payoff of an order and that of delay:

$$D(\zeta) = u_t(\zeta; \lambda_{t-1}, \mu_{t-1}) - w_t(\zeta; \lambda_{t-1}, \mu_{t-1}).$$

By definition of ϕ_t, $D(\zeta) < 0$ for all $\zeta \in (\phi_t, 1 - \lambda_{t-1}]$, and its derivative is not equal to 0 at the point $\zeta = \phi_t$. Hence the graph of $u_t(\zeta; \lambda_{t-1}, \mu_{t-1})$ cuts that of $w_t(\zeta; \lambda_{t-1}, \mu_{t-1})$ from above at $\zeta = \zeta_t$: if the total quantity of orders is reduced from the equilibrium value ζ_t to a slightly smaller value ζ_t', the exercise value of the option, u, becomes strictly higher than the holding value w, and the optimal reaction of an individual is to speculate. The reaction is stabilizing in the sense that it operates as an increase in the aggregate quantity of orders[10] toward the equilibrium value ζ_t.

A general analysis is presented in Chamley (2003b). The properties of the model are described here within the context of an example.

16.1.3 An Example with Gaussian Noise

Assume that η has a normal distribution with variance σ_η^2. Let $v_t = \log(\mu_t/(1 - \mu_t))$ be the LLR between the two states. The Bayesian equation (16.4) takes the form

$$v_t = v_{t-1} + \lambda_t \frac{\theta_1 - \theta_0}{\sigma_\eta^2} \left(y_t - \lambda_t \frac{\theta_1 + \theta_0}{2} \right)$$

with $\lambda_t = \lambda_{t-1} + \zeta_t$, and $y_t = \lambda_t \theta + \eta_t$. The expected change of belief from period t to period $t + 1$ is measured by

$$(16.11) \quad E[v_{t+1} - v_t] = \begin{cases} \dfrac{\left(\theta_1 - \theta_0\right)^2}{2\sigma_\eta^2}(\lambda_{t-1} + \zeta_t)^2 & \text{in state } \theta_1, \\[2em] -\dfrac{\left(\theta_1 - \theta_0\right)^2}{2\sigma_\eta^2}(\lambda_{t-1} + \zeta_t)^2 & \text{in state } \theta_0. \end{cases}$$

We have seen before that the signal-to-noise ratio in the demand y_t increases with the fraction of active speculators, $\lambda_{t-1} + \zeta_t$. This property appears in the preceding expression, where the absolute value of the expected change of belief increases with the demand by speculators.

16.1.4 A Numerical Example

The graphs of the payoff of an order and that of waiting in the first period of a three-period game ($T = 2$) are presented in Figure 16.1 with the indicated parameter values.[11] The payoffs of an order and of delay in the first period are $u(\zeta)$ and $w(\zeta)$ for short.[12] There are three equilibria, but the middle equilibrium value of λ is unstable. The two stable equilibria are the zero equilibrium and an equilibrium in which a fraction of speculators purchase the asset. (For other values of the parameters, there may be more than one stable equilibrium where the mass of speculation is strictly positive.)

---

[10] The concept of stability remains informal here in that there is no room for an out-of-equilibrium ajustment process in real time.

[11] The probability α that a devaluation is triggered by the noise traders is less than 10^{-12}.

[12] Here $u(\zeta)$ and $w(\zeta)$ are computed on a grid for $\zeta \in [0, 1]$ of width 0.02. The first step is the computation of $U_2(\lambda, \mu)$ and $V_2(\lambda, \mu)$ on a grid of values $(\lambda, \mu) \in [0, 1] \times [0, 1]$.

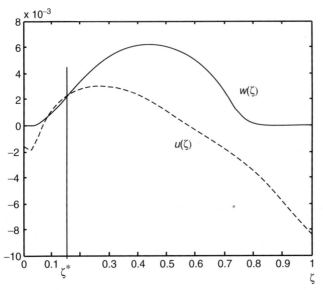

Figure 16.1 Payoff of immediate attack (u) and of delay (w). ζ is the fraction of speculators who buy the foreign exchange in the first period. The payoff of attacking in the first period is decreasing and negative if ζ is small, because of the foregone interest and the exchange rate, which increases with ζ. When ζ is sufficiently high, the payoff is increasing because the market price gives a strong signal about the high state (if that state is the true state). Parameters: belief of the high state, $\mu_1 = 0.05$; height of the band in the peg, $\gamma = 0.025$; rate of the devaluation, $A = 0.275$; supply elasticity, $a = 1$; standard error of the noise trade, $\sigma_\eta = 0.08\overline{X}$; masses of speculators in the two states, $\theta_0 = 0.7\overline{X}$ and $\theta_1 = 1.3\overline{X}$; interest rate per period, 0.15 percent.

When ζ is small, the value of a buy order is a decreasing function of ζ: a higher mass of speculation raises the price of the asset, but because this mass is still small, it does not provide much information on the state, and the gross payoff of an order remains low.

When ζ is sufficiently large, the price conveys an informative signal on the high state if it is the true state. The anticipation that such information will be provided at the end of the first period and will generate a successful continuation of the attack in period 2 raises the value of a purchase order above the value of the option of delay. The gain of buying early compensates for the risk of finding out at the end of period 1 that the state is bad and enduring a capital loss in period 2.

16.1.5 Defense Policies

A defense policy is successful if it abolishes the coordination equilibrium associated with a speculative attack. Three types of policies are considered: (i) widening the band of fluctuations, (ii) stabilizing the exchange rate through trading, and (iii) random interventions. For each policy it is assumed that the central bank cannot observe the state θ.

WIDENING THE BAND OF FLUCTUATIONS

Widening the band while keeping the rate of devaluation unchanged is equivalent to an increase in γ. In the present model, if $\gamma = A$, there is no capital gain if a devaluation takes place, hence no expected profit. If the attack fails, however, there is a capital loss. Hence, there is no speculative attack in an equilibrium. By continuity, that property holds if $\gamma^* < \gamma \le A$ for some γ^* ($0 < \gamma^* < A$). A speculative attack can be prevented by a suitable widening of the band of fluctuations.

A relevant episode occurred at the end of July 1993 with the speculative attack against the French franc, which was part of the ERM (Exchange Rate Mechanism). The regime had margins of 2.25 percent on each side of a reference level. After trying unsuccessfully to ward off the speculators through trading, the central banks of the monetary union raised the bands of fluctuations to 15 percent. The change of regime stopped the attack,[13] as illustrated in Figure 1 of Obstfeld (1996).

STABILIZING THE EXCHANGE RATE THROUGH TRADE INTERVENTION

There are two types of trade interventions by the central bank, those that are *deterministic* and predictable, and those that are *random* and surprise the speculators. A trade policy that is determined by the exchange rate is predictable by rational agents. As an example, assume that the central bank supplies a quantity of foreign currency according to the linear rule

$$(16.12) \quad S_B = b(p-1) \quad \text{with} \quad b > 0.$$

With $b > 0$, the central bank attempts to reduce the fluctuations of the exchange rate. Such a policy requires a positive level of reserves R. The problem of defense is interesting only if the reserves cannot prevent a speculative attack under perfect information, i.e., if $R < \theta_1 - \overline{X}$ (as in Obstfeld, 1996). Such a constraint imposes a restriction on the stabilization policy. Because $S_B \le R$ for all values of $p < 1 + \gamma$, we must have $b \le R/\gamma$.

Speculators with rational expectations anticipate the policy. We assume accordingly that they know the value of the policy parameter b and know that the total supply of foreign exchange is equal to $(p-1)/a'$ with $a' = 1/(b+1/a) < a$. The

---

[13] The last exchange rate between the Deutsche mark and the French franc before the change of regime was at the top of the band at 3.4304. The day after the change of regime (August 2), the rate increased to 3.5080; it then fell to 3.46040 two days later. It then began to increase again and to hover around 3.50. However, by that time the information had probably changed. Agents expected the interest rate to be lowered in France to take advantage of the greater exchange rate flexibility and reduce unemployment. Eventually, the expectations were seen to be mistaken: such a policy was not conducted by the central bank. After hovering between 3.48 and 3.55 until the beginning of December, the exchange rate decreased steadily during the last month of the year to end at 3.40. In agreement with the policy interpretation in this chapter, after the exchange rate returned to its midband level, the central banks felt no need to reduce the bands back to the original 2.25 percent. The wider band contributed to the stabilization of the exchange rate. (For a discussion of the events see Buiter *et al.*, 1998.)

influence of the policy is the same as that of an increase in the supply elasticity of foreign exchange, or the liquidity of the market. A higher elasticity of supply enlarges the domain of beliefs in which a speculative attack may take place. In the present model, a central bank that reduces the fluctuations of the exchange rate does not alter the functioning of the exchange rate as a coordination device, but it reduces the risk taken by speculators. Such a policy facilitates speculative attacks.

When the price of the foreign currency rises (because of a noise shock or an attack), a central bank that conducts a deterministic (and predictable) policy should not sell the foreign currency, but it should *buy*.

RANDOM INTERVENTION

Trades by the central bank that cannot be predicted by speculators have to be random. Assume that the central bank supplies a random amount R, which is normally distributed $\mathcal{N}(0, \sigma_R)$ and set before the opening of the market. Rational speculators know the parameter σ_R but cannot observe R. The random trading by the central bank adds noise and thus reduces the information content of the price in the first period. Numerical simulations show that the smaller information reduces the possibility of coordination between speculators.

In the example of Figure 16.1, the speculative attack is eliminated when $\sigma_R \geq 0.06\,\overline{X}$. For a policy of random interventions, some reserves are required (because the foreign currency does have to be sold at times), contrary to the policy of deterministic trade. However, these reserves may be significantly smaller than what would be required under perfect information. This is an important implication of the present model for policy. By trading in a nonpredictable manner, the central bank can prevent speculators from coordinating an attack. The amount of reserves required for this policy can be smaller than what would be required if speculators had complete information on their total resources.[14]

THE INTEREST RATE

Raising the interest rate is a standard defense policy. Numerical simulations (in Chamley, 2003b) show that this policy is effective in the context of the model. For the parameters of Figure 16.1, an increase of the interest rate from 0.15 to 0.25 percent defends the regime. The policy is effective because it raises the cost of "communication" through the price at the beginning of an attack.[15]

---

[14] In the example of Figure 16.1, the central bank needs a level of reserves equal to $R = 0.12\overline{X}$. (The normal distribution can be considered as an approximation of a distribution where the trade by the central bank is bounded.) If all speculators have knowledge of the high state and attack, the central bank's reserves R are too low to fend off the attack: $\theta_1 - \overline{X} = 0.3\overline{X} > R$.

[15] If the parameters of the model and the beliefs are such that there is an attack by all speculators and it must succeed or fail in the first period, raising the interest rate is significantly less effective (Chamley, 2003b).

16.2 **Information Delays in Financial Markets**

The aggregation of private informations about the fundamental value of an asset is an important theme in finance. In the standard framework, the uncertainty is about the future real payoffs that are generated by the underlying physical capital. Can there be multiple equilibria that generate different amounts of information?

The answer is negative in the standard CARA–Gauss model where the state is the value of an asset, because the multiplier from the private information of an agent to his demand is independent of the precision of the public information (Section 15.1.1).[16] The answer may, however, be positive in the CARA–Gauss model when the state is defined by the mass of agents. There may be one equilibrium with a low price because agents are unsure about their total mass (which is positively related to the price in the future), and another where the demand of each agent is large and the variance about the future demand and hence the future price is low; a large mass of agents who "come out of the woods" in the present provides a strong signal about the demand in the future.

In this section, the value of an asset depends on the quantity of funds available for its purchase. The uncertainty about the value of the asset is driven by the uncertainty about the demand for it in the future. In order to sharpen the analysis, agents have no private information of any kind.

As in Chapter 6 on delays, the information is generated by the market when agents reveal their existence by taking an action. The uncertainty may be self-fulfilling: the uncertainty on the quantity of available funds reduces the demand for the asset and thus the information content of the equilibrium price, leaving the uncertainty significant. Are there two equilibria, one with low demand and low information, and the other with high demand and low uncertainty? The present model provides a positive answer.

16.2.1 **The Model**

There are two periods and an asset with an uncertain return after the second period. There are two types of traders: rational agents – *agents* for short – and noise traders. Agents are identical and have a demand for the asset in periods 1 and 2 that is driven by a utility function with CARA normalized to one. An agent is negligible with respect to the set of agents, which forms a continuum of mass θ. The value of θ defines the state of nature. It is realized before the first period and fixed for the two periods. It is drawn from a normal distribution[17] $\mathcal{N}(m_\theta, \sigma_\theta^2)$ and is not observable.

---

[16] Multiple equilibria appear in models of financial markets when agents pay a fixed cost of entry and the variance of the asset decreases with increasing number of agents (Pagano, 1989a, 1989b), and in non-Gaussian models (Barlevi and Veronesi, 2000).

[17] The agents' belief about θ incorporates the information of an agent that comes from his very existence. (See the example of identical beliefs in Section 2.3.2.)

THE MARKET IN PERIOD 2

The value of the asset in period 2, p_2, is an increasing function of the mass of agents θ (which is the same as in the first period). For simplicity, we assume[18] a linear relation

$$(16.13) \quad p_2 = a + b\theta + \epsilon,$$

where ϵ is a normal random variable $\mathcal{N}(0, \sigma_\epsilon^2)$, and where σ_ϵ^2 and the parameters a and b are publicly known.

THE MARKET IN PERIOD 1

The supply of the asset is endogenous in period 1 and assumed to be of the form[19] $\beta(p_1 - \bar{p})$, where p_1 is the price in the first period and $\bar{p}$ a parameter. The demand by an agent in period 1 is

$$(16.14) \quad x = \frac{E[p_2|p_1] - p_1}{\text{Var}(p_2|p_1)},$$

and the equation of the market equilibrium in period 1 is

$$(16.15) \quad \theta x + \eta = \beta(p_1 - \bar{p}),$$

where η is the demand of the noise traders, which is distributed $\mathcal{N}(0, \sigma_\eta^2)$.

16.2.2 Equilibria

Because all agents have the same demand, the value of x in the first period is commonly known. Using equation (16.13) for the price p_2 in the second period, we have $E[p_2] = a + bE[\theta]$ and $\text{Var}(p_2) = b^2 \text{Var}(\theta)$. Rational agents use their observation of the equilibrium price p and their knowledge of the equilibrium equation (16.15) to update their probability distribution on θ. In the equilibrium equation (16.15), agents know the right-hand side. The observation of the equilibrium price p_1 is therefore equivalent to the observation of the "order flow" $Y = x\theta + \eta$, which is a noisy signal on θ, which is itself informationally equivalent to the variable

$$(16.16) \quad Z = \frac{Y}{x} = \theta + \frac{\eta}{x}.$$

The signal-to-noise ratio depends on the individual demand x. If x is small, the noise η dwarfs the endogenous component $x\theta$ in the demand Y – or the variance of η/x is large in Z – and the signal-to-noise ratio is small. A higher demand x by all agents reduces the variance of θ and therefore has a positive effect on the demand of any

[18] Equation (16.13) can be viewed as the linearization of an equilibrium equation of a CARA–Gauss market: $\theta(\bar{\xi} - p_2)/\sigma_\xi^2 + \eta' = K$, where the payoff ξ per unit of the asset after period 2 is $\mathcal{N}(\bar{\xi}, \sigma_\xi^2)$, and η' is a random exogenous demand.

[19] This function can be justified by Tobin's q-theory with a quadratic adjustment term.

single agent. This property of strategic complementarity will be critical for multiple equilibria.

Following the observation of the price p_1 or equivalently of Z in (16.16), the distribution of θ is updated from $N(m_\theta, 1/\rho_\theta)$ to $N(\tilde{\mu}_\theta, 1/\tilde{\rho}_\theta)$ with

$$(16.17) \quad \tilde{\rho}_\theta = \text{Var}(\theta \mid p_1) = \rho_\theta + \rho_\eta x^2,$$

and

$$\tilde{\mu}_\theta = E[\theta \mid p_1] = \gamma \cdot \frac{Y}{x} + (1 - \gamma) m_\theta, \qquad \gamma = \frac{\rho_\eta x^2}{\rho_\theta + \rho_\eta x^2}.$$

Replacing Y/x with the expression in (16.16), we obtain

$$E[\theta \mid p] = \gamma(\theta - m_\theta) + m_\theta + \frac{\gamma}{x}\eta.$$

Using equation (16.13) for the price p_2 in period 2, we have

$$E[p_2 \mid p_1] = a + b E[\theta \mid p_1],$$

$$\text{Var}(p_2 \mid p_1) = \sigma_\epsilon^2 + \frac{b^2}{\tilde{\rho}_\theta} = \sigma_\epsilon^2 + \frac{b^2}{\rho_\theta + \rho_\eta x^2}.$$

Substituting in the demand function in (16.14), we obtain

$$x = \frac{\rho_\theta + \rho_\eta x^2}{\sigma_\epsilon^2 (\rho_\theta + \rho_\eta x^2) + b^2}$$

$$\times \left(a + b \left(\frac{\rho_\eta x^2}{\rho_\theta + \rho_\eta x^2}(\theta - m_\theta) + m_\theta + \frac{\rho_\eta x}{\rho_\theta + \rho_\eta x^2}\eta \right) - p_1 \right).$$

Because in the equilibrium equation (16.15) we have $\theta x + \eta = \beta(p_1 - \bar{p})$, by substitution of p_1 in the previous equation, the equilibrium is characterized by the solution in x of the equation

$$(16.18) \quad x = \frac{\rho_\theta + \rho_\eta x^2}{\sigma_\epsilon^2 (\rho_\theta + \rho_\eta x^2) + b^2}$$

$$\times \left(A + b \left(\frac{\rho_\eta x^2}{\rho_\theta + \rho_\eta x^2}(\theta - m_\theta) + \frac{\rho_\eta x}{\rho_\theta + \rho_\eta x^2}\eta \right) - \frac{\theta}{\beta}x - \frac{\eta}{\beta} \right),$$

with $A = a + b m_\theta - \bar{p}$.

For each realization of the random variables (θ, η), an equilibrium is determined by the solution in x of equation (16.18). The price p_1 is then determined by the equilibrium equation

$$p_1 = \bar{p} + \frac{x\theta + \eta}{\beta}.$$

We consider the particular realization of the random variables (θ, η) that is equal to

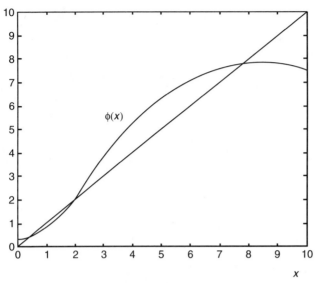

Figure 16.2 Multiple equilibria in the financial market. Parameters: $A = 2$, $\rho_\theta = 5$, $\rho_\eta = 10$, $b = 6$, $\rho_\epsilon = 10$, $\beta = 10$, $m = 1$.

the means $(m_\theta, 0)$. Equation (16.18) becomes

$$(16.19) \quad x = \phi(x) = \frac{\rho_\theta + \rho_\eta x^2}{\sigma_\epsilon^2(\rho_\theta + \rho_\eta x^2) + b^2}\left(A - \frac{m_\theta}{\beta}x\right).$$

The solutions of this equation are roots of a polynomial of degree 3. An example of the graph of $\phi(x)$ is presented in Figure 16.2.

The shape of the graph of ϕ can be understood intuitively in the important case where the supply of the asset is highly elastic and the precision ρ_θ of the information about the mass of agents is low. If β is very large, on any finite interval for x the function $\phi(x)$ is approximated by

$$\psi(x) = \frac{\rho_\theta + \rho_\eta x^2}{\dfrac{\rho_\theta + \rho_\eta x^2}{\rho_\epsilon} + b^2} A.$$

This function is strictly positive at $x = 0$. If ρ_θ is small, ψ is itself approximated by

$$\tilde{\psi}(x) = \frac{\rho_\eta x^2}{\dfrac{\rho_\eta}{\rho_\epsilon} x^2 + b^2} A,$$

which is convex near $x = 0$ and tends to a limit A/σ_ϵ^2 from below when $x \to \infty$. It therefore has an inflection point. One can show the next result as an exercise.

PROPOSITION 16.1 *If the elasticity of supply of capital (β) is sufficiently large and the precision ρ_θ on the mass θ of rational agents is sufficiently small, there are values of the other parameters of the model such that for a set of realizations of (θ, η) that includes an*

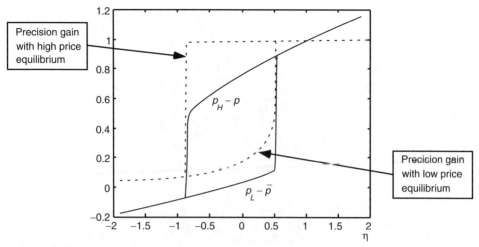

Figure 16.3 Equilibrium prices. The parameters are the same as in Figure 16.2. p_H and p_L are different equilibrium prices when the exogenous demand η is between -0.5 and 0.5. The precision gain is $1 - \rho_\theta/\tilde{\rho}_\theta$, where $\tilde{\rho}_\theta$ is the precision after the observation of the equilibrium price in the first period.

open neighborhood of the mean $(m_\theta, 0)$, there are three equilibrium levels of the demand. The low and the high values are stable.

The equilibrium prices are represented as function of the noise demand η in Figure 16.3 for the realization $\theta = m_\theta$. For a large and significant interval of values of η there are two equilibrium prices. When η is negative and low, the high price disappears and the low price is the only equilibrium price. When the shock is positive and large, the low price disappears.

MULTIPLE EQUILIBRIA AND INFORMATION

The information conveyed by the market is measured by the increment of the precision about θ following the market observation. It is obtained from (16.17) and is equal to

$$\tilde{\rho}_\theta - \rho_\theta = \rho_\eta x^2.$$

When there are two equilibria, the equilibrium with the high price (and a higher level of demand x) generates a higher level of information: the increment in precision can be very different in the two equilibria. The reduction of the variance of θ as a proportion of the initial variance $1/\rho_\theta$ is represented in Figure 16.3. One verifies that in the equilibrium with a high price (and high demand), the price reveals the value of θ with near perfection. The equilibrium with a low price does not convey much information.

Equilibrium prices are represented in Figure 16.4 for other realizations of the mass of rational agents θ and of the noise η. When both θ and η are positive and sufficiently large, the high price is the only equilibrium price. When θ and η are negative, the equilibrium has a unique price, which is low.

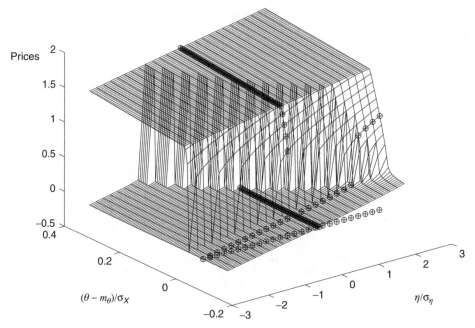

Figure 16.4 Equilibrium prices as functions of the mass of agents θ and the noise demand η. Parameters: $\rho_\eta = 10, \sigma_\theta = 0.3, \rho_\epsilon = 11.1, A = 3, \beta = 10, b = 10$.

The figure highlights the values of the prices for θ and η equal to their means m_θ and 0. A constant level of prices for $\theta = m_\theta$ is also highlighted as a reference: one can verify that the low price is an increasing function of the shock η.

16.3 The Crash of a Bubble

A bubble occurs when an asset that yields no real dividend has a positive price. The equilibrium price is positive because agents expect it to appreciate, on average. Under reasonable conditions, however, the price is subject to an upper bound. When the price reaches the upper bound (an event that must occur in finite time), no further appreciation is possible and the high price is not sustainable in an equilibrium. It is therefore not sustainable in the previous period, and, by backward induction, in any period, including the first one. This argument, stated informally, is the main one against the existence of bubbles with rational agents.

An examination of famous bubbles in the past shows that they always originated with some genuine good news. The spectacular rise of the price of John Law's company in 1719 was supported by some real events: he gained control of all tax collections, all foreign trade, and the central bank. The critical issue is the transition from a fundamental rise of the price to a bubble. During the recent boom of new technology stocks, no one questioned the emergence of new opportunities. The concern was about the magnitude of these opportunities. For some, the Dow should have risen to 30,000; for others, the market was already much above the value of the fundamentals.

In other terms, a critical issue is the lack of common knowledge about the onset of a price rise that is not due to fundamentals.

The lack of common knowledge about the timing of the beginning of a bubble is the central problem in the paper by Abreu and Brunnermeier (2003). Removing the common knowledge and introducing some simplifying assumptions, they show how a bubble may occur although all agents know that a crash will eventually take place. Their model is also a contribution to the analysis of social interactions when there is no common knowledge about the "first period."

THE MODEL

An asset has a fundamental price, which grows at the rate g in a first interval of time $[0, \theta]$; after time θ, the price grows at the rate of the market $r < g$. The first phase can be justified by the gradual arrival of good news about the future profits generated by the asset.[20] The realization of θ is random and is distributed according to a Poisson process with parameter λ per unit of time. Agents do not observe θ perfectly. After time θ the price continues to rise at the pre-θ rate g, which is higher than the fundamental rate r, unless a crash occurs, as will be defined below. If a crash takes place at time t, the price drops, by assumption, to the fundamental price at time t. Let $p(t)$ be the *bubble price* at time $t > \theta$: $p(t) = p(\theta)e^{g(t-\theta)}$. Because the fundamental price at time t is $p(\theta)e^{r(t-\theta)}$ when a crash takes place, the price loses a fraction $\beta(t-\theta)$ of its value with

$$\beta(t - \theta) = 1 - e^{-(g-r)(t-\theta)}.$$

There is no microeconomic foundation of the market that determines the price of the asset. The price depends on the actions of agents as follows. The asset is held at the beginning of time by a continuum of agents of mass one. Each agent holds a fixed amount of the asset, which can be normalized to one (as in the model of speculative attacks, Section 16.1). An agent can trade between the asset and the market (which earns the rate r) at any time. The present discussion is simplified, with no loss of substance, by assuming that the strategy of the agent is about the timing of the sale of his holding.

An essential purpose of the model is to represent the gradual acquisition of private information and the absence of common knowledge. At the time θ when the phase of above-market growth stops, a constant flow of information begins: the mass of informed agents at time $t > \theta$ is $(t - \theta)/\sigma$. When an agent becomes informed at time t, he learns that the market price is above the fundamental, i.e., $\theta < t$. For simplicity, the flow of newly informed agents is taken as constant at the rate of $1/\sigma$ per unit of time, until all the agents are informed, at time $\theta + \sigma$. This generating

---

[20] This phase corresponds to the rise due to fundamentals (e.g., the beginning of John Law's company). A growth rate g higher than r can be justified only by a sequence of good surprises if agents have rational expectations. One surprise would generate only one jump of the price.

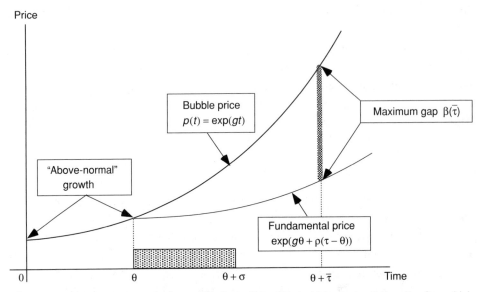

Figure 16.5 The evolution of price and information. The bubble starts at time θ, after which the fundamental price grows only at the rate r, smaller than the bubble rate g. The bubble price cannot be higher than an exogenous multiple of the fundamental price. For an interval of length σ, agents become informed in a constant flow. At time $\theta + \sigma$ all agents are informed that the bubble is taking place. The bubble may go on after time $\theta + \sigma$ because of the lack of common knowledge.

process implies that the reception of the "informed" signal at time t is equivalent to the information that $\theta \in [t - \sigma, t]$, a piece of information that leaves a significant uncertainty about the information of others.

The crash occurs when the first of the following two conditions is met:

(i) the fractional gap between the bubble price and the fundamental price, $\beta(t - \theta)$, reaches a maximum value $\bar{\beta}$, a fixed parameter;
(ii) the mass of agents who have sold the asset reaches the critical mass κ, which is a fixed parameter.

In case (i), the crash is exogenous. Because the gap $\beta(t - \theta)$ is an increasing function, there is a value of time, $\bar{\tau}$, such that $\beta(\bar{\tau}) = \bar{\beta}$. The bubble can last at most $\bar{\tau}$ units of time: a crash occurs exogenously at time $\theta + \bar{\tau}$ if the mass of agents who have sold at that time is smaller than κ. The structure of the model is illustrated in Figure 16.5.

THE TRADING STRATEGY IN EQUILIBRIUM
We consider only symmetric PBEs. Without loss of generality, we assume that, in an equilibrium, the strategy of an agent who is newly informed at time t_i is to hold until time $t_i + \tau^1$ and to sell at time $t_i + \tau^1$. Given the flow of newly informed

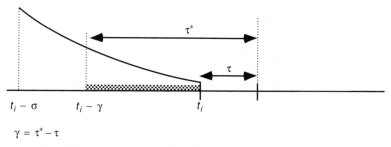

$$\gamma = \tau^* - \tau$$

Figure 16.6 The sequence of critical instants.

agents, the mass of sales at time $\theta + \tau$ is $\max((\tau - \tau^1)/\sigma, 0)$. There are two possible cases:

(i) if $(\overline{\tau} - \tau^1)/\sigma < \overline{X}$, then the amount of sales is smaller than the critical value at the maximum duration of the bubble: an exogenous crash takes place;

(ii) if the previous inequality is not satisfied (with the strategy τ^1 endogenously determined), then a crash takes place endogenously at time $\theta + \tau^*$, where the length of time τ^* satisfies $(\tau^* - \tau^1)/\sigma = \kappa$.

The agent holds the asset as long as the probability of a crash is sufficiently small compared with the capital gain if no crash takes place. The main inference problem is to determine the probability of a crash at the time $t_i + \tau$. The crash occurs at time $t_i + \tau$ if $\theta = t_i - (\tau^* - \tau)$, where the duration of the bubble, τ^*, is exogenous or endogenous (Figure 16.6). Before time $t_i + \tau$, the distribution of θ for the agent is the exponential distribution truncated to the interval $[t_i - (\tau^* - \tau), t_i]$. The instantaneous probability of θ around $t_i - (\tau^* - \tau)$ is given by the next lemma.

LEMMA 16.2 *Consider an agent who is informed at t_i that the bubble started in the interval $[t_i - \gamma, t_i]$. His instantaneous probability that $\theta = t_i - \gamma$ is $\pi(t_i - \gamma) = \lambda/(1 - e^{-\lambda\gamma})$.*

The proof uses the exponential density of θ, $e^{-\lambda t}$, truncated on the interval $[t_i - \gamma, t_i]$. Figure 16.6 may help to visualize the various dates that have to be tracked. The instantaneous probability is an increasing function of τ: the probability of the crash, conditional on no crash before, increases with time.

Arbitrage

An agent holds on to the asset for a while after being informed of the bubble, because he estimates rationally that few agents have become informed yet, or that the gap of the bubble price has not widened significantly. An agent sells the asset at time $t_i + \tau$ when the instantaneous return from the market, $rp(t_i + \tau)$, becomes identical to the instantaneous return of holding the asset, that is $gp(t_i + \tau) - \pi(\tau^* - \tau)\beta(\tau^*)p(t_i + \tau)$, where τ^* is the delay between θ and the time of the crash.

The differential yield between holding and selling is

$$(16.20) \quad U(\tau; t_i) = \left(g - r - \pi(\tau^* - \tau)\beta(\tau^*)\right)p(t_i + \tau),$$

which is a decreasing function of τ. The optimal strategy τ^1 is defined by the arbitrage equation $U(\tau^1; t_i) = 0$. By use of Lemma 16.2, τ^1 is solution of

$$(16.21) \quad g - r = \frac{\lambda}{1 - e^{-\lambda(\tau^* - \tau^1)}}\beta(\tau^*).$$

THE EXOGENOUS CRASH

The case of an exogenous crash is sufficient to highlight the main properties of the model. An exogenous crash takes place if the mass of agents who have sold at time $\theta + \overline{\tau}$, where $\overline{\tau}$ is determined by the maximum price gap, is smaller than κ. Given the strategy τ^1 of the agents, this condition is equivalent to

$$(16.22) \quad \frac{\overline{\tau} - \tau^1}{\sigma} < \kappa.$$

The value of τ_1 is determined by (16.21) where τ^* is replaced by $\overline{\tau}$. An exogenous crash takes place if that value of τ^1 is greater than $\overline{\tau} - \sigma\kappa$. The solution τ^1 is a decreasing function of the parameter λ: if λ is smaller, the probability of the onset of the bubble is smaller. An informed agent knows that the bubble takes place, but the lower value λ raises the probability that θ occurred recently (see Figure 16.6) and that a crash occurs later: the agent holds the asset for a longer time. The condition for an exogenous crash can thus be replaced by the condition $\lambda < \overline{\lambda}$ with $\overline{\lambda}$ the solution of

$$(16.23) \quad g - r = \frac{\overline{\lambda}}{1 - e^{-\overline{\lambda}\kappa\sigma}}\beta(\overline{\tau}).$$

THE ENDOGENOUS CRASH

The characterization of an endogenous crash is adapted from that of the exogenous crash by replacing the exogenous length $\overline{\tau}$ with the endogenous time τ^*. The inequality in (16.22) is replaced by an equality (the mass of sales at the time of the crash is exactly κ):

$$(16.24) \quad \begin{aligned} \tau^* - \tau^1 &= \sigma\kappa, \\ g - r &= \frac{\lambda}{1 - e^{-\lambda(\tau^* - \tau^1)}}\beta(\tau^*). \end{aligned}$$

The necessary and sufficient condition for the existence[21] of such a crash is that $\tau^1 < \overline{\tau}$. We have seen that this condition is equivalent to $\overline{\lambda} < \lambda$, where $\overline{\lambda}$ is defined in (16.23).

[21] The equilibrium solution is nontrivial only if newly informed agents hold the asset for a positive length of time, which is the case if $\lambda < \lambda^*$ for some value $\lambda^* > \overline{\lambda}$.

DISCUSSION

Let us consider the exogenous crash, which contains the main features of the model. The bubble ends with a crash, and the price returns to the fundamental, with probability 1. The model seems to solve the problem of backward induction when a crash must take place. However, a careful examination shows that this is not the case.

The standard argument against bubbles with rational agents is that the ratio between the bubble price and a variable that grows with the economy must be subject to an upper bound. Suppose that the economy is growing at the rate $n < r$ (on an efficient path), and that there is an arbitrarily large value A such that $p_0 e^{gt} < A e^{nt}$. Such a property contradicts the assumptions of the model of Abreu and Brunnermeier: the inequality implies that a crash must occur no later than T such that $p_0 e^{gT} = A e^{nT}$, and this property is *common knowledge*. An essential feature in the model is that the growth rate of the bubble price is strictly[22] higher than $r + \alpha$, where $\alpha > 0$.

The answer to the bubble problem by Abreu and Brunnermeier is not different, essentially, from that by Blanchard (1979). In the model of Blanchard, the bubble returns to the fundamental through a crash, which occurs in a Poisson process. The end of the bubble occurs with probability 1. As long as the bubble goes on, the growth rate is above the rate of return of the market. The argument requires that no upper bound exist on the bubble price. In the model of Blanchard, the growth rate of the bubble price must be higher than the market rate to compensate for the probability of the crash, as all agents are informed. In the model of Abreu and Brunnermeier, the growth rate of the bubble price does not need to be as high, because only a fraction of the agents are informed.

---

[22] If one admits that g decreases over time and $g \to r$, the holding length of time tends to 0. If agents sell as soon as they are informed, the equilibrium is trivial: agents hold the asset only while they are not informed.

References

Abreu, D. and M. K. Brunnermeier (2003). "Bubbles and Crashes," *Econometrica*, **71**, 173–204.

Admati, A. (1985). "A Noisy Rational Expectations Equilibrium for Multi-asset Securities Market," *Econometrica*, **53**, 629–657.

Admati, A. and M. Perry (1991). "Joint Projects without Commitment," *Review of Economic Studies*, **58**, 159–276.

Aghion, P., P. Bolton, C. Harris, and B. Julien (1991). "Optimal Learning by Experimentation," *Review of Economic Studies*, **58**, 621–654.

Akerlof, G. (1970). "The Market for 'Lemons': Quality Uncertainty and the Market Mechanism," *Quarterly Journal of Economics*, **84**, 488–500.

——— (1980). "A Theory of Social Custom, of Which Unemployment May Be One Consequence," *Quarterly Journal of Economics*, **94**, 749–775.

Allen, B. (1982a). "Some Stochastic Processes of Interdependent Demand and Technological Diffusion of an Innovation Exhibiting Externalities Among Adopters," *International Economic Review*, **23**, 595–607.

——— (1982b). "A Stochastic Interactive Model for the Diffusion of Information," *Journal of Mathematical Sociology*, **8**, 265–281.

Anderson, L. (2001). "Payoff Effects in Information Cascade Experiments," *Economic Inquiry*, **39**, 609–615.

Anderson, L. R. and C. A. Holt (1996). "Classroom Games: Informational Cascades," *Journal of Economic Perspectives*, **10**, 187–193.

——— (1997). "Information Cascades in the Laboratory," *American Economic Review*, **87**, 847–862.

Aoyagi, M. (1998). "Equilibrium Delay in a Simple Dynamic Model of Investment," *Economic Theory*, **12**, 123–146.

Arthur, B., Y. M. Ermoliev, and Y. M. Kaniovski (1983). "A Generalized Urn Problem and Its Applications," *Kibernetika* (Transl. in *Cybernetics*), **19**, 61–71.

——— (1986). "Strong Laws for a Class of Path-Dependent Stochastic Processes with Applications," in *Stochastic Optimization: Proceedings of the International Conference, Kiev, 1984*, I. Arkin, A. Shiraev, and R. Wets, eds. New York : Springer-Verlag.

Arthur, B. and D. Lane (1994). "Information Contagion," in *Increasing Returns and Path Dependence in the Economy*, B. Arthur, ed. Michigan University Press, 69–97.

Aumann, R. (1976). "Agreeing to Disagree," *The Annals of Statistics*, **4**, 1236–1239.

Avery, C. and P. Zemsky (1995). "Multi-dimensional Uncertainty and Herd Behavior in Financial Markets," *American Economic Review*, **88**, 724–748.

Bala, V. and S. Goyal (1994). "The Birth of a New Market," *Economic Journal*, **104**, 282–290.

——— (1995). "A Theory of Learning with Heterogeneous Agents," *International Economic Review*, **36**, 303–323.

——— (1998). "Learning from Neighbours," *Review of Economic Studies*, **65**, 595–621.

——— (2000a). "A Noncooperative Model of Network Formation," *Econometrica*, **68**, 1181–1231.

——— (2000b). "Social Learning and Network Formations," mimeo. Eramus University, Rotterdam.

——— (2001). "Conformism and Diversity under Social Learning," *Economic Theory*, **17**, 101–120.

Banerjee, A. (1992). "A Simple Model of Herd Behavior," *Quarterly Journal of Economics*, **107**, 797–817.

Banerjee, A. and D. Fudenberg (1995). "Word-of-Mouth Learning," mimeo, MIT; in *Games and Economic Behavior*, forthcoming.

Bar-Ilan, A. and A. Blinder (1992). "Consumer Durables: Evidence on the Optimality of Doing Nothing," *Journal of Money Credit and Banking*, **24**, 253–272.

Barlevi, G. and P. Veronesi (2000). "Information Acquisition in Financial Markets," *Review of Economic Studies*, **67**, 79–90.

Batchelor, R. and D. Pami (1992). "Conservatism and Consensus-Seeking among Economic Forecasters," *Journal of Forecasting*, **11**, 169–181.

Battacharya, G. and G. Simons (1996). "Informational Cascades in Informal Markets," *Journal of Economics*, Missouri Valley Economic Association, **22**, 47–55.

Becker, G. (1991). "A Note on Restaurant Pricing and Other Social Influences on Prices," *Journal of Political Economy*, **99**, 1109–1116.

Benabou, R. and G. Laroque (1992). "Using Privileged Information to Manipulate Markets: Insiders, Gurus and Credibility," *Quarterly Journal of Economics*, **107**, 921–958.

Benassy, J.-P. (1982). *The Economics of Market Disequilibrium*, New York: Academic Press.

Bernheim, D. (1984). "Rationalizable Strategic Behavior," *Econometrica*, **52**, 1007–1028.

Berry, D. A. (1972). "A Bernoulli Two Armed Bandit," *Annals of Mathematical Statistics*, **43**, 871–897.

Berry, D. A. and B. Fristedt (1985). *Bandit Problems: Sequential Allocation of Experiments*, London: Chapman and Hall.

Besley, T. and A. Case (1993). "Modeling Technology Adoption in Developing Countries," *The American Economic Review, Proceedings*, **83**, 397–402.

———— (1994). "Diffusion as a Learning Process: Evidence from HYV Cotton," manuscript, Princeton, NJ: Princeton University, Department of Economics.

Bikhchandani, S., D. Hirshleifer, and I. Welch (1992). "A Theory of Fads, Fashion, Custom and Cultural Change as Informational Cascades," *Journal of Political Economy*, **100**, 992–1026.

———— (1998). "Learning from the Behavior of Others: Conformity, Fads, and Informational Cascades," *Journal of Economic Perspectives*, **12**, 151–170.

Binmore, K. (1987). "Modeling Rational Players: Part 1," *Economics and Philosophy*, **3**, 179–214.

Black, F. (1988). "An Equilibrium Model of the Crash," in *NBER Macroeconomics Annual 1988*. Cambridge, MA: MIT Press, 269–275.

Blackwell, D. (1951). "Comparision of Experiments," in *Proceedings, Second Berkeley Symposium on Mathematical Statistics and Probability*. Berkeley: University of California Press, 93–102.

Blanchard, O. (1979). "Speculative Bubbles, Crashes and Rational Expectations," *Economic Letters*, **3**, 387–389.

Blanchard, O. and N. Kiyotaki (1987). "Monopolistic Competition and the Effects of Aggregate Demand," *American Economic Review*, **77**, 647–666.

Blanchard, O. and M. Watson (1982). "Bubbles, Rational Expectations and Financial Markets," in *Crises in the Economic and Financial Structure*, P. Wachtel, ed. Lexington Books, 295–316.

Blau, P. (1954). "Patterns of Interaction among a Group of Officials in a Government Agency," *Human Relations*, **7**, 337–348.

Bliss, C. and B. Nalebuff (1984). "Dragon Slaying and Ballroom Dancing: The Private Supply of a Public Good," *Journal of Public Economics*, **25**, 1–12.

Blume, L., D. Easley, and M. O'Hara (1994). "Market Statistics and Technical Analysis: The Role of Volume," *Journal of Finance*, **49**, 159–181.

Brandenburger, A. and B. Polak (1996). "When Managers Cover Their Posteriors: Making the Decisions the Market Wants to See," *RAND Journal of Economics*, **27**, 523–541.

Brunnermeier, M. (2001). *Asset Pricing under Asymmetric Information – Bubbles, Crashes, Technical Analysis and Herding*, Oxford University Press.

Bryant, John (1987). "The Paradox of Thrift, Liquidity Preference and Animal Spirits," *Econometrica*, **61**, 1231–1235.

Buiter, W., G. Corsetti, P., and A. Pesenti, eds. (1998). *Financial Markets and European Monetary Cooperation: The Lessons of the 1992–1993 Exchange Rate Mechanism Crisis*, New York: Cambridge University Press.

Bulow, J. and P. Klemperer (1994). "Rational Frenzies and Crashes," *Journal of Political Economy*, **102**, 1–23.

——— (1999). "The Generalized War of Attrition," *American Economic Review*, **89**, 175–189.

Burguet, R. and X. Vives (2000). "Social Learning and Costly Information Acquisition," *Economic Theory*, **15**, 185–205 (first version, 1995).

Burke, E. (1790). "Reflections on the Revolution in France." In *The Works of the Right Honourable Edmund Burke, vol. 2*, London: Henry G. Bohn, 1864, pp. 515–516.

Burnum, J. F. (1987). "Medical Practice à la Mode: How Medical Fashions Determine Medical Care," *New England Journal of Medicine*, **317**, 1220–1222.

Business Week (1995). "Did Dirty Tricks Create a Best-Seller?" August 7, 22–24.

Business Week (1996). "A Star is Reborn," July 8, 102–106.

Cao, H. H. and D. Hirshleifer (2000). "Conversation, Observational Learning, and Informational Cascades," mimeo, Ohio State University.

Caplin, A. and J. Leahy (1993). "Sectoral Shocks, Learning and Aggregate Fluctuations," *Review of Economic Studies*, **60**, 777–794.

——— (1994). "Business as Usual, Market Crashes and Wisdom after the Fact," *American Economic Review*, **84**, 547–564.

——— (1998). "Miracle on Sixth Avenue: Information Externalities and Search," *Economic Journal*, **108**, 60–74.

Carlsson, H. (1989). "Global Games and the Risk Dominance Criterion," mimeo, University of Lund.

Carlsson, H. and M. Ganslandt (1998). "Noisy Equilibrium Selection in Coordination Games," *Economic Letters*, **60**, 23–34.

Carlsson, H. and E. van Damme (1993a). "Global Payoff Uncertainty and Risk Dominance," *Econometrica*, **61**, 989–1018.

——— (1993b). "Equilibrium Selection in Stag Hunt Games," in *Frontiers of Game Theory*, Binmore K., A. Kirman, and A. Tani, eds. Cambridge, MA: MIT University Press.

Çelen, B. and S. Kariv (2002a). "Observational Learning under Imperfect Information," mimeo, New York University.

——— (2002b). "Distinguishing Informational Cascades from Herd Behavior in the Laboratory," mimeo, New York University.

——— (2002c). "An Observational Test of Learning under Imperfect Information," mimeo, New York University.

Chamley, C. (1999). "Coordinating Regime Switches," *Quarterly Journal of Economics*, **114**, 869–905.

——— (2003a). "Delays and Equilibria with Large and Small Information in Social Learning," *European Economic Review*, forthcoming.

——— (2003b). "Dynamic Speculative Attacks," *American Economic Review*, forthcoming.

——— (2003c). "Cascades and Slow Social Learning," mimeo, Boston University.

——— (2003d). "Learning the Demand and Multiple Equilibria in Financial Markets," mimeo, Boston University.

Chamley, C. and D. Gale (1994). "Information Revelation and Strategic Delay in a Model of Investment," *Econometrica*, **62**, 1065–1085.

Chari, V. V. and P. Kehoe (1998). "Hot Money," mimeo, Federal Reserve Bank of Minneapolis (revised 2001).

——— (2000). "Financial Crises as Herds," mimeo, Federal Reserve Bank of Minneapolis, University of Minnesota.

Chari, V. V. and P. J. Kehoe (2003). "Hot money," *Staff Report 228*, Minneapolis, MN: Federal Reserve Bank of Minneapolis.

Chassin, M. R., R. H. Brook, R. E. Park, J. Keesey, A. Flink, J. Kosecoff, K. Kahn, N. Merrick, and D. H. Solomon (1986). "Variations in Use of Medical and Surgical Services by the Medicare Population," *New England Journal of Medicine*, **314**, 285–290.

Cherkaou M. (1992). "Mobilité," in *Traité de Sociologie*, R. Boudon, ed., Paris: Presses Universitaires de France.

Choi, J. P. (1997). "Herd Behavior, the 'Penguin Effect', and the Suppression of Informational Diffusion: An Analysis of Informational Externalities and Payoff Interdependency," *Rand Journal of Economic*, **28**, 407–425.

Chwe, M. S. Y. (2001). *Rational Ritual: Culture, Coordination, and Common Knowledge*, Princeton, NJ: Princeton University Press.

Clark, T. N., ed. (1969). *Gabriel Tarde: On Communication and Social Influence*, Chicago: University of Chicago Press.

Coleman, J. (1966). *Medical Innovation: A Diffusion Study*, New York: Bobbs-Merrill.

Coleman, J., E. Katz, and H. Menzel (1957). "The Diffusion of an Innovation among Physicians," *Sociometry*, **20**, 253–270.

Condorcet, Jean-Antoine-Nicolas de Caritat, Marquis de (1785). *Essai sur l'application de l'analyse à la probabilité des décisions rendues à la pluralité des voix*, Paris: De l'Imprimerie royale.

Conley, T. and C. Udry (2000a). "Learning about a New Technology: Pineapple in Ghana," mimeo, Yale University.

———— (2000b). "Social Learning through Networks: The Adoption of New Agricultural Technologies in Ghana," mimeo, Yale University; *American Journal of Agricultural Economics*, forthcoming.

Conlisk, J. (1980). "Costly Optimizers versus Cheap Imitators," *Journal of Economic Behavior and Organization*, **1**, 275–293.

Cooper, R. (1994). "Equilibrium Selection in Imperfectly Competitive Economies with Multiple Equilibria," *Economic Journal*, **104**, 1106–1122.

———— (1999). *Coordination Games: Complementarities and Macroeconomics*, New York: Cambridge University Press.

Cooper, R. and A. John (1988)."Coordinating Coordination Failures in Keynesian Models," *Quarterly Journal of Economics*, **103**, 441–463.

Corsetti, G., A. Dasgupta, S. Morris, and H. S. Shin (2000). "Does One Soros Make a Difference? A Theory of Currency Crises with Large and Small Traders," *Review of Economic Studies*, forthcoming.

Crawford, V. and J. Sobel (1982). "Strategic Information Transmission," *Econometrica*, **50**, 1431–1451.

Cremer, J. (1995). "Arm's Length Relationships," *Quarterly Journal of Economics*, **110**, 275–295.

Deckel, E. and M. Piccione (2000). "Sequential Voting Procedures in Symmetric Binary Elections," *Journal of Political Economy*, **108**, 34–55.

Diamond, D. and P. Dybvig (1983). "Bank Runs, Deposit Insurance, and Liquidity," *Journal of Political Economy*, **91**, 401–419.

Diamond, P. (1982). "Aggregate Demand Management in Search Equilibrium," *Journal of Political Economy*, **90**, 881–894.

Diebold, F., G. Rudebusch, and D. Sichel (1993). "Further Evidence on Business Cycle Duration Dependence," in *Business Cycles, Indicators and Forecasting*, J. Stock and M. Watson, eds. Chicago: The University of Chicago Press, 255–280.

Dixit, A. and R. Pindyck (1994). *Investment under Uncertainty*, Princeton, NJ: Princeton University Press.

Dodd, S. C. (1955). "Diffusion is Predictable," *American Sociological Review*, **20**, 349–396.

Drèze, J. (1972). "Econometrics and Decision Theory," *Econometrica*, **40**, 1–18.

Durkheim, E. (1897). *Le Suicide: Etude de Sociologie*, Paris: Alcan. Translation (1951), *Suicide*, by J. A. Spaulding and G. Simpson, New York: The Free Press.

Easley, D. and N. Kiefer (1988). "Controlling a Stochastic Process with Unknown Parameters," *Econometrica*, **56**, 1045–1064.

Eichengreen, B., A. Rose, and C. Wyplosz (1996). "Contagious Currency Crises," NBER Working Paper No. 5681.

Ellison, G. and D. Fudenberg (1995). "Word of Mouth Communication and Social Learning," *Quarterly Journal of Economics*, **109**, 93–125.

Evans, G. (1983). "The Stability of Rational Expectations in Macroeconomic Models," in *Individual Forecasting and Aggregate Outcomes: "Rational Expectations" Examined*, R. Frydman and E. S. Phelps, eds. New York: Cambridge University Press, 69–94. (Mimeo in 1981.)

Farrel, J. and G. Saloner (1985). "Standardization, Compatibility and Innovation," *Rand Journal of Economics*, **16**, 70–83.

Feder, G., R. Just, and D. Silberman (1985). "Adoption of Agricultural Innovations in Developing Countries: A Survey," *Economic Development and Cultural Change*, **33**(2), 255–298.

Festinger, L. (1957). *A Theory of Cognitive Dissonance*, Stanford, CA: Stanford University Press.

Filardo, A. (1994). "Business-Cycle Phases and Their Transitional Dynamics," *Journal of Business & Economic Statistics*, **12**, 299–308.

Forbes, K. (1999). "The Asian Flu and Russian Virus: Firm-Level Evidence on How Crises Are Transmitted Internationally," mimeo, MIT, Sloan School.

Forbes, K. and R. Rogobon (1999). "Measuring Contagion: Conceptual and Empirical Issues," mimeo, MIT.

Foster, A. and M. Rosenzweig (1995). "Learning by Doing and Learning from Others: Human Capital and Technical Change in Agriculture," *Journal of Political Economy*, **103**, 1176–1209.

Foster, D. and S. Viswanathan (1993). "The Effect of Public Information and Competition on Trading Volume and Price Volatility," *Review of Financial Studies*, **6**, 23–56.

Fudenberg, D. and J. Tirole (1991). *Game Theory*, Cambridge, MA: MIT Press.

Freedman, D. A. (1965). "Bernard Fredman's Urn," *Annals of Mathematical Statistics*, **36**, 956–970.

Gale, D. (1995). "Dynamic Coordination Games," *Economic Theory*, **5**, 1–18.

Gale, D. and S. Kariv (2002). "Bayesian Learning in Social Networks," mimeo, New York University.

Gardner, M. (1970). "The Fantastic Combinations of John Conway's New Solitaire Game of Life," *Scientific American*, **223**, 120–123.

Geanakoplos, J. (1992). "Common Knowledge," *Journal of Economic Perspectives*, **6**, 53–82.

——— (1994). "Common Knowledge," in *Handbook of Game Theory, Volume 2*, R. J. Aumann and S. Hart, eds. New York: Elsevier Science B.V.

Genotte, G. and H. Leland (1990). "Market Liquidity, Hedging and Crashes," *American Economic Review*, **80**, 999–1020.

Gersho, A. and D. Mitra (1975). "A Simple Growth Model for the Diffusion of a New Communication Service," *IEEE Transactions on Systems, Man, and Cybernetics*, **SMC-5**, 209–216.

Glazer, J. and A. Rubinstein (1996). "What Motives Should Guide Referees? On the Design of Mechanisms to Elicit Opinions," *Journal of Economic Theory*, **79**, 157–173.

Glosten, L. and P. R. Milgrom (1985). "Bid, Ask and Transaction Prices in a Specialist Market with Heterogeneously Informed Traders," *Journal of Financial Economics*, **17**, 71–100.

Glover, A. (1938). "The Incidence of Tonsillectomy in School Children," *Proceedings of the Royal Society of Medicine*, **31**, 1219–1236.

Gonzalez, F. (1999). "Why Getting into a Recession is Easier Than Getting Out of It," mimeo, University of British Columbia.

Goodwin, R. (1951). "The Non-linear Accelerator and the Persistence of Business Cycles," *Econometrica*, **19**, 1–17.

Goyal, S. (1999). "Networks, Learning and Equilibrium," Inaugural Lecture, Erasmus University.

Goyal, S. and F. Vega-Redondo (1999). "Learning, Network Formation and Coordination," mimeo, Erasmus University.

Gradstein, M. (1992). "Time Dynamics and Incomplete Information in the Private Provision of Public Goods," *Journal of Polical Economy*, **100**, 581–597.

Granger, G. G. (1956). *La Mathématique Sociale du Marquis de Condorcet*, Paris: Presses Universitaires de France.

Granovetter, M. (1973). "Strength of Weak Ties," *American Journal of Sociology*, **78**, 1360–1380.

Griliches, Z. (1957). "Hybrid Corn: An Exploration in the Economics of Technical Change," *Econometrica*, **25**, 501–522.

——— (1960). "Hybrid Corn and the Economics of Innovation," *Science*, **25**, 501–522.

Grimmet, G. R. and D. R. Stirzaker (1992). *Probability and Random Process*, New York: Oxford Science.

Grinblatt, M., S. Titman, and R. Wermers (1995). "Momentum Investment Strategies, Portfolio Performance and Herding: A Study of Mutual Fund Behavior," *American Economic Review*, **85**, 1088–1105.

Grossman, S. (1976). "On the Efficiency of Competitive Stock Markets where Agents Have Diverse Information," *Journal of Finance*, **31**, 573–585.

—— (1981). "An Introduction to the Theory of Rational Expectations under Asymmetric Information," *Review of Economic Studies*, **48**, 541–559.

—— (1988a). "An Analysis of the Implications for Stock and Futures Price Volatility of Program Trading and Dynamic Hedging Strategies," *Journal of Business*, **61**, 275–298.

—— (1988b). "Insurance Seen and Unseen: the Impact on Markets," *Journal of Portfolio Management*, **14**, 5–8.

Grossman, S. and J. E. Stiglitz (1980). "On the Impossibility of Informationally Efficient Markets," *American Economic Review*, **70**, 393–408.

Guesnerie, R. (1992). "An Exploration of the Eductive Justifications of the Rational Expectations Hypothesis," *American Economic Review*, **82**, 1254–1278.

—— (2002). "Anchoring Economic Predictions in Common Knowledge," *Econometrica*, **70**, 439–480.

Guesnerie, R. and J.-C. Rochet (1993). "(De)stabilizing Speculation on Futures Markets: An Alternative View Point," *European Economic Review*, **37**, 1043–1063.

Gul, F. and R. Lundholm (1995). "Endogenous Timing and the Clustering of Agents' Decisions," *The Journal of Political Economy*, **103**, 1039–1066.

Hägerstrand, T. (1953). *Innovation, Diffusion as a Spatial Process*, Chicago: University of Chicago Press.

Halberstam, D. (1991). *The Next Century*, New York: Morrow.

Hamilton, J. (1989). "A New Approach to the Economic Analysis of Nonstationary Time Series and the Business Cycle," *Econometrica*, **57**, 357–384.

Hanson, W. and D. Putler (1996). "Hits and Misses: Herd Behavior and Online Product Popularity," *Marketing Letters*, 297–305.

Harris, C. and B. Nalebuff (1982). "Dragon-Slaying and Ballroom Dancing: The Private Supply of a Public Good," *Journal of Public Economics*, **25**, 1–12.

Harsanyi, J. C. (1973). "Games with Randomly Disturbed Payoffs: A New Rationale for Mixed Strategies Equilibrium Points," *International Journal of Game Theory*, **2**, 1–23.

Harsanyi, J. C. and R. Selten (1988). *A General Theory of Equilibrium Selection in Games*, Cambridge, MA: MIT Press.

Hauser, J., G. Urban, and B. Weinberg (1993). "How Consumers Allocate Their Time When Searching for Information," *Journal of Marketing*, **60**, 50–68.

Heidhues, P. and N. Melissas (2003). "Equilibria in a Dynamic Global Game: The Role of Cohort Effects," mimeo, University of Leicester.

Hellwig, M. (1980). "On the Aggregation of Information in Competitive Markets," *Journal of Economic Theory*, **57**, 76–93.

—— (1982). "Rational Expectations Equilibrium with Conditioning on Past Prices: A Mean-Variance Example," *Journal of Economic Theory*, **26**, 279–312.

Hendricks, K. and D. Kovenock (1989). "Asymmetric Information, Information Externalities, and Efficiency: The Case of Oil Exploration," *RAND Journal of Economics*, **20**, 164–182.

Hicks, J. R. (1939). *Value and Capital*, Oxford, England: Clarendon.

Hill, B. M., D. A. Lane, and W. D. Sudderth (1980). "A Strong Law for Some Generalized Urn Processes," *Annals of Probability*, **8**, 214–226.

Hirshleifer D. and I. Welch (2002). "An Economic Approach to the Psychology of Change: Amnesia, Inertia, and Impulsiveness," *Journal of Economics and Management Strategy*, **11**(3), 379–421.

Holmström, B. and J. Ricart i Costa (1986). "Managerial Incentives and Capital Management," *Quarterly Journal of Economics*, **101**, 835–860.

Holt, C. A. and L. R. Anderson (1996). "Classroom Games: Understanding Bayes' Rule," *The Journal of Economic Perspectives*, **10**(2), 179–187.

Huck, S. and J. Oechssler (1998). "Informational Cascades with Continuous Action Spaces," *Economics Letters*, **60**, 163–166.

—— (2000). "Informational Cascades in the Laboratory: Do They Occur for the Right Reasons?," *Journal of Economic Psychology*, **21**, 661–671.

Huynh, H.-L. and R. Rosenthal (2000). "Waiting for the Good Doctor: Information in Queues," mimeo, Boston University.

Jacklin, C., A. Kleidon, and P. Pfleiderer (1992). "Underestimation of Portfolio Insurance and the Crash of October 1987," *Review of Financial Studies*, **5**, 35–63.

Jackson, M. and A. Wolinsky (1996). "A Strategic Model of Social and Economic Networks," *Journal of Economic Theory*, **71**, 44–74.

Jeanne, O. and P. Masson (2000). "Currency Crisis, Sunspots, and Markov-Switching Regimes," *Journal of International Economics*, **50**, 327–350.

Jeitschko, T. and C. Taylor (1999). "Local Discouragement and Global Collapse: A Theory of Information Avalanches," *American Economic Review*, **91**, 208–224.

Jones, S. R. G. (1984). *The Economics of Conformism*. Oxford, England: Blackwell.

Jun, B. and X. Vives (1996). "Learning and Convergence to a Full-Information Equilibrium Are Not Equivalent," *Review of Economic Studies*, **63**, 653–674.

Katz, M. L. and C. Shapiro (1986). "Technology Adoption in the Presence of Network Externalities," *Journal of Political Economy*, **94**, 822–841.

Kennedy, R. (2002). "Strategy Fads and Competitive Convergence: An Empirical Test for Herd Behavior in Prime-Time Television Programming," *The Journal of Industrial Economics*, **50**, 57–84.

Khanna, N. (1998). "Optimal Contracting with Moral Hazard and Cascading," *Review of Financial Studies*, **11**, 557–594.

Kiefer, N. (1989). "A Value Function Arising in the Economics of Information," *Journal of Economic Dynamics and Control*, **13**, 201–223.

Kirman, A. (1993). "Ants, Rationality, and Recruitment," *Quarterly Journal of Economics*, **108**, 137–156.

Kiyotaki, N. (1988). "Multiple Expectational Equilibria under Monopolistic Competition," *Quarterly Journal of Economics*, **103**, 695–713.

Krishna, V. and J. Morgan (1998). "A Model of Expertise," mimeo, Pennsylvania State University and Princeton University.

Krugman, P. (1996). "Are Currency Crises Self-fulfilling," in *NBER Macroeconomics Annual*, Cambridge, MA: MIT Press.

Kuran, T. (1987). "Preference Falsification, Policy Continuity and Collective Conservatism," *Economic Journal*, **97**, 642–665.

——— (1995). *Private Truths, Public Lies: The Social Consequences of Preference Falsification*, Cambridge, MA: Harvard University Press.

Kyle, A. (1985). "Informed Speculation and Imperfect Competition," *Review of Economic Studies*, **56**, 317–356.

——— (1989). "Continuous Auctions and Insider Trading," *Econometrica*, **53**, 1315–1335.

Kyle, S. Albert (1985). "Continuous Auctionis and Insider Trading," *Econometrica*, **53**, 1315–35.

Lee, I. H. (1992). "On the Convergence of Informational Cascades," *Journal of Economic Theory*, **61**, 395–411.

——— (1998). "Market Crashes and Informational Avalanches," *Review of Economic Studies*, **65**, 741–759.

Leibniz, G. W. (1998). Philosophical Text. Richard Francks, R. S. Woolhouse (Ed.) Oxford Philosophical Texts, Oxford, UK: Oxford University Press.

Leland, H. (1988). "Portfolio Insurance and October 19th," *California Management Review*, **30**, 80–89.

Leland, H. and M. Rubinstein (1988). "Comments on the Market Crash: Six Months Later," *Journal of Economic Perspectives*, **2**, 45–50.

Lewis, C. (1969). "Variations in the Incidence of Surgery," *New England Journal of Medicine*, **281**, 880–884.

Lohmann, S. (1994a). "Information Aggregation through Costly Political Action," *American Economic Review*, **84**, 518–530.

——— (1994b). "Dynamics of Informational Cascades: The Monday Demonstrations in Leipzig, East Germany, 1989–1991," *World Politics*, **47**, 42–101.

Luft, H. (1980). "The Relationship between Surgical Volume and Mortality: An Exploration of Causal Factors and Alternative Models," *Medical Care*, **18**, 940–959.

Luft, H., J. Bunker, and A. Enthoven (1980). "Should Operations Be Regionalized? The Empirical Relation between Surgical Volume and Mortality," *New England Journal of Medicine*, **301**, 1364–1369.

Lukes, S. (1972). *Emile Durkheim: His Life and Work*, New York: Harper & Row.

Lumet, S. (1957). *Twelve Angry Men*, film directed by Sidney Lumet, writing credits by Reginald Rose.

Madrigal, V. and J. Scheinkman (1999). "Price Crashes, Information Aggregation and Market-Making," *Journal of Economic Theory*, **75**, 16–63.

Mansfield, E. (1961). "Technical Change and the Rate of Imitation," *Econometrica*, **29**, 741–766.

Manski, C. (1993a). "Identification of Endogenous Social Effects: The Reflection Problem," *Review of Economic Studies*, **60**, 531–542.

——— (1993b). "Adolescent Econometricians: How Do Youths Infer the Returns to Schooling," in *Studies in Supply and Demand in Higher Education*, C. T. Clotfelter and M. Rothschild, eds. Chicago: University of Chicago Press.

Marx, K. (1867). *Das Kapital*.

Matsumura, T. and M. Ueda (1996). "Endogenous Timing in the Switching of Technology with Marshallian Externalities," *Journal of Economics*, **63**, 41–56.

Matsuyama, K. (1991). "Increasing Returns, Industrialization and Indeterminacy of Equilibrium," *Quarterly Journal of Economics*, **106**, 617–650.

McLennan, A. (1984). "Price Dispersion and Incomplete Learning in the Long Run," *Journal of Economic Dynamics and Control*, **7**, 331–347.

Mc Pherson, K., J. E. Wennberg, O. B. Hovind, and P. Clifford (1981). "Regional Variations in the Use of Common Surgical Procedures: Within and Between England and Wales, Canada, and the United States of America," *Social Science in Medicine*, **15A**, 273–288.

——— (1982). "Small-Area Variations in the Use of Common Surgical Procedures: An International Comparison of New England, England and Norway," *New England Journal of Medicine*, **307**, 1310–1314.

Meyer, M. and J. Vickers (1997). "Performance Comparisons and Dynamic Incentives," *The Journal of Political Economy*, **105**, 547–581.

Milgrom, P. (1981). "Good News and Bad News: Representation Theorems and Applications," *Bell Journal of Economics*, **12**, 380–391.

Milgrom, P. and J. Roberts (1990). "Rationalizability, Learning, and Equilibrium in Games with Strategic Complementarities," *Econometrica*, **58**, 1255–1277.

Milgrom, P. and N. Stokey (1982). "Information, Trade and Common Knowledge," *Journal of Economic Theory*, **26**, 17–27 (1982).

Milgrom, P. and R. Weber (1982). "A Theory of Auctions and Competitive Bidding," *Econometrica*, **50**, 1059–1122.

Minehart, D. and S. Scotchmer (1999). "Ex Post Regret and the Decentralized Sharing of Information," *Games and Economic Behavior*, **27**, 114–131.

Morris, S. (1999). "Political Correctness," Cowles Foundation Discussion Papers 1242, Cowles Foundation, Yale University: New Haven, CT: Yale University Press.

——— (1999). "Approximate Common Knowledge Revisited," Papers 987r, Yale Economic Growth Center, Yale University: New Haven, CT: Yale University Press.

——— (2001). "Political Correctness," *Journal of Political Economy*, **109**, 231–265.

Morris, S. and H. S. Shin (1998a). "Unique Equilibrium in a Model of Self-Fulfilling Currency Attacks," *American Economic Review*, **88**, 587–597.

——— (1998b). "A Theory of the Onset of Currency Attacks," in *Asian Financial Crisis: Causes, Contagion and Consequences*, P.-R. Agenor, M. Miller, D. Vines, and A. Weber, eds. Cambridge, England: Cambridge University Press.

——— (2000). "Global Games: Theory and Applications," mimeo, paper presented at the World Congress of the Econometric Society, Seattle.

Moscarini, G., M. Ottaviani, and L. Smith (1998). "Social Learning in a Changing World," *Economic Theory*, **11**, 657–665.

Motulsky, A. G., R. L. Bennett, A. Bittles, L. Hudgins, S. Uhrich, D. Lochner Doyle, K. Silvey, R. Scott, E. Cheng, B. Mc Gillivray, R. Steiner, D. Olson (2002). "Genetic Counseling and Screening Consanguineous Couples and Their Offspring: Recommendations of the National Society of Genetic Counselors," *Journal of Genetic Counseling*, **11**, 97–119.

Munshi, K. (2002). "Social Learning in a Heterogeneous Population: Technological Diffusion in the Indian Green Revolution," mimeo, University of Pennsylvania.

Munshi, K. and J. Myaux (2002). "Development as a Process of Social Change: An Application to the Fertility Transition," mimeo, University of Pennsylvania.

Murphy, K., A. Shleifer, and R. Vishny (1989). "Industrialization and the Big Push," *Journal of Political Economy*, **97**, 1003–1023.

Muth, J. (1961). "Rational Expectations and the Theory of Price Movements," *Econometrica*, **29**, 315–335.

Nasar, S. (1993). "The Economics of Wait and See," *The New York Times*, May 12.

Neeman, Z. and G. Orosel (1999). "Herding and the Winner's Curse in Markets with Sequential Bids," *Journal of Economic Theory*, **85**, 91–121.

Obstfeld, M. (1986). "Rational and Self-Fulfilling Balance-of-Payments Crises," *American Economic Review*, **76**, 72–81.

——— (1996). "Models of Currency Crises with Self-Fulfilling Features," *European Economic Review*, **40**, 1037–1047.

Okuno-Fujiwara, M., A. Postlewaite, and K. Suzumura (1990). "Strategic Information Revelation," *Review of Economic Studies*, **57**, 25–47.

Ottaviani, M. and A. Prat (2001). "The Value of Public Information in Monopoly," UCL Economics Discussion Paper 98-16, 1998; *Econometrica*, forthcoming.

Ottaviani, M. and P. Sørensen (1999). "Professional Advice," mimeo, London Business School.

——— (2000). "Herd Behavior and Investment: Comment," *American Economic Review*, **90**, 695–704.

——— (2001). "Information Aggregation in Debate: Who Should Speak First," *Journal of Public Economics*, **81**, 393–421.

Ottaviani, M. and P. Sorensen (2000). "Herd Behavior and Investment: Comment," *American Economic Review, vol. 90*, **3**, pp. 695–704.

Ozkan, G. and A. Sutherland (1995). "Policy Measures to Avoid a Currency Crisis," *Economic Journal*, **105**, 510–519.

Pagano, M. (1989a). "Endogenous Market Thinness and Stock Price Volatility," *The Review of Economic Studies*, **56**, 269–287.

——— (1989b). "Trading Volume and Asset Liquidity," *The Quarterly Journal of Economics*, **104**, 255–274.

Pearce, D. (1984). "Rationalizable Strategic Behavior and the Problem of Perfection," *Econometrica*, **52**, 1029–1050.

Persons, J. and V. Warthers (1995). "Boom and Bust Patterns in the Adoption of Financial Innovations," *The Review of Financial Studies*, **10**, 939–967.

Phelps, C. (1992). "Diffusion of Information in Medical Care," *Journal of Economic Perspectives*, **6**, 23–42.

Phillips, D. P. (1974). "The Influence of Suggestion on Suicide: Substantive and Theoretical Implications of the Werther Effect," *American Sociological Review*, **39**, 340–354.

Piketty, T. (1995). "Social Mobility and Redistributive Politics," *Quarterly Journal of Economics*, **110**, 551–584.

Prendergast, C. (1993). "A Theory of 'Yes Men,'" *American Economic Review*, **83**, 757–770.

Prendergast, C. and L. Stole (1996). "Impetuous Youngsters and Jaded Old-Timers: Acquiring a Reputation for Learning," *Journal of Political Economy*, **104**, 1105–1134.

Rauch, J. (1993). "Does History Matter Only When It Matters Little? The Case of City Industry Location," *Quarterly Journal of Economics*, **108**, 843–867.

Reinganum, J. (1990). "The Timing of Innovation: Research, Development and Diffusion," in *Handbook of Industrial Organization*, R. Schmalensee and R. Willig, eds. Amsterdam: North Holland, 849–908.

Rochet, J.-C. and J.-L. Vila (1994). "Insider without Normality," *Review of Economic Studies*, **61**, 131–152.

Rodionova, Y. and J. Surti (1999). "Speculative Currency Crises in a Dynamic Setting," mimeo, Boston University.

Rogers, E. M. (1995). *Diffusion of Innovations*, 4th edition, New York: Simon & Schuster.

Romer, D. (1993). "Rational Asset-Price Movements without News," *American Economic Review*, **83**, 1112–1130.

Rothschild, M. (1974). A Two-Armed Bandit Theory of Market Pricing," *Journal of Economic Theory*, **9**, 185–202.

Rousseau, Jean-Jacques (1762). *Le Contrat Social*. Translation, University Press of New England, Hanover, NH: 1994.

Ryan, B. and N. Gross (1943). "The Diffusion of Hybrid Seed Corn in Two Iowa Communities," *Rural Sociology*, **8**, 15–24.

Salop, S. (1987). "Evaluating Uncertain Evidence with Sir Thomas Bayes: A Note for Teachers," *The Journal of Economic Perspectives*, **1**, 155–160.

Scharfstein, D. and J. Stein (1990). "Herd Behavior and Investment," *American Economic Review*, **80**, 465–479.

Schelling, T. (1978). *Micromotives and Macrobehavior*, New York: Norton.

Shiller, R. J. (2000). *Irrational Exuberance*, Princeton, NJ: Princeton University Press.

Smith, L. and P. Sørensen (1996). "Pathological Outcomes of Observational Learning," mimeo, MIT.

———— (1997). "Rational Social Learning with Random Sampling," mimeo, University of Michigan.

———— (2001). "Pathological Outcomes of Observational Learning," *Econometrica*, **68**, 371–398.

Sunstein, C. R. and T. Kuran (1999). "Availability Cascades and Risk Regulation," *Stanford University Law Review*, **51**, 683–768.

Tarde, Gabriel (1900). *Les Lois de l'Imitation*. Translation, *The Laws of Imitation*, by E. C. Parsons (1962), Gloucester, MA: Peter Smith.

Thompson, W. R. (1933). On the likelihood that one unknown probability exceeds another in view of the evidence of two samples, Biometrika, **25**, 285–294.

Tocqueville, Alexis de (1856). *L'Ancien Régime et la Révolution*, Robert Laffont, ed. (1986).

Trueman, B. (1994). "Analyst Forecasts and Herding Behavior," *Review of Financial Studies*, **7**, 97–124.

Vayda, E. (1973). "Comparison of Surgical Rates in Canada, England and Wales," *New England Journal of Medicine*, **289**, 1224–1228.

Vives, X. (1990). "Nash Equilibrium with Strategic Complementarities," *Journal of Mathematical Economics*, **19**, 305–321.

———— (1993). "How Fast Do Rational Agents Learn?" *Review of Economic Studies*, **60**, 329–347.

———— (1995). "The Speed of Information Revelation in a Financial Market Mechanism,"*Journal of Economic Theory*, **67**, 178–204.

———— (1996). "Social Learning and Rational Expectations," *European Economic Review*, **40**, 589–601.

———— (1997). "Learning from Others: A Welfare Analysis," *Games and Economic Behavior*, **20**, 177–200.

Wang, J. (1994). "A Model of Competitive Stock Trading Volume," *Journal of Political Economy*, **102**, 127–168.

Welch, I. (1992). "Sequential Sales, Learning, and Cascades," *Journal of Finance*, **47**, 695–732.

———— (2000). "Herding among Security Analysts," *Journal of Financial Economics*, **58**, 369–396.

Wennberg, J. and A. Gittelsohn (1973). "Small Area Variations in Health Care Delivery," *Science*, **182**, 1102–1108.

Zeira, J. (1994). "Information Cycles," *Review of Economic Studies*, **61**, 31–44.

Zhang, J. (1997). "Strategic Delays and the Onset of Informational Cascades," *RAND Journal of Economics*, **28**, 188–205.

Zwiebel, J. (1995). "Corporate Conservatism and Relative Compensation," *Journal of Political Economy*, **103**, 1–25.

Author Index

Subject Index

Warning:

The following material contains graphic sexual content meant for mature readers. *Haunting Love Alley* has been rated E–rotic by a minimum of three independent reviewers.

Ellora's Cave Publishing offers three levels of Romantica™ reading entertainment: S (S-ensuous), E (E-rotic), and X (X-treme).

S-*ensuous* love scenes are explicit and leave nothing to the imagination.

E-*rotic* love scenes are explicit, leave nothing to the imagination, and are high in volume per the overall word count. In addition, some E-rated titles might contain fantasy material that some readers find objectionable, such as bondage, submission, same sex encounters, forced seductions, and so forth. E-rated titles are the most graphic titles we carry; it is common, for instance, for an author to use words such as "fucking", "cock", "pussy", and such within their work of literature.

X-*treme* titles differ from E-rated titles only in plot premise and storyline execution. Unlike E-rated titles, stories designated with the letter X tend to contain controversial subject matter not for the faint of heart.

Haunting Love Alley

ഌ

Dedication

❧

We'd both like to dedicate this story to our spouses.
They tolerate our weird ways and our increased telephone bills
and for that we are eternally grateful.

A Personal Acknowledgement from
Sahara Kelly and S.L. Carpenter

❧

This book was completed in early August of 2005, prior to the disastrous arrival of Hurricane Katrina. We chose Louisiana as the setting for our story because it is a state rich in history and legend, blessed with traditions and a past that has strongly influenced its present.

Devastation notwithstanding, we believe the spirit that made Louisiana unique has not been diminished, but is still strong—especially within the hearts of those who call its bayous and allées home. Time has demonstrated that the passion for this land burns hotter than the summer sun, as disasters have swept across the delta before now, but never lessened the allure of its character. We are confident that Louisiana and New Orleans will recover and prosper once more, becoming the charmingly exciting and mysterious places that possess a magic all their own. Someday we would like to visit and find out for ourselves…

Authors' Note

❧

The Ghost Orchid referred to in this story is a real flower that probably originated in South America long ago. Also called the Frog Orchid, it blooms during the summer months, producing white flowers with two elongated petals—not unlike frog's legs.

Although it was discovered and officially named in 1844, we have taken liberties with the timing of that discovery, since it is likely this flower existed and thrived long before that date. The Ghost Orchid is an epiphyte—a plant that derives its nutrients from the air, not the earth. Thus it grows as a small bundle of roots clinging to a convenient tree. When in flower, its white blossom hovers high above the ground and has been described as "dancing on moonlight" like the ghosts after which it is named.

Unfortunately, it is found today only in South Florida's Fakahatchee Strand (and possibly deep in the Everglades) and is on the endangered species list. Propagated by the giant sphinx moth—another Florida native—it is a treasure that may well be lost within a generation or two, since its growth in controlled environments has thus far proved unsuccessful.

Chapter One
Early 1800s Louisiana

ಐ

"*Baptiste?*"

She forced the word past lips that were swollen and stiff with her own blood.

"I'm here, *cherie.*"

And he was. A warm palm soothed her cheek, gently brushing away a lock of her hair and then returning with a cool cloth to ease her pain.

"I'm glad." Her *homme de nuit* was with her. *Man of the night.* As dark as the shadows that hid the bayou, with a voice deeper than the inky black waters, Baptiste certainly lived up to the name she'd bestowed upon him.

"Shhhh…" He wiped her face again, careful not to touch the cuts or bruises and somehow she managed a smile. How she relished his caress, and how familiar to her it was now. As familiar as his scent, his smile, the length of his arousal and the height of her passion as he thrust himself to the hilt inside her.

He was her deepest desire, the father of her child and the only man in this world she had ever loved—*would* ever love. With one small exception. "Baptiste, is *he* all right?"

"Etienne?" The question needed no answer. "Yes, he'll soon be well away from here. Heading north with Louise. We will go north too, my love, and we'll meet them in Virginia. It is all arranged. As soon as you are healed."

She drew in a breath, wincing as knives of pain sliced through her chest. "It's a wonderful dream, Baptiste. A wonderful dream."

She felt the light splash of tears on her face as he bent closer. "Shhh." He stilled her once more with the lightest brush of his lips across hers.

"I will not be going north." She struggled to speak. "I will be with you in spirit, my love, but not in this body."

"Ahhh, Claudine…"

She opened her eyes with difficulty, the swelling forcing her to squint to make out his face. "Don't cry, my love. My only love." A sigh crossed her lips. "Baptiste. Promise me something…" Her voice firmed a little as she found a reserve of inner strength. There was a task she must accomplish before surrendering to her fate.

"Anything, *cherie*. Name it."

"Do not avenge me, please?" She held her breath as silence fell in the room. "I mean it, Baptiste. No *gris-gris*. No Voudou punishment. Monsieur Franklin has powerful friends and much influence. Too much influence. He would wreak havoc on my girls, my servants…then he'd hunt down you and Etienne… I could not stand it, my love."

"Ahh, *cherie*, what you ask, it is so difficult."

Claudine could hear the pain in his voice. "I know. But you must promise me. It is all I ask." She groped for his hand. "That, and your love. Forever."

His hand clasped hers, and she took comfort from the warmth of his skin. She always had. One look into his liquid black eyes and she had been lost to this man, willingly giving her body and her heart to him knowing he would cherish her forever.

As the madam of an elegantly isolated "house", Claudine Lavalieres had made her own rules. The

"Lavalieres" place had become known to one and all as "Love Alley" in a simple corruption of the French pronunciation and the function of the estate.

Her choice of lovers was hers alone, as was her right. She cared deeply for her girls, and kept as clean and respectable a house of ill repute as possible in these days of disease and negligently disreputable personal behaviors. Drunkenness was not acceptable, violence against her girls resulted in immediate removal from the premises and her prices were high, but not out of keeping with the current market. She'd rather charge a little more for her girls and ensure clients who could pay. It was better to be on the higher-priced end of this market. It deterred those Claudine considered unwelcome guests.

All had been smooth sailing until Lloyd Franklin had arrived at Love Alley. His first few visits had been unremarkable, although his eyes began to follow Claudine with a somewhat unnerving intensity. She'd ignored it, preferring to believe he simply admired her features.

But it was more and within a few months he made his desires plain. He wanted to fuck Claudine. And he considered that it was his right to do so, since he could afford any price she named. His determination to take the madam to bed had turned sour when he'd been refused, resulting in his anger, his obsession with her and his discovery of her secret "family"—Baptiste and their son, Etienne.

Franklin's fury exploded, but Claudine knew none of this when she'd admitted him to Love Alley earlier that evening. He was a wealthy member of Louisiana society, and she saw no reason to refuse him admittance. His money was as good as anybody else's, and if he found a girl he really liked, then all well and good. He would return regularly, as did several other gentlemen from the area around Bayou Chanson.

No, she'd not guessed at the depth of Franklin's fury— he'd hidden it well until they were alone. And then...

She shuddered as she pushed the images away from her mind. He'd beaten her, raped her then beaten her again. There had been no mercy and she'd smelled the fumes of brandy beneath his minty tongue.

Alcohol and thwarted desire had driven him to the brink, and the knowledge of her affair with Baptiste had pushed Lloyd Franklin over the edge of sanity. He'd sated his lusts within her body, and sated his fury with his fists.

Then he'd left, calmly flicking a few coins on the bedside table.

And Claudine had been forced to endure. One cry, one scream of pain and the servants would have come running— along with Baptiste. The result would have been instant death for Franklin. Of that, Claudine had no doubt.

And life would have ended for Baptiste too. Inevitably he would have been hunted down and slaughtered. Along with their son, Etienne.

Their passion was forbidden, their love an abomination in the eyes of Louisiana.

For Baptiste was a black slave.

And Claudine had given him her heart.

* * * * *

Baptiste choked back his grief as he held his love and watched her life ebb slowly away.

How could he promise not to avenge her? She was his goddess, his woman, his life, the mother of his child—how could he possibly allow her killer to walk free? He did not understand how a man could do this to a woman and still call himself a man.

He ached to put his strong hands around Lloyd Franklin's neck and choke the life out of him, slowly and inexorably. To watch the awareness in his eyes as he stared into Baptiste's face, shared Baptiste's pain and sorrow.

And yet he knew he *would* promise her this. Franklin's punishment would come at the hands of the Lord—or somebody else. Just not him. Because he would stand by his word.

Because he loved her beyond reason, beyond sanity. Because his life had been nothing before she entered it, and other than his son, there would be little to care for after she departed.

"I love you, *chère*. More than words can express." His hand lay dark against the pale whiteness of her shoulder, the bruises and blood an obscene slash of color that had no place on her perfect body.

She managed another smile, her green eyes glinting through the swollen folds of her eyelids. "I know. And I love you. I gave you my heart when we first loved, Baptiste. I have never regretted it."

"I promise, on our love, that I shall not avenge you, Claudine, though my heart breaks to make this vow." The words were dragged from his throat as his grief poured through him.

She eased down slightly into her pillows. "Thank you, *mon amour*. Thank you."

For a second or two Baptiste's vision blurred as tears flooded his eyes and he thought his woman shimmered oddly in his arms. Then his focus returned and he knew the end was near. Her injuries were severe, too severe for even *his* magic to heal.

"Give me your mouth, Baptiste. I have a long journey ahead of me. I would start it with your lips on me...on our special place…" She was weakening, yet strong enough to ask for his kiss.

He leaned to her and gently pressed his lips to hers, then moved, easing her tattered gown from her body. Her breasts were bruised, but there was one spot, just beneath her left nipple, where her heart beat and where Baptiste now ran his tongue softly against the thready pulse. The skin was silk to his touch, unmarred by violence, a pure place of passion, desire and everlasting emotions.

"Ahhh." She sighed, her chest rising shallowly as her breath rattled awkwardly in her throat.

Baptiste's agony swept through him, a fiery eruption of pain. He reached for his amulet, a small locket containing an even smaller bag of mysteries. He had never taken it off in his entire life.

He would now.

Calling on his Voudou gods all the way up to Maitresse Erzulie, along with every incantation and blessing he knew, Baptiste opened the locket and held the tiny bag to the lips of Claudine Lavalieres as she fought for the last moments of her life.

"Breathe your desire, *mon ange*. Tell your passion to the ancient gods, and I promise you our love will never *ever* die. I won't lose you to something as simple as death. We *will* be together again. *Always*." The need in him burned, the room around him faded and all he could see was a strange light shining on Claudine's face as she moved slightly toward his hand.

"I love you, Baptiste. I will love…you…for ev…"

The light flared brilliantly, blinding Baptiste. He blinked, surprised by the heat that the amulet was radiating as he held it to Claudine's lips.

As it faded, he realized that Claudine's soul was fading with it. Her body was still, her pulse gone, her breasts unmoving.

He closed the locket and folded it into her cooling hand, cupping it with his own warm ones. "Your spirit lives on, *chère*. Our love lives on. Forever."

There was no answer, and in truth Baptiste expected none. He knew. His soul cried out its grief and found an answering cry boiling deep in his lungs.

Baptiste, runaway slave from Haiti, servant of Claudine Lavalieres, father of her child and *Papa Lo* to the local Voudou community, opened his mouth wide and roared out a desolate scream of mourning.

Two hundred years into the future, a woman shuddered awake, the sound of his cry ringing in her ears. There were tears on her cheeks as she sobbed, the loss of the woman in her dream too real to be dismissed.

"Fucking *hell*." Through her grief, Cory Lavalle once again cursed her "gift". If only her psychic skills worked as well for her clients as it did in her dreams.

Determinedly, she blew her nose and shrugged away the images of a dying woman and her devastated lover. Who they were or why she kept dreaming about them, she had no frickin' idea.

And it was getting on her damn *nerves.*

Chapter Two
Present day

ಐ

Her long soft hair tangled between his fingers as her lips wrapped around his cock. The constant pull of his flesh in her mouth begged for him to let go. She was merciless.

He groaned loud and all the nerves in his body electrified and jolted through his bones to his spine. She released him from the suction of her mouth.

All his muscles loosened and he lay back on the fluffy satin bedspread, closing his eyes on a thought. *Mmm...my fantasies are made of times like these when an exotic woman shows pleasure beyond compare.* Peeking through slitted eyelids he saw long black hair dangling over her face and brushing over his stomach and thighs like the softest paintbrush. It tickled and caressed all at once. The addition of her licking his burning flesh only added to the extreme bliss he was feeling.

Louis was naked, aroused and crossing the line of having his soul ripped from his body in a passionate seduction of the mind and spirit.

Swirling in the comfort of his passion, he felt a gentle tug around his wrist. With a sigh he smiled then filled his lungs with the fragrance of the woman's body as she hovered above his head. He could feel the heat radiate from her skin followed by the wetness of her pussy on his abdomen as she straddled his body.

He felt another tug on his other wrist. He cleared his mind and realized she'd strapped his wrists to the brass headboard. Before he could open his eyes, she lowered a sheet of silk over his forehead, blinding him.

Dropping a gentle kiss onto the thin fabric, she whispered with their lips touching, "Just relax. Every fantasy has its price."

Louis jerked his arms forward. The headboard held him firm and he was blind to what she was doing. All he could do was lie there and wait. He couldn't scream or fight it. He was seduced, taken advantage of and now helpless.

Louis licked his now dry lips. The silk remained over his head and his panting and struggling only got him hotter and more uncomfortable.

He couldn't hear anything in the room except a scratching sound. The light could barely penetrate the silk but he could see there was brightness around him.

After a grating rasp echoed around his ears, he recognized the sound. It was wooden matches being struck.

Oh shit, she's going to burn my house down and leave me in it.

He felt a finger press against his lips. He was to remain silent. He wanted to ask what she was doing—what she wanted? He was dumbfounded and stripped of all his barriers and inhibitions.

Shaking his head, Louis thought he might be able to get the silk off his head. Then it suddenly became dark. Only the dim remnants of lights could be seen through the fabric.

Oh fuck. Now what?

Louis felt the bed move. Then he felt smooth skin brushing against his tied arms. Inhaling, he knew what was above him. She squatted down, resting her wet pussy on the silk fabric above his face. Her arms held her weight just inches from him and the headboard creaked as she lowered herself.

He pushed his tongue out into the fabric and along the wet slit of her cunt. The scent and taste of a woman were his weakness. How a woman's cunt smelled during arousal was the simplest and best aphrodisiac and his cock sprang back to life. She was playing with him.

Louis could hear the muffled moans as he continued to flick his tongue at her. Like eating pussy through panties, the fabric became the only barrier between them. He could taste her juices as they soaked through.

With a deep, lustful moan, he felt her lower more and squish the lips of her pussy against his face as she wiggled her tightened ass.

Louis was in heaven but he was fighting the hell his cock felt because he was aroused beyond any boundaries and limits of need. As she slid her pussy from his face, the silk stuck to her wet cunt. Like peeling a blanket off a bed, Louis could suddenly see what was around the room. There were candles on every table, mantle and along the dresser. They reflected in the mirror dazzling him, and he could barely see the woman standing at the dresser and pouring something into her hand. She looked into the mirror as his vision cleared and he saw her stare back at him.

She turned, moving toward him, her hair hanging long and dark along her body. The space between her legs glistened from the flickering light of the candles as they shone on the wetness welling from her cunt.

She held her hand above his head and Louis could smell the sweet fragrance of wine.

She lowered it to his chest and let a few drops fall from her palm onto his skin. The cool wine almost sizzled against the heat of his flesh. She dribbled a few more drops onto his stomach and then poured the rest of her handful onto his throbbing cock. The splash trickled between his legs, cooling the inferno in his balls.

Jerking hard on the ropes, Louis said nothing, knowing his eyes were saying everything that needed to be said.

She just kept her hair hanging over her face and the glittering of the whites of her eyes pierced through the darkness and into Louis' mind.

Moving to the foot of the bed, she reached over to the dresser and grabbed the bottle of wine, then stepped onto the bed and stood over Louis. Admiration flooded him as he looked up to the statuesque frame above him. Her eyes twinkled through the darkness. She threw her head back, exposing her breasts and tilted the wine bottle onto her chest letting the red liquid slowly trickle down her breasts and between her legs. The wet trails down her thighs and calves were a sweet blend of the wine and her pussy and offered a bounty Louis ached to taste.

She took a long swallow of the wine, letting some fill her mouth as she finished off the liquid.

She tossed the bottle aside and it thumped against the wooden floor.

Lowering down, her hair fell back to her sides and covered their bodies in a blanket of black curls. Their flesh met in a wet blend of sweat and wine. She slid up Louis' chest and to his face. With a deep kiss she let the wine trickle to his mouth, quenching part of his thirst.

She reached her damp hand to his eyes and brushed them closed.

All Louis could feel was the moisture of their skin melting together. His cock was throbbing and he strained not to explode. His mouth opened and a gasp left his body as she lowered her tight cunt down the thickened shaft of his cock.

Paradise wasn't far away.

Louis breathed out and tugged his arms forward, trying to grab some control. She had him tied and locked inside her vise. The inner walls of her cunt caressed his skin with each plunge in. The lips clung tight and dared him to leave as she rose up. He felt her hair falling against his skin and pulling off as she rode him.

This was torture and Louis was about to break. Everything she was doing was what he'd dreamed a woman would do to him. The dark hair, the wine, the ties around his wrists — everything that made him crazy, she was doing, except for one thing.

When she did it, he lost control.

Leaning back, she stretched the opening of her pussy tight against the stiffness of his pulsing cock. She moved her hand behind her and flicked her fingertips against the tight, rough skin of his balls sending him over the edge.

"Sir, please wake up. You're scaring some of the other passengers." The flight attendant tried to be as polite as possible even though she was clearly observing the rather large protrusion straining into the fabric of Louis' black slacks. "Perhaps you'd like a second pillow for your lap?"

Louis turned twelve shades of red and sat up straighter in his seat. Fortunately, the plane was more than half empty given the odd timing of this red-eye flight to Louisiana.

The attendant walked back toward him and stopped in the aisle. She kneeled down and handed him a small piece of paper. "Um, I'm in town for the weekend. A layover." She giggled. "If you don't have a room, well, after listening to you moan like that, I thought you might — you know — need someone?" She smiled and Louis watched her walk away.

Nice ass. He read the phone number, then slipped it into his shirt pocket.

Now that was a dream!

* * * * *

Cory Lavalle pressed her hand to her forehead in an attempt to push away the headache that had been threatening her all day. It was midafternoon, her spirits were as heavy as the clouds that roiled overhead and she seriously considered indulging herself in a nice long cry.

She had no clients for the rest of the week. Not one. Zippo. *Nada*. Not a solitary soul wanting to know their future, their past or their present.

Truth be told, Cory wasn't a very good psychic. She knew it, and apparently most of her customers knew it. Or rather the people who would have been customers if she'd been any good, knew it.

Whatever. She shut up her desk with resignation. The tiny corner in the darkest end of her friend Eileen's clothing store wasn't exactly the choicest location on Bourbon Street. But then again, neither she nor Eileen could afford Bourbon Street rents.

At least they were company for each other when it was quiet, like now, but unlike their usual banter, Cory and Eileen were both somber and disinclined to chat. Eileen was getting over the latest in a long series of dating disasters. And Cory?

Cory was flat-out depressed.

Lavalle women had been possessed of "second sight" for as long as she could remember. There had always been one woman in every generation who was in touch with another world, one unseen by regular mortal eyes.

Her elderly Aunt Carolina had been the last, and also the one to stare at Cory and pronounce *her* the next in the line of succession. It was a moment that had scared the crap out of Cory, who was all of thirteen at the time and wanted a real boyfriend or breasts a hell of a lot more than some weirdo psychic gift.

But she hadn't argued, since she knew—had known for some time—that her *Tante* Carolina was right.

Cory could *see*. Sometimes little more than a faint coloration in the air surrounding somebody. Most times, nothing at all.

But other times—those were the times when her hair stood on end all over her body. When visions of the past mingled with the present, when voices long dead whispered secrets into her brain and when her nights became journeys into times and places unknown to her.

She'd gone to college and majored in history, learning a lot about Louisiana, its past and its people. She'd planned to teach, but found there was no major in one very essential part of that career—patience.

So after a brief stint in a library doing research for a novelist, Cory decided to cash in on her gift and the Lavalle name, which was not unknown in New Orleans. Several people had become clients, most of them relatives. For some reason, Cory had much better luck with her "sight" when she was related, albeit distantly, to these people.

She often wondered if it had more to do with inherited genetic memories than a gift of psychic abilities.

Whatever it was, it served her reasonably well and she had eked out a living for the past six months giving readings and making predictions. The latter made her uncomfortable, since the future was—in her opinion—as yet unformed. She never hesitated to tell her clients exactly that.

Today, though, she wasn't going to be able to tell anybody anything, since there was nobody on her appointment schedule at all. It was distressingly blank.

The rumble of thunder echoed around her skull and she winced. "Eileen, I'm outta here. Okay with you?" She emerged past the blue-black velvet draperies and into the store.

"Sure thing, Cory-honey. Wish I could go too." The pale blonde-haired figure of Eileen Morrisey emerged from a rack of dresses to a flash of lightning and a louder rumble of thunder. "Isn't likely we'll get many customers for the rest of *this* day."

Cory grimaced. "Yeah. Well, I'll see you tomorrow, *chère*." She left Eileen with the traditional Creole endearment and pushed the door open into a torrent of rain. "*Sheeeeit.*"

It was the ultimate insult. Her waist-length black hair would frizz something fierce if she got it soaked and didn't dry it right away, and her shoes—*hah*. These tropical downpours flooded the sidewalk in seconds.

They were new leather mules. Cory narrowed her eyes, removed her shoes and tucked them under her arm. Barefoot, she paddled her way down to the end of the street, carefully watching where she stepped and trying to stay under the shop awnings as much as possible.

She was wet, miserable, had a headache and didn't have a dime to spare. Life was about as much fun as this thunderstorm and just as grey.

She had no idea that before too long the blinking light on her answering machine would signal the beginning of possible salvation. Nor could she see that she was about to embark on an adventure that had been two hundred years in the making.

For the sad thing was, Cory couldn't *see* for herself at all. When it came to her own personal aura and future, she was totally and completely blind.

It didn't worry her one bit, however. There were much more pressing things in her life, like how she was going to meet the next rent payment without dipping further into her cherished savings account, and whether the water had spotted the leather on her new shoes.

And overriding all those considerations was the question of whether she had any of her headache pills left. A migraine was walloping up a thunderous roll of pain behind her left eye and she wanted nothing more than to curl up someplace dark and silent and sleep it off for about eight hours.

Creeping onto her bed and ignoring the pile of wet clothes on the floor, Cory reached for her bedside table and found her pills. Thankfully there were several left, and she took one, swallowing it down with a grimace.

She left the bottle out as a reminder to herself to refill the damn thing before she ran out, then surrendered to the drum solo in her skull and lay down closing her eyes.

There was nothing worse, in Cory's opinion, than a goddamned migraine.

Chapter Three

∾

The dream crept over her like snowflakes, kissing various parts of her skin awake. Or *sort of* awake. The sort-of state that isn't really awake, but more than sound asleep and snoring. An odd in-between world where the unreal seems real.

And the kisses seemed *soooo* real.

They began at her toes, little brushes of something that might have been lips and by the time they reached her thighs she was thrumming with delight. She tried to part her legs in eager anticipation, only to feel the pressure firming and moving higher, heat spreading low in her belly as her navel was explored and the kisses lingered just beneath her breasts.

As is so typical in the surreal world of dreams, Cory couldn't move. She wanted to, badly. She wanted to grind her hips in invitation. She wanted to reach for whoever it was that peppered her skin with tiny licks, flares of fire from a tongue that never stayed in one place long enough.

And when that tongue and those lips found her nipple, she wanted to scream and leap with pleasure. But she could not—she was held captive by her imagination and her desires. She couldn't even open her eyes.

She could only *feel*.

And there was so much to feel. A warm weight, moving, sliding over her prone body, arousing every single inch of skin with just the right combination of pressure and heat. Firm lips parted to expose hard teeth, allowing nibbles and nips to drive Cory even higher along this wild and wonderful path.

For some reason her dream lover seemed enchanted with her left breast. Time and time again the kisses returned to the exact spot that magnified every single shiver and shudder that coursed through her. A tiny congregation of nerve endings right below her left nipple that so few of her past lovers had ever bothered to explore. But this dream of hers…well, who or whatever it was, it *knew*.

It knew to the millimeter where to stroke, to suckle the sensitive skin. It knew precisely how hard to bite, and where to soothe. And when it finally retreated from her breast and slithered down over her body to settle between her legs, Cory wanted desperately to sob out a breath of eager desire.

But it caught in her throat, rendering her mute. Again she was restrained, again she was forced to rely on her other sense — the sense of touch.

And the first touch she felt was breath — warm breath — dusting across the hairs on her mound and dappling over her pussy enticingly.

Strangely, she wanted more. Cory had no objections to oral sex, but in the past had preferred to get straight down to business. Her lovemaking technique was pretty simple — put the right thing in the right hole and repeat as often as both deemed necessary.

She'd never even imagined that foreplay could arouse her so explosively. That every iota of her being would resound with the need to be sucked, to be fucked. There was no escaping the inexorable climb. The tongue wandered erotically around the hills and valleys of her pussy lips, pausing in some spots and caressing others with a wet heat that flooded through her veins.

She felt her juices welling free of her cunt, dripping over her skin in a wave of lust, of need. Her ass clenched fiercely and little electric tingles began to ignite her spine. She was going to orgasm, to come against the face of this dream lover with the oh-so-skilled mouth.

With a mighty effort, Cory opened her eyes on her dream. For the fraction of a second before waking, she stared at a face between her legs. The features were indistinct, the hair a blur. But the eyes...

One was *blue*—the other was *grey*. And they were staring at her over her own pussy.

She snapped into awareness, wet and poised to climax. Her bedroom was dark and empty, and her bed a tumbled mess where she'd kicked the sheets away. She had no choice—her desire was too intense to go unrelieved.

Without conscious thought she slid her hand to her mound and beyond, finding the soaking and hot folds of her cunt. It took less than a moment to brush her fingertips delicately across her aroused clitoris.

And less than a heartbeat for her to come.

Quite a bit more time had to elapse before Cory realized her migraine was completely gone.

* * * * *

Sitting on a red-eye with a hard-on wasn't Louis' idea of fun. His recurrent dream was getting more and more intense. It had started after the death of his grandfather and had been going on for several weeks.

He had been closer to his grandfather than to his Army father. Louis grew up moving from country to country but had settled in with his grandfather at the age of twelve. His grandfather Franc was a shrewd but honest businessman and had made his fortune in real estate. He told Louis tales of his childhood, one that had been spent traveling up and down the Mississippi River. Each time Franc told the stories to

Louis, the boy eagerly promised his grandfather he would go there one day.

After finishing up his latest home restoration project in Chicago, he rushed to his grandfather's side in New York, and was there when he passed away. After the funeral he called his job foreman and told him he would be gone for a while. He trusted the guy to clean up all the loose ends of Louis' business in Chicago. He also told him not to set up any more jobs until he heard from Louis.

He was going to honor his vow to his grandfather and was thrilled to discover that the will contained a very personal bequest—quite a lot of money and a parcel of land with an old house and all its outer amenities in the depths of Louisiana.

Louis was wide awake now after his nap, and a glance at his watch told him there were still about two hours left on his flight. Since the seat beside him was empty he tugged his briefcase from the overhead compartment and opened the thick stack of papers the lawyer had loaded onto him after he'd signed the final deed to the land and the house. For a moment or two, he wished his parents could have lived to join him. But he was pretty much the last of his line.

Love Alley? That's a weird name for a house.

He sorted through papers, bypassing the boring ones that had nothing to tell him and going for the ones that might give him an idea of what he was going to find waiting in Louisiana.

Ahh. A Surveyor's Report. Louis felt optimistic, then sighed as he realized he was holding something that must be at least a hundred-odd years old.

Concerning the lot of land bounded easterly by Bayou St. Jacques; to the northerly and northwesterly by Bayou St. Gilles; to the southwesterly by the toll pike road to New Orleans; to the westerly by the Emperor Bayou. Said lot comprised of approximately 40 hectares, containing one large dwelling and associated smaller dwellings. Quarters for housing up to 50 slaves are located to the south of the main dwelling and separated by sufficient distance to ensure privacy.

This dwelling is commonly known by its nickname — "Love Alley".

There it was again. Love Alley. The survey told him nothing he could use and the names of the bayous meant nothing to him at this point. They might not even exist today, since Louis knew that a lot of Louisiana was a swamp that was changing almost daily.

He continued his investigation of the paperwork, thumbing through endless legal documents, some old, some more recent. Apparently the fact that Louisiana still followed the Napoleonic legal code meant that twice as many papers had to be filed.

He sighed again, ready to give up, when the title of one sheet caught his attention.

A Brief Recounting of the History of Love Alley. It was a reprint of an article by a local historian.

Louis settled down to read.

Deeded to the Lavalieres family in the last part of the eighteenth century, the property was developed by Emile Lavalieres into a thriving estate. Shipping interests, made feasible by the network of navigable bayous leading to M. Lavalieres, provided much of the income necessary to keep the family well financed, and it wasn't until Emile's death in 1792 that events took a downturn for the Lavalieres.

Emile's son, Georges, died within months of his father, a victim of the annual outbreak of yellow fever. Other Lavalieres family members also succumbed, and eventually the title reverted to Osmonde Lavalieres who lived long enough to deed the property to his daughter Claudine on his death.

Louis glanced out the window of the plane but barely noticed the clouds and the dawn sky, since his thoughts were in the past. He figured it was probably unusual for a woman to inherit property. It must have been quite a valuable estate. Otherwise Osmonde Lavalieres would never have considered trying to preserve it by making such a dramatic move. He returned to the story, his interest caught.

By this time (approximately 1805), there was little money left, and Claudine set about maximizing her investment in order to survive. She converted the estate into a brothel, and capitalized on both its proximity to New Orleans and its private location. Within a few short months, her clientele was established, the money rolled in and the estate quickly became known locally (and affectionately) as Love Alley *in a salute to its new role within the community and a corruption of the French surname of its current mistress.*

At around this time, unusual events occurred, giving rise to the so-called Mystery of Love Alley. Claudine Lavalieres was, allegedly, a sharp and responsible madam, running a well-organized brothel. She was acutely aware of financial matters and invested her profits with an eye to the future.

At some point during 1808 Claudine Lavalieres disappeared.

Louis sat up straight and reread the words. A smart and clever woman had disappeared, leaving a profitable venture behind her. He narrowed his eyes. It didn't feel right to him. He read on.

There were many rumors within the community surrounding Love Alley. Some said she had died in childbirth, others that she had been murdered by a disgruntled customer. Still others averred that she had fled with a lover, possibly a slave, to the greater freedom and acceptance of the North.

Whatever the reason, Claudine Lavalieres completely and utterly disappeared, never to be seen again. With her went the good fortune that had blessed Love Alley.

The property passed into the hands of a far distant relative who professed distaste for the Southern climate. It fell rapidly into disrepair, and was rescued in the late eighteen-hundreds by the skin of its archeological teeth. The deed to the property became part of a poker game pot on a Mississippi riverboat and here this reporter notes an interestingly coincidental piece of trivia. The winning hand that secured the pot, and Love Alley, was a full house – three Queens high. Once again it appears the ladies came to the rescue of Love Alley. The new owner did his best to restore some of the grandeur before his death.

Since then, the estate has been sadly neglected, and only the circumstance of it having been constructed from some of the finest native woods has kept it intact.

In 1942..."

Louis stopped reading. The more recent events had been relayed to him by his grandfather's attorney. There was no need to go into that portion of the history. It was dull and didn't involve a profitable brothel and its vanishing madam.

Why on Earth would Claudine Lavalieres hightail it out of a place where she had a good income and probably a pretty secure future? It made no sense, and the more Louis thought about it, the more he began to believe that there probably had been some foul play involved.

If the house was big enough to be a brothel, then it was probably worth quite a bit of ready cash, even two hundred years ago, and would certainly be worth killing for.

He shrugged. He was no historian and couldn't begin to guess at motives for a mystery that happened some two centuries in the past. What he could guess at, and with reasonable accuracy, was the building itself and how it must have appeared back then.

The paper crackled and he turned it over curiously. Attached to the back with a yellowing piece of tape was what looked like a page torn from an old magazine. On it was a faded picture of a painting, obviously hung on somebody's wall for many years. The text was torn, the artist's name illegible and the paper itself beginning to show signs of advanced age.

But the image of the painting itself was intact, as were the words beneath...*Love Alley.*

Louis stared at it. White pillars soared to the eaves and there were the traditional porches surrounding both the ground and the first floors. Long windows would let in whatever breezes were out there when it got hot, and elegantly worked shutters stood ready to guard against bad weather. There were neatly clipped bushes lining the grassy walkway to the huge double doors that dominated the front of the house.

It was very much a typical "plantation" type of building—square, white, classy and very elegant. Heavy magnolias had scattered their petals like southern snow over the lush green walk, or "alleé" as Louis knew they were called. It was where the phrase "Alley" came from in so many of these old homes and their charming names. Rows of trees were planted to line the path leading to the house, a dramatic piece of landscaping that also provided cool walks and a measure of shelter from harsh winter winds.

Even then—at the time the picture was painted—heavy swags of Spanish moss cascaded from the trees, adding the unique touch of magic that said "the Old South" so clearly.

It was beautiful. Louis stared at it, struggling with the thought that it was now actually *his*.

He wondered if he could come close to restoring it, if the records of the parish might contain some architectural information. Then he wondered if there was anything at all left standing, given the passage of years and the wild Louisiana weather.

"Ladies and gentlemen, this is your captain speaking. We are about to begin our descent to the Louis Armstrong New Orleans International airport. The current weather conditions are a balmy eighty-four degrees with a humidity level off the scale." The captain sounded amused. "So I hope you're wearing washable clothing."

Louis gulped. This was going to be an interesting experience for him.

"We estimate touchdown in approximately twenty minutes. If there are any changes we'll let you know right away. Would the flight attendants please prepare the cabin for landing."

This, realized Louis as he tightened his seatbelt, tucked his folding tray back into place and returned his seat to a locked and upright position, was *it*.

Love Alley — here I come.

Chapter Four

❧

It was the oddest feeling.

Something was watching him, but he couldn't figure out where the *something* was.

It was Louis' third day at Love Alley and already he was crazy about the place, even though he'd had to improvise a lot of basic living needs like a small refrigerator, some wiring that would never pass inspection and a large piece of wood over one window on the ground floor.

It didn't matter — the house had woven a spell on him as soon as he'd crossed the rickety threshold.

The double doors had opened onto a scene that wasn't as bad as it could have been. There were cobwebs, of course. Some rot — less than he'd expected — and evidence that some squatters had tried to trash the place at some point in time, but surprisingly they'd given up.

The water worked, with some encouragement, and after a little wizardry with an out–of-date and definitely not-up-to-code fuse box, Louis had some light at night.

The kitchen was the most habitable, and one room upstairs seemed usable, so Louis camped out in those two locations while he worked on repairing the stairs and getting a bathroom into some kind of working order. The toilet flushed but made a noise that reminded him of some kind of horrible creature drowning in mud. Added to that was a water hammer in the plumbing system that threatened to shatter the porcelain tub.

Time passed very quickly once he'd stripped off his traveling clothes, thrown on one of his several pairs of cutoff jeans and thrown his heart into his new home.

But it hadn't taken too long for this odd itch at the back of Louis' neck to begin, a feeling that he wasn't alone.

He'd disposed of the various species of wildlife that had decided to make their nests and homes inside the house, and thanked his lucky stars that none of them were deadly. He was actually a little surprised that there'd been so few, since it was clear that the area had had little, if any, human occupation for quite some time.

The downstairs window was fixed, thanks to a couple of hours of fighting with an annoyingly stubborn sash weight, and his fudged-up electrical supply was maintaining the little fridge and providing him with cream for his coffee, ice cubes, water and cold beer. All the essentials of life.

He was amazingly content, had rapidly slipped into the rhythm of life in the bayou and was enjoying the early morning chores and work he'd begun, finding the short rest occasionally accompanied by a snooze in the late afternoon heat of the steamy day.

He'd just finished clearing out all the debris from the room he was planning on using as his master bedroom when the weight of the air settled on his bare shoulders and he wiped the sweat from his eyes.

It was late—time for that break.

Perhaps now was a good moment to head out back of the house and snoop around the grounds—something Louis hadn't had a chance to do yet. He knew there was an old, broken-down kind of jetty affair, boards that led out to the murky water and had crumbled at the end, leaving a stark little path to nowhere in particular.

He grabbed a cold bottle of water from his little fridge and left the house, wincing as the air hit him in the face like a wet rag. It was hot in the house, but outside—where the sun really went to work—it was close to unbearable.

The shade of the bayou was a welcome relief, and Louis gladly swatted away the few mosquitoes for the price of cooler air. They'd come back in droves at sundown, he knew, but for now they were little more than a mild nuisance.

Standing at ease on the ruined dock, in his cutoff jeans and not much else, Louis had no idea what a delectably male picture he presented.

Somebody else did.

* * * * *

Honey Treadwell knew a fine piece of male ass when she saw one.

She should, since she'd been married twice, engaged four times and selected her lovers as carefully as she did her divorce lawyers.

And what she stared at as she quietly poled her pirogue down the bayou made her mouth water.

Strong shoulders reflected the dappled sunlight, and an equally strong chest rose and fell as he sniffed in lungsful of the bayou air. His legs were tanned and muscular and rippled with masculinity as he raised one work-booted foot, resting it on a broken post.

She glanced at his dark hair, noted that it was a little longer than usual, mentally applauded and moved on. Downwards to those real nice cutoffs that hugged just about everything a girl could ask for. Tight.

A word that could not only describe the fit of his ragged jean shorts, but also his ass, which she duly noted as he turned to watch a butterfly. And when he turned back…well, *fuckin' A, and hey hey heyyy!* There was one real nice package just begging to be petted lurking behind his faded fly.

She licked her lips and poled more noisily. If this was her new neighbor, then damned if she wasn't about to develop a *lot* more of that Southern hospitality than she had up to now.

Pulling down her miniscule tank top to make sure her breasts showed to their best advantage, Honey pasted an alluring smile on her face and let her pole splash in the water, scaring a few egrets into clattering flight.

He jumped, and Honey's grin grew even bigger as she watched the bulge in his shorts expand at the sight of her itty-bitty top and her plentiful titties. Both top and tits had been carefully designed to complement each other and it would appear the sizeable financial investment was paying off.

"Hi sugar. You look like you havin' a fine ol' time jus' starin' at this ol' bayou." The voice oozed with Southern charm, something Honey had perfected over the nine years since she'd moved to Louisiana from New Jersey.

"Er…hello?" Puzzlement, surprise and a host of other emotions chased themselves across his handsome face, and Honey was pleased to note he was having a hard time dragging his gaze from her breasts.

Her nipples hardened. "I'm your neighbor, sugar. Name's Honey. I'm as sweet as those magnolias and real sticky at times, too." She laughed at his expression. "Don't mind me. I live a couple turns down the bayou there. That makes us neighbors, sugar, so I figured I'd just do the neighborly thing and come right on over to make you feel welcome."

He extended a firm hand as she navigated the little boat efficiently up to the ruined dock. "Nice to meet you, Honey. I'm Louis. Louis Beekman. I didn't realize I had neighbors here."

Honey managed to slide a portion of her skin over his hand and arm as she stepped from the boat. It was a very nice sensation. The feel of his body lived up to the look of his body, and her pussy throbbed in pleasant anticipation.

Oh chèr. You an' me is going to make the beast with two backs. An' it'll be sensational.

"I'm afraid there's not much at the house right now, but I can offer you a soda or a beer if you'd like?"

"Oh I'd *like*. A long cool one'd slide down my throat like silk right about now…" She smiled politely and rested her hand on his arm as she picked her way over the rotting planks.

"Watch your step. These boards aren't safe. I have them on the list of things to be replaced. It's a pity too, since I reckon they're the original cypress. But time has really taken its toll down here." He glanced at her and looked embarrassed. "Sorry. I'm a renovator. Can't help loving all the stuff in this place, but I didn't mean to bore you."

"Oh sugar, you didn't bore me." *You could stand there and scratch your ear and you wouldn't bore me.* "So you gonna be renovatin' Love Alley, huh?"

"Yeah. Absolutely. It's a gorgeous old place with great bones."

"Great bones? You talk about it like it's a woman. A woman that needs the right man's touch." Honey managed to emphasize her point with her breasts, which were getting touched at that moment since she was squashing them "accidentally" into his chest. "Of course, most of us women surely do appreciate the touch of the right man."

Louis cleared his throat and blinked, stepping backwards hastily.

Which was a really bad thing to do given that he was standing on an old and rotting jetty.

He staggered and caught himself just before he toppled into the murky green bayou. But in doing so, he knocked Honey off balance.

Before she could stop herself, she was flying off the little pier to land flat on her back with a resounding splash. She had barely enough time to close her mouth before she went under.

Her brain worked even faster than her physical reflexes and she came up coughing and spluttering and playing the drowned maiden, even though she'd done no more than get a soaking — something she was quite used to.

But Louis didn't know that.

"Oh shit, oh *God* I'm sorry…" Louis was squatting down, arms outstretched, shorts cupping his sex in a mouthwateringly snug fashion.

Honey's mouth watered. She lifted her hand to her head in a delicate gesture. "Ohhhh *my*…"

As she'd hoped, strong arms swept her off her feet, picking her up like she was no more than a bunch of flowers. She so loved being carried around by arms like these. Restraining a purr of pleasure, she rested her head against hot flesh. "This is so kind of you, Louis. Such a silly thing, but it's knocked my breath quite out of my lungs."

"Ssshh." He strode to the house with Honey in his hold, barely checking his steps as he took her into the kitchen. "Now, are you sure you're all right?" He turned worried eyes on her.

She managed a shiver, and her nipples beaded up nicely. It was more a result of Louis than her dunking, but once again she rested secure in the knowledge that only *she* knew that. Louis, being a man, wouldn't have a clue.

Blessing the fundamental naiveté of the males of the species, Honey fluttered her eyelashes and looked down at her clothes. "I sure am a wet honey at the moment. And likely to make a puddle on your floor, Louis." *If you only knew the half of it.* "Might you have an old towel lyin' round someplace a gal could dry herself with?" *Your tongue would do nicely if all else fails. Or perhaps that itty bit of soft hair just above that intriguing zipper…*

"Of course. I know it's hot, but even so, standing round in soaking wet things probably isn't a good idea." Distractedly Louis rummaged through boxes and big green plastic bags, emerging at last with a huge yellow towel and a smile on his face. "Here we go. It's new, so it should be fine."

She took it from him, noting the price tag. He sure could afford the finer things in life if this was what he paid for his bath towels.

Honey's smile grew larger and her nipples got even harder. "Why, aren't you a darlin'?"

Louis looked absently around the kitchen. "Er…if you go upstairs there's a big room to the right at the top. Got a kind of old mirror thing in it. It's in better shape than the rest of them, and you can dry off in there if you'd like?"

"I surely do like, sugar. Top of the stairs to the right you say?"

"Yep. Watch the railing. It's a bit loose in places."

Honey nodded and carefully mounted the stairs. *Mission accomplished.* In a few short minutes she was gonna be as naked as a jaybird except for one expensive towel. Poor unsuspecting luscious Louis didn't stand a chance.

*   *   *   *   *

Once again Louis' neck itched like fury and he swung around, fully expecting to see Honey behind him. Or *someone* behind him. But there was no one there.

He frowned and pulled two cold sodas from the little fridge, opening one and taking a long drink. He was not a fanciful kind of man, imagining stuff like this. He was practical, commonsensical and down to earth.

Shrugging, he brushed it off once more. It was probably the heat or the humidity or he was coming down with a cold. Or maybe it was all the iced stuff he was drinking like a dying fish. Something…*anything*.

Anything other than the uncomfortable and disturbing feeling of a *presence* in the house. Because that was what it was. He'd slept well, exhausted to the bone for the first nights at Love Alley.

Last night he'd awoken an hour earlier than usual, soaked with sweat and with a hard-on that could've doubled as a flagpole outside the White House. He was used to morning stiffies, but this was…well, something to be proud of, he supposed.

The noise of Honey's footsteps upstairs jolted him back into reality and he resolutely ignored the feathering sensation down his spine. It was all crazy stuff, exaggerated by the heat and a sexy wet woman.

Who even now was stripping to the skin and drying that skin in his new bath towel. In spite of himself, Louis hardened inside his old cutoffs. Honey was well named, being a golden, creamy ice cream cone of sex that just begged for a lickin'. Her sandy-blonde hair was lighter in some places than others and touched her shoulders in a soft and tousled cloud that just asked for a man to run his fingers through it.

The rest of her matched up real nice too. Louis sucked down another sizeable swallow of soda. This woman had legs that wouldn't quit until they squeezed his ears, and breasts he'd like to devour for a month or so and then come back for seconds.

Okay. *Enough.* He was horny, sure. What guy wouldn't be when faced with an armful of hot wet woman? He had no friends in this place yet, no dates, and unless there were some cute girls at the lumber supply house, he wasn't likely to have any in the near future.

He was human, Honey was attractive and sending off "come and get me" signals like rockets on the Fourth of July. It was nature.

He sighed. Fucking a neighbor probably was a real stupid idea, since it might end up in some kind of bizarre bayou thing and his head would float up from a local gator's nest only to be identified by what was left of his teeth.

Especially if she was married. It occurred to him that he hadn't asked and she hadn't volunteered any information about her status.

Oh well.

Louis finished his soda and reached for another one, making a mental note to pick up more next time he went to town. Whatever was gonna happen would happen. He'd just relax and, like they said all the time in Louisiana, *laissez les bon temps roulées.*

Let the good times roll. Whether they involved rolling around with Honey remained to be seen.

He grinned.

And jumped when a shutter fell off the kitchen window with a huge crash.

Chapter Five

ജ

Honey ignored her surroundings—a dingy room that smelled musty with a big full-length mirror on a stand in one corner. Other than that, there wasn't much to see. A couple of suitcases lay awkwardly beneath the window, and it looked as though Louis might be planning on using this room as his bedroom, although right now there was only a lawn chair with a sleeping bag on it.

Honey had other ideas. She'd noticed a new hammock strung up on the shady side of the huge porch, and that would suit her just fine. She'd never done it in a hammock. Perhaps they could come up here later when the sun set and the bugs would make life pretty sucky for a couple of hours.

She shrugged. *Whatever.*

Peeling off the clingy wet tank, she thanked her lucky stars that she hadn't worn a bra that day. Her breasts were still damp and cool, their dark rose nipples standing proudly from the creamy mounds.

She cupped them with her hands, enjoying the feel of the silky skin weighing heavily in her palms. Her surgeon had really done an outstanding job.

A slight chill swept over her, reminding her that her shorts were sticking like wallpaper to her buttocks, and with a regretful sigh she stripped them off too. They really did make her ass look fine, but they had to go. There was no underwear beneath to worry about so she stood there nude and let the air sweep over her skin for a few moments.

Honey was a sensual woman. She loved her body, she loved men's bodies and she loved what they were capable of when the two got together.

Just thinking about having Louis' cock between her thighs got her wet. Thinking about his head between her thighs got her even wetter, and sent a shiver of delightful anticipation over her flesh.

Or was it anticipation? She slid her hands between her thighs to touch the slick of hot liquid that coated the folds of her smoothly shaved pussy. *Oh yeah, sugar. Honey's makin' honey.*

Standing there in the shadowy heat of the room, Honey caught a glimpse of herself in the mirror and stopped still, caught by the play of light and darkness over her body. She looked almost insubstantial — yet erotic. A symphony of curves and lines that flowed slowly — seductively — like the waters of the bayou outside.

Honey closed her eyes and let her fingers play around the center of her womanhood. Her clit responded to the slightest brush of air by shuddering and opening the floodgates of her sexual arousal even more. It was a moment to be treasured, relished, standing alone in Louis' bedroom, touching and stimulating herself in front of an antique mirror.

Or was she alone?

Awareness prickled her neck, making her turn quickly in the expectation of finding Louis watching her.

There was no one there.

She turned back to the mirror and what she saw choked a gasp from her throat.

She was wearing a *corset.*

Tentatively Honey ran her hands across her ribs in an attempt to touch the creamy satin or the stiffening seams, which ran to the base of her breasts and uplifted them into full swells of soft flesh.

She could feel nothing but her own skin, warm and silky beneath her fingertips.

No embroidered flowers twining around her hips, no lacing up from navel to chest—no corset at all. But it *was* there. She could *see* it.

What the fuck?

It straightened her posture, narrowed her waist, and thrust her breasts into erotic prominence. It heightened every single sensation that Honey was feeling, and although it did not exist, the corset seemed a part of her arousal—a tool of her sex.

She parted her thighs in a lascivious gesture, revealing the pink and shining folds of her aroused pussy, relishing the flood of excitement that rippled through her. This was the craziest shit, but nothing could prevent the wet heat from flowing down over her skin.

She stilled as the woman in the mirror breathed in and filled her lungs with a quivering rush of desire.

And two hands crept around her waist to clasp her breasts.

Honey surrendered. This might be some weird hallucination, but it was turning her on—*big*-time.

They squeezed tight—almost painfully tight—forcing her nipples into rock-solid peaks and then strumming them with fingers that seemed to know the exact amount of pressure to exert on the excruciatingly sensitive buds.

Warmth blossomed up and down her spine as something solid pressed against her.

A man.

Honey closed her eyes against the impossible vision in the mirror and leaned back a little, bringing more of her flesh into contact with the owner of the hands. And what hands they were.

They cupped and kneaded and stroked and pulled. They teased and tantalized and worked Honey's breasts until she was nearly weeping with need and thrusting her hips forward in a crazy attempt to come.

Flooded with crazed arousal, Honey panted. She burned, yearned and leaned every which way as she tried to touch herself since those strong hands wouldn't. But it was to no avail. Her arms seemed like lead weights, unable to move or reach for the clit that ached so ferociously.

"Oh God..." she sobbed and opened her eyes, seeing a twisting muddle of barely clothed woman in the mirror.

She saw something else, too.

There was a man's face leering at her over her shoulder. Long matted hair hung down either side of his face, pockmarks scarred one side of his cheek and an angry red scar sliced his lower lip neatly in two.

Honey nearly passed out, but managed to suck in enough air to scream. Without a second thought she ran. Down the stairs, past a dumbstruck Louis, heedless of the fact she was naked as a jaybird, she ran.

She didn't stop until she'd poled her pirogue out of sight of Love Alley.

In one of the small salons, a dusty portrait adorned a grimy and mold-covered wall. The barely legible caption read "M. Jean Argent, 1804". Instead of the usual formal expression, this portrait featured a harsh-faced man with a wicked smile.

A smile that curved around his scarred lower lip.

* * * * *

Louis was tired, sore from all the day's work, and as he saw a buck naked woman run screaming from his house his jaw dropped. He knew he probably ought to find out what the hell was going on with Honey, but she'd caught him completely by surprise. He stood on the porch and watched her remarkably fine ass as it bounced down the path to the bayou and disappeared.

He would've followed her, but common sense told him it wasn't wise to rush into an unknown bayou after a naked woman. And a splashing sound followed by the thunk of an oar told him she'd reached her pirogue.

Well. So much for a hot roll in the hay with my neighbor. Probably for the best, all things considered.

His hammock and the soda called to him silently. Not the type to go against such commands he obliged the little mental voices and popped open another cold one, swigging it down like a college senior with his first beer on a Friday night. He wondered if he'd ever be able to drink enough to cool his thirst.

The sun was lower now and slivers of light shone through the trees surrounding the house.

Louis knew that night was coming soon but he wanted to see the glorious sunset over the river. He had a front row seat and wouldn't have too long a wait. The inevitable mosquitoes would drive him indoors soon enough, but for now he climbed into the hammock that stretched across the porch and relaxed.

The sweat on his chest shimmered as he breathed and with each cleansing breath, Louis felt more relaxed and at home. Deep down he found he was probably a country boy trapped in a citified lifestyle.

Twilight crept over the bayou. It was still warm enough for Louis to rest shirtless in the open air. He hadn't felt this relaxed in quite a while. Life's daily chaos always interrupted times of great peace.

His eyelids became heavier by the minute and after one last glance at the sun setting over the trees, Louis looked up to see a few early sparkling stars in the sky. Sleep crept over him and he let it come, aware of that annoying itch again for a few seconds before sliding into unconsciousness.

Louis stretched his arms high above his head. A few cracks of his bones later he was comfortable with his fingers twined around the rope atop the hammock. He snickered thinking how this could be a sexy way to tie a woman down.

The breeze blew across the front of the house and as the leaves rustled against the wooden porch, Louis breathed in deeply. It was cleansing and pure. Not like that smoggy shit he breathed in the city.

Before his eyes closed he swore he saw something flicker through the window nearby. Two glistening visions of loveliness in white, with blonde hair.

He slept.

Inside the house, soft curls of mist formed low on the floor, whirling upwards as Louis snuffled into a deeper sleep. The wraiths took shape, faces forming atop the drifting clouds, female faces, surrounded by loose blonde curls.

Their bodies followed, lush and rounded, curvaceous in a way that contemporary women did their best to avoid. These were no wafer-thin impossibly slender models, these were warm, lusty and wantonly sensual girls.

"He's somethin', ain't he, Maxine?" The whisper was soft, slurred with the soft musical words of old Louisiana.

"He sure is, Mabel. He surely is."

Both Mabel and Maxine moved from the house to stare at Louis as he slept.

"You see how hard he worked, girl? See *them* hard parts there?" Maxine licked her lips.

"I see 'em, honey-chile. I knowed as soon as he started workin'. His smell woke me from my sleep."

"Mmm. He makes me *hungry*. He makes me *want* things. *Hot* things we ain't had for some long time now."

Maxine let her hand fall before her and dragged her fingertips up her body. Her eyelids fluttered as the tips brushed her pubic area. Her lace underwear floated over her skin, barely touching her. The outline of her shape was only visible when the fabric blew against her skin from the breeze. Her nipples became even more aroused and the pink lace revealed them risen and erect.

With the sun's glow dimming, and nighttime upon them, they watched Louis swaying slowly in the hammock as he slept.

In a flash Maxine and Mabel swept into Louis' body— becoming one with him.

* * * * *

Louis awoke feeling a nagging pull between his legs. He tried to reach downward but his hands wouldn't move—they were bound above his head. He was a captive in his own fantasy.

He looked down to see two blonde women pulling and jerking at his pants. They had bright blonde hair and were wearing old-fashioned lace undergarments. He struggled to free his hands but to no avail. Looking up he saw the beams of a darkened cellar and his arms bound with straps above his head. He was well and truly trapped.

The two women finally freed his pants and one pulled his cutoffs down along his legs, her nails dragging the soft skin of his inner thigh. Louis stood helpless and scared. But within seconds the fear in him changed to something else.

One blonde woman pulled her long hair to the side and Louis' eyes widened as she slowly drew his cock into her mouth.

Warmth shot through his body as the heat from her mouth made his blood boil. The other blonde had shorter hair but Louis could instantly see they were twins—nasty fucking little twins. Proving conclusively that there was a God and he did answer fantasy prayers.

Louis felt the velvety wetness of her mouth envelop his cock. No struggling to free himself...this was too good to be real. So, as every boy does when a sexy woman is kind enough to suck on his cock, Louis smiled and let her.

The other woman stepped behind him and pressed against his body. Her breasts molded to his back as he stood with arms bound above his head. Her breath brushed the thin hair on his neck as her hands caressed his back. Her fingertips dragged along his ribs and she kissed his shoulder. Louis moaned, falling willingly into the passion of the moment.

"I'm Mabel, an' that's my sister Maxine with your cock in her mouth." The husky voice sent a chill through Louis. "You got two of M'dame Claudine's best gals for yo' pleasure this evenin'."

Mabel lifted one hand up under Louis arm and she flicked her finger over his tight nipple. Maxine began to deep throat his cock, her saliva trickling along the base and onto his balls.

Louis' eyes fluttered. Something was different in this dream. Either the fact that there were two hot women taking him or because it seemed more real than any he'd ever had...he didn't know. It was wild, it was weird and it was pretty fucking wonderful, whatever it was.

Maxine slid down his body, her breasts rubbing his bare back. Soft kisses followed the dip of his spine and with Maxine sucking his cock, Louis was in ecstasy.

With a hard squeeze, Mabel grabbed Louis' ass and bit his hip. "Lordy, Lordy, I'm surely fixin' to enjoy fuckin' this guy. We all gonna have ourselves a private Mardi Gras..."

She released his ass and grabbed Maxine's hand, pulling her mouth from Louis' swollen cock.

The two girls stood together in front of Louis and painstakingly began to undress each other. Their eyes were focused on Louis—his eyes on their bodies. Mabel pushed the thin silken robe off Maxine's shoulders. It fell to the floor on a silent swirl of wind. She had on a corset that pushed her firm pale breasts upward. The pink nipples stood erect, just begging to be suckled. Louis' cock said all that needed to be said. It began to throb with anticipation.

Louis was being seduced with his full cooperation.

A wicked grin on her lips, Maxine turned her sister around to face Louis and stood behind her. Untying the white robe Maxine pulled it back, revealing Mabel's nude body to his appreciative eyes. He raised an eyebrow. *Wow. She's a real blonde.*

Mabel's knowing smile told Louis she was aware of his arousal. Maxine reached around her sister and held her close. Her hands stroked along Mabel's body, grasping her breasts and giving them a friendly squeeze. Mabel had one hand behind her, resting on her sister's leg. With her other hand, she caressed her own pussy.

Louis could only watch and beg with his eyes to be free of his bonds.

Mabel slid a finger into her pussy. Her eyes closed and she swirled it around the slippery entrance to her heavenly box.

Pulling it free, she opened her eyes and moved to Louis. Maxine turned and walked toward the darkness behind her.

Mabel held her glistening finger out just below Louis' nostrils. Breathing in, he could swear his lungs were filled with the fragrance of an angel.

Straining to free himself, he was crazed with lust and it only got worse when Mabel pressed her breasts against Louis' chest. They were warm and her hand lowered to his cock, stroking it slowly with her fingers. A deep moan rumbled through her body and Louis gasped when she squeezed hard.

"Oh sweet sugar man, I'm lookin' forward to this," Mabel groaned and began licking his chest.

She lowered herself before Louis and took over where her sister left off. Her mouth was wet and she sucked hard, drawing his length into her throat. She dropped her hand lower and began playing with her pussy again, moaning around Louis in her mouth.

Louis gulped and looked up to see Maxine's nude body moving nearer, carrying a chair with a high wooden back. She spun it around and sat down, quite ladylike, legs crossed at the ankles with her hand over her pussy. Louis was mesmerized when she spread her legs apart. His mouth watered and his mind raced with mindless excitement as Mabel began to fondle his balls as she sucked him.

When Maxine pulled her hand away from her pussy, Louis saw a shimmer of gold between her legs. She had inserted something into her pussy and the light reflected it just right to make it sparkle.

Maxine was putting on a show for Louis.

Mabel let Louis free and began to caress his legs and kiss him to prolong his excitement and torture.

Louis began to pant. He was so aroused he swore his mind would melt. His mouth hung open as Maxine pulled on the strand of beads she'd inserted into herself. Each bead would spread the opening slightly wider and she would shiver and shake as it closed back. Each bead made her more and more juicy. Her eyes closed, and Louis realized she too was being sensually tortured.

Maxine lured him in. In most dreams he would climb on top of her and fuck her into submission. But something about this fantasy was different. He wasn't the one in control of it— *they* were.

Mabel continued to massage Louis' legs as he stared at Maxine pulling the beads out of her soaked pussy. His arousal couldn't last much longer without him shattering into an explosion of massive proportions.

Maxine pulled the last few beads out with a quick tug, shuddering at the jolt of pleasure shooting through her body. Apparently she was now going to share that pleasure with him.

With hard tugs at the ties binding his wrists, Louis began to get scared. He couldn't free himself and Maxine was coming close with something leather in her hand. It was a long, thin piece of leather, smooth and stiff. She grabbed the chair as she walked toward him. The rumble of the chair's legs across the floor vibrated through him.

"Oh good girl. You brought your toys, *chère*." Mabel stood behind Louis. "My sister loves her toys, honey man. When I was wed, and she'd come to join us in bed, those toys sure did drive my poor husband near to crazy."

A tight black leather glove had materialized on Mabel's hand and she dragged it across Louis' chest. There was something sharp in each fingertip that scratched his chest.

His salty sweat seeped into the small wounds. "*Shit*, that burns..." Louis sucked in a breath between his clenched teeth.

Mabel reached down and grabbed his cock with the glove. It jerked to attention and Louis held his breath knowing that in that instant Mabel had complete control.

Maxine stood in front of Louis and licked her red lips, obviously craving his cock, staring as it protruded toward her. Louis could see that her pussy was extremely wet, her body primed and ready for sex. "Mmm. I want to fuck *so* bad." Her mouth uttered the words Louis wanted to hear.

Maxine handed the leather stick to Mabel, pushed the chair in front of Louis and turned it so the seat faced him. Her eyes looked approvingly over his body, stopping at the glisten of anticipation on the head of his cock. Leaning overand placing one hand on the chair for balance, Maxine flicked her tongue across the swollen head. Louis groaned as his cock throbbed with desire.

Then she turned around and pressed her back against his chest, molding into his frame. They were a perfect fit. The aroma of lust filled the air. Louis watched as Maxine knelt on the seat, positioning herself so that her smoldering pussy was only inches away from the head of his cock.

A swift, excruciating pain sliced through Louis. Mabel had slapped him low on his buttocks with the leather stick.

"Can't you see? She's offering herself to you. Look at that sweet pussy, begging you to fuck it. Now do as she asks." Mabel reached her arm back and swung the stick again, sending a shooting jolt of pain through his spine.

Louis' arms were aching from holding his body up for so long and he didn't need any more pain. "You fuckin' bitch, that *hurts*."

Mabel stepped closer and smacked Louis across the cheek with the black glove. "Nobody calls me a bitch.

Nobody." She wrinkled her nose. "What's wrong, honey? Too much for you?"

Moving purposefully behind Louis, Mabel reached her hand around him, grabbing his cock. She pointed the head downward directly at Maxine's eager cunt and moved her hand, pulling up and down on his shaft.

Louis could see his cock diving between Maxine's pussy lips. He wanted to sink into her so badly, he whimpered. "Oh, God. Let me fuck her. Come on, please—I'm sorry for what I said. I can't handle much more of this." He couldn't awaken from his dream, and wouldn't have even if given the chance. He was in tortured ecstasy.

Maxine's head turned toward him and he desperately shook the sweat from his face. She leaned her ass back and sighed—a joyful sound that matched what Louis was feeling—the thickness of his cock sinking within her walls. Walls that hugged him and clenched at him as Maxine experimented with her inner muscles.

Louis moaned feeling the tightness surround his cock with velvety smoothness. He pulled his ass back, letting his cock glide back out of Maxine's pussy.

Mabel reached her arm back and struck his ass again, making him grit his teeth. He knew what she wanted now—to dictate the sex between them. Obediently, he sank his cock back into Maxine.

Maxine's hair hung down, covering her face. Even though her expressions were hidden, her body language made it clear that her only concern was the man behind her plunging his firm, thick cock into her awaiting pussy. She reached one hand between her legs and began to massage her clit. The juices from her excitement coated Louis' cock and dripped from her pussy.

Each time Louis pulled back, Mabel would smack his ass with the stick, silently telling him to fuck Maxine harder and faster. Mabel was fingering her pussy as she watched Louis fuck her sister. He risked a glance at her and saw her pleasure as she released her own frustrations.

Louis began to pant and gasp. He couldn't hold back the oncoming urge to let loose. He was being whipped by one naked woman and fucking another. Everything a man craved was being fulfilled.

Maxine spoke with a low growl. "Oh, I'm gonna come. I'm so close. Just a few more strokes—"

Mabel knelt beside them slipping the leather toy between her own legs. Louis pulled back and as she furiously fucked herself, she reached up for Louis' cock, searching beneath it for his balls. Her fingers found him and she moaned—a sound of need and craving.

Maxine wiggled her ass, an invitation for Louis to return.

Mabel fondled his balls, nuzzling them and licking them.

Louis swore she could've swallowed them if she'd tried any harder.

Finally, she released his sac and pushed him back into Maxine. "Fuck—Maxine he's gonna come. Fuck him, *chère*. Fuck him *dry*. Take it all, girl."

Louis began to hammer back into Maxine. The boards above him creaked in protest against his powerful tugs as he fought to swing hard against Maxine's ass.

Mabel crawled behind Louis once more and raked his legs with the black glove. Louis leaned back and as he did so Mabel slid something between his ass cheeks and into his anus. It was slick and warm and he realized it was the leather stick.

Louis locked his muscles. He gasped and began to shiver. Violated by the stick, the rush of excitement to his cock made him swear the engorged head would blow off any second now. With a loud groan, Louis looked skyward.

Maxine began to shake and the inner walls of her pussy convulsed against Louis' hard cock. His heart pounded hard and fast in his chest. Teeth clenched, trying to prolong his release, Louis lost the battle. With a long, plunging thrust he let go. His seed gushed from his tightened balls, the spasms continuing for what seemed like an eternity.

Lost deep in his orgasm, he cried out and woke himself up.

"By God, boy. Dat must've been a good 'un." A cackle of laughter sounded right next to his ear.

Louis was disoriented, still shuddering from his climax and startled out of his wits. He jumped, forgetting he was in a hammock. It swiveled and spun, reacting to his jerky movements, and promptly dumped him upside down on the hardwood porch floor.

"Fucking *son of a...*" He winced and shook tears of pain from his eyes as his head met wood with a solid thunk.

"You all right, boy?"

A wizened face peered beneath the limp hammock, staring interestedly at him. Bright eyes creased into a grin and two teeth shone brightly in the dark face smiling at him. "You done hit dat head of yours one God almighty crack."

"No shit." Louis closed his eyes for a moment and checked his skull for blood.

"Don' be a baby. You'll live. Git your ass out from under dere and lemme look at you." The old woman straightened up with a grunt. She had something very colorful wrapped all over her in bits and pieces, held together with odd sparkling pins and jewelry. Even in the twilight she looked like an odd little blackbird dressed up for a night on the town.

"So you de new owner. *Monsewer Louieeee.*"

"Louis. Louis Beekman. And you are?" Louis tried to be polite. It wasn't easy since his vision was still a bit blurred from the incident with the hammock and the floor, not to mention one hellaciously fine orgasm and a pair of cutoffs that felt like they were lined with liquid detergent.

"Damn impressed, boy. You one mighty fine looker all right. No wonder Claudine's gals got to you." She laughed, proudly showing those two shiny teeth. Louis wondered if she had any more at home.

Then what she'd just said sank into his muddled brains. "Wait a minute here." His skin chilled in spite of the humid evening air. "*Claudine's gals*? I mean… *girls*?"

"Sho' nuf, sweet thing. Dey always did have an eye for de hard ones." Her eyes dropped to his lap where he was trying to nonchalantly hide a damp patch of denim. "An' dey always knew how to get him off, too."

Louis took a breath. This was freaking him out. Big-time. "Okay. Who the hell are you? And how do you know who was in my dream?"

The woman turned away. "I'm Zulee. Ever'body knows ol' crazy Zulee. Don' pay me no mind, boy." She walked toward the steps. "I'll be 'round some."

"Er, okay. Well. Nice to meet you, Zulee. But aren't you gonna tell me how…"

She stopped him with a movement of her hand. It was the oddest thing. For a brief moment she seemed taller and younger and Louis' voice died in his throat. Then she cackled again and he blinked, seeing only the old woman in the wild clothes. "Here, young 'un." She tossed something toward him. "When you ready, you call. She come. You need her, but you don' know it yet."

The floor creaked slightly under her bare feet as she left the porch and headed into the growing shadows of the Alley. "You don' know it *yet*—but you *will*."

Louis sighed. This was one damn weird load of shit. If he didn't know better, he'd think he was still dreaming. But there were no blondes anywhere, naked or otherwise, and his head was starting to ache where he'd hit it on the floor.

His shorts were beginning to stick to him in uncomfortably personal places and his stomach rumbled reminding him that soda was no substitute for solid food. He stood awkwardly and something fluttered to the floor.

He picked it up and carried it inside where he turned on one of the lights in the kitchen.

It was a business card. *"Cory Lavalle. Experienced Psychic Consultant. Discretion assured, results guaranteed."* The announcement was followed by a telephone number, New Orleans by the looks of it, and an address that was unfamiliar to Louis.

He snorted. Like a hot dream about two blonde babes was gonna freak him out. He'd been working too hard, was probably low on electrolytes with all the humidity and the sweating he was doing, and frickin' horny as hell.

Plus he was working in a place that used to be a whorehouse. It wasn't surprising he was experiencing some crazy sex fantasies. If he could get enough juice wired in for a halfway decent air conditioner, all this crap would probably evaporate along with the heat.

Louis shrugged and stuck the card up on the wall next to the cable company number and the utilities listings. He probably wouldn't use it, but it was polite to at least *keep* the damn thing. Plus that creepy old woman might come back, and she looked like just the type who'd check to see if he'd still got it.

As he locked up the house later that night, he realized he was completely exhausted from a day that had been a roller-coaster ride of sex and craziness. It certainly wasn't what he was used to, but would he have changed things if he could?

He looked around him as he switched off the lights and headed up the stairs to his makeshift bedroom.

Hell, no.

Chapter Six

ഔ

Within a few short days, Louis was starting to rethink his optimistic attitude about Love Alley and everything that went along with it.

"Fucking piece of goddamned — lousy worthless — motherfucking son of a — " The oaths flew fast and furious from his mouth as yet another power tool refused to work. First his circular saw had quit on him, chewing through wood rather than making a neat slice. He'd been reduced to his trusty old handsaw, which fortunately required no power other than that within his shoulders.

Which got sore pretty damn quick.

His chop saw had followed, along with any number of the modern gizmos that he'd had shipped to Love Alley for the renovation project. The power wasn't solely to blame, either, although he'd already ordered enough replacement fuses to power half of New Orleans, and used up nearly all of 'em.

They blew out on a regular basis whenever he plugged in anything resembling a useful piece of equipment. Sometimes they blew out when the little fridge clicked on, and sometimes they blew out just for the hell of it.

He'd managed to get his "bedroom" — for want of a better word — into almost habitable condition, and there were now mesh screens over the tall windows. He was hoping they would allow him a night's rest undisturbed by mosquitoes. The shutters had been repaired, so in the event of a bad storm, he could protect what little furniture he had.

In a fit of energy, he'd broken through a wall from his room to the bathroom next door, so he had the beginnings of a master suite well underway. They would have been even more well underway if his frickin' tools had worked.

Louis sighed as the eighth drill bit snapped like chalk. Sure, this old cedar was hard wood. It had to be to withstand Louisiana weather. But shit, it was like goddamned iron sometimes. He was working on a lovely piece of molding he'd found dumped in an empty room. Miraculously it was unbroken and he was attempting to place it over where the bed would be.

He reached into his tool belt and pulled out his trusty standby—a very basic screwdriver and a couple of wood screws. Perhaps there was enough of a starter hole pre-drilled…

He held the molding in place and spent a moment or two lost in admiration of whoever had painstakingly carved the acanthus leaves and dogwoods that intertwined throughout the heavy decoration. "Shit. You're a beauty all right." He shoved a screw between his lips, put the other one where he'd tried to drill a hole and started tightening it.

Apparently the gods of carpentry approved. The screws sank silently home and the piece graced the wall above where his bed would eventually stand.

"Perfect, chèr. Quite lovely."

"It is, isn't it? Nothing like a good screw to…" Louis automatically turned around to answer the comment that had echoed the exact thought in his brain.

There was nobody there.

"Jesus H. I am losing my mind, that's for sure." Louis shook his head and moved on to his next chore. Bad enough that he was struggling every day with annoying problems— he didn't need to start hearing voices on top of it.

A thunderstorm the following afternoon revealed two places where the roof leaked. No real surprise, but something Louis could have done without. One leak was in the center of the living room, the other above his bed. A wet night that turned his mattress into a sponge.

He really could have done without a toolbox that seemed to prefer the porch.

He damn well *knew* he'd taken the thing into the kitchen, but when he looked for it later, was it there? *Noooo.* It was out on the fucking *porch*. The tools stayed with him, but the box? It was like it had other ideas.

Louis couldn't help but notice the whole frickin' house seemed to have its own ideas. If he found something that clearly belonged to a certain room it would refuse to be installed anywhere but where the house wanted it—in that certain room. This wasn't a bad thing, since Louis was doing his best to restore the original beauty to this charming old lady.

But it could be fucking annoying at times.

The weather was unpredictable but hot. Always hot. Lung-strangling, soakingly humid and hot. Louis got used to sticking a few of his T-shirts in a bucket of cool water and then slipping them on during the day to keep his body temperature semi-stable, but even this didn't work on the worst days.

That's when he was forced into less physical pursuits, like going through some of the ancient chests that had lain untouched in a storage area under the eaves. He'd rescued them from an imminent soaking and tugged them to a dry area, eventually bringing one or two downstairs where it was cooler and he could spend a restful hour or so checking them out.

The first two were full of junk, and mostly unusable junk at that. There was a pot and a couple of spoons that might be of interest to local historians, and some faded and stained pieces of fabric. Used to saving things for historical society types, Louis already had a neat pile of artifacts that would go to the local authorities if they wanted any of them.

He enjoyed touching the past like this, but every time he did that annoying itch came back and several times he actually glanced over his shoulder. He just *knew* somebody was watching — but as always there was nobody there.

Louis was a practical man. He loved working with his hands and building things. He had little time for fairy tales, had never read a ghost story and if anybody had asked him he'd probably have dismissed the whole idea of the psychic world as something that was directly related to the quality of the bourbon a person was drinking at the time. But as the days lingered on and his problems compounded themselves, he was forced to rethink that assessment.

And he didn't like it one little bit.

The last straw came unexpectedly when he was enjoying a quiet read of *Architect's Weekly* in his bathroom. Being a male, and in full possession of the "don't bother to change the roll until it's empty" gene, he reached for the toilet paper only to discover that yes, it was indeed, empty.

He sighed. His supplies were on the other side of the bathroom next to the almost-ready claw-footed tub he was plumbing in.

Folding his magazine he was about to do the only thing he could do, when a voice sounded in the silence. "*Here you go, chèr.*" A fresh roll of toilet paper toppled from the stack and quietly tumbled over itself to come to rest at Louis' feet.

It could've been the wind.

It could've been a small earthquake.

It could've been some enormous barge causing a wake on the river that traveled up into the bayou.

Louis knew, with a horrible certainty, that it wasn't any of these things.

"*Oh fuck.*" With trembling hands, Louis finished up his bathroom business and rushed downstairs to the kitchen. Yep—it was still there. The card with that psychic's number on it.

He stared at it, not knowing who else to call, or what else to do. Explaining that he had a haunted bathroom with self-delivering toilet paper wasn't gonna cut it with any city agency he could think of.

His cell phone was on the counter and he reached for it, turning it on. There was barely enough power for a signal, but Louis figured he should be able to get one call out before recharging it. He dialed the psychic's number.

"*Hi. You've reached my answering machine. I'm a damn good psychic, but even I can't tell why you're calling—you'll have to do that. Leave the usual stuff, and I'll get back to you? Thanks.*"

It was a warm voice, accented a little with the Southern softness that Louis found so seductive when spoken by a woman. And this woman did it really well. He took a breath and waited for the beep.

"Hello. Damn, I hate these machines. My name is Louis and I got your number from—um—er—well, this woman gave me your card and said I'd need you. And I do. Need you that is." He winced. *God, I'm sounding really fucking stupid here.* "Look, I don't know if I believe in this stuff, but there's some really weird things happening and I guess I didn't know who else to call."

Well, that's real gracious, asshole. She'll come running out here when she hears that.

"Sorry. I didn't mean to sound stupid. Anyway, I live at a place called Love Alley and my phone number—well, I'll have to leave my cell phone number since I don't have a working landline yet. Can you call me please? Thanks." Louis left his number and closed his phone.

He shrugged as he plugged his charger into one of the outlets that actually worked. The woman was probably a nutcase anyway. She'd have to be if that Zulee recommended her. Talk about freaky. Determinedly, he dismissed his lingering concerns about rolls of toilet paper that moved around of their own accord, wild-eyed old women who made jokes about his sex life and all the craziness.

He had a house to renovate. His house.

He went to find his chisel and his tape measure.

Once again, his toolbox wasn't where he'd left it. Louis sighed. He knew exactly where it was.

On the fucking *porch*.

And as he reached it, the final fuse blew out, taking his cell phone charger with it.

* * * * *

Cory noticed the blinking red light on her answering machine as soon as she got home that night. It had been a long, fruitless day, and she'd been reduced to bagging clothes and cleaning out the fitting rooms for Eileen in an effort to stay awake.

Apparently the denizens of the "otherworld" were quiet, and not a darn soul needed a psychic consultation. Which sucked for Cory's business.

Perhaps the message would be good news. Like she'd won a gazillion dollars in some lottery she'd never entered. She giggled at herself and hit the "play" button.

"Hello. Damn, I hate these machines. My name is Louis and I got your number from..."

Cory staggered as an odd heat crashed into her body like a physical collision with something resembling a brick wall. Her guts churned and she literally panted, trying to get air into her lungs.

What the fuck?

The message had ended, so she rewound it and tried to listen to it again, holding on to the doorjamb this time in case the earthquake or whatever it was hit her once more.

It didn't. This time the message played through and she was calm enough to be able to jot down his phone number.

But two words rang loudly in her ears. *Love Alley.*

She'd been there once when she was a child with her mother. She barely remembered it, but knew of course that there was family history there. Her mother had been more impressed with the visit than Cory had, and all she recalled was a lot of really big trees and the sweet pecans she'd bought to bring home. They'd stuck together in the bag.

She grinned at the childhood memory.

So apparently Love Alley had an owner who needed her help. And he had her business card, too. That was odd. Cory kicked off her shoes and wandered around her apartment, doing routine things, all the while turning over the thought of Love Alley in her mind.

Finally, she poured herself a well-deserved mint julep and settled in her favorite chair with an old photo album her aunt had given her a while ago. Perhaps there were some photos of Love Alley in it.

She wasn't convinced that going out there was the best thing, although God knew she needed the job. Cory was a firm believer in letting her psychic skills help her make decisions since they seldom steered her wrong. And how better to stimulate them than by looking at pictures of Love Alley? The reaction that guy's voice had caused was certainly out of the ordinary, but it could be just the effects of being overtired and stressed.

The mint julep soothed and cooled her, and she casually thumbed through the well-worn album, smiling at the old-fashioned black and white photos of people dressed in clothes that Eileen would probably love to get her hands on. Talk about retro styles.

Some were relatives she knew, others were strangers. All seemed happy to smile at the camera, although there were a few grumpy children who looked less than thrilled at the whole thing.

She turned a page and stopped short. Her fingertips tingled and the hairs on her arms stood up. Her mother was smiling at her, relaxed and leaning up against a porch railing.

Cory knew, with a rock-solid certainty, that this picture was taken at Love Alley. The pleasure-pain of seeing her mom's face would have given her pause. She still missed her every day and probably always would. But it was more than grief at the loss of a parent.

This was a shiver of the psyche, a ripple in that place that only Cory could see and feel. She closed her eyes for a moment or two, trying to nail down the source of this odd sensation. As was her habit, she "unclicked" the real world, separating herself from it in a maneuver that was as natural to her as scratching an itch would be to everyone else. Disconnected from outside distractions, she could focus her psychic talents and "see".

There was nothing to see, however. Not this time. Just the vague grey mists of another place out of any known dimensions and the glitter of mystic images too faint to identify. Frustrated, Cory prepared to drop back into reality.

But before she could, a voice spoke quite clearly to her.

[I need you there, chère. It's a matter of family honor. Our family. Don't fail me? Don't fail us?]

Cory gulped back a sound of surprise. Hearing voices wasn't something she was used to, being a very visual psychic most of the time. This voice wasn't messing around. It was clear, female, slightly accented—European maybe or French—and the urgent note of pleading could not be denied.

She opened her eyes, fighting for balance, for that comforting feeling of having her mental feet back on the ground. The picture on her lap swam into focus and for an instant in time there was a face behind her mother's shoulder. A beautiful woman, hair dark and coiled in a very old-fashioned style.

But what caught Cory's attention was the woman's eyes. Brilliant green, they shone with life and the fire of passion. Then the image was gone, the photo normal and Cory's senses settled back into their customary places.

Well, fucking hell.

She sat there, stunned, staring at the perfectly ordinary photograph, and seeing nothing at all. Her brain seethed, struggling to adapt to the new information and process it into something usable.

One thing was clear. She *had* to go to Love Alley. There was no question in her mind, and the sooner the better. Her confusion was turning into an itch—a drive to be there, to go *now*. It was a compulsion she knew well, a focus of her psychic senses on something important, something large and something that absolutely positively had to be followed through to its conclusion.

She picked up her phone and dialed the number that Louis, whoever he was, had left. She got his voice mail. Stupid idiot had probably turned off his cell phone. Politely, Cory left her name and number along with her declared intention of stopping by Love Alley at her earliest opportunity. She mentioned the following afternoon, ending by saying that if she didn't hear to the contrary, she'd assume that time was acceptable.

Her psychic nerves were quiet now, no disturbances ratcheted up her stress levels. In fact, she felt rather relaxed — as if a weight had been lifted from her shoulders.

It was very evident that going to Love Alley was the right thing to do, and she spared a moment as she got ready for bed to wonder why she hadn't been back there for so long. She knew it had fallen into disrepair, information like this being passed around like desserts at holiday gatherings. But recently she couldn't recall much of anything being said about the current owner, or anybody named Louis.

He sounded okay. Not from Louisiana, that was for sure. *And how the hell did he get my card?*

That was a question that would have to wait until she met the man himself on the following day. With all the excitement of a child on Christmas Eve, Cory snuggled into her bed. This was going to be an adventure and one that involved her family.

Two things guaranteed to bring a smile to her face. The smile was still there as she fell asleep.

Chapter Seven

∞

Unaware that there was another woman planning a trip to Love Alley that same day, Honey Treadwell slid into her bikini and mentally girded her loins. She had some serious damage control to do, and a rather embarrassing exit to *undo*. Plus there was one helluva hottie just waitin' for a fuckin'.

And she aimed to be the fuck*ee*. Or fuck*er*. *Whatever*.

She just wanted a piece of that sex on the hoof known as Louis the luscious. So what if her dreams had been plagued by the vision of a scarred face with hands that knew how to tweak her nipples? It was simply because she was horny.

She was always horny, of course, but this was…well, it was probably something to do with the alignment of the planets. She just knew she was hot to trot and trotting would be one delicious pleasure with her new neighbor.

Lascivious thoughts brought the heat to her pussy as she hopped into her pirogue and began poling down the familiar bayou waters. She'd slicked enough body lotion on her to grease a herd of pigs, topped it with a dab of suntan lotion so that she wouldn't get tan lines or—God forbid—*wrinkles*, and touched her breasts with her favorite perfume.

It was still early enough that the mosquitoes and bugs wouldn't be a problem and she had no intention of returning until daylight tomorrow. Mr. Nice Body was in for a long hard ride tonight, and no mistake about it. Her bikini bottom rubbed softly against her mound and she smiled as the heat rose through her cunt.

Oh yeah, baby. We're cookin' now.

The heat shimmered through the low hanging foliage, a caress of moisture that added to the sensual arousal flooding Honey. The dabs of fabric that masqueraded as a bikini seemed to abrade her breasts, making her nipples sensitive and hard beneath the silky stuff.

She couldn't help but remember the feel of that...that *thing,* that wild and crazy moment when she'd fought off the urge to scream and come like gangbusters. That face, harsh and ugly and...and sexy.

Yeah, okay. Sexy in a horrible rough sort of way. The corset thing, too, tight and constricting and exciting. Lulled by the heat and the rhythmic swish of the waters, Honey let her mind drift along with the slow current, wondering what it would be like to lie in the bed of a man like that.

Thinking about Louis had gotten her aroused. Thinking about *him,* scars and all, got her shivering and wet—aching almost—and needy in a way she wasn't quite sure she liked. She had no idea what the fuck had happened in Louis' bedroom, or what she'd seen in that mirror. It sure as hell wasn't her.

But the things she'd felt—the things those hands had done with just a fondle and a pinch—*fuck.* If it had been a real moment, instead of a heat-induced hallucination of some sort, Honey knew she'd have been on her back with her legs spread in no time flat. And from that point on, she had a sneaking feeling there would have been no limits to what that man demanded.

And no limits on what she would have surrendered.

Her thighs grew clammy as her juices soaked her bikini and dampened her skin. She was more than ready to take on Louis. He'd do just as well.

At least she told herself so. His jetty was in sight now, and she brushed away the thought that he probably wouldn't be as good as her imaginary villain. Louis was real. So was his cock. That was all that counted today.

That was all she wanted. A good fuck.

* * * * *

If he'd thought about it, Louis would probably have said a good fuck was pretty high on his list of things to do as well. But since he was knee-deep in sanding the bottom of a couple of doors and trying to get them the same dimensions, the issue hadn't actually crossed his mind for a couple of hours.

Until he saw Honey. And wondered why she'd plastered some black electrical tape over her breasts and pussy.

After he'd blinked away the sawdust, he realized she was wearing something that could have passed for a bikini or a couple of pot holders. Whatever it was, it didn't look too secure.

Her breasts were glowing and all but popping out to say hello, her nipples hard buds revealed by the clingy top. The rest of her was mostly naked, with just one small black triangle modestly hiding her pussy. A part of his mind spared a nod of awe to the engineering principles that kept the thing in place. The rest of his mind just stood there and drooled.

This probably wasn't a neighborly call to borrow a cup of mint julep. This was a flat-out "*I'm here to do you*" visit. There was no mistaking it.

Louis swallowed awkwardly, not quite knowing where to look other than at her crotch or her breasts. "Uh…hi."

She smiled sweetly. "Well, hi yourself, darlin'. I figured I surely oughta come over heah and tell y'all how sorry I am for running out on you like I did." She batted her eyelashes and walked closer, reaching out and brushing a drop of sweat off his chest with a fingertip.

"You just got me so excited I din' know if I was comin' or goin'…" She paused and giggled. "I think it was closer to comin' if you get my meanin'."

She wiggled her hips just in case Louis hadn't got her meaning. He had.

"Anyhoo, in spite of that, I'm heah now. I'm sure hopin' we can kinda pick up where we left off. Gettin' to know each other, that is." She lifted her fingertips to her lips and licked off the bead of his sweat. "Mmm. Bayou sweet, *chèr*."

Louis' throat moved as he swallowed again. He knew by this point he should be as hard as a rock and ready to rip off that tiny bit of nonsense prior to fucking Honey Treadwell long and hard.

Which was clearly just what she wanted.

But something was interfering with the natural order of things and his cock barely managed an interested twitch. He would have started to tremble at that if he hadn't been holding a heavy door steady with one hand and his planer in the other. His very sharp planer. Perhaps it was the distraction of his tools that was damping down the hormones.

It certainly couldn't be this sexy curvaceous blonde in the itty-bitty black bikini.

Could it?

Carefully, Louis put down his planer and tugged another sawhorse beneath the door to steady it. Then he turned to see that Honey was headed inside the house where it was a little cooler. The black strip of fabric that separated her smooth buttocks danced from side to side as she walked, and made Louis sweat some more.

But still didn't get anywhere near as aroused as he would have expected.

He followed her into the shade of the large hall, glad the portable fan he'd bought was still circulating some air. Perhaps he had one stable electrical circuit at last. The whirr of the blades was a quiet accompaniment to the lazy hum of crickets and he had no problem hearing Honey call him. "Louis, *chèr*, c'mere…"

He found her in a small room staring at an old and darkened painting. "You know who this is?" She pointed at the scarred face.

"Er…no?" He leaned over her shoulder. "There's a caption here…" He rubbed a bit of grime off the small plaque. "M. Jean Argent, 1804. Whoever that was."

"I can see that." Honey's voice was sharp and had lost a little of its Southern drawl. "I need to know who he is."

"It's '*was*', Honey. Judging from his clothes and the age of the frame, he's got to have been painted a couple of hundred years ago, maybe." Louis stroked the wood surrounding the painting. "This is original. Hand-carved. The detail puts it definitely in the late seventeen hundreds, maybe early eighteens. That would be my best guess. I'm no expert on the art, just the woodwork."

With a visible effort, Honey turned away from the painting and faced Louis, the heat from her body brushing his. "Well, never mind him." She licked her lips. "Although he seems like someone who could give a woman what she needed…"

Louis looked at the man's face, noting the raggedly cut hair, and the scar that creased a full lower lip. "You think so?"

"Mmm hmm." Honey brushed her fingertips up Louis' biceps. "It would be nice to have a man like that around." The fingertip went back down and then came back up again to trace his pectoral muscle. "You look like that sort of man, too, Louis." This time the fingertip found his nipple and played with it.

"I do?" *I don't have any scars on my lips.* Louis gulped, uncomfortable now, and not from the fit of his shorts, but from a desire to retreat from that persistent finger before it slid downwards and stripped him naked.

"Yeah, you do, sugar." The accent was back. "You look like a man who's got what it takes to make a woman scream and get all crazy, you know?"

Sure enough, the finger was moving lower, tracing the line down his chest toward his belt. "Uhh...well..."

Louis took a step backwards but she followed him like a well-trained dance partner. "Don't be all modest 'bout it, *chèr*. You're a real man and I'm a real woman. We could have fun exploring..." The finger found his navel and toyed with it. "...the..." It dipped beneath his waistband and popped the snap securing it. "...possibilities..."

Louis grabbed her wrist before she could discover he wasn't wearing anything under his shorts but his skin. He had a bad feeling that a guy going commando was an open invitation to assault from this Southern belle.

And he *so* didn't want to be assaulted. Perhaps the heat had sapped all his testosterone. Perhaps he was coming down with a cold. Whatever it was, he knew without question that he just wasn't interested in fucking Honey Treadwell.

Since she had the opposite goal, this was going to be one interesting piece of fancy footwork.

Louis moved to the right, Honey followed.

He stepped to the left, she mimicked his actions, and smiled. The moonwalk move crossed his mind but he'd left his dancing shoes somewhere else.

He turned away and she rubbed her breasts over his back. "C'mon, Louis *chèr*. Let's go upstairs and get naked. You know I wanna fuck you. You wanna fuck me too. It's all part of the natural way down here in the bayou." Her hands slid around his waist and back down beneath the waistband of his shorts.

It tickled and Louis jumped, freeing himself again. "Uh…look Honey, I don't really…er, we haven't…"

She chuckled. "What? We haven't been formally introduced?" She reached to her neck and untied the thin strand of black silk. The top sagged down revealing her breasts, nipples hard and erect at their peaks.

"Here. Louis, meet my tits. Girls, this is Louis. He's gonna put those lovely lips of his on you and suck you and make us *all* real happy." She pushed her chest out.

Oh look — twins! was his first thought. His next was to run screaming from the room, which really wasn't an option.

He jumped a foot in the air when a loud knocking echoed through the house and offered up a prayer of thankfulness as Honey quickly retied her bikini. Whoever was at the front door, he didn't care. They'd obviously come straight from his guardian angel, and he intended to make sure that they stayed.

Somebody had to protect him from Honey Treadwell.

* * * * *

The house lured Cory with a strange siren song, which resounded deep in her gut and made her palms itch. She paused on the alley, standing in the shade provided by the old trees and staring at a masterpiece of eighteenth century architecture.

For a few moments the air stilled, the birds fell quiet and even the bees stopped buzzing. The odd silence made Cory uneasy in that unique way that only she possessed — she was about to catch a glimpse of *something*. A look past a curtain that was never meant to be lifted. A glimpse at something yet to come or some other thing long passed.

A soft breath of air crossed the alley and suddenly Cory could see the house as it had once been, complete with carriages, horses and people coming and going.

The lamps were being lit and a shriek of laughter came from an open upstairs window. It was promptly followed by a mostly naked woman running out of one of the sets of French doors onto the balcony that ringed the second floor. After her came a totally naked man with outstretched arms, who pursued his prey around the corner of the house, his cock a light shadow bobbing against the darkness of his pubic hair.

Cory was scared to move — to *breathe* — lest she break the spell that held her transfixed at the threshold of this passageway back through time. She knew quite well what she was seeing. She needed no guidebook or historical document to tell her that this was Love Alley in its glory days — a whorehouse of parish-wide renown.

As Cory watched, the rattle of a carriage crunched down the gravel driveway and stopped in front of the grand entrance. It disgorged four or five well-dressed gentlemen, laughing and removing their jackets as they mounted the steps to the porch.

The large double doors were thrown open and Cory's mouth dropped as a woman moved through them, arms lifted in welcome. Even from this distance, Cory could see the glitter of amazing emerald green eyes.

"*Bonsoir, Messieurs. Entrez-vous.* Welcome to Love *Allée.*"

Rich and velvety, her voice reached Cory along with a wave of nausea. It was the voice she'd heard not so long ago, and it took her off guard with its warmth and its familiarity.

Lightheaded, she staggered, catching her balance on the hard bark of an old tree. The rough surface scratched her hand, and as her eyes watered, the air shimmered and the vision disappeared as rapidly as it had appeared.

Cory sagged against the trunk. That was one helluva thing.

Moments like this drained her, caught her off guard and reminded her of her gift. They were seldom as detailed or as vivid as this one had been though. It was as if the past had deliberately waited, sharpening its edges, purifying its colors—just waiting for Cory to set foot on Love Alley ground.

The house had poured itself into those few brief moments, as alive and as real as anything Cory could have reached out and touched. She would never be able to look at it again without remembering that vision.

It took a lot of courage for her to continue her stroll down the alley of trees toward the front door. She almost checked for carriages as she crossed the drive, paved now though, and with a few weeds poking up here and there.

The shrubs—neatly groomed mounds of flowers back then—were now huge and shaggy tumbles of dying branches. Cory wanted to grab a trimmer and shape them, return them to the spectacular glory she recalled from her mental images.

As the wood squeaked beneath her feet she realized there were other things that needed some restoration. But...time had passed and taken its toll. No one knew that better than Cory.

She reached out and picked up the heavy wrought iron door knocker, letting it fall back with a loud clang.

The door swung open almost immediately, and Cory found herself face-to-face with one of the best-looking men she'd seen in quite some time. Longish dark hair brushed his shoulders, and he wore nothing more than a rather snug pair of well-worn cutoffs with an open waistband. She didn't get chance to check out much else though, since as soon as he laid eyes on her he silently mouthed the word "help" and took her in his arms.

"What's your name?" He hissed the question under his breath.

"Er...Cory." She had to think for a minute.

"*Cory...sweetheart*...I can't believe you're here. At last. I've missed you so much." He pulled her close, an intriguing fragrance of man and sawdust encompassing her. Out of the corner of her eye, she noticed a blonde almost wearing a bikini and staring at them with her mouth open. Cory had little time to evaluate the situation, however, since a firm hand slipped to her chin and turned her face upwards. "I don't think I could've lasted another day without my fiancée at my side."

Stunned, Cory stood there as this lovely man proceeded to kiss the crap out of her.

There was no delicate foreplay...this was an *open-your-mouth-and-get-ready-to-fuck* type kiss. Tongues twined, interplaying with a suddenly dexterous skill that astounded Cory. He tasted of sweet man and tart lemonade with a hint of toothpaste, a seductively unique flavor.

She found herself breathless, not so much from the unexpected assault on her lips as from the sensation of rising desire that billowed up from her toenails to her eyebrows and swamped her with a passionate heat the likes of which she'd never envisioned in her wildest sexual fantasies.

Her brain swirled and shut down conscious thought, leaving her adrift in a sea of visions that mostly involved her and him and a lot of naked skin.

She felt her hands move over his arms to his shoulders and his neck, fingers digging into his muscles and finally twining through his damp hair. He groaned a little, deep in his throat, a sound that was echoed within Cory. She pressed herself against him, as his hold on her tightened.

They were flame to kindling, cock to pussy. Superheating, approaching-the-red-line, pussy. If this went on for one minute more, Cory was going to forcibly strip him and fuck him right there with the front door open and the sun shining on them, mosquitoes be damned.

As her wits gathered up their panties from the floor of her mind, Cory realized that she was in the arms of the new owner of Love Alley. The man who had requested her help.

Before she succumbed once more to the lure of his kiss, she realized something else too.

He had unusual eyes. One was blue and the other was grey.

Chapter Eight

2∽

Honey was enraged.

Here she was all dressed up, or barely dressed, with nobody to fuck. With a snide glare she looked at Cory. "*Fiancée*? As in getting-married-type *fiancée*?" She put her hands on her hips and frowned at them.

The frown grew deeper as Cory struggled to drag her gaze away from Louis. "Um, yes. I was...away on a trip and just got back." Her voice was soft and within seconds she was back staring into Louis' eyes. He hadn't looked away from her face, a dreamy expression curving his lips. Honey pouted as Cory reached back up and kissed him again. This time it was her move, not his.

Louis and Cory ended their kiss but stayed locked together in their own private world, which completely excluded Honey. She could almost see the connection between them, something magical and mystical.

"I know you. I remember those eyes." Cory caught her breath and shivered.

Honey sneered. "I should hope so. At least *I* managed to remember the eyes of the guys I married." She was totally furious. There was no way she would be brushed aside again. *That's twice by the same man in a week.* She'd showed him all her goodies and he didn't even want a taste. This was totally unacceptable and the absolute last straw. *I am so out of here.*

Without a look at either Cory or Louis, Honey stalked past them and marched out the door. She turned back to mouth a Southern version of *fuck you*, when her foot slammed into a toolbox on the porch. Honey fell forward and collided with a man walking up the steps.

With a grunt and a thud they both tumbled onto the grass in a heap.

Honey ended up on top of the man, rubbing the bump on her head she'd gotten from hitting the dirt. A vibration echoed against her body as she pushed herself up. The man's face was snugly resting under her naked breasts. Her insubstantial top had twisted as she fell giving the man full access to her large, not-quite-natural assets. He was definitely getting an eyeful—and a mouthful.

Honey straddled him, sitting up and quickly pulling her bikini top back into place over her bare breasts.

"Don't cover those beauties up on my account. I was just thinking I suddenly had a craving for milk." It was a deep voice and tickled her ass as it reverberated through his chest and into Honey.

"Ah'm sooo sorry, *chèr*..." Honey began to move and looked at the man's face. A beard covered his chin but when Honey saw the look in his eyes, she began to stammer and forgot all about her bayou drawl. "Oh my God, *you*—you...you're the man in that picture...the one I saw in the mirror...*oh my God.*"

Honey was almost beside herself with shock as her entire being became hot and aroused. The small, tight bikini bottom couldn't contain the sudden wetness from her body.

She crawled off him rapidly and scooted back against the porch stairs.

The front door opened and Louis looked out, an expression of surprise on his face as he saw Honey climbing the stairs ass-backward and a man getting up from the ground. "Who the fuck are you?" Louis looked at him.

Straightening, he brushed off his coveralls. He was a very large man, realized Honey, easily six-foot-six or so, with a short tidy beard cut tight to his face and curly brown hair. He had a light scar on his cheek that his beard didn't completely cover. "Maurice Silver. Nick from the lumberyard sent me. Said you needed some woodcarving done."

"I saw him in the mirror the other day, Louis. That day I ran out naked and screaming. I couldn't tell you because it sounded stupid, but it was *him*. I'm sure of it." Honey couldn't drag her gaze from Maurice. "Well, it looked *sort* of like him. Maybe." Her voice trailed off. The intensity of this man peeled away every layer of her brazen façade.

"You always run around naked? I'm gonna have to hang around here more often." Maurice grinned and his smile made her cunt ache.

She sighed. Something about him got to her. Almost like the man she'd seen in the reflection and in the picture. Something that was an odd blend of spiritual and fiendishly sexual.

"Well I've never seen him before, but if Nick says he's okay..." Louis raised an eyebrow at her and turned to Maurice. "Hi. I'm Louis Beekman and this is my place. I'm renovating it and asked Nick to get me a detail woodcarver for all the inside finish stuff. He said you were the best, and I trust his word. I don't care too much about the cost, because I want perfection. I'm restoring, not updating."

Maurice nodded. "Good for you. Not enough folks appreciate fine craftsmanship these days." He pointed to his truck. "Let me go grab my bags and tools. Trust me. When I get done, this place will look just like the whorehouse it once was." And he walked away.

Cory stepped from the house onto the porch beside Louis. "Who's that?"

"That's Maurice—he's a detail woodcarver. Nick said he redid a few other places like this and his work is impeccable."

She nodded. "You can't go wrong if Nick recommended him. Everybody 'round here knows Nick and how picky he is about his workers." She paused. "Louis—I was watching him from inside the house. I don't know how to say this, but he's not alone." Cory's voice was hushed, but Honey heard it. An odd chill ran down her spine.

"Not alone? Like married?"

"No, it's like somebody is within him. Somebody...something...I'm not sure." She shook her head. "I can't describe it. I just *know*. There's *an air* about him that's unusual."

Honey stood up, watching Maurice as he pulled bags and a few red toolboxes from the back of his truck. "Well, whatever that air is, it's damned appealing. I'm going to find out all I can about this guy." She tugged her thong comfortably around her ass and squared her shoulders.

Look out, Maurice. Honey's comin'.

With any luck.

* * * * *

Louis raised an eyebrow and felt a sharp elbow in the ribs as Cory noticed his amusement. "If anyone can, *you* can, Honey." Louis turned to Cory, pasting innocence over his face. "*What*?"

She shook her head and walked back inside Love Alley.

Louis watched for a moment or two as Honey strutted toward Maurice and his truck. *The poor guy won't know what hit him.* He turned and followed Cory into the house.

The foyer was empty and he wondered where his newfound *fiancée* had gone. There were a few things he figured he'd better explain or apologize for. Walking into the small salon he found her staring at the painting hanging on the wall. The painting that had so fascinated Honey earlier.

He quietly walked up behind Cory and looked over her shoulder. Yep, same guy. He glanced at Cory's face. Her eyes were wide and vague as she fixated on the painting. She must have sensed him, though, since she spoke to him in a low voice.

"This portrait. The man in this painting—he is a lot like Maurice. Look at his face, Louis. Do you see it? Can you *feel* it?"

Louis leaned back and took a good long look, not at the man in the painting, but at Cory. Her profile, the slope of her breasts within her blouse, the roundness of her ass just begging to be groped—he could very easily imagine having that entire package wrapped tightly around his body like a blanket. She was the epitome of eroticism and Louis tumbled into lust without a second thought.

As he stared, there was a low, drawn-out moan echoing in the room.

"Did you hear that? It was his spirit awakening." Cory breathed the words into the silence that followed.

"Nah, it was my stomach. I'm hungry. Let's get some lunch."

Louis grinned as Cory snorted her disgust. "Look, I suppose I should introduce myself. I'm Cory, Cory Lavalle. The psychic you called."

"I figured as much." Louis led the way into the kitchen, then paused. "Did you say Lavalle? That sounds familiar."

"Yeah. My ancestors owned this place. Long before yours got their hands on it."

He turned. "You mean Claudine, don't you? The whore?"

A shutter banged harshly against the wall as Cory frowned and straightened her spine. "I beg your pardon. Claudine was *not* a whore. She ran the most successful brothel in the parish. Back then it was an honorable accomplishment for anybody, let alone a woman."

Louis shrugged and ushered her into the kitchen. "Well, whatever. It's the past. Long gone."

"Oh no, Mr. Beekman. You're quite wrong." Cory lifted her chin and looked down her nose at him. "I'm a psychic. I can assure you that the shades of the past are all around us. Especially here."

"Yeah, okay." Louis rummaged in the fridge and pulled out two cold sodas and a large sandwich he'd made earlier. "Wanna split a ham and cheese on whole wheat?" He opened another cabinet. "I've got chips too."

Quickly separating the two halves of the sandwich and dumping chips from a bag next to them on paper plates, Louis fixed lunch. "There. Sorry it's informal, but right now it's the best I can do."

Cory sighed and sat down, munching on a chip. "How'd you find me?"

"Uhh..." He thought rapidly. "Your card. It's on the wall."

"That's odd." She sipped her soda through rather nice lips. Familiar lips.

Louis let himself watch her as she ate, wondering why he should feel this sense of familiarity. She'd said earlier she knew him—knew his eyes. And in all honesty he felt sort of the same thing. Her thick black hair fell to the middle of her back, a long braid of darkness.

Her skin was clear and rich, like *café au lait*. Where the hell that phrase had come from, he had no idea, but it fit her to a tee. Her eyes were large and dark, and when she looked at him in inquiry, his voice dried up in his throat.

He coughed a little to clear it. "Never know what you'll find in old houses like this."

She turned the conversation general, asking about his work and how he'd ended up at Love Alley, laughing as he told her about the poker game. "So it all comes down to a turn of the card. Three queens, huh?"

"Yep. Strictly chance." He finished his chips. "So how'd you get to be a psychic? You graduate from Ghost U.?" He laughed at his own joke.

Cory's face turned chilly. "No."

Uh oh. Note to self. Don't kid about this psychic crap around Cory. "Sorry, I didn't mean to sound like an ass. I'm just not used to this sort of thing."

She pushed her chair back. "Perhaps you should show me the house, Mr. Beekman."

"Um, okay." The temperature had dropped twenty degrees on the strength of her displeasure alone.

Her frosty attitude lasted all of five minutes however. Each room they entered seemed to entrance her, each painting, each window, every fireplace and lintel held a fascination for her. "This house sings, Louis." She whispered the words.

Aha. Back to "Louis". He mentally gave himself a high five. "It does?"

"Oh yes." She paused in the foyer, resting her hand on the top of the banister. "It is happy you're here. It wants caring for, tending, loving hands restoring it..." She ran her palm appreciatively over the softly glowing wood.

Louis rather wished she'd run her hands over him—just like that. He had something every bit as hard as that wood right about now. A few minutes of watching Cory stroke the banister had done more for his libido than half an hour of Honey and her thong bikini.

"It's called a dollop of cream."

"What?" Cory looked at him in confusion.

"That molding you're...fondling. One name for it is a dollop of cream." He smiled as she ran a finger around the swirl of wood, which really did resemble cream when spooned thickly onto something. It was an attempt to distract himself, Louis knew.

To calm the rising desire that threatened to pop out of his shorts and embarrass both of them. It didn't help much that she looked about as lickable as a Popsicle and just as tasty. One snap at the back of her neck and a couple more at her waist and those breasts would burst free into his—

"There are many voices here." She sighed as she found the broken piece of the railing. "*So* many voices."

"Would you—" Louis' voice squeaked. He cleared his throat and tried again. "Would you like to see upstairs?"

She was already on the first step. "It's changed from what I remember when I visited as a child. Empty. It used to have some of the original furniture in it." She glanced over her shoulder. "Did you find anything of value? Any pieces that might have come from an earlier time?"

"Not much furniture, no." Louis followed her swaying ass, barely covered by her short denim skirt. The halter top left her back bare, and he drooled at the thought of running his tongue down her smooth spine and beneath that waistband.

"Umm..." He dragged his thoughts out of her clothes and back to the subject. "There're several chests and boxes. I pulled them free of a leak in the eaves and stored them here." He nodded to a side room. "Haven't gotten around to fixing this one up yet, but it's dry."

Cory darted in and gazed around her, excitement shimmering from every pore. "Oooh. Look." She touched the old trunks with a gentle hand. "This one..." Her eyes drifted shut. "A young girl. She's missing her family, but she's happy here."

"Ahh." Louis wisely kept his mouth shut.

"And here..." Another box, this time more of a battered suitcase. "A servant I think. A man, anyway."

"Seriously, Cory. How come you're psychic?" Louis was genuinely curious. Whether he believed or not, she clearly did and he wondered about the intensity of her beliefs.

"Seriously?" She glanced quickly at him then away again. "In my family, there's one in every generation. Has been for as long as anyone knows."

"Really?"

"Yep. *Tante* Carolina was the last one and she told me I was next when I was a teenager. I knew she was right. And when the time comes, I'll be the one to recognize the next Lavalle woman with the...the gift."

"So do you see visions and stuff?" Louis pursued his thoughts, but found his words falling on deaf ears.

Cory was delightedly prowling the room, finding first one thing then another, touching them all regardless of the dirt. "Oh wow." She pulled out a small flat box. "Would you look at this?"

Her eagerness tugged at Louis and they both moved to the window where the sunlight illuminated Cory's burden. "It's old, probably 1930s or so." She gingerly lifted the lid and spread the opened box flat on the floor, lifting out a folded and beautifully decorated piece of thin wood. "It's an original Ouija board."

"Oh cool. We used to have fun with these in college." Louis watched her put the little carved thing in the center of the numbers and letters. "You ever play strip Ouija?" He waggled his eyebrows.

It was an offhand remark meant as humorous, but as soon as the words were out of his mouth, the heat level in the room shot up. Cory's eyes met his and something arced between them that felt like captured lightning.

His cock thrummed, his hands itched to touch her and for an instant in time she was naked on top of him. Then he blinked. *That* was the familiar memory. His dream on the airplane.

The woman in it had been Cory.

They both jumped as a bolt of genuine lightning flashed outside and the crack of thunder that followed shook Love Alley.

Okay. Enough of this psychic shit. This is too much like a Hollywood movie to be real.

* * * * *

Honey ignored Louis and Cory as they went back into Love Alley.

All she wanted to do was watch as Maurice opened the large steel box on the inside of his truck bed. His muscles flexed and Honey found herself staring wide-eyed at the big man. He had sharply cut muscles from all his hard work and he hummed with pure strength.

Honey felt a savagely strong twitch of arousal. She licked her lips and swallowed, oddly uneasy because for the first time in a long while, she didn't know what to say. She settled for the obvious. "So those are your tools, huh?"

Looking back with a puzzled glance Maurice answered her. "No, I'm unloading fireworks for a circus."

Honey rolled her eyes realizing the stupidity of her question. "I'm sorry, I was just trying to make conversation. My name's Honey, by the way. Honey Treadwell."

"What's your real name?" He asked the question without looking at her.

"That *is* my name. Why would you think it wouldn't be?" She was a little perturbed by his odd words.

"I don't know. Honey is a cute name but for some reason I see you as being more of an Alice." He continued pulling the woodcarving tools from his truck.

A chill crept through Honey in spite of the heat and humidity. She shivered and found herself unable to move. "Who *are* you? How did you know that?"

"Know what?"

"How the *fuck* do you know my name? *Nobody* knows that my first name is Alice. I dropped it close to twenty years ago." A cloud rolled over the sun, casting shadows and an odd light over the man in front of her. A question rolled from her lips in a hushed whisper. "*What do you want?*"

Turning to face her, Maurice looked into her eyes. "You know what I want. You felt it when you saw me. I don't want your money or your house—nothing material. I want to possess *you*." He stepped closer. "After we fuck, I will own you."

Her knees weakened and a rush of heat filled her cunt, lighting a powerful fire and sending hot juices flowing. He touched something within her—a complete release of her lustful essence. She wanted *him*. For some unfathomable reason he caused an inner rage of desire she'd never felt before.

Barely able to speak, Honey fought to remain calm. "You know…we have time…we could go over to my house and…"

Maurice grinned and put his large hands on her shoulders. "Not now. I have to work. I will come for you, Alice. I will come for you, and you will come when I let you." He paused. "Wait for me tonight. I want you wet, I want you ready and I want you naked. We will fuck like animals and I won't be gentle. I'm gonna call you Honey around everyone else. But when I want something, I will call you Alice. Now go home. *Alice.*"

Honey gazed at him, confused, befuddled and horny. She ached for this man, ached to have him take her any way he wanted. And the sooner the better.

She looked at him, his chest, his shoulders, his air of masculinity, and she yearned. But he made a hand gesture like he was shooing away a puppy. To her surprise, she found herself turning to leave. He had her obeying his commands, and they had only just met.

What is it about this man? Why does he have this power over me?

She paused and looked back at him. "Where do you live?"

"Why?" Maurice clanged the tailgate shut on his truck.

"Just curious. I know most folks hereabouts."

"Mostly the other side of N'Awlins, but I'm renting a houseboat moored up on Bayou St. Jacques. Doing some carpentry on it in exchange for room and board for a while. You'll see."

"I will?"

"Yeah. You will. If I decide to let you." He hefted his tools over his shoulders and headed toward Love Alley. "Remember. Be ready for me tonight."

A flash of lightning from across the bayou lit up his face as he turned away from Honey and she shuddered at the lust she saw in his gaze. She'd be ready. She'd be naked, in bed, out of bed, on the floor, up a tree…any way he wanted. He could have her.

She bit her lip. It wouldn't really be a case of him *having* her. It would be more a case of him *taking* her, since she knew he was a man who would not argue nor demand. He would simply *take*.

And she knew she was eager for every single minute of it.

Honey turned to her pirogue as thunder rumbled distantly over the swamps. A storm was coming. Time to go home.

And wait.

Chapter Nine

ഔ

The storm turned the skies to lead and broke in its full fury over Love Alley as Louis hurried to put buckets under the worst of the leaks — the one over his bed.

"It's only water." Cory leaned against the doorjamb and watched him in amusement.

"Yes, but it doesn't belong on my mattress. It's wet enough in this place already." Sweat beaded on Louis' skin and trickled down over his body, emphasizing his maleness. Cory appreciated the picture he made. He sure was one sweet-looking piece of man.

And she still hadn't come to terms with the fact that he'd been part of one of the most intensely erotic dreams she'd had in quite some time.

"Look, I'd better head off home." She sighed. "If you don't mind, I'd like to come back with a few odds and ends that might help me figure out what's going on here. And then perhaps you can tell me what you've experienced?"

Louis frowned. "In this weather?"

She smiled and repeated herself. "It's only water."

Louis looked out of the window and waved his hand at the torrential sheets that blanked the view. "So was the iceberg that sank the Titanic."

"Tourist." She grinned at him and headed downstairs for her purse and her keys, only to be brought up short at the sight of Maurice tidying his tools.

"Er, hi."

"You thinking of going someplace?" His words were abrupt, but Cory didn't sense a threat, just a natural reserve.

"Yeah. I'm headin' for home. New Orleans."

"Don't bother." Maurice nodded outside. "Levee's out just past the bayou bridge. They were workin' on it when I drove in and told me that if we got this rain today it'd be out for a bit. Tough job, that. Fixin' levees."

Louis came up behind Cory, his warmth dusting her naked back. "Trouble?"

She turned to him. "Um…Maurice says there's some local flooding on the roads. Happens a lot 'round here."

"Fact of life when you're next to a river, I guess." Louis wrinkled his nose. "You sure?" He glanced at Maurice.

"Yep."

"Well, there you are. You'll have to stay a bit I guess."

Cory could have sworn there was a distinct smirk lingering around his lips. She ignored it and looked at Maurice once more. "So where are you going?"

"I'm renting a houseboat on Bayou St. Jacques. I can get there if I go now." He nodded to Louis. "Got the pattern and measurements for that dado rail in the dining room. Figured I'd start with that, since a lot of the decorations are repeated in other rooms. If you don't see me, don't worry. I do a lot of the carving off-site. It's quiet. I can concentrate." His eyes drifted over Cory. "Pretty women distract me."

"Um, thanks." Surprisingly, Cory blushed at the compliment.

Louis' hand came up and rested possessively on her shoulder and her cheeks burned even more. She could feel her nipples hardening at just the brush of his palm. What the hell would happen if anything *else* of his ever touched her, she couldn't begin to imagine.

"Okay, Maurice. You know this stuff better than I do. Drive carefully." Louis politely opened the door and then closed it after Maurice as he dashed through the downpour to his truck. "Interesting man."

Cory pursed her lips. "There's an aura around him. I wish I could get a handle on it."

"Don't I have an aura?" Louis pouted and led her back into the kitchen, where the lights flickered and immediately went out. "Shit."

"Yes. You have an anti-electrical aura apparently." Cory giggled and perched on a chair while Louis fussed with matches and candles. "How many fuses have you blown out anyway?"

"Enough to support half of Chicago, I'm thinking." He growled the answer as he tried to light a candle and glue it to the countertop.

"Oh for God's sake, give me that." Cory took the candle and carefully dripped a few blobs of hot wax onto the lid of an empty jar of salsa. Then she touched the base of the candle to the liquid and let it solidify. "*Voila*. Instant candlestick."

Her gaze fell on the old box she'd brought down from the attics. "Hey. Since I'm stuck here, do you want to start on a little research?"

Louis blinked then smiled—a rather wickedly attractive smile. "What did you have in mind?"

She ignored the little dance of pleasure that rippled through her body and pointed to the table. "Over there. I'll set up the Ouija board."

"Oh." Louis was definitely crestfallen, but he cleared off the remains of lunch, grabbed a couple more beers, restocked the little fridge in the hopes it would keep the drinks cool at least, and came over to sit opposite Cory. He stared at the board.

"Okay. So what now?"

"Shhh. I'm concentrating." And it was frickin' hard too, with Louis in all his gorgeous manliness an arm's length away. Cory sighed and focused, opening that little door in her mind to another place, another dimension.

[*He's goin' to make you happy, petite. Be happy. Help me be happy.*]

The words were as clear as a bell and, startled, Cory glanced at Louis. He was studying the board interestedly, running his fingers over the carved planchet. Obviously he hadn't heard the voice.

She "listened" again but there was nothing, just the odd turbulent hum of that other world. There were definitely *things* in this house, old things, happy and sad things, closer to the surface than Cory was used to, but her relationship to the Lavalieres line could account for it.

She sensed no threat, just an unsettled — *unfinished* — sort-of emotion. And there was an undercurrent of arousing sexuality running strongly through it all. Her panties were damp after just opening her psychic senses to the house.

Or perhaps it was Louis who was responsible.

Whatever it was, Cory felt unusually sexy, and not a little horny.

She pushed it away and focused on the board. "Now," she said to Louis. "I want you to clear your mind, try not to think about anything in particular, and just rest all of your fingertips on the planchet. Do not push, do not hold it down. Just touch it."

"Yes, *Meeessssstreeessss.*" Louis chuckled as he answered in a Transylvanian accent.

Cory narrowed her eyes crossly. "Don't scoff. You may not have much experience in this area, but I have."

Louis looked penitent. "Sorry."

They both lowered their gazes to the planchet, the little carved triangle that would point out messages from beyond. It was warm to Cory's touch, although given the temperature outside that wasn't surprising.

What was surprising was the fact that the thing was dead in the water. Not a ripple, nor a twitch nor a tiny little shudder.

Nothing. Cory waited.

Nada. Zip.

Louis cleared his throat.

Still nothing happened, and Cory clenched her jaw. This was *so* not going to look good. What was worse, she could sense the house alive around her, host to many different spirits and souls from its past.

Yet not a one bothered to use this classic method of communication.

"Hmm." Louis broke the silence. "Perhaps they can't spell?"

"Aaargh." Cory tore her hands away from the planchet and leaned back in her chair. "This is absurd. It's never failed before. I don't understand it." She tipped her head back, closed her eyes and massaged her scalp. "This house is ready to talk. It wants to talk. So why the fuck isn't it?"

"Uhmm—"

"I swear they're here." Cory tugged on her hair in frustration. "I can hear them. I can sense them. This is just too—"

"Urgh. Ullffhhh—"

"*What*?" Wondering at the odd noises Louis was making, Cory sat back up and opened her eyes.

He was staring at the board, eyes wide, mouth open. Both hands were on the table at the edges, and he was rigid.

The planchet was moving.

All by itself.

"Well, that's better." Cory settled into her chair and reached for the pencil and paper she'd set next to her in preparation for just this event.

"Humplf. Ffflaaargh."

Louis was still astounded at the sight of the moving planchet, and Cory permitted herself a slight snicker. *So shall all unbelievers be punished.*

She busily wrote down the letters as the small device flew around the board, faster now, more assuredly spelling out its message. It was the first time Cory had watched one move unattended, free spinning, completely and absolutely under the control of unseen fingers.

As it paused Cory glanced at Louis, smiling at his confusion. "It's all right, Louis. It won't hurt you."

He blinked. "What's it saying?" The words were whispered from lips that had paled slightly. There were beads of sweat on his forehead, and Cory would have bet good money that the liquid would be cold not hot.

She suppressed a giggle. "You don't have to whisper, you know." She wrote more letters as the Ouija board continued its communication.

"Well?" Louis' voice was still a bit shaky, but growing more normal as he began to accept the phenomenon on his kitchen table.

"Okay." Cory leaned back as the planchet skidded to a halt. "Let's see what we've got here." She held the paper to the candle. "Oh."

"What?"

"Um…it's kinda X-rated. You blush easily?"

Louis raised his eyebrow. "No, do you?"

Cory swallowed. "Well, remember this is the board talking, not me, okay?"

"Just *read* it." Louis glared at her.

"Here goes." Cory blessed the shadows of the candlelight as she read the words. "Remember I'm trying to make sense of a less than literal communication here…"

"*Cory…*"

"Don't yell." She gulped as she held up the paper. "*Au dessous left nipple. Under the breast. C's favorite spot. Suck her there.*"

"Hmm." Louis' eyes drifted to Cory's breasts, and in spite of her determination, she knew her nipples were beading beneath her soft halter top. "Go on."

She quite failed to look at him. This was outrageous enough without having to watch his face at the same time. "*Fuck hard. Then love softly. Take what is yours. It is here. C loves B. Forever.*" She paused. "There is one more line."

"Go ahead." Louis sounded a little tense.

"*Find my soul. Bring me peace eternal. Au 'voir.*"

There was silence for a moment as both human occupants of the room considered the message sent them by the Ouija board. Then the skies opened once more and rain thundered down on Love Alley, drenching it with tears from the clouds.

* * * * *

The night had turned nasty with sheets of rain and lightning, which lit up the sky. The low rumble of thunder shook Honey to her core. She had sent her live-in housekeeper away and put on a thin silk negligee that really didn't cover anything. Maurice said he wanted her naked and she was two untied ribbons away from it.

She lay on the old antique couch, waiting patiently. She didn't know why. She'd never waited for a man before and wasn't quite sure why she was doing it now. It had always been her leading the way, her controlling the tempo and direction of a relationship. Something in Maurice broke every rule she had when it came to men. And she had only just met him.

The rain continued to make a splattering sound on the wood steps and after a while the sound soothed Honey. It was getting later and later, and no Maurice.

"Bastard stood me up. I knew he wouldn't show." She was angry and tired, and deep inside there was a definite twinge of disappointment.

A bright flash of light followed by a crackle of thunder exploded in the night air. Honey jumped and was suddenly in total darkness as the power went out.

"Oh fucking *great*. I send everyone home and now I have no power." Wandering around the room she lit some of her decorative candles and then walked over to turn on the gas fireplace.

It was getting a little cooler outside and she still had the front door ajar with the screen keeping the bugs out. Her night looked like it was a bust. With a sigh she was about to close the door when another flash of light lit the sky. Honey jumped as she saw the shadow of a man in front of her screen. As the thunder rumbled so did his voice.

"I see you were waiting up for me." It was Maurice.

Honey caught her breath. "Shit, you scared me."

"I thought I told you I wanted you to be naked. Why do you have that thing on? I want to see what I'm gonna be fucking." His words were coarse and harsh, but it made Honey moist between her legs.

Maurice pulled the screen door open and stepped in from the porch, closing both doors behind him and letting the darkness of the room envelop him. The only light came from the fire and candles. "You have anything to drink?"

"What would you like? I have white wine spritzer, some imported beer... "

"You have any whiskey? I hate taking shortcuts to drinking."

Honey bent down to look toward the back of the wet bar.

"Damn, you have a nice ass. Can't wait to start pounding on that later." Again his coarse comments cut through Honey's characteristic control and made her hot inside.

"I don't have any ice..."

Maurice interrupted her. "Just give me the bottle."

Honey walked up and handed Maurice the bottle as he stood dripping on her floor. She realized he'd walked from his truck to the house in the pouring rain. He was drenched—his clothes clinging to him like a layer of skin. The T-shirt outlined his broad chest and his jeans plastered to his hips.

"The fire." He nodded to the flames. "I need to dry off a bit."

Honey grabbed an afghan off the top of the couch and draped it over an expensive antique chair beside the fireplace. "This is a real nice chair. Why don't you sit here?"

Maurice stepped next to Honey and her breasts brushed against his wet skin. Jolts of electricity shot through her body. She wanted him more then any other man she had ever desired. She'd given up wondering why, she just knew she did.

Maurice plopped into the chair with a thud. He pulled his wet curly hair back with his hand and Honey watched as the muscles flexed on his arms. He seemed tired and Honey awkwardly tried to break the ice with small talk.

"So how long you been livin' around these parts?"

Maurice took a long, full drink from the bottle and swallowed. He shook his head. "I didn't come here to talk. Since you're sitting there, looking so fucking hot, why don't you show me your pussy?"

"Pardon me?" Honey blinked.

"Your pussy. I want to see it." He smiled and the glistening white of his teeth shone through his beard. "Show me *Alice*."

Honey melted. Her barriers were breaking down, one by one, useless in the face of the desire she felt for this man and the urge to please him. It was raw, uncivilized and the most exciting thing she'd done in her life. She sat on the couch, across from him and took a deep breath.

Maurice leaned back and watched as Honey spread her legs apart.

"Damn, that is one fine-looking pussy. Nice wet folds of flesh. They're shining in the firelight." Maurice's gaze was fixed on her crotch. "Open those lips Alice. I want to see more."

Honey swallowed and reached her hand down to do what he asked. Her fingertips slid easily along the slippery skin. She looked down and opened her labia revealing the pink flesh inside. Her body was burning with excitement that threatened to erupt.

"Mmm, mm, *damn*, I can't wait to sink my tongue into that thing. Do you want me to eat your pussy, Alice?"

Honey wanted to scream *yes*, but battled the urge. It would be too much like surrendering completely—and she wasn't quite ready to do that. Not *just* yet. "I like a man to lick my pussy." She became even more aroused by the thought of sitting on his face and grinding onto his tongue as it danced against her clit.

He took another drink from the bottle and wiped his mouth with the back of his hand. His demeanor hadn't changed but he seemed to be getting affected by Honey's exposure. "You know what I'd like to see? I'd love to watch you get yourself off. Do that for me, Alice. Show me how you play with your pussy and get yourself off."

"Is that what you want?" Honey wasn't quite sure she'd heard him. Her ears were buzzing with the heat that flooded her.

"Alice, I want to watch you fuck yourself with your fingers."

The direct command excited her to fever pitch. She'd never done this for a man before, never had a man ask this of her, but his interest spurred her on.

Honey sat back on the couch and breathed out—trying to calm her body before the storm she knew was coming. It had nothing to do with the weather, either, but everything to do with the man staring at her in the dim, flickering light. There was lust in his eyes and she could almost see a wicked aura to his mood. She was hotter than hot for him.

She let her fingers massage her pussy, the folds of flesh becoming slicker and more full as her arousal increased. Honey licked her lips and swallowed a gasp of excitement as she let her fingertip slip between the labia. Warmth flowed through her veins as the opening was breached. Her finger swirled around her cunt and the heightening of her desires made her begin to pant. Her pussy longed for the real thing, which was inside Maurice's pants. She wanted his thick cock, not her thin fingers.

"I'm not sure I can do this." Honey was wet and horny, but unaccustomed to taking matters into her own hands. Except for those times in the bathtub with her expensive showerheads.

"Come on, Alice. You've been a bad girl before, and I know you've fucked yourself before. Close your eyes and imagine what I tell you." His coarse words ripped at her need, opening up dark places with a key only he seemed to possess.

Honey closed her eyes and pictured Maurice in her mind as she heard his footsteps getting closer. She continued letting her fingers massage her soaking cunt.

"Can you see me, Alice?" His hot breath was next to her ear, making her shudder. He must be leaning over her, bending close. "I'm looking at you, wanting you, craving to bury my cock into that tight, sweet pussy."

Her fingers moved faster with the encouragement of his words guiding the images in her mind. She could see him fucking her. Her mind watched as he sunk into her inch by inch and when her fingertips brushed her clit, the inner muscles clenched the imaginary cock.

As she began to breathe faster she felt something—a pair of hands grasping her breasts. "I can't stand this fucking lacy thing. I want to see those big beautiful tits you smothered into my face earlier today." With a tug he pulled her negligee open, freeing her breasts as her nipples hardened into taut buds of sensation.

His rough hands rubbed against the softness of her skin and she moaned. "Can I open my eyes? I want…"

"*No.* Keep your eyes closed. You haven't come yet."

The mystery of what Maurice might be doing both tantalized her a little and sent a shiver of nerves through her body. He was stalking around her. Telling her what to imagine, talking to her like no man had ever talked to her before.

And she loved it, craved more of it and would've done anything he commanded without a blink. He'd found her weakness and she was riding a wave of arousal he had created within her cunt.

"Put two fingers inside because I have a big cock and plan to ride you hard. You like it hard don't you? You like it when a man hammers it home until his balls are slapping against you. I'm going to fuck you Alice. I'm going to fuck you until you beg me to stop, then I'm going to fuck you some more."

The raunchiness made Honey gasp. She longed for him now, almost angry that he wasn't already inside her. Her fingers furiously stroked against her clit as his words burned images into her mind of hard, rough sexual acts. Her peak was near.

"Alice, keep your eyes closed."

Curious, she did as she was told, straining her ears for a clue about what would come next.

Zzzzzzzzzip.

Oh God yes. He'd undone his pants and *now* she could have him.

"Damn Alice, you've gotten my cock real hard. It can't wait to fuck you." Maurice had a fiendish tone to his voice. He stepped next to Honey and rubbed the head of his cock along the line of her jaw. "You want to suck my cock, Alice? I'm a sucker for a good blowjob before sex. It makes me last longer when we get to the fucking. Seeing those big tits and that sweet pink pussy's made me hornier 'n hell."

With his hand he guided her head forward and she knew he was standing in front of her now. He opened his legs wide, forcing Honey's legs apart with his.

Finally Honey could stand it no longer, and she opened her eyes to see Maurice holding his thick cock in his hand. He tapped the head against her chin and then rested it against her lips. "Make me come with you, Alice."

A deep hunger filled Honey's body. It burned in her. She had a need to release her sexual desire and make this man understand how painful her need was.

She closed her eyes and frantically rubbed on her clit, finding her juices flowing like a river and her mouth watering for her first taste of him. Her lips parted and she let Maurice's long cock glide into her mouth. At first she gagged as the wide head touched the back of her throat, but then she found her pace and let her tongue learn him.

Letting him out a bit she kept one hand playing with her cunt and lifted the other to his balls. Like a virtuoso she played his instrument with great expertise. His groans of pleasure were the chorus for the crescendo of the music she played. "Fuck Alice, mmm, baby you suck *good*. Damn, if you do this with your mouth I can just imagine what you're gonna do with your pussy."

Honey was beside herself. She was feeling the spasms of her orgasm as it began to build deep within her.

Her mouth sucked in the saliva that trickled from the corners of her mouth. It was too much for her to handle and she began to clench her ass tight, trying to fight the inevitable. She was coming and wanted to take Maurice with her.

"Oh fuck Alice, you're going to make me—oh shit—*oh shit*—"

While her pussy creamed with her juices she grasped Maurice's balls in her hand and gently squeezed them and let him slide deep into her throat.

"Fuck baby." Maurice put his hand on the back of her head, pulling it closer to his body. Her lips locked tight around his cock and with a loud groan he spewed hot seed into her throat. Over and over he spurted the hot juice into her mouth.

She gulped and swallowed and gulped again, torn between the thundering orgasm sweeping through her cunt and the pulsing cock in her mouth. Her body clenched at her own fingers, wet and violent, and she fought for breath as Maurice's cock finally softened on her tongue. If she could have, she would have screamed.

Finally, staggering back a few steps and pulling free of her lips, Maurice sighed heavily and began to laugh.

Honey slumped into the couch and tugged the lace back over her breasts in a futile attempt to cover her nakedness. Eventually, she gave up and laughed too. "Damn, I can't believe I did that. We just met today. I feel like *such* a slut." It was a joking comment, but beneath it was a definite ring of truth. This *sooo* wasn't like her to act this way, but she didn't care. It felt fucking *great*.

"Hell, we just got started." Maurice left his pants undone and tugged on his cock a few times. He leaned over, grabbed the bottle of whiskey and motioned Honey to get up. "When I'm done with you Alice, you'll feel like a hooker after a bachelor party. Let's go upstairs. Now we *really* get to fuck."

* * * * *

Louis stared across the kitchen table at Cory, aroused, sweating and unable to keep his mind off her left breast. "So." He leaned in toward her. "Do you have a sweet spot under your left nipple?"

She fidgeted, blushed and refused to meet his gaze. "None of your business."

He leaned even closer. "Apparently, our spirit guides think it is."

"Well, they're nuts." Cory folded her arms protectively over her breasts.

"You haven't answered the question." A little smile crossed his lips. *God, I'd like to find out for myself.*

"This is ridiculous." Cory pushed herself roughly away from the table and stood, at the exact moment when a crooked cabinet door fell open and a half open bottle of wine tipped up, dousing her thoroughly. "Oh fuckin' *shit*."

She jumped, but could not avoid the shower of red liquid, which soaked her top, her skirt and clung to her hair.

Louis bit back a laugh. He was human and damn if she didn't look like a drowned rat, but it wasn't worth his life to laugh at her predicament.

"Shit shit *shit*. I'm soaked." She frowned at him, clearly indicating the whole thing was his fault.

"I'm so sorry, I thought that bottle was corked. And how the door opened, I have no clue." He stood and reached for paper towels. "Maybe it was one of your spirit buddies."

"Very funny." She dabbed ineffectively at her clothes. "*Eeeeuuch*. I'm stinking like a bar on Sunday morning."

Louis shook his head. "Upstairs. Just off my room you'll find the bathroom, remember? There's no shower, but a huge tub. And there should still be enough hot water left in the tank for a bath. I *think*. Dump your clothes in the sink to soak."

She sighed. "I don't have much choice. Okay. Thanks. I'll take another candle with me." With a little more mopping and dabbing, Cory squelched out of the kitchen and Louis heard the stair treads squeak as she went up to the second floor. Shortly thereafter, the loud hum of the water pipes replaced the silence as Cory turned on the faucets.

He looked back at the Ouija board. The hair on the back of his neck stood up as the planchet moved once more. He spelled out the words. *"Take her. Make her come. With mouth, with hands, with cock. I give her to you to fuck. And to love."*

Louis gulped back a gasp. This was major freaky shit, and he wasn't quite sure it was anything more than his own lusts translated into some sort of telekinetic energy. The damn thing started up once more.

"Don' forget de ass. Wimmen luv de ass."

His skin chilled as a rich masculine laugh echoed somewhere in the darkness, soft but clear. This was about as freaky as he ever wanted to get. He stared at the board, but it was still, sitting there looking just like most Ouija boards he'd ever seen.

Skeptical his entire life about things he couldn't actually hold in his hand, Louis was struggling with all of this...this...*otherworldly* stuff, but his practical mind simply couldn't ignore the evidence of his own eyes. Perhaps there was something more than he'd imagined up to now. Perhaps there were spirits, souls moving in another plane, touching his reality now and again.

Or perhaps it was just fucking hot, he was horny and an amazingly sexy woman was upstairs naked in his bath.

He wondered if she would *"luv de ass"*. His cock ached at the mere thought, and when he heard her call his name, something prompted him to think positively. He reached into his small travel bag and shoved a few condoms into his shorts pocket.

The boy scouts had the right idea. *Be prepared.*

Chapter Ten

80

Upstairs, lazing in the tub, Cory pondered the evening's events. She wondered who "C" and "B" were. Could it be Claudine herself?

The window above the bath slowly slid downwards, and Cory cursed, knowing an unscreened window was an open invitation to nasty biting bugs. She scrambled up through the bubbles and closed it.

There had been a small packet of bath salts resting atop the pile of towels, which had surprised Cory. She'd been even more surprised when she'd emptied a handful under the running water and the richly sensual fragrance of gardenias mixed with damask roses filled the air.

It was a scent that screamed sex and desire, and it made her want to stroke her hands over her body as she lay beneath the thick froth of bubbles. Ordinarily, she preferred simple perfumes—but this one was something else again. She squinted at the packet, but the name was smeared from either humidity or age.

Once more the window slid down and Cory sighed. "Hey Louis..." He must have a nail and a hammer or something.

She heard his footsteps pause outside the door. "You okay?"

"Yeah. The window keeps sliding down. You got a hammer and a nail? If you do, leave it outside and I'll fix it."

She heard him laugh. "You can't fix it with just a hammer and a nail. You'll ruin the sash."

"Shit."

"You decent?"

"I'm in the bath." She shook her head. What did he *think*?

"Well grab something. I'm coming in."

"*Nooo...*" Cory squawked and sank up to her chin beneath the water, praying it was milky enough to hide her, because the minute facecloth sure as hell wouldn't.

Louis walked in and looked at her with interest. "Damn. I was hoping for a quick flash." He grinned, robbing his words of anything but lighthearted humor. "Now. Where's this window? Ah, yeah. I see."

Afraid that he might *see*, Cory sank even lower, trying to breathe through her nose. "Can you fix it?" The water bubbled around her mouth.

"You know, you're gonna drown if you keep that up." Louis chuckled then stepped onto the edge of the bath.

"What the *hell* are you doing?"

He sighed. "Look honey, it's the only way I can reach this thing, okay? The sash is loose. I need to reattach the weight." He pulled on a dusty piece of rope and knotted things, leaning over and finally putting one foot on either side of the tub as he tried to slide the weight back into its groove.

Which gave Cory—looking upwards—a great view along his leg, inside his thigh, and up into places which should've been covered by underwear—but weren't.

Ohhh Mama.

He was thick, a solid length filling his shorts and she could almost glimpse his balls cradling that lovely cock. It was pretty amazing that she could see at all, since a warm heat was flooding her, the water caressing her pussy with softly moving fingers and she wanted to eat him whole.

Slowly, deliberately, she raised herself from the water, making barely a ripple as first her shoulders then her chest rose against the foam. She paused just before her nipples broke the surface.

"Looks like you've fixed it, then." Even her voice was sultry, and it surprised her with how natural it felt.

"I'm good at fixing things." He turned and stared down at her, freezing into immobility as he took in her revealed flesh. "Very good at fixing things."

"Really?" She licked her lips. "You good at other things too?"

The scent of the bubble bath was all around her, flooding her nose, making her a little lightheaded, and forcing her eyes back to his cock which was clearly growing harder beneath his shorts as her movements bared one breast for a brief second.

She wanted this man. Wanted him with every single fiber of her being. All other thoughts fled, chased away by the rising desire that flooded her. Images chased across her subconscious, naked images, tangled limbs, mouths and hands finding other mouths and hands—and bodies. She ached physically, her cunt screaming out its hunger for that cock.

The room seemed to sway and Louis lost his precarious balance, crashing into the tub and sending a spume of foam across the floor.

Cory rose to meet his fall, eagerly feeling the weight of his chest as he crushed her breasts and caught himself with his hands on the side of the tub. He slid down into the water and she parted her thighs, making room for him.

He lifted his head and stared at her, his lips just inches from her left breast. Then, without a word, he lowered his mouth to a place just below her nipple and sucked.

Cory screamed with ecstasy.

* * * * *

Louis was in heaven. He had an armful of naked writhing woman, with thighs that clutched at him and hands that reached for him. His lips had found *that* spot on her breast and she was rubbing her pussy against him with ferocious need.

He struggled to free himself of his shorts, throwing them away from the tub and hearing them plop wetly onto the floor. Finally he was naked, rubbing himself over Cory in his own frenzy, delighting in the scent of her, the feel of her and the eagerness with which she accepted his touch. His cock was harder than steel, and his heart thundered as he seized one breast and squeezed it roughly, nipping at the beaded tip and thrilling at the whimpers of pleasure coming from Cory's throat.

Her nails bit into his shoulders as she tried to pull him closer, her movements as desperate and yearning as the moans she tried so hard to stifle.

He slid a hand to her neck and grasped her chin, angling her mouth for his possession. And he kissed her. Hard.

Lips parted, teeth clashed and tongues savagely dueled for the prize — the taste of the other. She was sweet and spicy, and Louis ate at her mouth with no delicacy whatsoever, lost in the need to devour every fiber of her being.

Still her hips plunged, rubbing her mound against him, thrusting and pushing to get his body where she wanted it.

He kissed her some more, deliberately holding himself away, denying her the satisfaction she demanded, prolonging her sensual agony much as he was doing for himself.

Finally, the taste of her mouth imprinted on his soul, Louis drew back and stared at Cory. Her lips were red and swollen, her breasts high against his chest. Hard nipples dug against him and she mewled as he rubbed his own rough skin over them.

Sliding down, he ran his fingernails over her belly and around her hips, making her sigh and lift herself in offering. His mouth watered as he reached her pussy, hot and swollen between her thighs.

He took one of her legs and draped it over the side of the tub. The other he rested on his shoulder. She was spread wide, bared to his gaze and slickly wet with her own honeyed juices. He could smell her body over the scent of the flowery bath stuff, and he preferred her fragrance to any other he could remember.

He licked his lips in anticipation and bent his head to eat his fill. Once more Cory's cry filled the room.

The little bit of water left in the tub swished as Louis buried his face between her legs and learned her fleshy folds, finding the tiny nub of flesh hot and hard beneath the lips that welcomed his.

She panted and sighed and scrabbled for a hold on the tub, thrusting herself into his kisses, refusing to pull back as he let his tongue slide into her cunt. Louis realized he was possessed—he couldn't remember being this hard, this out of control during sex. He couldn't remember wanting to tear into a woman the way he was devouring Cory.

She trembled and shuddered and moaned and crashed into an orgasm around his face, her body clenching and releasing in a paroxysm of pleasure. He held on, urging her higher, as frantic now as she was.

Letting her slip free, he scrabbled outside the tub for his shorts and miraculously found a condom. She panted and watched him as he ripped the packet open and sheathed himself, her legs sliding down from his shoulder and the tub.

She spoke. One word. "*More.*"

And she meant it. Once was not enough, not nearly enough to quench the hunger that enveloped her. She still shuddered from the aftershocks of her first orgasm and yet she wanted more. She wanted that hardness deep inside her, filling her to overflowing.

He was sheathing himself, protecting them both, hard and thick and ready to oblige.

She spread herself in mute invitation as his cock found her wet folds and thrust roughly past them in a move that took her breath from her lungs. He felt — incredible.

And just as incredible was the rising heat that burgeoned through her cunt as he stretched her, plunging in and out, ravaging her, sending her to a new place where time and space merged into one place — the place where their bodies met.

Again and again they clashed, his pubic hair tangling with hers, his groin pressing her sensitive tissues, making her shiver and shake with an uncontrollable passion. The tub pressed hard against her spine, but no harder than his cock as it rammed into her, riding with her along this strange new road.

He paused, buried to the balls inside her, and shuddered, letting go as he exploded. She clamped down, feeling his throbbing heat as he came, wishing she could feel the boiling flood of his semen.

She cursed the condom, wild for more, out of her mind with some odd kind of driven desire. The scent of the bath salts made her lightheaded and she realized with astonishment that she was coming again, spasming around him, milking him, finding him still hard inside her.

Riding out her second climax, Cory wondered at the magic of it all, astounded at the depth of her responses, still thrumming with sexual energy and still ready to go on. She felt as if she could truly fuck this man forever.

He withdrew, fumbled with the condom and surprised her by reaching for another one. He'd come, but it hadn't been enough. For either of them.

This time, he spoke the word. "*More.*"

Cory knew with rock-solid certainty what *she* wanted. She hoped he wanted it too. Something she'd tried before, found interesting but not particularly fulfilling. This time, she knew it would be.

Cautiously, she rolled over in the bathtub and pulled in a towel to cushion her knees. On all fours she turned away from Louis, reached backwards and spread the cheeks of her ass.

There was nothing she would not do, no part of her body she wouldn't offer. No experience she would dodge. Not tonight. Not with him.

She wanted it *all*.

Louis found himself shaking as he rolled the second condom onto his still hard cock. Part of him was stunned at his abilities, another part just blindly followed his body's needs.

When Cory turned her back and offered him her ass, his heart nearly jumped from his chest. Tight rosy muscles beckoned him, and he slid his length between her legs, slicking her moisture over the sheathed tip. He couldn't resist the lure of claiming her this way.

"Are you sure?"

"God yes. *Please...*" She wiggled, and moved one hand to her breast beneath her. He followed suit, letting one hand find her clit as his cock pressed between her cheeks. She opened for him like a flower in the morning sunshine and he pushed slowly inwards, finding the snug passage welcoming him as he played gently with her clit.

She moaned again, a sound of deep pleasure, pressing herself backwards onto him even as he eased himself deeper. He steadied himself with one hand on her hip and began a slow thrust, loving the caress of her muscles as she clung to him, reluctant to let him leave her even for a second.

It was slower this time, more gentle, less frenzied but still heated...still taking them both to yet another orgasm. Louis could feel it, feel her body as it rose once more to a trembling pitch of madness, and his movements became faster, his balls slapping her body and adding to his own chaotic ride. He was drenched with sweat and her juices and wondered if his balls could possibly survive this insanity.

She panted, quick short breaths, and cried out his name. *"Louis—"*

He thrust his fingers into her cunt and his cock into her ass one last time. The dual intrusion was enough to send her flying and her whole body shattered around him.

Great clenching gasps told him she was there seconds before her muscles seized him in a rhythmic grip of iron, a velvet vise pulling him so deeply into her he lost sight of where he ended and she began.

And he let go.

His cock pumped what felt like geysers of semen, flooding the condom hotly and filling it, swirling around the tip of his cock in a boiling sea of life's essence. Her cunt spewed liquids that soaked his hand even as it seized his fingers, and her soft scream echoed the one caught in his throat.

He saw stars in front of his eyes, becoming dizzy and lost in the madness of the most incredible orgasm in the history of the world. His world, anyway.

Finally it eased, leaving him breathless and limp and very aware of the hard porcelain tub surrounding them. He sucked in a breath and moved, his cock slipping free of Cory's ass and her sigh following his movements.

"Oh *God*." It was a whisper as she uncramped her own body and tried to get out of the tub.

"Yeah." He disposed of the condom and turned to help her, finally digging up enough strength to lift her when her own legs seemed unable to support her weight.

Together they staggered to his bedroom where he pulled the bucket off the bed and flopped them both down. Thankfully the rain had eased, although at this point, he wouldn't have cared if they slept under a waterfall, as long as it was soft.

Cory was already asleep, and Louis nearly there. The odd flowery fragrance lingered a little around them, and just as Louis was dropping off, he could've sworn he heard a deep and laughing voice. *"Told you wimmen like de ass."*

* * * * *

Cory woke to the unfamiliar sound of birds chirping. They didn't chirp outside her apartment window, they coughed, hacked and occasionally squawked. Such was the cost of city living.

But this was a definite chirp, mixed with the occasional hum of crickets and the sharp-toothed buzz of a cicada.

When a definitely male snore joined the chorus, Cory awoke to the full realization of where she was. And what she'd done.

Holy fucking shit.

She cautiously and silently turned her head on the pillow to see one luscious length of naked man flat on his stomach beside her, facing away and snuffling quietly.

Okay. This is a dream. This cannot possibly be real.

The man shifted his position a little, and farted.

Okay. This is real. I have to get out of here.

Now.

Ignoring the lean length of tanned muscles and the nicely rounded un-suntanned buttocks, Cory crept slowly from the bed, holding her breath as an old floorboard squeaked under her feet.

She prayed he was one of those guys who could sleep through a cannonade outside his window. She didn't want to face him, speak to him or acknowledge the fact that she'd been a sex-crazed slut in his arms last night and come no less than *three* times.

Which was so far ahead of her personal best, she wondered if she'd imagined the whole thing.

Then an odd twinge in her thighs made her gasp and she knew it had been real. As real as Louis lying there amidst the rumpled covers, little shiny droplets of sweat already gathering at the base of his spine.

To her horror, Cory had to fight the urge to lean over and lick at the salty moisture. Backing from the bedroom, she blushed as she darted into the bathroom and retrieved her damp clothes from the towel rack where she'd hung them the night before.

They still bore the faintly pink marks of the wine bath she'd taken, but the hell with it. She couldn't drive home naked. And she simply *had* to get out of here.

With a sigh of relief she made it downstairs, fastening her halter as she did so. Stepping into the kitchen, the scent of coffee brought her up short.

"Mornin' *chère*. My my. You got de smell of Love Alley on you right enough."

An old and wizened woman was taking a large bubbling coffeepot off the makeshift stove and pouring the most fragrant stream of liquid into a large mug. In spite of her shock, Cory's mouth watered.

"Er…good morning to you too. Who are you? Louis' housekeeper or something?"

A couple of white teeth flashed against the woman's dark skin. "Hell no, *chère*. I ain't nobody's housekeeper. I jus' a frien' of Mr. Louis. Him with de real nice cock, eh?"

Cory blushed. "My name's—"

"I know who you is, gal. You a Lavalle. You got de sight, don' you?" The woman tapped her head, which was partially hidden under a wildly colored turban that looked mostly Hawaiian with a dash of Florida.

Surprisingly acute eyes surveyed Cory and she caught her breath for a second as she felt that look inside her secret places. This woman, whoever she was, knew about the gifts Cory had. She had touched them with a mere glance and made Cory regard her with a new respect—along with a great deal of caution.

"Uhh…yeah. You know about my family then?"

The woman pushed the mug toward Cory, ignoring the question. "Cream and sugar, *chère*?"

"Thanks." Cory found herself accepting the coffee. "This smells good."

The woman's mouth parted in a wicked grin. "Like you, *chère*. You smell of flowers an' lovin' and good strong man." She sniffed deeply. "You smell like a woman from dis' here place should smell."

Cory decided to pass on any further conversation of how she did or didn't smell. "Who are you? I'm sorry, I didn't catch your name."

"Didn' give it, *chère*." The woman cackled as she straightened one of the gazillion bead necklaces that piled around her scrawny cleavage. She must have been to every single Mardi Gras parade since the beginning of time. "But de Master—he knows."

"The Master?" Cory sipped her coffee. "My God, this is good stuff." She took another swig.

"I do make de good coffee, huh? Dey say dat 'bout me." She looked satisfied at Cory's praise. "Let's hope de Master likes it too."

Cory swallowed and heard a sound behind her. *Fuck it. Busted.*

"Zulee?"

It was Louis, and clearly he was as surprised as she was to find the old woman making him coffee in his kitchen. Cory half turned, to see him wearing only a creased pair of cutoffs, the waistband unsnapped, and with a real nice-looking stubbled chin thing going.

Shit. Cory's mouth watered and it had nothing to do with the coffee. She cleared her throat and turned back to Zulee. "So. You from around here?"

Zulee chuckled and poured a second mug for Louis. "You two found de magic of Love Alley, I'm guessin'."

"Sure did, Zulee." Louis leaned on the countertop and sipped his coffee while his eyes roamed over Cory. "She's a wild thing, ya know."

"*Me*?" Cory was outraged, embarrassed and very self-conscious. It was the first time in her life that anybody had described her as a "wild thing". She decided she rather liked it. "You were the one who started this whole thing by falling in the tub last night…"

"Oh yeah, like you weren't hot and waiting for me to do just that…"

"Pardon me, but you were the one with a boner hard enough to drill holes in cement…"

"Hah. And you were the one who brought those damn scented bubbles with you…just guaranteed to get a man's thoughts where they didn't ought to be."

"Did not!" Cory was irate. "Those were your bath salts, you asshole."

"Speaking of assholes…"

Cory shut her mouth with a snap.

"Bath salts, huh?" Zulee looked interested. "In a small paper packet, mebbe?"

Distracted, Cory looked at her. "Yeah. It was kinda faded and had flowers on it. Looked like lily of the valley and something else perhaps. Could've been gardenias—I'm not sure."

A slow smile spread over Zulee's face. "Well, well."

"*What?*" Cory drained her cup and slammed it down on the counter. "Enough with this crazy shit."

Zulee straightened, and suddenly the room seemed brighter, colors more vivid, sounds more distinct. "It's no shit, girl. Follow your sight. Trust in your visions. You here for a reason, *chère*. You got to find out what dat reason is." She turned to Louis. "And you got to help her, boy. You hear?"

She raised a bony finger and pointed it straight at Louis, who was staring at her intensely. "I hear." He answered quietly.

"Dem bath salts? Dey used to belong to Claudine. Her favorite. She swear up and down on de Bible dey make her horny." Zulee's eyes found Cory's and their gazes locked. "You got a link wit' her. Use it. Don' let family down."

She grinned and the world righted itself. "An' if you feel like dis here man can scratch dat itch of yours, den you go right ahead an' let him." She headed for the door. "Dis here's Love Alley. Seen a lot of dat good stuff. Time it saw more."

She paused, sniffing the morning air. "Seems like dere's some others doin' the same thing." Zulee chuckled. "Dat Honey's goin' to be sticky as her name dis' mornin'."

She was gone before Cory could say goodbye.

"God *damn*. She comes and goes like some sort of weird vision."

"Do not." Zulee was back, peering 'round the door. "Forgot. Lef' you a package, *chère*. Somethin' you need. Somethin' special for you to use. You know how." She nodded at the counter and then was gone once more.

Louis moved to the door and peered out, looking back over his shoulder at Cory in a rather embarrassed way. "Just checking."

"Good idea." Cory stepped to the counter and found a small package wrapped in brown paper behind the coffeepot. Carefully, she unwrapped it, gasping as she spread the contents on the stained counter.

"Hey…I recognize that." Louis came to stand behind her. "It's—"

"A Tarot deck." Cory finished for him. "The most beautiful one I've ever seen in my life." She let her fingers trail over the incredibly lush ornamentation and felt a shiver in her psyche. A ripple of awareness that caught her by surprise, startling her. "Louis, these are powerful cards."

He blinked. "Really?"

"Yeah." She turned and faced him. "Just who the *hell* is Zulee?"

Chapter Eleven

ဆာ

The sound of birds filled the morning air. A breeze rustled through the trees. Everything was peaceful, quiet and calm. Then it happened.

"Oh fuck, Maurice, I'm going to come again, oh shit, oh *shit…*"

Honey's voice was loud, loud enough to blare out of the bedroom window.

Maurice dripped with sweat and breathed hard. His hands groped at Honey's back as the loud *slap, slap, slap* of their bodies meeting echoed in the room. "Fuck, Alice, you are so damn *hot*. Shit — you're gonna make me bust a nut again." He sucked in air through his teeth, trying to hold back his orgasm.

The red marks on her skin were reminders of his hands holding on for dear life as they fucked through the night. Nothing was sacred, no positions not tried.

Honey's body began to shake as her cunt convulsed with her climax. Her mouth opened wide and her eyes closed tight as the wave of pleasure washed through her. She clearly didn't care how she looked, she just languished in the passion of the moment.

With a loud grunt and a final driving thrust, Maurice erupted into her dripping cunt. His seed spurted deep within the cavern of her lust. She oozed the mixture of their sex and it trickled along the soft surface of her inner thigh. She sure was fulfilled. His burning cock was a wonderful ache resulting from overuse.

Maurice had told her they were going to fuck. So that's what they did. They fucked until they were content, then they fucked some more.

"Well, I'm going to take a shower and get to work." Maurice scratched his ass while walking toward the bathroom.

Honey lay on her side, watching him, not knowing quite what to say. Finally, she figured she didn't need to say anything. She'd wanted a man for quite a while and Maurice was *all* man, who just happened to come with no strings attached. Even though she never trusted a man who said he was safe when it came to sex, something about Maurice was different. The way he looked at her. The way he treated her. He saw *inside* her, past her obvious assets and through into her heart. It felt *right* with him and when he assured her he'd been checked out as clean quite recently, she believed him. Just as he'd believed her.

It might end up as one of the stupidest and most naïve things she'd done in her entire life, but something was telling her that wouldn't happen. That this moment with this man was out of the ordinary, something special. For both of them.

There were no pregnancy worries thanks to her birth control shot, so her thoughts tumbled over the only question still unanswered—what happened next. She didn't know what to expect from him. His behavior bordered on cruel at times and he could have seemed quite an asshole to some women. But not to Honey.

From the bed she could see him through the tinted shower glass. She remembered all the rough edges of his large frame. How he'd held her, grabbed at her body and used her for all his sexual needs. They'd ended up using each other. Honey had used him to make her feel more like a real woman, not a token wife, girlfriend or random mistress. And he'd sure made her feel like a woman. A very well-lubed and stretched-open woman.

Before she dozed off to sleep, Maurice came out of the shower. He was naked and unashamedly dangling his assets in front of her. "Hey Alice, I almost forgot. Here's some money."

He stepped into his underwear by the bed as Honey blinked at the bills. "What's this for?"

"Buy something sexy for tonight. Maybe one of those little leather outfits."

"Maurice I don't need your money." Honey wasn't sure whether to be mad or not. Nobody'd ever given her money to get something for herself.

"So? You're buying it for me. I'm going to be the one seeing you in it. Surprise me. Tonight." He pulled his huge boots on and combed his wet hair back with his fingers.

"So you're just going to leave? No breakfast or anything?"

"I had my fill of eating pussy and sucking titties last night. I'll grab something on the way. Now get into the shower, Alice, you smell like me." With a firm smack on her ass he walked out of the room. Honey heard him close the front door behind him.

She felt a slight pain in her abdomen and cut loose a gasser. *Fuck. No dog to blame it on.* One of the drawbacks to indulging in anal sex raised its stinky head.

Honey decided Maurice was right. She *did* need a shower.

* * * * *

Louis stared at Cory as she stared back at him, all dark hair and soft brown skin. She'd asked him something, but the sun had slanted through the window seconds later and danced over her face, distracting him completely.

"Huh?"

She sighed. "I asked who Zulee is?"

"I don't know. She showed up one day, scared the shit out of me. She seems nice enough."

"She is more than she seems." Cory's eyes turned vague in that unique way she had. Louis watched, fascinated, as she examined things he could not see. "She has—"

"What? Like a wooden leg or something?" He wanted to hear her speak in that soft lilting accent and watch her lips move as they formed the words. He didn't give a rat's ass about this weird shit, but he did give a rat's ass, and the whole rest of the rat, for this incredible woman who'd rocked his world to its foundations last night.

He had never had sex like that before. *Ever*. Never felt the need to damn near devour a woman like a starved animal, never come *twice* like that and once in her *ass*, for Chrissake—it had been unique, and if he didn't know better, he'd say they'd both been under some sort of spell.

But of course, he didn't believe in any of that shit. Not at all. No sir. Not him.

He was far too practical to give any credence to psychic mumbo-jumbo.

Louis breathed in and shuddered as that particularly sensual fragrance swamped his nostrils once more. "Damn, woman. You still smell fabulous. What was in your bath stuff, anyway?"

"*My* bath stuff?" She gaped at him. "It was *your* bath stuff."

He snorted. "Was not. Do I look like the kind of guy who'd soak in bubbles?"

"It was sitting on top of your towels. I don't go visiting with bath salts in my bag." She looked skeptical. "Hey, I don't care if you go for that sort of thing. Not my business."

"I don't." He knew he was whining. "I do not go for *that sort of thing*. Those were not my bath salts. Most definitely *not*. Never seen 'em before in my life."

"Then who—" Cory paused. "Ah *shit*. This house is playing tricks, isn't it?"

Louis chuckled and poured himself more of Zulee's rich brew. "Look, call it whatever you want. All I know is that last night was a helluva ride. And when it comes to *tricks*…" He waggled his eyebrows suggestively and sipped from his mug.

Cory put her own cup down with a thud. "I'm outta here."

"No, wait. I'm sorry. That came out wrong." Louis scrambled to undo the damage he'd done with his flip comment.

"Yes it did." She gathered her things together. "You've got yourself one very haunted house, Mr. Beekman. I hope you enjoy it. And those who share it with you." She spun on her heel and headed for the door.

Louis jumped up after her. "Hey. Hold on. I'm sorry. Really. I didn't mean to be rude." He sighed and ran his hands through his hair. "I don't know what got into me last night, but whatever it was, I don't regret a minute of it." He grabbed her arm and held her, making her stop at the threshold. "Don't leave like this, Cory. Please. I need…"

She refused to look at him. "You need what? Certainly not a good fuck. You had that last night."

It was Louis' turn to be offended. "Now just a minute. I wasn't alone in that bathroom. And I didn't do anything you didn't want me to."

Cory's shoulders sagged. "Yeah. Okay. You're right. We both got—carried away there." She turned at last. "For the record, I don't do that shit with people I just met."

Her eyes were troubled as she stared at him. "I don't know why I did what I did last night. And I agree, we didn't do anything I didn't want."

Louis relaxed his grip. "So…er…you coming back?"

"For round two?" Her eyebrows lifted but a slight smile robbed her words of their sting.

"Cory, after last night I don't know what we could do that would qualify as round two." He had to laugh. "That was the hottest time I've ever spent with a woman in my entire life."

The house seemed to shimmer around them for an instant, and they both blinked as soft laughter threaded through the deserted rooms.

"Did you hear that?" Cory whispered.

"Yeah." Louis swallowed. "Yeah, I heard it. Same as I get the feeling somebody's watching me now and again. That itchy feeling on the back of my neck, you know?"

She nodded. "Yes. I know." She pulled free of his arm. "Put those Tarot cards away someplace safe. I'll come back. I don't think I have any choice."

"Tonight? This afternoon? When?" He didn't want to let her go. Didn't want to not feel her skin beneath his hands. Didn't want to miss a second of the expressions that crossed her face in a parade of delight. She was beautiful in a way he couldn't explain, and he wanted to examine this whole thing in minute detail. Preferably when they were both naked.

"I don't know. I'll call you."

"You can't. My frickin' cell phone's died and the battery charger's in never-never land somewhere." Louis shook his head. "Just come back, okay? I'll be here. I'll be waiting."

She nodded. "Okay."

He stood on the porch until he couldn't see her anymore then turned and went back inside to a house that now seemed oddly empty. He had chores and jobs to do, and they'd fill the time until she returned.

With a sigh he cleared away the coffee cups and decided to properly repair the bathroom window. If he could, of course. His toolbox was back where it seemed to think it belonged — on the front porch.

Louis rolled his eyes. "Look, I want to work and you're not making it easy for me. So quit fucking with my tools, okay?" He yelled and pointed at empty air and knew he must have looked like a complete idiot. But it made him feel better.

Or at least as good as he could feel without Cory beside him. Or beneath him. Or in front of him.

Another growing erection tingled inside his shorts, and Louis clenched his teeth. It was gonna be a helluva long day until she came back.

* * * * *

[You are coming back, chère, aren't you?]

The voice echoed in Cory's brain as she carefully drove around some leftover puddles on the road home.

[Please, chère. It's important.]

"Why?" She spoke aloud, answering the voice in the only way she knew how. "Tell me why? Who are you? Are you Claudine?"

[I cannot sleep apart from my love. Find my love, chère. I want to sleep now. With him. Forever.]

Cory swerved, trying to focus on her driving and keep the soft voice in the back of her mind. "I don't understand. Help me."

[You help me. C'est tu, chère. Seulement tu…]

The voice drifted away leaving Cory bereft and parked alongside a levee. "Only me, huh?" She'd translated the French easily, having grown up in that pidgin-language environment where French is blended musically into English and mixed with a N'Awlins drawl.

The problem with this whole being-psychic thing, decided Cory as she pulled back onto the road, was that ghosts were frickin' cryptic critters at the best of times. Never came right out and said what they meant.

She wished, just for once, that a spirit would tap her on the shoulder, point to a painting and say, "Excuse me, my secret will is taped behind that frame. Take the two pieces of backing paper off and there it is."

Or perhaps a visitation along the lines of, "I'd appreciate you filing suit against the Louisiana state highway department and stop them from excavating the spot where I happen to be interred."

That would work too. Something solid she could actually *do*, rather than vague and insubstantial messages that probably meant something, but nothing that was immediately apparent.

Cory's gift had bestowed upon her the ability to hear and occasionally communicate with lost souls. If they chose to communicate with her, that is. Actually, she'd had very little ghostly interaction—her strength lay in the area of psychic sensibility rather than spiritual contact. She could tell when somebody was worried, or sick, and now and again when somebody was lying.

She could see into the past at times, but never into the future. She could "sense" things about people and sometimes the things she sensed were from souls surrounding those people. Families who had one or two matters to settle before moving on to the next plane of existence.

Cory knew, without a doubt, that Love Alley was inhabited by denizens of the "otherworld". She could feel them, sense them on several levels, and this morning both she and Louis had heard them laugh.

She was apparently in routine contact with somebody — maybe Claudine Lavalieres herself — and that voice came through urgent and clear. When it frickin' chose to.

Cory sighed and found a parking space near her apartment. She knew exactly how this day was gonna turn out, for once having complete and utter faith in her ability to predict the next few hours.

She was going to go shower, throw a few things in a bag, grab more coffee, call Eileen and then get back in her car.

She was most definitely going back to Love Alley in an attempt to find out what the *fuck* was going on out there.

And she was most definitely going back to Mr. *Deee*-licious *Deee*-Louis Beekman. He'd said it was a night like no other for him. Well, hoo-rah. Because it had been a night like no other for her as well. And, okay yeah. She admitted it. She'd like another one, please.

Ghosts or no ghosts, *Louis* was real. And damn it, he was the best fuck Cory had ever had.

* * * * *

Louis finished up staining the downstairs kitchen cabinet and walked onto the porch. It was a hot day but the gods had been kind and the cool breeze swept through the heat. He downed his beer and tossed it into the blue recycle barrel. With all the beer and sodas he drank he figured he might as well recycle them or he'd end up making an even bigger hole in the ozone layer or something.

He heard Maurice's sander and opened the cooler to grab a couple more beers. He figured he might as well share.

He was also bored and the radio reception sucked. Louis had his fill of faith healers and bad music, his mind longed for some old-fashioned rock and roll.

"Heads up." Maurice caught the incoming beer Louis tossed to him. The fizzle of the top opening spewed a fine mist and Maurice took a long drink. "*Brrraaaaaappppp*. Ahhh, I needed that." The belch was impressive.

"That was about a seven on the burp scale." Louis sat on the tailgate of Maurice's truck looking over all the wooden molding he had cut. "Man, this is some nice work. You have enough for the house?"

"Yeah, think so."

"Umm, hey Maurice…um…I've got a question for you. You ever hear of an aphrodisiac? Something that drives a woman crazy?"

After another swig, Maurice looked at Louis. "Yeah , I've heard of those. I've got an aphrodisiac right here." He grabbed his crotch. "It's ten inches long."

"No you asshole. I mean like—like incense or something." Louis laughed as Maurice grinned at his remark. "Last night. I don't know what it was but, well, I had this woman acting a little odd. I didn't mind but shit, it was fucking *hot*. I'm just not used to a woman being that nasty after just meeting me. It was like she was—I don't know—like *craving* it."

The thoughts made Louis think about the night before and Cory's body rubbing his and that familiar twinge of arousal filled his body again. "Never mind. I feel stupid talking about this shit." He felt himself blush. He really didn't want to sound like a geek or diminish how fabulous it was. Cory deserved a little respect, which meant he wasn't going to talk about her like a guy in a gym after prom night.

"And the problem is?" Maurice was sarcastic, his tone telling Louis he was wondering why this was a problem.

"Man, I know you're talkin' about Cory. Don't worry I won't say anything. But, that is one fine lady. She comes from good genes—trust me. I was born and raised 'round here, even though I moved over to just outside the city a few years ago. I *know* that family. If a woman like that wants you, then don't think about it...just *do* it. I know I'd be all over that like butter on corn."

"Oh...it wasn't Cory. Er—it was this woman I picked up at that bar by the highway." Louis was a terrible liar.

Maurice looked at him and shook his head. "Hey Louis, relax. I don't care if you two hook up. Hell, it's good you did. Don't worry. I'm not the kind of guy to say shit to people. Kick a few hundred bucks more down after the job—a little extra beer money makes me forget things easier." He laughed and turned back toward the pile of wood. "But I do know that Cory's no more your *fiancée* than I am. News like that would've spread quicker'n summer lightning round these parts."

Louis gulped. "Does Honey know?"

Maurice grinned. "Nope. And after last night, I'm figuring it wouldn't matter much to her either way anymore."

"Whew. Okay then." Feeling a bit better, Louis took a breath, puffing his chest out at his conquest. Then something occurred to him. "What did you mean, good genes?"

"Are you stupid or what? This is Love—fuckin'—*Alley*, duhhh. This was *the* high-class whorehouse. Men came from all over the world to be here for one night. The women were beautiful, sexy and studied French techniques about sex. My great, great whatever grandfather came here all the time and the stories were passed down to my dad. He told me about it. About the Lavalieres. Cory's a Lavalle. They're part of the same family. She's a descendant of Claudine, the woman who was the madam here."

"I knew it was a bordello. Read about that on the plane coming here."

"Well it sure had a fine reputation hereabouts." Maurice leaned down to pick up some of the wood. He turned when he heard a shout from the river. It was Honey in her boat.

"What the heck is Honey doing here?" Louis sighed.

"I tell you Louis. That woman can *fuck*. I don't mean a quick roll in the hay. She fucks all night, every position, no holes untouched and I swear, she almost drained me. My balls are still sore."

Louis picked up some of the molding and walked beside Maurice up toward the house. He wasn't sure if he should ask the next question, because he didn't want to feel like a fool. But what the hell. "Cory thinks the house might have ghosts. Do you believe in ghosts?" Louis paused. "I don't. Or at least I didn't…"

"I've seen a lot of shit growing up down here. A lot of freaky shit. Never seen a ghost but that doesn't mean they don't exist. I *have* seen pink and purple dancing elephants though. Moonshine has that effect on you."

"Hi fellas." Honey appeared in front of them. "I thought y'all might want some lunch. I had my housekeeper make some sandwiches and figured I'd pop over to see if you were hungry."

Louis surveyed the basket. The rumble in his stomach answered her question. "Thanks Honey, I appreciate it. As soon as I get settled in here I'll have a big party for all the neighbors."

"What about you Maurice? Are you *hungry*?" Honey gazed at him.

Maurice was silent for a moment, gazing back at her. "Hey Louis, is it alright if I leave for a couple hours? I'll come back later and work extra on the molding in the living room."

Louis, busy with a mouthful of turkey sandwich, nodded.

Honey looked a little confused as Maurice ignored the food she'd brought. "Well come on, Alice, we need to go." He motioned to her boat with his hand.

"Er—sorry, Louis. Short visit I guess. Looks like I have somethin' to take care of…bye." Honey hurried away.

"*Mummmph, mumble, brruunch.*" He couldn't talk too clearly with food stuffed in his face. Louis watched as Maurice smacked Honey on the ass while she walked in front of him to the dock. They both stepped into the boat and Louis saw Maurice unfastening his pants. He said something to Honey, and without hesitation she kneeled down in front of him. Maurice took the handle of the pole and pushed them off into the bayou.

Hmm, looks like she's having tube steak for lunch. Louis finished his sandwich and chuckled.

Chapter Twelve

ஐ

Cory walked up the alleé under the oaks toward the house, struck anew by the beauty of the place and the peaceful heavy air of the late afternoon. She had her backpack this time, her hair was coiled up into a cool knot on the back of her head and her shorts and top were…adequate.

She'd even put a bra on, hoping to subdue her unruly nipples, which were displaying a distressing tendency to harden at the mere thought of this place—and its new owner.

Reaching the foot of the steps, she mentally smacked herself upside the head. She was here to settle unruly spirits and put things back in order, not get herself laid.

Riiiiight.

With a slightly apologetic grin at her own duplicity, she walked up to the open door and peered inside. "Helloooo?"

It was quiet, no tools whirring or buzzing anywhere, no strange laughter echoing around the empty rooms.

"In the kitchen." Louis' voice answered her call.

"It's me. Cory." The scent of fresh cut wood trickled up into her nostrils as she stepped around a small stack of molding, placed carefully to one side of the hall.

"Okay. C'mon in." Louis popped his head around the door. "Want a cold one?"

"Er…I'll take a soda for right now if you have one."

Louis bent to his tiny fridge. "Sure. Got one left. Remind me to get more next time I hit the supermarket."

"Yes dear." Cory chuckled.

Louis pulled out the last soda, shut the fridge door and laughed back. "Yeah, sorry. That was kind of a stupid thing to say, wasn't it?"

"No problem." Cory was already staring around the kitchen, her palms itching. "Look, I don't mean to be abrupt, but where'd you put those Tarot cards? I need to work with them a bit."

Louis looked puzzled, but pulled the deck from a drawer. "Here. You said put them someplace safe. They're fine." He passed them over to her and she crossed to the kitchen table, thankfully cleared of tools and empty beer cans.

Confidently, she opened the pack and pulled the cards free, glancing quickly at the surface to make sure it was spotless.

"You gotta *work* with them?" He sounded a little confused.

"Yeah."

Settling herself comfortably, Cory riffled her fingers through the familiar feel of the Tarot. A tingle brushed her skin—like feathers dusting over her body. She sighed, enjoying the knowledge that her psychic senses were on alert.

"So—like you have to warm 'em up, or what?" Louis pulled out another chair and settled himself next to her. "I've seen card dealers in Las Vegas before, I know how you all work."

"No. Sit there." She nodded at the seat directly opposite. "I need you across from me, not next to me."

"Yes, ma'am." Obediently Louis changed chairs. "Why?"

"Ssshh. I'll tell you in a minute."

Louis shushed, simply watching her and sipping his beer.

Cory shuffled the deck, spread them from left to right, then tipped them into the reverse setting, right to left. The cards felt right, and she opened her mind to the unseen world around them, waiting for the telltale itch of awareness.

It didn't take too long. On her third shuffle, the back of her neck prickled. The time was right. She took a drink from her soda, restacked the deck and pushed it across to Louis. "Shuffle, please. Several times."

"Okay…is this Texas hold-'em or five-card draw?" Louis did as he was told, finally pushing the deck back to Cory.

She nodded. "Now they're ready. Awakened. Know anything about Tarot cards?"

He shook his head. "Nope. I've seen 'em, but that's it."

She fanned the deck out on the table and pulled some cards free, setting them in front of Louis. "These are the *suit* cards. Wands, pentacles, swords and cups." Her fingertip tapped each colorful card in turn. "Sort of like hearts and clubs and so on. They're called the Minor Arcana."

Louis looked at them interestedly. "Wouldn't want to go all in with a handful of these."

Cory ignored him. "Each suit has meaning in the reading we're going to do, but I won't go into the details." She looked up. "And no, I wouldn't go all in either." She paused. "But then again, I don't gamble."

"Ah." Louis blinked. "Good to know. Guess being a psychic you wouldn't find too many people who'd want to play poker with you, huh?"

Cory rolled her eyes. "What*ever*." She pulled out more cards. "Now here—these are the *trump* cards. The equivalent of the face cards in a regular deck. It's the Major Arcana. We'll be using these to read from."

She showed Louis several of them. "Here's the Chariot, for example. And this..." She tapped another. "This is the High Priestess."

Louis leaned in. "Handy that they've all got labels on 'em."

"Yeah. But don't be misled. That's simply the name of the card, it's not the literal *meaning* of the card."

"Huh?"

Cory thought for a moment. "We're going to lay out these cards in a certain pattern. Their position in relation to each other can change the meaning of the reading. What would be a good card in one position can be a bad card in another position. And it's also affected by whether it's upside down or not. See?"

"No."

Cory pinched the bridge of her nose. "Okay. Let's skip the introductory lesson and just do it."

"Oh yeah, now you're talkin'!"

Something in Louis' tone caught her attention and she glanced up to see a heat radiating from the depths of his eyes. It took her no time at all to figure out where his thoughts were going and in spite of her firm resolution to be cool and professional, she blushed.

"But before we do..." He leaned across the table and reached for her head. "Take those pins out, please? You look nice, but that hair...it's pulled back so tight it's giving *me* a headache."

She gulped. "But...it's cool..."

"Pleeeease?"

She was completely helpless to resist the pleading in his tone. A few quick tugs and her hair tumbled down her back, soft tresses dusting her shoulders and adding to the warmth that was curling around low in her belly.

Enough, girl. You gotta focus here. "Better?"

Louis nodded and sat back with a smile. "Thanks. Okay let's do this card thing."

Cory took a deep breath. "Yeah. Let's."

* * * * *

"First, we need to find *you*."

Her words surprised him. He looked side to side, then replied, "Um, I'm right here."

"No, I meant in the cards. You are the *questioner* here, it's your house, your cards…we need to identify you."

"Oh." He sighed. This was all mumbo-jumbo to him, but she seemed pretty intense about the whole thing, so he was going to play along if it killed him. "What do I do?"

"Pick a card." Cory turned the deck facedown and spread it on the table.

He leaned in and carefully pulled one card loose with his fingers. "Here. This one."

She flipped it over, revealing seven ornate round things and a couple of naked people.

"Cool." Louis grinned in spite of himself.

She ignored it. "The seven of pentacles. Appropriate."

"Really?" He looked at the balls and the naked couple, biting back the dozen things he *soooo* wanted to say. *Relax, breathe and don't comment on trying the positions or the Kama Sutra references to the art.*

"Pentacles represent the realm of the physical. The material things in our lives. It's also about the manifestation of the material plane. A good card for you, given what you do." She glanced up. "It's telling us that you are a practical person who likes to see results. Things you can touch, accomplish, achieve with your own hands."

"No kidding." Louis kept his tone interested, even though he probably could have come up with the same thing given a few minutes. So far, she hadn't told him anything he didn't already know. "Do we find you now?"

"No, I'm doing the reading. My card won't appear."

"Oh." Louis was mildly disappointed, but kept silent and watched as she collected up the cards, setting his seven of pentacles to one side.

"If you have a question, now is the time to ask it."

Louis opened his mouth only to see her frown.

"Silently. In your mind. Ask the cards for an answer within your mind."

Yeah right. How long before I can get you naked and feel those long legs of yours wrapped around me?

The air in the house was hushed as she dealt a pattern onto the tabletop. Pretty soon he was going to have to turn on the lights, but for now the setting sun provided enough illumination for him to see her hands as they carefully positioned six cards faceup. It looked like a kind of cross when she'd finished. He did his very best to focus on the house and whatever had gone on there, but she was too damn distracting.

Like her hands, for instance.

She had nice hands. Long fingers with nails cut short and blunt, yet very much the hands of a woman. He knew how good they felt against his body and beneath the table his cock stirred.

Fuck, she was something *else*.

Unfortunately, it seemed like her mind was some*place* else at the moment. "There. That's it." She leaned back and blew air out through her teeth. "These are pretty damn impressive cards."

He stared at the jumble of colors and images. "How can you tell?"

"I feel them. They're talking already and we haven't even examined them."

He shook his head. This was *way* out of his experience. Give him a couple of tentacles and a hammer any day.

"Let's see what we've got here." Cory leaned in, studying the cards with intensity. "Hmm."

"Hmm? Is that a good hmm or a bad hmm?"

"Just a minute…"

Louis figured a helluva lot more than a minute had gone past when she finally sat back and looked up at him with an odd expression on her face.

"*What*? I didn't do anything. I shushed like you told me to…"

"The cards. They're telling a story." She blinked and he got the odd impression that now she was finally seeing *him*. Like she jerked herself back from wherever she'd been and found herself surprised to be sitting at a kitchen table.

Cory tapped the first card. "See this one? Underneath?"

He nodded. "Yep. It's…uh…the Moon, right?"

"Yes. This is where you are right now. Evolving. Still growing, still building, still working. Unfinished."

Louis looked around him at the chaos of renovation. "No shit."

"This card…" She ignored his comment and tapped the card that lay on top of the first one. "This is indicative of current influences. Things that may or may not help you."

"Okay." He stared down. "The Chariot."

"It's your will. Your determination to control things, to drive them where you believe they should go. This can help you achieve your goals, but sometimes it can represent a stubborn resistance to other ideas. Other *helpful* suggestions."

He couldn't miss the emphasis. "You mean like when you tell me about ghosts and stuff."

She snorted. "Maybe. We'll see. Let's move on." She pointed to the next card. "Here we have the distant past."

Even Louis sobered as he stared at the card he recognized immediately — *Death*. "Whoa. That isn't too good, is it?"

Cory's eyes softened. "Death is part of life, Louis. It's in all our pasts. We cannot escape the inevitability of it, or the finality of it as far as this existence is concerned." She glanced down again. "But here, in your past influences position, it's very strong. It's telling you of the cost of your inheritance. That at some time, somebody died, and the result has put you here, now."

"Well, yeah. I inherited this place from my grandfather."

She shook her head. "It's more than that. Further back than that. I don't know. Let's go on. We can come back to it if necessary."

Louis followed her hand as she moved to the next card, although his gaze kept straying back to that skeleton on horseback. A slight chill trickled down his spine. He shrugged it off. Too much beer and sun.

"Now we get to the recent past." Cory gestured to the card. "It's the High Priestess. A good strong card for this particular spot."

He shrugged. "Could it be you?"

Cory was silent for a moment. "Uh, yeah. I guess." She thought about it. "She represents the subconscious mind. And she's a balance — see the black and white columns either side of her? She's in between. Impartial."

"Hmm." Louis watched the pulse as it throbbed at the base of Cory's throat. *Impartial, huh? I don't think so.*

"She's the link between the conscious and the subconscious, so yes, I suppose in this particular pattern, it could well be me. And she is supporting you. Beneath you."

Cory realized what she'd said, and a slow flush of warmth spread from her breasts to her neck to her cheeks. "Uhhh…"

Louis smiled. He put every ounce of charm he had into it, too. "It's okay. I won't take that the wrong way." *The hell I won't.*

"Thanks." Hurriedly she moved on. "Now we get to your future influences. This one here—Justice."

"Well, that sounds official." Louis grinned, finishing off his beer.

"It's pretty clear."

"As mud. Care to explain?" He pushed back from the table and recycled the empty can. "And while you're at it, tell me if I'm ever gonna stop sweating." He grabbed another cold can and held it to his forehead.

Cory laughed. "You'll get used to it. We all do." She paused. "That is, if you decide to stay." Dark brown eyes met his. "Have you decided yet?"

Louis shook his head. "Not yet. I'm still working here. Gotta see what the end result looks like."

"Ah." Cory tilted her head. "Yeah. It fits. Seven pentacles, the Moon…"

"Right. So I'm a well-hung planet who likes to fix things."

She laughed again. "Sort of." Then she blushed and looked back down at the cards.

Louis would have given half his bank account to know what she was thinking right at that moment. Whatever it was that made her blush.

For once he wished for a few psychic skills of his own. He'd *really* like to read her mind.

* * * * *

Thank God he can't read my mind.

A sudden flash of his body, cock hard and balls oh-so-tempting, had stunned Cory into a quick eruption of heat. *Talk about well-hung.*

She hurriedly yanked her disobedient mind back to the table and the Tarot deck. Without a doubt there was a strong message here, and she only had four more cards to reveal. Then, perhaps, they'd be able to put it all together.

"Here's the last set. These four go here." She dealt the next four cards from the deck faceup, in a line, one above the other, to the right of the existing cards. "Now we're done."

"We are?" He looked at the cards, then at her.

Poor guy. He was really struggling with this, she knew. And he'd been a helluva lot more patient than a lot of her customers were. She smiled. "Yep. This lot should tie it all together. I hope. Bear with me, Louis. We'll make sense of it."

"I trust you." He grinned back as he popped another can. Damn, he was good-looking when he smiled like that. So unself-conscious, just enjoying the moment. Cory almost envied him that skill, since she seldom had the chance to purely have *fun*.

Once again her naughty thoughts rambled off into areas where both she and Louis were naked and having a great deal of fun.

She sighed. "Let's finish this." *Before I self-combust.*

"Okay. Oh…can I get you anything?"

Yeah. Fucked. "No thanks. I'm fine."

Louis sat back down at the table and looked at the last batch of cards. "Bottom up, huh?"

How she stopped her eyes from crossing, Cory never knew, but she did. She simply nodded and touched the lowest card. "This is you where you are right now. Within the current set of circumstances."

"Hell, that looks pretty bad."

She grinned. "It's not. It's the Tower. It symbolizes the jolt we get from understanding. You're beginning to understand this place, Louis. It's a good thing."

He looked unconvinced.

"Well, look, here in the next position is the World. This is kind of like what effect you'll have on those around you. It's representative of life. The cycles of life, the consistency of existence."

"Um…wanna translate that for me?"

The interpretation crashed into the back of Cory's neck like a physical blow. He was going to get her *pregnant*. She could possibly bear his child.

Shitfuck nooooo. I so *don't think so.*

She cleared her throat. "It's…er…it means that you'll be setting everything in order. Putting things that were wrong— right."

"I see."

No you don't. Because that ain't it. I wish it was, but it ain't.

She buried those thoughts in the basement of her brain and bravely soldiered on. "Almost done." She tapped the second to last card. "The Empress. Your hidden desires—"
Cory held up her hand. "Before you even say it, no, this doesn't mean you're looking for a woman. It means that

you're looking to find a way to heal the past. To solve whatever mystery lies here."

"I haven't admitted there is one, yet." Louis looked defensive. "Sure, there's been some odd stuff going on, but I'm still not positive—"

"Yes you are." Cory was staring him straight in the eyes. "You know, deep down inside, what's going on, you just don't want to admit it to yourself yet. But—" She lowered her head once more, "you will."

"Really?"

There was a silence for a moment. Cory swallowed, trying to rid her throat of the lump in it that had risen from her gut as she stared at the final card.

The *Lovers*.

How the hell was she going to interpret that for Louis, when all her instincts were screaming at her what it meant?

That she and Louis would be lovers again. *Often*. That passion would rise between them and work with the unseen world to correct a past injustice. That it needed both of them to work together, bringing their strengths to complement each other.

That they were both here, in this place at this time, to put the final words to a story which had clearly begun with a death a long time ago. And that the more they loved, the stronger the chances were that they'd accomplish this task.

She sighed.

Louis cleared his throat. "I recognize *that* card, too." He was staring at the linked and naked bodies.

"Figures." Cory almost groaned the word. She lifted her empty soda can and sighed. "Can I have a beer please?"

Louis almost jumped at the mundane question, but got her one from the fridge. She copied his earlier action and held it to her forehead, enjoying the cooling sensation. Finally, after she'd got her body under control and could deal with the moisture dampening her panties, she risked a look up at him.

"So. Here's what we've got."

He sat quietly, listening to her. He was a good listener, she realized. Funny, too. He was really one awful *nice* guy in a world where nice guys weren't exactly thick on the ground. Distracted again, she returned to the cards and forced herself to concentrate.

"You're here, with your particular skills and emotions, for a purpose. To right a wrong, correct an injustice— whatever it is—that happened in the past. It's connected with a death." She paused, gathering her impressions, her images, the psychic tingles that had flown up her arms from the Tarot cards.

"It's connected to this house, too. Very strongly. And, I guess, it's connected to me, as well, since I seem to be part of the picture." She rubbed her shoulder. "Jeez, I'm tired."

Louis pushed away from the table and came to stand behind her. Without asking, he pushed her hair aside and began to massage her neck, finding the exact spot that was aching. She closed her eyes and for a few moments just let her mind float, relaxing into the rhythmic motion of his hands.

Fuck, he had good hands.

"So I'm figuring here that we're talking about Claudine." His knuckles pressed either side of her vertebrae, easing the tension and setting up new ones. In places that weren't anywhere near her neck. "You're related to her, aren't you?"

"Yeah." Cory didn't even bother to ask how he knew. The touch of his fingers was too soothing, too pleasant, to disrupt. "Way back in the family tree. Claudine was one of the first Lavalieres to live here in Louisiana."

"And she died? Some kind of mystery, right?"

"So it's said." She leaned into his massage. "Shit, that's good."

"What do you know about her? I've only read a little bit about it."

"She ran Love Alley. Damn fine whorehouse, too, so they say. Anyway, she made the mistake of loving the wrong man, and refusing a rich man. After that, she was never heard from again."

"Hmm." Louis continued his firm touches, working down toward her shoulders now, stroking the bare skin of her upper arms and then returning to her neck once more.

Fuck. He's turning me on.

Big-time.

Cory opened her mouth to say something. She wasn't quite sure what it was going to be...possibly, "I don't think you should do that anymore", or maybe, "Don't stop doing that or I'll kill you", or—most likely—"Strip and fuck me. *Now*".

But before any words at all came out, there was a loud thumping sound from upstairs.

Louis' hands left her body and they both froze, listening.

It was Louis who broke the silence. "Oh *shit*. What now?"

Chapter Thirteen

෨

Two faces stared at each other, eyes wide.

Cory's were dark and nervous, and Louis figured his were pretty much the same except for their color. They both swallowed simultaneously, then Cory spoke. "You want to go find out what that was?"

"I have a choice? If I do, the answer is—not particularly."

She gave him a quick grin. "Me neither, but you know we're going to."

"You first."

"Uh uh. It's your house."

"Thanks a lot." He peered out of the kitchen doorway to see a perfectly normal-looking hall. Even the lights were working.

Grateful for small mercies he glanced up the stairs. "It came from up there, right?"

"Yep." She was close behind him and at any other time he would have spent a few moments wondering how to get her closer. But right now he was simply thankful for her presence.

The thump came again and they both jumped this time, the sound was loud and unmistakable. Something had fallen over.

"You know," began Louis, "I'm getting just a little bit tired of all this stuff. It never seems to frickin' *stop*..."

Cory nudged him toward the staircase. "It will. We just have to figure out what the house wants, is all."

"I asked it. It wouldn't tell me." He snorted, realizing how completely stupid that sounded. But in response to that insistent hand between his shoulder blades he walked to the stairs and put his foot on the first step. "Uh…I suppose you want me to go up here, right?" He tipped his head toward the second floor.

"Yep."

"You got a gun or a sword or a baseball bat handy?"

Cory sighed. "C'mon, Mr. Big Brave Man. Do your thing. I'll be right behind you."

And she was. As they mounted the stairs, Louis felt a hand grasp his back pocket. He paused and looked over his shoulder at her. "Scared?"

She glared at him. "Of course not."

He said nothing, just continued to hold her gaze.

"Oh, all *right*. Yeah. Just a wee bit."

"Me too." He reached down and unclasped her fingers from their death grip on his jeans, folding them within his palm instead. "Better?"

She nodded.

"Okay then. Let's go be brave ghostbusters." He mounted the stairs carefully, looking around him, trying to find the source of the noise. "It's probably only a shutter fell down or something."

"Sure." She squeezed his fingers tighter. "I'll bet that's what it is."

Their tentative perimeter check yielded nothing that looked like it could have thumped, bumped or dropped and the rooms were pretty much clear.

Pausing on the second floor, Louis raised an eyebrow. "Don't see anything, do you?"

Cory lifted her chin and stared at nothing in particular. He was starting to recognize that look as the one meaning she was off someplace else. Someplace he couldn't follow. Quietly, he waited.

"Up there." She indicated the small stairway leading to the attics.

Louis sighed. "Figures." He headed that way. "I haven't cleaned up here. It's pretty filthy."

Once again there was a soft thud, quieter this time. Two hands twitched and grasped each other tightly.

"We're on the right track." Cory's voice was quiet but encouraging.

"That's nice." Louis tried to keep his tone from being too sarcastic. This was so close to being a scene out of some horror movie that he'd started to sweat and it had nothing to do with the humidity.

They reached the top of the narrow stairs and stopped on the landing, surveying the small passageway from which doors led to tiny rooms and storage cupboards. A slight sound came from one of them.

"I'll bet it's a mouse or a squirrel or something." Louis moved to the door with a bravado that was all for show. It had nothing to do with how he actually felt, which could be described succinctly in two words. *Scared shitless.*

"Yeah, I'll bet you're right." Cory's body was now pressed tightly up against his back, adding to his tension.

Only this wasn't nerves, it was all a different kind of tension that started in his cock and progressed everyplace else quite rapidly. He tried to ignore the breasts brushing against his T-shirt and not breathe in too much of her womanly fragrance. He'd get dizzy for sure and do something stupid like strip her naked and lick her from head to foot.

Jerking his mind back from some pretty X-rated images, Louis pushed the door to a storage closet open, wincing at the loud and dramatic squeak.

"You could've oiled the frickin' hinges."

"Quit complaining. At least the stairs held." He peeked inside. "Ahhh." Pushing the door wide he led Cory in. "Here's our culprit."

A large chest had overturned and as it did so its lid had fallen off, spewing the contents over the floor. Some things had rolled to the far side of the little room, obviously making considerable noise as they did so.

"Wow. What the hell *is* all this stuff?" Cory stared at the pile of debris.

Louis shook his head. "Stuff. That's exactly what it is. *Stuff.* More leftover things from God-knows-when. I've dug through some of these storage boxes already. Not much in 'em worth keeping."

He bent to examine some odds and ends as Cory moved to the chest itself. "Ooooh."

He turned and snickered as she pulled out a long feather boa in an unlikely shade of pink and tossed it around her shoulders.

"Isn't this too cool?"

He thought for a minute. "I don't think I've ever seen a chicken that color."

"Philistine. Guys just don't *get* feathers." She fluffed the bits and pieces—and sneezed. "Okay. Dust and feathers. Not a good combination." The boa was returned to the chest. "Hmm." This time she'd found a bouquet of faded silk flowers.

Louis grinned as Cory rummaged with all the enthusiasm of a bargain hunter at a "reduced for clearance" sale. He knew the feeling—the ever-present possibility that there would be *treasure* tucked away in chests like this.

Sadly, there never was.

But Cory happily dug through the accumulated things that had once meant something to somebody. And Louis enjoyed watching her as she gently removed and replaced items that hadn't been touched for too many years to count.

"I think this was a woman's storage chest." She pulled out a faded and torn garment that was probably a corset of some sort. Creamy silk had spotted to brown in places, but the embroidered roses around the bottom edge were still red.

Louis raised an eyebrow. "Hmm. Bet you'd look good in that." His libido licked its lips.

"Riiiiight."

The corset went back in the box and Louis sighed.

Something caught his eye—a flicker of light on glittery thread. He reached over to a shadowy corner and picked it up.

"Hey. What's this?" He held it to the light so that Cory could see it.

She froze.

* * * * *

"Louis, put it down. Carefully."

Cory was pleased to see he obeyed her, gently lowering the item back to the floor. "So what the hell is it? Looks like a bag of marbles to me."

She shook her head. "It's a gris-gris."

"A *gree-gree*? What the fuck's a *gree-gree*?"

She stared at it as she moved to his side. "It's spelled G-R-I-S-G-R-I-S. It's a Voodoo artifact."

Louis tilted his head. "See, this is why I like having you around. You know shit like this."

She ignored him. "What I need to find out is if it's benevolent or not."

"So, ask it." He turned to the bag. "Are you a good gris-gris or a bad gris-gris?"

Once again, Cory paid no attention. Her focus was all on the small black velvet pouch and the decorations that glittered on the front of it. She moved closer, senses attuned to anything out of the ordinary, that special part of her mind opening to receive impressions.

She felt a soft pulsing warmth steal into her psyche and heaved a sigh of relief. "It's okay. It's a good gris-gris."

Louis moved to her side. "I thought Voodoo was dolls and pins and stuff."

She knelt on the floor, studying the embroidery. "Some of it is. This is more of a good luck charm. Something you'd carry with you to protect you from bad magic, or to bring love, money…that sort of thing."

"Aah." Louis looked knowledgeable. "Sort of a Voodoo version of a rabbit's foot?"

She chuckled. "Sort of. There may be one in there as a matter of fact."

Louis backed away a little. "Er…what exactly *is* in there?"

"Dunno." Cory shrugged. "Could be a variety of things depending on who made it and what they had in mind. Probably dried flowers, something of a lover's if it was a love gris-gris. Herbs, maybe some blessed dirt—there's no exact recipe."

"Ah." Louis raised an eyebrow. "Okay, so what do we do with it?"

Cory finally picked it up and stood, turning so that the light fully illuminated the little bag. "It's beautiful. See here?" She pointed at the tiny stitches. "That's the sign of the Goddess Erzulie. She is the earth-mother, if you will. The head honcho in Voodoo. Very powerful lady."

A distant rumble of thunder distracted both of them, and Cory's fingers tightened on the bag. "Shit. Here comes today's storm."

"Sounds like." Louis nodded and turned just as the lights in the room flickered and went out. He sighed. "I really would like to get some decent wiring into this place. Along with a set of twenty-first century circuit breakers."

She blinked into the darkness, her eyes adjusting to the total lack of light that had fallen within the small room.

"Don't trip, Cory. Give me your hand."

"I'm here." She moved toward him, still holding the gris-gris. It was too important a discovery to leave lying around on some attic floor.

"I've got a flashlight downstairs. If we can just find our way back out…"

Their bodies touched and Louis reached for her.

"Er…Louis?"

"Yeah?"

"That's my breast."

There was silence for a second or two. "So it is."

"Could we maybe get out of this stuffy room before we get personal?"

"We gonna *get* personal?"

Cory sighed. "We'll talk, okay? Let's just get out of here first." Slowly, Louis' hand peeled away from her breast. She rather missed the warmth and the really nice way it cupped her, but first things first.

Managing to find his hand, she linked their fingers.

And an odd light began to glow within the room — it was coming from the tiny gris-gris.

"What the *fuck*?"

Louis' whisper echoed her own thoughts at that exact moment. *What the fuck?*

The bag in her hand pulsed and heated. Convulsively she tried to drop it, but it wouldn't leave her grasp. She could only watch as the glow intensified, lighting her hand, then their bodies and finally the entire room.

A stream of glittering light began to spew from it, like waves of fairy dust freed onto a gentle wind. It swirled this way and that, uncertain at first, then with more definition, beginning to circulate around the two of them. A small tornado of dazzling stars that held them captive within its eye.

Cory blinked, her eyes blinded as the light grew more fierce. "Oh *shit*."

Louis' hand tightened convulsively on hers. "Don't let go."

"I won't."

She had no idea how long they stood in the middle of the brilliance, feeling nothing but the caress of the air on her cheeks. If she didn't have the evidence right in front of her face, she'd have dismissed the whole thing as some sort of hallucination.

But it was happening — the room swirled and heaved as the lights continued to surround them, a tube of painfully dazzling flashes.

Finally reality returned, Louis' hand still grasping hers, their feet on the floor, their eyes readjusting to the slowly fading light. The ring of stars disintegrated like leftover fireworks, dropping down in a circle around them and disappearing.

Neither moved. Neither spoke and neither barely breathed for a moment or two.

Then Cory's ears caught a sound.

Music. Voices.

The muted noises of *people* in Love Alley. A party going on beneath them in a house that should have been empty.

Beside her, Louis sniffed. "You smell that?" he said as his stomach grumbled.

"You *hear* that?"

"Fried chicken."

"People."

They looked at each other in bewilderment. Louis finally asked the million-dollar question. "What the fuck's going on?"

She shrugged her shoulders helplessly. "I don't know. But we won't find out just standing here."

Two gazes met. Neither moved.

Louis sighed. "You going to call me a fraidy cat or something? I suppose we have to do this, right?"

"Yeah." She swallowed down a lump of nerves. "Together. Don't let go my hand."

"Not a chance."

As their fingers locked tightly, they moved to the door. The gris-gris snuggled comfortably into Cory's free hand apparently unwilling to part from her. She sensed no threat from it, just a desire to be held. So she held it as Louis reached for the door.

And his hand passed right through it.

* * * * *

"Well this could be good or bad." Louis melted through the door. It didn't feel like he was walking through anything, but his eyes told him otherwise.

Pulling Cory along behind him, they both entered the hallway — and the past. The smells of the bordello seemed alive and fresh and were accompanied by moans of pleasure close by. Air that had been still and empty in their time now pulsed with music from downstairs.

"Now *this* could be a major cool effect for a movie." Louis saw lights coming from under doors in the passage. "You know what I think?"

"Yeah. I'm thinking it too." Cory's voice was hushed. "We're back in the past, right?"

"Looks like." He paused. "I don't think we're dead, are we?"

She shook her head. "Can't be. We didn't do anything that would have killed us." She stared at the small bag she still held in one hand. "It's this. The Voodoo amulet. I told you it was powerful."

"You weren't kidding." He touched another wall, fascinated as his hand disappeared then reappeared. "So. What now?"

Cory got an oddly self-conscious look on her face. "Er...we go look around?"

Louis was in favor of that plan. "Okay. I'm good with that. You think they can see us?"

"Hell, I don't even know if *I* can see us. So I guess there's only one way to find out."

"Okay. Don't move. Don't let go my hand. I'm gonna try an experiment."

From the room next to him, he could hear a deep growl followed by a soft whispery moan. It reminded him of the sounds Cory made when she came. Soft noises a woman lets free as she becomes wrapped up in the burst of passion's release. With a wicked grin he leaned toward the door beside him and carefully let his head pass through it to peek inside.

The light from an old-fashioned oil lamp illuminated the small room, leaving the corners in shadows. On the high, white, lace-covered bed a man's legs hung over the edge, his bare toes wiggling as they dangled loosely above the carpet. A woman sat upright from the pile of sheets and flesh. Her back was to Louis but he could see the tight black corset that laced up her spine, and the tangled mess of her long brown curly hair. She was straddling the man and pushed her weight up from him with her arms. From Louis' perspective he could clearly see the long length of the man's cock as it pulled free of her pussy. She lowered back down, grinding her ass against his legs and the lips of her pussy onto his cock.

She whispered into his ear. "You up for another round? I know I am."

He murmured back. "I'm not sure if I have another ten dollars, Lucille."

Louis automatically grabbed for his wallet. *Shit, I know I've got a fifty here somewhere.* He stared at the beauty of the woman as she clambered off the bed. Her body was pale and looked so pure—breasts perfect globes swinging free as she moved. Louis knew they couldn't be fake because there sure as hell wasn't any silicone this far into the past. The corset pushed them high and Lucille began to tug on the strings, tidying herself up a bit.

The man sat up, looked at the firm sensuality of this fine woman and obviously couldn't resist her.

"*Ooooff.*" Lucille's breath caught as the man grabbed her and pulled her back onto the bed.

"You win. Ma'am, you are just *too* beautiful to do without for another three weeks." With a long, lingering kiss he rolled on top of Lucille and smothered her with his mouth.

He raised his head up and stared into her face, "How much for the whole night?"

"Richard, for you I'll work something out with Claudine." Her voice, a sultry whisper of sexuality, came clearly to Louis' ears. He watched, spellbound, as she let her hands slide down Richard's body. With both hands she grabbed his ass and wrapped her creamy white legs around his torso — and moaned.

Louis found himself jerked from the room. Cory was frowning at him. "What's the matter with you? You keep squeezing my fingers. You know you're close to being a peeping Tom, for Chrissake." She paused. "What were they doing anyways?"

"Um — they were sleeping."

Cory snorted and tugged again, pulling him along the corridor once more. It was sort of like floating, only not really. They walked, but their feet weren't touching the floor. Louis was about to get disoriented when they heard a scream, quickly silenced by someone saying "*Shut up!*"

It was Cory's turn to ease her head through the wooden paneling and she almost pulled Louis with her but she jumped and froze as she saw the tail of a bull whip slice right through her face to slash against a man's reddened back. There was another stifled scream. It had been the man's yell Cory had heard from the corridor, and he was getting a whipping from a tall blonde woman. She was in a black corset, black stockings and long black satin gloves. She certainly seemed to know how to handle a whip—and other things.

With the man hunched over and naked, the blonde woman stepped closer and licked at his red wounds. Starting with the ones on his shoulders then squatting lower to lick the irritated flesh on the small of his back.

When the woman spun the man around, Cory swallowed. She wasn't one for watching other people get it on, but this particular scene and the graphic sexuality of it brought an uneasy urge swelling between her legs. The man's cock was enormous in girth and had an erection so hard it seemed like steel. The glistening tip seeped anticipation and the blonde obliged by licking the shaft with snake-like darts of her tongue.

The man was weakened and looked as if he was in pain but he sighed as she took his cock deeply into her mouth. His head hung forward and a grimace of what could have been agony or ecstasy washed across his face. He was on the verge. The sweat must have been burning across his irritated skin because he breathed through his teeth and his skin shone between the bruises.

"No more—I can't take any more." He uttered the words, gasping between each syllable.

Releasing him from her mouth, the woman looked angry. "I'll tell you when you've had enough."

Cory was part horrified, part mesmerized. She couldn't bear to see him like this or understand why she was so turned on by what she was watching. And she *was*, undoubtedly, turned on. Something about the raw brutality mixed with the sensual undercurrents was igniting her sex drive something fierce. Cory's body was on fire with desire.

She stared as the woman reached beside her and dipped her hand into a small container of a jelly-type substance. The blonde's eyes were hollow and expressionless. She knelt before the large man, his cock throbbing and swollen. She grabbed the shaft in one hand and swept her gleaming fingers between his legs, leaving smears of the slippery gel to mark her movements.

The man threw his head back as the blonde shoved her middle finger inside his ass and began to vigorously jerk the man off with her other hand. She flicked at the tip with her tongue and began to smile with what looked like delighted ecstasy as she controlled the situation.

Groaning, the man thrust his hips upwards as if fucking the air.

"Hey, what you doin' in here?" Louis finally looked in just in time to see the man spew his seed all over the blonde woman's black stockings. Over and over he blasted shots of semen from deep within his loins, spurting the creamy liquid in a stream that seemed to never end.

"Holy shit, a money shot!"

Cory blinked and ignored the joke. It may have been, as Louis said, a "money shot", but this wasn't a porn movie. It was real. Or at least it had been, two hundred years ago. The feel of Louis' hand within hers heated Cory's body. The sensuality of Love Alley and the activities of its residents was heating her mind.

Can spirits fuck? If this kept up for much longer, she was damn well gonna try and find out.

Chapter Fourteen

જી

Like a couple of kids in a candy store, Cory and Louis found themselves checking out Love Alley room by room and peeking at various couples in sexual acts. Most were the standard *man-on-top-get-it-over-with-quick* situations. But every now and then they'd catch something inspired and downright arousing.

Louis was the first to reach a room with a colored door and smiled. He envisioned something kinky and strange behind it and tugged Cory with him, living out a fantasy and going behind the green door.

Once inside, they both looked at each other with puzzlement. There was a one-legged woman in a camisole, a donkey, various marionette puppets and a midget in a tutu chasing a chicken around the room while singing old hillbilly tunes. And that was the more normal stuff. They couldn't understand the man pulling on a squirrel that was stuck on his cock nor the woman hanging upside down with flowers sticking out of her pussy like a vase.

This room was waaaay outside bizarre and they backed out of it simultaneously.

Moving on, Cory stopped suddenly at a white door with two etched stars on its surface—something different enough to make it stand out. Listening for a second, they heard a man's guttural groan followed by a giggle and a sucking sound. A woman's voice spoke softly from the room. "Mmm, it's my turn to have him." The voice was soft and very sexual.

"Hey—quit pulling on my arm." Louis complained as Cory pulled him into and through the white door.

Inside, the room was a heaven in white. The bed was covered in white and the sheer net drapes hanging around the bed shone brightly in the light of two lamps. The netting may have kept bugs outside the bed but it was a magnet to Cory. Louis followed as she moved to the bed and stared at the three people tangled together like a pretzel on top of it.

The back of a blonde woman's head popped up and she rolled to the side of the bed. Her pale skin almost blended into the white bed covering. In front of her was a couple in a sixty-nine position. The woman on top of the man was also a blonde and slobbering noisily on the man's cock. His skin was tanned, his body firm and the vision of the two women with this man was sex incarnate.

The man's hands groped and pulled on the woman's body, letting an occasional slurping sound loose as he devoured her pussy. The woman lying on the side began to fondle herself as she watched.

Louis noticed Cory lick her lips as she watched the tableau. *Fuck. I hope she's thinking what I'm thinking…*

When the woman sucking the guy pulled her head away from his cock and looked up, Louis suddenly got a *serious* hard-on. Memories darted through his body and his cock clicked into flashback mode with a mind of its own.

It was *Maxine*.

And sure enough, her sister Mabel was the other girl fondling her pussy, slipping her fingers in and out of her cunt. "C'mon Maxine *chère*, let me fuck him. Damn it, I wanna fuck him *now*."

Maxine licked her lips and shook her head. "Not sure I wanna let this big boy go. He's been away for a loooong time an' I reckon he got a lot of the good stuff, the man juices, just ready to let loose inside some nice sweet gal — like me."

The man groaned while Maxine tugged at his aching cock.

"Aww, c'mon sis, look—my little pussy has needs too. You have him tastin' yours, the least you can do is let him fuck mine." The banter between the sisters drove Louis wild and had the same effect on the man between them.

Louis was a goner. The twin blondes mesmerized him, just as they had done in his fantasy. Or *was* it a fantasy?

Why would the same two sexy women he'd dreamed about be the same two here fucking this man in a bordello? In the past? They'd said they were from Madame Claudine's, but he'd figured he'd imagined it.

Perhaps—just perhaps—he *hadn't.*

The questions began to rise, along with his own responses, when Mabel lowered her pussy onto the man's swollen cock.

It seemed that Cory wasn't exactly untouched by the display, either. Her hand began to sweat in Louis', and he swore he could scent her body. That unique fragrance that had burned itself into his sensory glands. He found himself looking away from the bed and watching Cory as she gazed at the women's faces contorting in pleasure.

Heat rose in her cheeks, her lips parted and the pulse at the base of her neck throbbed. A quick glance showed Louis nipples that were hard beads. She was as turned on as he was.

There were more moans from the bed as the three continued their sensual games. "Shit, talk about *déjà vu*—this is some *hot* sex." Louis blurted out the first thing that came into his head.

Cory turned to stare at him. "*Déjà vu*? Is there something you haven't told me about, Louis?"

She tugged him back through the door just as the groans increased in intensity. "Come on, I wouldn't want you to get any ideas in there."

"Too late."

Cory stopped dead in her tracks and Louis bumped into her. Apparently the whole *being-a-spirit* thing didn't apply to the two of them. "Oh my *God*."

Louis looked around. "What'd I miss? Triplets?"

She frowned. "Very funny." Then she waved her hand at a door. "I could *swear* I just saw Honey go into that room with a man that looked a helluva lot like *Maurice*."

"Now you're *really* seeing things." Louis tried to go back to the blondes' room for another peek, but Cory held on, keeping him back.

"Of *course* I'm seeing things. So are you. We're *both* seeing things. That was a real stupid thing to say." She sighed. "Sorry. This is so frickin' weird it's freaking me out."

Louis squeezed her hand, gently this time, offering comfort. "Yeah. All the sex aside, it is pretty fucked up, isn't it?"

"*Why* are we here, Louis? Did you ask yourself that? Are we supposed to meet someone, hear something, *see* something? What? We're here together, holding hands and can see the past. We're *in* the past." A note in her voice told Louis she was serious and he looked back at her.

"Did you ever think there might be a fundamental reason for all this strangeness and the otherworldly events in your house?" She stared at him.

He smiled. "And here I was just thinking we were getting a free peep show from the past. Of *course* this doesn't make sense, Cory. It is way beyond anything I've ever dreamed of."

Images of Mabel and Maxine darted into his brain, but he pushed them out again. *Uh uh. Best not to mention that. Women don't understand.* "Look, I just gotta go with it, you know? What other choice do we have?"

Louis knew he was right. He should probably have been a whimpering lump of terror by now, but something inside him held back the panic. Some certainty that whatever was happening to them wasn't going to hurt them. He'd lived with paranormal oddities since he'd arrived at Love Alley and not one had *ever* hurt him.

They'd brought him a dream-fantasy about the twins that had surpassed any he'd had in college—and they'd brought him Cory. Sure he'd had to chase his tools around, but overall he couldn't accept that they were in any danger.

"All right. So we've seen a shitload of hot sex, but this is the first time we've seen anybody that looks familiar." Cory moved to the door. "I'm wondering if it's a clue or something. If you're up for it, I reckon we should go find out." Cory pulled Louis' hand.

He almost grimaced at her choice of words. He was definitely *up for it*.

* * * * *

"Ah yes, it's been too long Alice. I missed having you." The bearded man stood behind the woman draped over the footboard.

Louis and Cory materialized in the room just as he began fucking her in the ass.

With the similarities between these two and the Honey and Maurice from the twenty-first century, it was difficult for Cory and Louis to stand there and watch as the man violently hammered into her. But she just whimpered and the euphoric look on her face did not speak of pain but a joyful pleasure. Her large breasts dangled from her chest as she propped herself up to take his cock.

"Yes Alice, that's my whore. You like your Captain fucking you like a whore, don't you?"

Instantly Cory looked at Louis. In unison they spoke. *"Captain?"*

"That's the captain from the portrait in that small room of yours. Remember?" Cory blinked. *"Now* I know why Maurice looked familiar."

Louis nodded. "Yeah, they must be related somewhere back in the family tree. Maurice told me he grew up around here."

The man began to growl as he pawed at Alice's ass and lower back. His knees bent as he thrust forward with a powerful force, every muscle on his body tensing as he reached the brink of his explosion. He threw his head back and with a groan he pulled free of her ass, spewing his seed on Alice's back. Over and over he gushed onto her bared skin. Alice slumped down onto the bed with a sigh, turned her head and smiled.

Louis dragged Cory from the room. *"Now* I've seen enough." His eyes glinted wickedly at her. "How about we go back and try some of the things those twins were doing?"

About to answer him, Cory paused. Which was probably a good thing, since she had a sneaking feeling her answer would have been "okay". Now *wasn't* the time. Or perhaps it was, since she had no idea which time they were actually in. Any more of this and her brain was going to fry.

A laugh distracted her and she glanced down to see a woman walking up the staircase.

Elegant and green-eyed, she was smiling, holding folds of her dress in one hand as she made her way to the second-floor landing.

"Claudine." Cory's hand twitched convulsively around Louis', and in her other hand the little amulet bag began to throb. "Louis, it's *Claudine.*"

Louis didn't answer. He too was staring at the beauty walking toward them. She turned and opened a door, passing quietly beyond and closing it behind her.

"Come on." Cory pulled at him. "This *has* to be why we're here."

"Not the twins?" His voice sounded a little wistful as he followed her.

"Shhh." Without hesitation Cory seeped through the walls of the room after Claudine, knowing that Louis would follow where she led. This was one time she was glad he didn't argue or stop to discuss the matter. Twins notwithstanding, she knew he was part of this whole— whatever it was. He had to be there, to see what she saw and hear what she heard.

"I know this room." Louis looked around. "This is the master bedroom, Cory. That molding—" He nodded to the heavily ornate wall decoration that loomed over the large bed. "I replaced that a few days ago. Right there, too."

"Yep." She nodded absently, her gaze fixed on Claudine as she moved around the room, dabbing a delicate lace handkerchief to her upper lip as she blotted the perspiration from it.

A touch of perfume from a large crystal bottle followed, flooding the air with the scent that was so familiar to both Cory and Louis.

"*Sheeeit*." Louis' fingers crushed Cory's. "It *was* her scent."

Heat boiled up inside Cory as that delicate floral fragrance curled around them. It had to be some kind of aphrodisiac. Or maybe it was just the man next to her.

She jerked her thoughts away from Louis and back to Claudine. The woman had straightened her appearance, sipped something from a glass next to her bed and smoothed

Slightly nauseous, Cory closed her eyes and focused on where her skin touched Louis'. Lights flickered behind her eyelids, whirling this way and that, adding to her confusion.

Her only constant was Louis, his hand still firmly clasped around hers. He was her lifeline, her anchor to whatever reality they would find themselves in.

As before, the experience eased, and Cory opened her eyes, only to shout as she thudded to the floor. In front of her, Louis was luckier—landing on his feet and rocking back against a wall.

He didn't go through it.

And Cory's knees were stinging.

"We're back. This is my room." Louis whispered the words. "Well hell." He sagged.

Cory looked up—straight into his fly. "So we are."

* * * * *

The look on Cory's face as she gazed at his crotch spoke volumes to Louis. Already stoked up to a highly aroused state of mind by their trip back in time, all she had to do was stare and lick her lips.

Bingo. He was harder than stone in two seconds flat. And ready to explode in less than three seconds more.

He groaned as her gaze met his for a brief moment then dropped down again. Deliberately she reached for his zip.

"*Louis...*"

"Yeah. Oh *God* yeah." He wouldn't beg—wouldn't whimper. He promised himself that even when she freed his cock and stroked it.

Okay, maybe one tiny whimper.

The sound became a groan as Cory licked him, learning him anew with her tongue, coating him with the hot wetness of her mouth.

"Shit..."

She scooted closer, the sound of her knees on the floor a sweet delight that permeated the darkness of the room along with the slight slurp she made as she pulled her mouth away then returned to swallow as much of him as she could.

Her fingernails scrabbled against his flesh as she hungrily tugged at his clothes, grabbing a breath and pulling his jeans to his thighs, taking his underwear with them. The wall behind him was hard against his spine and Cory — Cory was all softness and heat around his cock.

"Cory..." Her name was a moan of delight. She'd discovered how sensitive his balls were and was cradling them, moving her hand in concert with her mouth.

"Shut up. I've wanted to do this for — two hundred years." She grinned at him as she held his cock and dropped a kiss on the tip.

He felt a laugh bubble up in his throat and then she cupped him once more, moving her fingers behind his sac and stroking a place that brought tears of ecstasy to his eyes. She found each and every ridge and vein in his cock, treating them to the delicate attention of her tongue, lapping at him and sucking him with fierce enthusiasm.

Once again Louis saw lights flickering in front of him, but this time it had nothing to do with spooky time travel stuff. It had everything to do with an orgasm that was creeping inexorably around his groin and sucking his balls up into his spleen someplace as they swelled hotly.

"Jesus, woman..." He clenched his teeth. *"I can't..."*

Cory eased back. "Let go, Louis. Just let *go*."

Like he had a choice in the matter.

The adventures of the evening, the erotic images they'd seen, the scent of her body, the slip of her mouth along his cock—Louis was on a one-way ride and approaching the last station.

It was time to get off. Literally.

He squawked out a shout as he felt himself obey her command and *let go*. His legs tensed, his muscles locked and he thrust his cock forward, spurting into her mouth as she sucked him with all the eagerness of a new vacuum cleaner set on "high".

He was blind, helpless and totally lost in the orgasm that exploded from behind his eyebrows and shattered him with its intensity. Visions whirled through his mind, formless shades and colors, matching the rattle of his heart as he emptied himself into Cory.

Finally, she drained him dry and he slumped, his head falling backwards and thudding sharply into a panel behind him.

With a squeak and a rattle, a small section of wall swung open on the opposite side of the room.

Cory sat back on her heels. "Well, I'll be damned…"

Chapter Fifteen

ဆ

"Uhhh…I need a *nap*."

Louis sighed out the words as he pulled his pants back up and stared at the opening in the wall.

"Wuss." Cory dusted off her knees and rose to stand beside him. She was embarrassed, pleased that she'd rendered him limp and exhausted and privately astonished at herself.

She didn't mind oral sex, but this had been a case of serious hunger unlike anything she could've imagined. "Um, Louis…" She felt the color rise in her cheeks. "Look—about just now…"

He glanced down at her. "Yeah. That was the most incredible thing. *Incredible*." He reached out and brushed her cheek. The gesture was eerily like the one Claudine and Baptiste had exchanged and she shivered.

"I just don't want you to think—"

His finger on her lips stayed her words. "If you're thinking what I think you're thinking, then don't. Gimme a minute and I'll jump your bones and return the favor you just did for me. We're both adults, Cory. We're honest enough to admit that there's something special here between us— something that falls into the *I-can't-stop-lusting-after-you* category."

He eased away from the wall and studied the bit that he'd hit with his head. "You're stuck with me. I intend to make love to you, no perfume, no bordello visions, nothing but *us*. Are we clear on that?"

Cory nodded and cleared her throat. "Okay. Clear."

"Good. So all we have to do is decide when." He tapped and pulled and tugged, finally discovering a small patch of paneling that moved in and out when he pressed it. "I could go for it right now. But—knowing you—I won't get a minute's peace until we've explored that passage." He grinned. "Right?"

She wrinkled her nose. "You know me too well."

"So, let's do this." He crossed the room and peered into the opening. "We know how it opens. We don't know where it leads."

"Or if it leads anywhere. Things have changed a lot in two hundred years. Buildings fell down, got rebuilt—hell, I don't have to tell you that."

"True. But—and correct me if I'm wrong here—we got whooshed back in time for a reason. You said so."

"Yes."

"And this was about the only thing we didn't know existed, right?"

"Well, there were those blonde twins…" Cory snickered.

"Never mind them." Louis turned away hurriedly and grabbed a flashlight from his stash next to the bed. "Let's see what we've got here."

Cory peered over his shoulder as he moved into the darkness of a very small passageway. She closed the distance between them, liking the heat that radiated from his body.

And his scent. And the way his hair moved against his neck. And his unique eyes.

Face it girl. You're lost in this man.

She sighed.

"You okay?" Louis didn't wait for an answer, but was shining his light down a set of rickety steps. "These look sturdy enough, but be careful. Wait for me to test them first."

"Yessir, boss."

"Smart ass." He chuckled, but Cory noticed he placed his feet carefully and held on to the smooth wooden baluster that led downward.

She followed, doing as he'd told her and stepping cautiously onto old wooden stairs that looked worn down with time and the passage of many feet. "I'm thinking this would have been a convenient servant's entrance…"

Her voice was muffled by the close quarters of the walls and ceiling. Louis was stooping slightly and he grunted as they reached the bottom of the stairs. "That tall black dude must have had a helluva time getting through here."

"Baptiste. Yeah. He was Claudine's lover, I'm guessing."

"Ya think?" She felt him laugh silently. "Babe, it couldn't have been clearer if they'd painted a picture for us."

She opened her mouth to answer when Louis spoke again, an odd note in his voice. "And speaking of painting pictures…"

* * * * *

She took his breath away.

Her face, a pale oval in the brightness of his flashlight, the rest of her in shadows—just as they'd seen her in the past.

Just as she'd been painted.

"Oh my God…" Cory's whisper said it all. She was as stunned as Louis was.

The painting stood against one wall of the small space they found themselves in. There was a door leading somewhere, but it was barred and bolted, the rust thick on what had once been shiny metal. Louis doubted he or anyone else could get through it now. And it was absolutely impossible that anyone had used it for many years.

No, this room had probably been untouched since the painting was hidden — maybe two hundred odd years before.

"Hello Claudine." He stared at her once more. Green eyes twinkled back at him, the artist having captured the ethereal beauty and combined it with her grace and charm. It was a pretty good-sized oil on canvas, and Louis noted the delicate tracery of the frame even through the small damages that came from time and neglect.

"It's amazing." Cory moved closer. "This is in damn good shape considering its age." She extended one arm almost reverently. "It's her. So *much* her."

"Yeah." Louis exhaled through his teeth. This had been one helluva day and finding Claudine's portrait had just about put the cap on it.

"Louis…it shouldn't stay here…can we…" Cory paused.

He shrugged. "Sure. Gimme a hand." Tired though he was, Louis shouldered the portrait and they carefully made their way back up the narrow staircase, Cory holding the flashlight this time and making sure he handled the frame and its valuable contents with caution.

By the time they reached his room, he was sweating. "I'm real thankful Claudine ran a bordello not a music school. I'd have hated to lug a piano up those stairs." He flashed an aggrieved look at Cory.

"Oh stop complaining. Look. It was worth it…" And she placed the portrait under the light. "She was so lovely, wasn't she?"

There was a wistful note in Cory's voice that Louis caught immediately. He stood behind her and slid his arms around her waist. "Almost as lovely as her descendant." He rested his chin on Cory's shoulder, ducking his head so they could stare at the painting together.

The hair was coiled elegantly, just as they'd seen it, and the laughter was trapped forever in her green eyes by the talented hand of an unknown artist. Faint shadows of lace appeared around her chest and shoulders, but she'd been painted as the focus of a light—most of what surrounded her was in shadow.

"She was so in love." Cory stared at her ancestor. "I wonder what happened?"

Louis wondered too. "Given the times in which they lived, babe, she sure picked the wrong man to fall in love with."

"And it sounded as though they'd already had a child too."

Louis nodded. "Etienne, right?"

"Yep. I think I've heard that name someplace before. Probably way back in the family tree. It's odd..."

"What's odd Cory?" Louis rubbed his chin against her hair, loving the way it tangled in the stubble that had emerged on his chin over the last few eventful hours.

"Seeing my family history. I mean *really* seeing it, you know?"

He chuckled and tightened his arms. "It could have been stranger still. You could have been a descendant of those twins."

She elbowed him—and not gently. "Will you forget about those two, for Chrissakes?"

"It won't be easy."

Cory turned in his embrace and stared at him for a long moment, humor and exhaustion mingling in her eyes. "Ah *shit*. I want to fuck you, Louis. Drive the memories of those two blonde hookers right out of your mind. But right now I'm so damn tired I reckon I've forgotten how."

Louis soooo wanted to offer to refresh her memory. But even as the thought started, his body began to ache. He knew he had reached his limit as well. "So here's what we're gonna do." He released her and closed up the paneling, latching the little catch that secured it.

She watched him warily, raising one eyebrow as he slipped out of his shirt and jeans. "Take your clothes off."

"Pardon?"

"We're going to sleep. And that's all. *To sleep.*"

Her hands went to her shorts button. "*Perchance to dream?*"

"Huh?"

"Never mind. I guess you don't get to read much Shakespeare." Her top tangled in her hair and she swore.

Louis stepped to her side and freed her. "Sweetheart, you're rambling."

She yawned, a jaw-cracking gape that treated him to a glimpse of her tonsils. "Yeah. Sorry."

He pulled her onto the bed and pushed the covers back. The fan was circulating air above them thanks to the ultimate miracle—continued electricity. It wasn't cool by any means, but it was bearable.

The distant rumble of thunder sounded outside as Louis clicked off the light and snuggled Cory down next to him, spooning himself into her back.

"Louis—"

"Go to sleep."

"I didn't brush my teeth."

"Me neither. I won't tell if you won't." He found one rounded breast encased in the soft cotton of her bra and cupped it.

She sighed and settled herself. "That's nice."

"Mmm hmm." They were asleep within moments.

Across the room, Claudine's portrait kept watch through the night.

* * * * *

The scent of coffee and a soft rattling sound combined to drag Cory from a sound sleep. She opened her eyes and yawned.

"Mornin' chile."

The words were whispered, but made her jump all the same. "Holy *shit*."

Sitting on the floor, cross-legged by the bed, was Zulee. "'Bout time you opened dem eyes o'yourn." She picked up a mug and held it out. "Here."

"Uhh…" Cory's wits refused to gather themselves and she wondered if she should pinch herself. Automatically she took the mug, finding it hot to her touch.

Nope. This isn't a vision or a dream. It's fucking real.

"How…where…"

"I allus bring de mistress of Love Alley her morning drink, chile." Zulee sat back, her necklaces clattering a little against each other with the noise that had woken Cory.

"But I'm not…he should…" She glanced over at Louis, still deeply asleep.

"No matter." Zulee dismissed Louis. "Master needs de rest." She stared across the room. "You found her, den."

Cory shifted and sipped the coffee, almost purring as the strong and fragrant liquid slid down her throat. "God, this is good." She sipped some more. "Yeah. We found her last night down the bottom of a passageway."

"You done good." Zulee nodded in approval. "You de right one."

"For what?"

"For what needs to be done."

Cory rolled her eyes. "That's a *huge* help." She glanced at the portrait. "She's...she's spoken to me, Zulee. A couple of times. I've heard her voice, you know?"

Somehow, Cory knew that she didn't have to explain her gift to this unusual little woman. That Zulee would understand when she spoke of hearing a voice that had been silent for close on two hundred years.

"What she tell you?" Zulee looked interested.

Cory thought. "Something about helping her find her love. About being happy at last. It's...muddled."

Zulee nodded. "You gonna do it?"

"Do *what*? If I knew what to do I'd do it. It's frickin' frustrating, this whole damn thing. I'm getting all these messages from beyond and from the tarot and the Ouija board and none of them make fucking *sense*."

Cory angrily shoved a thick lock of hair back over her shoulder and finished her coffee. "If you know what the hell I'm supposed to do then I wish you'd just tell me. I'm going nuts with all this shit."

Zulee grinned. "You gotta listen wit' de heart, chile. She's tellin' you what to do. You jus' ain't listening right."

"Oh thanks a lot." Cory sighed.

"You here for a reason. *He* here for a reason." Zulee nodded at Louis who slumbered on, snoring a little, undisturbed by the conversation going on next to him. "All de pieces of de puzzle here for a reason."

"Okay. I'll buy that. I've seen enough to know there's a reason for most things, even though we don't know it at the time."

"So let Claudine talk to you some more, *chère*." Zulee's lined face cracked into a smile. "Dat woman got stories to tell...whooeeee." She fanned herself. "But dere's one big story dat needs *de end* written to it." Leaning over, she tapped Cory's chest. "In here, you got de answer."

"I do?"

"Sure t'ing, chile. An' you and him's gonna find it together." Her eyes drifted to Louis and she chuckled. "Looks like he's already dreamin' of doing somet'ing together wit' you."

Cory followed her gaze and noticed a quite delectable morning stiffy growing steadily between Louis' legs. "Probably dreaming about blonde twins." She put the mug back down on the tray sharply.

"Dose gals were..." Zulee stopped herself. "Never you min' 'bout dem." She waved her hand dismissively. "It's de here an' now you got to deal wit'. Use your brains an' your heart. An' *him*." She licked her lips. "If'n I had a few o' my years back..."

Something possessive raised its head within Cory. "Uh uh. He's mine."

Zulee grinned. "Yes he is, *chère*. Dat's good you know it." She stood. "Listen to Claudine. She got more to tell if'n you listen."

"But..."

"He gonna wake up soon. I go now. You t'ink 'bout what I said, chile." And quietly, with a last rattle of her wooden beads, Zulee slipped from the room.

Cory sighed. This was all too much for her. She needed answers, a shower and she absolutely needed to pee. This last was accomplished before anything else, making Cory a great deal more comfortable as she crept back into the master bedroom.

Louis—in that wonderful way men have—slept like the proverbial log, sprawled every which way, snuffling at regular intervals and generally ignoring the world around him.

He was hard now and Cory noticed a tiny smile on his lips as his eyelids flickered. *Yep. Definitely the twins.*

She paused by Claudine's painting. There hadn't been enough light last night to get a good look at it but now, as the sun rose outside, she could see it clearly.

The emerald green eyes were clear and brilliant, shining from a face that had the complexion of fresh cream. The lips were a natural rosy shade, with a slight gleam—perhaps from some old-fashioned salve or maybe just from Claudine licking them before sitting for the painting.

For the first time Cory noticed her jewelry. Pearl droplets hung from her earlobes, tiny points of light, emphasizing the nascent sheen of Claudine's skin. Around her neck was a fine silver chain ending in an ornate pendant.

Again, the skill of the artist was evident, since although this was a sizeable piece, it had faded into the background when placed beneath the face dominating the portrait.

Cory took a closer look at it. There were pearls—intertwined in vines of some sort—a delicate tracery of silver stems flowering into tiny diamonds at their tips. And in the center there was a silver oval with markings or engravings on it.

She leaned in for a closer look as a snort from behind her told her that Louis was waking up.

Absently she glanced at him. "Hey, you got a magnifying glass?"

* * * * *

Louis struggled back from the mists of sleep, pushing away dreams of women in corsets, lace sheets and blonde twins doing decadent things to his body.

He surfaced in time to hear a question that struck terror into his soul. He lifted the covers and glanced down. *Whew. Okay fella. She isn't asking about you.* His morning erection stood proudly away from his briefs. She wasn't going to need any kind of magnifying glass to find *that*.

With a sigh of relief he shoved himself up onto the pillows. "Huh?" It was the best he could do right at that moment.

"A magnifying glass. There's something I want to take a closer look at." She was sitting close to the painting.

"Uhh…"

"Oh never mind. It'll wait." She waved a hand to her side of the bed. "There's coffee over there on the floor."

"Mmmpf."

His head was foggy, his brains not quite making it to first gear yet and she was too damn bright-eyed and bushy-tailed for his comfort. He staggered to the bathroom, double-checked to make sure that time travel hadn't actually shrunk anything and ended up sitting on the unmade bed with a blessed cup of coffee in his hand as Cory continued to peer at the portrait.

"So." He sipped, letting the warm brew finish waking him up. "What ya got?"

Cory stretched, doing lovely things to her body. Who needed fancy underwear? The simple cotton briefs and bra were a miracle of delight all by themselves. Louis' cock agreed wholeheartedly.

"Dunno. A clue maybe. It's all so…*frustrating*, Louis, ya know?"

Louis, who was beginning to feel a healthy dose of frustration of his own, agreed. "Yeah. Anything I can do?"

She turned and looked at him.

He looked back.

And that was all it took. The heat between them blossomed and filled the room, sending a flush to Cory's cheeks and sweat to the back of Louis' neck. He put down his coffee.

"Come here." He held out his hand to her and she willingly moved to him, putting her palm against his. He tugged her closer and leaned forward, pressing his lips to the soft skin above her navel. "*Cory...*"

She sighed as he gently nipped her then licked the spot, slipping one hand around her to find her warm bottom beneath its cotton covering. It felt right, comfortable, familiar and arousing.

She was making that little noise he loved—a sort-of sighing whisper in back of her throat—that told him she was there with him, leaning in to his mouth as he found new places to kiss and lick and nibble.

He held her, bending her arm behind her, keeping her between his outspread thighs, standing before him and resting her free hand on his shoulder. He could smell her body, warm and womanly, sweetening with her particular spice as he ran his tongue beneath her breasts.

She giggled as he hit a ticklish spot and sighed once more as he moved on. Her buttock was flexing within his grasp now, her muscles responding as he aroused her. Louis found the elastic of her panties with his teeth and tugged on it, finally giving up. "Take these off."

He released her arm, shuddering with the force of his need as she immediately slid the white cotton to the floor and kicked it away. Her pussy hair gleamed dark in the sunshine, darker than the silky skin surrounding it but lighter than the hair falling down her spine. Fascinated, Louis stroked it gently, riffling his fingertips through it until they brushed the swollen lips beneath and she bit back a cry.

He knew where this was leading, what he was going to do. And he couldn't wait.

Grasping her ass he pulled her to his mouth.

"*Louis…*" Fingers scrabbled at his hair as he sucked her, learning each and every place that ratcheted up her breathing, probing her darkness, tasting her honey, licking her until she clenched her hands and almost tore at his scalp.

Her hips were thrusting into his face as he devoured her, drowning in the passion and desire of her pussy. She was a feast for his lips and his soul and he ate. Not his fill—he could never eat his fill of this woman. *His* woman.

But he let his senses absorb her responses, gauging from her sounds and her breaths how far along the road she had traveled. He wanted to take her all the way, but selfishly he knew he wanted to be there with her at the end.

Sweet, spicy, her flavor flooded his mouth as he teased her higher, loving the tears her cunt wept for him and the heat which boiled around his face. She shook and he knew she was close.

He eased back with a last long lick and lifted his gaze to her face. Desire was written in her parted lips, in the tongue that flicked over them and the flush that darkened her cheeks.

She bent her head and looked at him. "*Shit*, Louis…I *need* you. Don't stop now."

"I don't intend to." Louis released her and reached for his jeans and a condom. This wasn't going to end the way it had last night, with only one of them coming. This time, it was for them both.

She wriggled out of her bra as he sheathed himself and he could hear her breathing, ragged and harsh, as she watched him roll the thin latex over his cock. Just knowing she was watching did incredible things to him, making his hands shake and his brow sweat like crazy.

"Ready?" He spread his arms, inviting her to come to him.

"Oh yeah." Raspy, her voice cracked as she straddled him and put her knees either side of his hips on the bed.

"Do it, Cory. Do what feels good to you."

Gently she grasped his cock and put it right where he wanted it—at the opening of her cunt. Swollen and wet folds caressed him, an arousal all their own as she made sure she was comfortable. Her nipples grazed his body, her scent made his throat choke with lust and he was so *in the moment* with this woman that a tornado could have knocked the house down and he wouldn't have known it.

"*You* feel good to me." Cory lowered her body onto Louis, taking him deep, deeper inside her silky slick fire.

"Likewise, babe." He breathed her in, a symphony of sensual impressions—soft skin, boiling pussy, dark eyes and even darker hair. Her muscles flexed and eased as she rose and then lowered herself again, finding a rhythm that worked for her and drove him damn near insane.

His hands clasped her close to his chest and he found a nipple with his mouth, tugging on it as she moved, letting his hips thrust as much as they could in tandem with her ride.

The sunlight streamed in on them, isolating them in their own world of passion, warming Louis' back and shining on Cory's face. Her eyes were closed now as her body began to tremble once more and Louis knew from the tingling in his crotch that he was too damn close to stop now.

"Oh *God…*" Cory crashed down into him, grinding her clit against his body, forcing his cock as far inside her as it could possibly go.

And then she came, mammoth clamping spasms locking onto his cock, squeezing and releasing him with a savage stroke that sent him over the edge too.

Locked together they groaned and shuddered, throats making sounds that neither heard. His body quivering, Louis surrendered to the orgasm, a massive release of so much more than his come.

She'd taken him further than he could have ever imagined going with a woman. This was so much more than just *fucking*. The thought flashed through his head as she sagged against him with a groan.

"Holy *shit*, Louis…"

He couldn't have said it better himself. They tumbled back onto the bed, panting and sweaty. And he couldn't have been happier, either. He'd come, his woman was a useless sated lump of boneless exhaustion—all was right with the world.

Gently he eased them apart. "Don't move. Stay right there." He got up to dispose of the condom.

She snuffled. "Can't go anywhere. I'm dead."

He grinned as he returned from the bathroom. "You're a hell of a gorgeous ghost, then."

She stretched languorously, a cat begging to be stroked. "If this is heaven, bring it on. God, I feel good." She turned and smiled at him. "Thank you."

"My pleasure." He smiled back. "Believe me." His gaze wandered over her body, admiring the mounds of her breasts topped with nipples that were now soft and rosy from his mouth.

Her arms lay limply above her head and she idly twined her fingers in the wooden molding behind the bed. "Mmm. Must be this house. I swear I've *never* had sex that good."

"Uhh, I'd like to think I had something to do with it." Louis was mildly affronted. The house hadn't fucked her into this state, *he* had.

She opened her eyes. "You know what I mean."

"Yeah, but…"

Before he could continue his request for more and greater details on what an incredible lover he was, Cory's fingers twitched and there was a small snapping sound.

He looked up quickly, afraid the molding was going to drop on her.

It didn't, but something else did.

Her grasp had touched a piece of carving that released a little flower—it popped upwards and suddenly something small dropped onto the pillow beside her.

Cory jumped. "Oh crap…is it a bug?"

"I don't think so." Louis stared at it as it lay on the pillow. "No, it's not a bug."

Cory looked too. "Holy fucking *shit*…it's *Claudine's necklace.*"

Chapter Sixteen

ଚ

The sound of hammering echoed through the house.

Whap, whap, whap.

Peeling his eyelids open, Louis mumbled something about his mother and pulled the pillow over his head. Each time the thud of the pounding hammer collided with his eardrums, he jerked in reflex to the sound.

Motherfucker, now I have to get up. It had been such a lovely nap too.

The other side of the bed was empty, the indention of Cory's body still in the mattress. Louis rolled over and breathed in her scent from the pillow. Her hair always smelled good. With a little grin he moved his face lower in the bed and sniffed where her lower torso had rested after their early morning sex. *Mmm, smells like something marinated in pussy juice.*

Pussy was his favorite smell in the world.

Also the fresh scent of a new sports car...hot dogs at a baseball game...and the fragrance that spilled from a freshly poured glass of imported beer when eating a burrito. But pussy was his favorite by far. Especially Cory's pussy.

The banging shook Louis from his fantasy about Cory and the heaven between her thighs. Following his interrupted morning ritual he sat up, scratched his balls, walked to the bathroom and farted loudly as he peed. A scream rattled his brains as soon as he flushed the toilet.

Cory was in the shower and he'd just made her *hot*. Not the good kind of hot, the *I'm gonna kill you* kind of hot. "Woops, sorry, I...umm..." Louis rushed out the door.

He kicked at his clothes beside the bed then pulled them on—after giving them the "smell" test. His pants passed but his sticky T-shirt almost made him puke. Thank God he'd done some of the laundry. As he walked down the hall he heard Cory yell to him from the bathroom. "Louis? Don't forget to find me a magnifying glass."

Louis followed the hammering sound and hummed as he walked down the stairs to see Maurice working on the porch.

"Man, what a beautiful morning!" He spoke to deaf ears. Maurice was totally focused on his craft.

"Hey, I thought you were coming back later yesterday afternoon, Maurice?" Louis grabbed a bottle of water from the ice chest outside the door.

"I got tied up with something. Couldn't get out of it."

Louis shrugged. "Tied up? Is everything okay? You could have called, maybe I could have helped."

"No, I got *tied up*. Like with ropes, handcuffs. *Tied up*...get it?" Maurice shook his head at Louis.

Deciding to let that comment pass, Louis finished the water as they talked for a few more minutes. Today was going to be a hot one and Maurice was already beginning to sweat. He hissed in a breath between his teeth contorting his body and stretching. "Fuck this is starting to burn."

Peeling off his T-shirt and tossing it aside on the porch, Maurice saw his large frame already glistening with sweat as he turned back to start cutting the moldings.

"Shit, what happened to your back?" Louis looked at his skin and the multiple red marks across the bottom of Maurice's wide back.

"Honey got a little carried away with a tree switch last night. Damn Louis, I think I'm falling in love. She is the first woman I've met who's crazier in bed than me. She wants to fuck all the time and gets this little evil streak and wants to take control—" Maurice adjusted himself. "I'd show you what she did last night but it's embarrassing and fucking *itches* like mad. Word of advice—don't shave your balls."

"I'll take your word for it. Hey, you wouldn't happen to have a magnifying glass on you, would you?" Louis remembered what he was supposed to be doing.

"What's wrong? Your woman couldn't find your dick last night?"

"Ha ha ha. Very funny. She couldn't find it because it was stuck in her pussy." Louis puffed his chest with typical male bravado.

"Maybe she couldn't feel it inside so she was looking for the toothpick poking her instead." Maurice grinned and continued to work.

Louis looked around for the nearest piece of wood to crack over Maurice's head.

"You'll find one in the side drawer of my toolbox. I use it for detailing when I etch moldings." He paused as Louis found the magnifying glass. "Just remember to bring it back. My grandfather gave me that one."

"Well, well, lookie what we have here. Two hunks all ready to make me a Honey sandwich. Don't worry boys, I have all the juice you need to keep us slippery and happy." Honey appeared on the other side of the porch.

"Hello Honey. What brings you here so early?" Louis asked.

"Maurice left in such a hurry this morning, I was worried about him. I brought some salve for the little welts on his back. He was a bad boy last night. He got a little whuppin' for it." Honey grinned and winked at Maurice.

"Remind me to never be a bad boy around you," Louis joked.

"Sometimes being bad...is *gooood*." Honey's voice was seductive. She stepped toward Maurice and lightly stroked her fingertips along the marks on his back and side above his hips.

Maurice grimaced but didn't make a sound.

"Tonight I'll rub something special on these marks so you don't get scars. I found your boxers on the floor by the bed, by the way. You shouldn't walk around *commando* in tight jeans. Might make you itch more where we shaved last night." Her fingers followed the waistband of his jeans and tugged playfully at the button in front. "Come by at lunch and we can..."

She leaned in and whispered something in Maurice's ear. Louis couldn't hear what she was saying but seeing Maurice swallow hard and tighten the muscles in his neck gave him a pretty good idea.

After a soft pat on the front of Maurice's jeans, Honey turned and spoke to Louis. "Where's Cory? I wanted to ask her about reading my palm maybe, or telling my fortune." She smiled smugly. "Of course, I know there's a *real* man in my future."

Louis was spared having to answer as Cory herself came out of the house with her hand folded tight around something.

"Hey guys. Louis, you find a magnifying glass?"

"Yeah. Maurice had one. Why?"

"Come on, I'll show you." She turned and went back in the house followed by Louis, Maurice and Honey.

"*We* don't need a magnifying glass, do we big boy?" Honey's giggle made Louis roll his eyes. He didn't know whether to feel sorry for Maurice or not.

The sound of Maurice's hand smacking firmly against Honey's ass reassured him. Maurice had things under control.

Mostly.

*   *   *   *   *

A bubble of excitement welled up inside Cory as she pulled out chair and sat down at the kitchen table, carefully placing her little surprise on a white paper napkin.

"What's that?" Maurice leaned over.

"It belonged to Claudine Lavalieres, the owner of Love Alley a couple of hundred years ago."

"Wow. The hooker?" Honey stared at the tiny silver oval.

Cory frowned. "She was a businesswoman and my ancestor. Watch your mouth."

"Sorry." Honey wrinkled her nose. "That's real old, huh?" She leaned over the table.

"Yeah. Louis and I found her portrait in a hidden storage room. She was painted wearing this."

"So how'd you find it?" Maurice sounded interested.

"Er…" Cory glanced at Louis who gazed innocently back at her. "A little piece of molding got—moved. It popped open, and *bingo*."

Maurice's gaze traveled thoughtfully over the two of them but he said nothing. For which Cory was deeply grateful. Explaining that she was in a state of post-orgasmic bliss when she'd held on to the wood and accidentally slipped the catch would have been embarrassing to the max.

"Anyway…" She quickly diverted everybody's attention back to the necklace. "This is Claudine's. And it's got something engraved on it that I can't make out. Couldn't see it on the painting either."

"Oooh." Honey wriggled her ass on the chair. "Maybe it's a clue to like treasure or something." She glanced at Maurice. "Cool, huh?"

Cory smiled. Apparently the woman had forgotten her Louisiana drawl in the excitement, something that Cory rather liked since it turned Honey from a Southern siren into just an ordinary woman engrossed in an adventure.

A feeling she could share wholeheartedly.

Then she forgot all about Honey as Louis sat down next to her and handed her a magnifying glass. "Here you go."

Everybody fell silent as Cory studied the intricate carving on the little oval.

"Got a piece of paper?" She stared at the markings as Louis passed her a pencil and a notepad. "I still can't figure out what the hell this is…"

She carefully reproduced the engraving, slowly drawing the odd curved shape onto the paper and finally leaning back. "That's it." She sighed. "I dunno. Anybody got any clues?"

She pushed it in front of them and watched them all stare at it.

"Looks like one of those omega symbols." Louis tugged at his lower lip. "Think there was a fraternity for whores?"

"No." Cory rammed her elbow into his ribs making him grunt. "And even if there was, it would be a sorority, wouldn't it?"

"Damn." He grinned at her teasingly.

She couldn't help it. She grinned back. "Idiot."

"Wait a minute here." Maurice grabbed the pencil and did a little doodling of his own. "I've seen something like this before."

Cory blinked. "You have? Where?"

He was silent, hunched over the paper, turning it this way and that, until he sat back and looked up. "It's an orchid."

"What?" Cory's jaw dropped. "A *flower*?"

"Yeah." Maurice drew something else and turned it toward the rest of them. "It's *Polyrrhiza Lindenii*. Called either the Ghost Orchid or the Frog Orchid depending on the source. Doesn't grow 'round here anymore though. Only in Southern Florida."

Cory was staring at him with the same degree of fascination that Honey and Louis were showing. Total and absolute shock.

"You know about flowers?" Honey cleared her throat and tried again. "Uh...Maurice? *Flowers*?"

Louis snickered. "Funny. I didn't have you pegged for a guy who'd be into flowers." He paused. "You gay?"

Honey choked. "Uh...you're kidding, right?"

Cory stuck her tongue out at Louis. "Quit being such a *guy*. Just because somebody knows stuff about flowers doesn't make 'em anything but...er...interested in flowers, okay?"

Maurice, surprisingly, blushed. "It was a hobby of my mom's. I picked up a few things."

"No kidding." Louis stared at the picture Maurice had drawn, as did Cory. A small flower sat dead center of the page, with two long petals draping down from the underside of the flower.

"You know..." Maurice paused, as if in thought. "I reckon I saw one of these once."

"They're endangered though, aren't they? I've heard of the Ghost Orchid." Cory offered her two cents. "And we saw—er—*read* that they were Claudine's favorite flower way back when."

Louis' hand crept to her shoulder and squeezed. He was remembering, just as she was, the flowers that Claudine had had in her room.

"There was a place where I saw them. Years ago. They grow up in the trees, not on the ground, and when the wind blows…well, they dance around. Guess that's where they got their name."

Cory's skin chilled. "Maurice, could you find that place again?"

"Why? Is it important?"

Cory breathed in. "I don't know. No. Yes…*maybe*. I need to see it."

All eyes turned to Maurice. Who shrugged. "Well, hell. Let's go find out."

* * * * *

It took an hour of wandering through the bayous around Love Alley before Maurice finally stopped the little safari and scratched his head. "I'm thinking it was around here someplace."

Louis looked at the dense growth of God-knew-what that seemed pretty damned impenetrable to a city boy like himself. "I should've brought my machete."

"Stuff grows quickly hereabouts." Maurice wandered up and down a small path. "If it was left alone it'd all come back."

"You're an environmentalist at heart, aren't you?" Cory smiled at him.

"I love the bayou. Grew up here. Don't like stuff folks do to it. Take those levées. You stop the river from floodin', you're gonna lose all the alluvial deposits that enrich this part of the state…"

Honey moved to his side and ran her hand up his arm. "Talkin' like that, you're turning me on."

Louis struggled not to point out that simply saying "hello" to Honey was probably enough to turn her on. Cory's nails digging into his arm helped. He didn't need to be a psychic to know they were thinking the same damn thing.

He grinned down at her. "So what do you think? You feeling anything about this particular spot?"

She smiled back. "Thanks for asking that. You trust me now, don't you?"

"Always have, sweetheart." His hand slipped lower, their fingers interlacing. "You've never proved yourself wrong yet. I'm on board with this, whatever it is, wherever it leads. Love Alley may be in *my* name, but it's from *your* family."

Her gaze lingered on his face, happiness in her eyes. "Thanks, Louis."

"Hey—over here." Maurice beckoned. "I remember this tree…"

He led them down a shaded path, over massive gnarled roots and through a few muddy spots that made Honey shudder and pick her way carefully.

Mindful of the local residents, Louis picked his own path carefully too, cursing the television specials he'd watched that featured things like cottonmouth snakes and other assorted creepy crawlies.

None of which he wanted to accidentally tread on when he was this far from civilization.

Finally, Maurice stopped. "Here. It was here."

Ahead of them, Louis saw a small clearing and he blinked. Nothing grew there, no wild grasses or rambling weeds. The trees surrounding it were tall, shading most of it from the harsh rays of the midday sun.

"These trees used to be where those orchids grew. Not many of 'em, but I remember my grandpa tellin' me never *ever* to touch 'em." He sighed. "They're gone now. Too bad."

It was quiet, quieter here than in other places they'd walked through. The birds still sang and the mosquitoes buzzed, but it was sort of like a hush had fallen over this particular little spot. In spite of the heat and the humidity, Louis shivered.

Cory had stilled beside him and he sensed her emotions. "Cory?"

The others turned to look at her. "She okay?" Maurice raised an eyebrow.

"Dunno." Louis waited patiently.

"This is the place." Cory sighed the words and the air around them seemed to shudder slightly.

"All right..." Louis glanced around. After some of his experiences he had no clue what to expect next.

"I have to go in there." She released his hand.

"You sure?"

Her eyes were distant, that oddly unfocused expression that he was rapidly becoming familiar with. "Yes, Louis. I'm sure." She grasped the little necklace firmly in her palm and stepped forward.

Honey and Maurice made to follow her, but Louis' hand held them back. This was Lavalieres business and needed the hand of a Lavalle to finish it.

Somehow he *knew* that the only person who could take the final steps in this journey—which had lasted over two hundred years—was Cory.

And Cory *alone*.

* * * * *

The silver pendant warmed in her grasp as Cory stepped into the clearing. All around her, the shadowed bayou foliage rustled softly, barely moving in the heat of the day. Familiar sounds—the lapping of murky water, the chirping of an assortment of insects, the occasional hoot of a wading bird—echoed around her ears but made no impression.

She was watching the ground, sensing that which was there—but *not* there. Invisible waves of energy guided her steps, leading her to the very center and a tiny patch of moss glowing green in a ray of sunlight.

She bent down and reverently placed the pendant on top of it.

Within seconds a mist appeared around her feet, insubstantial at first then thicker, fuller, whirling into eddies and currents that had no relationship to the air in the rest of the clearing.

Cory moved backwards a pace or two, uncertain of her next move.

"Bonjour, chère."

This time the voice was real, as real as the mosquito biting her arm. She swatted the insect and stared at the mist as it strengthened into forms—two forms—human forms.

"Greetings, lil' one."

Eyes wide, she watched two bodies appear, arms intertwined, heads close to each other. "Oh my *God*…" She recognized them immediately, in spite of their vaporous appearance.

The first one. *"Claudine."* And the other. *"Baptiste."*

Claudine smiled. "Yes, *chère*. Together at last thanks to you."

Cory blinked as she realized the pendant had disappeared. "I don't understand any of this. Never have."

Claudine chuckled and snuggled into Baptiste's arms. "You know most of it. I died one terrible night. Killed by a savage man's hand, mourned by so many. It was a sad time at Love Alley."

Baptiste dropped a kiss on her head. "It was indeed, *mon amour*." He looked at Cory. "Part of all of us died that night. She took my heart and my love to her grave with her." He nodded down at the ground. "I laid her here to rest."

"Here? This is *your* grave?" Cory asked Claudine the question.

Claudine tilted her head. "And it should've been Baptiste's too. We discovered this spot. We came here to be alone—and to love. Ahh, we loved here so freely, *chère*. Giving all we had to each other surrounded only by my lovely bayou. It was a chance to leave all *that* behind, d'you see?"

Cory nodded. "Yeah. I can understand that, for sure." She remembered the noise and the music she'd seen in the past. Love Alley must have indeed been crammed full of people, no place for a truly private tryst between lovers. "So what happened?"

Claudine sighed. "My wonderful Baptiste saved my soul, Cory Lavalle. He was going to take it with him on his journey." Her eyes turned sad. "You must know how things were then. One like Baptiste—well, for him life was not easy." She pulled his arm tighter around her. "And our son Etienne. Had anyone known of him—it would have not ended well for either of them. Hatred roamed these bayous as easily as the 'gators, Cory."

Cory bit her lip. "Some places it still does, Claudine."

"I'm sorry to hear it. When there was such love here too." She shrugged. "Baptiste made me a promise that night before I passed. He fulfilled that promise. No revenge, just freedom for him and my son." She looked somber. "It was hard, but he kept that promise as I knew he would. My killer met his end soon enough."

Baptiste nodded. "He was a drunkard as well as a foul fiend of a man. Drinking does not mix with walking in the bayou."

"He fell in?" Cory's eyes opened wide.

Baptiste nodded again. "His death did not come from my hands or anybody else at Love Alley, but from his own stupidity and arrogance. Alligators—they do not care about money or influence, just their next meal."

Claudine sighed. "A fitting end for one such as he. But the damage was done to Love Alley."

Baptiste took up the story. "I couldn't get away as soon as I'd wanted. With Claudine gone, the house fell into chaos. Customers were everywhere, taking what they desired, many of them becoming the animals they were at heart." His lip curled in disgust. "I knew I had to flee—and quickly. I had concealed Claudine's necklace in a secret hiding place. If it was found on one like me, I'd be accused of stealing and shot immediately, without question. I'd planned on retrieving it just before we left."

A deep sigh made Cory's heart ache. "But something happened…"

"Yes. Many men came. There was noise, shouting, screaming…" He shook away the memory. "I had to get to Etienne—there was no time for anything else. I had to make a choice. I chose him."

"You chose correctly, my heart." Claudine turned her head on his shoulder and gazed at him. "Etienne was our love made real. You did the right thing."

Respectfully Cory gave them a moment before butting in with the first question that popped into her mind. "But...I still don't understand. What's with the necklace?"

Baptiste smiled. "It is Claudine's soul, *lil' one*. By finding it and bringing it here, you have freed her soul to join mine."

"Huh?"

His dark face glowed with joy. "She is with me again now, as it was meant. We are together for all eternity thanks to you."

"At the risk of repeating myself...huh?"

Claudine laughed, a lilting sound that warmed Cory's heart. "My Baptiste is an amazing man, *chère,* and not just in bed either." She nudged him. "Although I have to admit that there he is as a god."

"Only with you, my heart." Baptiste nuzzled her head.

"Excuse me." Loath to interrupt the moment, Cory still needed answers. "You were saying about the necklace?"

He looked up at her and smiled. "I had some powers of my own, *lil' one*. I wanted Claudine by my side for eternity. I made sure it would happen by placing her soul into the necklace."

"Ahh." Questions trembled on her lips, but for once they stayed there. Perhaps there were some things she was not meant to know.

"We needed to be reunited. And we needed the right person to accomplish that task."

Claudine took up the tale. "I waited. I waited alone, knowing that soon someone would come to my house and do what was needed." She sighed. "It was a long wait."

"And then I came along...or rather Louis did..."

"You had the *sight*. You are a Lavalieres by blood. And you loved." She smiled, a warm look that made her emerald eyes glow.

"It had to be the strongest love, *chère*." Baptiste nodded. "A passion to rival ours that would shake this house, dislodge its secrets and lead you here to this place."

Cory pursed her lips as she remembered exactly *how* they'd found the portrait and the necklace. And what she and Louis had been doing at the time. "Ah." What else could she say?

"Others stayed with me now and again." Claudine chuckled. "My girls. My friends. They visited, watched— waited with me. It helped."

"And then we arrived—"

"And everything was in place to finish the matter. To bring Claudine back to my arms for ever." Baptiste nodded. "Thank you, Cory Lavalle. It has been a long lonely wait, but now it's over."

"I still don't understand how—"

There was a sound behind the misty figures that attracted both their attention and Cory's. Another figure was materializing.

"We must go now, Cory. We are tired. We need to rest. Together." Claudine reached toward Cory. "Thank you, sweet child. From the bottom of our hearts. Thank you."

Cory reached out in her turn, only to see the mist begin to dissolve. "No, *wait...*"

"*Merci, chère. Merci...*"

The figures were gone, leaving Cory in the clearing facing someone or something that had stood behind them. She blinked. "*Zulee?*"

No longer a wizened old woman in a wild outfit, this was a tall and magnificent creature, skin glowing from within, eyes bright as the sun. Cory tried to focus on her, but it was like trying to stare at a light. She couldn't quite grasp any details.

Except a strong wave of power, the likes of which made her want to fall to her knees. "Who *are* you?"

"I have many names." Her voice chimed through the clearing, pure and musical, like a bell on a distant hill tolling the hours. "You know me as Zulee. They knew me as *Maitresse Erzulie.*"

Cory gasped at the words. She knew *that* name, for sure. The most powerful Voodoo goddess of all. "I...I..." Oh *shit*. What had she said to Zulee? Had she pissed off a supreme being by mistake?

The apparition smiled. "You have done well, Cory Lavalle. I've been waiting as well, keeping an eye on this place. Hoping that soon someone would come and settle the unfinished business that kept me here." She stretched and yawned, an oddly human gesture for a goddess. "It's been a helluva long wait too. Interesting at times, but mostly boring."

"Goddesses get bored?" Who knew?

Erzulie ignored the question. "Once that man arrived and finally followed my instructions to call you, I knew my wait was at an end. You two were clearly destined to end up in bed together."

"Did you fix it so we would?" Cory lifted an eyebrow.

Erzulie laughed. "*Chère*, I'm good — I'm not *that* good. I cannot command love or passion where there is none. You both did that on your own. And oh *my*, how you did *that* — "

Cory blushed. "Okay. Never mind *that*. So how — "

"Too many questions for which I have too few answers. Once there was real magic, Cory. There were people who believed that the impossible could become possible. A knowledge that floated on the bayou amongst its people the way trash floats on the bayou today. Once there were flowers, orchids even. Baptiste grew them just for Claudine. Now—poof. Endangered species." She sighed. "Too many changes now. Too much has been lost."

She pulsed with a strange light. "Sometimes I am sad at the end of the old ways. Other times I laugh to see the wonders that exist today." Her gaze caught Cory's and held it. "And always I rejoice when passion rises between lovers. When that heat devours them and turns them from rigid paths of technological torture and back into the old ways of bodies folding together in just the right pieces of a pattern. A simple wonder that has never changed—and I pray never will."

She began to float upwards, shimmering and gleaming brilliantly against the dappled shade of the bayou behind her. "The house is quiet now, Cory Lavalle. Its tenants will be able to sleep thanks to you and your lover. It has been a job well done and the end of the road has come upon us all."

Cory swallowed. "I want to know so much more—"

Erzulie smiled. "There is only one thing you need know. That man of yours is a good man, a sound man and he'll treat you well. He will love you and you will love him. 'Tis a gift you both give each other, child. Accept it, cherish it. Do with it what you will, but never doubt it."

"And you?"

"I intend to sleep for a while now. Do not forget me, Cory. I shall not forget you. You will not see me again, but perhaps I shall visit in a dream someday—"

She began to fade.

"I hope so." Cory meant it. So many questions still remained unanswered, but she knew in her heart that it would always be so. Mysteries would always be out there—

the fun was in working them through, not being given a cheat sheet to life.

"Thank you, *Maitresse*..."

"Go to your man, child. Fuck his brains out. *Laissez les bon temps roulées...*" She vanished with a throaty chuckle and Cory turned, leaving the clearing as she'd found it—empty and quiet.

The others were waiting silently, watching her as she walked back toward them. Louis held out his hand to her without a word. She took it, finding warmth and comfort in his touch.

"So? What the hell happened?" Honey couldn't hold the question back.

"Did you—*see* anything?" Cory's throat felt dry and she cleared it with a little cough.

"Just some fog or mist stuff, babe." Louis' arm snaked around her waist. "What *did* happen?"

Cory looked at them, faces eager, a need to share in the end of the adventure written clearly across them all. "Let's go back to Love Alley. *Boy*, do I have a story to tell you."

* * * * *

"So *that* is pretty much that." It was late now, the hours having passed quickly as the tale of Love Alley and its residents of so long ago had unfolded. The sun was setting, the cicadas buzzing, and it was a surprisingly ordinary setting for a ghost story.

Louis watched Cory as she finished her tale and leaned back in her chair. They were sitting around his kitchen table once more, in various stages of disbelief.

"I don't believe a word of it." Honey snorted. "Ghosts? Spirits? A love long dead? C'mon. It's the twenty-first century, for Chrissake. Things like that only happen in the movies."

Louis glared at her. "Oh really?" He paused. "*Alice?*"

Honey's jaw dropped. "How—*whaa*—" She turned accusing eyes on Maurice. "Did you—"

"Nope." He shook his head. "You may be from New Jersey, but I reckon you got Louisiana blood in you someplace, woman."

Cory raised an eyebrow at Louis and mouthed the words, "*New Jersey?*"

He shrugged back. He had no clue how to figure any of this out, but he believed every word Cory had told them. He'd seen too much to dismiss any of it at this point.

Honey was still sputtering with confusion and Maurice took pity on her. "Time to go." He grabbed her arm and tugged her from her chair. "We got business, Alice."

She opened her mouth to protest but shut it again as he stared at her. "Uh, yeah. We got business."

Louis and Cory stood too. "Okay. I guess we'll get back to work tomorrow, Maurice."

The man nodded as he led an unresisting Honey from the kitchen. "Yep. Tomorrow."

As one, the remaining couple moved to the window and watched them walk down the grassy expanse.

"Doesn't say much, does he?" Cory chuckled.

Louis watched Maurice reach down and firmly grab Honey's round ass. "Doesn't need to."

Honey's hand followed suit, grabbing Maurice by the buttocks. Thus linked, they disappeared from view. Cory's chuckle turned into a laugh. "Guess not." She began to clear up the empty soda cans from the table.

Louis stayed at the window and sighed.

"What?" Cory moved behind him, leaning against his back, all softness and curves where her breasts brushed against his spine.

"I was just thinking…" He stared outside. "The house. It's empty now. Quiet. The ghosts are all gone, haven't they?"

"Yep." She put her arms around him.

Louis sighed again. "It's kind of a shame. I'm happy everything turned out the way it did, but *damn*, I'm sure gonna miss those twins…"

He felt her body move as she laughed, then his own breath caught as two hands slid over his belly and up under his shirt. "You know, if you don't stop harping on about those frickin' twins, I'm gonna have to pay Honey a visit and borrow a few of her toys."

"*Really*?" Louis tried not to sound too interested, and failed. "Like what?"

"Hmm." Her fingertips found his nipples and pinched.

"Ouch." The little pain shot directly to his cock.

"Like her handcuffs. Maybe whatever she used on Maurice last night. I saw those marks. Wanna bet she whipped his ass too?"

"No bets. She probably did." He laughed.

"So perhaps you'd like it if you found yourself lashed to the bed…"

Louis' eyes crossed at the mere thought of it. "Depends on what comes next…"

"*You* would, babe. No question about it." She paused, her hands still against his skin. "Of course, there would only be *one* of me…" Her fingertips went exploring beneath the waistband of his jeans. "Think that would be enough?"

Louis grinned. "Dunno. We might have to spend several hours finding out."

"Yeah. At the very least." Cory rolled her eyes as he turned in her arms. He dipped his head to kiss her, promising himself she'd be rolling those eyes of hers more than once tonight.

And Louis Beekman was a man who *always* kept his promises.

About the Authors

෨

Sahara Kelly was transplanted from old England to New England where she now lives with her husband and teenage son. Making the transition from her historical regency novels to Romantica™ has been surprisingly easy, and now Sahara can't imagine writing anything else. She is dedicated to the premise that everybody should have fantasies.

S.L. Carpenter is a born and raised California man. He does both writing and cover art for novels as outlets for his overactive libido and twisted mind. His inspiration is his wife, who keeps him well trained. Writing is his true joy. It gives him freedom and expression for both his sensual and humorous sides.

Sahara Kelly and S.L. Carpenter welcome mail from readers. You can write to them c/o Ellora's Cave Publishing at 1056 Home Ave., Akron, OH 44310-3502.

Also by Sahara Kelly

ഔ

Tales of the Beau Monde 2: Miss Beatrice's Bottom
Tales of the Beau Monde 3: Lying With Louisa
Tales of the Beau Monde 4: Pleasuring Miss Poppy
Wingin' It

Also by S.L. Carpenter

∽

Betty And The Beast
Broken
Dark Lust
Detour (with Sahara Kelly)
In the End
Learning to Live Again
Partners In Passion 1: Eleanor and Justin (with Sahara Kelly)
Partners In Passion 2: No Limits (with Sahara Kelly)
Slippery When Wet
Strange Lust
Strange Lust 2
Toys 4 Us

Why an electronic book?

We live in the Information Age—an exciting time in the history of human civilization in which technology rules supreme and continues to progress in leaps and bounds every minute of every hour of every day. For a multitude of reasons, more and more avid literary fans are opting to purchase e-books instead of paperbacks. The question to those not yet initiated to the world of electronic reading is simply: *why?*

1. *Price.* An electronic title at Ellora's Cave Publishing and Cerridwen Press runs anywhere from 40-75% less than the cover price of the <u>exact same title</u> in paperback format. Why? Cold mathematics. It is less expensive to publish an e-book than it is to publish a paperback, so the savings are passed along to the consumer.

2. *Space.* Running out of room to house your paperback books? That is one worry you will never have with electronic novels. For a low one-time cost, you can purchase a handheld computer designed specifically for e-reading purposes. Many e-readers are larger than the average handheld, giving you plenty of screen room. Better yet, hundreds of titles can be stored within your new library—a single microchip. (Please note that Ellora's Cave and Cerridwen Press does not endorse any specific brands. You can check our website at www.ellorascave.com or

www.cerridwenpress.com for customer recommendations we make available to new consumers.)

3. *Mobility*. Because your new library now consists of only a microchip, your entire cache of books can be taken with you wherever you go.

4. *Personal preferences are accounted for*. Are the words you are currently reading too small? Too large? Too...**ANNOYING**? Paperback books cannot be modified according to personal preferences, but e-books can.

5. *Instant gratification*. Is it the middle of the night and all the bookstores are closed? Are you tired of waiting days—sometimes weeks—for online and offline bookstores to ship the novels you bought? Ellora's Cave Publishing sells instantaneous downloads 24 hours a day, 7 days a week, 365 days a year. Our e-book delivery system is 100% automated, meaning your order is filled as soon as you pay for it.

Those are a few of the top reasons why electronic novels are displacing paperbacks for many an avid reader. As always, Ellora's Cave and Cerridwen Press welcomes your questions and comments. We invite you to email us at service@ellorascave.com, service@cerridwenpress.com or write to us directly at: 1056 Home Ave. Akron OH 44310-3502.

Discover for yourself why readers can't get enough of the multiple award-winning publisher

Ellora's Cave.

Whether you prefer e-books or paperbacks, be sure to visit EC on the web at

www.ellorascave.com

for an erotic reading experience that will leave you breathless.